WHEN CORPORATE ACCOUNTABILITY MEETS TRANSITIONAL JUSTICE

Corporate malfeasance is omnipresent in situations of conflict and repression situations around the world, but efforts for corporate accountability by transitional mechanisms have been dispersed, meagre and unsuccessful. This book analyses the legal rationale behind integrating corporate accountability within the unique context of transitional justice, tracing these issues across international and national legal regimes. It offers a systematic inquiry into the precise legal possibilities and operational limits of access to remedy for victims of corporate abuses in transitions, and the corresponding obligations of states as designers of transitional measures. Providing a systematic and consolidated legal account of the convergence of corporate accountability and transitional justice, the book sketches a new imaginary of transitional justice, rooted in transformative approaches. It will be a valuable resource for academics, judicial and institutional actors, as well as victims and practitioners in the field of transitional justice and post-conflict reconstruction.

TAYGETI MICHALAKEA is an adjunct lecturer of International Law and Human Rights at the European Law and Governance School and Panteion University of Social and Political Sciences, and a postdoctoral researcher at the EU Horizon-funded project 'The Long Arms of Authoritarian States: Suppressing Independent Voices within and beyond their Borders.' Previously, she held advisory roles with international organizations and civil society, including the United Nations, the International Criminal Tribunal for the former Yugoslavia (ICTY) and Global Rights Compliance.

WHEN CORPORATE ACCOUNTABILITY MEETS TRANSITIONAL JUSTICE

International Law and National Practice

TAYGETI MICHALAKEA

CAMBRIDGE
UNIVERSITY PRESS

CAMBRIDGE
UNIVERSITY PRESS

Shaftesbury Road, Cambridge CB2 8EA, United Kingdom

One Liberty Plaza, 20th Floor, New York, NY 10006, USA

477 Williamstown Road, Port Melbourne, VIC 3207, Australia

314–321, 3rd Floor, Plot 3, Splendor Forum, Jasola District Centre, New Delhi – 110025, India

103 Penang Road, #05-06/07, Visioncrest Commercial, Singapore 238467

Cambridge University Press is part of Cambridge University Press & Assessment, a department of the University of Cambridge.

We share the University's mission to contribute to society through the pursuit of education, learning and research at the highest international levels of excellence.

www.cambridge.org
Information on this title: www.cambridge.org/9781009676823

DOI: 10.1017/9781009676847

When citing this work, please include a reference to the DOI 10.1017/9781009676847

First published 2025

Cover image: _The cover image is painted by Simón Carvajal Arango and belongs to MANIFIESTA FCC, a Colombian fashion company, led by young women, that supports, through design and storytelling, former guerrillas and victims of the armed conflict, in the framework of the Peace Agreement.

A catalogue record for this publication is available from the British Library

Library of Congress Cataloging-in-Publication Data
Names: Michalakea, Taygeti author
Title: When corporate accountability meets transitional justice : international law and national practice / Taygeti Michalakea.
Description: Cambridge, United Kingdom ; New York, NY : Cambridge University Press, 2025. | Includes bibliographical references and index.
Identifiers: LCCN 2025025950 (print) | LCCN 2025025951 (ebook) | ISBN 9781009676823 hardback | ISBN 9781009676861 paperback | ISBN 9781009676847 epub
Subjects: LCSH: Criminal liability of juristic persons (International law) | Social responsibility of business–Law and legislation | Transitional justice | Postwar reconstruction–Law and legislation
Classification: LCC KZ7082 .M53 2025 (print) | LCC KZ7082 (ebook) | DDC 345/.04–dc23/eng/20250730
LC record available at https://lccn.loc.gov/2025025950
LC ebook record available at https://lccn.loc.gov/2025025951

ISBN 978-1-009-67682-3 Hardback

To my father, absent but ever present, whose struggles for justice gave me the freedom to believe that another world is possible.

CONTENTS

PREFACE

Corporate malfeasance is omnipresent in conflict and repression situations, across different coordinates of time and space. From Palestine[1] to Ukraine,[2] Colombia,[3] Sudan[4] and the Congo[5] – just to name a few – businesses have been blamed and often found responsible for colluding with warring factions, sustaining war economies,[6] using the abusive state apparatus to secure their interests or financing and providing equipment to warlords or dictators.[7] Corporate complicity in atrocities seems to be the norm rather than the exception. But questions on their accountability, for cases in which their activities exacerbated, fuelled and contributed

1 According to the United Nations, a long list of companies is involved in Israel's illegal occupation of Palestine. United Nations Human Rights Council, human rights situation in Palestine and other occupied Arab territories, A/HRC/43/71, 28 February 2020.

2 Business and Human Rights Resource Centre, 'Ukraine: Global Outrage Over Russian Invasion Leads to Sanctions, Demands for Businesses to Divest', 7 March 2022, available at www.business-humanrights.org/en/latest-news/ukraine-global-outrage-over-russian-invasion-leads-to-sanctions-demands-for-businesses-to-divest/.

3 P. Wesche, 'Business Actors and Land Restitution in the Colombian Transition from Armed Conflict' (2021) 25 *The International Journal of Human Rights* 2, pp. 295–322.

4 In South Sudan, state forces launched attacks against civilians from oil companies' infrastructures. Human Rights Watch, 'Sudan, Oil, and Human Rights', 24 November 2003, available at www.hrw.org/reports/2003/sudan1103/.

5 UN Panel of Experts on the illegal exploitation of natural resources and other forms of wealth of the Democratic Republic of the Congo, Report on the illegal exploitation of natural resources and other forms of wealth of the Democratic Republic of the Congo DRC, S/2001/357, 12 April 2001.

6 See for example the illegal exploitation of natural resources that took place in Liberia and was recorded at the Truth and Reconciliation Commission's report. Truth and Reconciliation Commission of Liberia, Final Report, Volume 1, 156. See also R. Carranza, 'Plunder and Pain: Should Transitional Justice Engage with Corruption and Economic Crimes?' (2008) 2 *International Journal of Transitional Justice* 3.

7 A. Ramasastry and R. Thompson, *Commerce, Crime and Conflict: Legal Remedies for Private Sector Liability for Grave Breaches of International Law* (Fafo, 2006); J. Zerk, 'Corporate Liability for Gross Human Rights Abuses: Towards a Fairer and More Effective System of Domestic Law Remedies', Report prepared for the Office of the UN High Commissioner for Human Rights (2014).

to violence and repression, have only been asked marginally, during periods of transition. In practice, efforts towards corporate accountability (CA) are dispersed, meagre and unsuccessful despite their presumed importance in achieving the transition's goals.[8] In scholarship, little has been said on the integration of CA and transitional justice (TJ), and even less under a legal perspective.[9] Corporate accountability is not even conceived as an epistemic predicament of transitions, a gap that is accentuated by similar challenges in the field of business and human rights (BHR), making justice elusive, even more so in transitional settings. In the words of the International Commission of Jurists, 'the most acute challenges and needs in the area of business and human rights relate to the deficits both in ensuring the accountability of companies and in access to effective remedies for victims of abuse'.[10]

In response to this gap, this book examines the parameters of including CA within the scope of transitional mechanisms. Enriched by empirical analysis, historiographical approaches and an original theoretical vocabulary, it provides a systematic and consolidated legal account of the convergence of CA and TJ, and sketches a new imaginary of transitional justice, rooted in transformative approaches. It undertakes a comprehensive examination of the legal rationale behind integrating corporate accountability within the unique context of transitional justice, and knits an argumentative thread across varied legal regimes, as well as international and national experiences. It offers a consolidated and systematic inquiry into the precise legal possibilities and operational limits of access to remedy for victims of corporate abuses in transitions, and the corresponding obligations of states, as designers of transitional measures.

To accomplish that, the book relies on a granular analysis of relevant international and regional law, as well as national practice. While TJ is

[8] J. Sandt and M. Moor (eds.), *Peace, Everyone's Business! Corporate Accountability in Transitional Justice: Lessons for Colombia* (PAX, 2017).

[9] L. Payne, G. Pereira and L. Bernal-Bermúdez, *Transitional Justice and Corporate Accountability from Below: Deploying Archimedes' Lever* (Cambridge University Press, 2020); S. Michalowski (ed.), *Corporate Accountability in the Context of Transitional Justice* (Routledge, 2013); I. Pietropaoli, *Business, Human Rights and Transitional Justice* (Routledge, 2020).

[10] International Commission of Jurists, Needs and Options for a New International Instrument in the Field of Business and Human Rights, June 2014, p. 15. See also N. Sánchez et al., *Roles and Responsibilities of the Private Sector in Transitional Justice Processes in Latin America, The Cases of Colombia, Guatemala, and Argentina* (Due Process of Law Foundation, International Coalition of Sites of Conscience, 2020).

primarily a domestic exercise, recent research demonstrates that the 'blending of international and national law' is the right tool, which can ensure accountability for corporate perpetrators and relief for the victims, during transitions.[11] Crafting synergies across the two fields involves transcending conventional silos, and blending different legal regimes, at the international, regional and national level.

Furthermore, this inquiry takes a keen and yet innovative focus on the state, as the institutional driver of the transitional phase, but also considers the perspective of victims, whose experiences and demands are paramount for transitional justice. Are there any grounds for state obligations and corresponding victims' rights, vis-à-vis corporate malefactors during periods of transition? How should the legal imaginary be altered to meet the needs of the victims of corporate abuse, under a broader goal of transitioning out of conflict and repression? What were the challenges faced in practice where those two fields collided?

Revisiting the theory and practice of international and regional human rights and international criminal law, combined with a meticulous account of domestic praxis, the book presents a framework for understanding the issues mentioned earlier, moving at three different levels: doctrinal, theoretical and empirical. Substantiated by rich empirical evidence from diverse case studies, it systematizes doctrine, rearticulates theory and explores new legal rationales and normative accounts, under the windows of opportunity offered by TJ. In this way, the book convincingly challenges the mainstream paradigm of transitional justice,[12] and usual interpretations of applicable law, advocating for a paradigm shift towards transformative methodologies.[13]

The book unfolds in eight chapters structured in four different parts, each shedding light on distinct yet interwoven dynamics of the TJ–CA relationship. Part I of the book lays the foundation for understanding the

[11] Payne et al., *Archimedes' Lever*.

[12] The term mainstream or dominant transitional justice is borrowed by other scholars to denote the relatively narrower conception of transitional measures, focusing mainly on violations of civil and political rights and respective prosecutions. See D. Sharp, 'Interrogating the Peripheries: The Preoccupations of Fourth Generation Transitional Justice' (2013) 26 *Harvard Human Rights Journal* 149. See also P. McAuliffe, 'Transitional Justice's Expanding Empire: Reasserting the Value of the Paradigmatic Transition' (2011) 2 *Journal of Conflictology* 2, pp. 32–44.

[13] W. Lambourne, 'Transitional Justice and Peacebuilding After Mass Violence' (2009) 3 *International Journal of Transitional Justice* 1, pp. 28–48; P. Gready and S. Robins, 'From Transitional to Transformative Justice: A New Agenda for Practice' (2014) 8 *International Journal of Transitional Justice* 3, pp. 339–361.

complex interface between corporate malfeasance and transitional justice and situates it within dominant understandings of transitional theory and praxis. While the presence of corporate malefactors is pervasive in situations of conflict and repression, their inclusion within transitions is – if any – minimal and incommensurate. Critical transitional justice scholarship has marginally engaged with the topic, lacking a consolidated account and legal rationale. From the other side (and to the extent that they differ), business and human rights scholarship does not account for the particularities of providing remedies in the aftermath of conflicts. Chapter 1 concisely retraces the parallel but not intersecting development of theory and praxis in both fields and demonstrates the lack of integration into each other's normative architecture, vocabularies and institutional practices, substantiated by empirical evidence and a brief tour d' horizon.

Against this backdrop, a new imaginary of transitional justice requires corporate wrongdoers to be present in the topography of transitional justice, insofar as they were implicated in prior violence. Chapter 2 presents a normative understanding of such integration, assessed against the aims of TJ, namely accountability of the perpetrators, remedies for the victims and reconciliation. In cases of widespread corporate abuses during conflict or repression, the odds are that transitional justice can at least partially deliver those goals, insofar as it also includes corporate perpetrators. Furthermore, the proposed integration responds to persistent victims' calls for corporate accountability, situates the latter within the long-appraised discourse on 'root causes of violence' and inserts the much needed economic aspect in transitional praxis, equipping it better to address the multi-layered complexities of prior injustice, and making it more receptive to domestic predicaments (Section 2.2). The book then explores how the integration of CA and TJ can be translated in the vernacular of legal doctrine. Rather than embarking on companies' direct obligations, the inquiry puts under the spotlight states and their obligations, based on their leading position, as the institutional drivers of transitions and the corresponding rights of victims, whose experiences and demands are paramount for transitional justice. Those sets of rights and obligations are best performed via an amalgamation of different legal regimes in both the international and national levels and a blending of national and international law, as evidenced by different examples (Section 2.3).

Part II of the book explores corporate accountability vis-à-vis transitional criminal mechanisms and inquires how the latter's governing legal regimes accommodate (or not) a state obligation to prosecute and punish business entities. Although different transitional mechanisms are all based on the right to remedy, the challenges faced by each of them, when attempting to apply corporate accountability, are distinct, based on their specific operational parameters and normative underpinnings. For criminal measures, the main gap lies in the perception that prosecution and punishment of individual businessmen exhausts any potential relevant state obligation and the lack of conceptualization of corporate entities' prosecution as part of the transition. Accordingly, the book, firstly, makes a theoretical elaboration of the distinct nature of corporate crime from crimes of individual corporate officers, in qualitative and quantitative terms. Its distinctiveness is a first argument in favour of the punishment of the entire corporate entity rather than that of individual perpetrators.

The book, then, embarks on a scrupulous doctrinal examination of international criminal and international and regional human rights law, aiming to unearth elements of a state duty to prosecute and punish corporate entities.[14] Even if a standalone obligation in relation to corporate entities might not arise, yet it seems that in the face of corporate abuses, state duties do not end with individual prosecutions, particularly in light of the distinct nature of corporate crime. The absence of a respective international forum, despite various attempts for one, which the book retraces, does not detract from the conclusion that international criminal norms bind corporate actors, but rather points to the need for the establishment of such an institution. In addition, the book theorizes on two innovative and promising ideas. Firstly, the evolution of corporate criminal liability to an emerging principle of international law, which demonstrates that traditional barriers in the field of corporate criminal liability tend to be tempered, particularly so in the context of transitions. Secondly, it argues for a new conceptualization of CA within TJ, drawing on Teitel's 'right to accountability' in transitional periods.[15] The crystallization of that right, the enhanced position of the victim that it signifies and the departure of accountability from its secondary status

[14] Note that the state duty to prosecute and punish perpetrators of international crimes is the one that informs the establishment of criminal justice mechanisms, during transitions. See D. F. Orentlicher, 'Settling Accounts: The Duty to Prosecute Human Rights Violations of a Prior Regime' (1991) 100 *Yale Law Journal* 8, pp. 2537–2615; J. Malamud-Goti, 'Transitional Governments in the Breach: Why Punish State Criminals?' (1990) 12 *Human Rights Quarterly* 1.

[15] R. Teitel, 'Transitional Justice and Judicial Activism – A Right to Accountability?' (2006) 48 *Cornell International Law Journal*, p. 38.

demonstrate the magnitude of dissonance of corporate impunity during transitions and indicates the prevalence of holding perpetrators accountable over more technical and thus less important considerations. Considering the unique features of transitional periods, this chapter, also, explores the challenges of pursuing corporate accountability within their evolving dynamics and inherent constraints (Chapter 3).

Chapter 4 examines the application of modes of liability under international law, to corporate entities and corporate officials, the latter being useful for jurisdictions, where liability of the entity is ascribed through the conduct of its officials. It covers the main modes, namely direct and indirect perpetration, participation in group crimes, superior responsibility and complicity. The examination of these modes is empirically grounded on a rich historiographical and empirical account, from international, regional and domestic cases. The book gives a complete image of the attribution of liability to corporate entities, by analysing doctrinal and empirical examples of imputing acts and mental states necessary for each crime, from the individual to the entity. Section 4.3 examines domestic approaches in relation to corporate accountability through criminal mechanisms, with a focus on Argentina, a pioneering jurisdiction in this domain, and Colombia, a more recent and pertinent example. Both case studies, albeit confined to individual accountability of businesspersons, are noteworthy for pivoting our understanding of the various challenges encountered and for conversing and being influenced from judicial developments in foreign fora. In addition, the Argentinean example instantiates the blending of national and international standards, whereas the Colombian endeavours, especially with regards to 'civilian third parties', shed light on the interconnections between transitional and ordinary justice.

Part III of the book explores the field of reparations. Unlike criminal measures, the legal quandary with reparations measures lies on whether transitioning states have any duty to call on corporations to repair, as part of the states' overall duties during transition; and to include them, as debtors, in the design and delivery of reparations, as opposed to providing reparations themselves or hindering victims' efforts for adjudication, as was the case in South Africa. Legally, this would require that the overall reparative obligations of the state include an obligation to provide for victims of corporate violations redress avenues against corporate malefactors in domestic law, and particularly so during transitions.

The book embarks on a scrupulous doctrinal examination of relevant holdings of human rights bodies to extract and synthesize principles, and precedents. Having doctrinal elements as a point of departure, the book presents a novel theoretical framework, drawing on the exceptionality of TJ and the dialectical development of different state obligations, namely positive and remedial ones. A separate analysis is devoted to GNRs, where the book identifies their differential traits, in comparison to other reparations forms, that render them prone to including corporate accountability, namely their emphasis on addressing root causes, their preventive nature, their broadened scope and their departure from the strict requirements, typically associated with other reparative measures (Chapter 5).

Chapter 6 offers an account of court-ordered and administrative reparations that included corporate actors and tackles the common 'development'– oriented justifications against such efforts. It empirically analyses court-ordered reparations against corporate malefactors and explores the role of both national and foreign courts as valuable resources in the pursuit of justice. It highlights the different obstacles that have been faced, in cases arising out of transitioning states, with particular emphasis to the arduous challenge posed by the South African state's opposition to litigation. That opposition was based on developmental and investment concerns, which the book disavows in favour of more transformative approaches that challenge pre-existing structures of exclusion, marginalization and power, and can nest concerns over economic actors that anchor them. Administrative reparations that include corporate malefactors have been scarce, spearheaded again by Colombia. The last segment of Chapter 6 delves into the intricate process of land restitution in Colombia, where – in principal – a trailblazing regulation has been poorly implemented.

Part IV of the book focuses on Truth Mechanisms, and more specifically Truth and Reconciliation Commissions (TRCs), drawing from international law and domestic truth experiences. In the aftermath of widespread corporate violations during conflict or repression, excluding corporate harm from the scope of TRCs undermines the very goals of TJ, but also detracts much of truth's meaning as an entitlement to learn of events, reasons, circumstances and actors that produced significant harm.

Yet a different set of legal questions arises, namely the contours and content of truth, in the aftermath of violations and the extent of a relevant state duty to reveal the truth for corporate violations, as a matter of law. The book investigates relevant legal sources and case law of human rights bodies and emphasizes the evolution of 'a right to truth' in international law and its unrestricted nature, both of which place an unqualified focus on the importance of revealing the truth in its totality, countervailing other considerations invoked in relation to corporations. It critically assesses those two points against the common disregard of corporate malefactors in TRCs and their overriding by developmental concerns. The work of the TRCs of Colombia, East Timor and South Africa instantiates that analysis. Furthermore, drawing from the experiences of Mauritius and Sierra Leone, Chapter 7 analyses the collective dimension of the right to truth. The collective dimension is significant for corporate accountability purposes, as it widens the material scope of the truth itself to reach systematic patterns of abuse and distances it from strict human rights equation requirements.

Lastly, Chapter 8 explores the interaction between truth mechanisms and other transitional measures, highlighting synergies and challenges. While in Argentina (and more limitedly in Brazil) synergies were drawn and different reparation measures (funded by the state) and prosecutions were based on the moral capital of the truth efforts, this was not the case with other truth commissions. Usually, TRCs' recommendations in relation to corporate accountability rarely evolve to actual reparations or prosecutions. As illustrated by the Liberian and Tunisian examples, the TRCs were strong in providing substantial arguments for the inclusion of corporate actors in the transitional justice mechanism, but weak in procedurally paving the way to enforce that inclusion.

The book concludes by reflecting on the insights provided by the research. It assesses the political connotations of expanding the scope of transitional justice to cover corporate actors, particularly in an environment where economic actors are deeply enmeshed in conflict or repression and corporate impunity is the norm rather than the exception. Overall, the book informs us about the intricate issue of delivering justice for corporate violations, in societies that aspire to turn the page to past atrocities.

ACKNOWLEDGEMENTS

While my name is on the cover, this book would not have been written, were it not for the authors upon whose ideas I built mine, the guidance of my PhD supervisor Andrea De Guttry, and the help of all the academic and administrative personnel of Scuola Superiore Sant'Anna in Italy. The mentorship of Laura Bernal, from Javeriana University, was also invaluable – she navigated me through Colombia and its conflict during my time there, opening both her home and ideas to me. I am also deeply grateful to my editor, Tobias Ginsberg, and to the anonymous reviewers, whose insights and critiques helped shape this work.

This book, I have come to realize, was much more than the act of researching and writing. It was mainly about the 'homes' that sheltered my thoughts, hopes, discoveries and doubts while writing it. First and foremost, it is the 'home' I built in Pisa – Clara and Silvia, my two most treasured Italian legacies – along with Marie, Anna, Giorgos, Margarita, and Christina, all of whom shared the weight I carried while bringing this book to life. And, of course, Argyris, my companion, who first pulled me into academia, guided me with care and patience through my first years, and created more than beautiful memories in Italy and beyond. It is also the 'home' I built so far away from home, in Bogota, for few but crucial months; Sara, Alejandro, Edwin and Dario, who cared for me and helped me discover Colombia.

Finally, it is the 'home' I started from: my mom, who has struggled for my dreams to come true; my brothers Dimos and Christos – my oldest, eternal friends; my extended father's family, particularly Alekos, as well as Eleni, Kaiti and Eirini, all of them weaving my personal safety net. It is also my chosen family, sisters from another mother: Rozy lending hands and heart in every difficult turn, and there were many; Aggeliki and Stefania, loving, supporting and believing in me since kindergarten; Katerina, Kostantina, Anna, Eleni, Christina and Marina, who convert life's mundane moments into cherished ones. It is also Nikolas and

Christina, both instilling their distinct and necessary *joie de vivre*. For all those people, I am deeply grateful. It is not only the book – it is life itself that would have been poorer without them.

Lastly, this book would not have been possible without Manolis, who, through light and darkness, created the space I needed to write it.

PART I

Corporate Accountability and Transitional Justice
Untying the Gordian Knot

1

Of Absences and Invisibilities

1.1 Corporate Actors: From Palestine to Ukraine, History Repeats Itself

The story of corporate involvement in conflict and repression is far from novel, with a plethora of literature attesting to it. Records on the atrocities of the Nazi regime revealed names of companies,[1] like BMW, BASF or AEG – still thriving today – that were using forced labour from concentration camps. Others, like IBM, produced early computers that were utilized by the regime and contributed to the management of prisons and concentration camps.[2] Bayer supplied chemical and pharmaceutical products and conducted medical experimentation on detainees.[3] IG Farben created Zyklon B, used for the extermination of detainees. At the Nuremberg Tribunals, some businesspersons[4] were tried and convicted but they were, allegedly, released early and restored to similar positions in other companies.[5] Regrettably, the story has not ended at

[1] The terms company, corporate entity, corporation and business will be used interchangeably, to denote national or international business structures, with or without legal personality, including companies, cooperatives, associations, foundations and partnerships, exercising functions distinct from the individuals who compose it, for profit-seeking purposes. The only potential formations that are excluded from the current research are public companies.

[2] Jewish Virtual Library, 'Concentration Camps: List of Major Companies Involved in the Concentration Camps', available at www.jewishvirtuallibrary.org/list-of-major-companies-involved-in-the-concentration-camps.

[3] United States Holocaust Memorial Museum, Holocaust Encyclopedia, 'Bayer, Key Facts', available at https://encyclopedia.ushmm.org/content/en/article/bayer.

[4] The term businessperson includes the business owner, the manager or the representative, as well as the individual perpetrator, who physically committed the harmful act or the omission, on behalf of the corporate entity and who is usually brought to justice, instead of the entity as a whole.

[5] J. Diarmuid, *Hell's Cartel: IG Farben and the Making of Hitler's War Machine* (Metropolitan Books-Henry Holt and Company, 2008).

that point. From Palestine[6] to Ukraine,[7] Colombia,[8] Sudan[9] and the Congo[10] – just to name a few – businesses have been blamed and often found responsible for colluding with warring factions, sustaining war economies,[11] using the abusive state apparatus to secure their interests or financing and providing equipment to warlords or dictators.[12] Currently, the long-standing Israeli occupation of the West Bank and the Gaza Strip and the conflict that started in October 2023 are being carried out with corporate support. The United Nations Human Rights Council (UNHRC), already in 2016, published a database of all business enterprises engaged in Israeli settlement activity in the occupied Palestinian territories, deemed illegal under international law.[13] The list was updated in June 2023, with prominent business names featuring, but to no avail.[14] Corporate complicity in atrocities seems to be the norm rather than the exception,[15] and history is repeating itself across different coordinates of time and space.

At times, the involvement of corporations in conflict or repression has been direct,[16] when the harmful effects were known and foreseen, like in

[6] According to the United Nations, a long list of companies is involved in Israel's illegal occupation of Palestine. United Nations HRC, 'Human Rights Situation in Palestine', A/HRC/43/71.

[7] Business and Human Rights Resource Centre, 'Ukraine'.

[8] P. Wesche, 'Business Actors and Land Restitution in the Colombian Transition'.

[9] In South Sudan, state forces launched attacks against civilians from oil companies' infrastructures. Human Rights Watch, 'Sudan, Oil, and Human Rights'.

[10] UN Panel of Experts on the DRC, S/2001/357.

[11] See, for example, the illegal exploitation of natural resources that took place in Liberia and was recorded at the Truth and Reconciliation Commission's report. Truth and Reconciliation Commission of Liberia, Final Report, Volume 1, 156. See also Carranza, 'Plunder and Pain', pp. 310–330.

[12] Ramasastry and Thompson. *Commerce, Crime and Conflict*; Zerk, 'Corporate Liability'.

[13] UN, Human Rights Council, Resolution adopted by the Human Rights Council on 24 March 2016, A/HRC/RES/31/36, 20 April 2016.

[14] UN Office of the High Commissioner on Human Rights, update of database of all business enterprises involved in the activities detailed in paragraph 96 of the report of the independent international fact-finding mission to investigate the implications of the Israeli settlements on the civil, political, economic, social and cultural rights of the Palestinian people throughout the Occupied Palestinian Territory, including East Jerusalem, 30 June 2023.

[15] Corporate complicity is defined as the assistance or participation of economic actors in gross violations of human rights perpetrated by the state or state-like actors during authoritarian or civil conflict situations. Payne et al., *Archimedes' Lever*, p. 3.

[16] On the classification of corporate involvement, see A. Clapham and S. Jerbi, 'Categories of Corporate Complicity in Human Rights Abuses' (2001) 24 *Hastings International and Comparative Law Review* 339; F. Wettstein, 'Duty to Protect: Corporate Complicity,

2007, when Blackwater was sued, due to its employees' direct liability for extrajudicial killings and war crimes, in Iraq.[17] The same is the case of the Wagner Group, incorporated in Russia, which takes direct part in the current conflict in Ukraine, and beyond.[18] In other cases, the involvement was indirect, mainly when businesses supported the ability of the principal perpetrator to systematically violate human rights.[19] Perhaps one of the most characteristic cases was that of Unocal, a US corporation, which, in order to construct an oil pipeline in Myanmar, during the early 1990s, partnered with the local military and was, allegedly, complicit to widespread human rights abuses such as murder, rape and forced labour.[20] Cases filed before US Federal Courts found, among others, that Unocal aided and abetted the crime of forced labour.[21] In instances where corporate criminal liability was not incorporated in the domestic legal framework, individual businessmen were prosecuted. This was the case for Frans van Anraat, a Dutch businessman, known as 'Chemical Frans', who delivered a toxic substance to Saddam Hussein, used on the Kurdish population of Iraq. He was convicted by The Hague District Court of complicity in war crimes, for his essential contribution to the chemical warfare programme of Iraq.[22]

Yet, in other cases, companies have been accused of providing financial or technological assistance that caused, facilitated or exacerbated human rights abuses during periods of violence. By way of illustration, Danzer Group's senior manager faced a lawsuit alleging that the company's Congolese subsidiary provided payment, transport and logistical

Political Responsibility, and Human Rights Advocacy' (2010) 96 *Journal of Business Ethics* 33–47.

17 Most cases, regarding Blackwater, were settled out of court in January 2010, and the last remaining lawsuit was settled in January 2012. See Zerk, 'Corporate Liability'.

18 Office of the High Commissioner for Human Rights, 'Russian Federation: UN Experts Alarmed by Recruitment of Prisoners by Wagner Group', 10 March 2023, available at www.ohchr.org/en/press-releases/2023/03/russian-federation-un-experts-alarmed-recruitment-prisoners-wagner-group; Office of the High Commissioner for Human Rights, 'CAR: Russian Wagner Group Harassing and Intimidating Civilians', 27 October 2021, available at www.ohchr.org/en/press-releases/2021/11/car-russian-wagner-group-harassing-and-intimidating-civilians-un-experts; D. Walsh, 'Russian Mercenaries Are Driving War Crimes in Africa, U.N. Says', *The New York Times*, 27 June 2021.

19 Wettstein, 'Duty to Protect'.

20 Clapham and Jerbi, 'Categories of Corporate Complicity'.

21 *Doe I* v. *Unocal Corp*, 395 F 3d 932, 9th Cir (Cal), No 00-56603, 00-57195, 00-57197, 00-56628 (2002).

22 *Public Prosecutor* v. *Van Anraat*, LJN AX6406, The Hague District Court, 23 December 2005, at par. 17.

help to the police and military.[23] In Colombia, Chiquita and Drummond have been accused before US courts of providing financial support to paramilitary groups and employing them to kill labour leaders.[24] Amesys was brought before French courts for supplying surveillance technology to the Gaddafi's regime in Libya[25] and Qosmos to Al-Assad's in Syria.[26] More recently, the Russian aggression in Ukraine is reportedly heavily financed by various western companies that contribute through their taxes to Russia's operations, with over three and a half billion paid to the Russian state in profit taxes, in 2022 only.[27]

Lastly, corporations have profited from conflicts by remaining silent in front of serious abuses, in order to safeguard their stay in that country.[28] Without downgrading the involvement, Wettstein has categorized Shell's role in the 1995 execution of the Nigerian activist and playwright Ken Saro-Wiwa, as 'silent complicity'. Despite its direct connection to Wiwa's arrest, Shell remained idle before his undoubtedly unfair trial and execution, along with eight others, due to their opposition to environmental destruction by oil companies in the Niger Delta.

[23] The case was discontinued. European Centre for Constitutional and Human Rights, 'No Investigations Against Danzer Manager Over Human Rights Abuses Against Community in DRC', available at www.ecchr.eu/en/case/no-investigations-against-danzer-manager-over-human-rights-abuses-against-community-in-drc/.

[24] Zerk, 'Corporate Liability', p. 20. See also the criminal complaint filed against BNP Paribas for contribution to the Rwandan genocide. M. Kennedy, 'French Bank BNP Paribas Accused of Complicity in Rwandan Genocide', NPR, 29 June 2017, available at www.npr.org/sections/thetwo-way/2017/06/29/534865238/french-bank-bnp-paribas-accused-of-complicity-in-rwandan-genocide.

[25] Liberation, 'Libye: l'enquête visant la société française Amesys va se poursuivre L'entreprise est accusée de «complicité de torture» pendant l'ère Kadhafi', 15 January 2013, available at www.liberation.fr/planete/2013/01/15/libye-l-enquete-visant-la-societe-francaise-amesys-va-se-poursuivre_874118/.

[26] FIDH, 'France: Opening of a Judicial Investigation Targeting Qosmos for Complicity in Acts of Torture in Syria', 11 April 2014, available at www.fidh.org/en/region/europe-central-asia/france/15116-france-opening-of-a-judicial-investigation-targeting-qosmos-for-complicity; FIDH, 'Designation of Qosmos as "Assisted Witness" Constitutes an Important Step Forward in Case Underway', 20 April 2015, available at www.fidh.org/en/region/europe-central-asia/france/designation-of-qosmos-as-assisted-witness-constitutes-an-important.

[27] 'The Lucrative Business of Staying: Corporate Foreign Enables of the Kremlin's War', 4 July 2023, B4Ukraine, available at https://b4ukraine.org/what-we-do/business-of-staying.

[28] F. Wettstein, 'Silence as Complicity: Elements of a Corporate Duty to Speak Out Against the Violation of Human Rights' (2012) 22 *Business Ethics Quarterly* 37–61.

In sum, the quantity and severity of the cases are overwhelming. During his tenure, John Ruggie, Special Representative of the Secretary-General (SRSG) on human rights and transnational corporations, found that 'the most egregious business-related human rights abuses take place in conflict affected areas'.[29] Surprisingly – or not – while the coordinates of corporate abuse vary, across time and space, there is one unfortunate common feature. This is the absence of accountability of those corporations for their offences and, more generally, the absence of corporations from the topography of transitional justice.

1.2 Constructing Absences: (D)evolving Narratives in Transitional Praxis and Theory

Despite the abhorrent and severe nature of business involvement in violence, corporate accountability has not been embraced by transitional justice, the latter defined as 'the set of practices, mechanisms and concerns that arise following a period of conflict, civil strife or repression, and that are aimed directly at confronting and dealing with past violations of human rights and humanitarian law'.[30] In its over forty years' development,[31] transitional justice has experienced exponential growth, often described as an 'avalanche'.[32] Compared to that, the mechanisms established to realize the transition, namely court procedures, truth

[29] UN Human Rights Council, Report of the Special Representative of the Secretary-General on the issue of human rights and transnational corporations and other business enterprises, John Ruggie, 'Business and Human Rights in Conflict-Affected Regions: Challenges and Options Towards State Responses' (2011) A/HRC/17/32, at 1.

[30] N. Roht-Arriaza, 'The New Landscape of Transitional Justice', in N. Roht-Arriaza and J. Mariezcurrena (eds.), *Transitional Justice in the Twenty-First Century* (Cambridge University Press, 2006), p. 2. For other definitions, see R. Teitel, 'Theoretical and International Framework: Transitional Justice in New Era' (2003) 26 *Fordham International Law Journal* 4, 893; P. De Greiff, 'Theorizing Transitional Justice', in M. Williams, R. Nagy and J. Elster (eds.), *Transitional Justice* (NYU Press, 2012). Note also that Ruti Teitel arguably invented the term 'transitional justice' in 1991. R. Teitel, 'Editorial Note, Transitional Justice Globalized' (2008) 2 *International Journal of Transitional Justice* 1.

[31] Zunino locates the initial efforts in Argentina during the eighties and gives an overview of the history of the field; see M. Zunino, *Justice Framed: A Genealogy of Transitional Justice* (Cambridge University Press, 2019). Note that Elster contends that, in its essence, transitional justice existed since ancient times. J. Elster, *Closing the Books: Transitional Justice in Historical Perspective* (Cambridge University Press, 2004).

[32] J. Sarkin and T. Davi, 'Examining the Criticisms Levelled Against Transitional Justice: Towards an Understanding of the State of the Field' (2017) 11 *Human Rights & International Legal Discourse* 7, 12.

commissions and reparations, have engaged only sporadically with corporate accountability,[33] understood as different legal or non-legal ways to attach cost to a conduct.[34]

States and institutional designers of transitional processes are often unwilling or unable to include corporate entities, in the transitional landscape, choosing sometimes to totally disregard their malfeasance, and other times to hold only individual businesspersons accountable, such as their managers or owners. The prevalent post-violence discourse is premised on an assumed necessity of befriending business actors, for their role in 'pacifying the environment for investment' and in a potential future economic take-off.[35] To that geography, one should add corporate power, capable of blocking accountability efforts and directing the transitional discourse towards more favourable business outcomes.[36]

Truth and Reconciliation Commissions (TRCs) have engaged the most with corporate accountability, whereas in the field of reparations, the concept is practically unknown. In nineteen different countries, twenty-two TRCs investigated corporate entities for various abuses during conflict or repression.[37] Most of them were located in Latin America. In Brazil only, the Truth Commission named 123 companies as responsible for various human rights violations. In Argentina, different truth efforts examined companies' involvement in the military dictatorship and revealed that some company premises were used for torture, detention and kidnapping, such as the ones of Fiat car company, Ledesma sugar company, and others.[38] In the African continent, the South African

[33] For a codification of those efforts, see Payne et al., *Archimedes' Lever*, p. 287 *et seq.*

[34] For an analysis of the concept of corporate accountability, see N. Bernaz, 'Enhancing Corporate Accountability for Human Rights Violations: Is Extraterritoriality the Magic Potion?' (2013) 117 *Journal of Business Ethics* 494; Y. Farah, 'Toward a Multi-Directional Approach to Corporate Accountability', in S. Michalowski (ed.), *Corporate Accountability in the Context of Transitional Justice* (Routledge, 2013). For the concept of accountability in general, see D. Curtin and A. Nollkaemper, 'Conceptualizing Accountability in International and European Law' (2006) 36 *Netherlands Yearbook of International Law* 3–20, at 8.

[35] This was argued in Tunisia. See A. Guellali, 'Tunisia: Transitional Justice in the Crosshairs', Human Rights Watch, 8 September 2015.

[36] On corporate veto power, see Payne et al., *Archimedes' Lever*, pp. 113–161.

[37] Sandt and Moor, *Peace, Everyone's Business!*, p. 34.

[38] In 1983, the National Commission on the Disappearance of Persons (CONADEP) was established to investigate forced disappearances between 1976 and 1983. In 2013, the National Securities Commission (CNV) published a report regarding the adverse impacts of the dictatorship on the financial system. A further truth commission was established in 2016 to examine how banks supported the military dictatorship. Lastly, in 2015, the

TRC held the well-known hearings on businesses, and the commissions of Sierra Leone and Liberia were both mandated to investigate corporate entities involved in prior conflict.[39] In Asia, a similar effort was carried out by the Commission on Reception, Truth, and Reconciliation (CAVR) of East Timor.[40]

However, those positive contributions did not proceed smoothly. In some countries, amnesties, de facto or de jure, applying also to corporate perpetrators, were adopted, as in Brazil with the 1979 amnesty law.[41] In Argentina, a 2015 Senate-approved bill to establish a commission targeting economic complicity was eventually stalled.[42] Similarly, in Tunisia, while the various TRCs described the involvement of various corporations in Ben Ali's regime, the 2015 draft Economic and Financial Reconciliation Bill attempted to grant private persons involved in corruption the possibility of reconciliation.[43] The Liberian TRC, despite its legacy for engaging with corporate complicity in human rights violations, ultimately allowed them to avoid legal liability, in exchange for confessions and restoration of stolen goods,[44] but no companies came forth to confess any crime.[45]

Further to that, half of the TRCs that investigated corporate accountability and named corporate malefactors, failed to provide concrete recommendations on business remedies. By way of indication, the Guatemalan Commission for Historical Clarification (Comisión de Esclarecimiento Histórico (CEH)) referred to forty-five different corporate malefactors, but no specific recommendation was given and no prosecution or reparation involved corporate entities.[46] The South African TRC did make recommendations, but quite generic ones, alluding to companies' 'moral obligation' to support the country's reconstruction, including by means of a wealth tax and a one-off charge on their

Ministry of Justice and Human Rights published a vast report on corporate accountability for crimes against humanity. Sandt and Moor, *Peace, Everyone's Business!*, p. 70.

39 See Sections 7.4 and 8.2 of this book.

40 See Section 7.2 of this book.

41 Law No. 6.683 on Amnesty, 28 August 1979.

42 G. Pereira, 'Vaivenes en la responsabilidad legal de actores económicos por crímenes de lesa humanidad en Argentina', Agenda Estado de Derecho, 4 November 2020.

43 T. Michalakea, 'Anticorruption and Transitional Justice: A Distinction Without a Difference' (2022) 22 *Human Rights Law Review* 2.

44 Truth and Reconciliation Commission of Liberia, Final Report, Volume 2, p. 370.

45 M. Kersten, 'Legacies of Injustice in Liberia: Transitional Justice and Economic Crimes', Justice in Conflict, 16 February 2012.

46 Sandt and Moor, *Peace, Everyone's Business!*, p. 94.

revenue.[47] Broad labour and economic reforms, touching upon human rights issues, were proposed in Honduras, Paraguay and Ecuador.[48] The Brazilian TRC differed in that it explicitly recommended the prosecution of companies' violations.[49]

Even when TRCs provided specific recommendations regarding corporate wrongdoers, those were not respected. In East Timor, the CAVR acknowledged that 'business corporations who supported the illegal occupation of Timor-Leste, are obliged to provide reparations to victims'. However, the 2010 draft laws on reparations were never adopted.[50] The Liberian TRC recommended the creation of a Reparations Trust Fund, to be funded by restored funds and corporate taxes, but the fund was never created. Similarly, the recommendations of the Sierra Leonean TRC were finally not implemented.[51]

In terms of justice, the situation has been less promising, despite the legacy of Nuremberg, where forty-two corporate executives were tried for their involvement with the Nazi regime.[52] Different TRC reports across the globe identified 321 economic entities, but only twenty-two of them faced subsequent judicial action.[53] Most of those cases were against individual businesspersons, given that corporate criminal liability provisions are absent at the international level and in many national legal systems. In Argentina, where state policies and civil society movements were supportive, there have been various investigations and trials of company executives. Several trials have also been held in the framework of the Colombian transition, such as the ones against executives of Urapalma and the Córdoba Livestock Fund,[54] but the majority of them were pursued by victims and their families before domestic courts, and only targeted individual businesspersons and not business entities. Even worse, in East Timor, Sierra Leone and Guatemala, no prosecutions of

[47] South African Truth and Reconciliation Commission, Final Report, Volume 5, par. 39, pp. 318–319.

[48] Sandt and Moor, *Peace, Everyone's Business!*, p. 36.

[49] See Part II of this book 'Criminal Justice Mechanisms'.

[50] Amnesty International, 'Timor-Leste: Parliament Must Stop Ignoring Victims' Rights', Public Statement, 3 February 2012, available at www.amnesty.org/fr/wp-content/uploads/2021/06/asa570022012en.pdf.

[51] See Part IV of this book 'Truth Mechanisms'.

[52] W. Kaleck and M. Saage-Maasz, 'Corporate Accountability for Human Rights Violations Amounting to International Crimes: The Status Quo and Its Challenges' (2010) 8 *Journal of International Criminal Justice* 3, 699–724.

[53] Sandt and Moor, *Peace, Everyone's Business!*, p. 35.

[54] Payne et al., *Archimedes' Lever*, p. 261.

business entities took place. The prosecution of an executive of the Oriental Trading Company, recommended by the Liberian TRC, due to his involvement in war crimes and illegal arms deals with the Charles Taylor regime, was held, but outside the transitioning state.[55]

In response to those gaps, victims have often searched justice, on their own initiative, by filing cases in regional fora.[56] In cases where corporations were involved, victims usually resorted to foreign jurisdictions, as was the case with the lawsuit filed in Germany against an executive of the Danzer Group, for complicity in abuses of the Congolese security forces in 2011. The US jurisdiction has been extensively used due to the Alien Tort Claims Act (ATCA).[57] Among the most notable ATCA cases are those brought by Apartheid victims against Ford and IBM for their support and assistance to the South African Apartheid government in committing human rights violations,[58] as well as the lawsuit filed by the Ogoni people of Nigeria against Shell Oil for collaborating with the authoritarian regime's military and police in the murder of political activists.

The most meagre results can be found in the field of reparations, with the relevant examples in which victims were vindicated, being counted on one hand. In Germany, corporate reparations were paid to Jewish victims of slavery and forced labour in Auschwitz, as well as to non-Jewish victims, by IG Farben, Krupp, AEG-Telefunken, Daimler-Benz, Siemens and Rheinmetall.[59] In 1998, a Settlement Fund was established

[55] The trial was held in the Netherlands; see *Public Prosecutor* v. *Guus Kouwenhoven*, Judgment on the appeal in cassation against a judgment of 's-Hertogenbosch Court of Appeal, Case number 17/02109, 20/001906-10, 21 April 2017.

[56] An example of that are the cases filed by Guatemalans to the Inter-American Court of Human Rights. See IACtHR, *Plan de Sánchez* v. *Guatemala*, Judgement, IACHR Series C No. 105, 29 April 2004; IACtHR, *Río Negro Massacres* v. *Guatemala*, Judgement, Series C No. 250, 4 September 2012.

[57] United States Congress, 28 U.S. Code Part IV Chapter 85 § 1350. Under the ATCA, the United States has jurisdiction for civil actions brought by aliens for torts, committed in violation of the law of nations or treaties of the United States. A violation of the law of nations is the one which is contrary to a norm of customary international law. See *Sosa* v. *Alvarez-Machain*, 542 U.S. 692, 734–737 (2004). Even though ATCA is used in tort law cases, it utilizes criminal law standards and has been used against corporations, albeit increasingly being restricted. It is also to be noted that the ATCA litigation has not been successful. See Payne et al., *Archimedes' Lever*, p. 82; M. Kelly, 'Prosecuting Corporations for Genocide Under International Law' (2012) 6 *Harvard Law Policy Review* 339–367.

[58] In *re South African Apartheid Litig.* 617 F. Supp. 2d 228 (S.D.N.Y. 2009).

[59] P. Heinelt, *Financial Compensation for Nazi Forced Labourers* (Wollheim Memorial, 2010), pp. 44–45, available at www.wollheim-memorial.de/files/1066/original/pdf_Peer_Heinelt_Financial_Compensation_for_Nazi_Forced_Labourers.pdf.

by Swiss banks to provide compensation for retaining and concealing assets of Holocaust victims and for laundering Nazi profits of slave labour.[60] Two years after, in 2000, the 'Remembrance, Responsibility, and Future' Foundation was created by law, with funds by both companies and the government, to compensate forced labourers and other victims of abuses by German companies during the Nazi regime. However, in a subsequent circular, the Ministry of Finance clarified that the payments were 'voluntary without any legal obligations' arising thereof.[61] In 2008, as a form of symbolic reparation, Deutsche Bahn organized a memorial exhibition called 'Special Trains to Death'.[62]

In Argentina, despite extensive engagement by TRCs, it was the state that funded reparations programmes, and only few corporations granted compensation, on the basis of civil lawsuits filed against them.[63] In Brazil, Volkswagen and the Federal Public Prosecutor's Office in São Paolo reached an agreement for reparations to be granted to victims only in 2020. The company undertook to compensate the association of Volkswagen worker victims of the dictatorship, known as the Heinrich Hagge Association, and to grant four and a half million reais to the Federal University of São Paolo State to help identify victims buried in mass graves, and conduct research on the role of other companies in such human rights violations during this period.[64] Lastly, in South Africa, a voluntary Business Trust was created upon the recommendations of the TRC,[65] but the money received was used for tourism and educational development, rather than to benefit victims' communities.[66]

[60] U.S. Department of State, Office of the Special Envoy for Holocaust Issues, 'Swiss Bank Settlement', available at www.state.gov/swiss-bank-settlement/.

[61] Sandt and Moor, *Peace, Everyone's Business!*, p. 66.

[62] G. Pereira and L. Payne, 'Corporate Complicity in International Human Rights Violations' (2016) 12 *Annual Review of Law and Social Science* 63–84.

[63] See Section 6.1 of this book.

[64] The compensation to the Heinrich Hagge Association was more than five million euros. T. Ogier, 'In Brazil, It's Reparation Time for Volkswagen', Justiceinfo.net, 6 October 2020. See also the civil lawsuit filed against Volkswagen for its involvement in detaining and abusing twelve unionized workers; Deutsche Welle, 'Brazilian Lawsuit Against VW', 23 September 2015, available at www.dw.com/en/brazil-torture-lawsuit-against-vw/a-18731165.

[65] South Africa Truth and Reconciliation Commission, Final Report, Volume 5, para. 39, pp. 318–319.

[66] C. Sandoval and G. Surfleet, 'Corporations and Redress in Transitional Justice Processes', in S. Michalowski (ed.), *Corporate Accountability in the Context of Transitional Justice* (Routledge, 2013), pp. 101–102.

Against that background of inconsistent and inadequate efforts towards corporate accountability, there was an unexpected – but yet to bear significant fruits – shift in 2006, when the UN General Assembly adopted, without one dissenting vote,[67] the Basic Principles and Guidelines on the Right to a Remedy and Reparation for Victims of Gross Violations of International Human Rights Law and Serious Violations of International Humanitarian Law (Basic Principles).[68] They foresee that states should enable access to justice for victims seeking remedies and reparations. In cases where a person, a legal person, or other entity is found liable for a violation, such a party should provide reparation to the victim.[69]

Regrettably, around twenty years after, efforts can still be considered sketchy. Corporate complicity is still not conceived as an epistemic predicament of transitions, and authors argue that even human rights lawyers are not fully aware of its intricacies.[70] This is mirrored in the marginalization of the topic within transitional justice scholarship. The initial debates on peace versus justice[71] evolved into a series of multifaceted discussions, ultimately culminating to what Dustin Sharp called 'the fourth generation' of transitional justice.[72] The field's scholars and practitioners went into a mode of introspection concerning the nature of transitional justice, its imbalances and blind spots, accompanied by a new emerging consensus that new approaches were needed.[73] Some questioned the effectiveness of transitional justice,[74] while others lamented its

[67] C. Bassiouni, 'International Recognition of Victims' Rights' (2006) 6 *Human Rights Law Review* 203.

[68] UN GA, Basic Principles and Guidelines on the Right to Restitution, Compensation and Rehabilitation for Victims of Gross Violations of Human Rights and Serious Violations of International Humanitarian Law, UN Doc. A/RES/60/147, 16 December 2005 (Basic Principles).

[69] Basic Principles, Principle 15.

[70] Payne et al., *Archimedes' Lever*, p. 12.

[71] For more information on the truth versus justice debate, see M. Aukerman, 'Extraordinary Evil, Ordinary Crimes: A Framework for Understanding Transitional Justice' (2002) 15 *Harvard Human Rights Journal* 39–98. On retributive approaches to transitional justice, see Orentlicher, 'Settling Accounts'; Malamud-Goti, 'Transitional Governments in the Breach', p. 6. On restorative approaches, see J. Sarkin, *Carrots and Sticks: The TRC and the South African Amnesty Process* (Intersentia, 2004).

[72] Sharp, 'Interrogating the Peripheries'. For an overview, see Sarkin and Davi, 'Examining the Criticisms'.

[73] D. Sharp, 'What Would Satisfy Us? Taking Stock of Critical Approaches to Transitional Justice' (2019) 13 *International Journal of Transitional Justice* 3, 570–589, at 589.

[74] By way of indication, Wippman questions the efficacy of truth commissions and justice measures to remedy past violations. See D. Wippman, 'Atrocities, Deterrence, and the

narrow scope, which foregrounded civil and political rights violations,[75] by state and non-state armed actors,[76] while at times marginalizing questions of economic violence and structural injustice.[77] The technocratic character of the field and increased legalization and professionalization were placed under the spotlight as elements that decontextualized and ignored local context.[78] Yet others raised concerns on the field's underlying political connotations that project liberal democracy as the

Limits of International Justice' (1999) 23 *Fordham International Law Journal* 473. Sikkink argues that human rights prosecutions can help diminish human rights violations in the future. K. Sikkink and H. Joon Kim, 'The Justice Cascade: The Origins and Effectiveness of Prosecutions of Human Rights Violations' (2013) 9 *Annual Review of Law and Social Science* 1, 269–285. See also O. N. T. Thoms and J. Ron, 'State-Level Effects of Transitional Justice: What Do We Know?' (2010) 4 *International Journal of Transitional Justice* 329, 332; A. Macdonald, 'From the Ground Up: What Does the Evidence Tell Us about Local Experiences of Transitional Justice?' (2015) 1 *Transitional Justice Review* 3, 4; O. N. T. Thoms, J. Ron and R. Paris, *The Effects of Transitional Justice Mechanisms: A Summary of Empirical Research Findings and Implications for Analysts and Practitioners* (Centre for International Policy Studies, 2008); Sarkin and Davi, 'Examining the Criticisms'; K. Sikkink, *Evidence for Hope: Making Human Rights Work in the 21st Century* (Princeton University Press, 2017), p. 48; Sharp, 'What Would Satisfy Us?'.

75 E. Schmid, *Taking Economic, Social and Cultural Rights Seriously in International Criminal Law* (Cambridge University Press, 2005).

76 L. Moffett, *Reparations and War: Finding Balance in Repairing the Past* (Oxford University Press, 2023).

77 D. Sharp, 'Introduction: Addressing Economic Violence in Times of Transition', in Sharp (ed.), *Justice and Economic Violence in Transition* (Springer, 2013), p. 55; D. Sharp, 'Toward a Positive-Peace Paradigm for Transitional Justice' (2012) 35 *Fordham International Law Journal* 796; Z. Miller, 'Effects of Invisibility: In Search of the "Economic" in Transitional Justice' (2008) 2 *International Journal of Transitional Justice* 3, at 266; L. Arbour, 'Economic and Social Justice for Societies in Transition' (2007) 40 *New York University Journal of International Law and Politics* 1, at 1; J. Cavallaro and S. Albuja, 'The Lost Agenda: Economic Crimes and Truth Commissions in Latin America and Beyond', in K. McEvoy and L. McGregor (eds.), *Transitional Justice from Below, Grassroots Activism and the Struggle for Change* (Hart Publishing, 2008); D. Sharp, 'Economic Violence in the Practice of African Truth Commissions and Beyond', in D. Sharp (ed.), *Justice and Economic Violence in Transition* (Springer, 2013); Carranza, 'Plunder and Pain'; L. Laplante, 'Transitional Justice and Peace Building: Diagnosing and Addressing the Socioeconomic Roots of Violence through a Human Rights Framework' (2008) 2 *International Journal of Transitional Justice* 3, at 350.

78 B. A. Leebaw, 'The Irreconcilable Goals of Transitional Justice' (2008) 30 *Human Rights Quarterly* 1, at 95; R. Nagy, 'Transitional Justice as a Global Project: Critical Reflections' (2008) 29 *Third World Quarterly* 2, at 276; K. McEvoy, 'Beyond Legalism: Towards a Thicker Understanding of Transitional Justice' (2007) 34 *Journal of Law and Society* 4, at 412; R. Shaw, L. Waldorf and P. Hazan (eds.), *Localizing Transitional Justice: Interventions and Priorities After Mass Violence* (Stanford University Press, 2010).

sole goal of societies in transition.[79] This new phase of maturity led to the formulation of alternative imaginaries on what transitional justice should be. Mani situated transitional measures within a broader frame of social justice and redistribution to tackle inequalities.[80] Lambourne, Gready and Robins envisioned a more 'transformative' transitional justice as an emancipatory political project, able to fundamentally reshape prior structures.[81]

Still, engagement with corporate malfeasance and its subsequent inclusion in transitional justice has been marginal and inconsistent. Despite the significance of some efforts,[82] the combination of corporate accountability with transitional justice stands at the periphery of transitional theory, for the moment merely synthesizing disperse experiences. It arguably falls short of a solid and well-founded legal rationale and conceptual integration of the two strands.[83] Relevant contributions are geographically or substantially fragmented. Authors have been analysing diverse local experiences,[84] or different substantive angles of corporate

[79] C. Sriram, 'Justice as Peace? Liberal Peacebuilding and Strategies of Transitional Justice' (2007) 21 *Global Society* 4, at 591; A. Park, 'Peacebuilding, the Rule of Law and the Problem of Culture: Assimilation, Multiculturalism, Deployment' (2010) 4 *Journal of Intervention and Statebuilding* 4, at 415; H. Franzki and M. C. Olarte, 'Understanding the Political Economy of Transitional Justice', in S. Buckley-Zistel et al. (eds.), *Transitional Justice Theories* (Routledge, 2013), pp. 203–204; J. Bowsher, '"Omnus et Singulatim": Establishing the Relationship Between Transitional Justice and Neoliberalism' (2017) 29 *Law and Critique* 5.

[80] R. Mani, *Beyond Retribution: Seeking Justice in the Shadows of War* (Cambridge University Press, 2002), p 17.

[81] Lambourne, 'Transitional Justice and Peacebuilding After Mass Violence'; Gready and Robins, 'From Transitional to Transformative Justice'.

[82] Michalowski (ed.), *Corporate Accountability*; Pietropaoli, *Business, Human Rights and Transitional Justice.*

[83] A notable legal contribution is Aparac's book, which, however, deals only with justice mechanisms and not with truth or reparation. J. Aparac, *Business et droits de l'homme dans les conflits armés* (Larcier, 2021).

[84] For example, there are some contributions focusing on Colombia, Argentina, Nuremberg or South Africa; see S. Michalowski et al., *Entre coacción y colabouración. Verdad judicial, actores económicos y conflicto armado en Colombia* (Centro de Estudios de Derecho, Justicia y Sociedad, Dejusticia, 2018); L. Bilsky, *The Holocaust, Corporations, and the Law: Unfinished Business* (University of Michigan Press, 2017); G. Koska, 'Corporate Accountability in Times of Transition: The Role of Restorative Justice in the South African Truth and Reconciliation Commission' (2016) 4 *Restorative Justice* 1, 41; L. García Martín, *Transitional Justice, Corporate Accountability and Socio-Economic Rights, Lessons from Argentina* (Routledge, 2020); H. Verbitsky and J. P. Bohoslavsky (eds.), *Outstanding Debts to Settle: The Economic Accomplices of the Dictatorship in Argentina* (Cambridge University Press, 2015).

involvement in conflict or transition, such as financial complicity,[85] corporate complicity in natural resources' exploitation during conflict,[86] truth commissions[87] or corporate criminal liability.[88] Last but not least, Payne, Pereira and Bernal-Bermúdez, at their most recent book, offered significant sociological insight and identified obstacles blocking corporate accountability efforts, a topic that we will soon return to.[89]

What seems to be missing from the engagement so far and something which this book aims to contribute is a consolidated and granular account of the prescriptions of different areas of law that stand at the intersection of corporate accountability and transitional justice – that is to say, a more in-depth understanding of the legal technologies and operational limits of access to remedy for victims of corporate human rights abuse during transitions and the corresponding obligations of states as designers of transitional measures.

1.3 Consolidating Absences: The Business and Human Rights Field

The field of business and human rights has been steadily consolidating the last twenty years, as an umbrella field, consisting of different developments in national and international law and praxis addressing business-induced human rights abuses.[90] Determined, but failed,

[85] D. Gray, 'Devilry, Complicity and Greed: Transitional Justice and Odious Debt' (2007) 70 *Law and Contemporary Problems* 137–164; H. Verbitsky and J. P. Bohoslavsky (eds.), *Cuentas Pendientes Los Complices Economicos de La Dictadura* (Siglo Veintiuno Editores, 2013); A. Ramasastry, 'Secrets and Lies? Swiss Banks and International Human Rights' (1998) 31 *Vanderbilt Journal of Transnational Law* 325.

[86] E. E. Harwell and P. Le Billon, *Natural Connections: Linking Transitional Justice and Development Through a Focus on Natural Resources* (International Centre of Transitional Justice, 2009).

[87] P. Wesche, 'Business Actors, Paramilitaries and Transitional Criminal Justice in Colombia' (2019) 13 *International Journal of Transitional Justice* 478; S. Michalowski and J. P. Cardona Claves, 'Responsabilidad corporativa y justicia transicional' (2015) 11 *Anuario de Derechos Humanos* 173–182.

[88] J. Braithwaite and B. Fisse, *Corporations, Crime, and Accountability* (Cambridge University Press, 1993), pp. 141–145; J. Braithwaite, *Crime, Shame, and Reintegration* (Cambridge University Press, 1989), pp. 126–127; J. Kyriakakis, *Corporations, Accountability and International Criminal Law, Industry and Atrocity* (Edward Elgar Publishing, 2021).

[89] Payne et al., *Archimedes' Lever*.

[90] For an overview, see P. Muchlinski, 'The Impact of the UN Guiding Principles on Business Attitudes to Observing Human Rights' (2021) 6 *Business and Human Rights Journal* 2, 212–226.

initiatives during the seventies[91] passed the baton to the OECD Guidelines for Multinational Enterprises,[92] the International Labour Organization Tripartite Declaration of Principles Concerning Multinational Enterprises and Social Policy[93] and ultimately the UN Guiding Principles on Business and Human Rights (UNGPs).[94] While criticized for their parsimony in breaking new ground,[95] the UNGPs contributed to the currently negotiated draft Treaty on Business and Human Rights,[96] as well as to a 'galaxy' of other voluntary initiatives and instruments.[97]

Regrettably, none of the aforementioned documents is relevant for the subject of corporate accountability and transitional justice. The UNGPs and the OECD Guidelines refer to enhanced obligations of corporations to conduct human rights due diligence, when they operate amidst conflict, but do not refer to any state obligation or corporate responsibility during transition.[98] The Draft Treaty does not engage with transitional

91 See the Code of Conduct negotiated by UN Economic and Social Commission, Development and International Economic Cooperation, Transnational Corporations, E/1990/94, 12 June 1990; and the 2003 Norms on the Responsibilities of Transnational Corporations and Other Business Enterprises with Regard to Human Rights. Commission on Human Rights, Norms on the Responsibilities of Transnational Corporations and Other Business Enterprises with Regard to Human Rights, UN Doc. E/CN.4/Sub.2/2003/12/Rev.2, 26 August 2003.

92 They have been revised many times, the last one being in 2011 to align them to the UNGPs. OECD, *OECD Guidelines for Multinational Enterprises* (OECD Publishing, 2011).

93 International Labour Organization, *Tripartite Declaration of Principles Concerning Multinational Enterprises and Social Policy* (Geneva, 1977).

94 UN Human Rights Council, Guiding Principles on Business and Human Rights: Implementing the United Nations 'Protect, Respect and Remedy' Framework, A/HRC/17/31, 21 March 2011 [Guiding Principles].

95 S. Deva, 'Protect, Respect and Remedy? A Critique of the SRSG's Framework for Business and Human Rights', in K. Buhmann, L. Roseberry and M. Morsing (eds.), *Corporate Social and Human Rights Responsibilities: Global Legal and Management Perspectives* (Palgrave, 2011), pp. 108, 121; D. Wallace, *Human Rights and Business* (Brill Nijhoff, 2014), pp. 153–157.

96 UN Human Rights Council, 'Elaboration of an international legally binding instrument on transnational corporations and other Business Enterprises with respect to human rights', UN Doc A/HRC/RES/26/9, 26 June 2014.

97 E. Diggs et al., 'Business and Human Rights as a Galaxy of Norms' (2019) 50 *Georgetown Journal of International Law* 309.

98 G. Paul and J. Schonsteiner, 'Transitional Justice and the UN Guiding Principles on Business and Human Rights', in S. Michalowski (ed.), *Corporate Accountability in the Context of Transitional Justice* (Routledge, 2013), p. 74.

justice and only minimally refers to conflicts.[99] Corporate accountability in transitional contexts gained limited momentum, in 2022, as the UN Working Group on the issue of human rights and transnational corporations and other business enterprises issued a report entitled 'Implementing the Third Pillar: Lessons from Transitional Justice',[100] analysing how states have used transitional justice mechanisms to address business responsibility for their role in conflicts. Naturally, literature from the business and human rights field has only limitedly dealt with transitional justice, as described in Section 1.2. In addition, business and human rights scholarship has examined in isolation relevant angles that fall within the conceptual and legal parameters of transitions, albeit in isolation and not as conceptual part of transitional justice, such as corporate criminal liability for international crimes,[101] or civil liability for human rights abuses.[102]

The reliance on business and human rights instruments has proved to be problematic, especially in violent or repressive contexts. This can be attributed to their voluntary nature, the lack of monitoring mechanisms, the absence of reparation possibility, the absence of non-judicial grievance mechanism attached,[103] as well as the lack of government capacity or political will for their enforcement.[104] Potentially, due to those

[99] The EU proposal on regulating human rights and environmental due diligence, for the moment, seems to ignore the angle of conflict. European Commission, Proposal for a Directive of the European Parliament and of the Council on Corporate Sustainability Due Diligence and Amending Directive 2019/1937, 23.2.2022 COM(2022) 71 2022/0051 (COD), 23 February 2022. See also F. Bold, 'From Rushed Reactions to Proper Preparedness Corporate Due Diligence in Times of Armed Conflict', European Coalition for Corporate Justice, June 2022.

[100] UN Human Rights Council, Implementing the third pillar: lessons from transitional justice guidance by the Working Group Report of the Working Group on the issue of human rights and transnational corporations and other business enterprises, A/HRC/50/40/Add.4, 8 June 2022.

[101] Kyriakakis, 'Corporations, Accountability and International Criminal Law'; J. Stewart, *Corporate War Crimes: Prosecuting Pillage of Natural Resources* (Open Society Foundations, 2010); D. Stoitchkova, *Towards Corporate Liability in International Criminal Law* (Intersentia, 2010).

[102] G. Skinner, *Transnational Corporations and Human Rights: Overcoming Barriers to Judicial Remedy* (Cambridge University Press, 2020); D. Kinley (ed.) *Human Rights and Corporations* (Ashgate Pub., 2009); O. De Schutter (ed.), *Transnational Corporations and Human Rights* (Hart Publications, 2006); A. Clapham, *Human Rights Obligations of Non-State Actors* (Oxford University Press, 2006).

[103] With the exception of the OECD Guidelines and the IFC Performance Standards.

[104] For example, Deva argues that voluntary instruments and initiatives are not adequate in regulating corporate activities. S. Deva, 'The Zero Draft of the Proposed Business and

hurdles, victims, on their own initiative, have pursued litigation in foreign fora only to face further impediments. Most of the relevant cases that reached the court did not lead to an effective judicial remedy due to several barriers, namely the presumption against extraterritoriality,[105] the doctrine of *forum non conveniens*,[106] the lack of corporate criminal liability provisions in some jurisdictions,[107] the structure of the corporate group,[108] the difficulties in gathering evidence,[109] the cost of bringing transnational litigation and the enforcement of remedies.[110] As for criminal liability, in the international plane, apart from the ad hoc tribunals, which have occasionally dealt with the issue,[111] the statute of the International Criminal Court (ICC) excludes corporate actors.

A commonly used forum by victims in the aftermath of violence has been the US Courts pursuant to the ATCA, allowing for civil actions brought by aliens for torts, committed in violation of the law of nations or treaties signed by the United States.[112] Despite the lack of judgments

Human Rights Treaty, Part I: The Beginning of an End?' Business & Human Rights Resource Centre Blog, 14 August 2018.

105 *Kiobel* v. *Royal Dutch Petroleum Co.* 133 S. Ct. 1659, 1665 (2013), p. 1669; *Daimler AG* v. *Bauman*, 571 U.S. 117 (2014); note that this was not the case for all the lawsuits that were combined in this litigation.

106 *Gulf Oil Corp.* v. *Gilbert*, 330 U.S. 501 (1947); *Aguinda* v. *Texaco, Inc.*, 303 F.3d 470 (2d Cir. 2002); *Bhopal* v. *Union Carbide Corporation*, 809 F.2d 195 (2d Cir. 1987); *Canadian Association against Impunity* v. *Anvil Mining Ltd.* Québec Court of Appeal, Canada, Case No 500-09-021701-115, 24 January 2012.

107 Ramasastry and Thompson, *Commerce, Crime and Conflict*.

108 For example, the issue of limited liability of the parent company was illustrated by the position adopted by the courts in the Netherlands after several claims were brought against some businesses in the Shell group. The court ultimately held that under the applicable Nigerian tort law, parent companies have no obligation to prevent their subsidiaries from inflicting damage on others through their business operations. *Oguru and Efanga et al.* v. *Royal Dutch Shell PLC and Shell Petroleum Development Company of Nigeria LTD*, The Hague Court of Appeal, ECLI:NL:GHDHA:2021:132, 29 January 2021, at 3.26–3.34.

109 For example, the *Sinaltrainal et al.* v. *Coca Cola* case was dismissed because the court held that the plaintiffs' evidence did not suffice to allege war crimes under international law. *Sinaltrainal et al.* v. *Coca Cola Company et al.*, No. 06-15851, (US District Court, 2009).

110 N. Roht-Arriaza, 'Reparations Decisions and Dilemmas' (2004) 27 *Hastings International and Comparative Law Review* 166.

111 On 2 October 2014, the Appeals Panel of the Special Tribunal for Lebanon ruled in the New TV S.A.L. case that the Tribunal has jurisdiction over legal persons in contempt proceedings. See Part II of this book, 'Criminal Justice Mechanisms'.

112 See Section 1.2.

favourable to victims,[113] the ATCA litigation was providing an avenue of hope. Lamentably, it also seems to have reached an impasse, after the *Kiobel* and *Jesner* cases. In *Kiobel*, the court held that victims' claims must touch and concern the US territory with sufficient force to displace the presumption against extraterritorial application.[114] In *Jesner*, it was decided that foreign corporations cannot be sued under the ATCA.[115] On top of those theoretical and practical barriers, one has to consider that the business and human rights discourse focuses primarily on the Global North countries. Its contribution to and engagement with transitional justice has been, overall, quite limited.

113 Payne et al., *Archimedes' Lever*, p. 82; Kelly, 'Prosecuting Corporations for Genocide Under International Law'.

114 *Kiobel* v. *Royal Dutch Petroleum Co.*, 133 S. Ct. 1659, 1665 (2013), p. 1669.

115 *Jesner* v. *Arab Bank*, PLC, 584 U.S. (2018).

2

Challenging the Invisible

Who, How and Why

2.1 Re-Charting the *Topoi* of Transitional Justice: The Contours of a New Imaginary

Amidst an unsettled and patchy background, a new imaginary of transitional justice would require corporate wrongdoers to be present in the *topoi* of transitional justice, insofar as they were implicated in prior violence, as a way to ensure the very aims of transition, namely accountability of the perpetrators, remedies for the victims and ultimately reconciliation.[1] Such inclusion is both rooted in and looking up to holistic understandings of transitional justice[2] that defy the mainstream paradigm that narrows itself to the confines of achieving liberal democracy but not full justice for victims.[3] It also challenges rigid conceptions of transitional geography that obscure continuities of violence and exclusion and apply narrowly to state perpetrators and gross civil and political rights violations, putting aside structural violence, social injustice and other kinds of perpetrators, like corporations.[4] Thus, it shifts the focus towards embracing transformative visions, entwining transitional justice within the broader scope of social justice[5] by unearthing the actors that anchored prior violence.

[1] United Nations, Guidance Note of the Secretary-General, United Nations Approach to Transitional Justice, March 2010.

[2] Mani, 'Beyond Retribution', p. 17.

[3] The terms 'mainstream', 'paradigmatic' or dominant transitional justice are borrowed by other scholars to denote the relatively narrower conception of transitional measures, focusing mainly on violations of civil and political rights and respective prosecutions. See Sharp, 'Interrogating the Peripheries'. See also McAuliffe, 'Transitional Justice's Expanding Empire', pp. 32–44.

[4] Nagy, 'Transitional Justice as a Global Project', 275–289.

[5] Lambourne, 'Transitional Justice and Peacebuilding After Mass Violence'; Gready and Robins, 'From Transitional to Transformative Justice'; A. C. Nowak, 'Accommodating

In practice, this entails that the corporate entity, involved in prior violence or repression, should face criminal court proceedings, provide reparations to victims and that truth about their misdeeds becomes part of official accounts, as the transitioning state implements measures to prevent similar abuses from reoccurring. To that end, some might focus on potential direct obligations of corporations to repair, but this might yield no results, especially within transitions. Corporate malefactors are not considered participants in peace negotiations but rather subjects under state authority. Corporate entities certainly have increasing power, both political and economic, but they have not been conceded – yet – the power to institute, operate and implement judicial and quasi-judicial measures, such as those included in transitional processes. Focusing on direct corporate obligations to repair would be a purely theoretical exercise, as the status of corporations in international law is currently ambiguous and national frameworks usually envision corporate wrongs as a mere civil law violation. Also, its implementation would be postponed to a rather distant future, given that there is no hint of remedy obligations in the current state of international law. The draft treaty on business and human rights does not refer to obligations of corporations, and the EU due diligence guidelines are seemingly not including conflict situations. Similarly, and most importantly, it is doubtful whether any corporate human rights (or other) obligations will have any tangible impact. As Baars has powerfully pointed, the corporation is in essence a 'structure of irresponsibility',[6] through the legal technologies of separate legal personality and limited liability. Not much hope can be placed on corporate activities being pivoted on human rights, even under the most stringent legal enforcement, given that at their core, corporations were created in order to accumulate power without responsibility.

In contrast, putting the state and its obligations under the spotlight might have more traction, due to its leading position as the institutional driver of the transitional phase. It is the transitional authorities who are responsible for designing and implementing reparations, justice and truth measures. It is them who should spearhead a process that will ultimately enable reconciliation, peace and democracy, and it is also them that should signal a closure of the anteceding violence or repression

Social Justice Into Transitional Justice Mechanisms: The Case of Northern Uganda' (2011) 1 *International Journal of Rule of Law, Transitional Justice and Human Rights* 107.

[6] G. Baars, *The Corporation, Law and Capitalism* (Brill, 2019), pp. 74–75; D. Whyte (ed.), *Crimes of the Powerful: A Reader* (Open University Press, 2008), p. 104.

and a new beginning. In this new beginning, legality, rule of law and justice play a fundamental role. Otherwise, there would be no difference between the old and new regime. In addition, unlike situations of active conflict and lawlessness, in non-violent yet transitioning times, the state authorities bear the burden of coordinating the necessary mechanisms that allocate responsibility to perpetrators and relief to victims.

By focusing on states, a range of questions arise. Do they have any legal obligation to include corporate malefactors in the design and implementation of transitional measures, as debtors of respective responsibilities? Are there any legal grounds, for the inclusion of corporations in processes of reparations, truth, justice and guarantees of non-repetition? Do those grounds provide for state obligations vis-à-vis corporate malefactors during periods of transition? Is there an obligation of the transitioning state to compel corporate malefactors into providing reparations to their victims? Is there any similar state obligation to prosecute corporate wrongdoers or to involve them in truth processes? Also, is there a state obligation to take measures, in the form of guarantees of non-repetition that involve the regulation of corporate malfeasance? How has relevant practice unfolded and been operationalized, amidst the challenges and windows of opportunity of transitional justice? And finally, how should the legal imaginary be altered to meet the needs of the victims, under a broader goal of transitioning out of conflict and repression?

Re-charting the *topoi* of transitional justice requires exploring those questions outside the confines of the mainstream transitional justice paradigm. First, by investigating the full scale of abuses that led to or took place during the conflict, taking into account the intricacies of corporate involvement in conflict. While businesses certainly commit physical integrity violations, they often fuel conflict or repression via violations of socio-economic rights,[7] as was the case with corruption in Tunisia. Corporate involvement in conflict or repression might take

[7] Under socio-economic rights violations, this book also classifies economic crimes, like corruption. Corruption, for example, has been linked to the enjoyment of human rights. See E. Schmid, 'War Crimes Related to Violations of Economic, Social and Cultural Rights' (2011) 71 *Heidelberg Journal of International Law* 3, 540; R. Duthie, 'Transitional Justice, Development, and Economic Violence', in D. Sharp (ed.), *Justice and Economic Violence in Transition* (Springer, 2013), 1; Carranza, 'Plunder and Pain', 327–328; I. Bantekas, 'Corruption as an International Crime and Crime Against Humanity: An Outline of Supplementary Criminal Justice Policies' (2006) 4 *Journal of International Criminal Justice* 3, 466–484.

different forms, such as direct or indirect action, assistance or participation; provision of services and resources to abusive states; provision of logistical and financial assistance to human rights abusers; and complicity in human rights abuses by virtue of investing in states with poor human rights records.[8] Going beyond that traditional classification, a broad exploration necessitates establishing the threshold of engagement based on the link of the abuse to the conflict and repression, insofar as this abuse went beyond immoral forms of doing business, into breaches of international and national legal frameworks.[9] In other words, the aim should be to grasp and examine corporate entities that were involved in conflict or repression, their abuses fuelling or exacerbating them – in short, when their operations intersected with violence or authoritarianism, by way of complicity to violations carried out in armed conflicts or by authoritarian regimes.[10]

Such '*re-charting*' requires, also, to step beyond the typical inquiries of business and human rights literature. To begin with, this is because transitional justice as an institutional arrangement to address unique contexts of violations offers windows of opportunity into conceptually broader understandings, consonant to its goals and the particular context. For that to take place, one should not confine oneself either to the remedies that states should grant for their own failures, or to their traditional protective obligations (typically examined by the business and human rights field), but rather to engage with the rather niche integration of protective and reparative duties, under the light of various soft law instruments and in analogy to arguments coming from international criminal and international humanitarian law. Next, taking into

[8] Zerk, 'Corporate Liability', p. 16; A. Clapham, 'Extending International Criminal Law Beyond the Individual to Corporations and Armed Opposition Groups' (2008) 6 *Journal of International Criminal Justice* 899.

[9] The book does not investigate different patterns of corporate involvement in conflict. For these types of patterns, see UN Office of the High Commissioner for Human Rights, 'Improving Accountability and Access to Remedy for Victims of Business-Related Human Rights Abuse', A/HRC/32/19, 10 May 2016.

[10] Payne et al. define it as follows: '*When economic actors participate directly or indirectly in the human rights violations carried out in armed conflicts or by authoritarian regimes, their actions constitute corporate complicity in those violations for which victims demand accountability. The use of the term "complicity," means that individual economic actors are not acting on their own. Instead, they form part of the violent structure in which human rights violations occur in authoritarian regimes and armed conflicts. They are directly or indirectly involved in the violations, not as individual citizens, but as economic actors.*' Payne et al., *Archimedes' Lever*, p. 5.

account the various mechanisms used during transitions, corporate accountability in that phase should be navigated beyond judicial processes (that are the main focus of business and human rights literature), into reparations, truth and guarantees of non-repetition. It should, also, synthesize rather than fragment different fields of international and national law, in a multi-layered investigation spanning across different regional and domestic systems – both in the Global North and the Global South, able to grasp their nuances and trace their development.

Accordingly, the specific set of accountability mechanisms that require consideration, and are examined in this book, originates from transitional justice processes, but goes beyond artificial geographical and time zones, to cover measures adopted many years after the transitional moment, or in fora other than the domestic one, insofar as they emerged due to violence or repression. Particularly, the concept of corporate accountability is used to capture the ways of attaching cost to a conduct that might not be limited to legal liability.[11] It includes a range of ways that a company is held to account, by an independent and impartial external party or body. The form of accountability depends on the normative source of the claim and can include strict forms of accountability like criminal, civil and administrative, to milder ones, such as settlements and truth commissions. In addition, a full assessment necessarily goes beyond formal cases that ended in victims' favour, to include references to prejudgment processes and claims,[12] as well as informal restorative and reparative initiatives.[13]

One might wonder why those wrongs should be addressed by transitional justice and not ordinary justice, and even before that, whether transitional justice is even efficient.[14] To the latter, Sikkink's note on the efficacy of human rights can be illuminating, in counter-asking

[11] Bernaz, 'Enhancing Corporate Accountability for Human Rights Violations'; Curtin and Nollkaemper, 'Conceptualizing Accountability', 8; Farah, 'Toward a Multi-Directional Approach'.

[12] W. Felstiner, R. Abel and A. Sarat, 'The Emergence and Transformation of Disputes: Naming, Blaming, Claiming' (1980) 15 *Law and Society Review* 3, 631–654.

[13] G. Dancy et al. 'Behind Bars and Bargains: New Findings on Transitional Justice in Emerging Democracies' (2019) 63 *International Studies Quarterly* 1, 1–12. See also J. Goodstein and K. Butterfield, 'Extending the Horizon of Business Ethics: Restorative Justice and the Aftermath of Unethical Behaviour' (2010) 20 *Business Ethics Quarterly* 3, 453; Braithwaite, *Crime, Shame, and Reintegration*, 126–127.

[14] Wippman, 'Atrocities, Deterrence, and the Limits of International Justice'; Sikkink and Joon Kim, 'The Justice Cascade', pp. 269–285; Thoms and Ron, 'State-Level Effects of Transitional Justice', 332; Macdonald, 'From the Ground Up'; Thoms, Ron and Paris,

'compared to what'.[15] Extrapolating a similar conclusion, it seems that despite the shortcomings of transitional measures, their absence might have more detrimental effects. Even if wanting, transitional justice cannot be classified single-handedly as worthless.[16] Coming back to the former question, which saddles on the debate among scholars on the exceptional or ordinary character of transitional justice,[17] transitional measures are best considered as 'adapt[ed] existing institutional arrangements in countries to address unique contexts of violations'.[18] It is exactly this link of corporate malfeasance with 'unique contexts of violations' due to conflict or repression that dictates their inclusion in transitional justice rather than ordinary justice.[19] Transitional justice, involving an array of possibilities and variants of responsibility and infused with exceptionality, might be better suited to address the intricate ways in which involvement in conflict or repression plays out, to compromise conflicting priorities and offer new and much needed conceptualizations, while at the same time looking towards the future.[20]

Placing the emphasis on law during transitions has been criticized for undermining the political aspect of the transitional experiments.[21] However, the problem is not with law and human rights per se but with

'The Effects of Transitional Justice Mechanisms'; Sarkin and Davi, 'Examining the Criticisms'.

15 Sikkink, *Evidence for Hope*, 48.

16 Sharp, 'What Would Satisfy Us?', 570–589.

17 Bell and Gray vouch for the exceptional character of transitional justice, as opposed to Posner and Vermeule. C. Bell, 'Transitional Justice, Interdisciplinarity and the State of the "Field" or "Non-Field"' (2009) 3 *International Journal of Transitional Justice* 1, 21; D. Gray, 'Extraordinary Justice' (2010) 62 *Alabama Law Review* 1, 55; Teitel, 'Editorial Note'; E. Posner and A. Vermeule, 'Transitional Justice as Ordinary Justice' (2004) 117 *Harvard Law Review* 3, 761–825.

18 Payne et al., *Archimedes' Lever*, p. 17.

19 See Payne et al. arguing that corporate accountability should be included in transitional justice, when prior violence could not have been possible without corporate contributions. Payne et al., *Archimedes' Lever*, p. 14.

20 Wesche, 'Business Actors, Paramilitaries and Transitional Criminal Justice in Colombia', 492.

21 McEvoy, 'Beyond Legalism'. For example, Snyder and Vinjamuri argue that criminal measures hamper forgiveness and reconciliation. J. Snyder and L. Vinjamuri, 'Trials and Errors: Principle and Pragmatism in Strategies of International Justice' (2004) 28 *International Security* 5–44. See more broadly, M. Mutua, 'The Ideology of Human Rights' (1996) 36 *Virginia Journal of International Law* 589, 592; D. Kennedy, 'The International Human Rights Movement: Part of the Problem?' (2002) 15 *Harvard Human Rights Journal*, at 101, 109–110.

the depoliticized way in which 'justice' can operate.[22] Judicial processes should not be viewed, aphoristically, as antithetical to political ones. This is because access to courts empowers individuals, so that they can also form part of the political discourse. Additionally, decisions of human rights and criminal courts respond directly to political and legal institutional failures and do not arise out of a vacuum.[23] Striking a compromise among political and legal accountability will always be a matter of context, but, as Teitel successfully pointed, 'a worked-out political consensus on what is just' cannot be automatically displaced in favour of other agreements, regardless of their political legitimacy.[24]

In addition, focusing on the law has the potential to elucidate persistent epistemic and empirical challenges. This is because, despite high-level paeans to the need for remedies, the precise meaning of the right to remedy corporate-induced violations and its performance during transition times remain contested, poorly understood and thus inapplicable. As Payne, Pereira and Bernal-Bermúdez noted, even human rights lawyers lack the relevant knowledge,[25] knowing that legal meaning will also allow assessment of states' compliance to legal prescriptions, when they decide on reparations for corporate wrongs or when they merely prosecute individual businessmen instead of business entities. In reverse, it will facilitate an evaluation of potential claims of victims against their states to include corporations in the remedy process, as debtors of reparations. A scrupulous legal examination that offers nuances and theoretical backing can in fact enforce victim's claims. An obligation of the state is meaningless without an enforceable right for the addressees and primarily the victims. Considering the ever-increasing institutional and scholarly calls for more victim-centred transitional measures, looking at legal duties of states can serve the goal of putting victims at the epicentre of attention.

2.2 Contesting Marginalization: The Why

There is, however, a lingering question as to the reasons for inserting corporate accountability in transitional topography. Does it suffice that corporations have not been systematically included in TJ theory and

22 Nagy, 'Transitional Justice as a Global Project', 279.
23 Teitel, 'A Right to Accountability?'.
24 Ibid., p. 422.
25 Payne et al., *Archimedes' Lever*, p. 13.

praxis, so far? Amidst a variety of abuses lining to be remedied, what is the value of prioritizing corporate ones? And after all, are not corporate entities needed to reconstruct the transitioning state and financially stabilize it?

Starting from the fundamentals, transitional justice aims to facilitate successful transitions, by achieving accountability for the perpetrator, justice for the victims and reconciliation.[26] As will be elaborated in the sections following, in cases of widespread corporate abuses during conflict or repression, the odds are that those goals can at least partially be delivered, insofar as transitional mechanisms also include corporate perpetrators. Such an engagement responds to calls for visibility of the victims and accountability of the perpetrators. Furthermore, it touches upon the long-appraised discourse on 'root causes of violence'[27] and animates the economic 'phantom' of transitional justice,[28] equipping it to better address the multi-layered complexities of prior injustice. Ultimately, corporate accountability in transitional times can seemingly feed into efforts to make transitional experiments more receptive to domestic politics and predicaments.

2.2.1 *The Goals of Transitional Justice*

2.2.1.1 Identification and Accountability of Perpetrators

Accountability is a fundamental aim of transitional justice, delivered to different extents, by all transitional mechanisms. It enables and underpins the other aims of transitional justice, namely remedy and reconciliation, and is based on the identification of the perpetrator, which, in our case is the corporate entity.[29] The perpetrator's identification is

[26] United Nations, Guidance Note of the Secretary-General, United Nations Approach to Transitional Justice, March 2010.

[27] Mani, 'Beyond Retribution'; Sharp, 'Introduction: Addressing Economic Violence in Times of Transition'.

[28] Miller, 'Effects of Invisibility'.

[29] Various difficulties emerge in respect to the identification of the responsible entity, in view of changes in the corporate structure. This issue has been raised with respect to Aker's acquisition of Lundin company, after its top officials were charged by Swedish prosecutors for war crimes in Sudan. The controversy stems from the fact that the merger purportedly leaves only the assets necessary to satisfy future criminal fines, thus depriving victims from the possibility to seek compensation before civil courts. See Pax for Peace, 'Did Aker BP Breach Key Human Rights Standard When Taking Over Lundin's Oil Business', 30 May 2022, available at https://paxforpeace.nl/news/did-aker-bp-breach-key-human-rights-standard-when-taking-over-lundins-oil-business/. For a relevant analysis

important for allowing remedies and justice to unfold their retributive, deterrent and compensatory functions.[30] It is to be noted that the accountability of the corporate entity is assessed, as opposed to different options that are usually selected in transitional contexts, namely no accountability at all, the state assuming liabilities, and individual businesspersons doing so; for each mechanism, the options being different.

In its criminal manifestation, effective accountability can only be achieved by successfully bringing perpetrators before the courts.[31] Otherwise, what would the purpose of establishing criminal tribunals be? In the absence of any prosecutions, accountability and retribution remain unattained – a straightforward conclusion. When transitioning states pursue criminal action against individual businesspersons, rather than corporate entities, the complexities of the situation intensify, but what remains the same is that accountability as a goal of transitional justice is undermined. This is because, as will be demonstrated in Section 3.1, individual accountability of the businessperson does not adequately respond to corporate crime, which is a distinct form of deviance different from the aggregate of individual crimes, carrying its own blameworthiness.[32] For this reason, it should entail its own accountability, separate from the one of the businesspersons, capable of aligning to the reality of corporate structures[33] and taking into consideration the specific

on the necessity of human rights' due diligence processes and remedies during corporate insolvency proceedings, see E. Vaccari and T. Van Ho, 'Insolvency Law Through the Lens of Human Rights Theories', in E. Ghio et al. (eds.), *Re-Examining Insolvency Law and Theory. Perspectives for the 21st Century* (Edward Elgar Publishing, 2023), pp. 190–215.

[30] It is important to note that remedies and reparations have multiple functions, namely restorative, retributive, remedial and deterrent. D. Shelton, *Remedies in International Human Rights Law* (Oxford University Press, 2005), p. 10.

[31] Orentlicher vests criminal justice mechanisms with retributive goals, while other authors argue for a restorative approach. Orentlicher, 'Settling Accounts'; J. Llewellyn and D. Philpott (eds.), *Restorative Justice, Reconciliation, and Peacebuilding* (Oxford University Press, 2014); L. Laplante and K. Theidon, 'Truth with Consequences: Justice and Reparations in Post-Truth Commission Peru' (2007) 29 *Human Rights Quarterly* 228; T. Phillips and M. Albon, 'When Prosecution Is Not Possible: Alternative Means of Seeking Accountability for War Crimes', in B. Cooper (ed.), *War Crimes: The Legacy of Nuremberg* 244 (TV Books, 1999); L. Mallinder, *Amnesty, Human Rights and Political Transitions: Bridging the Peace and Justice Divide* (Hart, 2008); M. Freeman, *Necessary Evils: Amnesties and the Search for Justice* (Cambridge University Press, 2009); L. Vinjamuri and J. Snyder, 'Law and Politics in Transitional Justice' (2015) 18 *Annual Review of Political Science* 303.

[32] Stoitchkova, 'Towards Corporate Liability in International Criminal Law', p. 23.

[33] A. Ramasastry, 'Corporate Complicity: From Nuremberg to Rangoon – An Examination of Forced Labour Cases and Their Impact on the Liability of Multinational Corporations'

corporate culture that enabled the abuses.[34] Further to that, the prosecution of the individual businessperson, and in general its inclusion in the transitional process, is already taking place, albeit with many difficulties. What is missing is theoretical and practical engagement with business entities, as a whole.[35]

Holding a single individual, or the so-called rotten apple, criminally accountable for the misdeeds of a corporate entity cannot fulfil the typical aims associated with criminal accountability, namely retribution and deterrence. Research shows that retribution and deterrence of corporate criminality are fostered when the entity as such is held to account,[36] especially when it was the specific corporate culture that enabled the commission of abuses.[37] The mere conviction of individual employees does not incorporate adequately the greater harm that a collectivity is able to provoke and there are cases where it is difficult to isolate the specific contribution of separate corporate agents to a crime and apportion liability thereof.[38] Also, individual accountability does not guarantee the non-repetition of the violation on behalf of the corporation, since the latter, as an entity, continues to exist even if an agent is convicted,[39] and its 'criminogenic' culture is unaffected.[40] In reverse, the reputational losses incurred when convicting an entity[41] have widespread

(2002) 20 *Berkeley Journal of International Law* 91; J. Coffee, 'No Soul to Damn: No Body to Kick – An Unscandalized Inquiry Into the Problem of Corporate Punishment' (1980) 79 *Michigan Law Review* 386.

34 B. Fisse and J. Braithwaite, 'The Allocation of Responsibility for Corporate Crime: Individualism, Collectivism and Accountability' (1988) 11 *Sydney Law Review* 468, 494.

35 Thus, this book will only refer to convictions of individual businesspersons, to the extent that they reveal useful insight for the subject at hand.

36 S. Beale, 'A Response to the Critics of Corporate Criminal Liability' (2009) 46 *American Criminal Law Review* 1481, at 1484–1485.

37 Fisse and Braithwaite, 'The Allocation of Responsibility for Corporate Crime', p. 494.

38 Ramasastry, 'From Nuremberg to Rangoon'; Coffee, 'No Soul to Damn'; M. Pieth and R. Ivory, 'Emergence and Convergence: Corporate Criminal Liability Principles in Overview', in M. Pieth and R. Ivory (eds.), *Corporate Criminal Liability: Emergence, Convergence, and Risk* (Springer, 2011), pp. 3, 4–5.

39 Ramasastry writes that similarly a corporate conviction might not deter the individual and that, therefore, a parallel approach to both agent and entity is needed. Ramasastry, 'From Nuremberg to Rangoon'.

40 J. Braithwaite, *Corporate Crime in the Pharmaceutical Industry* (Routledge & Kegan Paul Books, 1984), p. 308.

41 Empirical criminological studies of corporate crime underline the importance of reputational loss rather than the fear of criminal liability as of higher deterrent value. B. Fisse and J. Braithwaite, *The Impact of Publicity on Corporate Offenders* (State University of New York Press, 1983).

deterrent[42] and retributive functions,[43] not only in and of themselves but also because they presumably threaten individual prosecutions.[44] Thus, corporate criminal liability holds higher possibilities of incentivizing the corporation to change its policies, culture and structure than individual prosecutions do.[45]

Similarly, absent corporate accountability and identification of perpetrators, truth mechanisms are deprived of their potential to offer healing to victims, by acknowledging the harm suffered and most importantly the perpetrator of that harm. The acknowledgement that flows from the work of TRCs, although typically associated with restorative justice, serves also retributive purposes in that it illuminates the harm in its totality, primarily in terms of its perpetrator and accordingly directs the prosecutions and reparations that the state will decide to pursue.[46] But if there is no reference to perpetrators, how can acknowledgement even initiate? And, in that case, how can the prospect of non-recurrence materialize? Acknowledging the entity as the perpetrator and not presenting it as the deviance of one single individual bears high symbolic significance that can remove the victim from the position of powerlessness, especially considered against potent corporate actors.

The identification of perpetrators is also significant for reparations, in that it conditions their foundational components to materialize, namely responsibility of the perpetrator, acknowledgement of victims' suffering and remedy of the harm.[47] The exclusion of corporate actors from the

[42] It should, however, be noted that there are scholars arguing that in conflict situations, the deterrent value of punishment is uncertain. M. Drumbl, 'Collective Violence and Individual Punishment: The Criminality of Mass Atrocity' (2005) 99 *Northwestern University Law Review* 539, at 589.

[43] S. Ratner, 'Corporations and Human Rights: A Theory of Legal Responsibility' (2002) 111 *Yale Law Journal* 443, at 478.

[44] H. Ball and L. Friedman, 'The Use of Criminal Sanctions in the Enforcement of Economic Legislation: A Sociological View' (1965) 17 *Stanford Law Review* 197, at 215.

[45] R. Slye, 'Corporations, Veils, and International Criminal Liability' (2008) 33 *Brooklyn Journal of International Law*, at 962, 963.

[46] N. Valji, *Trials and Truth Commissions: Seeking Accountability in the Aftermath of Violence* (Centre for the Study of Violence and Reconciliation, 2004), p. 3; C. Fernandez Torne, *Accountability, a New Framework to Assess the Impact of Truth Commissions* (Institut Català Internacional per la Pau, 2015).

[47] In transitional settings, accountability and responsibility for offences is achieved not only through criminal justice measures but also via the provision of reparations by the respective actor. P. De Greiff, 'Introduction Repairing the Past: Compensation for Victims of Human Rights Violations', in P. De Greiff (ed.), *The Handbook of Reparations* (Oxford University Press, 2006), pp. 494–495; Walker states that

reparations' field undercuts their corrective justice origins, which dictate that the wrongful act should be remedied by those responsible[48] and thereby link accountability of the perpetrator to victims' redress.[49] It is the element of 'the responsible actor paying' that distinguishes reparations as a separate form of accountability, different from charity or philanthropy.[50] If the state or the individual businessperson grants reparations for corporate violations, then the element of responsibility is absent, diluting as a result the other foundational elements, particularly the element of 'acknowledgement of victims suffering', as this fulfils its symbolic value only when the harm is presented in its totality, primarily by including the perpetrator.[51] The benefits of ordering the perpetrator to provide reparations for the recovery of the victim are recognized and corroborated by Article 75 of the ICC Statute that foresees reparation by the convicted person.

'[r]eparations are made when those who are responsible for repair of a wrong intentionally give appropriate goods to victims of wrongs in a specific act (or process) that expresses acknowledgement of the wrong, responsibility for the wrong or its repair, and the intent of rendering just treatment to victims in virtue of wrongful treatment'. M. Walker, *What Is Reparative Justice?* (Marquette University Press, 2010), p. 19. See also L. Moffett, 'Beyond Attribution: Responsibility of Armed Non-State Actors for Reparations in Northern Ireland, Colombia and Uganda' in N. Gal-Or, C. Ryngaert and M. Noortmann (eds.), *Responsibilities of the Non-State Actor in Armed Conflict and the Market Place: Theoretical Considerations and Empirical Findings* (Brill, 2015). For an opposite view that in transitional justice reparations are given by the wrongdoer already and this should change, see L. May, 'Reparations, Restitution, and Transitional Justice', in L. May and A. Forcehimes (eds.), *Morality, Jus Post Bellum, and International Law* (Cambridge University, 2012), pp. 32–48. See also Public Submission on reparations issues, Situation in the Democratic Republic of the Congo in the ICC, *Prosecutor* v. *Thomas Lubanga Dyilo*, International Centre for Transitional Justice, ICC-01/04-01/06, 10 May 2012; and ICC, *Prosecutor* v. *Thomas Lubanga Dyilo*, Situation en République démocratique du Congo, Decision establishing the principles and procedures to be applied to reparations, ICC-01/04-01/06-2904, 7 August 2012, par. 179.

48 The law of remedies was initially applied to acts between individuals. Shelton, *Remedies in International Human Rights Law*, pp. 9, 65.

49 The underlying notions of reparations can be traced back to the Aristotelian concept of corrective justice, which promotes restitution to the *status quo antes* as a way to correct the injustice that the defendant inflicted on the plaintiff and re-establish equality. L. Moffett, 'Transitional Justice and Reparations: Remedying the Past?', in D. Jacobs et al. (eds.), *Research Handbook on Transitional Justice* (Edward Elgar Publishing, 2017).

50 Ibid.

51 Public Submission on reparations issues, Situation in the Democratic Republic of the Congo in the Case of the *Prosecutor* v. *Thomas Lubanga Dyilo*, International Centre for Transitional Justice, ICC-01/04-01/06, 10 May 2012.

Overall, the accountability of the corporate entity is crucial for the practical impact that it has on retribution, deterrence and non-repetition. Without a tangible cost to their malfeasance, why should perpetrators halt their abuses? In fact, research suggests at least a correlation between corporate impunity and the recurrence of corporate crimes. By way of indication, Bayer has committed crimes during the Holocaust and in Guatemala; BNP Baripas during the Holocaust, Iraq and the Rwandan civil war; Chase Bank during the Holocaust and the South African Apartheid; Commerce Bank during the Holocaust and South Africa; and Ford in the Holocaust, the Argentinean and Brazilian military dictatorships.[52]

In addition, corporate accountability is fundamental for the compensatory function of remedies, served by all different measures. In terms of criminal measures, the criminal liability of the entity should be juxtaposed to that of mere individual businesspersons. There is no need of analysis of cases where neither the entity nor the individuals involved are held liable, as this completely eliminates compensatory functions. Convictions of businessmen for the harm inflicted by corporate structures will most probably not serve its compensatory function, as illustrated by the case against oil palm businessmen of Urapalma SA in Northern Colombia, for forcible displacement of Afro-Colombian communities, in collaboration with paramilitary squads. The court convicted the individuals, but its orders for compensation to each forced displacement victim were ultimately left unfulfilled, even though they were minimal.[53] Contrary to convictions of individual businesspersons, decisions against corporate entities order satisfactory amounts of compensation. For example, in the context of ATCA litigation, three Cuban plaintiffs in the *Licea* v. *Curacao Drydock Co* case were awarded $80 million in damages,[54] whereas even in the cases that settled, plaintiffs are usually awarded large sums of compensation.[55]

[52] Payne et al., *Archimedes' Lever*, p. 118.

[53] The court awarded £5,300 to each victim of forced displacement. Sandt and Moor, *Peace, Everyone's Business!*, pp. 146–149.

[54] *Licea* v. *Curacao Drydock Co*, 584 F. Supp. 2d 1355 (S.D.Fla. 2008).

[55] Among the cases that the amounts are known, 6 million dollars settlement was reached in *Siderman de Blake* v. *Republic of Argentina*, 965 F.2d 699 (9th Cir. 1992); 175,000 dollars per plaintiff in the *Abdullahi* v. *Pfizer, Inc.* 562 F.3d 163 (2d Cir. 2009); 15.5 million dollars settlement in *Wiwa* v. *Shell*, 2009 U.S. App. LEXIS 11873 (2d Cir.) (3 June 2009); In *Doe I* v. *The Gap, Inc.* No. CV-01-0031, 2001 WL 1842389 (26 November 2001), *Does I* v. *The Gap, Inc.* No. CV-01-0031, 2002 WL 1000068 plaintiffs were awarded attorneys'

In the field of reparations, it might be the state that assumes the costs of corporate violations. But in that case, the compensatory function will most probably weaken,[56] given that transitional states usually struggle to secure the costs of reparation measures, and lack of funding is a common reason for ignoring TRC recommendations.[57] As was witnessed in South Africa, the state might assume responsibility to repair without in reality having the capacity and willingness to do so. This endangers a second victimization of the victims, who, in the case of South Africa, resorted to foreign courts to vindicate their rights. TRCs' contribution to compensation is more limited due to their recommendatory character, but along with bringing corporate accountability to public attention, they can also order the recovery of illegally obtained corporate assets and create synergies with other reparative processes.

2.2.1.2 Putting an End to Victims' Neglect

Authors contend that transitional processes are usually top-down measures,[58] run by elites,[59] along with international organizations and global civil society, carrying specific norms, practices and preconceived ideas on how the process should unfold. More often than not, the process is pioneered by a group of transitional justice professionals or otherwise 'experts',[60] with wanting knowledge of the local context and even more wanting idea of whether and how they should take it into account. Both experts and institutions seem 'occasionally externally imposed'.[61] The language used is primarily one of law,[62] with criminal justice and

fees of 3,150,000 dollars and expenses in the amount of 4,687,651,97 dollars. One of the lowest awards was granted in re *XE Services Alien Tort Litig.* 665 F. Supp. 2d 569 (E.D. Va. 2009), where plaintiffs received maximum 30,000 dollars for claims for injuries, and 100,000 dollars in case of death.

56 De Greiff states that one of the principles that should govern reparations is munificence. For an analysis of those principles, see De Greiff, 'Introduction'.

57 Segovia mentions that the effectiveness of reparation programs is correlated to the transitional country's socio-economic development. A. Segovia, 'Financing Reparations Programs: Reflections from International Experience', in P. De Greiff (ed.), *The Handbook of Reparations* (Oxford University Press, 2006).

58 R. Paris, 'Saving Liberal Peacebuilding' (2010) 36 *Review of International Studies* 337, at 363.

59 Sarkin and Davi, 'Examining the Criticisms', 16.

60 S. Lefranc and F. Vairel, 'The Emergence of Transitional Justice as a Professional International Practice', in L. Israël and G. Mouralis (eds.), *Dealing with Wars and Dictatorships: Legal Concepts and Categories in Action* (Springer, 2013).

61 Sriram, 'Justice as Peace?' 591.

62 McEvoy, 'Beyond Legalism'.

tribunals leading the way. The toolbox or 'post-conflict checklist'[63] is complemented by a range of typically replicating measures, including security sector reform, trials, demobilization, disarmament, and reintegration programs and truth commissions.

This approach has been strongly criticized for disregarding victims, marginalizing local perceptions of justice and contextual factors.[64] Victims of corporate abuses are one such category, whose will has been disregarded. Victims of civil and political rights' violations, by business entities or with their significant contribution, often remain marginalized. But the victims' gap in the field of economic and social rights is even wider. Such victims are twice as invisible; not only have they suffered economic and social rights violations, which usually remain out of purview for transitional mechanisms, but they are also victims of corporate perpetrators.

Research on victims' needs in relation to corporate accountability during transition is absent, due to institutional and epistemological deficiencies, which silence them further and deny the possibility to express and vindicate their needs.[65] Assumptions can be drawn by analogy, from the literature on victims of ordinary corporate crime, which contends their common need to 'face the corporation'.[66] The same conclusion can be drawn by the many cases that have been brought before domestic and foreign fora by victims of corporate human rights violations, during conflict or repression, demonstrating their increasing quest for corporate accountability.[67] The expressed requests of the

[63] D. Sharp, 'Beyond the Post-Conflict Checklist: Linking Peacebuilding and Transitional Justice Through the Lens of Critique' (2013) 14 *Chicago Journal of International Law* 1.

[64] T. Longman et al. 'Connecting Justice to Human Experience: Attitudes Toward Accountability and Reconciliation in Rwanda', in E. Stover and H. Weinstein (eds.), *My Neighbor, My Enemy: Justice and Community in the Aftermath of Mass Atrocity* (Cambridge University Press, 2004), p. 206; S. Engle Marry, 'Transnational Human Rights and Local Activism: Mapping the Middle' (2006) 108 *American Anthropologist* 1, at 38–51; M. Mutua, 'Never Again: Questioning the Yugoslav and Rwanda Tribunals' (1997) 11 *Temple International & Comparative Law Journal*, at 167, 168.

[65] This has been named as an 'epistemic injustice' for victims of corporate crimes. It creates a vicious cycle, whereby the victims themselves fail to perceive victimization in an appropriate manner. G. Forti, 'Introduction', in G. Forti et al. (eds.), *Victims and Corporations. Legal Challenges and Empirical Findings* (Wolters Kluwer, 2018).

[66] The evidence proves that if there is one need in common, it is that 'all victims want to talk to the corporation'. I. Aertsen, 'Restorative Justice for Victims of Corporate Violence', in G. Forti et al. (eds.), *Victims and Corporations. Legal Challenges and Empirical Findings* (Wolters Kluwer, 2018), p. 239.

[67] See, for example, the many cases referenced by Zerk, 'Corporate Liability'.

victims, such as to collaborate with the investigators or participate in trials, posit that their underlying need is justice and compensation, as well as ascertainment of the truth.[68] More often than not, this is done at great financial and personal cost, and amidst an intimidating ambience. Against a background of top-down transitional justice measures, local business and human rights practice can be considered as resistance to the hegemonic paradigm and can enhance a bottom-up perspective.

This should be assessed against the privileged position that usually corporations find themselves during transitions, primarily those whose operations intersected with the conflict. Businesses have, most probably, more financial and legal resources than the victims, and they can use public relations and lobbying campaigns to their favour. According to Payne, Pereira and Bernal-Bermúdez, corporate 'veto power' is a weighty factor that has hindered advancements in the field of business and human rights, both internationally and domestically.[69] Instead of following the limiting narration of the mainstream transitional paradigm, an honest and emancipatory transitional praxis would need to follow a multitude of approaches, taking notice of different forms of violence and victimhood, including corporate one.

In what concerns victims, the identification of the corporate perpetrator serves the restorative aims of transitional justice and focuses the attention to their needs, fostering the potential for a successful outcome of the transition.[70] For criminal measures, those restorative aims materialize, when the perpetrator is brought to court and victims receive acknowledgement and disclosure for the harm suffered,[71] including by confronting the perpetrator. The validation of their experiences that

[68] G. Forti et al., *Victims and Corporations. Legal Challenges and Empirical Findings* (Wolters Kluwer, 2018), pp. 196, 239.

[69] On corporate veto power, see Payne et al., *Archimedes' Lever*, pp. 113–161.

[70] K. McEvoy and L. McGregor, 'Transitional Justice from Below: An Agenda for Research, Policy and Praxis', in K. McEvoy and L. McGregor (eds.), *Transitional Justice from Below, Grassroots Activism and the Struggle for Change* (Hart Publishing, 2008); J. Méndez, 'Victims as Protagonists in Transitional Justice' (2016) 10 *International Journal of Transitional Justice* 1, at 1–5; S. Robins, 'Failing Victims? The Limits of Transitional Justice in Addressing the Needs of Victims of Violations' (2017) *Human Rights and International Legal Discourse*, at 41–58.

[71] Hayner analyses the importance of disclosure for victims of torture. P. Hayner, 'The Contribution of Truth Commissions', in B. Duner (ed.), *An End to Torture: Strategies for its Eradication* (Zed Books, 1998).

comes with criminal trials offers healing for the victims,[72] who see justice delivered[73] and feel that their cause is being heard by states, society and the international community. The same flows from the recognition coming from truth commissions,[74] contingent upon the recognition of the violation in its totality, including by identifying the corporate entity as the perpetrator, and its crime as distinct from an individual's crime.[75] In reverse, impunity of the perpetrator perpetuates the cycle of trauma of the victim, functioning as a second injury,[76] which hinders the healing process.[77] By absolving corporations from their responsibility, truth commissions can bring about what Bakiner termed 'negative judicial impact by promoting impunity'.[78]

Reparations, from their part, are formed by three components: responsibility, acknowledgement of victims' suffering and remedy. As explained previously, the identification of the perpetrator is a synonym to satisfying the first component, but, in what concerns victims' needs, it brings about acknowledgement and can, thus, lead to their recovery.[79] Reparations are also important for the public message that they convey.[80] When the public narrative created following corporate violations does not recognize that the harm suffered was the result of specific violations originating

[72] N. Kritz, 'Coming to Terms with Atrocities' (1998) 59 *Law and Contemporary Problems* 4. However, opposite position is held by A. Boraine, 'Introduction', in A. Boraine et al. (eds.), *Dealing with the Past: Truth and Reconciliation in South Africa* (Institute for a Democratic Alternative for South Africa, 1994).

[73] H. Kury et al., 'The Position of the Victim in Criminal Procedure – Results of a German Study' (1994) 3 *International Review of Victimology* 1–2; J. O'Connell, 'Gambling with the Psyche: Does Prosecuting Human Rights Violators Console Their Victims' (2005) 46 *Harvard International Law Journal* 295.

[74] D. Kaminer et al., 'The Truth and Reconciliation Commission in South Africa: Relation to Psychiatric Status and Forgiveness Among Survivors of Human Rights Abuses' (2001) 178 *British Journal of Psychiatry* 4, at 373–377.

[75] For an analysis of that argument, see Section 3.1 of this book.

[76] The Redress Trust, *Torture Survivors' Perceptions of Reparation Preliminary Survey* (REDRESS, 2001), p. 27.

[77] S. Robins, 'An Assessment of the Needs of Families of the Missing in Nepal' (2009) *SSRN Electronic Journal* 1, at 27.

[78] O. Bakiner, 'Truth Commission Impact: An Assessment of How Commissions Influence Politics and Society' (2014) 8 *The International Journal of Transitional Justice* 6–30.

[79] L. Bosire, 'Overpromised, Under-Delivered: Transitional Justice in Sub-Saharan Africa' (2006) 3 *International Center for Transitional Justice* 5; N. Sveass and N. J. Lavik, 'Psychological Aspects of Human Rights Violations: The Importance of Justice and Reconciliation' (2000) 69 *Nordic Journal of International Law* 43, at 35–52.

[80] B. Hamber, 'Repairing the Irreparable: Dealing with the Double-Binds of Making Reparations for Crimes of the Past' (2000) 5 *Ethnicity & Health* 3–4, at 215–226.

from specifically named corporate actors, then victims are deprived of acknowledgement, disclosure and social restatement.[81] While not in relation to corporate actors, the importance of acknowledgement and the public message conveyed was evident in Argentina, where the Madres de Plaza de Mayo rejected reparations, because the narrative accompanying them was not recognizing the extent of their children's harm.[82]

Overall, by including corporate entities in the transitional processes as duty holders, victims of their abuses can overcome the so-called victims' gap, particularly present in cases of corporate abuses.[83] The lack of recognition of the violations in their totality, or the invisibility of victims of corporate abuses, contravenes fundamental principles of transitional justice,[84] but also risks disaggregating victims,[85] to the detriment of corporate ones. That disaggregation perpetuates social marginalization and exclusion.[86] The victim can be fully dignified and reinstated at their public standing only when society recognizes the harm suffered, but most importantly the entity that induced that harm. In that way, recognition can restore also the lost trust across society, strengthen social ties and ethical values, enable the empowerment and reintegration of the victim[87]

[81] See also B. Hamber, 'The Dilemmas of Reparations: In Search of a Process-Driven Approach', in K. De Feyter, S. Parmnetier, M. Bossuyt and P. Lemmens (eds.), *Out of the Ashes: Reparation for Victims of Gross and Systematic Human Rights Violations* (Intersentia, 2005), p. 141.

[82] Instead, it was linked to a narrative which was legitimizing state's use of torture and disappearances of their children and grandchildren. C. Moon, 'Who'll Pay Reparations on My Soul? Compensation, Social Control and Social Suffering' (2012) 21 *Social and Legal Studies* 2, at 194.

[83] J. Nolan, 'The Corporate Responsibility to Respect Human Rights: Soft Law or Not Law?', in Bilchitz and S. Deva (eds.), *Human Rights Obligations of Business: Beyond the Corporate Responsibility to Respect* (Cambridge University Press, 2013); A. Ramasastry, 'Corporate Social Responsibility Versus Business and Human Rights: Bridging the Gap between Responsibility and Accountability' (2015) 14 *Journal of Human Rights* 2; N. Bernaz, *Business and Human Rights History, Law and Policy – Bridging the Accountability Gap* (Routledge, 2017).

[84] On transitional justice's potential to make victims visible, see P. De Greiff, 'The Future of the Past: Reflections on the Present State and Prospects of Transitional Justice' (2020) 14 *International Journal of Transitional Justice* 2, 251–259.

[85] P. De Greiff, 'Justice and Reparations', in P. De Greiff, *The Handbook of Reparations* (Oxford University Press, 2006).

[86] C. Sandoval (ed.), *Adverse Consequences of Reparations Briefing Paper No. 6* (2011) Essex Transitional Justice Network.

[87] Especially if there is victim participation in the procedures, Roht-Arriaza, 'Reparations Decisions and Dilemmas', 160; The Redress Trust, 'Torture Survivors' Perceptions', p. 23.

and contribute to conditions of security and justice that allow social relations.[88]

2.2.2 Plato's Cave and the Shadows of Partial (In)justice: Root Causes and Structures

As per Professor Ruggie, the business-related human rights violations during periods of violence are the most egregious of them all.[89] However, similarly to Plato's cave allegory, the shadows of those abuses are not visible in the wall of transitional justice. One is left to wonder how transitional measures can achieve their goals of justice, accountability, even reconciliation, if a large segment of really serious abuses remain unaccounted for. In Iraq, for example, Blackwater committed war crimes against civilians.[90] Can those crimes remain unaccounted for and a transition to a peaceful society still be achieved? When corporate entities provide fundamental assistance to other actors, like the military or the police to directly commit abuses,[91] is not their contribution a serious crime to be addressed? In an opposite scenario, when business involvement in conflict is disregarded, then suffering is passed on to the 'new' state,[92] with lasting effects on perceptions of justice and reconciliation, like in South Africa, with the long-lasting debate over corporate reparations.[93]

Rather, corporate accountability forming part of the transitional topography would indicate a fuller understanding of prior injustice at all its different levels and manifestations, than the one usually acknowledged by dominant paradigms. This is, first, evidenced in the field of civil and political rights violations, but also in the less mainstream field of

[88] Referring to benefits of reparations in general, Speech of Sergio Garcia Ramirez, president of the Inter-American Court of Human Rights, see C. Grossman et al., 'Reparations in the Inter-American System: A Comparative Approach Conference' (2007) 56 *American University Law Review* 6, 1375–1468.

[89] UN HRC, A/HRC/17/32, at 1.

[90] Zerk, 'Corporate Liability'.

[91] Fafo, *Business and International Crimes. Assessing the Liability of Business Entities for Grave Violations of International Law* (Fafo, 2005), p. 29.

[92] Nagy pointed that in South Africa, where certain crimes were presented merely as context, then suffering is passed on to the 'new' state. Nagy, 'Transitional Justice as a Global Project', 276; M. Mamdani, 'Reconciliation Without Justice' (1996) 46 *South African Review of Books* 3–5.

[93] R. Nagy, 'Post-Apartheid Justice: Can Cosmopolitanism and Nation-Nuilding Be Reconciled?' (2006) 40 *Law and Society Review* 3, 623–652.

economic and social rights. Civil and political rights are undisputedly at the core of transitional measures. However, without corporate accountability, even this undeniable focus can devolve into a sort of cherry picking. To put words into context, in Colombia, the Special Jurisdiction for Peace (Jurisdicción Especial para la Paz or JEP), established after the 2016 Peace Accords, opened investigations for illegally perpetrated deaths in Cesar, Antioquia, Catatumbo, Casanare, Meta and Huila, but only for those deaths that were committed by agents of the state,[94] given that it did not have the mandate to prosecute corporate entities. While acknowledging the complexity and the constraints of such an endeavour, the record of injustice being registered is in some instances incomplete considering the well-known corporate involvement in killings in those regions?[95]

But addressing physical violence or civil and political rights' violations is not the only condition for a society to move forward. As UN High Commissioner for Human Rights, Louise Arbour has noted, 'transitional justice is poised to make the gigantic leap that would allow justice, in its full sense', including violations of economic and social rights.[96] For the moment, transitional experiences, despite their heterogeneity, 'consistently focus on civil and political rights, especially forced disappearances, execution, and torture'.[97] But to address those violations in their full spectrum, more often than not, corporate accountability is

[94] For an account of the cases, see Colombia Peace, 'What Macro-Cases Has Colombia's Special Jurisdiction for Peace (JEP) Opened?', 13 March 2020, available at https://colombiapeace.org/what-macro-cases-has-colombias-special-jurisdiction-for-peace-jep-opened/.

[95] Dejusticia, *Cuentas Clara, El papel de la Comision de la Verdad en la develacion de la responsabilidad de empresas en el conflict armado colombiano* (Dejusticia, 2018). Although the TRC investigated corporate involvement, justice measures did not focus on them. See also Part IV of this book on 'Truth Mechanisms' describing the Colombian Truth Commission Report's revelations on links between the paramilitaries and the business sector, as well as Part II on Criminal Justice Mechanisms, Section 4.3.2 on Colombia's JEP.

[96] L. Arbour, 'Economic and Social Justice for Societies in Transition', speech at New York University of Law School, 2006, p. 2, available at https://nyujilp.org/wp-content/uploads/2013/02/40.1-Arbour.pdf. Note also that in 2010, the UN Secretary-General released a Guidance Note on the United Nations Approach to Transitional Justice calling on the UN to 'ensure transitional justice processes and mechanisms take account of the root causes of conflict and repressive rule, and address violations of all rights, including economic, social and cultural rights'. Guidance Note of the UN Secretary General, United Nations Approach to Transitional Justice (March 2010).

[97] Cavallaro and Albuja, 'The Lost Agenda'.

necessary.[98] This is, first, because private actors often commit them. Ignoring the perpetrator and usually the violation altogether leads to a lesser image of prior injustice and to marginalization of its victims. Going back to the Colombian example, the Special Jurisdiction for Peace investigated, among others, forced displacement of Afro-Colombian communities. Again, that was examined to the extent that it was carried out by members of the armed forces or paramilitary groups, despite evidence submitted regarding the involvement of corporate entities, such as Prodeco, Drummond Ltd., Chiquita Brands International Inc. and Dole Food Company.[99]

Further to that, socio-economic rights' violations by corporate malefactors, often serve as the basis of subsequent infringements of civil and political rights, by both state and corporate actors. For example, the transitional measures in Tunisia, Côte d'Ivoire and Gambia, while attempted to redress violations of economic rights, including corruption, disregarded the corporate supply of said corruption, despite the fact that it greatly enabled repression and propelled further violations of civil and political rights.[100] In reverse, acknowledging corporate malpractice can expose the collaboration between economic actors and political elites that violently reproduced socio-economic inequalities,[101] and engaged in diverse violations. It seems to be the 'missing piece of the puzzle, to pursue the full spectrum of justice and remedy for authoritarian and civil conflict periods'.[102] Absent corporate accountability, transitional justice may risk consolidating artificial zones of impunity,[103] and recognizing an

[98] Schmid, *Taking Economic, Social and Cultural Rights Seriously*, p. 306; Pietropaoli, *Business, Human Rights and Transitional Justice*, p. 15.

[99] Civil society organization Corporate Accountability Lab has submitted the relevant evidence to the JEP, to serve the latter's ongoing investigations into human rights abuses. See Corporate Accountability Lab, 'Submission of Report on Role of Economic Actors in the Armed Conflict to the Special Jurisdiction for Peace in Colombia', 25 October 2022, available at https://corpaccountabilitylab.org/calblog/2022/11/9/cal-provides-more-evidence-of-corporate-complicity-in-armed-conflict-to-colombian-peace-tribunal.

[100] Michalakea, 'Anticorruption and Transitional Justice'; P. Maguchu, *Transitional Justice and Socio-Economic Rights in Zimbabwe* (T.M.C. Asser Press, 2019), at 71–76; R. Carranza, *Truth, Accountability, and Asset Recovery: How Transitional Justice Can Fight Corruption* (International Centre for Transitional Justice, 2020), p. 2.

[101] Payne et al., *Archimedes' Lever*, p. 12; Bowsher, 'Omnus et Singulatim'.

[102] J. P. Bohoslavsky and V. Opgenhaffen, 'The Past and Present of Corporate Complicity: Financing the Argentinean Dictatorship' (2010) 23 *Harvard Human Rights Journal*, 157–203, at 160.

[103] Nagy, 'Transitional Justice as a Global Project', 276.

incomplete picture of prior injustice, which could potentially endanger its own goals.

At a second level, corporate accountability can address the increasing calls for transitional justice to tackle root causes of violence and repression. It is alleged that a narrative about conflict or repression that superficially stays only on the dominant band of violations of civil and political rights and international humanitarian law, while absolutely necessary, does not suffice to ensure sustainable and long-lasting peace and democracy.[104] If the conditions that precipitated violence or repression in the first place are left intact, the chances of a successful transition become meagre and conflicts reignite within, on average, five years of their cessation.[105]

Corporate misconduct can be easily understood as a 'root cause', if one sees the war economies that flourish alongside and sustain violence and repression.[106] In 2001, the UN Panel of Experts on the illegal exploitation of natural resources and other forms of wealth of the Democratic Republic of the Congo powerfully described the involvement of private entities in illegal natural resource exploitation that fuelled and exacerbated conflict in several regions of the Congo.[107] Pillage, corruption and illegal natural resource exploitation are varieties of socio-economic violence[108] that enable the maintenance of systems of abuse.[109] Not engaging with those aspects of conflict or repression risks the credibility and viability of the whole transitional experiment.[110]

In his theory on the bureaucratic authoritarian state, Guillermo O' Donnell illustrated how corporate malfeasance is deeply enmeshed with

104 Sharp, 'What Would Satisfy Us?'; Miller, 'Effects of Invisibility', 268; T. Addison, 'The Political Economy of the Transition from Authoritarianism', in P. De Greiff and R. Duthie (eds.), *Transitional Justice and Development. Making Connections* (Social Science Research Council, 2009).

105 P. Collier and A. Hoeffler, 'On the Incidence of Civil War in Africa' (2002) 46 *Journal of Conflict Resolution* 13, 17; A. Suhrke and I. Samset, 'What's in a Figure? Estimating Recurrence of Civil War' (2007) 14 *International Peacekeeping* 195.

106 See, for example, the illegal exploitation of natural resources that took place in Liberia and was recorded at the Truth and Reconciliation Commission's report. Truth and Reconciliation Commission of Liberia, Final Report, Volume I, 156. See also Carranza, 'Plunder and Pain', 310.

107 UN Panel of Experts on the DRC, S/2001/357.

108 Sharp, 'Introduction: Addressing Economic Violence in Times of Transition'.

109 Schmid, *Taking Economic, Social and Cultural Rights Seriously*.

110 R. Mani, 'Dilemmas of Expanding Transitional Justice, or Forging the Nexus between Transitional Justice and Development' (2008) 2 *International Journal of Transitional Justice* 253, 235.

authoritarian regimes. He established that the collusion of businesses and repressive states was inherent in the growth of authoritarian regimes in Latin America.[111] By developing hand in hand with violence or repression, corporate wrongdoers are able to accumulate wealth and power at every turn of the conflict. As such, corporate abuse during those periods becomes a structural issue. Corporations' position at the top of a presumed hierarchy of power gives them the opportunity to shape and maintain the structural dynamics that repress some and create socio-economic inequalities;[112] in short to contribute to and profit from structural violence.[113] Further, their structurally hierarchical position enables corporate malefactors to consolidate their power in the aftermath of conflict[114] and influence the design of transitional measures. In Tunisia, for example, the business association, UTICA, even received the Nobel Peace Prize for facilitating the National Dialogue. Under those circumstances, it is only natural that corporations elude accountability.

Vasuki Nesiah has attributed the crisis of legitimacy and effectiveness of the field of transitional justice, to persisting hierarchies of power and structures of impunity.[115] This is corroborated, again by the Tunisian example, where corruption was much heralded, albeit the fight against it did not include corporate perpetrators. Presently, almost a decade after the revolution, corporate accomplices remain active in the country and most importantly corruption does not seem to have receded, resulting in recurring local anticorruption movements.[116] Placing corporate

[111] G. O'Donnell, *Modernization and Bureaucratic-Authoritarianism: Studies in South American politics* (Institute of International Studies, University of California, 1973).

[112] Bowsher, 'Omnus et Singulatim'.

[113] According to Galtung, structural violence not only harms people but also prevents them from realizing their potential as political and social subjects. See J. Galtung, 'Violence, Peace, and Peace Research' (1969) 6 *Journal of Peace Research* 3, 167–191.

[114] For example, in Tunisia, it has been demonstrated that economic elites, by purchasing Ben Ali's confiscated assets, accumulated more wealth as a result of the anticorruption efforts and accessed key political positions. See M. Oubenal, 'The Political Economy of Business Elites in Tunisia: Actors, Strategies and Identities' (2018) Working Papers 1273, Economic Research Forum, at 10.

[115] V. Nesiah, 'Transitional Justice Practice: Looking Back, Moving Forward', Scoping Study, Impunity Watch Research Report (May 2016), p. 5.

[116] J. Murphy and O. Brindusa Albu, 'The Politics of Transnational Accountability Policies and the (Re)construction of Corruption: The Case of Tunisia, Transparency International and The World Bank' (2018) 42 *Accounting Forum* 1, 32–46. See also the persistence of those movements, the Petrofac and Kamour Movements created in 2016 and 2017, demanding the respective companies to provide employment and contribute to development but also accountability for corruption. International Centre

accountability in the transitional discourse would be a call to dismantle those dynamics. In turn, deconstructing structural patterns of exclusion and inequality opens the possibility of reconstructing socio-economic equality, in line with social justice prerogatives.[117] It ensures non-repetition to a larger extent, but also comes closer to transitional justice, as a transformative project,[118] aiming to 'distribute' rather than solely to 'retribute'.[119]

At a last and broader level, corporate accountability in transitional justice conveys a public message of commitment to justice,[120] fight against impunity,[121] and respect of rule of law.[122] It signifies that no person or entity is above the law and that the transitioning society has truly turned the page to injustices and impunity. Leaving corporate

for Transitional Justice, 'Work, Freedom, Dignity for Young Tunisians, the Revolution Was Not Only About Accountability for Corruption' (2020) 15; Yom et al. 'Youth Politics in the Middle East and North Africa' (2019) *Project on Middle East Political Science* 16.

117 Andrieu noted that transitional justice should come closer to social justice. K. Andrieu, 'Civilizing Peacebuilding: Transitional Justice, Civil Society and the Liberal Paradigm' (2010) 41 *Security Dialogue* 537, at 544; P. Arthur, 'How "Transitions" Reshaped Human Rights: A Conceptual History of Transitional Justice' (2009) 31 *Human Rights Quarterly* 321, at 325–326, 359.

118 Gready and Robins, 'From Transitional to Transformative Justice'; Lambourne, 'Transitional Justice and Peacebuilding After Mass Violence'.

119 Mani, 'Beyond Retribution'.

120 For reparations as commitment to justice, see transcript of speech of Darren Hutchinson at Grossman et al., 'Reparations in the Inter-American System', at 1405.

121 Impunity has been defined as 'the impossibility, *de jure* or *de facto*, of bringing the perpetrators of human rights violations to account – whether in criminal, civil, administrative or disciplinary proceedings and to making reparations to their victims'. See UN Commission on Human Rights, Question of Impunity of Perpetrators of Human Rights Violations (Civil and Political Rights), revised final report prepared by Mr Joinet pursuant to Sub-Commission decision 1996/119, E/CN.4/Sub.2/1997/20/Rev.1, 2 October 1997 ('Joinet report'), par. 17–25. See also A. Eide, 'Preventing Impunity for the Violator and Ensuring Remedies for the Victim' (2000) 69 *Nordic Journal of International Law*, at 1–10.

122 Corporate accountability contributes to rule of law by satisfying victims' legitimate expectations for remedies and rehabilitating the legal order that was violated. Regarding victims' expectations, see M. Walker, *Moral Repair* (Cambridge University Press, 2006). For the links of rule of law and transitional justice, see UN Security Council, Report of the Secretary-General, the rule of law and transitional justice in conflict and post-conflict societies, UN Doc. S/2004/616, 23 August 2004. However, a stream of scholarship considers rule of law and transitional justice as two distinct fields that can obstruct each other. P. Mcauliffe, *Transitional Justice and Rule of Law Reconstruction: A Contentious Relationship* (Routledge, 2013), p. 3. For an overview of the content of rule of law, see J. Maravall and A. Przeworski (eds.), *Democracy and the Rule of Law* 68 (Cambridge University Press, 2003), p. 4.

malefactors – or any malefactor – unpunished would signal that some groups have more privileges than others and that injustice persists despite the presumed end of violence or repression. It is only reasonable that such impunity does not communicate a credible message for the establishment of the rule of law, access to justice and, ultimately, the change that transitions themselves are supposed to embody.

The contribution of corporate accountability, during transition, to justice and rule of law outweighs the often-cited discourse of its drawbacks on development and investments, during those periods.[123] The hidden assumption is that corporations will divest if some of them are held to account. Several TRCs and respective transitional governments preferred to abstain from corporate accountability and replace it with developmental measures on behalf of corporations. The underlying tension locates justice, truth and reparations as dynamics which are opposing future development and economic prosperity. However, considering justice as an opposing dynamic to development and prosperity can be easily refuted by a reverse argument. Namely, there is no evidence to suggest that lack of accountability leads to increased investments. By way of illustration, the minimum accountability imposed on corporations (in the form of wealth tax, insofar as that can correspond to a degree of accountability) by the South African Truth and Reconciliation Commission has not benefited the economic indicators of the country. In fact, South Africa continues to be riddled with poverty and inequality. Besides, one can wonder how allowing harmful investments to continue with impunity into conflict zones can result in development and peace stabilization. No transitional state can reasonably argue that impunity aligns with its transition goals or that it can attract responsible investors while allowing grave violations to go unaddressed. In reverse, a state complying with rule of law and pursuing justice against any malefactor seems better equipped to ensure the stability required for investments.

[123] The criminalization of corporate identity has been blamed of causing larger economic disruptions in transitional societies than the criminal prosecution of individuals. Speech of Jaime Malamud Goti during the Conference on 'Transnational Business and International Criminal Law', held at Humboldt University Berlin, 15–16 May 2009 in J. Geneuss et al. 'Core Crimes Inc.: Panel Discussion Reports from the Conference' (2010) 8 *Journal of International Criminal Justice*, 3, at 957–977; De Greiff and R. Duthie (eds.), *Transitional Justice and Development. Making Connections* (Social Science Research Council, 2009); L. Laplante, 'On the Indivisibility of Rights: Truth Commissions, Reparations, and the Right to Development' (2007) 10 *Yale Human Rights and Development Law Journal*, at 141–177.

2.2.3 Replacing Liberal Confines with Spaces of Contestation

Scholars have noted that transitional policies, despite being presented as a politically neutral 'toolbox',[124] or an 'a-historical and pre-political' means to an end,[125] are in fact imbued with politics. Several foundational elements of the dominant transitional paradigm have been attributed to liberal thinking. Dustin Sharp linked the historic marginalization of economic violence to a transition paradigm borrowed by Western liberal democracy.[126] Franzki, Olarte and Bowsher heavily criticized transitional measures for their decontextualizing impacts that insulate economic issues from contestation.[127] Others pointed to the depoliticizing effects of the prevailing legal tools[128] and the professionalization of the field.[129] At last, Andrieu has noted that what comes to be designed and implemented is 'an extensive part of the liberal peace "package"'.[130]

The marginalization of corporate accountability seems to rubber-stamp that tendency. This is primarily because it contributes to the exclusion of the economic sphere from contestation, which according to Marks is a propensity of liberalism.[131] Furthermore, it presents an

[124] Park, 'Peacebuilding, the Rule of Law and the Problem of Culture', 415; Lundy and McGovern note that wide political questions are presented as politically and economically neutral by transitional justice initiatives. P. Lundy and M. McGovern, 'Whose Justice? Rethinking Transitional Justice from the Bottom Up' (2008) 35 *Journal of Law and Society* 265, at 273, 276–277; Leebaw, 'The Irreconcilable Goals of Transitional Justice', at 95; Robins examines how wide-ranging political questions are shoehorned into narrow legal questions; see Robins, 'Transitional Justice as an Elite Discourse: Human Rights Practice: Where the Global Meets the Local in Post-Conflict Nepal' (2012) 44 *Critical Asian Studies* 1, 3.

[125] O. J. Sending, 'Why Peacebuilders Fail to Secure Ownership and Be Sensitive to Context' (2009) 8 Norwegian Institute of International Affairs: Department of Security and Conflict Management, Security in Practice Working Paper No. 755.

[126] Sharp, 'Introduction: Addressing Economic Violence in Times of Transition', pp. 796–801.

[127] Franzki and Olarte, 'Understanding the Political Economy'; Bowsher, 'Omnus et Singulatim', 83–106.

[128] B. Rajagopal, 'Invoking the Rule of Law in Post-Conflict Rebuilding: A Critical Examination' (2008) 49 *William & Mary Law Review* 1347, at 1349.

[129] See Wilson who discussed the creation of the 'global reconciliation industry'. R. A. Wilson, 'Anthropological Studies of National Reconciliation' (2003) 3 *Anthropological Theory* 3, at 367–387. In a similar vein, Bell et al. examined the emphasis of transitional language to 'professionalism', 'efficiency' and 'modernisation' – C. Bell et al., 'Justice Discourses in Transition' (2004) 13 *Social and Legal Studies* 3, at 305–328.

[130] Andrieu, 'Civilizing Peacebuilding', 541.

[131] S. Marks, *The Riddle of All Constitutions. International Law, Democracy and the Critique of Ideology* (Oxford University Press, 2000), pp. 70–74.

erroneous account of corporate malfeasance as a mere aberration of an otherwise healthy system. Absent corporate accountability, the responsibility lies solely with state or armed non-state actors, which is right, but not solely. To rub salt to the wound, corporate entities usually oscillate between victims' and saviour status and the prevailing discourse is about the need for business investments to facilitate economic recovery.[132] This signals an approach that matches liberal thinking in that it considers the state as the entity to be disciplined, as the source of all wrongs and the private sector as an immaculate actor that should only be concerned with operating in the newly established open economy, oblivious about its past malfeasance.

By way of illustration, the Tunisian transitional example, while in principle pioneering, as it included anti-corruption within the transitional scope, yet focused exclusively on Ben Ali and his entourage's corrupt activities and left out of its purview the supply dimension of corruption. Thus, corruption was mainly ascribed to state domination in the economic and political realm. Simultaneously, the private sector, which was active during the previous regime, was considered beyond blame, as if it was coerced into corrupt practices due to its relation and alleged subordination to the state.[133]

However, the liberal underpinnings of transitional justice stymies in-depth debate and political negotiation of the tensions, trade-offs and dilemmas of the transitional period,[134] with repercussions for the aims of transitional justice and the society at large. It presents the structures of power and impunity, mentioned in Section 2.2.2, as irrelevant to transitional politics.[135] To make things worse, liberal measures have potentially destabilizing effects, given that the accompanying economic measures entail rapid liberalization that post-violence countries cannot support.[136]

Against this background, corporate accountability can contribute to expanding the horizon of possibilities for people to choose from, without their options being channelled into a specific set of premeditated

[132] Indicatively, see the example of Tunisia in Section 2.2.2.

[133] Michalakea, 'Anticorruption and Transitional Justice'.

[134] Leebaw, 'The Irreconcilable Goals of Transitional Justice'.

[135] With reference to the same in South Africa, see E. Christodoulidis and S. Veitch, 'Reconciliation as Surrender: Configurations of Responsibility and Memory', in F. Du Bois and A. Pedain (eds.), *Justice and Reconciliation in Post-Apartheid South Africa* (Cambridge University Press, 2009), pp. 9, 18.

[136] R. Paris, 'International Peacebuilding and the "Mission Civilisatrice"' (2002) 28 *Review of International Studies* 637, 639.

assumptions.[137] Given that post-conflict policies can be instrumental in bolstering future power arrangements,[138] allowing them to be contested gives the possibility of choice and negotiation over specific measures, but also over their accompanying political and economic parameters. Opening up the discussion on economic choices and policies associated with corporate accountability or impunity has also the potential to neutralize the liberal confines of mainstream transitional justice,[139] envisioning market-oriented economies and western liberal democracies as the irreplaceable key to peace.[140] Through it, it is left for the people to decide among different possibilities and varieties of remedy to be questioned, in line with local priorities and needs. After all, by allowing options to be contested and negotiated, it has the potential of rendering transitional justice into an emancipatory project.

2.3 Contesting Silos: The How

2.3.1 The Separate Significance of International and National Legal Frameworks

Transitional justice is primarily a domestic political exercise, despite tendencies to portray it as an international bureaucratic experiment.[141] National laws and processes present the necessary flexibility and reflexivity to calibrate expectations and externally imposed prescriptions,[142] bringing them closer to the particularities of each context, on which justice in transition depends. Domestic laws and practice are instrumental in balancing interests and domestic priorities and taking context into account.[143] This is best illustrated in the context of amnesties, where local needs to advance peace, in many cases, overrode international law standards.

137 Nagy, 'Transitional Justice as a Global Project', 276.

138 Sriram, 'Justice as Peace?', 587–588.

139 Lundy and McGovern, 'Whose Justice?'; R. Paris, 'Peacebuilding and the Limits of Liberal Internationalism' (1997) 22 *International Security*, at 54, 56.

140 Ibid.; Sriram, 'Justice as Peace?'.

141 Franzki and Olarte, 'Understanding the Political Economy'.

142 Sriram, 'Justice as Peace?', p. 591.

143 Shaw, Waldorf and Hazan, 'Localizing Transitional Justice', 3; A. Hinton, 'Introduction: Toward an Anthropology of Transitional Justice', in A. Hinton (ed.), *Transitional Justice: Global Mechanisms and Local Realities After Genocide and Mass Violence* (Rutgers University Press, 2010), pp. 2 and 17; R. Falk, 'Reparations, International Law, and Global Justice: A New Frontier', in P. De Greiff, *The Handbook of Reparations* (Oxford University Press, 2006), p. 491.

National laws and processes are also fundamental in the field of business and human rights, for their contribution of grassroots elements. Levit qualifies the field as a bottom-up law-making process that departs from 'on the ground experiences' that coalesce and 'gel as law'.[144] Furthermore, national developments in business and human rights, especially during transitional periods, have fostered a doctrinal convergence across jurisdictions, which influences not only other domestic jurisdictions[145] but also general international law.[146]

Perhaps counterintuitively for critical transitional justice scholarship,[147] and while paying due respects to the significance of national law, the integration of corporate accountability with transitional justice benefits also from international law. To begin with, scholars argue that remedies for corporate abuses have been hindered due to the absence of international law, with national processes oftentimes unable to grapple with multinational actors, let alone in fragile contexts of transitions.[148] While acknowledging the absence of a relevant international treaty, international law is, still, seemingly better equipped to tackle the power asymmetries among host states and big corporate actors, as it is insulated

[144] J. Levit, 'Bottom-Up International Law-Making: Reflections on the New Haven School of International Law' (2007) 32 *Yale Journal of International Law*, at 409.

[145] Especially for the jurisprudence of the US courts in ATCA cases, see D. Scheffer, 'The Impact of the War Crimes Tribunals on Corporate Liability for Atrocity Crimes Under US Law', in C. Walker-Said and J. Kelly (eds.), *Corporate Social Responsibility? Human Rights in the New Global Economy* (University of Chicago Press, 2015), pp. 163–164.

[146] For example, some authors seem to consider corporate accountability as a rule of customary law. See Clapham, 'Extending International Criminal Law'; Ramasastry, 'From Nuremberg to Rangoon', 91; V. Nerlich, 'Core Crimes and Transnational Business Corporations' (2010) 8 *Journal of International Criminal Justice* 3, 895–908. Some authors seem to accept that there is an emerging trend and an 'expanding web of liability for business entities implicated in international crimes'. See A. Ramasastry et al., 'Translating Unocal: The Expanding Web of Liability for Business Entities Implicated in International Crimes' (2009) 40 *George Washington International Law Review*, at 856; J. Kyriakakis, 'Prosecuting Corporations for International Crimes', in L. May and Z. Hoskins (eds.), *International Criminal Law and Philosophy* (Cambridge University Press, 2010), p. 342. It is to be noted that the Appeals Panel of the STL held that national laws are 'sufficiently similar' to signify a trend, and 'indeed, corporate liability for serious harms is a feature of most of the world's legal systems and therefore qualifies as a general principle of law'. See STL, Case Against New TV S.A.L. and Karma Mohamed Tahsin al Khayat, STL-14-05/PT/AP/ARI26.1, Decision on Interlocutory Appeal Concerning Personal Jurisdiction in Contempt Proceedings, 2 October 2014, par. 51 and 67.

[147] For the discourse on the marginalization of local input, see Engle Marry, 'Transnational Human Rights and Local Activism'; Mutua, 'Never Again'.

[148] Deva, 'The Zero Draft of the Proposed Business and Human Rights Treaty'.

from the political manipulations that often ravage domestic judicial procedures. Also, international law remains important as a check and balance, because its remoteness from domestic considerations can limit political agendas about transitional measures,[149] and particularly the competing priorities of economic development.[150]

Most importantly, research shows that for corporate impunity to be overcome during transition, a set and clear international framework is required.[151] Clarity over the applicable international law can lend legitimacy to transitional states that try to enforce those rules, particularly in transitional times.[152] This is because it enables four – crucial for the integration of corporate accountability and transitional justice – factors to become operative. Those factors include strong civil society demand,[153] strong domestic judicial leadership and institutional innovators, strong international pressure and weak veto players. That framework will empower international pressure and civil society demand and will underpin local institutional innovators' work. Diverse approaches on corporate accountability in transition, developed globally or regionally, like the one adopted by the Malabo Protocol, can potentially infuse new understandings and inspire developments.[154] Further, civil society and

[149] Falk, 'Reparations, International Law and Global Justice'. See also R. Camilo and Q. Villamarin, 'Shredded Colombia's Special Jurisdiction for Peace in an Increasingly Illiberal Context of Misinformation and Backlash' (2022) 20 *Journal of International Criminal Justice* 1–28.

[150] This is without ignoring international law's own political underpinnings; see Franzki and Olarte, 'Understanding the Political Economy'.

[151] Payne et al., *Archimedes' Lever*. Note also that Merwe and Lykes link the corporate accountability deficit during transitions to the lack of a clear regulatory framework. See H. Merwe and M. Brinton Lykes, 'Transitional Justice and Corporate Accountability: Introducing New Players and New Theoretical Challenges' (2022) *International Journal of Transitional Justice* 16, at 291–297.

[152] Kyriakakis, 'Corporations, Accountability and International Criminal Law', p. 238.

[153] D. Becker, 'Civil Society and Transitional Justice: Possibilities, Patterns and Prospects' (2003) 2 *Journal of Human Rights* 3, at 297–313. See also Sikkink, who emphasizes key individual activists and their linkages to domestic and international human rights organizations as advancing the accountability demand. K. Sikkink, 'The Age of Accountability: The Global Rise of Individual Criminal Accountability', in F. Lessa and L. Payne (eds.), *Amnesty in the Age of Human Rights Accountability: Comparative and International Perspectives* (Cambridge University Press, 2012). See also F. Lessa et al., 'Overcoming Impunity: Pathways to Accountability in Latin America' (2014) 8 *International Journal of Transitional Justice* 1, at 75–98.

[154] T. Michalakea, 'Article 46C of the Malabo Protocol: A Contextually Tailored Approach to Corporate Criminal Liability and Its Contours' (2018) 7 *International Human Rights Law Review* 2, 225–248.

institutional innovators, with and through this clear international framework at hand, can amplify local demands and pressure for change.[155] It should not be forgotten that even outside the field of corporate accountability, international law has triggered developments in essential issues of transitions, such as amnesties,[156] or rules establishing criminal jurisdiction,[157] and through its interpretation and development by regional human rights systems, it has arguably led different governments to establish massive reparations programmes.[158]

2.3.2 *Beyond Silos: Blending Insights from National and International Law*

Yet neither the international nor the national seem to suffice, in isolation, when one attempts to legally engage with corporate accountability during transitional justice. Recognizing the limitations of both national and international law[159] and avoiding romanticizing them,[160] Payne, Pereira and Bernal-Bermúdez found that the right tool to advance corporate accountability, during transition, is the combination of domestic laws

155 M. Keck and K. Sikkink, *Activists Beyond Borders: Advocacy Networks in International Politics* (Cornell University Press, 1998).

156 Domestic civil society in Latin America advocated against amnesties for torture, disappearance and crimes against humanity. But the Inter-American Court, using international humanitarian and human rights law, put pressure on states of the region to refrain from amnesties for those type of crimes. In addition, Engstrom analyses the regional impact of cases before the IACtHR; see P. Engstrom, 'The Inter-American Human Rights System: Notable Achievements and Enduring Challenges', in C. Lennox (ed.), *Contemporary Challenges for Understanding and Securing Human Rights in Practise* (University of London Press, 2015).

157 The absence of set international rules on universal jurisdiction halted the efforts of the Spanish judiciary to hold Pinochet accountable for violations that took place during the Chilean dictatorship.

158 Argentinean courts carried out 'truth trials' in the aftermath of Carmen Aguiar de Lapacó case, which was brought before the Inter-American Commission on Human Rights. De Greiff, 'Introduction', fn. 23; E. Lutz and K. Sikkink, The Justice Cascade: The Evolution and Impact of Foreign Human Rights Trials in Latin America' (2001) 2 *Chicago Journal of International Law* 1, at 1–34; K. Sikkink, *The Justice Cascade: How Human Rights Prosecutions Are Changing World Politics* (Norton, 2011).

159 For example, in Argentina, domestic criminal law was not sufficient. See Sandt and Moor, *Peace, Everyone's Business!*, p. 73.

160 O. Richmond, 'The Romanticisation of the Local: Welfare, Culture, and Peacebuilding' (2012) 44 *The International Spectator* 149, 160, 166–168; T. Donais, 'Empowerment or Imposition? Dilemmas of Local Ownership in Post-Conflict Peacebuilding Processes' (2009) 34 *Peace and Change* 3, at p. 21.

with international norms.[161] Even if actors like civil society or victims are weak, in terms of influence, the right tool in their hands, what they called 'the blending of the national and the international', can reverse their weakness, lift the 'Archimedes' lever' and ultimately ensure accountability for the perpetrators and relief for the victims.[162]

Evidence from across various transitional experiments corroborate the methodological advances brought by that blending of laws. One successful manifestation was the Techint case in Argentina. Enrique Roberto Ingegnieros, an employee of steel company Techint S.A., which had a pivotal role in the Argentine dictatorship, disappeared from the factory during the military dictatorship in Argentina.[163] His daughter, Maria Gimena Ingegnieros, asked compensation from the company before civil courts, for its failure to ensure the safety of its employee. The legal basis drew from an innovative combination of Argentinean labour law, regarding workers safety, along with international human rights law regarding disappearance as a crime against humanity, with the international segment being used to overcome the domestic statute of limitations. Ingegnieros' claim was accepted by the Appeals Court in 2015, and Techint was ordered to pay compensation. The appeals judge referred to the UN Draft Norms, as well as to the Nuremberg trials, and used a hybrid form of domestic and international legal tools.[164] Likewise, the Vildoza case in Argentina, regarding theft of property from victims of Argentinean repression, used an innovative blending of domestic money laundering legislation with international human rights law.[165] In Colombia, the case of Urapalma, against palm oil company's executives, for the forced displacement of Afro-Colombian communities, along with paramilitary forces in the late 1990s, relied heavily on international human rights law not only in substance but also in terms of expanding

[161] Payne et al., *Archimedes' Lever*; Sandt and Moor, *Peace, Everyone's Business!*, p. 32.

[162] For further information on the different forms of interaction between international and national systems, see Part II (Section 4.2) and Part III (Section 6.1). See also Payne et al., *Archimedes' Lever*, chapter 5 'Justice from Below', p. 214 *et seq.*

[163] V. Paulon, 'Acindar and Techint: Extreme Militarization of Labour Relations', in H. Verbitsky and J. P. Bohoslavsky, *Outstanding Debts to Settle: The Economic Accomplices of the Dictatorship in Argentina* (Cambridge University Press, 2015), pp. 174–185.

[164] Regrettably, the case was reversed by the Supreme Court, allegedly due to the less favourable environment created by the election of the Macri government. Payne et al., *Archimedes' Lever*, p. 237.

[165] Note that the case was dropped, as the unit dedicated to investigating it was dismantled. See Sandt and Moor, *Peace, Everyone's Business!*, p. 52.

prosecutors' investigations that have corporate accountability implications. Rather than only pursuing violations of paramilitary groups, in 2016 Colombia's national prosecutor's office determined that financing paramilitary forces constitutes a crime against humanity, and thus it is not subject to statutes of limitations.[166]

Beyond legal instruments, blending is also about the fora being resorted to. Cases against corporations arising out of transitional states have extensively used litigation in foreign states, oftentimes multi-forum litigation or regional bodies. This has stimulated impact, within domestic jurisdictions and has expedited progress and constructive dialogue among different approaches to the issue. In the case of Urapalma, the Inter-American Commission ordered the Colombian state to investigate the role of palm oil companies in the human rights violations of displaced Afro-Colombian communities.[167] The trial of Ford Motor Company executives in Argentina included both domestic and foreign trials before the US courts. The same took place in the Chiquita Brands case in Colombia. Both sparked domestic developments, analysed in Section 2.3. The ATCA cases are particularly important in that respect. Even if not ending successfully, yet they incorporate not only the foreign element but also the element of international law, given that the ATCA grants to US federal courts original jurisdiction over any civil action brought by a foreign national for a tort in violation of international law.[168] The Special Tribunal for Lebanon, in the New TV S.A.L., used a mix of national and international law,[169] interpreted 'persons' to include corporations and convicted two companies rather than the individuals representing the companies.[170] Lastly, the Malabo Protocol is also expected to contribute to domestic advancements in terms of corporate accountability.[171]

In terms of truth commissions, the TRCs that most seminally engaged with corporate accountability drew their mandate from a combination of national and international law. The Truth and Reconciliation

[166] See Part II of this book on 'Criminal Justice Mechanisms'.

[167] Ibid.

[168] See (n 72) of Section 1.2.

[169] Statute of the Special Tribunal for Lebanon, Article 2. See also M. Kelly, *Prosecuting Corporations for Genocide* (Oxford University Press, 2016), p. 69.

[170] STL, Case Against New TV S.A.L. and Karma Mohamed Tahsin al Khayat, STL-14-05/PT/AP/ARI26.1, Decision on Interlocutory Appeal Concerning Personal Jurisdiction in Contempt Proceedings, 2 October 2014, par. 51 and 67.

[171] Michalakea, 'Article 46C of the Malabo Protocol'.

Commission of South Africa drew heavily in its mandate and its interpretation from international law.[172] The TRCs of Sierra Leone and Liberia performed their mandate on the basis of national and international law.[173] Lastly, and maybe more innovatively, the Commission on Reception, Truth and Reconciliation (CAVR) of East Timor recommended reparations to be granted by the business sector. The Commission founded this obligation on national law but also on the principle of international responsibility recognized in the international customary law of torts.[174]

2.4 Concluding Remarks

Corporate involvement has been a persistent parameter in situations of violence across the world, evidenced also at the recent conflicts in the Palestinian territories and Ukraine. Widespread evidence registers the often-vital role of business actors in triggering, exacerbating and sustaining violence, through various means, and complex networks of complicity with other actors. Despite the abundance of relevant awareness and knowledge, the accountability of corporations is inconsistently being dealt with, during periods of transition. Efforts seeking to hold corporations accountable and deliver justice to victims of their abuses have been limited and lack significant success. Few scattered efforts of Truth Commissions exist, but they have not usually culminated in tangible outcomes. The criminal cases that have been filed targeted mainly corporate officials and not the corporate entities as such, whereas in the field of reparations, relevant instances are extremely scant. Equally, scholarly contributions on the integration of corporate accountability and transitional justice are scarce, a gap that is further compounded by similar challenges in the field of business and human rights (BHR), making justice elusive, even more so in transitional settings.

[172] Truth and Reconciliation Commission of South Africa Report, Volume One, indicatively, pp. 64, 66, 70.

[173] The Truth and Reconciliation Commission Act of Sierra Leone, 2000, Part III, Article 6 (1); Act to Establish the Truth and Reconciliation Commission of Liberia of 12 May 2005, Article IV, Section 4, enacted by the National Transitional Legislative Assembly, 12 May 2005.

[174] *Chega!*. Report of the Commission for Reception, Truth and Reconciliation in Timor-Leste (CAVR), 2005 ['CAVR Report'], part 11: 'Recommendations', under 12.10 Financing. However, note that finally the Commission did not name specific companies to grant those reparations, but rather the business sector as a whole.

In that context, a new imaginary of transitional justice would require corporate wrongdoers to be present in its topography, insofar as they were implicated in prior violence, as a necessary precondition for achieving transitional goals, namely accountability of the perpetrators, remedies for the victims and reconciliation. By excluding accountability of some actors – for the purposes of this book, corporations – accountability itself as a core aim of transitional justice is undermined, which, in turn, affects its other objectives. The identification of perpetrators is a crucial aspect of remedies, allowing them to perform their functions, whether they relate to acknowledgement, retribution, deterrence or compensation. In addition, holding corporations accountable would better align to victims' demands, who increasingly seek justice against them, as evidenced by multiple cases filed at their initiative. Centring on victims' vindications would bestow transitional justice with a more bottom-up character, addressing the dominance of top-down approaches, while also strengthening the victims' position vis-à-vis powerful corporate actors.

The integration of corporate accountability in transitional mechanisms would also achieve a more complete understanding of the parameters of prior injustice. Unlike mainstream transitional justice which limits itself in civil and political rights violations of state and armed non-state actors, the proposed integration would highlight the wrongdoings of corporate entities, typically associated with a broader range of violations, including socio-economic ones. Even more important, such an endeavour would bring to the fore the so-called root causes that led, exacerbated or maintained violence and repression, in which corporate malfeasance is often an intricate part. Lastly, corporate accountability within transitions could unlock discussions on associated socio-economic issues, related to power, marginalization and impunity. This could spark a more pluralistic debate on future political and economic choices, expanding the range of possibilities for people to choose from, but also stimulate discussions on the nature of transitional justice itself, as a project underpinned by liberal principles.

In more operational terms, the proposed integration would be better anchored in transitional states and their respective obligations, instead of companies' potential direct obligations. This is because states hold a leading position, as the institutional drivers of transitions and their obligations align to the rights of victims, whose experiences and demands are paramount for transitional justice. Important questions would thus centre on the examination of legal grounds in favour of potential state obligations and corresponding victims' rights vis-à-vis corporate malefactors during periods of transition. Having said that, the proposed convergence of corporate accountability and transitional justice necessitates a robust theoretical framework and clarification of its legal parameters. While transitional justice is typically better addressed by politics, focusing on the law can elucidate persistent epistemic and empirical challenges that dominate those fields separately, as well as their integration. Despite high-level paeans to the need for remedies, the precise meaning of the right to remedy corporate-induced violations and its performance during transition times remain contested, poorly understood and thus inapplicable.[175] Clarifying the law would, thus, benefit transitional states, when they implement their potential obligations and design transitional measures, but also when they assess their compliance to those obligations. In addition, an in-depth theoretical framework would also strengthen the potential claims of victims against their states to include corporations in the remedy processes.

Furthermore, while transitional justice performs better when rooted in domestic experiences and legal realities, recent research demonstrates that accountability of corporate malefactors during transitions relies on 'blending of international and national law'.[176] A well-defined international framework and practice, in conjunction with their domestic counterparts, is the best tool to trigger international pressure, foster civil society demand and institutional designers' work, in the area of corporate accountability during transitions. Accordingly, the next parts will revisit the theory and practice of international and regional human rights and international criminal law, and provide an account of domestic transitional praxis, in order to present a framework for understanding the inclusion of corporate accountability in criminal justice mechanisms, truth commissions and reparations. They will delineate the legal possibilities and operational limits of access to remedy for victims of corporate abuses in transitions and put forward developing interpretations of the corresponding obligations of states, as designers of transitional measures. Crafting synergies across the two fields involves transcending conventional silos, and blending different legal regimes and discourses, at the international, regional and national level. In this way, this book aspires to convincingly challenge the dominant paradigm of transitional justice, and conventional interpretations of applicable law, advocating for a paradigm shift towards emancipatory transitional practice, which places deeper questions of economic power, violence and impunity at its core.

[175] Payne et al., *Archimedes' Lever*, p. 13.
[176] Ibid.

PART II

Criminal Justice Mechanisms

3

Deciphering the State Duty to Prosecute and Punish Corporate Entities and Its Contours in International Law

3.1 Understanding Differences: Corporate and Individual Crimes

Criminal measures taken during transitions are mostly blind to economic actors that were implicated, in one form or the other, in prior conflict or repression. In the current conflict in the Gaza Strip – although not yet at the stage of transition – this inertia to examine the corporate angle led over 600 justices, judges, lawyers and legal scholars to issue a common appeal detailing the serious international humanitarian and human rights law violations that take place in Gaza, with the complicity of businesses.[1] Across different transitional experiments, scarce efforts have reached the level of official charges being pressed against businessmen, and even fewer led to the perpetrators' convictions.[2] Colombia and Argentina are seminal exceptions, as businessmen were and are still targeted by criminal justice mechanisms. Yet, even in those cases, it was the individual business persons who were prosecuted, and sometimes punished, and not the corporate entities.

The overall tendency of transitional states to ignore corporate malefactors might flow from domestic criminal law principles, oftentimes lacking corporate criminal liability provisions (CCL). Usually, however, corporate impunity is a pattern observed irrespective of the existence or not of CCL. For example, the Tunisian criminal code foresees entity liability for money laundering and corruption, but it was not used by the transitional mechanisms that targeted the array of companies involved in Ben Ali's corruption web. Besides, all domestic jurisdictions

[1] Open Letter from Scholars and Practitioners to Corporations Engaged with and in Israel, including in West Bank Settlements, 3 April 2024, available at https://docs.google.com/forms/d/1pbUKHJQdQ1GoJxHa-2oNOM_zh7jaUWgXavPBygpC-hU/viewform?edit_requested=true.

[2] See Payne et al. classifying the cases, depending on their outcome, along an accountability scale. Payne et al., *Archimedes' Lever*, pp. 223–261.

foresee liability of natural persons, including business persons, but those provisions have rarely been put to work during transitions. Transitional criminal measures against economic entities, either in the face of their managers or representatives or against the entity as a whole, seem to be the exception rather than the norm.

In addition to the situation on the ground, insights from international law regarding transitional states' duties to consider corporate actors, in their strategies, yield to perfunctory arguments. Well-wishers rush to say that international criminal law regulates solely individual conduct and thus no other obligation arises for respective states than to punish individuals. Ecopetrol company argued before the Colombian Truth Commission that the conspiracy of its officials with the paramilitaries was merely individual conduct that has been punished as such by courts, and no issue can arise for the company itself.[3] Others add that the conviction of individuals suffices for the purposes of international criminal law and there is no need to further convict the entity, even when corporate criminal liability provisions are in place. Thus, states might consider that the prosecution of individual business persons exhausts their duty to prosecute, during periods of transition.[4]

Transitional states mostly opt against any prosecution of economic actors, while few of them choose to go after the business persons, running those corporations that committed abuses.[5] If one, then, attempts to insert corporate accountability in transitional justice, as a matter of law, it is necessary to justify the prosecution of the entity, as opposed to no prosecution at all, as well as the prosecution of the entity as opposed to that of the business person. In both instances, the absence of corporate accountability from transitional mechanisms and its parallel substitution by prosecutions of individual business persons demonstrates a lack of understanding of the distinct nature of corporate crime, deserving its

[3] Comisión para el Eclarecimiento de la Verdad, la Covivencia y la No Repetición, Hay futuro si hay verdad: Informe Final, Tomo 4. *Hasta la guerra tiene límites: violations de los derechos humanos, infractions al derecho international humanitariano y responsabilidades colectivas, Primera edition* (Comisión de la Verdad, 2022), p. 960.

[4] Ramasastry and Thompson, *Commerce, Crime and Conflict*, pp. 15–16. To that, one should add the view of Jaime Malamud-Goti arguing that corporate prosecutions might cause larger economic disruptions in transitional societies than the criminal prosecution of individuals. Speech of Jaime Malamud-Goti during the Conference on 'Transnational Business and International Criminal Law', held at Humboldt University Berlin, 15–16 May 2009 in Geneuss et al., 'Core Crimes Inc.: Panel Discussion', pp. 957–977.

[5] Payne et al., *Archimedes' Lever*, pp. 223–261.

self-standing punishment, cumulatively, or at least independently, to the punishment of individual persons. This is justified on the basis of the distinct nature of corporate offences in qualitative and quantitative terms. Corporate crimes, framed as either human rights violations or criminal or civil offences, constitute a distinct form of criminality and cannot be equated to single crimes of individual perpetrators or corporate managers, because they differ in their essential features, namely the perpetrator, the means, motivations and characteristics.[6] In addition, corporations can commit crimes, not only of small scale but also of mass atrocity and transnational scale.[7]

In the case of corporate crime, the perpetrator is a legal entity, with separate personhood, different from the sum of their individual members. Also, corporate crime relies on the means that can be secured by the entity and, thus, has much more detrimental capacity than individual crimes. It uses a combination of various eventualities and capacities, the so-called instrumentality,[8] all of which are part of the corporate structure and the prevailing culture. Moreover, the motivations to carry out criminal activities are different, when the perpetrator is a legal person, in the sense that they are affected and framed by the company's organizational characteristics.[9] Scholars have argued that the

[6] C. Wells, *Corporations and Criminal Responsibility* (Oxford University Press, 2005), pp. 66–67; P. French, *Collective and Corporate Responsibility* (Columbia University Press, 1984). For a concise overview of collective responsibility variants in philosophical as juxtaposed to legal writings, see E. Van Sliedregt, *The Criminal Responsibility of Individuals for Violations of International Humanitarian Law* (T.M.C. Asser Press, 2003), pp. 349–352.

[7] W. Huisman, 'Corporations and International Crimes', in A. Smeulers and R. Haveman (eds.), *Supranational Criminology: Towards a Criminology of International Crimes* (Intersentia, 2008), p. 197; E. Black, *IBM and the Holocaust: The Strategic Alliance between Nazi Germany and America's Most Powerful Corporation* (Crown Publishers, 2001).

[8] Instrumentality is a term that has been used since Nuremberg to denote the use of corporate entity for the commission of crimes. *United States* v. *Carl Krauch* in 8 *Trials of War Criminals before the Nuremberg Military Tribunals Under Control Council Law No. 10* (1952) [Farben Vol. 8], 1084.

[9] R. C. Kramer, 'Corporate Crime: An Organisational Perspective', in P. Wickman and T. Daley (eds.), *White-Collar and Economic Crime. Multidisciplinary and Cross-National Perspectives* (Lexington Books, 1982). For information on the existing theoretical models explaining corporate crime focusing on motivation, opportunity and control, see generally W. Huisman, *Between Profit and Morality. Background Factors of Regulatory Compliance and Violation by Corporations* (Boom Legal Publishers, 2001); M. B. Clinard and P. C. Yeager, *Corporate Crime* (Free Press, 2000); D. V. Cohen, 'Ethics and Crime in Business Firms: Organisational Culture and the Impact of Anomy' (1995) 6 *Advances in Criminological Theory* 183.

profit orientation of corporations suffices to create incentives for illegal behaviour.[10] Others have pointed to the structure and idiosyncrasies of the corporation that influence, to a large extent, its choices.[11] Lastly, the differentiating function of corporate crime is that it is being carried out 'on behalf' and not only within an organization, justifying the illustrative assertion that 'managers murder and corporations kill'.[12]

On that basis, criminological literature has long accepted that corporate deviance is a distinct form of criminality, classified under organizational deviance.[13] A similar concept is the one of 'system criminality', used to explain 'the phenomenon that international crimes are often caused by collective entities in which individual actors of these acts are embedded'. According to that theory, responsibility for system crimes, including corporate ones, shall be attached to the 'system' rather than the individual, insofar as individuals committed offences, acting as part or on behalf of a group or organization, and the collective entity was the causal mechanism of the crimes, either changing the normative climate within the collectivity or through different ways of collaboration, such as providing goods or funds for other groups and individuals.[14]

Those essential differences necessitate and justify separate prosecution and punishment of the entity, as opposed to that of the individual perpetrator or the corporate manager, with the necessary attributes to

[10] E. D. Helihy and T. A. Levine, 'Corporate Crisis: The Overseas Payment Problem', in E. Bittner and S. L. Messinger (eds.), *Criminology Review Yearbook II* (Sage, 1980). For an opposite opinion, see K. Jamieson, *The Organisation of Corporate Crime* (Sage, 1994).

[11] M. Punch, 'Suite Violence: Why Managers Murder and Corporations Kill' (2000) 33 *Crime, Law and Social Change* 243, at 245. For other factors that comprise corporate culture and can affect corporate crime, see R. Chen, 'Organisational Irrationality and Corporate Human Rights Violations' (2009) 122 *Harvard Law Review* 1931 at 1934–1937.

[12] M. Punch, 'Why Corporations Kill and Get Away with It: The Failure of Law to Cope with Crime in Organizations', in A. Nollkaemper and H. Van der Wilt (eds.), *System Criminality in International Law* (Cambridge University Press, 2009), pp. 42–68.

[13] The concept of 'organisational deviance' was first captured by Ermann and Lundman. See M. D. Ermann and R. J. Lundman, 'Deviant Acts by Complex Organizations: Deviance and Social Control at the Organizational Level of Analysis' (1978) 19 *Sociological Quarterly* 1, at 55–67. It was then expanded by Sherman and Shover who clarified that individual deviance within the organisation and deviance on the part of the organisation itself are different issues. L. Sherman, *Scandal and Reform* (University of California Press, 1978) and N. Shover, 'Defining Organisational Crime', in M. D. Ermann and R. J. Lundman (eds.), *Corporate and Governmental Deviance: Problems of Organisational Behaviour in Contemporary Society* (Oxford University Press, 1978).

[14] A. Nollkaemper and H. Van der Wilt (eds.), *System Criminality in International Law* (Cambridge University Press, 2009), p. 1.

address that specific crime. The individual action that amounted or contributed to the crime cannot always be abstracted from other elements of the crime or might not separately reach the necessary threshold of illegality. Merely convicting the individuals who staff the structure will, in essence, leave its detrimental potential unaffected and undeterred, since new people can take their place, who will be bred in the same culture. Empirical evidence proves that corporate impunity has allowed the same corporations to commit crimes across times, regions and wars. This is the case of Bayer that has committed (either as a direct perpetrator or an accomplice) crimes during the Holocaust and in Guatemala; BNP Paribas has committed crimes during the Holocaust, Iraq and Rwanda; Chase Bank during the Holocaust and in South Africa; Commerce Bank during the Holocaust and in South Africa; and Ford in the Holocaust, Argentina and Brazil.[15]

Corporate liability will presumably respond better to corporate crime than individual prosecutions, as it aligns to the reality of corporate structures[16] and takes into consideration the specific corporate culture that enabled the commission of abuses.[17] It arguably generates incentives for corporations to supervise their employees from a better position than the state and to develop a culture of compliance.[18] It has also been claimed that corporate prosecutions are preferred by companies themselves who demand clarity and hard law standards.[19] In short, the aforementioned differences underscore the conceptual distinction between individual and corporate crime. Properly acknowledging this

[15] Payne et al., *Archimedes' Lever*, p. 118.

[16] Ramasastry, 'Corporate Complicity: From Nuremberg to Rangoon', 91; Coffee, 'No Soul to Damn'.

[17] Fisse and Braithwaite, 'The Allocation of Responsibility for Corporate Crime', p. 494.

[18] International Commission of Jurists, *Report of the ICJ Expert Legal Panel on Corporate Complicity in International Crimes: Corporate Complicity & Legal Accountability*. Vol. 2 (International Commission of Jurists, 2008), p. 9 [ICJ Report]. On the issue of corporate prosecutions creating disincentives for corporations, see Kelly, 'Prosecuting Corporations for Genocide', p. 4.

[19] M. Gjølberg, 'Explaining Regulatory Preferences: CSR, Soft Law, or Hard Law? Insights from a Survey of Nordic Pioneers in CSR' (2011) 13 *Business and Politics* 2, 1–31; Clapham, 'Extending International Criminal Law', 899–926; S. Chesterman, 'The Turn to Ethics: Disinvestment from Multinational Corporations for Human Rights Violations – The Case of Norway's Sovereign Wealth Fund' (2008) 23 *American University International Law Review* at 577–615. Of course, this is not always the case; see, for example, the opposition of corporate lobbies to recent attempts to introduce binding legislation at the national or international level in the case of the C-300 Bill in Canada, of the Devoir de Vigilance law in France and the BHR international treaty.

distinction is the necessary stepping stone for taking effective legal action, whether by developing new approaches and measures or by applying existing ones to address the particularities and unique nature of corporate crime, including during transitions.

3.2 Deciphering a State Duty to Prosecute Entities in International Criminal Law

3.2.1 The Perceived Limits of ICL

The regulation of international crimes,[20] by the respective international criminal and humanitarian law conventions and customary law, affirms that there is a state obligation to prosecute and punish their perpetrators, although the content of such an obligation is contested.[21] In delineating the contours of such duty, a landmark point is the entry into force of the ICC Statute.[22] Its preamble clearly articulates the duty of state parties to exercise criminal jurisdiction over those responsible for international crimes.[23] It therefore binds state parties to prosecute the crimes covered by the Statute.[24] As for states' non-parties, it is still important in proving broad acceptance by the international community of such a duty in relation to genocide, crimes against humanity and war crimes and thus fortifies the respective customary law duty. Beyond the ICC Statute,

[20] There is no universal definition of what exactly can amount to international crimes. Cassese proposes several common cumulative factors to identify international crimes. A. Cassese and P. Gaeta, *Cassese's International Criminal Law* (Oxford University Press, 2013), pp. 37–57.

[21] N. C. Sánchez and R. Uprimny, *The Challenges of Negotiated Transitions in the Era of International Criminal Law in Beyond Binary Securing Peace and Promoting Justice after Conflict* (Dejusticia Collection, 2019), p. 18 *et seq*; P. Seils, *Squaring Colombia's Circle: The Objectives of Punishment and the Pursuit of Peace* (International Centre for Transitional Justice, 2015), p. 6.

[22] While some scholars might tend to argue that the ICC is an international court which cannot form part of domestic transitional processes, this book assumes that the ICC in fact affects transitional societies and influences the delivery of justice. See also the former ICC Prosecutor Luis Moreno Ocampo arguing that his office prevents and deters future violence. L. Moreno Ocampo, 'Building a Future on Peace and Justice', Keynote Address at the Building a Future on Peace and Justice Conference, Office of the ICC Prosecutor, 24 June 2007, at 8–9. See also L. Moreno Ocampo, 'Transitional Justice in Ongoing Conflicts' (2007) *International Journal of Transitional Justice* 1, at 25–27.

[23] ICC Statute, par. 4–6 of the Preamble.

[24] D. Robinson, 'Serving the Interests of Justice: Amnesties, Truth Commissions and the International Criminal Court' (2003) 14 *European Journal of International Law* 3, at 491–493.

treaty[25] and customary law[26] oblige states to enact criminal legislation for the prosecution and punishment of perpetrators of war crimes, crimes against humanity, genocide and torture. According to recent research, 86 per cent of the UN member states have criminalized one or more international crimes under their national law.[27] This state obligation is further strengthened by the *aut dedere aut judicare rule*[28] that has been

25 For an analysis of the respective treaties, see Orentlicher, 'Settling Accounts'; D. F. Orentlicher, '"Settling Accounts" Revisited: Reconciling Global Norms with Local Agency' (2007) 1 *International Journal of Transitional Justice* 1; N. Roht-Arriaza, 'State Responsibility to Investigate and Prosecute Grave Human Rights Violations in International Law' (1990) 78 *California Law Review* 449–513; J. Méndez, 'Accountability for Past Abuses' (1997) 19 *Human Rights Quarterly*; R. Aldana-Pindell, 'In Vindication of Justiciable Victims' Rights to Truth and Justice for State-Sponsored Crimes' (2002) 35 *Vanderbilt Journal of Transnational Law* at 1399; C. Bassiouni, 'Accountability for Violations of International Humanitarian Law and Other Serious Violations of Human Rights', in C. Bassiouni (ed.), *Post-Conflict Justice* (Brill Nijhoff, 2002); N. J. Kritz, 'Progress and Humility: The Ongoing Search for Post-Conflict Justice', in C. Bassiouni (ed.), *Post-Conflict Justice* (Transnational Publishers, 2002), at 56; Y. Naqvi, 'Amnesty for War Crimes: Defining the Limits of International Recognition' (2003) 85 *International Review of the Red Cross* at 599.

26 For the customary norms, see Bassiouni, 'Accountability for Violations of International Humanitarian Law and Other Serious Violations of Human Rights', at 26; J. Henckaerts and L. Doswald-Beck (eds.), *Customary International Humanitarian Law*, Vol. I (International Committee of the Red Cross, 2005). However, it is to be noted that other scholars have argued that there is no consolidated practice to support the formation of a customary rule. K. Ambos, 'The Legal Framework of Transitional Justice', in K. Ambos et al. (eds.), *Building a Future on Peace and Justice: Studies on Transitional Justice, Conflict Resolution and Development* (Springer-Verlag Berlin Heidelberg, 2009), p. 30. As for the argument that the duty has the status of general principle of law (Article 38 (c) ICJ Statute), Ambos argues that state practice is either missing or contrary. But as Cassese noted, general principles are not strictly state practice, but they rather represent rules of the most significant 'common points' of law. See Cassese and Gaeta, *Cassese's International Criminal Law*, p. 151.

27 Amnesty International, *Universal Jurisdiction: A Preliminary Survey of Legislation around the World – 2012 Update* (Amnesty International, 2012).

28 Universal jurisdiction should be distinguished from the principle of *aut dedere aut judicare*. The *aut dedere aut judicare* (extradite or prosecute) rule establishes an obligation of states to either exercise jurisdiction over certain crimes or to extradite such person. If it chooses to exercise jurisdiction, it can do so on the basis of universal jurisdiction, but also on other jurisdictional principles. See International Law Commission, the obligation to extradite or prosecute (*aut dedere aut judicare*) Final Report of the International Law Commission (2014) *Yearbook of the International Law Commission*, Vol. II (Part Two), par. 18. The principle of *aut dedere aut judicare* overlaps with universal jurisdiction when a state has no other nexus to the alleged crime or to the suspect other than the mere presence of the person within its territory. M. Inazumi, *Universal Jurisdiction in Modern International Law: Expansion of National Jurisdiction for Prosecuting Serious Crimes Under International Law* (Intersentia, 2005), p. 122.

incorporated in more than seventy treaties[29] and is, also, part of customary law, at least for international crimes.[30] Bassiouni has argued that the *jus cogens* character of the prohibition of international crimes yields an *erga omnes* obligation of states to either extradite or prosecute the alleged offenders.[31]

Overall, the obligation to prosecute and punish is robust, in what concerns individual perpetrators of international crimes, given international criminal law's focus on individuals. This would also apply to individual business persons, insofar as the businesses that they own, manage or represent were involved in international crimes. In fact,

[29] Among those treaties, the ones that are important for the purposes of the criminal strand of transitional justice are the four Geneva Conventions of 1949 and Additional Protocol I, as well the Genocide Convention. See C. Bassiouni and E. Wise, *Aut Dedere Aut Judicare: The Duty to Extradite or Prosecute in International Law* (Martinus Nijhoff Publishers, 1995) at 73. Note that Mitchell claims that the number of treaties specifically providing for 'extradite or prosecute' are considerably lower. C. Mitchell, *Aut Dedere, aut Judicare: The Extradite or Prosecute Clause in International Law* (Graduate Institute Publications, 2009), chapter 1.

[30] Some authors consider that there is a general customary obligation to extradite or prosecute; see Bassiouni and Wise, *Aut Dedere Aut Judicare*. Other writers opine that state practice or *opinio juris* are insufficient to support such an obligation. See L. S. Sunga, *The Emerging System of International Criminal Law, Developments in Codification and Implementation* (Kluwer Law International, 1997), at 254; G. Gilbert, *Transnational Fugitive Offenders in International Law: Extradition and Other Mechanisms* (Martinus Nijhoff Publishers, 1998), at 322. For the rule as applying to war crimes and torture, see ICTY, *Prosecutor* v. *Tihomir Blaskic*, Judgment, IT-95-14-AR (18 July 1997), par. 29. Note also that the fourth report of the ILC on the obligation to extradite or prosecute proposed a draft article on international custom as a source of the obligation. See Special Rapporteur Zdzislaw Galicki, fourth report on the obligation to extradite or prosecute (*aut dedere aut judicare*), General Assembly, 31 May 2011, A/CN.4/648. However, this was not well received by neither the Commission nor the Sixth Committee, emphasizing the lack of unanimity on the subject. See Yearbook of the International Law Commission, 2011, Vol. II, Part Two, A/CN.4/SER.A/2011/Add.1, paras. 320, 326; General Assembly, Report of the International Law Commission on the work of its sixty-third session, Topical summary of the discussion held in the Sixth Committee of the General Assembly during its sixty-sixth session, 20 January 2012, A/CN.4/650, par. 48. However, even the most stringent authors have accepted that in respect to those specific crimes, there is evidence suggesting existing or emerging customary obligations. See Mitchell, 'Aut Dedere, Aut Judicare'.

[31] For a detailed analysis of the concepts of *erga omnes* obligations, *jus cogens* status and their interrelation to international crimes, see C. Bassiouni, 'Searching for Peace and Achieving Justice: The Need for Accountability' (1996) 59 *Law and Contemporary Problems*, at 17. However, Miles Jackson says that the absolute character of a right does not immediately translate to an absolute character of the rights it gives rise to. But this is said for human rights. M. Jackson, 'Amnesties in Strasbourg' (2018) 38 *Oxford Journal of Legal Studies* 451.

transitional criminal measures have already included individual business persons, in Colombia, Argentina and elsewhere. This will certainly affect the entity, but only to a limited extent, given that the acts of individual business persons are qualitatively and quantitatively different from those of the entity per se, as explained in Chapter 2. In order for punishment to fulfil its retributive and deterrent goals, prosecution and punishment has to be imposed upon the entity in addition to the business person.[32]

Opponents of corporate prosecutions argue that no obligation arises from international criminal law for respective states than to punish individuals, because international criminal law is focused on individuals only and thus their prosecution suffices for state duties to be exhausted, even when the respective state has corporate criminal liability provisions in place.[33] They contend that international criminal law includes no hints on handling corporate entities,[34] especially in the absence of respective adjudicative fora. In this line of thinking, the Nanterre Tribunal dismissed a case against Alstom and Veolia companies, filed by the Palestine Liberation Organization due to aiding and abetting Israel's occupation and commission of war crimes in western Jerusalem, by contributing to the construction and operation of a light-rail project in the city. The court found that the relevant rules of international law could be violated only by respective states and not corporations.[35] In opposition to corporate criminal liability, others argue that the *aut dedere aut judicare* rule does not apply in cases of corporations, as they are not extraditable. Extradition of corporate entities will, certainly, have to follow some analogous treatment to individual ones,[36] but it seems to be a rather technical issue. Equally the absence of adjudicating international forum, at least in what concerns international crimes, is not an insurmountable obstacle, in view of universal jurisdiction. Rather, the gist of those arguments stands on whether international criminal law affords prohibitions to corporations, in addition to individuals. The litmus test would

[32] See also Section 2.2 of Part I.

[33] Ramasastry and Thompson, *Commerce, Crime and Conflict*, 15–16.

[34] The argument that international criminal law does not apply to corporations was used by the Defence in the STL case against New TV S.A.L. and Karma Khayat. See N. Bernaz, 'Corporate Criminal Liability Under International Law: The New TV S.A.L. and Akhbar Beirut S.A.L. Cases at the Special Tribunal for Lebanon' (2015) 13 *Journal of International Criminal Justice*.

[35] Association France–Palestine Solidarité 'AFPS' v. Société ALSTOM Transport SA, Case No. 11/05331, Versailles Court of Appeal, 22 March 2013.

[36] Kelly, 'Prosecuting Corporations for Genocide', p. 164.

require that corporate entities are bound by international criminal law prohibitions. If this is suggested by a normative interpretation of the law,[37] then, coupled with the analysis of Chapter 2 on the different nature of corporate crime, it could reasonably be argued that transitional states should consider adopting criminal measures towards corporate entities, cumulatively or independently to their obligations in relation to individual corporate officials, when they commit international crimes.

3.2.2 *Corporate Entities and International Crimes' Prohibitions*

An inquiry into whether prosecution and punishment should be interpreted to cover corporate entities, in addition to individuals, based on international criminal law,[38] pivots on whether those entities should be bound by that field of law. This is because the existence or not of corporate obligations under international criminal law shapes the existence or not of any respective state obligation to hold them accountable as entities, beyond the responsibility of their representatives or employees.[39]

[37] There is an ongoing theoretical debate regarding the relationship between interpretation and modification of rules in international law. A comprehensive analysis of this debate falls beyond the scope of this book. For the purposes of this discussion, the terms are used interchangeably to describe the normative trajectory that the law should follow. For more information on the debate, see O. Dörr and K. Schmalenbach, Article 32. Supplementary means of interpretation in O. Dörr and K. Schmalenbach (eds.), *Vienna Convention on the Law of Treaties* (Springer, 2012), pp. 579–633; S. Kadelbach, 'The International Law Commission and Role of Subsequent Practice as a Means of Interpretation Under Articles 31 and 32 VCLT' (2018) 46 *QIL, Zoom-in* 5–18. In addition, for the formation of international legal duties on the basis of international treaty and customary law, see J. Crawford, *Brownlie's Principles of Public International Law*, 8th Edition (Oxford University Press, 2012), p. 20.

[38] This book does not deal separately with international humanitarian law, given that international humanitarian law instruments are enforced through respective international criminal law ones. Furthermore, it is noted that international humanitarian law (IHL) provides relatively limited tools for transitions out of totalitarian situations, which do not rise to the threshold of armed conflicts. In addition, beyond private security companies, it would be rather difficult to argue and prove that corporations operating in conflict zones are parties to the conflict. While in principle IHL can bind corporate actors as long as they participate in hostilities, the criteria for the application of the obligation to repair refer to traits pertaining only to non-state armed groups and not to corporate entities. This can be attributed to the fact that addressing non-state armed groups' violations in armed conflicts is higher in the priority scale than corporate actors. Lastly, IHL does not provide justiciable rights or any equivalent tool that can be used against non-state actors. A. Panepinto, 'The Right to the Truth in International Law: The Significance of Strasbourg's Contributions' (2017) 37 *Legal Studies* 742.

[39] Nerlich, 'Core Crimes and Transnational Business'.

As Orentlicher notes, the fact that international criminal law imposes obligations on its subjects, currently individuals, makes them liable to criminal punishment, and imposes respective obligations on states.[40] This chapter will argue that the internal bifurcation of criminal law norms (explained later) and the corporations' capacity to actually violate those norms suggest that international criminal law obligations should be interpreted and developed to bind corporations, and not only individual persons, meaning that state prosecution should also cover them. This normative proposition is further reinforced by references to established international criminal law topics, such as the issues of amnesties, universal jurisdiction and the *nullum crimen sine lege* principle.

The capacity discourse has been presented by scholars and courts as a compelling rationale and strong indication, providing support for the view that international criminal law imposes substantive obligations on corporations, and not only natural persons.[41] It has served as a stepping stone and necessary assumption for arguing that international criminal law should also apply to corporate entities. If corporations lacked the capacity to commit international crimes, there would be little practical basis for extending the reach of international criminal law to include them. Notably, it was the capacity discourse that was used to prove that other entities beyond individuals and states – that is, armed non-state actors – are bound by customary law,[42] with the ICC clarifying that the capacity to carry out an attack is the primary requirement for conviction, albeit in relation to armed non-state groups and not corporations.[43] The reference to the capacity discourse in relation to non-state actors other than corporations is important, as it can be used for analogous

[40] Orentlicher, 'Settling Accounts', 2552.

[41] The issue of corporate criminal capacity transpires the debates of corporate criminal liability for both domestic and international crimes and is quite evident in the Anglo-American tradition which accepts corporate capacity to harm. See Kyriakakis, *Corporations, Accountability and International Criminal Law*, p. 231. See also T. Weigend, 'Societas Delinquere Non Potest? A German Perspective' (2008) 6 *Journal of International Criminal Justice* 5, at 927; Clapham, 'Extending International Criminal Law'; 'Discussion: International Trends Towards Establishing Some Form of Punishment for Corporations' (2008) 6 *Journal of International Criminal Justice* 947, at 952.

[42] See K. Fortin, *The Accountability of Armed Groups Under Human Rights Law* (Oxford University Press, 2017), chapter 10.

[43] The ICC in relation to crimes against humanity and armed non-state actors has clarified that the primary requirement is a capacity to carry out an attack of the scale required by Article 7 of the Rome Statute. See, for instance, ICC, *The Prosecutor* v. *Katanga*, Judgment, ICC-01/04-01/07, 7 March 2014 [Katanga Trial Judgment].

argumentation in the case of corporate entities. Both corporations and armed non-state groups are legal entities outside the traditional subjects upon whom international law is applicable and the developments concerning the one can potentially be useful for the other.

Andrew Clapham has suggested that the capacity of corporations to breach international criminal law norms arguably suffices to prove that international criminal law should be interpreted as imposing substantive obligations on corporations.[44] Specifically for war crimes, the capacity of corporations to commit them seems to be accepted by the *rationae materiae* formulation of the prohibition, which focuses on the act and not the perpetrator, thus leaving open the possibility that non-state actors do commit them.[45] Looking closely to the formulation of the prohibition on war crimes during non-international armed conflicts, it posits that among the perpetrators can be a non-state actor, given that the conflict is non-international.[46] This interpretation lays the groundwork for an extension of the prohibition's scope to potentially include corporate entities and opens the door for them to fall under the prohibition as well.[47]

In terms of case law, the – extensively used – US ATCA litigation has stepped on the assumption that private actors do have the capacity to violate international norms along with state officials,[48] and that US corporations can be liable under the ATCA for complicity in serious human rights violations.[49] The hurdles posed by Kiobel in ATCA claims

[44] Clapham, 'Extending International Criminal Law'; 'Discussion: International Trends Towards Establishing Some Form of Punishment for Corporations' at 952.

[45] It is interesting to note that even jurisdiction granting statutes do not limit the persons who can violate those prohibitions. See Rome Statute of the International Criminal Court, 1 July 2002, 2187 U.N.T.S. 90, Article 8; ICTY Statute, UN Doc S/RES/827, adopted 25 May 1993, Article 3; ICTR Statute, UN Doc S/RES/955, 8 November 1994, Article 4.

[46] Common Article 3 of the Geneva Conventions.

[47] To the extent that it can be relevant, the assumption of corporate capacity transpired the communication to the ICC by Palestinian human rights organizations in 2018, where they claimed that 'high-level Israeli officials, and individuals associated with corporations that are extracting and destroying Palestinian natural resources [and are committing] the war crimes of extensive destruction and appropriation of property, pillage, and destruction and seizure of property'. See Al Haq, Palestinian Human Rights Organizations Submit File to ICC Prosecutor: Investigate and Prosecute Pillage, Appropriation and Destruction of Palestinian Natural Resources, 26 October 2018, available at www.alhaq.org/advocacy/6144.html.

[48] *Kadic* v. *Karadzic* 70 F.3d 232 (2d Cir. 1995).

[49] The Supreme Court's decision in *Sosa* v. *Alvarez-Machain* affirmed that corporate liability exists under ATCA but limited its application to violations of 'specific, universal,

did not question the issue of corporate capacity, but were centred on the connection of the claims to US territory.[50] Also, the Supreme Court of Canada has held that private corporations in Canada can commit violations of customary international law and can be held accountable for the violations of their subsidiaries outside Canada.[51] Similarly, the Nuremberg tribunals also constructed their logic on the assumption that corporations have the capacity to commit harm. It is notable that in the Farben case, the tribunal opined in favour of corporate criminal capacity to commit war crimes and stated:

> [W]here private individuals, including juristic persons, proceed to exploit the military occupancy by acquiring private property against the will and consent of the former owner, such an action not being expressly justified by any applicable provision of the Hague Regulations, is in violation of international law ... Similarly where a private individual or a juristic person becomes a party to unlawful confiscation of public or private property by planning and executing a well-defined design to acquire such property permanently, acquisition under such circumstances subsequent to the confiscation constitutes conduct in violation of the Hague Regulations.[52]

As Kyriakakis notes, despite the fact that the court did not have jurisdiction over entities, it set precedent over capacity and liability, considering that its holdings and statements should be understood alongside the whole range of measures – beyond court-ordered ones – to include administrative dissolution and other measures that targeted

and obligatory' laws of nations. *Sosa* v. *Alvarez-Machain*, 542 US 692 (2004). Note, however, that the appropriate standard for determining third-party liability has never been conclusively determined. See also K. Golden, 'License to Kill? Corporate Liability Under the Alien Tort Claims Act?' (2012) *In the Balance* 14. For an overview of US cases using the ATCA, see Ramasastry and Thompson, *Commerce, Crime and Conflict*, at 20–23.

50 In the *Kiobel case*, the court held that the claims must touch and concern the US territory with sufficient force to displace the presumption against extraterritorial application. *Kiobel* v. *Royal Dutch Petroleum Co.*, 133 S. Ct. 1659, 1665 (2013), p. 1669. Furthermore, in the *Jesner* case, it was decided that foreign corporations cannot be sued under the ATCA, but the issue of US corporations remains to be decided. *Jesner* v. *Arab Bank*, PLC, 584 US (2018).

51 *Nevsun Resources Ltd.* v. *Araya*, 2020 SCC 5, [2020] 1 SCR 166, 28 February 2020. See also other cases against corporations for international crimes, referred in International Bar Association, IBA War Crimes Committee shines a light on corporate liability cases, 25 November 2022, available at www.ibanet.org/IBA-War-Crimes-Committee-shines-a-light-on-corporate-liability-cases.

52 Farben Vol. 8, at 1132, 1133.

economic entities.[53] Under this holistic perspective, Nuremberg seemingly considered entities capable of committing those crimes.

Regarding the internal bifurcation of criminal law norms, scholars indicate that those norms are constituted by a first sub-norm, containing the substance of the prohibition, and a second attaching the consequence of a potential violation, namely liability of the offender, the so-called jurisdiction-creating norm.[54] The fact that there is no jurisdiction-creating norm for corporations does not mean that the first norm of substantial prohibition does not extend to them, especially taking into consideration universal jurisdiction, analysed subsequently. Besides, international humanitarian law norms, which can be considered as the substance of the prohibition, can bind corporate actors as long as they participate in hostilities. The distinction was clear in the IG Farben case before the US Military Tribunal. The court declared that Farben was responsible for plunder of public or private property, stating that 'with reference to the charges in the present indictment concerning Farben's activities in Poland, Norway, Alsace-Lorraine, and France, we find that the proof establishes beyond a reasonable doubt that offenses against property as defined in Control Council Law No. 10 were committed by Farben (. . .)'.[55] However, the Tribunal lacked jurisdiction over the corporation itself. This reflects the aforementioned bifurcation of legal norms, given that while the corporation was deemed capable of committing crimes and held accountable for them, meaning that such conduct was considered prohibited, there was no norm vesting the Tribunal with relevant jurisdiction. Arguably, the absence of the jurisdiction-creating norm operates at a different level from the former substantive norm, and in no way negates its legal validity.[56]

Regarding crimes against humanity, their substantive prohibition extends to corporations – again despite the lack of a competent forum to convict them. This is because the prohibition is absolute,[57] and

[53] Kyriakakis, *Corporations, Accountability and International Criminal Law*, p. 90.

[54] Nerlich, 'Core Crimes and Transnational Business'; Kyriakakis, *Corporations, Accountability and International Criminal Law*, pp. 240–241. See also the contribution of Florian Jessberger in the Conference on 'Transnational Business and International Criminal Law', in Geneuss et al., 'Core Crimes Inc.: Panel Discussion', p. 967.

[55] Farben Vol. 8, at 1139.

[56] This same logic has also been put forward by the International Court of Justice. See ICJ, *Jurisdictional Immunities of the State* (*Germany v. Italy: Greece Intervening*), Judgment of 3 February 2012, par. 58.

[57] Absolute liability attached to crimes against humanity based on Article 33 of ICC Statute which rejects superior order as a plausible defence.

nothing in its formulation hints to the exclusion of any actor from it. The ad hoc tribunals have already considered that entities are capable of committing crimes against humanity,[58] whereas the Nuremberg tribunal blamed specific corporations for those crimes.[59] Recently, the Draft Articles prepared by the UN International Law Commission categorically accepted that companies can violate the prohibition of crimes against humanity and established a duty of states to prosecute and punish legal persons.[60]

Corporations can, also, violate the prohibition on genocide. The International Court of Justice (ICJ) has accepted that the act of genocide can be committed by non-state 'persons or entities'.[61] Being even more vocal, the International Criminal Tribunal for Rwanda (ICTR) held that the radio company RTLM explicitly called for the extermination of the Tutsi ethnic group and incited genocide through radio emissions.[62] However, deprived of jurisdiction to convict corporations, it found guilty only two corporate officials of RTLM.[63] As was the case with the previous crimes, the prohibition of genocide is an absolute prohibition of the act, notwithstanding the perpetrator.[64] Remarkably, Article 4 of the Genocide

[58] ICTY, *Prosecutor* v. *Tadic*, Case No. IT-94-1-T, Judgment, 7 May 1997, par. 654 [Tadic Trial Judgment]; ICTY, *Prosecutor* v. *Kunarac*, Case No. IT-96-23-A, Judgment, 12 June 2002, par. 96; ICTR, *Prosecutor* v. *Akayesu*, Case No. ICTR 96-4-T, Judgment, 2 September 1998 [Akayesu Trial Judgement] par. 580.

[59] Farben Vol. 8, at 1135 and 1139; *United States* v. *Alfried Krupp* 9 Trials of War Criminals Before the Nuremberg Military Tribunals Under Control Council Law No. 10 (1952), [Krupp case] at 1376.

[60] International Law Commission, Crimes Against Humanity: Texts and Titles of the Draft Preamble, the Draft Articles and the Draft Annex Provisionally Adopted by the Drafting Committee on First Reading, Rep. on the Work of Its Sixty-Ninth Session, UN Doc A/ CN.4/ L.892, at 6 (2017); General Assembly, Third report on crimes against humanity, Special Rapporteur Sean D. Murphy, A/CN.4/704, 23 January 2017.

[61] ICJ, *Application of the Convention on the Prevention and Punishment of the Crime of Genocide* (Bosnia and Herzegovina v. Serbia and Montenegro), Judgment, ICJ Reports 2007, p. 43, par. 393; ICJ, *Order on Request for the Indication of Provisional Measures in Case Concerning Application of the Convention on the Prevention and Punishment of the Crime of Genocide* (Bosnia and Herzegovina v. Serbia and Montenegro), 1993, *International Legal Materials*, 32(3), 888–902, par. 52.

[62] ICTR, *Prosecutor* v. *Nahimana*, Case No. ICTR 99-52-T, Judgment, 3 December 2003, par. 552, 949, 952–953.

[63] Ibid., par. 973–974.

[64] The same applies to the statutes of the ad hoc tribunals but not to the Rome Statute. See M. Kelly, 'The Status of Corporations in the Travaux Preparatoires of the Genocide Convention: The Search for Personhood' (2010) 43 *Case Western Reserve Journal of International Law*, at 484.

Convention obliges states to punish perpetrators without distinguishing natural from judicial persons.[65]

As for torture, while the act per se was initially conditioned on state involvement, this requirement is yielding to a less state-centred approach.[66] Seminal cases such as the *Sadiq Shek Elmi* v. *Australia* have pointed out that actions by non-state actors could, under certain circumstances,[67] be included under the scope of the definition of torture.[68] The Committee against Torture has acknowledged instances where non-state actors carry out torture.[69] In addition, the Committee has accepted that

[65] Stating that 'persons committing genocide shall be punished, whether they are constitutionally responsible rulers, public officials or *private* individuals'. UN General Assembly, Convention on the Prevention and Punishment of the Crime of Genocide, United Nations, Treaty Series, Vol. 78, p. 277, 9 December 1948. See also Kelly, 'The Status of Corporations'.

[66] Article 1 of the Convention requires the instigation or consent or acquiescence of a public official or other person acting in an official capacity. Accordingly, the Committee at the beginning found that activities of non-governmental entities do not fall under the scope of the definition of torture. UN Committee against Torture (CAT), *G.R.B.* v. *Sweden*, Communication No. 83/1997, CAT/C/20/D/083/1997, 15 May 1998, par. 65. However, it is to be noted that according to the *travaux preparatoires*, the justification for the nexus with the state was that it can reveal a pattern of abuse and a state apparatus that does not function properly. Furthermore, during the *travaux preparatoires*, several governments advocated unsuccessfully for an extension of the definition covering also private individuals. M. Nowak, *UN Convention against Torture, A commentary* (Oxford University Press, 2008), pp. 30, 77.

[67] For example, when the non-state actors have effective control and the central government is absent (*Sadiq Shek Elmi* v. *Australia*, CAT/C/22/D/120/1998, 25 May 1999) or when they carry out deportation of foreigners or detention facilities. [Consideration of Reports Submitted by States Parties under Article 19 of the Convention, Second periodic report of the United Kingdom of Great Britain and Northern Ireland and dependent territories, CAT/C/SR.234, 22 November 1995.].

[68] UN CAT, 'Sadiq Shek Elmi v. Australia'; UN CAT, *Dzemajl et al.* v. *Yugoslavia*, CAT/C/29/D/161/2000, 2 December 2002.

[69] UN CAT, Concluding Observations on the third periodic report of Croatia, CAT/C/CR/32/3 (2004), par. 8; UN CAT, Concluding observation on the Philippines in 2016, CAT/C/PHL/C/3; UN CAT, Concluding observations on the initial report of Iraq, CAT/C/IRQ/CO/1; UN CAT, Conclusions and recommendations, United States of America, CAT/C/USA/CO/2, 25 July 2006. This also stems from the fact that the Convention prohibits any state entity from committing torture or from being involved ('instigation of or with the consent or acquiescence') in acts of torture. However, for being involved in something, it means that someone else is committing it, proving as such that the norm can be violated by entities other than the state. Confirming the latter, the Committee against Torture has stated that state failure to provide remedies to torture victims 'enables non-State actors to commit acts impermissible under the Convention with impunity', and that 'the State bears responsibility' where it fails 'to exercise due diligence to prevent, investigate, prosecute, and punish such non-State officials or private actors' for violating

the prohibition of torture binds private and public institutions alike, which can violate the torture prohibition but cannot be held liable under it.[70] It has held that each state party should prohibit, prevent and redress torture and ill-treatment in all contexts, where the failure of the state to intervene would encourage the danger of privately inflicted harm.[71] Lastly, Article 4 of the Convention against Torture provides that states shall criminalize torture and ensure that penalties 'apply to an act by any person which constitutes complicity or participation in torture'. Corporations have been convicted for torture primarily in the United States under the ATCA,[72] but also in Europe.[73]

Lastly, extrajudicial killings are absolutely prohibited by international law, irrespective of who is committing them. The Principles on the Effective Prevention and Investigation of Extra-legal, Arbitrary and Summary Executions accept that the crime can be committed by actors other than the state and thus the prohibition can be violated by any actor, as long as the state consents or acquiesces.[74] Therefore, the state's obligation to prosecute and punish covers every actor that can commit the specific crime. The UN Special Rapporteur on Extrajudicial, Summary or Arbitrary Executions accepted that extrajudicial executions can be committed by both state and non-state actors[75] and explicitly classified cases of corporate misconduct as amounting to extrajudicial

the torture prohibition. UN CAT, General Comment No. 2 par. 18, UN Doc. CAT/C/GC/2, 24 January 2008.

70 Brief of Yale Law School Centre for Global Legal Challenges as Amicus Curiae in Support of Petitioners, Supreme Court of the United States, case *Esther Kiobel et al.* v. *Royal Dutch Petroleum Co., et al.*, and *Asid Mohamad et al.* v. *Palestinian Authority*, Nos. 10–1491 and 11–88 (*Yale Brief Kiobel*); Brief of Yale Law School Centre for Global Legal Challenges as Amicus Curiae in Support of Petitioners, Supreme Court of the United States, case *Joseph Jesner et al.* v. *Arab Bank*, PLC, Nos. 16–499 (*Yale Brief Jesner*).

71 UN CAT, 'General Comment No. 2', par. 15.

72 *Al Shimari* v. *CACI Premier Tech.*, Inc., 840 F.3d at 151, 162.

73 See *Guerrero* v. *Monterrico Metals* PLC [2009] EWHC (QB) 2475. See also the cases against *Amesys* and *Qosmos* in France, in Section 4.1.5, Part III of this book.

74 Principles on the Effective Prevention and Investigation of Extra-legal, Arbitrary and Summary Executions, UN Doc. E/RES/1989/65, 24 May 1989.

75 HRC, Report of the Special Rapporteur, Mission to the Philippines, UN Doc. A/HRC/8/3/Add.2, 16 April 2008, par. 5; HRC, Report of the Special Rapporteur on extrajudicial, summary or arbitrary executions, UN Doc. A/HRC/14/24, 20 May 2010, par. 45, 46(d); Report of the Special Rapporteur, Civil and Political Rights, Including Questions of Disappearances and Summary Executions, Commission on Human Rights, UN Doc. E/CN.4/2005/7, 22 December 2004, par. 69.

killings.[76] More recently, he proposed that 'the same precautionary principle applied to State law enforcement officials must also apply to private actors' including private security providers.[77] Notably, also the ICTR has accepted that extrajudicial killings can be carried out with the complicity or acquiescence of the state, thus accepting that the principal perpetrator may be non-state actors.[78]

The foregoing resonates within the context of the current Israeli attack at the Gaza strip. The preliminary ruling by the ICJ accepted that Israel's actions are plausibly genocidal.[79] In early 2024, the UN High Commissioner for Human Rights noted that the 'extensive destruction of property, not justified by military necessity and carried out unlawfully and wantonly, amounts to a grave breach of the Fourth Geneva Convention and a war crime'.[80] Reportedly, all those actions have been facilitated by various companies.[81] Israel has received tons of weapons, primarily from the US, but also from France, Germany, the UK, Sweden, Japan and elsewhere. While there is no international forum-creating norm for corporate implication and facilitation in those crimes, the ICC[82] and

[76] 'Oil companies have long been accused of complicity in actions involving human rights violations including extrajudicial executions.' Report of the Special Rapporteur, Mission to Nigeria, Commission on Human Rights, UN Doc. E/CN.4/2006/53/Add.4, 7 January 2006, par. 86; Report of the Special Rapporteur, Communications to and from Governments, Human Rights Council, UN Doc. A/HRC/8/3/Add.1, 30 May 2008, par. 308–310.

[77] Report of the Special Rapporteur, Extrajudicial, Summary or Arbitrary Execution, UN Doc. A/71/372, 2 September 2016, par. 62.

[78] ICTR, *Prosecutor* v. *Kayishema et al.*, Case No. ICTR 95-1-T, Trial Judgment 21 May 1999, par. 140. Human rights courts have also accepted that non-state actors can commit extrajudicial executions and that the state's duty to investigate those violations includes those cases as well. IACtHR, *Case of the Mapiripán Massacre* v. *Colombia*, Judgment, 15 September 2005, Ser. C, No. 134, par. 110, 123, 138; ECtHR, *Ergi* v. *Turkey* (App. No. 23818/94), Judgment of 28 July 1998, par. 398; ECtHR, *Finucane* v. *United Kingdom* (App. no. 29178/95), Judgment of 1 July 2003, paras. 10, 84.

[79] ICJ, *Application of the Convention on the Prevention and Punishment of the Crime of Genocide in the Gaza Strip*, South Africa v. Israel, Order of 26 January 2024.

[80] UN Human Rights Office Press Release, 'Turk Warns Israeli Extensive Destruction Near Gaza Border "Grave Breach" of Geneva Conventions, Possible War Crime', 8 February 2024, available at www.un.org/unispal/document/turk-warns-israeli-extensive-destruction-near-gaza-border-grave-breach-of-geneva-conventions-possible-war-crime-8feb2024/.

[81] American Friends Service Committee, 'Companies Profiting from the Gaza Genocide', 28 May 2024, available at https://afsc.org/gaza-genocide-companies.

[82] ICC Prosecution request pursuant to Article 19(3) for a ruling on the court's territorial jurisdiction in Palestine, No. ICC-01/18, 20 December 2019, par. 95.

various other authoritative sources[83] have made it clear that Israel's actions are illegal and is reasonable to assume that companies that assist them also engage in illegal activity.[84] In that respect, the United Nations Human Rights Council, in its resolution 31/36, updated in 2023, created a list of 'business enterprises [that] have, directly and indirectly, enabled, facilitated and profited from the construction and growth of the Israeli settlements in the Occupied Palestinian Territory', which is illegal according to international law, and arguably amounts to war crimes under the ICC Statute.

The fact that corporations can commit international crimes and should be bound by the substantive prohibition of international criminal law obligations seems to address the litmus test mentioned in Chapter 2. That chapter concluded that the main argument against corporate prosecutions is rooted in the perceived absence of obligations for corporations, on the basis of international criminal law. However, according to the aforementioned, corporations are not only capable of committing international crimes but also are seemingly covered by the substantial prohibitions enshrined in international criminal law. This could potentially impact the way the respective state obligations should be perceived, formed and structured in relation to corporations, including in periods of transition.[85] Kyriakakis pointedly mentions that

> [a] convincing case [on the basis of the internal bifurcation of criminal law norms] exists that corporations have the same core obligations under international criminal law that apply to other private non-state actors, and that international law permits corporations being held liable by a competent institution when they are breached. This is notwithstanding the fact that a positive principle of corporate criminal liability has yet to emerge under customary international law.[86]

Although presently there are no established obligations, corporate capacity to do harm and the expansion of international criminal law's substantive prohibitions over corporations suggest a certain direction of state obligations *de lege ferenda*. In other words, domestic jurisdictions in the performance of their duties to prosecute and punish, or in the design

[83] 'Statement of the UN Special Rapporteur on the Situation of Human Rights in the Palestinian Territory', 9 July 2021, available at www.ohchr.org/en/press-releases/2021/07/occupied-palestinian-territory-israeli-settlements-should-be-classified-war.

[84] I. Pietropaoli, 'Obligations of Third States and Corporations to Prevent and Punish Genocide in Gaza', Al Haq Organization, 5 June 2024.

[85] Orentlicher, 'Settling Accounts', 2552.

[86] Kyriakakis, *Corporations, Accountability and International Criminal Law*, p. 242.

and delivery of transitional criminal justice mechanisms, should consider that corporations are seemingly prohibited from committing international crimes. For the aforementioned conventions to have meaning, the duty of the state to prosecute and punish should be reformulated to mirror that prohibition,[87] either cumulatively or independently from state obligations in relation to individual corporate officials. None of the international instruments cited earlier excludes non-state actors from the actual commission of the crime. While not providing for private entities' liability, the conventions accept that commission of the violation can be carried out by private actors and their prohibitions are formulated according to the act that is prohibited *rationae materiae* and not according to the actor who is performing it. Authors have emphasized that the absence of enforcement mechanisms does not detract from the conclusion that international criminal norms bind corporate actors.[88] Instead, the fact that no international forum has jurisdiction over corporations, weights in favour of respective state obligations to that end; otherwise, perpetrators would be left unpunished. In that respect, it is interesting to note that even SRSG Ruggie, typically against law-based approaches, took a different stance in relation to corporate international crimes. Although he did not promote the existence of a respective state obligation, he noted that long-standing debates over the binding force of international crimes' prohibitions for corporations are yielding to new realities and that 'the absence of an international accountability mechanism . . . does not preclude the emergence of corporate responsibility today'.[89]

In light of this, states that foresee corporate criminal liability provisions could arguably conduct those prosecutions, without making a distinction between natural and legal persons,[90] provided that they have incorporated international criminal law into their domestic statutes.[91]

[87] 'Yale Brief Kiobel'; 'Yale Brief Jesner'.

[88] B. Stephens, 'The Amorality of Profit: Transnational Corporations and Human Rights' (2002) 20 *Berkeley Journal of International Law* 45.

[89] HRC, Business and Human Rights: Mapping International Standards of Responsibility and Accountability for Corporate Acts, Report of the Special Representative of the Secretary-General on the Issue of Human Rights and Transnational Corporations and other Business Enterprises, UN Doc. A/HRC/4/035, 9 February 2007, paras. 20, 21.

[90] Ramasastry et al., 'Translating Unocal', 871; Ramasastry and Thompson, *Commerce, Crime and Conflict*, pp. 15–16.

[91] By way of illustration, this was the case with the investigations carried out in France against Qosmos and Lafarge companies for their complicity in crimes allegedly committed in Syria. See Section 4.1.5 of this book.

Most importantly, if international criminal law is interpreted as binding corporate entities and if states provide for CCL in their domestic legislation, then the obligation to prosecute and punish corporate entities should be additional to that of individual business persons, and the latter cannot substitute the former. For states that do not recognize domestically corporate entities as persons for the purposes of criminal law, international criminal law cannot be considered as imposing them an obligation to adopt CCL, but the aforementioned suggest that they should do so and offer direction on the future development and effective articulation of respective laws and transitional measures. In both cases, the adoption or use of CCL would be advisable when a corporation has committed an international crime, but no individual business person can be held liable, because their activities separately do not reach the necessary threshold. Otherwise, the state would be effectively obliged to leave the crime unaddressed. This occurs often in transitional contexts, due to the various limitations on state duties and the challenges of transitions. Although transitional times call for nuances in the formulation and prioritization of duties, it is important to recognize that under positive international law, leaving those crimes unaddressed would be particularly severe, given the *jus cogens* character of international crimes, and the *erga omnes* duty to prosecute and punish the alleged offenders.[92]

Besides, international criminal law has already considered obligations for non-state actors, namely individuals. Thus, the paradigm shift required to 'fit' corporate entities is smaller than in other fields, such as human rights law.[93] Also, as mentioned earlier, the discourse on the capacity of non-state actors to commit crimes has already been used in order to bypass personality issues in the international sphere, namely in the case of Armed Non-State Actors. By analogy, it is suggested that personality issues should be bypassed also in domestic law or that CCL provisions should be adopted.

Going even further, the discussion on amnesties can lend additional arguments. The prohibition of amnesties, undoubted by legal

[92] For a detailed analysis of the concepts of *erga omnes* obligations, *jus cogens* status and their interrelation to international crimes, see Bassiouni, 'Accountability for Violations of International Humanitarian Law and Other Serious Violations of Human Rights', 393–397.

[93] L. Van den Herik and J. Letnar Cernic, 'Regulating Corporations Under International Law: From Human Rights to International Criminal Law and Back Again' (2010) 8 *Journal of International Criminal Justice*.

scholarship, at least in what concerns blanket ones,[94] is grounded on the abhorrent nature of international crimes.[95] Under the same reasoning that applies to the prohibition of international crimes, amnesties are banned on the *rationae materiae* basis of the abhorrent nature of the act, meaning that their prohibition can also extend to cases when the offender is a corporation, given that the nature of the crime and the underlining justification of the norm remain the same. If the crime was so heinous that individual perpetrators cannot be amnestied, then the same should apply when an equally heinous crime was committed by a company. That should be viewed under the light of the analysis carried out in the first segment of this chapter, regarding the distinct nature of corporate crime, as opposed to the crime of the individual business person. Under that reasoning, leaving the corporation unpunished, even if the business person is prosecuted, amounts to de facto amnesty for the corporate crime. This conclusion is clear, given that the absence of corporate prosecutions saddles upon a generalized lack of measures to tackle corporate malfeasance, fostering a widespread perception of corporate impunity, seemingly equivalent to de facto corporate amnesty. The significance of this argument lies not in drawing direct analogies with other cases of amnesties, but in recognizing the broader implications of the absence of corporate prosecutions, which resembles the effects of amnesties. While accepting that the necessary requirements set by international law for amnesties might often not be met in cases involving corporations, and that the issue of amnesties is continuously raising hurdles in transitional spaces, there is notable symbolic significance in reframing our understanding and utilizing potentially relevant concepts, particularly one as significant as amnesties. Acknowledging that corporate impunity can in some cases rise to the level of amnesty – albeit one that does not meet legal requirements – carries significant symbolic force, by emphasizing the severity of the situation and, thus, paving the way for constructive discussions.

[94] The national practice of blanket amnesties is rare, and various courts have declared them illegal. Ambos, 'The Legal Framework of Transitional Justice', pp. 58–60; C. Stahn, 'Complementarity, Amnesties and Alternative Forms of Justice: Some Interpretative Guidelines for the International Criminal Court' (2005) 3 *Journal of International Criminal Justice* 695–720, at 704. Many authors have dealt with the issue of amnesties in transitional justice: see Mallinder, *Amnesty, Human Rights and Political Transitions*; Freeman, *Necessary Evils*; Vinjamuri and Snyder, 'Law and Politics in Transitional Justice'.

[95] G. Werle, *Principles of International Criminal Law* (TMC Asser, 2005), p. 65.

Importantly, the fact that corporate entities can commit international crimes and the affirmation that they are covered by the substantive prohibition even if a corresponding forum is missing could lend support to the idea that upon the establishment of an adequate forum, this norm can be enforced, without a breach of the *nullum crimen* principle,[96] as long as domestic law was accessible and foreseeable.[97] The justification is that such legislation will not create new crimes, but will just enable national courts to apply the relevant rules of international law criminalizing the conduct.[98] This was the conclusion in two cases against legal persons, from the Special Tribunal for Lebanon (STL), the *New TV S.A.L.* and *Akhbar Beirut S.A.L.*[99] In both cases, the Appeal Chambers, deciding on the Interlocutory Appeals Concerning Personal Jurisdiction in Contempt Proceedings, found that there is no breach of the *nullum crimen sine lege* principle, given that their interpretation of the applicable rules 'does not create a new offence where before there was none'[100] and considering that 'the status of the perpetrator, legal or natural person, is not an element of the crime of contempt'.[101] Therefore, if an offence existed before its specific commission, then it cannot be deemed unforeseeable or inaccessible, and the alleged perpetrator should have been aware of the international prohibition,[102] especially in view of the fact that the status of the perpetrator is not an element of the crime.

[96] Nerlich, 'Core Crimes and Transnational Business'.

[97] ECtHR, *Kolk and Kislyiy* v. *Estonia*, App. Nos. 23052/04, 24018/04, Judgment of 17 January 2006, par. 9; ECtHR, *Streletz, Kessler, and Krenz* v. *Germany*, App. Nos. 34044/96, 35532/97, & 44801/98, Judgment of 22 March 2001, par. 89.

[98] Article 15(2) of the ICCPR further legitimizes the prospect of trying and punishing conduct which is criminal 'according to the general principles of law recognized by the community of nations'. For further analysis, see M. Nowak, *UN Covenant on Civil and Political Rights – A Commentary* (Engel, 1993), p. 360.

[99] For an analysis of those cases, see Bernaz, 'Corporate Criminal Liability Under International Law'.

[100] STL, Case Against New TV S.A.L. and Karma Mohamed Tahsin al Khayat, STL-14-05/PT/AP/ARI26.1, Decision on Interlocutory Appeal Concerning Personal Jurisdiction in Contempt Proceedings, 2 October 2014, par. 85.

[101] STL, Decision on Interlocutory Appeal concerning personal jurisdiction in contempt proceedings, Akhbar Beirut S.A.L. and Ibrahim Mohamed Al-Amin (STL-14-06/PT/AP/AR126.1), Appeals Panel, 23 January 2015, par. 3. This conclusion of the Appeals Chamber should not be watered down or confused with the trial judgment in the New TV S.A.L. case, which held that there is no international consensus on attributing corporate liability. See STL, Al Jadeed [CO.] S.A.L./NEW T.V. S.A.L. (N.T.V.) Karma Mohamed Tahsin Al Khayat, Case No. STL-14-05/T/CJ, Trial Chamber Judgment, 18 September 2015, par. 56.

[102] In addition, the state is required to have ratified the respective international treaty, as well as to have incorporated the prohibition of international crimes into its domestic

Similar conclusions were made in Nuremberg,[103] where substantive justice was selected at the expense of strict legality.[104] Although the defence foregrounded the argument of *nullum crimen sine lege*, arguing that the crimes charged to the defendants were not crimes at the time of their commission, the Tribunal rejected this positivist interpretation and stated that where the 'attacker must know that he is doing wrong, and so, far from it being unjust to punish him, it would be unjust if his wrong were allowed to go unpunished'.[105] For the tribunal, the aforementioned principle was one of law and not of justice and, thus, it could be overridden by a higher principle of justice.[106]

Nowadays, the various laws establishing due diligence obligations for companies to be informed on the repercussions of their operations, as well as on domestic and international laws,[107] as well as the informative role of civil society are factors that would most probably provide evidence of knowledge and foreseeability of the laws on behalf of the company and potentially weaken the defence of non-retroactivity.[108] The dearth of relevant cases and scholarship, along with the economy of the current book, prevents a more detailed analysis at this stage, other than its occurrence in the Argentinean transition that will be examined further. As a cautionary note, it should be emphasized that the *nullum crimen sine lege* principle, as a fundamental guarantee of due process, should be adhered to. This will most probably pose a challenge for transitional states lacking corporate criminal liability provisions, but the exceptional circumstances and opportunities of transitions might assuage some of these difficulties.

Lastly, developments such as the increasing number of states that adopt CCL legislation and most importantly the principle of universal jurisdiction can be important for the future development of the

legislation. V. Spiga, 'Non-Retroactivity of Criminal Law: A New Chapter in the Hissène Habré Saga' (2011) 9 *Journal of International Criminal Justice* 1, p. 16.

103 Judges grounded the criminalization of certain conduct, such as aggression, in the existence of an international rule, regardless of the lack of any corresponding rule in domestic law. Kyriakakis, *Corporations, Accountability and International Criminal Law*.

104 Cassese and Gaeta, *Cassese's International Criminal Law*, pp. 38–39.

105 *United States* v. *Goering*, Judgment, 49, International Military Tribunal, 1 October 1946.

106 J. Kolieb, 'Through the Looking-Glass: Nuremberg's Confusing Legacy on Corporate Accountability Under International Law' (2017) 32 *American University International Law Review* 2, at 595.

107 'Guiding Principles', UN Doc. A/HRC/17/31, Principles 17–21, 23.

108 Note that according to Spiga, this defence has rarely been successful. Spiga, 'Non-Retroactivity of Criminal Law'.

obligation to prosecute and punish corporate entities. The principle of universal jurisdiction enables states to exercise jurisdiction over crimes solely on the basis of their abhorrent nature, irrespective of the locus of commission or the nationality of victims or perpetrators.[109] It is foreseen by respective treaties for war crimes,[110] torture,[111] enforced disappearances[112] and piracy.[113] In addition, states are authorized to exercise universal jurisdiction for *jus cogens* crimes,[114] and crimes provided for in customary international law,[115] thus allowing genocide and crimes against humanity to be prosecuted, irrespective of where they were committed.[116] It is exactly the *jus cogens* character of those core crimes that forms the basis for the exercise of universal jurisdiction, because it creates a shared interest of the international community to prevent and

109 For the differences between universal jurisdiction and the principle of *aut dedere aut judicare*, see Section 3.2.1.

110 Article 49 Geneva Convention for the Amelioration of the Condition of the Wounded and Sick in Armed Forces in the Field of 1949 (75 UNTS 31), Article 50 Geneva Convention for the Amelioration of the Condition of Wounded, Sick and Shipwrecked Members of Armed Forces at Sea of 1949 (75 UNTS 85), Article 129 Geneva Convention relative to the Treatment of Prisoners of War of 1949 (75 UNTS 135) and Article 146 Geneva Convention relative to the Protection of Civilian Persons in Time of War of 1949 (75 UNTS 287).

111 UN General Assembly, Convention Against Torture and Other Cruel, Inhuman or Degrading Treatment or Punishment, United Nations, Treaty Series, Vol. 1465, p. 85, 10 December 1984, Article 5(2).

112 International Convention for the Protection of All Persons against Enforced Disappearance, 2716 UNTS 3, UN Doc. A/RES/61/177, 20 December 2006, Article 9(2).

113 UN Convention on the Law of the Sea, 1833 UNTS 397, 21 ILM 1261 (1982), 10 December 1982, Article 105; UN Convention on the Continental Shelf, United Nations, UNTS 499, p. 311, 29 April 1958, Article 19.

114 C. Schwöbel-Patel, 'The Core Crimes of International Criminal Law', in K. Jon Heller et al. (eds.), *The Oxford Handbook of International Criminal Law* (Oxford University Press, 2020).

115 C. Bassiouni, 'Universal Jurisdiction for International Crimes: Historical Perspectives and Contemporary Practice' (2002) 42 *Virginia Journal of International Law* 81; A. Zimmermann, 'Violations of Fundamental Norms of International Law and the Exercise of Universal Jurisdiction in Criminal Matters', in C. Tomuschat and J.-M. Thouvenin (eds.), *The Fundamental Rules of the International Legal Order. Jus Cogens and Obligations Erga Omnes* (Martinus Nijhoff Publishers, 2006), p. 351. For arguments against the customary status, see C. Ryngaert, *The Principles of Extraterritorial Criminal Jurisdiction* (Oxford University Press, 2008).

116 Kelly, 'Prosecuting Corporations for Genocide', p. 161. See also Joint Separate Opinion of Judges Higgins, Kooijimans and Buergenthal, ICJ, *Case Concerning the Arrest Warrant of 11 April 2000* (Democratic Republic of the Congo v. Belgium) and SCSL, *Prosecutor* v. *Kallon*, Decision on Challenge to Jurisdiction: Lomé Accord Amnesty (Appeals Chamber), 13 March 2004, paras. 67–70.

punish them,[117] and in fact several states have adopted national legislation in that respect.[118] Authors, like Bassiouni and Wisse, suggest that the exercise of universal jurisdiction is not a possibility granted to states but, instead, is an obligation to investigate, prosecute and punish perpetrators of core crimes.[119] This means that if relevant laws with regards to international crimes and CCL exist, then any state has the authority to investigate, prosecute and punish corporate entities for core crimes committed abroad, even if neither they nor the victims have the respective nationality and irrespective of where the crimes occurred.[120] In 2002, Burmese victims accused the French company, Total, of complicity in crimes against humanity committed by the Burmese military, in relation to the construction and operation of the Yadana Gas Pipeline in Myanmar. The complaint was filed before Belgian courts and was based on the – back then in force – Belgian Law on universal jurisdiction.[121] Universal jurisdiction can be used within the transitional discourse, if not to contribute to transitional goals, then at least as a pressure point for transitioning states that often tend to undermine corporate prosecutions. By allowing the possibility that a corporation's wrongdoing – although marginalized within the transitional state – could be prosecuted in another forum, it illustrates that although the enforcement forum may be relative, the prohibition against committing international crimes remains absolute and anchors the way that corporate prosecutions should be conceptualized and developed. Moreover, the potential for prosecution in another forum under universal jurisdiction relativizes the strength of the *nullum crimen sine lege* principle, since it is probable

[117] Bassiouni, 'Universal Jurisdiction for International Crimes', 148–149; ICTY, *Prosecutor* v. *Anto Furundzija*, IT-95-17/1-T, Judgment of 10 December 1998 ('Furundzija Trial Judgment').

[118] Ramasastry and Thompson, *Commerce, Crime and Conflict*, pp. 15–16; Amnesty International, *Universal Jurisdiction*.

[119] Bassiouni and Wise, *Aut Dedere Aut Judicare*; but see Ryngaert analysing that under the Lotus judgment, what needs to be proven is that no rule prohibiting universal jurisdiction needs to crystallize. Ryngaert, *The Principles of Extraterritorial Criminal Jurisdiction*.

[120] For the problems arising out of universal jurisdiction in relation to corporate crimes, see P. Macklem, 'Corporate Accountability Under International Law: The Misguided Quest for Universal Jurisdiction' (2005) 7 *International Law Forum du droit international* 281–289; C. Ryngaert, 'Accountability for Corporate Human Rights Abuses: Lessons from the Possible Exercise of Dutch National Criminal Jurisdiction Over Multinational Corporations' (2018) 29 *Criminal Law Forum*, pp. 1–24.

[121] The case was dismissed for lack of standing of the plaintiffs. See Zerk, *Corporate Liability*, p. 20.

that globalized multinational corporations operate in jurisdictions where CCL laws already exist, rendering the invocation of the aforementioned principle futile.

3.2.3 Beyond and Before the ICC Shadowing Tower

Any discussion on corporations and international criminal law cannot but pay due respects to the Nuremberg precedent.[122] It was there that it was first discussed to hold an additional international trial for 'businesses or businessmen', which would target individuals as well as entities.[123] But the plan of a second trial did not materialize, drifting away the idea of corporate prosecutions.[124] In its place, the United States and the United Kingdom, under Control Council Law No. 10, which authorised the occupying powers to try suspected war criminals in their respective occupied areas,[125] conducted trials, including against industrialists who collaborated with the Nazi regime. Those tribunals did not have jurisdiction over corporate entities, so they tried individual business persons, but corroborated the 'symbiotic relationship between big business and a criminal regime which could not have survived without the former's unfaltering support'.[126]

The US Military Tribunal held three cases against industrialists. In the *Trial of Carl Krauch and Twenty-Two Others*, also known as IG Farben,[127] thirteen of twenty-four high-level members of IG Farben industrial concern, a German conglomerate of chemical and pharmaceutical firms, were found guilty of war crimes and crimes against humanity, through the plunder and spoliation or slave labour of civilians from German occupied territories and of German nationals.[128] In the

[122] K. R. Jacobson, 'Doing Business with the Devil: The Challenges of Prosecuting Corporate Officials Whose Business Transactions Facilitate War Crimes and Crimes Against Humanity' (2005) 56 *A. F. L. Revenue* 167, 230–231.

[123] J. A. Bush, 'The Prehistory of Corporations and Conspiracy in International Criminal Law: What Nuremberg Really Said' (2009) 109 *Colom LR* 1094, 1105, at 1113.

[124] Pietropaoli, *Business, Human Rights and Transitional Justice*, p. 28.

[125] Control Council Law No. 10, Punishment of Persons Guilty of War Crimes, Crimes against Peace and Against Humanity, 20 December 1945 [Control Council Law No. 10].

[126] H. van der Wilt, 'Corporate Criminal Responsibility for International Crimes: Exploring the Possibilities' (2013) 12 *Chinese JIL* 43, 52.

[127] Farben Vol. 8.

[128] All were acquitted of the charges of crimes against peace and conspiracy to commit crimes. Although four of the accused had participated in the rearmament of Germany, the fact that they were not military experts meant that they could not have known that

Trial of Alfried Felix Alwyn Krupp von Bohlen und Halbach and Eleven Others, also known as Krupp, employees of Krupp factories in Germany were found guilty of war crimes and crimes against humanity by participating in plunder and spoliation, and all but one were found guilty for the employment of 'prisoners of war, foreign civilians and concentration camp inmates under inhuman conditions in work connected with the conduct of war (. . .)'.[129] Lastly, in the *Trial of Friedrich Flick and Five Others*, also known as Flick,[130] Friedrich Flick and Otto Steinbrinck, high-level officials of the Flick Concern of industrial enterprises, including coal and iron plants, were convicted of using slave labour, plundering, and spoliating, as well as of financial support and membership to the SS. Similarly, the British Military Tribunal, in the *Trial of Bruno Tesch and Two Others*, also known as Zyklon B,[131] charged Bruno Tesch, the owner Tesch & Stabenow, a company that supplied the Auschwitz concentration camps with Zyklon B, a pesticide used by the Nazis in the gas chambers, as well as the company's manager and chief technician, for the supply of poison gas 'used for killing allied nationals interned in concentration camps, knowing that it was so to be used'.[132]

The legacy of the Nuremberg trials first lies in that they took for granted the responsibility of the respective business entities. It was on that assumption that they convicted individuals.[133] As per Ramasastry, the industrialist judgments 'reveal[s] an underlying implication that the corporations for which they worked had also committed international war crimes'.[134] Although the prosecution was required to prove 'that an individual defendant was either a participant in the illegal act or that, being aware thereof, he authorized or approved it',[135] individual criminal

they were aiding Germany in preparing for an aggressive war and consequently lacked the required mental element. Farben Vol. 8, at 36–37.

129 Krupp case, at 69, 70.

130 *United States* v. *Friedrich Flick* in 6 Trials of War Criminals before the Nuremberg Military Tribunals Under Control Council Law No. 10 (1952) (Flick case).

131 Trial of Bruno Tesch and Two Others in Law Reports of Trials of War Criminals, The United Nations War Crimes Commission, Vol. 1 (1947) 93 (Zyklon B case).

132 Zyklon B case, 93–103.

133 Ramasastry, 'Corporate Complicity: From Nuremberg to Rangoon'; Bernaz, 'Corporate Criminal Liability Under International Law' at 321; Pietropaoli, *Business, Human Rights and Transitional Justice*, p. 27.

134 A. Clapham, 'The Question of Jurisdiction Under International Criminal Law Over Legal Persons', in M. Kamminga and S. Zia-Zarifi (eds.), *Liability of Multinational Corporations Under International Law* (Kluwer Law International, 2000), pp. 139, 140.

135 Farben Vol. 8, 1153; Ramasastry, 'Corporate Complicity: From Nuremberg to Rangoon'.

responsibility was constructed as derivative of a corporation's collective responsibility for a crime. In the *Farben* case, it was because of Farben's liability that individual directors were convicted by virtue of their affiliation with the company.[136] The court noted that 'while the Farben organization, as a corporation, is not charged under the indictment with committing a crime and is not the subject of prosecution in this case, it is the theory of the prosecution that the defendants individually and collectively used the Farben organization as an instrument by and through which they committed the crimes enumerated in the indictment'.[137] Farben was deemed to have been used as a vehicle for the defendants, who acted through its 'instrumentality'.[138] Even fervent opponents of such a reading of the Farben case note, with surprise, that the corporation itself was represented by an attorney during the trial, who gave a closing argument, on behalf of Farben.[139]

A further legacy of Nuremberg is that the tribunals considered corporate entities as capable of committing international crimes. In *Farben*, businesses were considered able of violating international norms and engaging in illegal behaviour.[140] The Tribunal noted: 'Auschwitz was financed and owned by Farben.'[141] It added, 'if not actually marching with the Wehrmacht, Farben at least was not far behind'.[142] In Krupp, the court held that the company had violated the Hague Regulations, when it seized and confiscated property in occupied countries.[143] Overall, corporate criminal liability was seriously explored, and while it was not adopted, it was never rejected as impermissible under international law. In adopting a systemic approach to corporate crime, the trials of German industrialists highlighted the relationship between corporate activities

[136] Ramasastry, 'Corporate Complicity: From Nuremberg to Rangoon'. Note, however, that Heller argues the opposite and stresses out that nothing in the judgments supports the idea that a corporation's collective intent was attributed to individuals. See K. J. Heller, *The Nuremberg Military Tribunals and the Origins of International Criminal Law* (Oxford University Press, 2011), p. 253.

[137] Farben Vol. 8, 1108.

[138] Farben Vol. 8, 1084.

[139] Heller, *The Nuremberg Military Tribunals*, p. 253.

[140] F. Jessberger, 'On the Origins of Individual Criminal Responsibility Under International Law for Business Activity: IG Farben on Trial' (2010) 8 *JICJ* 3, at 783.

[141] Farben Vol. 8, at 1183–1184.

[142] Ibid.

[143] Krupp case, at 1351–1352.

and the commission of war crimes and crimes against humanity, and drew important conclusions thereof.[144]

The Nuremberg legacy was complemented by the Japanese courts and the Batavia Temporary Court Martial, in the former Dutch East Indies, present-day Jakarta. The latter was established by the Dutch colonial powers and the Allied powers to adjudicate less serious crimes than the ones of the International Military Tribunal for the Far East. One of those trials was against Washio Awochi, a Japanese hotel entrepreneur, convicted and sentenced to ten years' imprisonment for war crimes, under public international law. His crime consisted of employing young girls and forcing them into prostitution, under threat of violence.[145] Regarding Japanese courts, thirteen economic actors underwent trial by the Fukuoka District Court. Mitsui was convicted for slave labour, albeit only on first instance, and Mitsubishi and Nishimatsu companies reached settlements including apologies and compensation to slave labourers and the construction of a monument.[146]

The discussion on legal persons and international crimes was reignited in 1981, when the Ad Hoc Working Group of Experts on Southern Africa proposed an international penal tribunal for the suppression and punishment of the crime of apartheid with competence over legal entities.[147] This was based on the recognition by the Apartheid Convention that corporations, like other organizations, are capable of committing the crime of apartheid, albeit the liability that it attached was individual.[148] The experts accepted that international criminal law attaches primarily individual liability, but foregrounded a 'quasi-criminal responsibility' for corporate entities, including fines and punitive damages.[149]

Presently, the aforementioned efforts and discourse surrounding them seem to be sidelined. The absence of an international forum to try corporate malefactors has been wrongly perceived as amounting to an overall invisibility of corporate entities from the purview of international

[144] Pietropaoli, *Business, Human Rights and Transitional Justice*, p. 29.

[145] Case No. 76 Trial of Washio Awochi X II Law Reports of the Trials of War Criminals 122; F. Borch, *Military Trials of War Criminals in the Netherlands East Indies 1946–1949* (Oxford University Press, 2017).

[146] The Mitsui Judgment was reversed on appeal. Payne et al., *Archimedes Lever*, pp. 73–74.

[147] Implementation of the International Convention on the Suppression and Punishment of the Crime of Apartheid, UN Doc E/CN.4/1426, 19 January 1981, Draft Convention Articles 4–6.

[148] Ibid., Articles 1, 3 and 10.

[149] Ibid., pp. 58–60.

criminal law, while the lack of ICC jurisdiction over those entities has removed the leverage of complementarity from any potential plea for domestic corporate prosecutions. However, one has to remember first that the absence of enforcement mechanisms does not detract from the conclusion that international criminal norms bind corporate actors, which was analysed in Chapter 2.[150] Secondly, jurisdiction over corporations was excluded by the ICC Statute not due to oppositions in terms of substance but rather because of technical considerations, and primarily due to concerns over how complementarity will unfold.[151] But, to quote the STL prosecutor, 'international tribunals have repeatedly eschewed narrow, technical interpretations in favour of broader, pragmatic interpretations in the spirit of the fight against impunity, to carry out that fight as effectively as possible'.[152]

Today, with the increasing number of states adopting CCL provisions, those fears seem to be obsolete, and many advocate for an expansion of ICC jurisdiction over corporations,[153] especially in view of the 2016 inclusion of corporate crimes in the prioritization strategy of the court.[154] Notably, already since 2005, former Chief Prosecutor of the Special Court for Sierra Leone, David Crane, asserted that conflicts, like the one in Sierra Leone, do not only include combatants but also external players like corporations.[155] Similarly, ICC Prosecutor Moreno Ocampo, in 2003, asserted that investigation of the financial aspects of the alleged

150 Stephens, 'The Amorality of Profit'.

151 Clapham, 'The Question of Jurisdiction Under International Criminal Law', at 171; J. Kyriakakis, 'Corporations and the International Criminal Court: The Complementarity Objection Stripped Bare' (2008) 19 *Criminal Law Forum*, at 115–151.

152 He also referred to the UNGPs, STL, Case Against New TV S.A.L. and Karma Mohamed Tahsin al Khayat, STL-14-05/PT/AP/ARI26.1, Decision on Interlocutory Appeal Concerning Personal Jurisdiction in Contempt Proceedings, 2 October 2014; Bernaz, 'Corporate Criminal Liability Under International Law', p. 324.

153 J. P. Calderon Meza, 'ICC Personal Jurisdiction on Corporations for Criminal Liability and/or Civil Liability for Reparations' (2021) *Harvard International Law Journal*; J. Kyriakakis, 'Article 46C: Corporate Criminal Liability at the African Criminal Court' in C. Jalloh, K. Clarke and V. Nmehielle (eds.), *The African Court of Justice and Human and Peoples' Rights in Context: Development and Challenges* (Cambridge University Press, 2019).

154 In 2016, the 'Policy paper on case selection and prioritization' mentioned crimes occurring in the context of land grabbing by multinational corporations. ICC, Office of the Prosecutor, Policy Paper on Case Selection and Prioritisation, 15 September 2016.

155 D. Crane, 'Dancing with the Devil: Prosecuting West Africa's Warlords – Building Initial Prosecutorial Strategy for an International Tribunal After Third World Armed Conflicts' (2005) 37 *Case Western Reserve Journal of International Law* 1.

atrocities will be crucial for the prosecution of crimes already committed in the DRC, as well as to prevent future crimes.[156] The most significant and recent development has been the insertion of a CCL provision in the Protocol on Amendments to the Protocol on the Statute of the African Court of Justice and Human Rights ('Malabo Protocol').[157] While it remains to be seen how corporate jurisdiction will unfold, it is interesting to note that this initiative emerged in the African context, ravaged by violent conflicts, where corporate complicity to international crimes has been widely recorded.[158]

3.2.4 *Corporate Accountability as an Emerging Trend*

A state obligation to prosecute and punish corporate perpetrators of international crimes, particularly during transitions, can be related to the observation that criminal punishment of business entities for core international crimes has seemingly developed to a trend across national jurisdictions. Some authors seem to consider it as a rule of customary law,[159] but the required threshold seems difficult to attain. The consideration of corporate accountability for core crimes as general principle of law, according to Article 38 of the ICJ statute, might be more pertinent.[160]

156 Chatham House, 'Business and International Crime: What Are the Relevant Legal Principles Relating to the Responsibility of Companies and CEOs for Violations of International Criminal Law?' (2006), available at www.chathamhouse.org/sites/files/chathamhouse/public/ Research/International%20Law/ilp230206.pdf.

157 'Draft Protocol on Amendments to the Protocol on the Statute of the African Court of Justice and Human Rights', AU Doc. No. STC/Legal/Min. 7(1) Rev.1 (14 May 2014), adopted by the Decision on the Draft Legal Instruments (30 June 2014) AU Doc. No. Assembly/AU/Dec.529 (XXIII), Article 46C.

158 Michalakea, 'Article 46C of the Malabo Protocol', at 225–248.

159 Ramasastry, 'Corporate Complicity: From Nuremberg to Rangoon', 91; Clapham, 'Extending International Criminal Law'; Nerlich, 'Core Crimes and Transnational Business'.

160 General principles have been considered to derive from a comparison of various systems of municipal law, or directly from international legal relations, in addition to municipal law sources. H. Thirlway, *The Sources of International Law* (Oxford University Press, 2015), p. 93. According to Bassiouni, both approaches have been used by the ICJ and the PCIJ. C. Bassiouni, 'A Functional Approach to "General Principles of International Law"' (1990) 11 *Michigan Journal of International Law* 768, at 772–773. See also Méndez, 'Accountability for Past Abuses', p. 263; B. Simma and P. Alston, 'The Sources of Human Rights: Custom, Jus Cogens and General Principles' (1989) 12 *Australian Yearbook of Int'l L*, at 772.

An examination of relevant instruments and practice demonstrates a rise in the demands for corporate criminal liability over the last decades,[161] in contrast to the traditional view of classifying corporations as non-accountable, 'next to animals, children and the insane'.[162] Various international and regional instruments recognize corporate criminal accountability and urge states to adopt respective measures.[163] While the United Nations Guiding Principles on Business and Human Rights (UNGPs)[164] refer to criminal law only as a possibility,[165] a combined reading of Articles 4, 15 and 22 of the UN Basic Principles on the Right to a Remedy and Reparation ('Basic Principles') suggests that prosecution of perpetrators, as a form of reparation encompasses criminal measures against corporate legal persons.[166] The 'Impunity Principles'[167] prepared by Professor Diane Orentlicher and adopted by the Commission on Human Rights in 2005 are equally important for transitional societies, for articulating a seemingly unqualified duty of the state to investigate and prosecute perpetrators, without narrowing their focus to natural

161 C. Caeb, 'The Shifting Sands of Corporate Liability Under International Criminal Law' (2016) 49 *The George Washington International Law Review.*

162 C. Wells, *Corporate Criminal Liability*, Paper written for the ICJ Expert Legal Panel on Corporate Complicity in International Crimes, p. 33.

163 There are at least seventeen multilateral international instruments providing for corporate criminal liability, while before 1997 there was none. See, indicatively, Council of Europe, Council Recommendation (EC) No. R (88) 18 of 20 October 1988; the Basel Convention on the Control of Transboundary Movement of Hazardous Wastes and their Disposal, Articles 2(14), 4(3), 9, 22 March 1989, 1673 U.N.T.S. 57; the Bamako Convention on the Ban and Import Into Africa and the Control of Transboundary Wastes Within Africa, 29 January 1991 reprinted in 30 I.L.M. (1991). See 'Discussion. International Trends Towards Establishing Some Form of Punishment for Corporations' at 949.

164 'Guiding Principles', UN Doc. A/HRC/17/31.

165 It is worth recalling the SRSG's view, who, while typically against law-based approaches, took a different stance in relation to corporate international crimes. He noted that long-standing debates over the binding force of international crimes' prohibitions for corporations are yielding to new realities and that 'the absence of an international accountability mechanism … does not preclude the emergence of corporate responsibility today'. HRC, 'Business and Human Rights: Mapping International Standards of Responsibility', paras. 20, 21. It is also interesting to note that the Commentary to the UN Guiding Principles cites nine times criminal law as a potential implementation mechanism.

166 'Basic Principles', UN Doc. A/RES/60/147, Principles 4, 15, 22.

167 Report of the independent expert to update the set of principles to combat impunity, Diane Orentlicher. Addendum: Updated Set of principles for the protection and promotion of human rights through action to combat impunity. E/CN.4/2005/102/ Add.1: 8 February 2005 ('Impunity Principles'). Their precursor was the report prepared by Louis Joinet, the so-called Joinet Report.

persons.[168] To that, one should add the 2016 resolution of the European Parliament on corporate liability for serious human rights abuses in third countries,[169] and the 2016 Recommendation of the Committee of Ministers of the Council of Europe on human rights and business,[170] which explicitly mention criminal law.

In the realm of international courts, a relatively recent decision of the STL Appeals Panel represents this broader trend towards holding corporations accountable for international crimes.[171] It found that 'the term "person" in a legal context can include a natural human being or a legal entity (such as a corporation)'. The Appeals Panel confirmed that there has been a concrete movement on an international level backed by the United Nations for corporate accountability for human rights, which manifests in state practice providing for corporate criminal liability.[172] It also held that national laws are 'sufficiently similar'[173] to signify a trend, and 'indeed, corporate liability for serious harms is a feature of most of the world's legal systems and therefore qualifies as a general principle of law'.[174]

Demands from victims and civil society are also rife and play a crucial role in shaping a bottom-up, victim-centred approach to transitional justice. Various NGOs have long pled for corporate accountability for companies involved in grave crimes against Palestinians,[175] whereas just days after the Russian invasion in Ukraine, a large coalition was formed

[168] See principle 19 of the Impunity Principles. The Joinet Report stated that the right to effective remedy implies that all victims shall have the opportunity to assert their rights and receive a fair and effective remedy, ensuring that their oppressors stand trial and that they obtain reparation. Joinet Report, par. 26–27.

[169] European Parliament resolution of 25 October 2016 on corporate liability for serious human rights abuses in third countries (2015/2315(INI)) (2016).

[170] Recommendation of the Committee of Ministers of the Council of Europe on human rights and business, CM/Rec (2016)3, 2 March 2016.

[171] STL, Case against New TV S.A.L. and Karma Mohamed Tahsin al Khayat, STL-14-05/PT/AP/ARI26.1, Decision on Interlocutory Appeal Concerning Personal Jurisdiction in Contempt Proceedings, 2 October 2014. It is to be noted that this case sparked controversy. However, it deserves to be mentioned, as its findings were corroborated by the STL, Decision on Interlocutory Appeal concerning personal jurisdiction in contempt proceedings, Akhbar Beirut S.A.L. and Ibrahim Mohamed Al-Amin (STL-14-06/PT/AP/AR126.1), Appeals Panel, 23 January 2015. For an analysis of both cases, see Bernaz, 'Corporate Criminal Liability Under International Law'.

[172] Ibid., par. 46, 50, 52.

[173] Ibid., par. 51.

[174] Ibid., par. 67.

[175] By way of indication, see Al Haq and Lawyers for Palestinian Human rights, both having distinct projects on corporate accountability.

advocating for business disengagement from international crimes.[176] Also, victims' groups continuously approach the ICC. In 2014, Cambodian villagers filed a communication before the ICC alleging that the local 'ruling elite', along with companies, committed 'widespread and systematic' land grabbing using violence and forcible relocation against the population.[177] In 2017, another complaint was filed before the ICC, alleging that Chiquita Brands International incurs accomplice responsibility for crimes against humanity committed by Colombian paramilitary groups.[178] The most significant development, in the international sphere, has been the insertion of a CCL provision in the Malabo Protocol, which foresees criminal jurisdiction over corporations by the African Court of Justice and Human Rights (ACJHR).[179]

Similar developments take place in the domestic sphere.[180] Increasingly, civil law jurisdictions are establishing corporate criminal liability schemes in their domestic criminal codes,[181] catching up with their common law counterparts.[182] Several of them provide additionally for corporate criminal liability for genocide, crimes against humanity and

[176] See B4Ukraine website available at b4ukraine.org/.

[177] Communication under Article 15 of the Rome Statute of the International Criminal Court, the Commission of Crimes Against Humanity in Cambodia July 2002 to Present, available at www.fidh.org/IMG/pdf/executive_summary-2.pdf.

[178] The contribution of Chiquita corporate officials to crimes against humanity in Colombia, Article 15 Communication to the International Criminal Court, May 2017, available at www.fidh.org/en/region/americas/colombia/human-rights-coalition-calls-on-icc-to-investigate-role-of-chiquita.

[179] Draft Protocol on Amendments to the Protocol on the Statute of the African Court of Justice and Human Rights, AU Doc. No. STC/Legal/Min. 7(1) Rev.1 (14 May 2014), adopted by the Decision on the Draft Legal Instruments (30 June 2014) AU Doc. No. Assembly/AU/Dec.529 (XXIII), Article 45 and 46C ('Malabo Protocol').

[180] A survey conducted in 2016 by Clifford Chance asserts that most jurisdictions have CCL. Clifford Chance, Corporate Criminal Liability, April 2016; M. Engelhart, 'Corporate Criminal Liability from a Comparative Perspective', in D. Brodowski et al. (eds.), *Regulating Corporate Criminal Liability* (Springer, 2014), pp. 54–55.

[181] Limiting the application of the principle of *societas delinquere non potest*, which means that a legal entity cannot be blameworthy; Ramasastry mentions as examples France, the Netherlands, Canada, Switzerland, Austria, Belgium, India, Norway, Iceland, South Africa, New Zealand, Australia, Myanmar, Finland, Denmark, China, Philippines, Lithuania; Moldova, Albania, Romania, Singapore, Spain and Japan. See Ramasastry and Thompson, *Commerce, Crime and Conflict*. See also Linklaters, Global Guide: Corporate Criminal Liability, available at www.linklaters.com/insights/publications/corporate-criminal-liability-guide/global-guide-corporate-criminal-liability.

[182] Slye mentions that corporate criminal liability is found as early as 1670 in the civil law jurisdiction of France. See Slye, 'Corporations, Veils, and International Criminal Liability'. See also J. Kyriakakis, 'Corporate Criminal Liability and the ICC Statute:

war crimes.[183] The Special Representative of Human Rights and Transnational Corporations and Other Business Enterprises has also acknowledged the increase in the number of jurisdictions that accept corporate criminal liability.[184] Various national action plans[185] and NGO reports[186] rely on the effectiveness of criminal law against corporate wrongdoing. The ATCA litigation,[187] despite the hurdles posed by the *Kiobel* precedent,[188] confirms the increase of the demands for corporate accountability, when corporations facilitated the commission of international crimes.[189]

These developments do not yet rise to the level of a customary norm of corporate criminal liability, but they can be regarded as steps towards the development of general principles of law, according to Article 38 (1) (c) of the ICJ statute.[190] According to the International Law Commission, general principles of law are derived from national legal systems and include diverse legal issues, such as right to access an enclaved territory,

The Comparative Law Challenge' (2009) 56 *Netherlands International Law Review* 333, at 336–339.

183 Ramasastry and Thompson, *Commerce, Crime and Conflict*, pp. 15–16.

184 UN Special Representative of the Secretary-General on the issue of human rights and transnational corporations and other business enterprises; John Ruggie, Protect, Respect and Remedy: A Framework for Business and Human Rights, UN Doc. A/HRC/8/5, 7 April 2008, par. 74.

185 For example, see the national action plans of Italy, Denmark and Sweden, available at www.ohchr.org/EN/Issues/Business/Pages/NationalActionPlans.aspx.

186 International Corporate Accountability Roundtable and Amnesty International, the Corporate Crimes Principles, Report (October 2016).

187 United States Congress, 28 US Code Part IV Chapter 85 § 1350. Under the ATCA, the United States has jurisdiction for civil actions brought by aliens for torts, committed in violation of the law of nations or treaties of the United States. A violation of the law of nations is the one which is contrary to a norm of customary international law. See *Sosa* v. *Alvarez-Machain*, 542 US 692, 734–737 (2004). See further elaboration in Section 3.2.

188 In the *Kiobel* case, the court held that the claims must touch and concern the US territory with sufficient force to displace the presumption against extraterritorial application. *Kiobel* v. *Royal Dutch Petroleum Co.*, 133 S. Ct. 1659, 1665 (2013), p. 1669. Furthermore, in the *Jesner* case, it was decided that foreign corporations cannot be sued under the ATCA, but the issue of US corporations remains to be decided. *Jesner* v. *Arab Bank*, PLC, 584 US (2018).

189 See other important cases: *Wiwa* v. *Shell*, No. 08-1803-cv, 2009 WL 1560197 (2d Cir. 3 June 2009); *Bowoto* v. *Chevron*, No. C 99-02506 SI, 2006 WL 2455752 (N.D. Cal. 22 August 2006); *Xiaoning* v. *Yahoo! Inc.*, No. 07-CV-02151 (N.D. Cal. 30 July 2007); *Doe* v. *Nestle, S.A.*, No. 05-CV-05133 (C.D. Cal. 14 July 2005)], *Doe I* v. *Unocal Corp.*, 395 F.3d 932 (9th Cir. 2002).

190 *Joseph Jesner et al., Petitioners* v. *Arab Bank, PLC*, On a Writ of Certiorari to the United States Court of Appeals for the Second Circuit Brief of Amici Curiae of Comparative Law Scholars and Practitioners in Support of Petitioners, No. 16–499.

exclusion of illegal evidence, duress as a complete defence and various others. According to the Commission, those principles are identified under a two-pronged procedure. First, those principles need to exist in various different legal systems of the world and, second, they need to be transposed to the international legal system.[191] In what has to do with corporate criminal liability, although the second step of transposition is currently missing, the first one regarding the existence of said practice in different parts of the world is increasingly present. While not reaching yet that level, it appears that developments are moving in the direction of corporate liability for international crimes evolving to a general principle, albeit the exact forms of liability that states decide to implement might vary.[192]

At a minimum, they certainly demonstrate an emerging trend and an 'expanding web of liability for business entities implicated in international crimes'.[193] This means that states that 'like to see themselves as contributing to an international lawful order' should consider adopting measures to show respect to those principles.[194] Especially in cases of transition, where massive crimes take place, a 'government [...] can and should be judged by how much it attempts to do to comply with these principles'.[195] Corporate criminal liability legislation and investigation of corporate entities would certainly demonstrate such compliance and most importantly would serve as a necessary stepping stone towards establishing a binding international legal obligation. Each move along this path could potentially have implications for victims' rights and for states' responsibilities in holding corporate wrongdoers accountable.

Further, those developments signal a doctrinal convergence of elements in legal systems worldwide, ranging from domestic to international

191 International Law Commission, Report to the United Nations General Assembly, A/78/10, 2023, chapter IV, General principles of law, Conclusions 4 and 5. See also International Law Commission, second report on general principles of law by Marcelo Vázquez-Bermúdez, Special Rapporteur, UN GA, A/CN.4/741, 9 April 2020, par. 19.

192 STL, Case Against New TV S.A.L. and Karma Mohamed Tahsin al Khayat, STL-14-05/PT/AP/ARI26.1, Decision on Interlocutory Appeal Concerning Personal Jurisdiction in Contempt Proceedings, 2 October 2014, par. 67; Kyriakakis, *Corporations, Accountability and International Criminal Law*, p. 241.

193 Ramasastry et al., 'Translating Unocal', at 856; Kyriakakis, 'Prosecuting Corporations for International Crimes', at 108, 111; Kyriakakis, 'Corporate Criminal Liability and the ICC Statute', at 342. SRSG Ruggie also used that phrase, SRSG report, UN Doc. A/HRC/4/035, 9 February 2007, par. 22.

194 Méndez, 'Accountability for Past Abuses', 263.

195 Ibid.

legislation, which in turn can influence other domestic jurisdictions.[196] In addition, it demonstrates that the issue of personality and subjectivity of corporations for the purposes of international and national law tends to be tempered. That should be interpreted as a suggestion for the adoption of domestic CCL provisions to states that have not already done so. Further to that, the doctrinal development proves the beginning of a shift for the international dialogue as well, given that various authors advocate for the expansion of the ICC jurisdiction to cover corporate actors.[197] Domestic developments will likely impact the priorities of the international criminal law agenda and possibly bring the issue at the forefront, given that the gradual convergence of laws and concepts annuls the complementarity concerns, which hindered the inclusion of CCL to the Rome Statute.[198]

3.3 What about Victims? A New Landscape of the Right to Justice in International Human Rights Law

According to international human rights law, the obligation to prosecute and punish is robust, in what concerns individual perpetrators, in a similar way as with international criminal law.[199] When it comes to corporate entities, well-wishers might claim that international and regional human rights law regulate state conduct, and thus, in principle, they do not create any obligation for corporate actors, but it is a noticeably shrinking circle of authors still clinging to it.[200] In view of the

196 Especially for the jurisprudence of the US courts in ATCA cases, see Scheffer, 'The Impact of the War Crimes Tribunals on Corporate Liability for Atrocity Crimes Under US Law', pp. 163–164.

197 Calderon Meza, 'ICC Personal Jurisdiction on Corporations'.

198 Presumably, the jurisdiction over corporations was not included in the ICC Statute not due to oppositions in terms of substance but rather due to technical considerations. Clapham, 'The Question of Jurisdiction Under International Criminal Law'; Kyriakakis, 'Corporations and the International Criminal Court'.

199 For an elaborate account of the state obligation to investigate and prosecute, see Bassiouni, 'Accountability for Violations of International Humanitarian Law and Other Serious Violations of Human Rights', 3; Orentlicher, 'Settling Accounts'; Orentlicher, '"Settling Accounts" Revisited'; Roht-Arriaza, 'State Responsibility to Investigate and Prosecute'. Marginal scholarly voices claim that investigation, prosecution and punishment are not exclusive sanctions. J. Gavron, 'Amnesties in the Light of Developments in International Law and the Establishment of the International Criminal Court' (2002) 51 *ICLQ* 91–117, at 99.

200 M. Karavias, *Corporate Obligations Under International Law* (Oxford University Press, 2013).

increasing corporate political and economic power,[201] most authors argue that corporate human rights duties do not depend on their international legal subjectivity[202] but rather on their capacity to violate them[203]; that corporations fall under the 'every organ of society' clause of the UDHR[204]; and that other non-state actors, like ANSAs, are bound by international human rights law.[205] Recent developments, notably the UN Guiding Principles and the negotiated treaty on business and human rights, have seemingly outgrown any resentment.

The additional contribution of international human rights law in relation to the inclusion of corporate accountability in transitional criminal mechanisms lies at the emergence of the so-called right to justice. Shifting the lens to the victims, international and regional human rights law suggest a new landscape, much more fertile for corporate criminal accountability purposes, at least during transitions. This is because a right to justice is steadily emerging, according to the case law of human rights bodies, which brings new considerations at the forefront. The HRC, while asserting that the right to remedy does not give rise to a corresponding right to see another person prosecuted,[206] accepts that serious violations

201 J. Paust, 'Human Rights Responsibilities of Private Corporations' (2002) 3 *Vanderbilt Journal of Transnational Law* 5, at 801, 802; F. Wettstein, *Multinational Corporations and Global Justice* (Stanford Business Books, 2009), p. 18; S. Joseph, *Corporations and Transnational Human Rights Litigation* (Hart Publishing, 2004).

202 J. Knox, 'Horizontal Human Rights' (2008) 102 *American Journal of International Law* 1, at 19–20; S. Kobrin, 'Private Political Authority and Public Responsibility: Transnational Politics, Transnational Firms, and Human Rights' (2009) 19 *Business Ethics Quarterly* 3, at 356; Ratner, 'Corporations and Human Rights', pp. 496–497.

203 Clapham, *Human Rights Obligations of Non-State Actors*, pp. 69–70; P. Alston, *Non-state Actors and Human Rights* (Oxford University Press, 2005).

204 A. McBeth, 'Every Organ of Society: The Responsibility of Non-State Actors for the Realization of Human Rights' (2008) 30 *Hamline Journal of Public Law and Policy* 1. Similar argument by Report of the Special Rapporteur on extrajudicial, summary or arbitrary executions, Philip Alston, Mission to Sri Lanka, E/CN.4/2006/53/Add.5, 27 March 2006. In addition, it is argued that corporate entities are bound by human rights law when it is also *jus cogens* obligation.

205 Fortin, *The Accountability of Armed Groups Under Human Rights Law*, p. 98; Clapham, *Human Rights Obligations of Non-State Actors*, p. 82; Moffett, 'Beyond Attribution', pp. 323–346; A. Clapham, 'Focusing on ANSAs', in A. Clapham and P. Gaeta (eds.), *The Oxford Handbook of International Law in Armed Conflict* (Oxford University Press, 2014); D. Murray, *Human Rights Obligations of Non-State Armed Groups* (Hart Publishing, 2016), p. 75; L. Zegveld, *Accountability of Armed Opposition Groups in International Law* (Cambridge University Press, 2002), p. 149.

206 HRC, *H.C.M.A.* v. *the Netherlands*, UN Doc. CCPR/C/35/D/213/1986, Views of 30 March 1989, par. 11.6. However, in the following case, the applicant grounded a right 'to see another person criminally prosecuted' on Article 14(1) of the Covenant,

require criminal remedies.[207] Similarly, the ECtHR, while initially reluctant to provide for an individual right to criminal justice for violations of the rights included in the Convention,[208] later accepted that the enforcement of criminal justice when those violations take place is necessary for the effectiveness of remedies.[209] The Inter-American Court[210] and the Commission[211] have clearly expounded a victim's right to justice in cases of serious violations, grounded on a combination of the right to fair trial under Article 8 and the right to judicial protection under Article 25, which includes prosecution and punishment.[212] The African Charter on Human and Peoples' Rights contains a provision stating that 'every

which guarantees the right to a fair trial. See HRC, *S.E.* v. *Argentina*, UN Doc. CCPR/C/38/D/275/1988, Views of 26 March 1990, par. 5.5. Note also that, initially, criminal justice was only considered as a precondition for civil redress. HRC, *Rodriguez* v. *Uruguay*, UN Doc. CCPR/C/51/D/322/1988, Views of 19 July 1994, par. 6, 14.

[207] The HRC recognized that non-criminal remedies do not satisfy the threshold of 'adequate and effective' repair of the harm suffered by victims of serious violations such as those of the right to life. HRC, *Bautista de Arellana* v. *Colombia*, UN Doc. CCPR/C/55/D/563/1993, Views of 27 October 1995, par. 8; HRC, *Coronel* v. *Colombia*, UN Doc. CCPR/C/76/D/778/1997, Views of 24 October 2002, par. 6.2.

[208] ECtHR, *Perez* v. *France* (App. No. 47287/99), Judgment, Merits, 12 February 2004, par. 70.

[209] ECtHR, *Nikolova and Velichkova* v. *Bulgaria* (App. No.7888/03), Judgment (Merits and Just Satisfaction), 20/12/2007, par. 55; ECtHR, *Kaya* v. *Turkey* (App. No. 22729/93), Judgment (Merits and Just Satisfaction), 19 February 1998, par. 107; ECtHR, *Bitiyeva and X* v. *Russia* (App. Nos. 57953/00 and 37392/03), Judgment (Merits and Just Satisfaction), 21 June 2007, par. 156; ECtHR, *Keenan* v. *United Kingdom* (App. No. 27229/95), Judgment (Merits and Just Satisfaction), 3 April 2001, par. 122.

[210] IACtHR, *Castillo-Páez* v. *Peru*, Judgment (Reparations and Costs), ser. C no 34, 27 November 1998, par. 106.

[211] IAComHR, Case 11.725. *Carmelo Soria Espinoza* (Chile), 19 November 1999, par. 86–91; IAComHR, Case 11.228, 11.229, 11.231, 11.182, *Meneses Reyes, Lagos Salinas, Alsina Hurtos and Vegara Inostroza* v. *Chile*, 15 October 1996, par. 67–71; IAComHR, Case 10843, *Garay Hermosilla* v. *Chile*, 15 October 1996, par. 68–72; IAComHR, Case 10.488, *Ignacio Ellacuría, S. J. et al. (El Salvador)*, 22 December 1999, par. 189–196; IAComHR, Case 11.654, *Riofrio Massacre* (*Colombia*), 6 April 2001, par. 64–76; IAComHR, *Lucio Parada Cea, et al.* v. *El Salvador*, Case 10.480, Report No. 1/99, 27 January 1999, par. 124–129.

[212] IACtHR, *Durand and Ugarte* v. *Peru*, Series C No. 68, 16 August 2000, par. 130; IACtHR, *Blake* v. *Guatemala*, Series C No. 36, Judgment of 24 January 1998, par. 97; IACtHR, *Villagran Morales et al.* v. *Guatemala*, Series C No. 63, Judgment of 19 November 1999, par. 225; IACtHR, *Las Palmeras* v. *Colombia*, Judgment (Merits), Series C No. 90, 6 December 2001, par. 65; IACtHR, *Juan Humberto Sanchez* v. *Honduras*, Judgment (Preliminary objections, Merits, reparations and costs), Series C No. 99, 7 June 2003, par. 121–136; IACtHR, *Myrna Mack Chang* v. *Guatemala*, Judgment (Preliminary objections, Merits, reparations and costs), Series C No. 101, 25 November 2003, par. 200–211.

individual shall have the right to have his cause heard'.[213] In addition, soft law instruments conceptualize the victims' right to justice.[214] The 'Impunity Principles' explicitly conceived a right to justice separate from the right to remedy and devoted eleven principles to the duties of the states and the rights of the victims, while they restricted any potential justification limiting the right to justice.[215]

Further foundations of the right to justice can be found in the incremental strengthening of the position of the victims in criminal justice processes.[216] While for many years the main focus of international criminal law has been the accountability of the individual perpetrator, there are lately various signs of an enlargement of that focus to encompass victims' needs, as well.[217] Human rights bodies acknowledge victims' rights to participate in criminal proceedings.[218] Also, national

[213] Article 7.

[214] 'Basic Principles', UN Doc. A/RES/60/147, Principle 22 (f).

[215] Impunity Principles, Principle 19; Joinet Report, par. 26–27.

[216] For an overview of international criminal law from the perspective of victims, see G. Musila, *Rethinking International Criminal Law: Restorative Justice and the Rights of Victims in the International Criminal Court* (Lambert Academic Publishing, 2010); R. Henham, 'Some Reflections on the Role of Victims in the International Criminal Trial Process' (2004) 11 *International Review of Victimology* 1; M. Funk, *Victims' Rights and Advocacy at the International Criminal Court* (Oxford University Press, 2010); S. Karstedt, 'From Absence to Presence, From Silence to Voice: Victims in Transitional Justice Since the Nuremberg Trials' (2010) 17 *International Review of Victimology* 9; R. Henham, 'Conceptualizing Access to Justice and Victims' Rights in International Sentencing' (2004) 13 *Social and Legal Studies* 27.

[217] S. J. Ochoa, *The Rights of Victims in Criminal Justice Proceedings for Serious Human Rights Violations* (Brill Nijhoff, 2013), at 101–103; Aldana-Pindell, 'In Vindication of Justiciable Victims' Rights'. For an overview of the ICC redress regime, see C. McCarthy, 'Victim Redress and International Criminal Justice Competing Paradigms, or Compatible Forms of Justice?' (2012) *Journal of International Criminal Justice* 10, 351–372; L. Zegveld, 'Victims' Reparations Claims and International Criminal Courts' (2010) 8 *Journal of International Criminal Justice* 79; C. Ferstman, 'The Reparation Regime of the International Criminal Court: Practical Considerations' (2002) 15 *Leiden Journal of International Law* 667; E. Kristjansdottir, 'International Mass Claims Processes and the ICC Trust Fund for Victims', in C. Ferstman et al. (eds.), *Reparations for Victims of Genocide, War Crimes and Crimes against Humanity* (Martinus Nijhoff, 2009) 167.

'Discussion: International Trends Towards Establishing Some Form of Punishment for Corporations' at 965.

[218] The ECHR has held that the state obligation to protect the right to life demands the effective access of victims to the investigation but has not accepted a right to participate in criminal proceedings. ECtHR, *Case of Ogur* v. *Turkey* (App. No. 21594/93), Judgment of 20 May 1999, par. 92; ECtHR, 'Kaya v. Turkey', par. 107; ECtHR, *Mckerr* v. *United Kingdom* (App. No. 28883/95), Judgment (Merits and Just Satisfaction), 4 May 2001,

jurisdictions increasingly accept the victim's right to participate in criminal proceedings, amidst varying national approaches.[219] Lastly, several UN documents address criminal justice as a function of victims' redress, thereby underlining the link among victims' rights and criminal justice.[220] The right to justice should, further, be seen under the light of what Teitel termed the right to accountability in transitional periods, consisting of a set of obligations of the successor state to ensure accountability

par. 111–115; ECtHR, *Paul and Audrey Edwards* v. *United Kingdom* (App. No. 46477/99), Judgment (Merits and Just Satisfaction), 14 March 2002, par. 69–73; ECtHR, 'Bitiyeva and X v. Russia', par. 156. The Inter-American system has considered victims' participation in criminal proceedings as deriving from the right to fair trial but also from the right to judicial guarantees. IACtHR, 'Blake v. Guatemala, Judgment', par. 96; IACtHR, 'Villagran Morales et al v. Guatemala', par. 227; IACtHR, *Paniagua Morales and others* v. *Guatemala* (Judgment) Series C No. 37, 8 March 1998, par. 153; IACtHR, *Case of Caracazo* v. *Venezuela* (Reparation), Judgment of 29 August 2002, Series C No. 95, paras. 118, 143; IACtHR, 'Durand and Ugarte v. Peru', par. 129; IACtHR, *Rochela Massacre* v. *Colombia*, Judgment (Merits, Reparations and Costs), 11 May 2007, Series C No. 163, par. 195; IAComHR, 'Garay Hermosilla v. Chile', par. 63; IAComHR, *Mendoza et al.* v. *Uruguay*, Cases 10.029, 10.036, 10.145, 10.305, 10.372, 10.373, 10.374 and 10.375, Report No. 29/92, OEA/Ser.L/V/II.83 Doc. 14 at 154 (1993), 2 October 1992, par. 40–46; IAComHR, 'Carmelo Soia Espinoza (Chile)', par. 81. The Commission has also recognized the need to allow victims to participate in the proceedings regardless of the criminal model adopted (IAComHR, 'Garay Hermosilla v. Chile', par. 64, and IAComHR, 'Lucio Parada Crea et al. v. El Salvador', par. 119). The African Commission included victims' rights in criminal proceedings within the concept of fair trial rights, in the Principles and Guidelines on the Right to a Fair Trial and Legal Assistance in Africa.

219 It should be noted that victims' rights in criminal proceeding have traditionally been recognized in civil law countries, but it is not a common concept in common law countries. See M. Chiavario, 'Private Parties: The Rights of the Defendant and the Victim', in M. Delmas-Marty and J. R. Spencer (eds.), *European Criminal Procedures* (Cambridge University Press, 2002), at 542–547. However, the emergence of international and regional standards on the issue has led to gradual convergence in favour of the recognition of victims' rights to participate. Aldana-Pindell, 'In Vindication of Justiciable Victims' Rights'.

220 Commission on Human Rights, Question of the Violation of Human Rights and Fundamental Freedoms in Any Part of the World with Particular Reference to Colonial and Other Dependent Countries and Territories: Extrajudicial, Summary or Arbitrary Executions. Report by the Special Rapporteur, Mr Bacre Waly Ndiaye, submitted to Commission on Human Rights Resolution 1993/71, UN Doc. E/CN.4/1994/7, 7 December 1993, par. 688–699. The General Assembly has confirmed the importance of prosecution for the effective remedy of the victims on occasion of the Khmer Rouge Trials. UN GA, Khmer Rouge Trials, UN Doc. A/RES/57/228, 27 February 2003, at 1. The same also applies to consideration regarding other ad hoc tribunals.

for the perpetrators of serious crimes.[221] Its blueprint can be witnessed in both treaties[222] and case law of human rights bodies.[223]

The discourse on the right to justice offers a new analytical frame for corporate accountability in transition. First, the enhanced position of the victim in criminal procedures demonstrates increased attention to victims' needs. One of those needs, as evidenced by the multiplicity of cases brought in domestic and international fora, is the accountability of corporate perpetrators. Further to that, the emergence of the right to accountability entails a departure of accountability from its secondary status, as an obligation that is triggered upon the breach of a primary international obligation. It is arguably approximating an autonomous primary obligation itself,[224] at least for victims of war or repression. Its primary status, though, can more smoothly support its application against both private actors, since primary rights are already protected against acts committed by private persons, through the respective positive duties.[225] Human rights bodies and courts have held that they are to be performed against acts committed by both public and private persons.[226] Conversely, the lack of CCL legislation, or the unwillingness to enforce it, will essentially deny victims of their right to justice.

221 Teitel, 'Transitional Justice and Judicial Activism'.

222 Arguably, the International Convention for the Protection of All Persons from Enforced Disappearance and Article 7 of the ICC Statute define as an element of forced disappearance the refusal of the state to acknowledge the deprivation of the disappeared.

223 IACtHR, Velásquez-*Rodriguez* v. *Honduras* (Judgment), Series C No. 4, 1 126, 29 July 1988; ECHR, *Finogenov and Others* v. *Russia* (App. Nos. 18299/03, 27311/03), Judgment of 20 December 2011, par. 273.

224 Teitel, 'Transitional Justice and Judicial Activism'.

225 For an analysis, see C. Bakker, 'Duties to Prevent, Investigate and Redress Human Right Violations By Private Military and Security Companies: The Role of the Host State', in F. Francioni and Ronziti (eds.), *War by Contract: Human Rights, Humanitarian Law and Private Contractors* (Oxford University Press, 2011), p. 130.

226 See, indicatively, UN HRC, General Comment No. 31 [80], the nature of the general legal obligation imposed on States Parties to the Covenant, CCPR/C/21/Rev.1/Add.13, 26 May 2004, par. 8, 17; HRC, *Delgado Paez* v. *Colombia*, UN doc. CCPR/C/39/D/195/1985, Views of 12 July 1990; the Inter-American Court of Human Rights has ruled that the state violates its positive obligations when it does not protect the population against acts of non-state actors. IACtHR, *Pueblo Bello Massacre* v. *Colombia*, Series C No. 140, Judgment of 31 January 2006, par. 140, 226–259; IACtHR, 'Velásquez-Rodriguez v. Honduras', Judgment, par. 18; for the ECtHR, *Mccann and Others* v. *the United Kingdom* (App. No. 18984/91), Judgment (Merits and Just Satisfaction), 27 September 1995, par. 161; for the AfComHPR, see AfComHPR, *Zimbabwean Human Rights NGO Forum* v. *Zimbabwe*, 245/2002, ACHPR 73, Judgment of 25 May 2006, par. 143, 155, 160; AfComHPR, *Commission Nationale des Droits de*

What is more, the reinforced status of accountability demonstrates its increasing importance for transitional settings and by implication proves the magnitude of dissonance of corporate impunity with that imperative. It signifies a recognition of the prevalence of holding perpetrators accountable over more technical and thus less important considerations. This is evident by the fact that the right to accountability developed in order to bypass evidentiary issues with violations, such as disappearances when it was not possible to attribute them to the state.[227] It was thus an alternative way to find the state responsible, even when the first abuse could not be established as an internationally wrongful act. In an analogous way, the existence or not of CCL legislation, as a technical and thus less important issue, should not stand in the way of accomplishing accountability for egregious acts, and ultimately achieving peace, justice and reconciliation. It also denotes an enlargement of the focus of criminal justice, which in turn signals a shift of criminal law from mere accountability to pragmatic instrumentalism, where the focus is on the utility of punishment in achieving greater policy objectives.[228] This means that new considerations are put at the forefront of criminal justice and can potentially override the long-standing reticence against CCL.

3.4 Corporate Prosecutions and the Limits of Transitional Justice Periods

A new imaginary of transitional justice would locate corporate wrongdoers in the topography of transitional justice, insofar as they were implicated in prior violence. As discussed in Part I of this book, this would render the transitional endeavour better equipped to achieve its goals, namely accountability of the perpetrators, remedies for the victims, reconciliation and ultimately peace. In cases of widespread corporate abuses during conflict or repression, the odds are that transitional justice can at least partially deliver those goals, insofar as it also includes corporate perpetrators. Furthermore, the proposed integration would respond to persistent victims' calls for corporate accountability, as well as to the long-appraised discourse on 'root causes of violence'. It would

l'Homme et des Libertes v. *Chad*, Communication 74/92, 9th Annual Activity Report (2000) AHRLR 66, 11 October 1995.

[227] Teitel, 'Transitional Justice and Judicial Activism' at 392.

[228] 'Discussion: International Trends Towards Establishing Some Form of Punishment for Corporations' at 965.

insert the much needed economic aspect in transitional praxis, equipping it to better address the multi-layered complexities of prior injustice, and making it more receptive to domestic predicaments, insofar as those concerned corporate wrongdoing.[229]

Criminal justice mechanisms are a foundational pillar of transitional efforts and are associated with states' international obligations to investigate, prosecute and punish perpetrators of international crimes.[230] The inclusion of corporate malefactors in those mechanisms would play a significant role in achieving the aforementioned transitional objectives. But such inclusion would not be without controversy. The first challenge[231] thereof would focus on the existence or not, and contours of a potential state duty to investigate, prosecute and punish corporate entities.[232] It seems to be uncontested that the state duty to investigate, prosecute and punish perpetrators of international crimes is not limited to individual combatants,[233] as other actors can also bear criminal responsibility for international crimes, including economic actors,[234] insofar as they are among those most responsible for those crimes. This is corroborated by the various domestic and international courts that, since Nuremberg, have prosecuted economic actors[235] and seems to have straightforward implications for individual business people. For corporate entities, the law is not yet settled, but as examined in Chapters 1 and 2, different arguments suggest an approach that should also include those

229 For an elaborate account of those arguments, see Part I, Section 2.2.

230 Special Rapporteur on the Promotion of Truth, Justice, Reparation and Guarantees of Non-Recurrence, Report of the Special Rapporteur on the Promotion of Truth, Justice, Reparation and Guarantees of Non-Recurrence, UN Doc. A/HRC/48/60, 9 July 2021.

231 Note that this chapter presents a selection of challenges, as it is not possible to have an exhaustive account. Another pertinent challenge that is analysed in Part II Section 4.1.5.3 on financial complicity has to do with where to draw the line between appropriate business practices and those complicit to international crimes. See S. Michalowski, 'Doing Business with a Bad Actor: How to Draw the Line Between Legitimate Commercial Activities and Those That Trigger Corporate Complicity Liability' (2015) 50 *Texas International Law Journal* 403.

232 It is to be noted that this challenge does not apply to individual business persons who, like any natural person, are subject to the jurisdiction of ordinary criminal courts, thereby indirectly implicating also the corporate entity. The latter, as a distinct person, might be subject to ordinary courts, in states with relevant provisions or by civil courts.

233 Kyriakakis, *Corporations, Accountability and International Criminal Law*, p. 221.

234 S. Michalowski, 'Approaches to Criminal Responsibility of Economic Actors in Transitional Justice Processes: Lessons from Colombia' (2024) 55 *Columbia Human Rights Law Review* 2, at 488.

235 For an examination of those cases, see Sections 3.2.3, 4.1 and 4.2 of Part II.

entities. According to Section 3.2.2, corporate actors can seemingly commit the most serious crimes during conflict or repression. Various corporate entities have committed, through diverse modes of participation, genocide, war crimes and crimes against humanity. Despite the absence of an international forum with jurisdiction over those crimes, corporate entities seem to be covered by the substantive prohibition of international crimes.[236] In the most recent conflict in Palestine, several companies are providing Israel with weapons and military equipment despite the interim order by the ICJ determining that there is 'real and imminent risk' of irreparable harm to the rights of the Palestinians in Gaza to be protected from genocide.[237] Those companies supply weapons, while knowing how they will be used, therefore risking complicity to genocide charges for the entities and the personnel involved.[238]

A further challenge pertains to the rationale for resorting to transitional courts instead of ordinary ones. Transitional justice is inherently limited to the most responsible actors and the most serious crimes, and it is not settled that including corporate accountability cases does not overstretch those limits. It might be argued that amidst a period requiring resolution of intricate problems, with limited resources and increased tensions, cases against corporations might be better addressed by ordinary courts. To that, one should add the usual discourse on corporate contribution to development, which usually makes governments shy away from discussions on corporate accountability, let alone through criminal measures.[239] Thus, a crucial issue is whether the investigation and prosecution of corporate entities should happen in the framework of transitional mechanisms rather than ordinary justice, given that a transitional state might plausibly argue that its obligation to investigate, prosecute and punish is exhausted insofar as proceedings have started before ordinary courts against corporate perpetrators.[240] This question holds practical value for a hypothetical scenario where a transitional state has

[236] See Section 3.2.2 of Part II.

[237] The court also found that 'at least some of the rights claimed by South Africa and for which it is seeking protection are plausible'. See International Court of Justice, Interim Order, Application of the Convention on Prevention and Punishment of the Crime of Genocide in the Gaza Strip (*South Africa v. Israel*), par. 54, 74.

[238] Pietropaoli, 'Obligations of Third States'.

[239] Wesche, 'Business Actors, Paramilitaries and Transitional Criminal Justice in Colombia', p. 479.

[240] Michalowski, 'Approaches to Criminal Responsibility', p. 486.

CCL provisions in place, but it is debated whether to include corporate entities in transitional criminal tribunals. Beyond that, this discussion carries considerable symbolic significance for the broader integration of corporate accountability into transitional justice.

In legal terms, international law does not oblige states to include third-party actors in transitional mechanisms, as long as ordinary criminal courts take hold of the relevant cases.[241] However, the Inter-American Court of Human Rights, in the *Vereda la Esperanza* v. *Colombia* case, held that a violation of the obligation to investigate, prosecute and punish can be substantiated when ordinary courts are slow in opening investigations of cases that have been referred to them by special tribunals.[242] It can thus be concluded that the inclusion of economic actors in transitional mechanisms is required to meet a state's obligation to investigate, prosecute and punish, as long as not including them would result in impunity for economic actors who hold increased criminal responsibility. In other words, such inclusion seems necessary when ordinary justice does not offer effective alternatives, which would be unsurprising in transitional contexts, where resources are limited, the rule of law and institutions are weakened and there is often a substantial backlog of cases.

Beyond the strictly legal considerations, including corporate entities in transitional criminal mechanisms, instead of relegating them to ordinary courts, holds significant symbolic importance. This is, primarily, because such inclusion acknowledges the principal role of corporate entities in prior conflict or repression. As extensively documented, corporate activities might frequently be part of violence or intersect with the underlying causes of conflict or repression, fuelling, exacerbating or maintaining them. Assigning those cases to ordinary courts conveys the message that corporate involvement was tangential to the conflict, a mere anomaly of an otherwise well-functioning system. Instead, placing them under the auspices of transitional justice acknowledges their substantial role and significance in the prior situation, as well as the potential contribution of their accountability for achieving the aims of transitional justice. It, thus, holds greater potential of averting similar cases in the future.

In addition, assigning corporate accountability cases to transitional courts, alongside other cases related to past atrocities, rather than

[241] Ibid., p. 490.

[242] IACtHR, *Vereda La Esperanza* v. *Colombia*, Preliminary Objections, Merits, Reparations and Costs, Series C No. 341, 31 August 2017, par. 235, 236.

separating them and handling them exclusively in ordinary courts, has important implications for transitional justice's ability to construe the past and construct a holistic narrative of prior violence, along with its complexities, including the actors and dynamics involved, rather than a simplistic and linear account.[243] As the UN Special Rapporteur on the Promotion of Truth, Justice, Reparation and Guarantees of Non-Recurrence noted, mass violations rely on the coordination of various actors and the support of economic and political actors and accordingly necessitate a prosecutorial strategy able to tackle those intricate webs.[244] In an opposite scenario, where the complicated phenomenon of violence is fragmented, with some perpetrators allocated to specialized courts and others – potentially collaborators of the former – to ordinary courts, then what results is a disjointed judicial narrative.[245] This fragmentation appears inadequate to address a multifaceted yet single phenomenon, as it creates differing dynamics,[246] emphasizes the importance of some actors at the expense of others and ultimately makes the ground fertile for corporate impunity to prevail.[247]

Professor Michalowski eloquently demonstrated those points, using the example of the two Colombian transitional justice efforts.[248] The first one, under the Justice and Peace Law 975/2005, created special criminal justice mechanisms with limited jurisdiction over demobilized paramilitaries. The role of economic actors was relegated to the context within

[243] For the interpretation of past crimes taking place in forums of communication such as courts of law, truth commission and other, see S. Buckley-Zistel, 'Detained in Hohenschönhausen. Heterotopia, Narratives and Transitions from the Stasi Past in Germany', in S. Buckley-Zistel and S. Schäfer (eds.), *Memorials of Violence in Times of Transition* (Intersentia, 2013).

[244] Report of the Special Rapporteur on the promotion of truth, justice, reparation and guarantees of non-recurrence, to the Human Rights Council, UN DOC. A/HRC/27/56, 27 August 2014, par. 72.

[245] Michalowski, 'Approaches to Criminal Responsibility', at 461.

[246] D. M. López and J. P. Vera Lugo, Actores económicos, formación de Estado y justicia transicional: Comentarios críticos desde Colombia, 20 *IdeAs* 2022.

[247] R. F. Layús, 'Just Collateral Damage? Accountability of Economic Elites in Peacebuilding and Transitional Justice in Colombia' (2024) 49 *Peace & Change* 3, at 223–241; Michalowski, 'Approaches to Criminal Responsibility', at 460; Michalowski et al., *Entre Coacción y Colabouración*, pp. 131–132.

[248] Michalowski, 'Approaches to Criminal Responsibility'; See also Wesche, 'Business Actors, Paramilitaries and Transitional Criminal Justice in Colombia'; J. A. Tobar Torres, 'Responsabilidad corporativa en procesos transicionales de paz: Entre la judicialización y la autorregulación. Elementos de análisis desde el caso colombiano' (2019) 17 *Estudios Constitucionales* 2.

which the crimes of paramilitaries took place,[249] and relevant cases were referred to ordinary justice, with few resulting in actual criminal trials.[250] For Michalowski, deferring those cases to ordinary courts was problematic in that it created a fragmented approach to the conflict and backgrounded key contributors to it. In addition, relegating the involvement of corporate actors to the context, while still speaking of it, raised due processes concerns, given that statements were made without respecting the evidentiary standards used in criminal proceedings.[251] The case of the Chiquita Brands company is illustrative. Charges against it for supplying arms to paramilitary groups, although fundamental for the maintenance of the conflict, were brought before ordinary courts, as opposed to the crimes of the company's collaborators who were decided by specialized courts. Even worse, the judges of the ordinary courts who assumed competence for the company lacked a comprehensive understanding of the conflict and of Chiquita's role within it.[252]

In contrast, the Colombian transitional justice process that was based on the Peace Agreement of 2016 between the government and the FARC foresaw the creation of the Special Jurisdiction for Peace (JEP), with jurisdiction to punish those with the greatest responsibility for the most serious and representative crimes, including economic actors, who voluntarily submitted to it.[253] This focus on the nature and gravity of crimes and the responsibility of perpetrators leveraged a different investigative strategy, centred on identifying patterns of violence and synthesizing information on the motivations of various actors and structural alliances between them for the most serious crimes.[254] To satisfy those requirements, investigations and prosecutions refrained from fragmenting the conflict across different courts, including for economic actors. There was,

[249] Michalowski, 'Approaches to Criminal Responsibility', p. 459.

[250] For an explanation of the inaction of the ordinary jurisdiction, see L. Bernal-Bermúdez and D. Marín Lopez, 'Los Empresarios en la Guerra: Elementos de la Verdad Judicial Sobre la Complicidad Empresarial en Colombia', in N. Sanchez et al. (eds.), *Cuentas Claras* (Dejusticia, 2018), p. 65.

[251] S. Michalowski et al., *Los terceros complejos: la competencia limitada de la Jurisdicción Especial para la Paz 50* (Dejusticia, 2019).

[252] Michalowski, 'Approaches to Criminal Responsibility', p. 463.

[253] For an overview of the process, see M. Valiñas, 'The Colombian Special Jurisdiction for Peace' (2020) 18 *Journal of International Criminal Justice*, at 452–453. See also H. Olasolo and J. Ramirez Mendoza, 'The Colombian Integrated System of Truth, Justice, Reparation and Non-Repetition' (2017) 15 *Journal of International Criminal Justice*, at 1011.

[254] Michalowski, 'Approaches to Criminal Responsibility', p. 469.

thus, the possibility to present a much fuller image of the conflict, and a unified judicial truth.

Importantly, leaving corporate entities outside the scope of transitional criminal justice measures means that they are deprived of the criminal benefits usually associated with them, which raises difficult questions regarding the proportionality of punishment and the equal treatment of actors that have been central to the conflict or repression.[255] A system allowing combatants to profit from transitional mechanisms and receive lesser penalties from what they would have received were they to be tried by ordinary courts, while prohibiting corporate entities – usually the combatants' collaborators – from doing so, would treat stakeholders unequally and seriously risk its legitimacy. In addition, by excluding corporate entities from transitional criminal mechanisms, they are forced to resort to ordinary justice mechanisms, usually associated with harsher penalties for the same wrongs. In turn, this provides no incentives to those entities to reckon with their past, and to avert the repetition of the same wrongs in the future. As a result, corporate impunity is exacerbated, and victims' satisfaction is shrunk even more,[256] altogether putting the realization of the aims of transitional justice at risk.

One might tend to argue that the role of corporate actors in conflict or repression, while widely recorded, is still an issue of contestation, as businesses are not a unified and homogenous group. Indeed, it is certain that while some businesses profit from violence, others take every step possible not to be implicated in it. Still, excluding businesses altogether from transitional mechanisms does not seem to offer any adequate solution or even the necessary nuance in the treatment of corporate actors. Rather, a more plausible answer seems to be the one followed by the Colombian Final Peace Agreement which adopted a differentiated approach and clarified that economic and other third-party actors might have been victims of the conflict but also possibly perpetrators.[257] Another widely held argument, especially prominent in Colombia, was that criminalizing corporate actions is unnecessary amidst an environment where the primary focus should be on former combatants who bear

[255] Michalowski and Cardona Chaves, 'Responsabilidad Corporativa y Justicia Transicional', pp. 173–182.

[256] Michalowski, 'Approaches to Criminal Responsibility', p. 464.

[257] Final Agreement for the Termination of Conflict and the Construction of Stable and Lasting Peace, FARC-EP, Government of Colombia, 11 December 2016, p. 189. For an analysis, see Michalowski, 'Approaches to Criminal Responsibility', p. 476.

the primary responsibility and are favoured, through benefits, by transitional mechanisms in order to achieve peace.[258] To this debate, as well, no solution would be offered by excluding corporate actors altogether, but rather by including them under a scheme of differentiated responsibility, similar to the approach already applied to former combatants.

The debate on whether to prosecute corporate entities for their implication in conflicts and repression is admittedly a difficult one to settle, partly because it saddles on the already existing debate on peace versus justice.[259] In its simplified form, this debate embodies the choice between granting amnesties to former combatants and securing peace or pursuing accountability and risking the usually fragile peace processes.[260] Negotiators are called to make hard decisions among incommensurable goods,[261] and disagreements arise on whether retribution is the most appropriate way to respond to the wrongdoing or whether it fits into a broader demand of justice.[262] This debate can also emerge in terms of corporate accountability, as the inclusion of corporate actors in criminal mechanisms might multiply already existing tensions, increase polarization and endanger the transitional process. Those risks can be further aggravated by corporations' economic strength and political connections.[263] Those dynamics have been evident during the peace negotiations in Colombia. The balance between prosecutions and amnesties has

258 Michalowski, 'Approaches to Criminal Responsibility', p. 476.

259 For more information on the cardinal transitional debate over justice versus peace, see M. Aukerman, 'Extraordinary Evil, Ordinary Crimes'. For the peace versus justice approaches, see C. S. Nino, 'The Duty to Punish Past Abuses of Human Rights Put into Context: The Case of Argentina' (1991) 100 *The Yale Law Journal* 8, at 2619–2640, J. Zalaquett, 'Balancing Ethical Imperatives and Political Constraints: The Dilemma of New Democracies Confronting Past Human Rights Violations' (1992) 43 *Hastings Law Journal* 1425. On retributive approaches to transitional justice, see Orentlicher, 'Settling Accounts'; Malamud-Goti, 'Transitional Governments in the Breach', at 6. On restorative approaches, see Sarkin, *Carrots and Sticks*.

260 H. Yusuf, 'Peace Versus Justice and Rule of Law Debates in Transitions', in H. Yusuf and H. van der Merwe (eds.), *Transitional Justice Theories, Mechanisms and Debates* (Routledge, 2021).

261 M. Pensky, 'Amnesty on Trial: Immunity, Accountability and the Norms of International Law' (2008) 1 *Ethics and Global Politics* 1.

262 C. Murphy, *The Conceptual Foundations of Transitional Justice* (Cambridge University Press, 2017), p. 1.

263 See the analysis of Payne et al. on corporate veto power. Payne et al., *Archimedes' Lever*, pp. 113–161.

been considered delicate,[264] and the campaign against the ratification of the final peace agreement during the 2016 referendum was allegedly orchestrated, among others, by businesses that were named as financial supporters of paramilitary groups during the armed conflict. They were provisions concerning economic actors that changed thereafter.[265] Similarly, in Tunisia, a draft Economic and Financial Reconciliation Bill, offering the possibility of reconciliation to private actors involved in corrupt activities, was presumably the fruit of intense lobbying by the business sector.[266]

Attempting to prosecute such powerful actors, particularly within transitional justice, transpired by the logic of limited prosecutions, could overwhelm the criminal mechanisms, potentially already burdened by the volume and complexity of cases. As a first step, it would thus be advisable to avoid horizontal prosecutions of business actors and instead develop a prioritization strategy, potentially focusing criminal measures on the most responsible actors and the most serious crimes, including those of corporations. Depending on the gravity of their crimes, corporations could be included in the competence of criminal tribunal, not in a voluntary way as in Colombia, but rather under mandatory terms,[267] while not losing sight of the specific features of each transition and avoiding additional risks to the usually already tense transitional dynamics. At the same time, less grave corporate violations could be addressed by other transitional mechanisms. Corporate accountability will arguably be better tackled by multiple transitional measures, capable of maximizing the efficacy of any single measure and of tempering each one's inherent limitations.[268] One such limitation of criminal measures is that they move away from broad patterns of complicity, due to the inability of a criminal law model to deal with tiers of moral blameworthiness.[269] Approaching corporate accountability during transitional times through

[264] 'Symposium on the Colombian Peace Talks and International Law' (2016) 110 *AJIL Unbound* 161; R. Urueña, 'Prosecutorial Politics: The ICC's Influence in Colombian Peace Processes, 2003–2017' (2017) 111 *AJIL* 104.

[265] Michalowski, 'Approaches to Criminal Responsibility', p. 473.

[266] Michalakea, 'Anticorruption and Transitional Justice', p. 14.

[267] Michalowski, 'Approaches to Criminal Responsibility'.

[268] Kyriakakis, *Corporations, Accountability and International Criminal Law*, p. 177.

[269] N. Roht-Arriaza, 'Why Was the Economic Dimension Missing for So Long in Transitional Justice? An Exploratory Essay', in H. Verbitsky and J. P. Bohoslavsky (eds.), *Outstanding Debts to Settle: The Economic Accomplices of the Dictatorship in Argentina* (Cambridge University Press, 2015).

an ecological vision, namely a logic of multiple justice modalities that are complementary to each other, seems capable of addressing the complexities of corporate involvement in conflict.[270] Broadly speaking, a combination of different measures against corporate malfeasance under each transitional pillar would presumably be able to ensure the largest possible protections,[271] under a varieties of remedies approach,[272] that could maximize the efficacy of each single measure and mitigate their limitations.[273]

The peace versus justice debate was relevant for transitional justice since its inception and due consideration should always be afforded to it and its implications. Nevertheless, its invocation regarding the intersection of corporate accountability and transitional justice should not serve to obscure other underlying tensions and overshadow more 'mature' questions that have emerged alongside the field's development.[274] According to Teitel, unlike before, the current dilemmas of transitional justice concern more comprehensive issues than simply holding accountable the predecessor regime and are shifted into how to heal an entire society and incorporate diverse rule-of-law values.[275] For Sharp, the current fourth generation of transitional justice engages more with issues that were previously relegated to the field's peripheries, like economic justice, while the debates and dilemmas of previous eras – like the peace versus justice one – remain relevant and occasionally intractable.[276] It seems that in this new phase of maturity, the debate of truth versus justice tends to be tempered, as truth and justice are not mutually exclusive objectives. Rather, as the UN Secretary General noted, 'justice,

[270] Kyriakakis, *Corporations, Accountability and International Criminal Law*, p. 216.

[271] Report of the Special Rapporteur on the Promotion of Truth, Justice, Reparation and Guarantees of Non-recurrence, to the Human Rights Council, UN DOC. A/HRC/21/46, 9 August 2012, par. 21–27.

[272] T. Olsen, *Seeking Justice. Access to Remedy for Corporate Human Rights Abuse* (Cambridge University Press, 2023), chapter 2.

[273] Kyriakakis, *Corporations, Accountability and International Criminal Law*, p. 177.

[274] See Sharp discussing the phases of maturity of transitional justice. Sharp, 'Interrogating the Peripheries'.

[275] R. Teitel, 'Transitional Justice Genealogy' (2003) 16 *Harvard Human Rights Journal* 69, at 77. However, the turn into the inclusion of socio-economic rights with the transitional remit as well as of corporate actors is associated with a shift of transitional justice away from a more retributive or restorative understanding towards a more distributive approach.

[276] Sharp, 'Interrogating the Peripheries'.

peace and democracy are not mutually exclusive objectives, but rather mutually reinforcing imperatives'.[277]

In an era of peace and justice considered mutually reinforcing imperatives, re-inserting an antagonistic relationship between them could mask or divert attention from discussions with deep-seated economic and political repercussions, hinder a clearer understanding of current realities and limit opportunities for meaningful action. It is widely accepted that the economic orthodoxy favoured by governments translates into a reluctance to confront business interests,[278] and even when there is evidence of their complicity to abuses, states prefer to envisage corporate actors as playing a key role in their efforts to rebuild post-conflict societies, particularly with regard to achieving the new regime's socio-economic or developmental objectives.[279] Oftentimes, transitional governments try to befriend businesses for their presumed contribution to economic development or as was argued in Tunisia for their future role 'pacifying the environment for investment' and in a potential future economic take-off.[280] In addition, they tend to avoid challenging their interests, including of those who collaborated or profited from previous injustice, presumably because they have the power to undermine the transitional efforts.[281] In light of those, the peace versus justice debates, while undoubtedly significant, should be analysed in parallel and not in place of other fundamental concerns that have struggled to gain attention. Those include questions around the reasons why the business sector might have the aforementioned capabilities and whether this reflects structural and power hierarchies reminiscent of the very issues that initially prompted the need for transition. Illustratively, such an argument perceiving corporate accountability as antithetic to peace was

[277] 'The Rule of Law and Transitional Justice in Conflict and Post-Conflict Societies', UN Doc. S/2004/616, par. 1. See also Biggar noting that the aims of justice, peace and truth are interrelated, and they might be served by different mechanisms. N. Biggar, 'Making Peace or Doing Justice: Must We Chose?', in Nigel Biggar (ed.), *Burying the Past: Making Peace and Doing Justice After Civil Conflict* (Georgetown University Press, 2003), pp. 3, 7–16.

[278] Kyriakakis, *Corporations, Accountability and International Criminal Law*, p. 182.

[279] C. Abrahams, 'Lessons from the South African Experience', in S. Michalowski (ed.), *Corporate Accountability in the Context of Transitional Justice* (Routledge, 2013), pp. 153–154.

[280] This was argued in Tunisia. See Guellali, 'Tunisia: Transitional Justice in the Crosshairs'.

[281] P. McAuliffe, 'Rhetoric and Realpolitik: Interrogating the Relationship between Transitional Justice and Socio-Economic Justice' (2012–2013) 23 *Finnish Yearbook of International Law*, at 239–307.

voiced by South African Minister of Justice Penuell Maduna.[282] Despite the widely recorded corporate implication in Apartheid, Maduna launched a fervent opposition to Apartheid victims' lawsuits in the US. He exonerated corporations and stated that reparations have already been adequately addressed by the TRC,[283] and measures have been taken by the state despite wide evidence to the contrary. In light of those, litigation efforts were, for him, only a threat to reconciliation efforts.[284] In hindsight, Maduna's arguments seem unsubstantiated and unconvincing. It, rather, appears that they served to mask his politico-economic vision of future recovery and prosperity, being contingent on those same corporations and their investments.[285] His fondness of the corporations sued in the US was later corroborated by him being hired by one of them as their lawyer.[286]

Notably, the framing of a particular problem can be traceable to a historically and theoretically conditioned awareness of it.[287] Putting one debate or the other in the forefront mirrors one's understanding of conflict and repression, as well as of transitional priorities.[288] It further reveals how one evaluates the mainstream transitional justice paradigm, which determines future possibilities for alternative action. In this context, overlooking essential questions on socio-economic issues, including corporate power and impunity, and allowing debates about peace versus justice to dominate the intellectual and practical space appears to ignore the critical shortcomings of transitional justice, especially those related to its liberal underpinnings and may, thus, lead to inadequate and incomplete future responses. As Lai suggests, taking corporate accountability seriously during transitional justice means altering the way that we

[282] Ministry of Justice and Constitutional Development, Republic of South Africa, Declaration by Justice Minister Penuell Maduna, on Apartheid Litigation in the United States, 11 July 2003, available at www.gov.za/sites/default/files/gcis_document/201409/apartheid1.pdf.

[283] Ibid., par. 10.

[284] Ibid., par. 10–13.

[285] P. Bond and K. Sharife, 'Apartheid Reparations and the Contestation of Corporate Power in Africa' (2009) 36 *Review of African Political Economy* 119, at 120.

[286] Ibid.

[287] R. W. Cox, 'Social Forces, States and World Orders: Beyond International Relations Theory' (1981) 10 *Millennium – Journal of International Studies*, at 128.

[288] See Atteberry who argues that the conception of history that transpires transitional justice has led to its inability to address issues relating to the economy. J. Atteberry, 'Turning in the Widening Gyre: History, Corporate Accountability, and Transitional Justice in the Postcolony' (2019) 19 *Chicago Journal of International Law* 333, 337–344.

perceive of it, as structuring factor of war related violence, but also as a broader issue of political economy.[289] To that respect, Franzki and Olarte rightly caution that instead of framing the 'demands to address socio-economic dimensions of past conflict again as a post-political claim to inform a consensus among a peace-willing community', the transitional justice discourse should make the leap forward and subject to public debate questions about the role of social justice in the institutional design of society, economic self-determination and the means to achieve it, as well as issues of economic democracy.[290] In that framework, corporate accountability would be incorporated into transitional criminal mechanisms, not only to assign responsibility to specific enterprises but also to foster discussions on corporate power, especially as it relates to threats to peace. It is these broader questions, carrying significant socio-economic implications, that should not be overshadowed by the peace versus justice discourse, usually framed in non-political terms.

Overall, incorporating business entities within the scope of work of transitional criminal mechanisms seems necessary, but also challenging. Holding corporations accountable before criminal mechanisms can potentially contribute towards a more comprehensive form of justice that mirrors and acknowledges a wider form of prior injustice and achieves increased satisfaction for victims' rights. In addition, it can potentially address the structural and economic dimensions of violence particularly so where economic activities are 'written into the logic of the conflict itself'.[291] Yet the issue is far from settled, as many important questions persist and answers to them depend on the particularities of each context and the applicable legal system.

[289] D. Lai, 'Beyond Context: Taking Political Economy Seriously in the Study of Corporate Accountability' (2024) 29 *New Political Economy* 3, 385–399.

[290] Franzki and Olarte, 'Understanding the Political Economy', p. 210.

[291] D. Sharp, 'Economic Violence in the Practice of African Truth Commissions and Beyond', pp. 87, 107.

4

Operational Insights

Balancing National and International Elements

4.1 Modes of Liability

Corporate entities have long been associated with international crimes[1] – from actively engaging in criminal acts, as private military and security providers, to pillaging and plundering natural resources in war zones, forcibly removing population for mining, using forced labour or providing funds and equipment to warring parties,[2] trading with warring counterparts and sustaining conflicts.[3] Corporate implication to international crimes has ranged along a wide spectrum, spanning from active participation to complicity and enabling presence in a warring environment. Attributing crimes to corporate entities presupposes some clarification of modes of participation, which, despite their long-standing use, have been a source of confusion, for courts and scholars alike. The following part will examine the modes of liability that are applicable to corporate entities and have been used at the international and national planes. Jurisdictions that allow for corporate criminal liability will be in a position to use them in corporate prosecutions, similarly to when they prosecute individuals.[4] A pertinent example could be that of Ukraine. The Ukrainian Criminal Code was recently amended to introduce quasi-

[1] 'Workshop' in (2008) 6 *Journal of International Criminal Justice* 5, at 899–979; Transnational Business and International Criminal Law, Special Issue (2010) 8 *Journal of International Criminal Justice* 3.

[2] For a typology of corporate complicity in international crimes, see 'ICJ Report', pp. 37–43; Kaleck and Saage-Maasz, 'Corporate Accountability for Human Rights Violations Amounting to International Crimes', pp. 700–709.

[3] Final Report of the Panel of Experts on the Illegal Exploitation of Natural Resources and Other Forms of Wealth of the Democratic Republic of Congo, UN Doc. S/2002/1146, 16 October 2002.

[4] W. Schabas, 'Enforcing International Humanitarian Law: Catching the Accomplices' (2001) 83 *International Review of the Red Cross* 842, at 454.

criminal liability for corporations.[5] They can now become subject to criminal sanctions in case their executives or other authorized persons commit specifically listed crimes, including propaganda of war, war crimes and crimes against humanity.[6]

The modes, discussed in Chapters 5–8, are functionally classified under international law's categorization, in order to systematize dispersed approaches under a common understanding, and also to identify international legal approaches and case law of the ad hoc courts and the ICC that can be useful as customary practice for domestic jurisdictions. Insights from international criminal law are useful, given that domestic jurisdictions rarely have the requisite legal framework or willingness to hold corporations criminally liable, particularly for crimes committed abroad, risking that victims of those crimes remain without resource to justice. The application of modes of liability under international law to individual corporate officials is examined to the extent that it is useful, particularly for jurisdictions, where liability to the entity is ascribed through the conduct of its officials. It is also useful for jurisdictions where corporate criminal liability does not exist, and therefore prosecution of the business person might be the only viable option to – at least indirectly – hold corporations accountable.[7] Issues relating to determination of the 'mental element' of a business corporation are examined in Section 4.2.

4.1.1 Direct Commission of Crimes: From Nuremberg to the Wagner Group

Responsibility for direct commission of a crime attaches to an individual who physically completed all material elements of the underlying crime without involving anyone else,[8] with intent and/or knowledge.[9] The value

[5] See Criminal Code of Ukraine, Articles 963 *et seq.*, available at http://zakon5.rada.gov.ua/laws/ show/2341-14/page3.

[6] D. Kamensky, 'Introducing Corporate Criminal Liability in Ukraine: Terra Incognita' (2020) 46 *Stetson Law Review*, p. 90.

[7] N. Farrell, 'Attributing Criminal Liability to Corporate Actors' (2010) 8 *Journal of International Criminal Justice* 3, pp. 873–894, at 875.

[8] G. Werle and F. Jessberger, *Principles of International Criminal Law* (Oxford University Press, 2014), p. 524.

[9] Regarding the status of direct commission in international law, the Tadić Appeal Judgment named it the default understanding of commission. See ICTY, *Prosecutor v. Tadić*, Case No. IT-94-1-A, Appeal Judgment, 15 July 1999 (Tadić Appeal Judgment), par. 188; STL, Interlocutory Decision on the Applicable Law: Terrorism,

of direct commission for corporate crimes is doubtful, not only because corporations rarely commit international crimes on their own but also because direct commission per se is less relevant to tackle intricate international crimes that are rarely the result of insulated individual efforts.[10] Evidence suggests that direct commission of international crimes by corporate entities has been less prevalent than other forms of participation, mainly focused on cases of private military and security companies, whose activities might qualify as 'direct perpetration' of an international crime.[11] One such instance might be the one of Wagner Group and its involvement in the Ukrainian conflict. Wagner Private Military Company was incorporated in St. Petersburg, Russia, in the beginning of 2023.[12] Although the lines of command are blurred and the group is state sponsored, one could suggest that achieving the confiscation and freezing of the company's assets would require charges to be brought against it, in addition to Putin and Yevgeny Prigozhin, its alleged late front man.[13] This, of course, is a theoretical exercise, as it is well known that Wagner Group was created precisely to absolve the Russian state from any responsibility. However, rumours of ruptures between Prigozhin and the Russian president, before the death of the former, hint towards independent responsibilities for Wagner, in addition to its acting as shield for the state.

Conspiracy Homicide, Perpetration, Cumulative Charging, Appeals Chamber, STL-11-01/1/I/AC/R176bis, 16 February 2011, par. 216.

10 Kelly, 'Prosecuting Corporations for Genocide', p. 82.

11 Few cases can be found in modern times. For example, the case brought before US courts against Blackwater alleging direct liability for extrajudicial killings and war crimes following the actions of Blackwater employees in Iraq in 2007. Also, the case brought before the same courts by a group of Iraqi nationals against defence contractors, CACI and Titan, alleging torture, war crimes, crimes against humanity, sexual assault and cruel, inhuman and degrading treatment at Abu Ghraib prison in Iraq. See Zerk, 'Corporate Liability', pp. 17–18.

12 The Moscow Times, 'Wagner Group Becomes Legal Entity in Russia', 17 January 2023, available at www.themoscowtimes.com/2023/01/17/wagner-group-becomes-legal-entity-in-russia-bbc-a79967.

13 Office of the High Commissioner for Human Rights, 'Russian Federation: UN Experts Alarmed by Recruitment of Prisoners by Wagner Group', 10 March 2023, available at www.ohchr.org/en/press-releases/2023/03/russian-federation-un-experts-alarmed-recruitment-prisoners-wagner-group; Office of the High Commissioner for Human Rights, 'CAR: Russian Wagner Group Harassing and Intimidating Civilians', 27 October 2021, available at www.ohchr.org/en/press-releases/2021/11/car-russian-wagner-group-harassing-and-intimidating-civilians-un-experts; D. Walsh, 'Russian Mercenaries Are Driving War Crimes in Africa, U.N. Says', *The New York Times*, 27 June 2021.

Back in Nuremberg, corporate involvement in Nazi atrocities was conceptualized more clearly. Although, the distinction between principals and accessories and modes of responsibility were not the main oeuvre of the court,[14] Control Council Law No. 10 specifically provided that any defendant whose actions fell within the parameters of Article II (2) was 'deemed to have committed' as principal a war crime, crime against humanity or crime against peace.[15] Thus, forty-two industrialists were convicted of war crimes and crimes against humanity, because their activities intersected, to a lesser or bigger extent, with the Nazi regime. The industrial cases tried by the United States military courts started with the *IG Farben* case. Thirteen out of twenty-four high-level officials of the chemical and pharmaceutical industries conglomerate were found guilty of war crimes and crimes against humanity, through plunder and spoliation, or slave labour of civilians from German-occupied territories and of German nationals.[16] In the *Flick* case, officials of a coal and steel industries conglomerate were convicted of war crimes and crimes against humanity, in the form of slave labour, plunder and financial support of the SS atrocities.[17] Lastly, employees of *Krupp* steel and arms factories in Germany were found guilty of war crimes and crimes against humanity by participating in plunder and spoliation of private property in territories seized by the Nazis, and all but one were found guilty for the employment of 'prisoners of war, foreign civilians and concentration camp inmates under inhuman conditions in work connected with the conduct of war'.[18] Similarly, the British Military Tribunal convicted Bruno Tesch, the owner of Tesch & Stabenow, as well as the company's manager and chief technician, Karl Weinbacher, for the war crime of supplying a commodity used for mass extermination, in violation of Article 46 of the Hague Regulations of 1907. Tesch's company supplied the Auschwitz concentration camps with Zyklon B, a pesticide used in

[14] Heller notes that investigating modes of responsibility in Nuremberg judgments is an exercise in frustration. Heller, 'The Nuremberg Military Tribunals', p. 252.

[15] Control Council Law No. 10.

[16] All were acquitted of the charges of crimes against peace and conspiracy to commit crimes. Although four of the accused had participated in the rearmament of Germany, the fact that they were not military experts meant that they could not have known that they were aiding Germany in preparing for an aggressive war and consequently lacked the required mental element. Farben Vol. 7, pp. 36–37.

[17] Flick case, p. 1187 *et seq.*

[18] *Krupp* case, at 1327.

the Nazi gas chambers, 'for killing allied nationals interned in concentration camps, knowing that it was so to be used'.[19]

4.1.2 *Indirect Perpetration: Control Over an Organization*

A form of principal liability that can be more suitable for corporate involvement in international crimes than direct commission is 'indirect perpetration', as introduced by Article 25(3) (a) of the ICC Statute,[20] and particularly its 'control over an organization' variant. Under the latter, a person is liable as principal perpetrator of a crime, because they used their control over an organization as a vehicle to assure that the crime will occur. According to the ICC, such organization should consist of an organized and hierarchical apparatus of power, which the indirect perpetrator controls, securing the execution of the crime by almost automatic compliance.[21] In addition, they must have acted with intent and knowledge, as per Article 30 of the ICC Statute,[22] coupled with any specific mental elements required for the crime and, most importantly, awareness of the existence of the organization and their authority over it, including through automatic compliance with orders.[23] The ICC has already used this mode, in the case of Joshua Arap Sang, a corporate executive and head of a radio station, in Kenya. Sang was charged with indirect co-perpetration of crimes against humanity, because as part of a

[19] Tesch and Weinbacher were convicted and sentenced to death, while Drosihn was acquitted. *Zyklon B* case, pp. 93–103.

[20] Indirect perpetration means that a person commits a crime by using another person as a tool for such commission. ICC, *Katanga and Ngudjolo Chui*, Pre-Trial Chamber I, Decision on the Confirmation of Charges, ICC-01/04–01/07-717, 30 September 2008, par. 499.

[21] Ibid., par. 500–518; ICC, *Ruto, Kosgey and Sang*, Decision on the Confirmation of Charges, ICC-01/09-01/11-373, 23 January 2012, par. 292 and 313; ICC, *Ntaganda*, Pre-Trial Chamber II, Decision on the Confirmation of Charges, ICC-01/04-02/06-309, 9 June 2014, at par. 104; ICC, *Gbagbo*, Pre-Trial Chamber I, Decision on the Confirmation of Charges, ICC-02/11-01/11-656-Red, 12 June 2014, par. 230; ICC, *Hussein*, Pre-Trial Chamber I, public-redacted version of 'Decision on the Prosecutor's application under article 58 relating to Abdel Raheem Muhammad Hussein', ICC-02/05-01/12-1-Red, 1 March 2012, par. 35; ICC, *Abu Garda*, Pre-Trial Chamber I, Decision on the Confirmation of Charges, ICC-02/05-02/09-243-Red, 8 February 2010, par. 246.

[22] The indirect perpetrator must act with intent to generate the objective elements of the crime, or with awareness that their acts will bring those elements. See ICC, 'Katanga, Chui Confirmation of Charges', par. 536. However, perpetrators need not know all the underlying details of the crimes that will be committed. ICC, 'Katanga Trial Judgment', par. 1415.

[23] ICC, 'Katanga, Chui Confirmation of Charges', par. 534, 536.

group of persons, acting with a common purpose, he committed or contributed to the commission of crimes against humanity during the post-electoral violence of 2007–2008.[24] He allegedly used his radio programme and broadcasted coded messages that led to furthering ethnic tensions murder, forcible transfer, persecution and attacks.[25]

Scholars have suggested that this mode of liability might be valuable in attaching responsibility to business officials, who committed crimes through the instrumentality of a business organization.[26] Swart opined that it is pertinent for corporate liability purposes, as it signifies a shift from naturalistic to social conceptions of action in criminal law.[27] The concept seems also to resonate with the holdings of the industrialist cases at Nuremberg.[28] Although the Nuremberg trials did not explicitly use the modern modes of liability, yet their holdings can be functionally classified according to the modes.[29] The American Military Tribunal in *Farben* considered that the company was used as a vehicle for the defendants and noted that 'all of the defendants, acting through the instrumentality of Farben and otherwise with diverse other persons'.[30] It went further to note that 'while the Farben organization, as a corporation, is not charged under the indictment with committing a crime and is not the subject of prosecution in this case, it is the theory of the prosecution that the defendants individually and collectively used the Farben organization

[24] ICC, 'Ruto, Kosgey and Sang, Decision on the Confirmation of Charges'.

[25] The charges were vacated, due to insufficient evidence. ICC, *Prosecutor* v. *William Samoei Ruto and Joshua Arap Sang*, ICC-01/09-01/11, public-redacted version of Decision on Defence Applications for Judgments of Acquittal, 5 April 2016.

[26] J. Kyriakakis, 'Developments in International Criminal Law and the Case of Business Involvement in International Crimes' (2012) 94 *International Review of the Red Cross* 887; A. Clapham, 'The Complexity of International Criminal Law: Looking Beyond Individual Responsibility to the Responsibility of Organizations, Corporations and States', in R. Chandra Thakur and P. Malcontent (eds.), *Sovereign Impunity to International Accountability: The Search for Justice in a World of States* (United Nations Press, 2004), p. 239. However, Olasolo describes why it is difficult to transpose this theory to corporations. H. Olasolo, *The Criminal Responsibility of Political and Military Leaders as Principles to International Crimes* (Hart Publishers, 2009), pp. 116–134 and 302–330.

[27] 'Discussion: International Trends Towards Establishing Some Form of Punishment for Corporations', pp. 950–951, 958.

[28] Jacobson, 'Doing Business with the Devil'.

[29] On the notion of functional equivalence, see K. Zweigert and H. Kötz, *An Introduction to Comparative Law* (Oxford University Press, 1998).

[30] Farben Vol. 8, p. 1084. Note that other times the Tribunal found that the organization was acting through individuals, pp. 1147 and 1152.

as an instrument by and through which they committed the crimes enumerated in the indictment'.[31]

A close examination of relevant domestic and international theory and case law corroborate the amenability of such mode to corporate malfeasance. First, the important – for this mode – concept of control has been used flexibly by the ICC. Different factors have been considered to compensate in cases of absence of strict organizational discipline and control.[32] In spite of opposing views, Nuremberg, as well, interpreted the 'control' requirement, in what concerned industrialists, as their capacity to 'shape and influence' due to their economic status, rather than their capacity to actually control and direct.[33] Corporate crime literature has already highlighted that components of indirect perpetration through an organization are amenable to corporate crime, particularly so, because of their ability to harness resources,[34] and the 'fungibility' of their personnel. Corporations as independent legal entities continue to exist, even if their officials change.[35] Importantly, German case law – where the notion first emerged[36] – has ruled that various kinds of organizations can satisfy the control requirement, including business enterprises. Companies, although lacking the stringent hierarchical structures and discipline of military groups, have been considered to constitute organizations for the purposes of this theory.[37] According to the German Federal Court of Appeals, 'the problem of responsibility for leading business enterprises could also be solved that way'.[38]

31 Farben Vol. 8, p. 1108.

32 A. Kiss, 'Indirect Commission', in M. Cupido et al. (eds.), *Modes of Liability in International Criminal Law* (Cambridge University Press, 2019), p. 39.

33 Note, however, that those articulations were made in relation to the crime of aggression in the Farben and Krupp cases, for which industrialists were acquitted. K. J. Heller, 'Retreat from Nuremberg: The Leadership Requirement in the Crime of Aggression' (2007) 18 *The European Journal of International Law* 3, at 483.

34 M. Osiel, *Making Sense of Mass Atrocity* (Cambridge University Press, 2009), p. 95.

35 Braithwaite and Fisse, *Corporations, Crime and Accountability*, pp. 17–58.

36 E. Van Sliedregt and L. Yanev, 'Co-Perpetration Based on Joint Control Over the Crime', in M. Cupido et al. (eds.), *Modes of Liability in International Criminal Law* (Cambridge University Press, 2019), pp. 85–120.

37 Bundesgerichtshof, Judgment of 26 July 1994, in 40 Entscheidungen des Bundesgerichtshofes in Strafsachen (1995) 218–240, at 237. See commentary of the case in T. Weigend, 'Perpetration Through an Organization: The Unexpected Career of German Legal Concept' (2011) 9 *Journal of International Criminal Justice* 1, 91–112.

38 Weigend, 'Perpetration Through an Organization', fn. 32. The presiding judge of the court's panel who coined this phrase later revealed that the court intentionally used this

4.1.3 *Participation to a Group Crime*

Participation to group crimes has been criminalized by the statutes of both the ad hoc tribunals and the ICC, albeit under different modes of liability.[39] The ad hoc tribunals tackled participation in group crimes by the structure of 'joint criminal enterprise' (JCE), considered to be customary international law.[40] Under the ICC Statute, liability for participating in a group crime is foreseen for principal perpetrators in Article 25 (3) (a) on co-perpetration, and for accessories in Article 25(3) (d) on common purpose liability.

JCE liability, rooted in conspiracy-based theories of liability,[41] attaches to a person for the commission of a specific crime or for their assistance or contribution[42] to the execution of a common plan, design or purpose.[43] Its *mens rea* requirements depend on the category of joint criminal enterprise under consideration,[44] but are seemingly higher than

formulation in order to extend the notion of perpetration through an organization to business enterprises.

39 According to Vest, the basic and systemic forms of JCE are covered by Article 25(3) (a) ICC Statute on perpetration. H. Vest, 'Business Leaders and the Modes of Individual Criminal Responsibility Under International Law' (2010) 8 *Journal of International Criminal Justice* 3, 851–872, at 865.

40 A. Sanders, 'New Frontiers in the ATS: Conspiracy and Joint Criminal Enterprise Liability After Sosa' (2010) 28 *Berkeley Journal of International Law* 619. See also the same corroborated by Prosecutor in ICTY, Tadić Appeal Judgment; and In Re South African Apartheid Litigation, 617 F.Supp.2d 228, 263 (S.D.N.Y., 2009) ('Re South African Apartheid Litigation'). According to Kelly, the customary law status of JCE is not imperilled by the fact that some countries do not allow it. See Kelly, 'Prosecuting Corporations for Genocide'; A. Marston Danner and Jenny S. Martinez, 'Guilty Associations: Joint Criminal Enterprise, Command Responsibility, and the Development of International Criminal Law' (2005) 93 *California Law Review* 75, 104.

41 Sanders, 'New Frontiers in the ATS'; Kelly, 'Prosecuting Corporations for Genocide', p. 104.

42 The contribution of an individual accused need not be necessary or substantial, but it should at least be a significant contribution to the crimes. See ICTY, Judgment, *Krajišnik* (IT-00-39-A), Appeals Chamber, 17 March 2009, at 215.

43 Note also that the persons forming the group need not be organized in a military, political or administrative structure. Also, there is no necessity for the criminal purpose to have been previously arranged or formulated. It may materialize at a different time period and be inferred from the facts. Tadic Appeal Judgment, par. 227; ICTR, Judgment, *Ntakirutimana and Ntakirutimana* (ICTR-96-10-A, ICTR-96-17-A), Appeals Chamber, 13 December 2004 (Ntakirutimana Appeal Judgment), par. 466. It is also not necessary that the accused's participation passes the 'but-for' threshold. See Tadic Appeal Judgment, par. 199.

44 Whether it is a basic, systemic or extended form of JCE, see L. Yanev, 'Joint Criminal Enterprise', in M. Cupido et al. (eds.), *Modes of Liability*.

aiding and abetting. However, authors contend that JCE can be successfully transposed to business activity.[45] Notably, former Chief Prosecutor of the Special Court for Sierra Leone David Crane has argued that corporations are often involved in conflicts 'in a type of joint criminal enterprise' with combatant parties.[46] Plaintiffs in the Khulumani litigation added a joint criminal enterprise theory of corporate involvement, in addition to the aiding and abetting one. To substantiate that mode, they alleged, among others, that Barclays National Bank was an active participant to the South African Defence Advisory Board through the bank's director, Basil Hersov. By forming a joint criminal enterprise and collaborating in that way with the Apartheid regime and supplying it with funds, the bank allegedly intentionally strengthened the local security forces in maintaining Apartheid while knowing that the latter will commit criminal acts.[47] The case against the banks was dismissed, because no legal link could be established between the loans and human rights violations.[48] However, as will be explained in Section 4.1.5, that judgment relied on misinterpretation of previous case law.[49]

From its part, the ICC case law has held that co-perpetration, under Article 25(3) (a) of the statute requires knowledge, contribution to a common plan and joint control over the crime.[50] Co-perpetration might be difficult to sustain for corporate actors, although the issues around the control requirement, analysed in Chapter 3, might be applicable here as well.[51] Again, the case of the Wagner Group is one that can less problematically satisfy the requirements of this mode. Corporate liability seems simpler under Article 25(3) (d) of the ICC Statute, which foresees holding a person liable, if they intentionally contributed to the commis-

[45] Farrell, 'Attributing Criminal Liability to Corporate Actors', at 878; Justice Ian Binnie, 'Legal Redress for Corporate Participation in International Human Rights Abuses' (2009) 38 *Summer Brief* 44, 48; ICJ report, p. 27; Kelly, 'Prosecuting Corporations for Genocide', p. 108; Vest, 'Business Leaders and the Modes of Individual Criminal Responsibility', 868.

[46] Crane, 'Dancing with the Devil'.

[47] Bond and Sharife, 'Apartheid Reparations and the Contestation of Corporate Power in Africa', pp. 115–125.

[48] In 'Re South African Apartheid Litigation', p. 269.

[49] S. Michalowski, 'No Complicity Liability for Funding Gross Human Rights Violations?' (2012) 30 *Berkeley Journal of International Law* 451.

[50] Van Sliedregt and Yanev, 'Co-Perpetration'.

[51] This is because control of an organization stems from the control over the crime theory developed in German legal doctrine. Van Sliedregt and Yanev, 'Co-Perpetration'.

sion of a crime,[52] by a group of persons acting with a common purpose, aiming to further the crime or the criminal purpose, or knowing that the group intended to commit such crime.[53] The amenability of this mode to corporate structures relies on different facts: first, it requires contribution, but less than the substantial contribution criterion of aiding and abetting, and applies to different forms of involvement, including provision of resources or tacit or explicit encouragement of a crime.[54] Secondly, its *mens rea* standards do not require that the accused shares the group's common purpose,[55] but it is sufficient that they make an intentional contribution. Thirdly, common purpose has been accepted by courts,[56] even in cases where just an element of criminality was present, without the need that it covers the commission of the exact crime.[57]

Liability theories related to JCE, conspiracy and common purpose have been used against individual businessmen in Nuremberg and Colombia, but also before the ICTR. Starting from the latter, the indictment against Félicien Kabuga, founder of the radio station RTLM, stated that he acted with others in a manner that furthered hatred and violence against the Tutsi community and that he and others agreed to disseminate anti-Tutsi messages with the goal to eliminate them. It further alleged that Kabuga was liable for these crimes based on his participation in a joint criminal enterprise with others involved in RTLM's operations, as well as aiding and abetting the criminal conduct of RTLM journalists, Interahamwe, and others, whose crimes were assisted or instigated by RTLM broadcasts.[58]

In the *IG Farben* case,[59] the first to hold individuals accountable for their economic activities under international criminal law, Count 5 of the

[52] It is required that the accused influenced the commission of the crime, but the latter does not need to depend on that contribution. ICC, 'Katanga Trial Judgment', paras. 1632–1633.

[53] ICC, *Blé Goudé*, Pre-Trial Chamber Decision on the Confirmation of Charges, ICC-02/11-02/11, 11 December 2014, par. 173.

[54] ICC, 'Katanga Trial Judgment', par. 1635; ICC, *Mbarushimana*, Chamber Decision on the Confirmation of Charges, ICC-01/04-01/10, 16 December 2011, par. 277.

[55] ICC, 'Mbarushimana, Decision on the Confirmation of Charges', par. 272–275, 289; ICC, 'Katanga Trial Judgment', par. 1631.

[56] On the exact contours of common purpose, see M. Cupido, 'Group Acting with a Common Purpose', in M. Cupido et al. (eds.), *Modes of Liability*, p. 329.

[57] ICC, 'Mbarushimana, Decision on the Confirmation of Charges', par. 271.

[58] *Prosecutor* v. *Félicien Kabuga*, Prosecution's Second Amended Indictment, Case No. MICT-13-38-PT, 1 March 2021.

[59] Farben Vol. 8; *United States* v. *Carl Krauch* in 7 Trials of War Criminals before the Nuremberg Military Tribunals under Control Council Law No. 10 (1952) (Farben Vol. 7). Note that those analogies are made under the concept of functional equivalence.

indictment read that industrialists had participated in 'a common plan or conspiracy to commit, or which involved the commission of, crimes against peace (including the acts constituting war crimes and crimes against humanity which were committed as an integral part of such crimes against peace) as defined by Control Council Law No. 10'.[60] That count was dismissed because the court held that the same issues were already addressed, under the mode of 'connected with plans or enterprises' to commit war crimes and crimes against humanity.[61]

Lastly, in the corporate trials in Colombia, albeit against individual persons, the concept of *concierto para delinquir*, akin to common purpose liability and conspiracy, is widely used.[62] It centres on those who came to an agreement, whether under the auspices of an organization or not, with the objective of committing an indeterminate number of crimes and is punishable with three to six years of imprisonment.[63] It has been used for businessmen who established or financed paramilitary groups. By way of indication, Arnulfo Peñuela Marin, director of a private security firm that functioned as an intermediary between the paramilitaries and Chiquita, was convicted, by the Supreme Court of Antioquia, for conspiring with the United Self-Defense Forces of Colombia (AUC), a right-wing paramilitary group.[64]

4.1.4 Superior Responsibility

Superior responsibility encapsulates a specific form of omission liability for military and civilian superiors, foreseen in the statutes of the ad hoc

60 Farben Vol. 7, p. 146. Heller explains that according to the London Charter, conspiring to commit crimes against peace was a crime in itself, but conspiring to commit war crimes or crimes against humanity was a mode of participation in those crimes. Law No. 10 foresaw conspiracy as an independent crime with regard to crimes against peace but gave no indication that conspiring to commit war crimes or crimes against humanity was an independent crime. See Heller, 'The Nuremberg Military Tribunals'.

61 Farben Vol. 8, pp. 1127–1128. See Heller, 'The Nuremberg Military Tribunals', p. 275; Bush, 'The Prehistory of Corporations'.

62 For the controversies of this concept, see E. Cote-Barco, 'Complicidad, responsabilidad penal de directivos empresariales y violaciones de Derechos Humanos cometidas por grupos armados ilegales: lecciones del Derecho Penal Internacional para Colombia' (2019) 68 *Vniversitas* 138.

63 Wesche, 'Business Actors, Paramilitaries and Transitional Criminal Justice in Colombia', p. 487.

64 Juzgado Segundo Penal de Circuito Especializado de Antioquia, Arnulfo Peñuela Marín y otro, Rad. 050003107002200900031, Medellın (4 August 2010); Tribunal Superior de Antioquia, Sala de Decision Penal, Arnulfo Peñuela Marín y otro, Rad. 050003107002200900031, Medellın, 17 April 2012.

courts, the ICC and various domestic jurisdictions.[65] Beyond the superior–subordinate relationship and the necessary knowledge, this mode of responsibility relies, primarily, on the failure of the superior to take the necessary and reasonable measures to prevent the criminal act or punish the perpetrator.[66]

If the theoretical leap from the required military or civilian contexts to the corporate one can be made, this mode of responsibility can be amenable to corporate contexts. Applying, for example, the ICC standard to contexts of corporate crimes, the corporation would be liable for acts of those under its 'effective authority and control' where it 'knew, or consciously disregarded information which clearly indicated, that the subordinates were committing or [were] about to commit such crimes'[67] and where 'the crimes concerned activities that were within the effective responsibility and control of the superior'. Like in indirect perpetration though an organization, analysed in Section 4.1.2, there is no principled legal reason why the notions of control and authority required by superior responsibility cannot apply to corporate entities. Relatedly, the Montreux Document on pertinent international legal obligations and good practices for states related to operations of private military and security companies during armed conflict foresees the responsibility of superiors in the context of those specific companies.[68] Going further, Ratner has argued that an entity per se can be responsible as a superior, having state officials as subordinates, when, for example, companies use state military forces to secure land for their operations and those forces

[65] M. Jackson, 'Command Responsibility', in M. Cupido et al. (eds.), *Modes of Liability*; Y. Dinstein, 'Command Responsibility', in F. Lachenmann and R. Wolfrum (eds.), *The Law of Armed Conflict and the Use of Force: The Max Planck Encyclopaedia of Public International Law* (Oxford University Press, 2017), p. 4; G. Mettraux, *The Law of Command Responsibility* (Oxford University Press, 2009), pp. 5–11.

[66] ICTY, *Delalić et al.*, Trial Chamber Judgment, IT-96-21-T, 16 November 1998, par. 346; ICTY, *Prosecutor* v. *Orić*, Appeals Chamber Judgment, IT-03-68-A, 3 July 2008, par. 18. There is, of course, the implicit requirement that the subordinate commits the underlying crime; see K. Ambos, *Treatise on International Criminal Law – Volume 1: Foundations and General Part* (Oxford University Press, 2013), p. 200.

[67] The knowledge standard was also used in the International Military Tribunal for the Far East (IMTFE) in *re Soemu Toyoda* case. For an elaboration on the use of the knowledge standard, see Kelly, 'Prosecuting Corporations for Genocide', pp. 94–96.

[68] International Committee of the Red Cross, Montreux Document on pertinent international legal obligations and good practices for states related to operations of private military and security companies during armed conflict, par. 27.

commit international crimes. Notably, the knowledge standard that underlies it is a flexible one.[69]

Kelly has argued that 'command responsibility is possibly the legal mechanism to make this [hold corporations liable for complicity] happen'.[70] This is because command responsibility theory is the conceptual cousin of *respondeat superior*,[71] a theory commonly used for the imputation of crimes to corporate entities, on the basis of unlawful acts committed by employees.[72] Unlike *respondeat superior*, command responsibility is even better equipped, because it does not allow for a due diligence defence,[73] often put forward by corporations. The draft paragraph on corporate entities that was proposed to be included in the ICC Statute entrenched the *respondeat superior* concept and thus resonates with superior liability. It provided for trying 'legal persons, with the exception of States, when the crimes were committed on behalf of such legal persons or by their agents or representatives'.[74]

In fact, elements of superior responsibility have been used in international and domestic cases that dealt with corporate officials, and primarily the failure to prevent element. For example, the ICTR held Alfred Musema, the manager of Gisovu Tea Factory, responsible for genocide, both individually and as a superior, for the actions of his employees.[75] The court held that while having authority and control over the employees of the factory, he failed to take the necessary and reasonable measures to prevent their participation in genocide, as well as to punish them.[76] Musema's effective control was inferred by his social and economic influence and his superior position, able of appointing and

[69] Ratner, 'Corporations and Human Rights', pp. 504–506; Kelly, 'Prosecuting Corporations for Genocide', p. 99, drawing analogies between *respondeat* superior and superior responsibility.

[70] Kelly, 'Prosecuting Corporations for Genocide', p. 101.

[71] Ibid., at 99.

[72] Variants of this principle are used in various jurisdictions, including South Africa, the US, the UK, Canada, Australia, Israel and France. For an overview, see Wells, 'Corporations and Criminal Responsibility', pp. 66–67, 73, 77.

[73] I. Bantekas, 'The Contemporary Law of Superior Responsibility' (1999) 93 *American Journal of International Law*, at 573, 585. For an overview of the handicaps to the due diligence defence for corporate crimes, see B. Choudhury and M. Petrin, *Corporate Duties to the Public* (Cambridge University Press, 2019), p. 183 *et seq.*

[74] Clapham, *Human Rights Obligations of Non-State Actors*, p. 30.

[75] ICTR, *The Prosecutor* v. *Alfred Musema* (Judgment and Sentence), ICTR-96-13-T, 27 January 2000 (Musema Trial Judgment).

[76] Ibid., paras. 892–906, 914–915, 919–920, 924–925, 936 and 950–951.

dismissing employees.[77] Due to his position and authority over the employees, he was considered capable of taking the necessary measures to prevent and punish the use of factory vehicles for the commission of crimes, something that he did not do.[78] Similarly, while not on exact superior liability basis, Obed Ruzindana, a local prestigious businessman from Kibuye, was held responsible for not deterring perpetrators of massacres, while in a position to do so.[79] He was convicted of genocide for the crimes committed in Bisesero, Rwanda, between 9 April and 30 June 1994.

In the well-known Dutch criminal case against Kouwenhoven, owner of the Royal Timber Corporation and head of the Oriental Timber Cooperation (OTC), the accused was charged with war crimes in Liberia and Guinea, and violation of the Dutch arms embargo, pursuant to Security Council Resolutions. He was acquitted on charges of war crimes but convicted for his involvement in illegally supplying the Liberian regime with weapons, shipped through OTC's ships and ports. In relation to war crimes, he was also prosecuted under a subsidiary charge, as a superior, for acts committed by his subordinates.[80] It was alleged that although he had respective management powers, he had failed to prevent or punish the employees who had committed the wrongs.[81] Although witness statements identified him as the head of the company, the court was not convinced beyond reasonable doubt and dismissed that charge.[82] In another domestic Swiss case, Bührle, head of the Swiss arms manufacturer Oerlikon-Bührle, was convicted of illegal arms-dealing with the Apartheid regime and sentenced to prison for eight months.[83] Although the court could not establish that

[77] J. A. Williamson, 'Command Responsibility in the Case Law of the International Criminal Tribunal for Rwanda' (2002) 13 *Criminal Law Forum* 365–384, at 370–372. Other authors do not agree with this conclusion; see A. Zahar, 'Command Responsibility for Civilian Superiors for Genocide' (2001) 14 *Leiden Journal of International Law* 591–616, at 601–604.

[78] ICTR, 'Musema Trial Judgement', par. 880, 984; ICJ Report, p. 35.

[79] ICTR, *Prosecutor* v. *Obed Ruzindana*, ICTR-96-10-T and ICTR-96-1-T, 1 June 2001.

[80] This mode of responsibility is stipulated in Article 9 of the Dutch Criminal Law in Wartime Act.

[81] L. Van den Herik, 'The Difficulties of Exercising Extraterritorial Jurisdiction: The Acquittal of a Dutch Businessman for Crimes Committed in Liberia' (2012) 9 *International Criminal Law Review*, pp. 211–226.

[82] Court of Appeal, The Hague, 10 March 2008, Case No. BC6068, par. 9.21.

[83] P. Davison, Dieter Bührle: Controversial arms dealer, *The Independent*, 18 December 2012.

the defendant ordered the sale of weapons himself to areas forbidden by Swiss law, due to embargo, it ruled that given that he knew of those orders and due to his unique position in the company, he would have been obliged to prohibit these deliveries immediately.[84] Closing with Nuremberg, in *United States* v. *Flick*, Flick was convicted for war crimes and crimes against humanity, among other charges, because he failed to prevent the criminal acts of Weiss, one of his subordinates. The Tribunal found that Weiss used forced labour to increase production goals of railroad carriers, but Flick did nothing to prevent that despite knowing it.[85]

4.1.5 Complicity

The concept of corporate complicity has been researched extensively,[86] due to its alleged pertinence for the business and human rights discourse,[87] and has been the subject of a separate report by the Special Representative of the Secretary-General on the Issue of Human Rights and Transnational Corporations and Other Business Enterprises, John Ruggie.[88] Human rights scholars have classified complicity in direct, indirect and silent, and parallels to that framework can be drawn with respect to international criminal law.[89]

[84] Entscheidungen des Schweizerischen Bundesgerichts, Vol. 96 (1970), Part IV 155 *et seq.*

[85] Flick case, pp. 1187, 1202.

[86] ICJ Report; Clapham, 'Extending International Criminal Law'; Ramasastry, 'Corporate Complicity: From Nuremberg to Rangoon'; Stephens, 'The Amorality of Profit'; Schabas, 'Enforcing International Humanitarian Law'.

[87] According to SRSG Ruggie, most of the over forty Alien Tort Claims Act (ATCA) cases brought against companies in the United States concerned alleged complicity. Moreover, the Office of the High Commissioner for Human Rights (OHCHR) for the Special Representative, documented that 41 per cent of the 320 cases alleged indirect forms of company involvement in various human rights abuses. Report of the Special Representative of the Secretary-General on the issue of human rights and transnational corporations and other business enterprises, Addendum, Corporations and human rights: A survey of the scope and patterns of alleged corporate-related human rights abuse, A/HRC/8/5/Add.2., 23 May 2008.

[88] Report of the Special Representative of the Secretary-General on the Issue of Human Rights and Transnational Corporations and other Business Enterprises, John Ruggie, Clarifying the Concepts of 'Sphere of influence' and 'Complicity', A/HRC/8/16, 15 May 2008 ('SRSG, Sphere of influence and Complicity').

[89] Clapham and Jerbi, 'Categories of Corporate Complicity'; Ramasastry, 'Corporate Complicity: From Nuremberg to Rangoon'. The same division is also espoused by the UNGPs, the Global Compact and the OECD Guidelines. However, Steward opined that the standards employed by international criminal law cannot be transposed to

Scholars and case law converge that corporate complicity in international crimes generates liability when some elements are present, namely the crime, the contribution of the accomplice and intent or knowledge.[90] A commonly used form of complicity – for corporate accountability purposes – is aiding and abetting, capturing various forms of assistance provided to the principal perpetrator of an international crime.[91] It has been criminalized under the statutes of ad hoc criminal tribunals, the ICC Statute[92] and customary international law,[93] but, despite its long-standing use, both its *actus* and *mens rea* requirements have been interpreted differently by various international fora.

For the ad hoc tribunals, the conduct element of 'aiding and abetting' can include both actions and omissions,[94] with 'substantial effect on the perpetration of the crime'.[95] From its part, the ICC requires simply

international human rights law. J. G. Stewart, 'Complicity in Business and Human Rights' (2015) 109 *Proceedings of the ASIL Annual Meeting* 181.

90 Ramasastry and Thompson, 'Commerce, Crime and Conflict'. See also Huisman and van Sliedgart, who argue that the causation standard should be lower to engage more detached forms of involvement and that proximity should be approached with caution when used as an indicator of criminal liability. W. Huisman and E. van Sliedregt, 'Rogue Traders: Dutch Businessmen, International Crimes and Corporate Complicity' (2010) 8 *Journal of International Criminal Justice* 3, at 803–828. For an overview, see 'ICJ Report'.

91 While aiding and abetting are usually classified together as a single form of accomplice liability, initially it corresponded to two discrete activities. According to the Akayesu Trial Chamber, 'aiding means giving assistance to someone. Abetting, on the other hand, would involve facilitating the commission of an act by being sympathetic thereto'. 'Akayesu Trial Judgement', par. 484. Note that although the anticipated crime must have been committed, the physical perpetrator need not have been tried or identified. G. Boas, J. Bischoff and N. Reid, *International Criminal Law Practitioner* (Cambridge University Press, 2008), p. 318.

92 See Stephens for other relevant conventions. Stephens, 'The Amorality of Profit'.

93 M. Ventura, 'Aiding and Abetting', in M. Cupido et al. (eds.), *Modes of Liability*.

94 See, indicatively, ICTY, *Prosecutor* v. *Popovic*, Case No. IT-05-88-A, Appeals Judgment, 30 January 2015; ICTR, *Prosecutor* v. *Kalimanzira*, ICTR-05-88-A, Appeals Judgment, 20 October 2010; ICC, *Prosecutor* v. *Bemba*, Case No. ICC-01/05-01/13, 19 October 2016 (Bemba Trial Judgment).

95 ICTY, 'Furundzija Trial Judgement', par. 249. See also ICTY, *Prosecutor* v. *Simić*, Case No. IT-95-9-A, Appeal Judgment, 28 November 2006, par. 85; ICTY, *Prosecutor* v. *Tihomir Blaskic*, IT-95-14-A, 29 July 2004 (Blaskic Appeal Judgment), par. 45; ICTY, *Prosecutor* v. *Mitar Vasiljevic*, IT-98-32-A, 25 February 2004 (Vasiljevic Appeal Judgment), par. 102. Note that in their former jurisprudence, the ad hoc tribunals required actions with specific direction to assist. However, this was later overturned; see J. G. Stewart, Judicial Rejection of 'Specific Direction' is Widespread, 23 December 2015, available at http://jamesgstewart.com/judicial-rejection-of-specific-direction-is-widespread/. Also, note that the International Law Commission's commentary to the 1996 Draft Code of Crimes against the Peace and Security of Mankind required 'significant facilitation of the crime' (Draft Code of Crimes against the

'effect', rejecting its substantial character since 2016.[96] Even under a substantiality requirement – good as it may be for avoiding trivial prosecutions – it would not be necessary to prove that the crime would not have occurred without this assistance.[97] Vest notes that for corporate aiders and abettors, the substantiality requirement does not put an insurmountable hurdle, since it prevents only minimal assistance from being penalized.[98]

Regarding the requisite *mens rea* for aiding and abetting liability, the ad hoc courts opted for a threshold of knowledge that one's actions will assist the perpetration of a crime,[99] including for specific intent crimes.[100] In contrast, the ICC Statute, in its limited jurisprudence on the topic, has set the threshold higher and requires that the aider and

Peace and Security of Mankind, Report of the ILC on the work of its 48th session, UN Doc. A/51/10, 6 May–26 July 1996, at 24, par. 10.) For an elaboration of the substantial effect requirement, see Vest, 'Business Leaders and the Modes of Individual Criminal Responsibility', at 857.

96 ICC, 'Bemba Trial Judgment'; ICC, *Prosecutor* v. *Al Mahdi*, Case No. ICC-01/12-01/15, Decision on the Confirmation of Charges, 24 March 2016. The issue of substantial effect was discussed by the Pre-trial Chamber I in Mbarushimana and the Trial Chamber I in Lubanga, but only as *obiter dicta*, in relation to other considerations. ICC, 'Mbarushimana, Decision on the Confirmation of Charges'; ICC, *Prosecutor* v. *Lubanga*, Case No. ICC-01/04-01/06 A 5, Judgment on the Appeal of Mr Thomas Lubanga Dyilo against his Conviction, 1 December 2014, par. 468.

97 'ICJ Report', p. 19.

98 Vest, 'Business Leaders and the Modes of Individual Criminal Responsibility', p. 858.

99 ICTY, 'Furundzija Trial Judgement'; ICTY, Blagojevic and Jokic, IT-02-60-A, Appeals Judgment, 9 May 2007, par. 127; ICTY, 'Simić Appeal Judgement', par. 86; ICTY, 'Blaskic Appeal Judgement', par. 45–46; ICTY, 'Vasiljevic Appeal Judgement', par. 102. However, see Michalowski analysing few isolated judgments that tried to establish some form of intent requirement for aiding and abetting liability. S. Michalowski, 'The Mens Rea Standard for Corporate Aiding and Abetting Liability Conclusions from International Criminal Law' (2014) 18 *UCLA Journal of International Law and Foreign Affairs* 2, 237–274, at 251. Note that sharing the same intent as the perpetrator is not necessary for aiding and abetting, for which knowledge is sufficient. Sharing the same intent applies to liability as a co-perpetrator. ICTR, 'Ntakirutimana Appeal Judgment', par. 499; ICTY, *Prosecutor* v. *Vasiljevic*, Case No. IT-98-32-T, Judgment, 29 November 2002, par. 171; ICTY, *Prosecutor* v. *Aleksovski*, Case No. IT-95-14/1-A, Judgment, 24 March 2000, par. 162–163; ICTY, *Prosecutor* v. *Perisic*, Case No. IT-04-81-A, Appeal Judgment, 48, 28 February 2013. The described *mens rea* threshold was applied also regarding aiding and abetting specific intent crimes. Farrell, 'Attributing Criminal Liability to Corporate Actors', at 882.

100 Similarly, for specific intent crimes, it is not necessary that the aider and abettor shares the specific intent but must know of the principal perpetrator's intent. ICTY, 'Prosecutor v. Blagojevic and Jokic, Appeal Judgment'; ICTY, 'Aleksovski Appeals Judgment', par. 162. See, further, Kelly, 'Prosecuting Corporations for Genocide', p. 102.

abettor provide assistance '"for the purpose of facilitating" the commission of a crime'.[101] Scholars seem to converge that despite the significance of the ICC Statute, the *mens rea* requirement for aiding and abetting under international law is one of knowledge, as developed by the ad hoc courts.[102] Some confusion, however, remains due to – widely contested – ATCA jurisprudence,[103] arguing that the purpose test is the one reflecting customary international law.[104] Courts have used various contextual elements to infer knowledge in cases where corporations are involved, such as the context of a transaction, if this is the aiding and abetting act[105]; the volume of production and direction of shipments,[106] particularly when the products are lethal and can be used for unlawful activities[107]; and the position and experience of the accomplice in the company.[108] Notably, scholars have advocated for a lower threshold of negligence, in cases that involve business-induced abuse, as it is allegedly

[101] ICC, 'Bemba Trial Judgment'; see also ICC, 'Mbarushimana, Decision on the Confirmation of Charges', par. 281.

[102] Farrell, 'Attributing Criminal Liability to Corporate Actors', at 886–889; Kyriakakis, 'Developments in International Criminal Law', at 998. See also Schabas in that the ICC threshold confuses intent and motive. W. Schabas, *The UN International Criminal Tribunals* (Cambridge University Press, 2006), p. 307; Vest, 'Business Leaders and the Modes of Individual Criminal Responsibility', p. 862.

[103] Note that some ATCA tribunals have followed the purpose standard (*Doe* v. *Nestle* (9th Cir., Sept. 4, 2014); *Aziz* v. *Alcolac, Inc.*, 658 F.3d 388 (4th Cir. 2011); *Presbyterian Church of Sudan* v. *Talisman Energy*, 582 F.3d 244, 259 (2d Cir. 2009); *Mastafa* v. *Chevron Corp.*, 770 F.3d 170, 193–96 (2d Cir. 2014)). Others have opted for a broader kind of conduct based on knowledge (*Doe VIII* v. *Exxon Mobil Corp.*, 654 F.3d 11 (D.C. Cir. 2011); *Cabello* v. *Fernández-Larios*, 402 F.3d 1148, 1161 (11th Cir. 2005); *Du Daobin* v. *Cisco* (D. Md., Feb. 24, 2004).)

[104] Michalowski, 'The Mens Rea Standard for Corporate Aiding and Abetting', p. 264; Farrell, 'Attributing Criminal Liability to Corporate Actors', pp. 886–889.

[105] The context of the business transaction would also be relevant. For example, during World War II, it was apparent to the officials of Farben enterprise in Germany that they did not have enough labour to use in the two coal mines they acquired to support their Auschwitz plant; therefore, they would have to use slave labour. Farben Vol. 8, p. 1187; 'ICJ Report', p. 24.

[106] *Farben* Vol. 8, p. 1169; *Zyklon B* case, p. 101; Also, in the *Van Anraat* case, the court paid attention to the significant amount of the TDG chemical provided to Hussein. *Public Prosecutor* v. *Van Anraat*, LJN BA6734, The Hague Court of Appeal, 9 May 2007 (*Van Anraat* case), par. 12.5.

[107] *Zyklon B* case, p. 101.

[108] *United States* v. *Ernst von Weizsaecker Trials of War Criminals*, Vol. XIV (1952) (Ministries Case), p. 622. Also see the assessment of the liability for each of the defendants in the *Farben* case.

more adequate as a mental state for failures to perform due diligence requirements.[109]

The Nuremberg tribunals have provided important lessons in terms of the knowledge threshold and how to infer it, on behalf of a corporate actor. In the *Zyklon B* case, the court heavily engaged in identifying whether Bruno Tesch knew of the purpose of the poisonous gas he supplied to the Nazis, in order to convict him of war crimes.[110] His knowledge was proven by travel reports provided by his assistant, recording a meeting with members of Wehrmacht, exchanging views on the most hygienic way to kill Jews, whether by shooting or gas.[111] In the *Flick* case, the Tribunal held that 'one who knowingly by his influence and money contributes to the support thereof must, under settled legal principles, be deemed to be, if not a principal, certainly an accessory to such crimes'.[112] Knowledge was seemingly inferred from the nature of the SS themselves,[113] and by the fact that such large amounts of money cannot be spent solely for cultural purposes.[114] Similarly, in the *Van Anraat* case, the Dutch court held that Van Anraat, at the very least, must have known that the mustard gas would be used not only in the Iran–Iraq war but also upon Kurdish civilians.[115]

The ATCA litigation, despite the aforementioned confusion on the required mental element, has been leading the way in developing a doctrine of corporate complicity for multinational corporations that collaborate with repressive governments. While it is tort litigation, reference to it is important because it uses international criminal law standards. It is also highly influential for the scholarly discussion on corporate complicity in human rights violations, as well as for jurisdictions that do not draw a clear distinction between criminal and civil

109 However, in the framework of human rights law and not international criminal law. Stewart, 'Complicity in Business and Human Rights'.

110 Zyklon B case, pp. 93–102.

111 Ibid, p. 95.

112 Flick case, p. 1217. Note, however, that according to Burchard's interpretation, the liability of the defendants is based on their membership in the SS and cannot provide any guidance as to the standards that apply with regard to liability as an accessory to the crime. C. Burchard, 'Ancillary and Neutral Business Contributions to "Corporate-Political Core Crime"' (2010) 8 *Journal of International Criminal Justice* 919, pp. 936–937.

113 *Flick* case, at 1216–1123. See also Michalowski, 'No Complicity Liability for Funding', 477.

114 *Flick* case, at 1217, 1220.

115 *Van Anraat* case, par. 12.1.1.

proceedings.[116] The *Kadic* v. *Karadzic* judgment, recognizing jurisdiction over private actors who committed international law violations along with state officials,[117] passed the baton to the *Unocal* litigation, where the tribunal set the precedent that US corporations can be liable under the ATCA for complicity in serious human rights violations.[118] In *Wiwa* v. *Shell*, that holding was extended to foreign corporations, if they had 'continuous and systematic ties to the US'.[119] Even more pertinent for transitional praxis, recent ATCA litigation on forced labour during World War II held that legal persons bear the same obligations as natural persons regarding serious violations of international law.[120] But the question of whether, according to the ATCA, these obligations amount to corporate liability for violations of international criminal law has not yet been settled. One controversy is whether corporate accomplice liability presupposes that the corporation is the addressee of the obligation that was breached. Some judges reply affirmatively.[121] Others support that the underlying prohibitions of international crimes apply equally to every actor, be it natural or legal person.[122] An unfortunate turn were the *Kiobel* and *Jesner* cases. In *Kiobel*, the court held that any ATCA claims must touch and concern the US territory with sufficient force to displace the presumption against extraterritorial application.[123] In *Jesner* v. *Arab Bank*, it was decided that foreign corporations cannot be sued under the ATCA,[124] but the issue of US corporations remains to be decided.

[116] Several countries adopt a mixed approach, allowing victims, to seek damages during the criminal trial, as civil parties.

[117] *Kadic* v. *Karadzic* 70 F.3d 232 (2d Cir. 1995).

[118] However, because the parties settled, the appropriate standard for determining third-party liability was never conclusively determined. *John Doe I, et al.* v. *Unocal Corp*. et al., 395 F.3d 932 (9 Cir. 2002). Also, the Supreme Court's decision in *Sosa* v. *Alvarez-Machain* affirmed that corporate liability exists under ATCA, but limited its application to violations of 'specific, universal, and obligatory' laws of nations. *Sosa* v. *Alvarez-Machain*, 542 U.S. 692 (2004).

[119] In 2009, Shell settled with the claimants in the Wiwa case for $15.5 million. *Wiwa* v. *Royal Dutch Shell*, 226 F.3d 88 (2000).

[120] See *In re World War 11 Japanese Forced Litigation*, 164 F. Supp. 2d 1160 (N.D. Cal. 2001). For a brief account of the litigation, D. Caron and A. Schneider, 'U.S. Litigation Concerning Japanese Forced Labour in World War II' (2000) 5 *ASIL* 18.

[121] Judge Katzman opinion in the case of *Presbyterian Church of Sudan* v. *Talisman Energy*, 582 F.3d 244, 259 (2d Cir. 2009).

[122] Justices Kagan, Sotomayor and Ginsburg in the oral arguments of Jesner stressed that international law identifies the wrong, and domestic legal systems provide the remedies when that norm is violated.

[123] *Kiobel* v. *Royal Dutch Petroleum Co.*, 133 S. Ct. 1659, 1665 (2013), p. 1669.

[124] *Jesner* v. *Arab Bank, PLC, 584 U.S. (2018).*

A close examination of the relevant case law demonstrates different kinds of acts or omissions that have led to complicity charges, namely the provision of material or other assistance, the collusion with repressive governments to extract profits, and financial complicity, with a special reference to banks' complicity.

4.1.5.1 Providing Material and Other Assistance to Perpetrators

A significant strand of cases deals with corporations that knowingly provided different forms of assistance to the principals of international crimes, and they are commonly classified in business and human rights scholarship as 'direct complicity' cases.[125] To be substantiated, that form of complicity requires intentional participation of the accomplice,[126] and knowledge of the foreseeable harmful outcome,[127] but not necessarily any intention to do harm.[128] A corporation that participated in human rights abuses by assisting to their commission can be held complicit in those abuses, irrespective of whether it intended the actual harm, as long as it could have been foreseen that the assistance will lead to harm.

The aforementioned assistance can take the form of direct contribution to violations, and several cases, originating in transitional spaces, have been brought against companies for contribution to kidnappings, forced disappearances, torture or killings. Two important cases against car manufacturers arose from the Argentinean dictatorship. In 2004, a lawsuit was filed before US courts against Daimler, alleging that its subsidiary, Mercedes Benz Argentina, was complicit with the dictatorship in kidnapping, torturing and killing employees.[129] In the same year, another complaint was filed against Ford Motor and Ford Motor Argentina in the US District Court of Los Angeles, alleging that the companies' managers conspired with the dictatorship, in illegally

125 Clapham and Jerbi, 'Categories of Corporate Complicity'.

126 *Tadic Trial Judgment*, par. 674.

127 Note that, as discussed previously, the required mental element, particularly in relation to aiding and abetting, remains unsettled, with great confusion stemming from the multi-disciplinarity of the business and human rights field. See, for example, Stewart, 'Complicity in Business and Human Rights'.

128 Clapham and Jerbi, 'Categories of Corporate Complicity'.

129 *Daimler AG* v. *Bauman et al.*, No. 11-965, 134 S. Ct. 746 (2014). The Supreme Court decided that it had no jurisdiction to hear the case in 2014.

detaining, torturing and killing employees.[130] Both cases did not move forward. The former because the Supreme Court held that it had no jurisdiction to try the case and the latter was withdrawn, due to the developments in *Kiobel*. In a more recent, yet similarly unfortunate, case, a criminal investigation was initiated in Switzerland against Argor-Heraeus SA, a gold refinery corporation, for its alleged complicity in pillage in the Democratic Republic of Congo.[131]

Various cases have also been brought before international courts, on the basis of complicity, by providing the necessary means to principals of international crimes. The British Military Tribunal, in the Trial of Bruno Tesch and Two Others, known as *Zyklon B*,[132] charged Bruno Tesch, the owner of Tesch & Stabenow, a company that supplied the Auschwitz concentration camps with Zyklon B, a pesticide used in the gas chambers, as well as the company's manager and chief technician, for the supply of poison gas 'used for killing allied nationals interned in concentration camps, knowing that it was so to be used'.[133] In the ICTR case against Bagaragaza, Director General of OCIR/Thé, the government office controlling the Rwandan tea industry and vice president of Banque Continentale Africaine au Rwanda, the court convicted him of aiding and abetting the génocidaires. It found that as director of the tea industry office, he controlled eleven tea factories, which employed approximately 55,000 persons. Despite having the power to do so and being aware of the genocidal intent, he did not prevent staff from committing genocide. Further, Bagaragaza approved that vehicles and fuel from the Rubaya and Nyabihu Tea Factories be used to transport militia members for the attacks, that the attackers be provided with weapons, which he had allowed the army to conceal at the tea factories in 1993, and that

130 Verbitsky and Bohoslavsky, *Outstanding Debts to Settle*, p. 165. The case was withdrawn because it had to be heard first in Argentina.

131 The case was, however, closed due to lack of evidence in 2015. Business & Human Rights Resource Centre, 'Swiss General Attorney Not to Prosecute Argor-Heraeus over Refining of Alleged Pillaged Gold by Illegal Armed Group in Rep. Dem. of Congo' 2 June 2015. Another class action suit was brought in a Canadian court against Argor-Heraeus SA for complicity in human rights abuses, by providing logistical support to the Congolese army who committed serious abuses in the town of Kilwa, DRC in 2004. See L. Payne and G. Pereira, 'Accountability for Corporate Complicity in Human Rights Violations: Argentina's Transitional Justice Innovation?' in Verbitsky and Bohoslavsky, *Outstanding Debts to Settle*.

132 *Zyklon B* case.

133 Tesch and Weinbacher were convicted and sentenced to death, while Drosihn was acquitted. *Zyklon B* case, pp. 93–103.

personnel from the factories participate in the attacks. He further financed the purchase of alcohol to motivate the Interahamwe in order to motivate them to continue with the killings in the Kabaya and Bugoyi areas.[134]

Domestic jurisdictions – outside the transitional framework – have also engaged with corporate assistance – particularly material one – to international criminals. Most of them have not been successful when they were directed against a company, in contrast to the ones against individual business persons. Various such efforts have arisen out of the long-standing Israeli occupation of the Palestinian territories and the associated international crimes, usually carried out with the necessary material and logistical assistance by companies. In the Netherlands, a case had been filed against Lima Holding B.V. for the alleged complicity of its subsidiary (Riwal) in humanitarian law violations committed by Israel in the Occupied Palestinian Territories. The company was accused of having provided the necessary infrastructure for the construction of the wall, which the ICJ ruled as contrary to international law. Notably, the Dutch Foreign Minister reproached the company twice for its involvement in the construction of the wall.[135] However, the Dutch Public Prosecutor decided not to pursue the case, in view of the company's end of operations in Israel and Palestine.[136] While it was noted that Dutch legal persons are required to refrain from any involvement in such violations, it was decided that the company's contribution was minimal, raising concerns of improper reluctance to make politically charged decisions.[137]

In 2005, the parents of the American peace activist Rachel Corrie, and four other Palestinian families, whose relatives were killed and injured by Caterpillar bulldozers in 2003 during the demolition of houses in the Gaza Strip, brought a case against Caterpillar, before the US courts. The lawsuit was filed on the ground of aiding and abetting war crimes and serious human rights violations, using the ATCA and the TVPA. The

[134] ICTR, *Prosecutor* v. *Michel Bagaragaza*, Case No. ICTR-05-86-S, 5 November 2009.

[135] Al Haq, 'The Case Against Riwal: Corporate Complicity in International Crimes', 16 October 2010, available at www.alhaq.org/advocacy/7137.html.

[136] Dutch National Public Prosecutor's Office, Press Release, 'No further investigation into crane rental company', 14 May 2013.

[137] V. Azarov, 'Investigative or Political Barriers? Dutch Prosecutor Dismisses Criminal Complicity Case Against Riwal', 29 May 2013, available at https://rightsasusual.com/2013/05/29/investigative-or-political-barriers-dutch-prosecutor-dismisses-criminal-complicity-case-against-riwal/.

appeals court dismissed the case in 2007, stating that adjudicating the case would intrude upon the state's foreign policy.[138] A much more recent case from Palestine was initiated in France against Exxelia company. The company manufactures military components that enabled the Israeli army to strike the home of the Shuheibar family, killing three of their children and injuring other two, in July 2014 in Gaza. The criminal complaint was initiated by the family, who was summoned by the investigative judge in 2023 to testify.[139]

The French public prosecutor is also conducting investigations into Amesys company after civil society organizations on behalf of Libyan victims filed a criminal complaint in 2011. They alleged that it provided surveillance technology to the Gaddafi regime, used in the repression of opponents.[140] In 2017, another complaint was filed against Amesys' new configuration, Nexa Technologies, of complicity in torture and enforced disappearances committed in Egypt. The investigation ended with the indictment of corporate executives of the two companies.[141] A similar investigation was conducted against Qosmos company for complicity in human rights abuses, including torture for supplying surveillance technology to the Syrian government. The case was finally dismissed in 2020.[142] Most recently, but still unsuccessfully, a complaint was filed in France against TotalEnergies by two associations for 'war crimes complicity'. They alleged that the company assisted in the production of fuel, provided and used by Russian warplanes that have bombed Ukraine.[143]

[138] *Cynthia Corrie et al.* v. *Caterpillar Inc.*, US Court of Appeals for the Ninth Circuit, United States, CV-05-05192-FDB, 17 September 2007.

[139] Al Mezan Centre for Human Rights, Lawyers for Palestinian Human Rights, 'Bereaved Palestinian family gives significant evidence in Paris to investigating judge for unprecedented war crimes and corporate accountability case arising out of 2014 military attacks on Gaza', 3 August 2023, available at https://lphr.org.uk/wp-content/uploads/2023/08/Al-Mezan_LPHR-Statement-03-August-2023.pdf.

[140] Libération, 'Libye: L'enquête Visant La Société Française Amesys va Se Poursuivre', 15 January 2013; Business & Human Rights Resource Centre, 'Amesys Lawsuit (Re Libya)', 11 December 2013.

[141] Business & Human Rights Resource Centre, 'France: Judicial Investigation Opens into Amesys and Nexa Technologies' Surveillance Equipment Sales to Libya & Egypt Linked to Torture & Disappearances', 22 June 2021.

[142] Business & Human Rights Resource Centre, 'Qosmos lawsuit (re Syria)', 10 September 2013.

[143] The complaint was dismissed by prosecutors, see 'Charges Dismissed Against Total Energies for "Complicity" in Ukraine War Crimes', France 24, 16 January 2023, available at www.france24.com/en/europe/20230116-charges-dismissed-against-totalenergies-for-complicity-in-ukraine-war-crimes.

A stark and hopeful exception came from Belgium in 2019. In February of that year, the criminal court of Antwerp convicted three Flemish companies (AAE Chemie Trading, Anex Customs and Danmar Logistics) and two managing directors for shipping 168 tonnes of the chemical substance isopropanol to Syria between 2014 and 2016.[144]

Regarding individual offenders, Guus Kouwenhoven was convicted by Dutch Courts for complicity in war crimes during the conflict in Liberia. He had used his position as director of timber companies in Liberia to import weapons in the country, while he 'must have been aware' that 'in the ordinary course of events' those weapons would be used for the commission of war crimes.[145] Frans van Anraat was also convicted in the Netherlands as an accomplice in war crimes committed against the Kurds in Iraq in the 1980s, because he 'knowingly and in pursuit of profit' provided chemical weapons substances to Saddam Hussein.[146]

Against various procedural barriers,[147] a recent Swedish case stands out and bears some hope. In 2021, executives of the oil company Lundin Energy were formally charged by the Swedish prosecutor for aiding and abetting war crimes that occurred between 1997 and 2003 in today's South Sudan. It is alleged that Lundin Petroleum paid the Sudanese army and armed non-state groups to displace population, in order to continue exploration and production of oil in Block 5A concession, located in a disputed zone, where the government and rebel groups are fighting.[148] As a result, thousands of civilians were displaced, killed, tortured or otherwise suffered extreme violence. Lundin lawyers made several claims to quash the case, including that the involved Swedish ministers were biased, that the investigation violated Article 6 of the European Convention on Human Rights on fair and public hearing within a

[144] Syrian Archive, 'Antwerp Court Convicts Three Flemish Firms for Shipping 168 Tonnes of Isopropanol to Syria', 7 February 2019.

[145] The court found him liable both for crimes committed using the weapons he provided and for those which were enabled by the presence of a weapon, like pillage. He was arrested in South Africa. Information available at www.om.nl/vaste-onderdelen/zoeken/@101338/guus-arrested-south/. See also L. Van den Herik, 'The Difficulties of Exercising Extraterritorial Jurisdiction'.

[146] *Van Anraat* case.

[147] For an overview of those barriers, see Zerk, 'Corporate Liability', p. 20; International Federation for Human Rights, Corporate Accountability for Human Rights Abuses, A Guide for Victims and NGOs on Recourse Mechanisms, May 2016; Amnesty International, Injustice Incorporated (2014).

[148] European Coalition on Oil in Sudan, Unpaid Debt, The Legacy of Lundin, Petronas and OMV in Sudan, 1997–2003, June 2010.

reasonable time, that Swedish courts lacked jurisdiction and that the indictment was too vague to be actionable.[149] The crimes are prosecuted on the basis of universal jurisdiction. The trial started in September 2023 and at the time of writing is still ongoing. An aspect of it that has attracted attention has to do with the acquisition of Lundin company by Aker, after the charges were brought, as it raises significant issues of responsibility, in view of changes in the corporate structure and especially of the corporate capability to do so. The controversy stems from the fact that the merger purportedly leaves only the assets necessary to satisfy future criminal fines, thus depriving victims from the possibility to seek compensation before civil courts.[150]

4.1.5.2 Glaring Omissions and 'Business as Usual'

Aiding and abetting can also take place by omission, which is especially relevant in cases of businesses that operate amidst conflict, violence or repression and do nothing about it. Business and human rights scholars have categorised those cases as 'silent complicity'.[151] SRSG Ruggie noted that while those cases certainly raise moral and social condemnation (or even a responsibility to divest), legal responsibility seems to be difficult to establish for silent presence,[152] absent any obvious link of the violations to the corporate behaviour. The only exception he accepted is when silent presence amounted to substantial contribution to the crime, such as legitimizing or encouraging the crime, and the company knew of that encouragement.[153]

Contrary to the SRSG, international criminal law accepts that aiding and abetting can take place though omission,[154] if the accused has the

149 Business & Human Rights Resource Centre, 'Lundin Energy Lawsuit (Re Complicity in War Crimes, Sudan)', 1 September 2023.

150 See Pax for Peace, 'Did Aker BP Breach Key Human Rights Standard When Taking Over Lundin's Oil Business', 30 May 2022, available at https://paxforpeace.nl/news/did-aker-bp-breach-key-human-rights-standard-when-taking-over-lundins-oil-business/. For a relevant analysis on the necessity of human rights due diligence processes and remedies during corporate insolvency proceedings, see Vaccari and Van Ho, 'Insolvency Law Through the Lens of Human Rights Theories', pp. 190–215.

151 Clapham and Jerbi, 'Categories of Corporate Complicity'.

152 SRSG, 'Sphere of Influence and Complicity', par. 39.

153 Ibid.; 'Framework for BHR'.

154 ICTY, Milc Mrkšic et al., Case No. IT-95-13/1-A, Appeal Judgment, 5 May 2009, par. 103, 134; ICTY, 'Blaškic Appeal Judgement', par. 47; ICTR, Ferdinand Nahimana, Case No. ICTR-96-11A, Appeal Judgment, 28 November 2007, par. 482; ICTY, Radoslav Brđanin, Case No. IT-99-36-A, Appeal Judgment, 3 April 2007, par. 274; ICTR, André Ntagerura et al., Case No. ICTR-96-10A, Appeal Judgment, 7 July 2006, par. 335, 370;

ability and legal duty to act but failed to do so, or if the omission provided the necessary moral support to the principal perpetrator,[155] and under the same *actus reus* and *mens rea* requirements as a positive act.[156] Scholars suggest that aiding and abetting by omission should be seen as a general principle of law.[157] In cases regarding corporations, it appears that aiding and abetting via omission could take place, when the silence of a corporate entity could be interpreted as approval and moral encouragement to commit a crime. This is possible when a company has the political or economic influence, weight and authority over the principal perpetrators or, by reason of professional subordination, could prevent, stop or mitigate a crime but, nevertheless, refrains from any act.[158] Besides, the ICTY has held that presence may constitute complicity when it has a significant legitimizing effect on the perpetrator's conduct[159] or when along with superior status can amount to the necessary *actus reus* for aiding and abetting international crimes.[160] Also, the notion of 'sphere of influence' for assessing the authority of business actors, even by their mere presence, has been used by the ICTR in both the Ruzindana and the Musema judgments. Both defendants, while having the necessary authority – Ruzindana as a well-known and

ICTR, Akayesu Trial Judgment, par. 548; ICTR, *Prosecutor* v. *Kamuhanda*, Case No. ICTR-95-54A-T, Judgment, Trial Chamber, 22 January 2004, par. 597; ICTR, *Proseucutor* v. *Muvunyi*, Case No. ICTR-2000-55A-T, Judgment, Trial Chamber, 12 September 2006, par. 470; ICTR, *Prosecutor* v. *Bisengimana*, Case No. ICTR-00-60-T, Judgment, Trial Chamber, 13 April 2006, par. 34; *Prosecutor* v. *Mpambara*, Case No. ICTR-01-65-T, Judgment, Trial Chamber, 11 September 2006, par. 22.

155 ICTR, 'Prosecutor v. Kayishema et al.', par. 200; ICTR, 'Prosecutor v. Bisengimana, Trial Judgment', par. 34.

156 ICTY, 'Prosecutor v. Oric', Appeal Judgment, 3 July 2008, par. 43; ICTY, 'Blaškic Appeal Judgement', par. 47.

157 G. Werle, 'Individual Criminal Responsibility in Article 25 ICC Statute' (2007) 5 *Journal of International Criminal Justice* 4, at 966; M. Duttwiler, 'Liability for Omission in International Criminal Law' (2006) 6 *International Criminal Law Review* 1, at 60. For an opposing view, see A. Eser, 'Individual Criminal Responsibility (Art. 25)', in Antonio Cassese et al. (eds.), *The Rome Statute of the International Criminal Court: A commentary* (Oxford University Press, 2002), p. 819. For an analysis of responsibility by omission, see M. Jackson, *Complicity in International Law* (Oxford University Press, 2015).

158 'ICJ Report', p. 20.

159 ICTY, 'Tadic Trial Judgment', par. 688.

160 ICTY, *Prosecutor* v. *Kvocka*, Case No. IT-98-30/1-T, Trial Judgment, 2 November 2001, par. 257–261, summarizing the ICTY cases dealing with presence and accomplice liability. Also, 'SRSG, Sphere of Influence and Complicity', par. 40.

respected businessman,[161] and Musema as the factory's manager[162] – did nothing to prevent the participation in genocide, of people that they could influence. Aiding and abetting via omission was the basis of the criminal complaint filed in Germany against the senior manager of Danzer Group, a timber manufacturing company. It alleged the manager's complicity in violations committed by the local armed forces in Bongulu, Democratic Republic of Congo, in 2013, because he omitted to give local employees specific directions for cases of conflict, and he failed to prevent their abuses.[163]

Equally, the 'business as usual' defence, in the framework of aiding and abetting liability, does not seem to have gained traction. In cases where a company is aware of the impact of its actions in facilitating a crime, its intention to carry out normal business activities, like selling its produce, will not absolve it from liability, if it knew that the purchaser would use them to commit international crimes.[164] As Schabas has eloquently analysed, criminal intent is different and should not be confused with motives. Particularly for corporations, the motive is always profit and 'business as usual', but the intent is the one that interests international criminal justice.[165] Thus, the important factor to qualify routine business, as aiding and abetting, is the mental element.[166] Guiding principle 17 of the UNGPs seems also to hint to that direction, by foregrounding knowledge, as a way to avoid complicity.[167] By way of indication, the 'business as usual' defence was dismissed in the Van Anraat case in the Netherlands, regarding the supply of TDG chemical substances to Saddam Hussein. The judges opined that the huge amounts of TDG that Van Anraat delivered to Iraq could not be used for agricultural purposes

[161] ICTR, 'Prosecutor v. Obed Ruzindana'.

[162] ICTR, 'Musema Trial Judgement', paras. 880, 898–925, 936 and 950–951, 984.

[163] The Office of the State Prosecutor in Tübingen discontinued investigations. See ECCHR, 'No investigations against Danzer manager over human rights abuses against community in DRC', available at www.ecchr.eu/en/case/no-investigations-against-danzer-manager-over-human-rights-abuses-against-community-in-drc/.

[164] 'ICJ Report', p. 21; Kelly, 'Prosecuting Corporations for Genocide', p. 81. Michalowski notes that case law from ad hoc tribunals and the ATCA demonstrates that liability based on dual purpose acts is limited by requiring either that the assistance is significant or that the *mens rea* while carrying out the act was particularly disgraceful. Michalowski, 'Doing Business with a Bad Actor', pp. 403–464.

[165] Schabas, 'Enforcing International Humanitarian Law'.

[166] Farrell, 'Attributing Criminal Liability to Corporate Actors', p. 892.

[167] Guiding principle 17 imposes on corporations the responsibility to carry out human rights' due diligence in order to 'become aware of, prevent and address adverse human rights impacts'.

only and, therefore, were to be used at least partially by the armed forces.[168] Alfred Krupp was, also, convicted by the Nuremberg tribunal of plunder as war crime, for having taken over numerous factories, machines and other private property in territories seized by the Nazis,[169] despite the fact that he was merely interested in maximizing his profit. In the Apartheid litigation, the court held that simply doing business with a state or individual who violates the law of nations is insufficient to create liability under customary international law,[170] but accepted that this can be reversed if doing business, provides the 'tools, instrumentalities or services to commit (those) violations'.[171]

4.1.5.3 Financial Complicity

Financial complicity results from making funds available to those who commit gross human rights violations. It might apply to financial actors like banks, which will be examined separately at Section 4.1.5.4, as well as to other businesses not working in the financial sector. It has attracted limited academic research,[172] even though reports expound on the topic across the globe, since the 1970s.[173] That lack of attention might be attributed to the difficulty in proving the *actus reus* and causation elements, given that money is never the direct means to commit crimes, and it is difficult to connect to a particular human rights violation because of its fungibility.[174] In addition, financial complicity cases are analysed under the light of the *South African Apartheid Litigation*, where the US courts dismissed the case given that a legal link could not be

[168] *Van Anraat* case. See also H. van der Wilt, 'Genocide, Complicity in Genocide and International v. Domestic Jurisdiction: Reflections on the van Anraat Case' (2006) 4 *Journal of International Criminal Justice*, pp. 239–257.

[169] *Krupp* case, p. 1327.

[170] *Re South African Apartheid Litigation*, pp. 257–258; *Mastafa* v. *Australian Wheat Board Ltd and Banque Nationale De Paris Paribas*, 2008 WL 4378443 (SDNY), p. 4.

[171] *Khulumani* v. *Barclay National Bank*, 504 F.3d 254 (2d Cir., 2007), pp. 289–290.

[172] Notable exemptions are Ramasastry, 'Secrets and Lies?'; S. W. Scott, 'Note, Taking Riggs Seriously: The ATCA Case Against a Corporate Abettor of Pinochet Atrocities' (2005) 89 *Minnesota Law Review* 1497; Bohoslavsky and Opgenhaffen, 'The Past and Present of Corporate Complicity'; J. P. Bohoslavsky and M. Rulli, 'Corporate Complicity and Finance as a "Killing Agent": The Relevance of the Chilean Case' (2010) 8 *Journal of International Criminal Justice* 3, pp. 829–850.

[173] A. Cassese, Study of the Impact of Foreign Economic Aid and Assistance on Respect for Human Rights in Chile, E/CN.4/Sub.2/412, Vols. I–IV, 1978.

[174] For an elaborate account of financial complicity and its challenges, see Michalowski, 'No Complicity Liability for Funding', p. 452; Michalowski, 'Doing Business with a Bad Actor'.

established between commercial loans and specific human rights violations.[175] The *Doe* v. *Nestle* case has also been commonly referred to, mostly opposing financial complicity, as the court held that 'ordinary commercial transactions, without more, do not violate international law'.[176] However, Professor Michalowski, as will be analysed in Chapters 5–8, emphasizes the necessity of less sweeping accounts, based on examining closely the effect of financing to the offences carried out, the causation element and the *mens rea* of each financier, which would result in narrowing the accountability gap and providing respective incentives to businesses.

Despite the fact that existing case law is scarce and no clear principles can be dissected, it seems that the elements of 'aiding and abetting' could be amenable to financial complicity,[177] namely action with effect on the perpetration of the crime, along with knowledge that one's actions will assist the perpetration of an international crime.[178] Insofar as the financier's contribution had a substantial – yet not indispensable[179] – effect on the development of the financed activity,[180] and they knew of the criminal acts of the principal perpetrator and had sufficient proximity to them, then liability could be attached.[181] It is interesting to note that Article 25(3) (c) of the ICC Statute makes accessory to a crime liable if he or she 'aids, abets or otherwise assists in its commission or its attempted commission, including providing the means for its commission',[182] without however necessarily requiring providing the direct means in order to trigger complicity liability.[183]

175 Geneuss et al., 'Core Crimes Inc.: Panel Discussion'.

176 *Doe* v. *Nestle*, S.A., 748 F. Supp. 2d 1057 (CD. Cal. 2010), p. 1099.

177 Those elements were examined in Section 4.1.5 on complicity.

178 However, note that in *Cortie* v. *Caterpillar*, the court dismissed liability based on the seller's lack of specific intent to further the buyer's venture. See *Cortie* v. *Caterpillar, Inc.*, 403 F. Supp. 2d (W.D. Wash., 2005), at 1027.

179 ICTY, 'Furundzija Trial Judgement', par. 209.

180 Bohoslavsky and Opgenhaffen, 'The Past and Present of Corporate Complicity', at 172–173.

181 N. Bernaz, 'Establishing Liability for Financial Complicity in International Crimes', in J. Bohoslavsky and J. Letnar Černič (eds.), *Making Sovereign Financing and Human Rights Work* (Hart, 2014), pp. 61–76.

182 Rome Statute, Article 25(3) (c). See also 'Draft Code of Crimes Against the Peace and Security of Mankind'.

183 Michalowski, 'No Complicity Liability for Funding', p. 465. Note, however, that in *Doe* v. *Nestle and the South African Apartheid Litigation*, courts agreed that the *actus reus* test for liability was to provide the direct means. See 'Re South African Apartheid Litigation', par. 258; *Doe* v. *Nestle*, S.A., 748 F. Supp. 2d 1057 (C.D. Cal., 2010), p. 1099.

Liability would arguably be less challenging for those who provide funds out of personal affiliation, as in the case of Himmler's circle of friends, as opposed to financiers who provided funds in the framework of commercial transactions.[184] As Californian courts found, contrary to ordinary commercial transactions, liability clearly results from acts performed '*in a non-commercial, non-mutually-beneficial manner, as with the banker in the Flick Case who gratuitously funded the SS's criminal activities*',[185] although knowledge will still be important.[186] In contrast, concerning funding provided by doing business with a repressive or violent regime, liability would presumably attach if there is a distinction from ordinary commercial activities. To that respect, the International Commission of Jurists emphasized the importance of the financier's knowledge. It noted that the '*criminal liability of a financier will depend on what he or she knows about how his or her services and loans will be utilized and the degree to which these services actually affect the commission of a crime*'.[187]

The Nuremberg precedent was clear on financing responsibility, for entities other than banks. In the *Flick* case, Friedrich Flick and Otto Steinbrinck, leading officials of the Flick Concern and members of the Keppler Circle or Friends of Himmler, were held responsible for slave labour, plunder and participation to SS atrocities, including by contributing '*extensive financial and other support*' to the SS, while knowing their crimes,[188] and that such large amounts of money cannot be spent solely for cultural purposes.[189] The Tribunal did not specify the respective mode of liability but held that '*one who knowingly by his influence and money contributes to the support thereof must, under settled legal*

[184] Michalowski notes that one of the ambiguities of the Nuremberg precedent is whether the difference in outcomes in *Flick* and *Rasche* rests on the fact that Flick was accused of making personal financial contributions to Himmler in order to secure political favours, whereas Rasche was accused of making a commercial loan on behalf of Dresdner Bank. Michalowski, 'No Complicity Liability for Funding', at 478.

[185] *Doe* v. *Nestle*, S.A., 748 F. Supp. 2d at 1095 (CD. Cal., 2010).

[186] Note that Rasche was absolved of liability for making contributions to Himmler Circle of Friends because he did not know 'that any part of the fund to which the bank made contributions was intended to be or was ever used by Himmler for any unlawful purposes'. *Ministries* case, at 622.

[187] ICJ Report, pp. 39–40. Also Bohoslavsky and Rulli emphasized that the impact of funding depends on what the user of the service or consumer of the good plans to do with it. Bohoslavsky and Rulli, 'Corporate Complicity and Finance as a "Killing Agent"'.

[188] Flick case, at 1216–1123.

[189] Flick case, at 1217, 1220.

principles, be deemed to be, if not a principal, certainly an accessory to such crimes'.[190] Interestingly, the Tribunal did not find it necessary to establish whether those funds were spent 'on salaries or for lethal gas',[191] meaning that it did not consider it necessary to make direct links between the provision of the funds and the exact crimes committed.[192]

A more recent case on financial complicity is the French investigation against Lafarge, a cement company, for alleged complicity in crimes against humanity in Syria.[193] The investigation focuses on the large sums of money paid by the company to jihadist groups, including the Islamic State, in order to continue operating amidst conflict in North Syria. Initially, the lower court dismissed the charges, holding that the company's intention had to do with its operations and not with the commission of crimes. In September 2021, the Court of Cassation reversed that decision and held that the desire to keep the operations going is part of the motive of the company and should not be confounded to the required intention. Regarding the latter, it held that '[i]t is sufficient that he or she has knowledge that the principal perpetrators are committing or about to commit such a crime against humanity and that by his or her aid or assistance he or she facilitates its preparation or commission'.[194] Notably, in October 2022, Lafarge S.A. and its Syrian subsidiary admitted to have concluded revenue-sharing agreements with ISIS and agreed to pay $778 million in fines and forfeiture to the US authorities.[195] On 16 January 2024, the French Supreme Court confirmed the charges of complicity in crimes against humanity against Lafarge.[196]

190 Flick case, at 1217.

191 Flick case, at 1221.

192 Michalowski, 'No Complicity Liability for Funding', at 477.

193 ECCHR, 'Lafarge in Syria: Complicity in Human Rights Violations?' available at www.ecchr.eu/en/business-and-human-rights/lafarge-syria.html.

194 Cour de cassation, Arrêt de la Cour de Cassation, Chambre Criminelle, 7 September 2021, Pourvoi No. 19-87.367, par. 67. Note that in June 2023, the investigative judges closed the part of the case that concerned financing of terrorism. Information available at www.business-humanrights.org/en/latest-news/frances-lafarge-loses-ruling-in-syria-crimes-against-humanity-case/.

195 US Department of Justice, Office of Public Affairs, 'Lafarge Pleads Guilty to Conspiring to Provide Material Support to Foreign Terrorist Organizations', 18 October 2022, available at www.justice.gov/opa/video/lafarge-pleads-guilty-conspiring-provide-material-support-foreign-terrorist-organizations.

196 See Business and Human Rights Resource Centre, 'Lafarge in Syria: French Supreme Court issues decisive ruling on charges faced by the multinational', 16 January 2024, available at www.business-humanrights.org/en/latest-news/lafarge-in-syria-french-supreme-court-issues-decisive-ruling-on-charges-faced-by-the-multinational/. On 16 October 2024, Lafarge

Equally important have been efforts in the US against Chiquita brands for financing Colombian paramilitaries. An inquiry by the US Justice Department led Chiquita to plead guilty for financing the AUC, a right-wing paramilitary group in Colombia. Chiquita's sentence included a fine, other compliance requirements, five years' probation and the obligation to cooperate in the investigation.[197] Several lawsuits were then filed before US courts, by more than 200 victims of the paramilitaries, accusing Chiquita of financing torture, war crimes and other human rights abuses.[198] The court dismissed the ATCA and TVPA causes of action, on the basis of foreign policy implications, but the case is still ongoing on the basis of Colombian law,[199] and in March 2023, Chiquita was ordered to stand trial.[200] On 10 June 2024, in a groundbreaking verdict, a unanimous jury found Chiquita liable for over thirty-eight million in damages, for financing the murderous activities of AUC.[201] A further important contribution of the US cases is that it provided evidence and oral testimonies that led to domestic prosecutions in Colombia.[202] In 2009, another case arising from Colombia was filed under the ATCA before the US courts. The complaint alleged that

and four former executives were ordered to stand trial before the French criminal court for financing a terrorist organization and violating an embargo. See Business and Human Rights Resource Centre, 'France: Lafarge and Former Executives Set to Face Trial for Alleged Terrorism Financing in Syria', 16 October 2024, available at www.business-humanrights.org/en/latest-news/france-lafarge-and-former-executives-set-to-face-trial-for-alleged-terrorism-financing-in-syria/.

197 US Department of Justice, 'Chiquita Brands International Pleads Guilty to Making Payments to a Designated Terrorist Organization and Agrees to Pay $25 Million Fine', 19 March 2007.

198 Similar lawsuits against Chiquita alleging company's complicity in crimes committed by AUC in Colombia were filed in various other US federal courts, but in 2008 they were consolidated in one multidistrict trial, which transferred six separate lawsuits to the District Court for the Southern District of Florida.

199 For an overview of developments, see, Earthrights International, *Doe* v. *Chiquita Brands International*, available at http://earthrights.org/case/doe-v-chiquita-brands-international/.

200 Business and Human Rights Resource Centre, 'Chiquita Lawsuits (Re Colombia, Filed in USA by Colombian Nationals)', 14 November 2007, available at www.business-humanrights.org/en/latest-news/chiquita-lawsuits-re-colombia/; Earthrights International, 'Over 200 Colombian Plaintiffs File Claims for Torture and Killings Against Chiquita', 25 March 2020, available at https://earthrights.org/media_release/over-200-colombian-plaintiffs-file-claims-for-torture-and-killings-against-chiquita/.

201 In *re Chiquita Brands International Inc.* litigation, US District Court, Southern District of Florida, Case No. 08-MD-01916-MARRA, Verdict.

202 See, for example, the cases against Arnulfo Peñuela Marin and Luis Alberto Agudelo Jiménez, in Section 4.2.2.

Drummond Coal Company was complicit in the killings of union leaders in Colombia and made payments to the AUC paramilitary group to this end.[203] The case was finally dismissed due to presumed lack of jurisdiction by the US courts but stirred developments in Colombia, analysed in Section 4.2.2.

Although they face challenges, those precedents have laid the groundwork for alternative imaginaries to emerge and win an important part of common discourse. Indicative for that change is that few days after the Russian invasion in Ukraine, numerous civil society organizations from across the world united under the goal 'to block access to the economic resources behind the Russian aggression'.[204] Their research revealed that global corporations made over 200 billion in revenues through their local Russian subsidiaries – in 2022 only – and paid more than three billion in profit taxes to the Russian state, essentially financing its war machine.[205] They engaged in different types of advocacy in order to push economic actors to divest from Russia and their approach influenced other actors into speaking up, such as business association and investors' groups.[206] The pressure coming from various such advocacy efforts led 17 per cent of the western companies with Russian subsidiaries to completely exit Russia. Similar efforts have taken place in relation to other conflict spaces, such as Myanmar[207] and Palestine,[208] with differing and not always positive results. The importance of all those calls lies beyond their ability to bring about court cases in the shift of the public dialogue that they effectuate. They signal a growing acceptance of corporate financial

[203] International Network for Economic, Social and Cultural Rights 'Case Profile: Drummond Lawsuit (Re Colombia)', available at www.escr-net.org/node/365544.

[204] See the Global Business for Ukraine (GB4U) association, a consortium international and global companies, in support of Ukraine, its businesses and its economy. Information available at www.gb4u.org/.

[205] B4Ukraine & Kyiv School of Economics (KSE), The Business of Staying: A closer look at multinational revenues and taxes in Russia in 2022 available at https://b4ukraine.org/pdf/BusinessOfStaying.pdf.

[206] Investor Alliance for Human Rights, 'Investor Alert: Human Rights Risks Related to the Russian Invasion of Ukraine', 3 March 2022, available at http://investorsforhumanrights.org/news/investor-alert-human-rights-risks-related-russian-invasion-ukraine.

[207] Justice for Myanmar, 'Joint Civil Society Statement on Myanmar Military Coup', 3 February 2021, information available at www.justiceformyanmar.org/press-releases/joint-civil-society-statement-on-myanmar-military-coup; Htwe Htwe Thein and Sam Baron, 'Business Not as Usual: International Business and the Myanmar Crisis', 15 February 2024, available at http://asialink.unimelb.edu.au/insights/business-not-as-usual-international-business-and-the-myanmar-crisis.

[208] Pietropaoli, 'Obligations of Third States'.

involvement in conflict and repression and an ensuing concern over adequate responses by companies in those instances.

4.1.5.4 The Case of Banks

The contribution of banks to violent or repressive regimes has triggered various court cases. American, Austrian, French, German and Swiss banks were sued for providing funds to the Nazis, for not returning original bank deposits to victims and for using slave labour.[209] Likewise, banks were added as defendants in a US lawsuit against Ferdinand Marcos, long-time dictator of the Philippines.[210] Although in the beginning the ATCA lawsuit targeted Marcos himself,[211] for human rights abuses during the dictatorship, after his death, litigation continued against his estate and Swiss banks that plundered the national treasury by helping Marcos conceal his wealth. The court held that the banks acted as agents of the regime,[212] but the plaintiffs are to this day unable to access the funds in all three countries involved.[213]

Apartheid victims as well resorted against banks that financed the regime.[214] In 2002, the Khulumani support group sued twenty banks and companies in US federal courts, on the basis of their complicity in human rights abuses, against black South Africans during that time. Specifically, regarding banks, the plaintiffs claimed that between 1985 and 1993, they directly financed the regime's security forces, responsible for most atrocities. Given that other banks and governments

[209] In *re Austrian and German Bank Holocaust* litigation, No. 98 Civ. 3938 (S.D.N.Y. 7 March 2001); *In re Holocaust Victim Assets Litigation*, No. 96 Civ. 4849 (E.D.N.Y. 22 November 2000); *Bodner* v. *Banque Paribas*, 114 F. Supp. 2d 117 (E.D.N.Y. 2000). See also J. Authers, 'Making Good Again: German Compensation for Forced and Slave Labourers', in P. De Greiff, *The Handbook of Reparations*; B. Neuborne, 'Holocaust Reparations Litigation: Lessons for the Slavery Reparations Movement' (2003) 58 *N.Y.U. Annual Survey of American Law* 615, pp. 615–622; Ramasastry, 'Secrets and Lies?'

[210] J. Van Dyke, 'Promoting Accountability for Human Rights Abuses' (2005) 8 *Chapman Law Review* 153, p. 154.

[211] *Estate of Ferdinand Marcos Human Rights Litigation*, 94 F.3d 539, 542 (9th Cir. 1996).

[212] See *Hilao* v. *Estate of Marcos*, 95 F.3d 848, 855 (9th Cir. 1996).

[213] See Section 6.1 of this book.

[214] The *re South African Apartheid* litigation consists of two separate lawsuits that were consolidated: the *Khulumani* v. *Barclays* and the *Ntzebeza* v. *Daimler AG*. The initial complaints were filed in 2002 and have been amended many times. For an elaborate account of the litigation, see I. Gubbay, 'Towards Making Blood Money Visible: Lessons Drawn from the Apartheid Litigation', in J. Černič and P. Bohoslavsky (eds.), *Making Sovereign Financing and Human Rights Work* (Hart Publishing, 2014).

were boycotting any financial relation to the Apartheid and that the regime was financially unstable, they concluded that were it not for those banks' assistance, the Apartheid could not have survived for so long.[215] On 8 April 2009, the court dismissed aiding and abetting claims against banking defendants, because a legal link could not be established between commercial loans and specific human rights violations.[216] However, it has been argued that this sweeping holding was based in a misinterpretation of Nuremberg case law and specifically the *Ministries* case,[217] which is analysed further down.

More recently, in 2017, a complaint was filed before French authorities, against BNP Paribas, alleging complicity in genocide, crimes against humanity and war crimes, because it knowingly approved a transfer of $1.3 million from the Rwandan central bank to an arms dealer, despite the UN arms embargo and amidst the Rwandan genocide of 1994. The complaint alleged that those transfers would have financed the purchase of arms and contributed to the Rwandan genocide.[218] It referred to evidence proving the undoubted knowledge by the bank of the genocidal intentions of the authorities of the country for which it allowed the transactions.[219] Notably, this is not the first case that this bank is involved in. Cases have been brought against it in the US for payments made to the Hussein regime despite the UN's Oil for Food programme.[220] The bank has also pled guilty in the US for financing Sudan's government in its atrocities towards civilians in Darfur.[221]

4.1.5.4.1 The Ministries Case The most useful precedent regarding banks dates back to the Nuremberg times, in the cases against Karl

[215] 'Re South African Apartheid Litigation', pp. 103–125.

[216] Geneuss et al., 'Core Crimes Inc.: Panel Discussion'.

[217] *Ministries* case, at 621–622.

[218] M. Kennedy, 'French Bank BNP Paribas Accused of Complicity in Rwandan Genocide', NPR, 29 June 2017; Business and Human Rights Resource Centre, 'BNP Paribas Faces Accusations Over the Rwandan Genocide', 5 July 2017.

[219] Sherpa, CPCR and Ibuka, Rwandan Genocide: Sherpa, CPCR and Ibuka France launched a complaint against BNP Paribas on the basis of complicity in a genocide, in crimes against humanity and in war crimes. Press pack, available at http://media.business-humanrights.org/media/documents/d8eb055488d6e44342f5dd40ca8d1dfaeee56b0f.pdf.

[220] *Mastafa* v. *Australian Wheat Board* (n 393).

[221] See relevant documents and resources published by the US Department of Justice, available at www.justice.gov/archives/opa/documents-and-resources-june-30-2104-bnp-paribas-press-conference.

Rasche, member of the board of managers of the Dresdner Bank, and Emil Puhl, Deputy President of the Reichsbank. Karl Rasche was charged with different counts of war crimes and crimes against humanity, namely persecution of German nationals, atrocities against civilian populations, plunder, slave labour and membership in a criminal organization. Rasche was convicted for plunder and membership in a criminal organization, but it is the charges for which he was acquitted that bear more interest, namely providing loans for the construction of Auschwitz.[222] Count 5 concerned war crimes and crimes against humanity, for the loans given by Dresdner Bank to SS enterprises which employed inmates from concentration camps and resettlement programmes. Rasche was absolved of liability for making contributions to Himmler Circle of Friends because he did not know 'that any part of the fund to which the bank made contributions was intended to be or was ever used by Himmler for any unlawful purposes'.[223] But, regarding the loans made to SS enterprises, which employed slave labour and funded the Nazi resettlement programme, the Tribunal held that Rasche had the requisite knowledge, but again rejected liability because '*loans or sale of commodities to be used in an unlawful enterprise may well be condemned from a moral standpoint and reflect no credit on the part of the lender or seller in either case, but the transaction can hardly be said to be a crime*'.[224] Under Count 7, he was charged with war crimes and crimes against humanity in the context of slave labour for having 'participated in the financing of SS enterprises which used concentration camp labour on a wide scale and under inhumane conditions'.[225] In this count, he was acquitted because the prosecution did not 'show knowledge on the part of Rasche as to what was taking place in the SS enterprises with respect to slave labour'.[226]

Emil Puhl was convicted for his active role in arranging 'the receipt, classification, deposit, conversion and disposal of properties taken by the SS from victims exterminated in concentration camps'.[227] The tribunal acknowledged that '[Puhl's] part in this transaction was not that of mere messenger or businessman. He went beyond the ordinary range of his

[222] *Ministries* case, at 621 *et seq*, pp. 852–855.
[223] Ibid., at 622.
[224] Ibid. Rasche was also acquitted of the charge under Count 6 of funding agencies that were active in Germany's spoliation programme in Poland and Russia. See Michalowski, 'The Mens Rea Standard for Corporate Aiding and Abetting', pp. 237–274.
[225] *Ministries* case, at 853.
[226] Ibid., at 853–854.
[227] Ibid., at 609, 620–621.

duties to give directions that the matter be handled secretly by the appropriate departments of the bank'.[228] However, he was acquitted of financing enterprises that were primarily created to exploit slave labour, including the negotiation of a massive loan between the SS and DEST, a company specifically designed to utilize concentration camp labour. He was also acquitted of assisting DEST in 'securing additional large loans, obtaining reductions on interest rates on such loans, and receiving extensions of time for repayment, because it was doubtful whether defendant Puhl did more than act as a conduit in these particular transactions'.[229]

As Michalowski notes, this decision was interpreted wrongly by the Khulumani court,[230] other courts,[231] scholars and of course banks themselves[232] as implying that complicity liability for commercial loans is always excluded.[233] For her, the *Ministries* case is seemingly far more complicated and does not lend support to a sweeping understanding eliminating all liability for loans and other inherently neutral commercial goods.[234] While it is the second recital from the court's decision earlier that has attracted most attention and has been interpreted hastily, the first and third recital prove a more nuanced approach of the court on the issue. In fact, in Count 5 against Rasche, the court did not dismiss any liability but was not satisfied that his acts reached the necessary *actus reus* standard for aiding and abetting.[235] Count 7 was dismissed not because

228 Ibid., at 620–621.

229 Ibid., at 851–852.

230 *Khulumani* v. *Barclays National Bank Ltd.*, 504 F.3d 254, 292–293 (2d Cir. 2007); In 're South African Apartheid' litigation.

231 *Doe* v. *Nestle*, S.A., 748 F. Supp. 2d 1057, 1088–1090 (C.D. Cal. 2010); *Presbyterian Church of Sudan* v. *Talisman Energy, Inc.*, 582 F.3d 244, 259 (2d Cir. 2009); *Khulumani*, 504 F.3d at 276. See also S. Bhashyam, 'Knowledge or Purpose? The Khulumani Litigation and the Standard for Aiding and Abetting Liability Under the Alien Tort Claims Act' (2008) 30 *Cardozo Law Review* 245, p. 269.

232 Ramasastry mentions that the banks in the South African Apartheid litigation cited the Nuremberg holding on Rasche to support their innocence. Ramasastry, 'Secrets and Lies?'

233 Michalowski makes a further argument that antiterrorism jurisprudence does not support the view of the South African Apartheid litigation that loans are far removed from violations, since it casts a wide net for complicity liability. Michalowski, 'No Complicity Liability for Funding'.

234 Ibid., at 474.

235 Ibid. See also Farrell, 'Attributing Criminal Liability to Corporate Actors', pp. 887–888; K. Gallagher, 'Civil Litigation and Transnational Business' (2010) 8 *Journal of International Criminal Justice* 745, p. 763.

commercial loans are always exempt from liability, but rather because Rasche's knowledge or participation was not sufficiently proved.[236] In addition, the *Ministries* case has to be viewed under the light of Walter Funk's case. Funk, Minister of Economics and President of the Reichsbank, was convicted in the framework of *The Medical Trial* for war crimes and crimes against humanity, including for loans that furthered SS slave labour. This was based on the fact that as president of the Reichsbank, Funk was also indirectly involved in the utilization of concentration camp labour. Under his direction, the Reichsbank set up a revolving fund of 12,000,000 Reichsmarks to the credit of the SS for the construction of factories to use concentration camp labourers.[237] The issue of bank complicity is still pertinent in transitional settings, like in Argentina where victims of the dictatorship filed claims in Buenos Aires against a number of banks known to have financed the military junta, on allegations of corporate complicity to human rights abuses.[238]

4.2 Domestic Approaches

Several cases have been brought for violations linked to prior conflict or repression, either by authorities or by victims, in transitioning fora, or in foreign jurisdictions. The outcomes of those cases offered varying degrees of remedy to victims and put another brick in the wall of corporate accountability during transitions by – at least – furthering the understanding of the many challenges faced. The criminal cases – or those functionally classified under criminal mechanisms[239] – brought against corporations and corporate officials are quite dispersed, with multiple lessons to be learned, something that makes the task of a single condensed account arduous. Three facets of the various different examples deserve to be considered as future insights, namely the concerted efforts of victims and civil society in pursuing justice, the various innovations of domestic justice actors in corporate abuse cases and the developments that those efforts stirred, even when their immediate tangible result for the victims was limited.

236 Michalowski, 'No Complicity Liability for Funding', pp. 887–888; Gallagher, 'Civil Litigation and Transnational Business', p. 763.

237 *United States* v. *Brandt*, 1 Trials of War Criminals Vol. I (1949), at 171, 305–306 (The Medical Case).

238 R. Mattarollo, 'Los bancos de la dictadura', *Página 12*, 23 November 2009; H. Verbitsky, 'Los prestamistas de la muerte', *Página 12*, 16 March 2009.

239 Zweigert and Kötz, 'An Introduction to Comparative Law'.

A brief *tour d' horizon* cannot exclude Chile, where, albeit quite delayed, some limited results were levered through pressure from civil society and institutional innovators.[240] It was only in 2017 that the Supreme Court condemned businessman Francisco Luzoro Montenegro to twenty years in prison, as he was one of the landowners who, along with the military, exerted extreme violence and illegally dispossessed farmers of their land, in Paine, during the dictatorship.[241] In 2018, corporate executives of CMPC Paper Company were prosecuted for complicity in the Laja Rosendo case, where nineteen workers of the factory were executed by the police in 1973.[242] The company executives provided vehicles to the police, identified people to be murdered and participated in their executions.[243]

In addition, the Brazilian example is informative, for finding ways to circumvent legal barriers and deliver, if not criminal remedies per se, at least some degree of recognition for victims, and retribution for the offenders. In what Bohoslavsky calls 'truth trials', Brazilian prosecutors, barred from launching official action, due to amnesty laws, still decided to investigate Volkswagen subsidiary in São Paulo for complicity in crimes against humanity, in collaboration with the dictatorship. Volkswagen workers were the primary target of the Police Intelligence Agency, during the dictatorship, to whom the company donated 200 vehicles, and its premises to be used as detention and torture centres.[244] The prosecutors formed working groups to gather evidence and investigate those abuses. The public attention around the issue might have been one of the reasons why the company started negotiating a reparation plan with the state, in 2015.[245]

In the Congo, victims' herculean efforts to be repaired for corporate atrocities were fruitless despite spreading across different jurisdictions. On 25 April 2013, a complaint was filed before the German courts against a senior manager of Danzer Group, a Swiss and German timber manufacturer, for aiding and abetting gross human rights abuses, by

[240] Payne et al., *Archimedes' Lever*, pp. 263–266.
[241] Supreme Court, Case ref. Rol 1.568–2017, 16 November 2017.
[242] C. A. Concepción, Role No. Sección Criminal-Ant-174-2017, 15 March 2018.
[243] K. Fernández and S. Smart, 'Complicity of Companies in Chile's Current Human Rights Crisis', in L. Payne et al. (eds.), *Economic Actors and the Limits of Transitional Justice: Truth and Justice for Business Complicity in Human Rights Violations* (British Academy Scholarship Online, 2022).
[244] Sandt and Moor, 'Peace, Everyone's Business!', pp. 79–80.
[245] J. P. Bohoslavsky et al. (eds.), *Pinochet's Economic Accomplices: An Unequal Country by Force* (Lexington Books, 2020), p. 85.

providing financial and logistical assistance to the local police and military, during the attack at the Bongulu village, in 2011. The complaint was based on German laws relating to the duty of care of senior corporate managers to those affected by the actions of their staff, but the investigation was stopped by prosecutors' order in 2015. At the same time, a parallel trial was going on before military court in the DRC, against Danzer's former subsidiary SIFORCO, alleging that the latter aided and abetted the same abuses. In 2019, the court sanctioned the officers and imposed a fine on the government, but absolved the company from responsibility.[246]

Another multi-forum litigation arising from the Congo was the one against Anvil Mining Company, an Australian mining company allegedly complicit for a massacre committed by the Congolese army in Kilwa in 2004. A criminal trial in the DRC led to the acquittal of the victims, on charges of war crimes, during a trial that presented serious flaws and irregularities,[247] and was condemned by the UN.[248] In Canada, the Court of Appeal decided that Québec courts did not have jurisdiction, because there was no 'real and substantial link' of Anvil with the Province of Québec.[249] In Australia, a first investigation by Australian Federal Police was initiated in 2005, but no charges were filed.[250] In 2008, pre-action proceedings for discovery of documents by victims' lawyers were commenced in the Supreme Court of Western Australia by sixty-one victims, but the Congolese authorities did not allow them to travel and communicate with their clients back in the DRC.[251] However, the efforts before the

246 Business & Human Rights Resource Centre, 'SIFORCO lawsuit (re Dem. Rep. Congo, filed in Dem. Rep. Congo)', available at www.business-humanrights.org/en/latest-news/danzer-group-siforco-lawsuits-re-dem-rep-congo/.

247 Global Witness, RAID, ACIDH, 'The Kilwa Trial: A Denial of Justice', 17 July 2007, available at http://cdn2.globalwitness.org/archive/files/pdfs/kilwa_chron_en_170707.pdf.

248 J. Bavier, 'U.N. Denounces Congo's Anvil War Crimes Verdict', *Reuters*, 4 July 2007.

249 Specifically, in the DRC, where the harm occurred, or Australia, where the company's main office is located. *Anvil Mining Ltd.* v. *Association Canadienne Contre L' Impunite* (2012) J.Q. No. 368, 2012 QCCA 117, 24 January 2012, par. 103.

250 A. McBeth, 'Crushed by an Anvil: A Case Study on Responsibility for Human Rights in the Extractive Sector' (2008) 11 *Yale Human Rights and Development Law Journal*, p. 147.

251 R. Meeran, 'Tort Litigation Against Multinational Corporations for Violation of Human Rights: An Overview of the Position outside the United States' (2011) 3 *City University of Hong Kong Law Review* 1, at 1–41. See also J. Kyriakakis, 'Australian Prosecution of Corporations for International Crimes' (2007) 5 *Journal of International Criminal Justice*, at 809–826.

African Commission on Human and Peoples' Rights bore some fruits. The Commission held the DRC government responsible for the massacre and ordered it to prosecute and punish the staff of Anvil Mining.[252]

4.2.1 Argentina

Argentina is arguably pioneering the corporate accountability work. It was both victims and institutional actors who put efforts and resources towards corporate accountability, using innovative legal strategies, beyond the limits of criminal law, to achieve retribution for perpetrators and remedies for victims. In 2010, a special unit was created within the Ministry of Justice, Security and Human Rights, to examine crimes against humanity and economic actors during the Argentine dictatorship.[253] In 2015, the same ministry published a report on companies that participated in violations against workers during the dictatorship.[254] Arguably, almost all of the large entities identified in that report were subsequently investigated.[255]

Direct complicity in crimes was the basis of prosecution in the Ledesma sugar mill and the Ford Motor cases, albeit against individual corporate officials. In the Ledesma case, a senior official of Ledesma sugar mill was accused for complicity in kidnappings and killings along with four policemen during the 'Night of the Blackout' between 20 and 27 July 1976.[256] Further, officials of Ford Motor Argentina were accused in 2002 for assisting in the commission of torture and mistreatment by the military junta.[257] The prosecutor alleged that a detention camp was located in the company's premises,[258] but Ford admitted only to have asked for military protection. In 2006, the amnesty law was disbarred,

[252] AfComHPR, *Institute for Human Rights and Development in Africa and others* v. *Democratic Republic of Congo*, Communication 393/10, 18 June 2006.

[253] Ministerio de Justicia, Seguridad y Derechos Humanos, Resolución 3216/2010, 'Créase la Unidad Especial de Investigación de los Delitos de Lesa Humanidad Cometidos con Motivación Económica'.

[254] CELS, FLACSO-Argentina and the Truth and Justice Programme and Human Rights Secretariat, 'Business Responsibility in Crimes Against Humanity: The Repression of Workers During State Terrorism', November 2015.

[255] Sandt and Moor, 'Peace, Everyone's Business!', p. 73.

[256] Ibid., p. 49.

[257] Civil cases were also brought; see Verbitsky and Bohoslavsky, *Outstanding Debts to Settle*.

[258] 'Ford Sued Over Argentine Dictatorship Kidnappings of Union Members, Workers', *AFX News Limited*, 23 February 2006.

and in 2013, three former Ford managers were accused of crimes against humanity, by targeting union leaders for kidnapping and torture. They had permitted the establishment of a detention facility within the factory's grounds, for the purpose of interrogating the individuals who were abducted. In 2018, two of them were found guilty for complicity to the kidnapping and torture of twenty-four workers and were sentenced to prison.[259]

Juan Tasselkraut, Head of Production at the Mercedes Benz branch in González Catán, a province of Buenos Aires, was prosecuted for crimes against humanity committed against seven workers during the dictatorship. Initially the case was dismissed by the Federal Judge of San Martin,[260] but in October 2022, the Federal Court reversed its decision and convicted Tasselkraut for the kidnappings of two workers, but not for the disappearances of the other five.[261] Again, victims played an essential role, seeking justice against the firm and Tasselkraut in foreign jurisdictions, many years before the Argentinian cases. In 1999, when the amnesty law in Argentina was still in force, victims' families had filed a case against Tasselkraut, in Germany, but it was dismissed due to lack of evidence.[262] In 2004, they had resorted to Californian courts against Mercedes' parent company, Daimler, for its complicity to kidnap, detain, torture and kill employees, but the case was dismissed in 2014 due to lack of ties with the state of California.[263]

What makes the Argentinean approach distinct is also the innovative ways that judicial actors have approached the issue of corporate complicity to the dictatorship's abuses.[264] Cases have been addressed not only through criminal law but also on the basis of different domestic legal regimes. For example, company law was used in the lawsuit brought against Siderca for the disappearance of a former employee, Oscar

259 D. Politi, 'Argentina Convicts Ex-Ford Executives for Abuses during Dictatorship', *The New York Times*, 11 December 2018.

260 See also a complaint filed against the dismissal by the Secretariat of Human Rights. Secretaria de Derechos Humanos, 'La Secretaría de Derechos Humanos de la Nación apeló el sobreseimiento de un exgerente de Mercedes Benz en una causa por responsabilidad empresarial en delitos de lesa humanidad', 11 May 2022.

261 An appeal was filed at cassation level but was dismissed. K. Saucedo, 'Los crímenes de la dictadura y Mercedes Benz', Agencia de Noticias, Ciencias de la Comunicación, 27 April 2023.

262 G. Weber, 'Mercedes Benz: Industry and Human Rights', Le Monde Diplomatique, Southern Cone edition, Buenos Aires, December 2000.

263 *Daimler AG* v. *Bauman*, at 751.

264 Payne et al., *Archimedes' Lever*.

Orlando Bordisso. His wife successfully claimed that her husband disappeared after leaving work in 1977 and was granted compensation. Labour law has also been put at the disposal of transitional goals. The Worker Safety Law was used in the case brought against Techint SA by Maria Gimena Ingenieros. Her father disappeared on company premises, and she brought a case seeking compensation, for the company's failure to secure employees' safety, including to prevent disappearances. The defence put forward a statute of limitations claim. At this point, this case offered another innovative reasoning, which was later reversed. The lower court ruled that statutes of limitation do not apply to crimes against humanity, including to the said offence, which does not separately qualify as crime against humanity but is closely linked to it.[265] However, after considerable domestic debate, the Supreme Court stepped back and, in 2019, ruled in favour of the company, accepting to time-bar crimes against humanity claims.[266]

Claims have also been filed against several banks, alleging that they financed the military junta or were complicit in human rights abuses.[267] Martin Garragone, the son of a disappeared person, sued Citibank and the Bank of America, arguing that the banks provided loans to the regime, which were crucial for its existence, while knowing its abuses. The banks rejected the mediation offered, and the case is reportedly ongoing.[268] At the same time, investigations are being carried out into companies' involvement in illegal business transactions. In the *Papel Prensa* case, the heirs of the owner were forced to sell their company, which ended up being owned by the biggest Argentine print media, securing their monopoly of informing the people during the dictatorship.[269]

Lastly, the *Vildoza* case concerned the illegal appropriation of properties belonging to disappeared people, which were then sold to companies. The interesting element of this case is that money-laundering laws were put to use, to attribute liability for offences that took place many years

265 Camara Nacional de Apelaciones del Trabajo, Sala V, Ingegnieros, María Gimena c. Techint Sociedad Anónima Compañía Técnica Internacional s. accidente. Ley Especial, 2 February 2012.

266 Supreme Court of Justice of the Nation, Ingenieros, María Gimena c. Techint Sociedad Anónima Compañía Técnica Internacional s/ accidente – Ley Especial, 9 May 2019.

267 However, the claim is a civil one. Mattarollo, 'Los bancos de la dictadura'.

268 Payne and Pereira, 'Accountability for Corporate Complicity in Human Rights Violations'.

269 L. Castillo, 'Para Fresneda, la causa de Papel Prensa se encuentra cajoneada', Telam, 19 January 2014.

ago, where other laws would have failed due to statute of limitations. This is because profits from money laundering, in this case through the sale of the real estate, are still accrued to the benefit of individuals who committed the primary offence of seizing the property, making it possible to punish them for the current profit, while punishment for seizure of properties would have been time-barred.[270]

4.2.2 Colombia

In Colombia, corporate accountability made its way in the transitional justice debate, albeit unintentionally, during the first wave of transitional justice. The peace process with the United Self-Defense Forces of Colombia (AUC), led to the Justice and Peace Law 975/2005, which created the Justice and Peace Chambers inside the ordinary domestic judicial system, and a Justice and Peace Unit within the Attorney General's office.[271] The law ignored business malfeasance entirely, but the testimonies of paramilitaries, before the Chambers, revealed considerable business involvement in financing the AUC. That information led to requests filed with the ordinary justice system to carry out criminal investigations.[272] In 2015, a working group was created within the Justice and Peace Unit, to advance proceedings relating to financiers and supporters of paramilitary groups, including cases of big companies, across all big industry sectors such as banana, palm oil, agriculture, cattle ranching, mining and oil and gas.[273]

More than 300 criminal proceedings against businessmen were initiated, due to their linkages to paramilitarism,[274] but the actual convictions are very few.[275] One such case was the one against executives of palm oil

[270] Payne and Pereira, 'Accountability for Corporate Complicity in Human Rights Violations', pp. 29–46.

[271] Notable are also Law 1592/2012 and Decree 3011/2013, which introduced improvements, such as prioritization in the prosecutorial strategy and identification of patterns of criminality. This strategy is laid out in Directive 001 of 2012 of the Attorney General's office.

[272] Sandt and Moor, 'Peace, Everyone's Business!', p. 122.

[273] Resolution 3139 of 2015 by the Attorney General and Resolution 0429 of 2015 by the Director of Transitional Justice Management.

[274] Fiscalía General de la Nación, Dirección de Apoyo a la Investigación y Análisis para la Seguridad Ciudadana, En respuesta a su solicitud Rdo. 20182510002731, Oficio No. DAIASC-20320, Bogotá, D.C., 6 March 2018.

[275] Wesche, 'Business Actors, Paramilitaries and Transitional Criminal Justice in Colombia', p. 494.

companies, and particularly Urapalma S.A., where more than thirty business persons were convicted by the Criminal Court of Medellin, on the basis of associating with the AUC to forcibly displace members of the Afro-Colombian communities of Curvaradó and Jiguamiandó in the Department of Chocó.[276] The defendants received fines and prison sentences and were ordered to provide compensation to victims.[277] The court also ordered restitution of communal lands for members of the communities.[278]

In another well-known case, offshoot of the evidence revealed in the US lawsuit against Chiquita,[279] Arnulfo Peñuela Marin, director of a private security firm that functioned as an intermediary between the paramilitaries and Chiquita, was convicted for conspiring with the paramilitaries, by the Supreme Court of Antioquia.[280] In a rather contradictory move, that same year, the Medellin prosecutor's office closed the investigation against Banadex, Chiquita's subsidiary, alleging that the payments were made under extortion.[281] In 2023, Luis Alberto Agudelo Jiménez, a low-level security staff, was convicted for delivering cash payments to Chiquita. In parallel, Colombian attorney general filed charges for crimes against humanity against thirteen Chiquita officials.[282]

Along similar lines, the USA case against Drummond Coal Company for complicity in union leaders' killings and financing of the AUC[283] supplied evidence for domestic prosecutions. In February 2013, Jaime Blanco Maya, former contractor of Drummond, was convicted by the courts in Bogota to thirty-eight years in prison, for the assassination of two trade unionists of the Sintraminergética union. The victims were murdered in 2001, after leaving a meeting with Drummond officials,

[276] Juzgado Quinto Penal del Circuito Especializado de Medellín. Sentencia Rad. No. 201101799 de 30 de octubre de 2014.

[277] Ibid., pp. 349–356.

[278] Sandt and Moor, 'Peace, Everyone's Business!', p. 143.

[279] See Sections 4.1.3 and 4.1.5.3 of this book.

[280] Juzgado Segundo Penal de Circuito Especializado de Antioquia, Arnulfo Peñuela Marin y otro, Rad. 050003107002200900031, Medellín, 4 August 2010; Tribunal Superior de Antioquia, Sala de Decision Penal, Arnulfo Peñuela Marin y otro, Rad. 050003107002200900031, Medellín, 17 April 2012.

[281] 'Convivir en Urabá eran de las Auc: Tribunal Superior de Antioquia', *VerdadAbierta*, 19 April 2012.

[282] M. Evans, 'Chiquita's Bagman: Key Intermediary Sentenced in Paramilitary Payments Case', National Security Archive, 18 April 2023.

[283] The case was finally dismissed due to presumed lack of jurisdiction by the US courts. *Baloco, et al.* v. *Drummond Co., Inc., et al.*, No. 12-15268 (11th Cir. 2014). See also *Doe* v. *Drummond Co., Inc.*, No. 13-15503 (11th Cir. 2015).

where they advocated for better working conditions and, more specifically, for better catering services, provided by Blanco Maya.[284] The judge ordered prosecutors to investigate Drummond's president and several former employees to determine whether they had a role in the killings.[285] Most importantly, in 2021, the Colombian prosecutor's office indicted the current and former president of the Colombian subsidiary of Drummond, charging them with crimes against humanity for financing and supporting the AUC between 1996 and 2001.[286] Lastly, another landmark decision was reached in relation to the Fondo Ganadero de Cordoba (Livestock Fund of Cordoba), a land fund run by an association of cattle ranchers, which purchased more than 3,500 hectares of land from intermediaries of the paramilitaries. Its director, Benito Osorio Villadiego, was convicted for participation in a criminal enterprise and forced displacement.[287]

Colombia instituted a second transitional justice era, with the signing of the peace agreement with the Revolutionary Armed Forces of Colombia – People's Army (FARC-EP), the Final Agreement to End the Armed Conflict and Build a Stable and Lasting Peace.[288] The agreement set up an 'Integrated System of Truth, Justice, Reparation and Non Repetition', comprising of the Truth Commission, the Special Jurisdiction for Peace (JEP) and the Special Unit for Finding Missing Persons. After the debacle of the plebiscite, the agreement was finally passed by Congress in November 2016.[289] The creation of the JEP required statutory laws for its implementation. The law that concerned its procedural rules was adopted in 2018,[290] but the other concerning its

[284] Colectivo Abogados José Alvear Restrepo, Press Release 'Juzgado de la OIT ordena investigar a directivos de la Drummond por asesinato de sindicalistas', 7 February 2013.

[285] 'Top-Level Drummond Managers Charged with Financing Paramilitaries', Pax for Peace, 12 January 2021.

[286] Ibid.

[287] 'Compra irregular de tierras en el Fondo Ganadero de Córdoba', *Verdadabierta*, January 2014; Fiscalía General de la Nación, Ratifican condena de 19 años de cárcel a Benito Osorio Villadiego, expresidente del Fondo Ganadero de Córdoba, 18 August 2015.

[288] For an overview of the process, see Valiñas, 'The Colombian Special Jurisdiction for Peace', at 452–453. See also Olasolo and Ramirez Mendoza, 'The Colombian Integrated System of Truth, Justice, Reparation and Non-Repetition', 1011.

[289] Legislative Act 01/17, 4 April 2017, Diario Oficial (D.O.) 50196, Article 5 (Colom.) 'Jurisdiccion Especial para la Paz'. This legislative act amounted to a constitutional amendment. The amendment was enacted by Legislative Act 01 of 2017 on 4 April 2017 and approved by the Constitutional Court on 14 November 2017 (Sentencia C-674 de 2017).

[290] The JEP's procedural rules were adopted in Congress on 18 July 2018 (Ley 1922/2018).

establishment was gridlocked in Congress.[291] It took six months for the Duque administration to finally sign that law, with a lot of pressure from civil society and international aid organizations.[292]

Under the law, the JEP, as a new and separate domestic jurisdiction, using both international and domestic law,[293] is mandated to investigate, prosecute and punish violations of human rights and humanitarian law committed in the context of the armed conflict, or else crimes committed 'on occasion because of or directly and indirectly related to the conflict'. Those who confess the full truth about their crimes, before the JEP, receive lesser sanctions than what they would receive under the ordinary justice system.[294] The gist of the new system is that it affords this preferential treatment to former rebels and members of the armed forces but also to '*terceros civiles*', namely civilian third parties, in exchange for them clarifying the truth and assuming reparative responsibilities. Those civilian third parties can include individual businessmen, but not entities, given that according to Article 63 of Law 1957/2019, the JEP can only try natural persons.[295]

In order to fall under JEP's jurisdiction, perpetrators, including 'terceros civiles',[296] had to have an 'active or decisive' participation to the specific crimes covered by JEP's competence,[297] and to have a direct or indirect relation to the armed conflict.[298] The JEP's subject matter jurisdiction covers various acts related to the armed conflict, but importantly regarding business actors, it spreads to the acts 'of financing or collaborating with paramilitary groups, or with any other protagonist in the conflict', provided that they are not the result of coercion or have been subject to previous convictions.[299] Although in the beginning, '*terceros civiles*' were to be summoned by the JEP, this was later changed by the constitutional court. In its 2017 ruling, the constitutional court held that

291 Wesche, 'Business Actors, Paramilitaries and Transitional Criminal Justice in Colombia'.

292 L. 1957/19, junio 6, 2019, Diario Oficial (D.O.) 50.976.

293 Camilo and Villamarin, 'Shredded Colombia's Special Jurisdiction for Peace'.

294 Final Agreement to End the Armed Conflict and Build a Stable and Lasting Peace, November 2016, sec. 5.1.1.1.2. (Final Agreement).

295 Ley 1957/19, Article 63, par. 6.

296 S. Michalowski et al., *Guía De Orientación Jurídica, Terceros Civiles Ante La Jurisdiccion Especial Para La Paz* (Dejusticia, 2020).

297 Article 19 of the Final agreement; Article 19, Ley 1957/19.

298 Ley 1957/19, Article 63, par. 6.

299 Final Agreement, sec. 5.1.2., point 32.

terceros civiles cannot be summoned to the process but can only voluntarily present themselves before the system.[300]

Several businessmen have been accepted to the JEP, particularly those who were previously convicted for their allegiances to paramilitarism, as a result of the 'Justice and Peace' testimonies.[301] This is the case of Benito Osorio Villadiego, from the Fondo Ganadero de Cordoba, who submitted himself to the JEP, because, as mentioned earlier, was convicted for forced displacement of population.[302] Also, Jaime Blanco Maya, the former contractor of Drummond referred previously, who was convicted for murder,[303] submitted himself to the JEP, promising to clarify the truth on the relation of financing between the AUC and Drummond, between 1993 and 2002. He had also committed to carrying out 'Undertakings for Public Pardon', including two conferences in municipalities, where mines operated by Drummond are located, two newspaper publications and a monument to honour the victims.[304] Maya was conditionally released by the JEP, in October 2021, as his narrative was considered 'detailed and exhaustive in relation to his contribution of truth about his role' as an intermediary 'in the financing of the Juan Andrés Álvarez Front of the AUC by of the multinational Drummond and, in addition, exceeds the threshold of what was clarified in the ordinary justice by pointing out other companies that allegedly had a relationship of consideration with the AUC'.[305] Most importantly, the prosecutor's office indicted the current and the former president of the

[300] Article 63 of Act 1957 of 2019 adopted this revised version of the JEP's personal jurisdiction on the grounds that it violated their rights to a fair and impartial trial, in particular the principle of natural judge. Corte Constitucional, Sentencia C-332/17, Bogota D.C., 17 May 2017.

[301] See also cases of executives from the palm oil business in the framework of Macro Case Number 4 on the territorial situation in Urabá and Darién. See C. Quintero, 'Por primera vez los palmicultores hablarán ante la JEP sobre despojos en el Urabá' El Espectador, 12 May 2023.

[302] See 'Compra irregular de tierras en el Fondo Ganadero de Córdoba', *Verdadabierta*, January 2014; Fiscalía General de la Nación, Ratifican condena de 19 años de cárcel a Benito Osorio Villadiego, expresidente del Fondo Ganadero de Córdoba, 18 August 2015.

[303] JEP acepta a Blanco Maya para hablar de asesinato de sindicalistas, El Tiempo, 3 December 2019.

[304] J. Escobar Moreno, 'The Drummond Case Reaches the Special Jurisdiction for Peace', Colombia Support, 18 December 2019.

[305] Chamber for the Definition of Legal Situations of the Special Jurisdiction for Peace, Communicado 113, JEP Concede Libertad Condicionada A Jaime Blanco Maya, Excontratista De La Drummond, 20 October 2021.

Colombian subsidiary of Drummond, charging them with crimes against humanity for financing and supporting the AUC between 1996 and 2001,[306] based on testimonies from demobilized paramilitaries.[307] In this case, the defendants, Linares and Jimenez, chose not to present their cases to the JEP, but instead appealed the indictment.[308] Thus, the prosecutor confirmed the case in late May 2023.[309]

Colombia's transitional engagement with corporate actors has been a significant step forward, in both discourse and praxis, albeit suffering from severe limitations. The Justice and Peace Law excluded business actors from the transitional architecture, referring them to the ordinary justice system, which lacked necessary safeguards and was riddled with corruption. In the second wave, business lobbying managed to make their contributions voluntary, allowing them to allegedly use the system to avoid harsh convictions.[310] An overarching gap is the absence of corporate criminal liability legislation, which delimits corporate liability to individual actors, oftentimes low-level employees, whose conviction does not have the power to alter corporate culture on human rights abuses.[311] As a result, those with economic power and the lion's share of responsibility remained shielded behind corporate structures.

Overall, Argentina and Colombia offer two of the most significant and illustrative examples of inserting corporate accountability in the topography of transitional justice, each with its own set of particularities and challenges. In Argentina, no unified prosecutorial strategy or dedicated criminal justice mechanism for transitional justice was put in place. In Colombia, the first transitional effort excluded from its scope corporate malfeasance, but this changed in the second effort, which introduced the JEP with jurisdiction over economic actors. The JEP, while its jurisdiction was finally narrowed down to economic actors voluntarily submitting to it, prioritized an important number of cases involving individuals' economic activities.

[306] 'Top-Level Drummond Managers Charged with Financing Paramilitaries', Pax for Peace, 12 January 2021.

[307] Also, by testimonies of people submitted to the JEP. 'Directivos de Drummond irán a juicio por presunta financiación a paramilitares', El Espectador, 31 May 2023.

[308] 21 Years of Corporate Impunity – The Systematic Attempt to Eliminate a Union's Leadership in Colombia, Corporate Accountability Lab, 24 May 2022.

[309] L. Acosta, 'Colombia Accuses Drummond Executives of Funding Paramilitary Group', *Reuters*, 1 June 2023.

[310] Wesche, 'Business Actors, Paramilitaries and Transitional Criminal Justice in Colombia'.

[311] Sandt and Moor, 'Peace, Everyone's Business!' p. 148.

In both cases, persistent efforts by victims' groups and civil society played a crucial role in advancing corporate accountability and submitting lawsuits before different fora. Colombian groups also submitted relevant information to the ICC, where the situation of Colombia has been under preliminary examination since 2004. Another shared feature is the strong opposition of the business community in both cases, as well as the attachment of a part of judicial authorities to traditional barriers to corporate accountability.

An important legacy in both instances was that the legal debates and innovative strategies around corporate complicity spurred concrete legal reforms – in Argentina regarding the imprescriptibility of civil claims and labour law actions, and in Colombia regarding the procedural and evidentiary rules surrounding dispossession.[312] In addition, both cases emphasize the importance of coordinated efforts and of prosecutorial strategies that account for the responsibilities of all actors.[313] Colombia's experience particularly illustrates the need for specialized criminal justice measures in transitional periods, but also highlights the potential pitfalls of dissipating prosecutorial responsibilities across the ordinary and the transitional systems, as this can lead to fragmented investigations, a diluted understanding of the complex nature of the conflict and fosters corporate impunity, by depriving business of incentives to avoid wrongdoing.[314]

4.3 Concluding Remarks

Debates on corporate criminal accountability for violations during conflict or repression have been ongoing since Nuremberg. The prosecution of individual corporate agents for atrocious crimes is clearly prescribed in international law, but the same does not apply for corporate entities which have not been linked with transitional practice, in legal or conceptual terms. Sections 4.1–4.2.2 mapped the challenging path of including corporate entities in transitional criminal mechanisms on the basis of the theory and praxis of international law.

The first and fundamental challenge that was identified was that, for the state to have a duty to investigate, prosecute and punish corporate

312 Sánchez et al., *Roles and Responsibilities of the Private Sector*, p. 65.
313 Ibid.
314 Michalowski and Cardona Chaves, 'Responsabilidad Corporativa y Justicia Transicional', pp. 173–182.

actors in cases of international crimes, it must first be examined whether corporate obligations exist under international law, as the former would be an implication of the latter. In international criminal law, states are not currently required to investigate, prosecute and punish corporate actors, and corporate entities do not have relevant obligations. Nevertheless, certain elements indicate that the law should evolve in this direction, including the corporate capacity to commit atrocities and the substantial prohibition of international crimes covering legal persons, in addition to natural ones, despite the absence of a jurisdictional forum to try them. Developing a state duty to investigate, prosecute and punish corporate actors in cases of international crimes would disfavour the assertion that a state's obligations are fulfilled merely by prosecuting individual business persons. It will saddle on other arguments on the nature of corporate crime as distinct from the aggregate of individual crimes in terms of means, perpetrators, motivations and characteristics. As a distinct form of deviance, corporate crime should entail its own accountability, capable of aligning to the reality of corporate structures and take into consideration the specific corporate culture that enabled the commission of abuses.

In support of that interpretation of state duties, there is an increasing number of jurisdictions across the globe, as well as international instruments that recognize corporate criminal accountability. While those developments do not yet unequivocally change the status of corporate accountability, at a minimum, they demonstrate an emerging trend and an 'expanding web of liability for business entities implicated in international crimes'.[315] This means that states that aim to contribute to an international lawful order should consider interpreting their existing obligations to capture corporate liability or adopt measures to that respect. Corporate criminal liability legislation and investigation of corporate entities would certainly demonstrate the states' willingness to comply and would be an initial but necessary step towards establishing relevant international obligations in the future.

In addition, it is equally important to acknowledge the contribution to that direction of the emergence of the right to justice. This right is being steadily recognized as founded in the incremental strengthening of the position of the victims in criminal justice processes, and the centrality of

[315] Ramasastry et al., 'Translating Unocal', p. 856.

victims' needs in international criminal law. The contribution of the emergence of that right is that it signals a departure of accountability from its secondary status, and its presumed alignment with autonomous primary obligations. In turn, this can be interpreted as potentially facilitating its unfolding towards private actors, since primary rights are already protected against acts committed by private persons, through the respective state positive duties. What is more, the reinforced status of accountability demonstrates its increasing importance for transitional settings and, by implication, proves the magnitude of dissonance of corporate impunity with that imperative.

Another challenge faced in transitional spaces has to do with the rationale for resorting to transitional courts instead of ordinary ones. It might be argued that amidst a period requiring resolution of intricate problems, with limited resources and increased tensions, cases against corporations might be better addressed by ordinary courts. In legal terms, the inclusion of economic actors in transitional mechanisms is required to meet a state's obligation to investigate, prosecute and punish, as long as not including them would result in impunity for economic actors who hold increased criminal responsibility. Even more importantly, including corporate entities in transitional criminal mechanisms, instead of relegating them to ordinary courts, holds significant symbolic importance, as it acknowledges the principal role of corporate entities in prior conflict or repression, and emphasizes the potential contribution of their accountability in achieving the aims of transitional justice. It, thus, holds greater potential of averting similar cases in the future. As exemplified by the two transitional efforts of Colombia, assigning corporate accountability cases to ordinary courts hinders transitional justice from creating a comprehensive picture of the past and a consolidated judicial narrative.

Of course, the inclusion of corporate accountability cases should respect the limitations posed by the peace versus justice considerations. The inclusion of corporate actors in criminal mechanisms might multiply already existing tensions, increase polarization and endanger the transitional process. To avoid that, the corporate sector should not be addressed as a homogeneous group, but rather, as per the Colombian example, it would be plausible to legally acknowledge that they might have been perpetrators but also victims of violations and adopt a differentiated scheme of responsibility to reflect the different types of involvement. At the same time, less grave corporate violations could be addressed by other transitional mechanisms, putting in practice an ecological vision, namely a logic of multiple justice modalities that are complementary to each other, and capable of addressing the complexities of corporate involvement in conflict. Despite the importance of peace versus justice considerations, its invocation regarding the intersection of corporate accountability to transitional justice should be made with caution so as not to obscure other underlying tensions that focus on socio-economic issues and are being continuously sidelined, by being presented in post-political terms, resulting in inadequate future solutions.

As for the operationalization of corporate accountability before specialized criminal tribunals, the applicable modes of liability remain a challenging issue, as there is a wealth of interpretations by courts and scholars. The examination of those modes is more useful in unfolding different possibilities rather than favouring the use of one or the other mode. Besides, the choice among different modes would depend on the practical context of each instance of corporate involvement, determining which approach best suits the specific circumstances. Several of those modes present different promising aspects for corporate accountability purposes. Indirect perpetration as introduced by Article 25(3)(a) of the ICC Statute and particularly its 'control over an organization' variant seems to hold potential, at least in attaching responsibility to business officials who committed crimes through the instrumentality of a business organization. This is because the element of control has been flexibly used by the ICC, and its approach – resonating with the Nuremberg precedent – signifies a shift from traditional criminal law, adept to nest corporate accountability. Joint Criminal Enterprise liability can also show promise, since the contribution that it requires is limited to the execution of a shared plan, design or purpose and is related to conspiracy-based theories of liability. Common purpose liability under the ICC Statute seems to provide a streamlined approach, as it does not require that the accused shares the group's common purpose and less-than-substantial contribution. As for superior responsibility, provided that the theoretical leap from the required military or civilian contexts to the corporate one can be made, then a corporation could be liable for acts of those under its 'effective authority and control', insofar as the other requirements are fulfilled. Scholars have put forward superior responsibility also for its affinity to the theory of *respondeat superior*, which is commonly used for the imputation of crimes to corporate entities, on the basis of unlawful acts committed by employees.

Those being said, it is the concept of complicity and particularly aiding and abetting that attracts the most attention. Despite the existence of a wealth of case law on aiding and abetting, particularly coming from the USA under the ATCA litigation, further developments were paused due to the *Kiobel* and *Jesner* precedents. However, the amenability of aiding and abetting to corporate malfeasance appears promising in other jurisdictions. This is largely due to its knowledge-based *mens rea* requirement under customary international law, as well as the diverse range of actions that can fulfil its *actus reus* requirements, namely provision of material or other assistance, the collusion with repressive governments to extract profits, and financial complicity. A significant strand of complicity cases are the direct complicity ones which rest on aiding and abetting in the form of assisting, particularly in material or other terms, the principal perpetrator. Those are relatively straightforward, unlike their silent complicity counterparts, for which it is challenging to demonstrate the company's failure to act despite its ability or duty to do so; the moral support provided to the principal perpetrator by the omission; as well as to distinguish criminal intent from the motive of merely maximizing profit. Still, the most problematic cases are the ones of financial complicity. This is due to the difficulty in establishing the necessary legal link among the harm suffered and the funds provided to regimes violating human rights. Difficulties also lie in proving the *actus reus* and causation elements, given that money is never the direct means to commit crimes, and it is difficult to connect to a particular human rights violation because of its fungibility. In principle, aiding and abetting liability can attach to those cases, insofar as the normal requirements are met, but the well-known and often-cited judgment of the South African Apartheid litigation created confusion, as it dismissed the existence of legal links between commercial loans and the Apartheid violations, on the basis of a misinterpretation of the *Ministries* case at Nuremberg.

Lastly, the cases of Argentina and Colombia offer practical insight into the operationalization of corporate accountability in transitional justice, each with its own set of particularities and challenges. In Argentina, no unified prosecutorial strategy or dedicated criminal justice mechanism for transitional justice was put in place. In Colombia, the first transitional effort excluded from its scope corporate malfeasance, but the second effort allowed economic actors voluntarily to present themselves before the Special Jurisdiction for Peace. Both cases unfolded within the same framework of intense victim advocacy and growing corporate resistance, and both left different legal reforms as legacy. Most importantly, Colombia's experience vividly illustrates the need for specialized criminal justice measures in transitional periods and highlights the potential pitfalls of diffusing prosecutorial responsibilities across the ordinary and the transitional systems, leading to fragmented investigations, but also narratives about the prior violence.

PART III

Reparation Mechanisms

5

Calling Corporations to Repair

Insights from International Law

> Nothing can be so unjust as for a few persons abounding in wealth, to offer a portion of their excess for the formation of a company, to play with that excess, to lend the importance of their whole name and credit to the society, and then, should the funds of the incorporated body prove insufficient to answer all demands, to retire into the security of their unhazarded fortune, and leave the bait to be devoured by the poor deceived fish.
>
> Editorial, *Times* (London), 25 May 1824

5.1 The Traditional Reparation Formula and its Limited Impact on Corporate Malefactors

The term 'reparations' is used in two different contexts, which correspondingly define their form. The first one is that of international law, which includes restitution, compensation, satisfaction, rehabilitation and guarantees of non-repetition (GNRs). Those five different forms are used in the realms of public international law, international human rights, international criminal and international humanitarian law, albeit not always all of them together.[1] The second context is the one of transitions, where reparations are used in a narrower sense to denote attempts to provide benefits directly to victims, and are distinct from truth-telling and criminal justice, despite having the same legal basis. This book brings those two contexts together. While focusing on transitions, it does so from the lens of international law, and therefore neither of the two contexts can be used in isolation. It ascribes to reparations, a narrower

[1] Note, however, that in international human rights law, GNRs are usually classified as reparations, whereas in public international law, they are one of the consequences of the breach. In international criminal law, reparations include restitution, compensation and rehabilitation, while in international humanitarian law they mainly comprise restitution of properties and compensation.

meaning, than the one used in the juridical context, namely one of material and symbolic benefits to victims. Thus, truth-telling and criminal justice measures are analysed in separate chapters, their reparative aspects notwithstanding.[2] In addition, the current chapter uses the classification of reparation forms, according to international law, but since not all instruments and bodies explicitly refer to them, it classifies functionally equivalent information under those headings for reasons of homogeneity.[3]

Reparation mechanisms, in the aftermath of conflict or repression, have been considered as a primary condition for reconciliation, peace and security,[4] due to their ability to repair multiple registries of harm.[5] Beyond delivering individual redress,[6] they embody society's 'recognition, remorse and atonement' for the harm suffered,[7] communicate a new commitment to a system of human rights and rule of law,[8] and

[2] According to De Greiff, truth and justice measures are part of satisfaction. P. De Greiff, 'Justice and Reparations', in P. De Greiff (ed.), *The Handbook of Reparations* (Oxford University Press, 2006).

[3] On the notion of functional equivalence, see Zweigert and Kötz, *An Introduction to Comparative Law*.

[4] Speech of Sergio Garcia Ramirez, president of the Inter-American Court of Human Rights; see Grossman et al., 'Reparations in the Inter-American System'; Hamber, 'Repairing the Irreparable', at 218; Centre for the Study of Violence and Reconciliation (CSVR) and Khulumani Support Group, 'Survivors' Perceptions of the Truth and Reconciliation Commission and Suggestions for the Final Report, Submission to the South African Truth and Reconciliation Commission', 1998. On criticism to reparations, see B. Raftopoulos and A. Mlamba (eds.), *Becoming Zimbabwe: A History from the Pre-Colonial Period to 2008* (Weaver Press, 2009); S. Harring, 'German Reparations to the Herero Nation: An Assertion of Herero Nationhood in the Path of Namibian Development?' (2002) 104 *West Virginia Law Review*, at 393.

[5] De Greiff, 'Justice and Reparations'; P. De Greiff, 'Introduction Repairing the Past', in P. De Greiff (ed.), *The Handbook of Reparations* (Oxford University Press, 2006); Moffett, 'Transitional Justice and Reparations'.

[6] B. Hamber, 'Narrowing the Micro and Macro: A Psychological Perspective on Reparations in Societies in Transition', in P. De Greiff (ed.), *The Handbook of Reparations* (Oxford University Press, 2006), p. 566.

[7] D. Colleen et al., 'Reparations for Sexual and Reproductive Violence: Prospects for Achieving Gender Justice in Guatemala and Peru' (2008) *International Journal of Transitional Justice*, at 208.

[8] E. Klein, 'Individual Reparation Claims Under the International Covenant on Civil and Political Rights: The Practice of the Human Rights Committee', in A. Randelzhofer and C. Tomuschat (eds.), *State Responsibility and the Individual – Reparation in Instances of Grave Violations of Human Rights* (Martinus Nijhoff Publishers, 1999); The Redress Trust, Torture Survivors' Perceptions of Reparation Preliminary Survey (2001), p. 22. For the contribution of reparations to justice, see IACtHR, 'Myrna Mack Chang v. Guatemala', Concurring Opinion Judge Cançado Trindade, par. 46.

constitute a tangible manifestation of the state's efforts to remedy the harm suffered.[9] What is more, they reinstate victims as civil-rights holders in the new political order in equal terms with other citizens, in that their voices and interests have value.[10] As such, they serve justice not only on judicial standards of compensation, deterrence and retribution, but also, as De Greiff noted, on more political terms of recognition, civic trust and social solidarity.[11] In terms of forms, they include various measures ranging from restitution, like in the cases of land or liberty; rehabilitation, including medical and psychosocial services, for victims; satisfaction, such as measures for the search of the disappeared, apologies and memorials; and compensation for the harm suffered.[12]

In terms of legal basis, reparations can be traced back to the *Chorzów* case, where the ICJ ruled that the obligation to provide reparations is a sufficiently proven principle of international law, initially developed in the field of interstate relations, obliging a state, who acted wrongly to restore and remedy the injury caused to another subject.[13] According to the International Law Commission Articles on Responsibility of States for Internationally Wrongful Acts (ILC Articles), state responsibility is extended to human rights violations, and thus reparations are also owned for them.[14] The obligation of the state to repair in the transitional phase finds its legal corollary in international human rights law, in the right to

9 De Greiff, 'Introduction', p. 2.

10 L. Magarrell, 'Reparations in Theory and Practice' (2007) *ICTJ Reparative Justice Series*, p. 2; Gready and Robins, 'From Transitional to Transformative Justice'; T. Madlingozi, 'On Transitional Justice Entrepreneurs and the Production of Victims' (2010) 2 *Journal of Human Rights Practice* 2, at 213.

11 De Greiff, 'Justice and Reparations'; M. Du Plessis, 'Historical Injustice and International Law: An Exploratory Discussion of Reparation for Slavery' (2003) 25 *Human Rights Quarterly* 3, pp. 624–659.

12 For overview of reparation programs, see Special Rapporteur on the promotion of truth, justice, reparation and guarantees of non-recurrence, Practical experiences of domestic reparation programmes, A/HRC/42/45, 11 July 2019; Special Rapporteur on the promotion of truth, justice, reparation and guarantees of non-recurrence, Reparations for gross human rights violations and serious violations of international humanitarian law, A/69/518, 14 October 2014.

13 In the *Chorzów* case, reparation was defined 'as an attempt to as far as possible, wipe out all consequences of the illegal act and re-establish the situation which would, in all probability have existed if that act had not been committed', PCIJ, *Factory at Chorzów Case* (*Germany* v. *Poland*) (Merits), 1928 PCIJ (Series A) No. 17, at 47.

14 ILC, Commentaries on the Draft Articles on Responsibility of States for Internationally Wrongful Acts, Article 33, par. 3, Yearbook of the International Law Commission (2001) Vol. II, Part Two, at 95.

remedy.[15] International and regional human rights bodies and courts have held that the right to remedy entails the obligation of the state to provide reparations, including restitution, compensation, satisfaction, rehabilitation and GNRs.[16] Human rights jurisprudence and scholarship accept that to remedy a violation, one needs the procedural avenue to lodge a complaint, a procedure 'by which arguable claims of human rights violations are heard and decided, whether by courts, administrative agencies or other competent bodies', and an outcome, the substantial relief allocated.[17]

In what I will call the traditional reparation 'formula', the transitioning state undertakes to repair individual or collective harm, in a bipartite equation involving the state and the victim. In case of a corporate

[15] K. Ambos, 'The Legal Framework of Transitional Justice', pp. 19–103; H. Rombouts et al., 'The Right to Reparation for Victims of Gross and Systematic Violations of Human Rights', in K. De Feyter et al. (eds.), *Out of the Ashes: Reparation for Victims of Gross and Systematic Human Rights Violations* (Intersentia, 2005), p. 367.

[16] The Human Rights Committee has explained that the effective discharge of remedies requires reparation, which includes appropriate compensation, restitution, rehabilitation and measures of satisfaction, 'such as [. . .] guarantees of non-repetition'. 'HRC, General Comment 31', par. 16. The European Court of Human Rights has affirmed that states should provide reparations when they breach a Convention right. ECHR, Article 41. See also ECtHR, *Papamichalopoulos and others* v. *Greece*, Application No. 14556/89, Just Satisfaction Judgment, 31 October 1995, par. 34. The ECtHR, under a restrictive view on 'just satisfaction', has provided measures that can be classified under the traditional reparation forms. In the European human rights system, the pilot judgment procedure resembles GNRs as it is established in order to deal with systemic violations and cases of repetitive litigation, and not only to respond to the specific violation. The IACtHR has clearly stipulated the duty of the state to repair deriving from the state duty to provide effective remedies, which is grounded on a combined reading of Articles 25, 8(1) and 1 of the American Convention. At the African human rights system, the issue of reparations has attracted inconsistent attention. However, the Commission has held that the defendant state is responsible to provide reparations. The African Court on Human and Peoples' Rights (AfCHPR) is authorized under Article 27 of the Protocol on the Establishment of the African Court on Human and Peoples' Rights, to order compensation or reparation as remedy for a violation. See D. Shelton, *Remedies in International Human Rights Law* (Oxford University Press, 2005), p. 140.

[17] Shelton, *Remedies in International Human Rights Law*, pp. 7–9; T. Antkowiak, 'Remedial Approaches to Human Rights Violations: The Inter-American Court of Human Rights and Beyond' (2008) 46 *Columbia Journal of Transnational Law* 2, at 353; C. Tomuschat, 'Reparation for Victims of Grave Human Rights Violations' (2002) 10 *Tulane Journal of International and Comparative Law*, at 167–168. Note that the terms reparation, redress and remedy are used to denote both the procedural and the substantial aspect of reparations, often leading to terminological ambiguity. S. Haasdijk, 'The Lack of Uniformity in the Terminology of the International Law of Remedies' (1992) 5 *Leiden Journal of International Law*, at 250.

violation, it is the state, again, that bears responsibility, for omitting or failing to ensure and give effect to the norm that was violated, albeit not the perpetrator itself. The state obligation to ensure is enshrined in both international and regional human rights treaties, requiring states to adopt the necessary measures and exercise due diligence to protect rights, and prevent violations by non-State actors.[18] Accordingly, a failure to ensure gives rise to a violation on behalf of the state party to the treaty.[19] In that case, the state, at the transitional phase, would have to repair its own failure to 'ensure' by providing compensation, restitution, rehabilitation, satisfaction and GNRs to the victims. In fact, the report of the Sierra Leonean TRC perceived reparations as the primary responsibility of the government, even for human rights violations committed by non-state actors, because, according to it, states have an obligation to exercise due diligence to prevent violations by private persons, otherwise they are legally responsible.[20] Similarly, during the South African transition, government sources unequivocally stated that the successor government bears primary responsibility to improve through reparations the lives of victims, even when the abuse was carried out by corporate actors.[21]

To situate corporate malefactors and their accountability within transitions, one has to start from that traditional reparation formula. Do corporate malefactors fit within that formula or are they affected by its application? In fact, a closer examination demonstrates that some forms of reparations, even when delivered by the state, as part of the aforementioned 'formula', would, in practice, have the potential to reach corporate malefactors to varying degrees, without further ado. Even if

[18] Ratner, 'Corporations and Human Rights', p. 470; D. Chirwa, 'The Doctrine of State Responsibility as a Potential Means of Holding Private Actors Accountable for Human Rights' (2004) 5 *Melbourne Journal of International Law* 1, pp. 1–36.

[19] 'HRC, General Comment 31', par. 8; AfComHPR, 'Commission Nationale des Droits de L'Homme et des libertés v. Chad', par. 20. Note also that public international law and the ILC articles on state responsibility become relevant for corporate abuses, either because the corporate acts are attributable to the state or because the state failed to exercise due diligence and protect human rights against corporate abuses, according to its conventional or customary obligations to respect, protect and ensure human rights. See ILC, 'Commentaries on the Draft Articles on Responsibility of States for Internationally Wrongful Acts', commentary to Article 5.

[20] Sierra Leone Truth and Reconciliation Commission, *Final Report*, 2004, Vol. 2, chapter 1, par. 81.

[21] Ministry of Justice and Constitutional Development, Republic of South Africa, 'Declaration by Justice Minister Penuell Maduna on Apartheid Litigation in the United States', 11 July 2003, par. 6, available at www.gov.za/sites/default/files/gcis_document/201409/apartheid1.pdf.

provided by the state for its own failure to ensure, some measures, like GNRs, would theoretically and reasonably have direct or indirect effects on corporate perpetrators and the latter could be de facto included in them, as will be explained further. Conversely, other forms of reparation, such as compensation, when provided by the state only, would have no effect on the corporate perpetrator. The remaining forms of reparations fall within the spectrum, spanning various points along it.

More specifically, GNRs are forward-looking measures aiming to prevent future repetition of violations and dissuade perpetrators.[22] They can include common institutional reforms, personnel vetting to determine their suitability for public employment, adoption of laws and codes of conduct to define and regulate wrongful behaviour, trainings of security sector and justice sector personnel, awareness raising regarding the committed crimes, the list being endless. The obligation of the state to provide GNRs – in the aftermath of corporate violations during conflict or repression – will most probably have broad effects, able to reach the corporate perpetrator, as a matter of logic. Effective GNRs, in the aftermath of widespread corporate abuses, would have to rely on the establishment of the necessary legal and judicial framework that will avert the occurrence of the same type of violation in the future. To do that, GNRs reasonably need to include sanctions, monitoring and other regulation of corporate activities and misdeeds. Accordingly, the HRC has urged states to change their laws to provide remedies against corporate violations,[23] and the Inter-American Court has called states to implement GNRs in relation to non-state actors.[24] Similarly, the African Commission, upon finding of a violation, has ordered the creation of independent oversight bodies for the petroleum industry.[25] Due to its particularities, the topic of GNRs is examined separately, in Section 5.5.

[22] S. Vandegiste, 'Reparation', in D. Bloomfield et al. (eds.), *Reconciliation After Violent Conflict: A Handbook* (International Institute for Democracy and Electoral Assistance, 2003), p. 146; J. Schonsteiner, 'Dissuasive Measures and the "Society as a Whole": A Working Theory of Reparations in the Inter-American Court of Human Rights' (2011) 23 *American University International Law Review* 1, pp. 127–164.

[23] HRC, Concluding observations, Germany, UN Doc. CCPR/C/DEU/CO/6, 12 November 2012.

[24] IACtHR, *Albán-Cornejo et al.* v. *Ecuador* (Merits, Reparations and Costs) Series C No. 171, 22 November 2007, par. 119, 176.7; IACtHR, *Ximénes-Lopes* v. *Brazil* (Merits, Reparations and Costs), Series C No. 149, 4 July 2006, par. 246, 250; IACtHR, *Case of Suárez Peralta* v. *Ecuador* (Preliminary Objections, Merits, Reparations and Costs), Series C No. 261, 21 May 2013.

[25] AfComHPR, *Social and Economic Rights Action Centre and the Centre for Economic and Social Rights (SERAC)* v. *Nigeria*, Communication No. 155/96, Fifteen Annual Activity

Something similar takes place with restitution.[26] Assuming that the state failed to ensure a right against corporate abuse, or to exercise due diligence, then restitution to the *status quo antes* would require some sort of regulation of corporate activity that would, in turn, be able to ensure that right. For instance, human rights bodies have ordered restitution of lands to victims of displacement, which affected the new corporate owners, since they had to return the land illegally exploited. This was the case in the *Afro-Descendant Communities Displaced from the Cacarica River Basin* v. *Colombia*, where the Inter-American Court ordered Colombia to restitute the lands from where the victims were displaced and which was by then illegally exploited by corporate actors.[27] Similarly, in the *Endorois* case, the African Commission ordered Kenya to restitute the lands of the indigenous Endorois community, which was conceded to a private ruby mining company.[28] This was a measure that affected those corporate actors that were exploiting the land and rendered them de facto participants in the process. More generally, if the failure of the state consisted of lack of due diligence, then restitution would need to translate into diligently providing the necessary measures to regulate and control corporate activity. As an obligation of conduct, due diligence requires from the state to put in place the necessary procedures.[29] Insofar as corporate actors committed the violation, those

Report of the African Commission, 2001–2002, Annex V. The African Commission in General Comment 4 on victims of torture called states to reform laws so as to ensure that reparations are received from the corporate perpetrators. General Comment No. 4 on the African Charter on Human and Peoples' Rights: The Right to Redress for Victims of Torture and Other Cruel, Inhuman or Degrading Punishment or Treatment (Article 5), par. 45, 46 and 75.

26 Restitution aims to restore the status quo of the victim to the situation that existed before the violation took place. A. Buyse, 'Lost and Regained? Restitution as a Remedy for Human Rights Violations in the Context of International Law' (2008) 68 *Heidelberg Journal of International Law*, pp. 129–153.

27 IACtHR, *Case of the Afro-Descendant Communities Displaced from the Cacarica River Basin (Operation Genesis)* v. *Colombia* (Judgment) Series C No. 270, 20 November 2013.

28 AfComHPR, *Centre for minority rights development (Kenya) and minority rights group (on behalf of Endorois Welfare Council)* v. *Kenya*, Communication No. 276/03, dispositif, point (a). At the ECtHR, see the *Brumărescu* v. *Romania* case, where the restitution of property ordered by the Court affected the rights of the new tenant of the property. ECtHR, *Brumărescu* v. *Romania*, Application No. 28342/95, Just satisfaction, 23 January 2001, paras. 22–23.

29 D. Shelton, 'Private Violence, Public Wrongs, and the Responsibility of States' (1989) 13 *Fordham International Law Journal* 1, 17, at 23.

procedures would require their regulation and consequently the corporation would be affected.

Satisfaction is a form of public acknowledgement of the harm suffered,[30] with measures ranging from cessation of the violation, to verification of the facts, apologies, declarations restoring dignity, search for disappeared persons, judicial and administrative sanctions and other.[31] In this book, satisfaction does not include criminal justice and truth-telling,[32] which are analysed separately in the respective chapters. Scrutinizing the rest of satisfaction measures, such as public apologies,[33] memorials,[34] or publication of judgments,[35] one can easily discern the important role of the state as the one offering satisfaction. This is because satisfaction embodies an element of public acknowledgement to the victims for the harm suffered, while also attributing responsibility to the perpetrator.[36] Hence, it is debatable whether corporate malefactors can be affected by the traditional 'reparation formula', when the state is the one to provide satisfaction and public acknowledgement for its failure to ensure rights.

Rehabilitation is the process of restoring physical and psychological fitness that might address the individual, the family, local community and even society as a whole.[37] It depends on the needs of victims[38] and is usually comprised of medical, social and vocational aspects. The Chilean reparations scheme, which is considered one of the most successful ones, allowed beneficiaries to access social and medical services, psychological

30 Vandegiste, 'Reparation', p. 146.

31 'Basic Principles', UN Doc. A/RES/60/147, Principle 22. The list is not exhaustive.

32 De Greiff, 'Justice and Reparations'.

33 IACtHR, *Case of Barrios Altos* v. *Peru*, Series C No. 87, Reparations Judgment, 30 November 2001, par. 44e, operative par. 5e.

34 IACtHR, *Villagrán Morales et al.* v. *Guatemala*, Series C No. 77, Reparations Judgment, 26 May 2001, par. 103.

35 HRC, *Félix Enrique Chira Vargas-Machuca* v. *Peru*, CCPR/C/75/D/906 2000, Views of 26 July 2002, par. 10; IACtHR, Case *Trujillo Oroza* v. *Bolivia*, Series C No. 92, Reparations Judgment, 27 February 2002, par. 119. The ECtHR has often held that the condemnatory judgment is itself a satisfaction. ECtHR, *Golder* v. *United Kingdom*, Application No. 4451/70, Judgment of 21 February 1975, par. 46.

36 Public Submission on reparations issues, Situation in the Democratic Republic of the Congo in the case of the *Prosecutor* v. *Thomas Lubanga Dyilo*, International Centre for Transitional Justice, ICC-01/04-01/06, 10 May 2012.

37 Shelton, *Remedies in International Human Rights Law*, p. 275; Redress, *Rehabilitation as a Form of Reparation under International Law* (REDRESS, 2009).

38 Redress, *Reintegration and Reparation for Victims of Rendition and Unlawful Detention in the War on Terror: A European Perspective* (Workshop Report, 2008), p. 76.

counselling and educational opportunities.[39] Rehabilitation as a form of reparation can affect the corporate perpetrator, even when nominally provided by the state, depending on the specific measure chosen and the right that was violated. For example, the Inter-American Court has awarded rehabilitation measures, involving corporations, when it ordered the creation of development funds and programmes.[40] Notably, the new criminal section of the ACJHR will have jurisdiction over corporations and will be able to order directly the convicted person, natural or legal, to provide reparations to the victim, including rehabilitation.[41] However, considering that rehabilitation usually includes medical and psychological support and other types of social services,[42] engaging the corporate malefactor means transferring the cost of rehabilitation to it. This happened in the aftermath of the Marikana massacre in South Africa, at a mine owned by British company Lonmin. The company promised to finance the education for children of victims, albeit as a voluntary undertaking,[43] and not as part of the legal duty of the state to repair.

Lastly, compensation is the most commonly sought form of reparation in international practice,[44] and often reparations are, erroneously,

[39] E. Lira, 'Policy for Human Rights Violations in Chile', in P. De Greiff (ed.), *The Handbook of Reparations* (Oxford University Press, 2006).

[40] IACtHR, *Moiwana* v. *Suriname*, Judgment on Preliminary Objections, Series C No. 124, Merits, Reparations and Costs, 15 June 2005, paras. 213–215. In the *Yakye Axa* v. *Paraguay* case, the Court ordered the creation of a 'community development fund and program' as a non-pecuniary damage, and the provision of water, medical care and educational materials as 'other forms of reparation' (measures of satisfaction and guarantees of non-recidivism). IACtHR, *Yakye Axa Indigenous Community* v. *Paraguay*, Series C No. 125, Merits, Reparations and Costs, 17 June 2005, paras. 205–206, 221; IACtHR, *Sawhoyamaxa* v. *Paraguay*, Series C No. 146, Merits, Reparations and Costs, 29 March 2006, paras. 224–225, 229–233.

[41] Draft Protocol on Amendments to the Protocol on the Statute of the African Court of Justice and Human Rights, AU Doc. No. STC/Legal/Min. 7(1) Rev.1 (14 May 2014), adopted by the Decision on the Draft Legal Instruments (30 June 2014) AU Doc. No. Assembly/AU/Dec.529 (XXIII), Article 45 and 46C ('Malabo Protocol').

[42] Ensuring compensation, 'including relief and resettlement assistance' to victims of business-induced violations is also a measure of protection. It also includes cessation of the violation, investigation. AfComHPR, 'SERAC v. Nigeria', holdings.

[43] Mail & Guardian, Marikana, one year after the massacre, available at https://marikana.mg.co.za/.

[44] ILC, 'Commentaries on the Draft Articles on Responsibility of States for Internationally Wrongful Acts', Article 36(2), at 100.

equated to mere compensation.[45] Under international law, it covers any financially assessable damage, including proven loss of profits,[46] and has been awarded by various international courts.[47] In international human rights law, compensation covers both material and moral damage that is financially assessable,[48] including physical or mental harm; lost opportunities in terms of employment, education and social benefits; material damages and loss of earnings, such as loss of earning potential; moral damage; costs required for legal or expert assistance, medicine and medical services; psychological and social services; compensation for dispossessed people in case of spoliation; and damages to the 'life plan' of victims.[49] During transitions, the allocation of compensation has proved to be an arduous task resulting in amounts that the transitioning state cannot afford, due to difficulties in quantifying and evaluating harm, calculating compensation in terms of proportionality as well as due to the differences between the notions of loss and harm and their subsequent compensation.[50]

Compensation on behalf of corporate perpetrators can potentially cure those problems, assuming that corporate resources are sufficient and have been made available through laws or litigation. In those cases, they can be used to fund compensation awards, restitution in kind, rehabilitation programmes or measures of satisfaction, such as construction of memorials.[51] A number of lawsuits have ended with victims successfully receiving reparation, in the form of compensation by corporate entities that violated their rights, in the framework of war or repression. By way of illustration in the *Bodner* v. *Banque Paribas* litigation, US plaintiffs sued Paribas bank under the ATCA, for the war crime of looting their

[45] For a discussion of a model compensation programme for victims, see E. Lutz, 'After the Elections: Compensating Victims of Human Rights Abuses', in E. Lutz et al. (eds.), *New Directions in Human Rights* (University of Pennsylvania Press, 1989), p. 195.

[46] ILC, 'Commentaries on the Draft Articles on Responsibility of States for Internationally Wrongful Acts', Article 36.

[47] Compensation has been awarded by the International Tribunal for the Law of the Sea; the Iran-United States Claims Tribunal; the ICSID Tribunals. See commentary to ILC, 'Commentaries on the Draft Articles on Responsibility of States for Internationally Wrongful Acts', Article 36(2), at 100.

[48] 'Basic Principles', Principle 20.

[49] Shelton, *Remedies in International Human Rights Law*, pp. 291–353.

[50] De Greiff cites the findings of the Inter-American Commission and Court in cases of torture and disappearances in Peru, which, if followed by the Truth and Reconciliation Commission, would have cost more than the yearly national budget. De Greiff, 'Justice and Reparations'.

[51] Similar argument by Moffett, 'Beyond Attribution'.

possessions during World War II.[52] In the well-known *Wiwa* v. *Shell*, Nigerian plaintiffs received compensation (through settlement) from Shell company due to its complicity in various human rights abuses.[53] However, it should be noted that in legal terms, compensation for the failure of the state to ensure a right unfolds only between it and the claimant, even if the initial violation was committed by a non-state actor.

To sum up, individuals, whose rights have been violated, have the legal possibility to receive redress, by the state, given that treaties create primary rights only against the state. It can safely be concluded that corporate involvement in the overall reparative obligations of the state is a rather ad hoc exercise, with different forms of reparations impacting corporations to a different extent, even if provided by the state. At the same time, this impact on corporations does not seem to be the result of a state obligation, as a matter of law, but is rather a matter of coincidence and practical necessity. Some measures, like GNRs, depending on their content, could have direct or indirect effects on the corporate perpetrators and the latter could be de facto included in them, whereas others, like compensation, can be provided by the state only, without having any effect on the corporate perpetrator.

5.2 The Quandary

The quandary regarding reparations and corporate actors is not the same as in justice mechanisms. There the main difficulty lied in prosecuting the entity, instead of the individual. In the field of reparations, there is no need of criminalization; rather, the underlying violation, in most cases, corresponds to a civil law violation. Given that private entities are subject to civil law in all jurisdictions, the attribution of civil fault to the entity is, in theory, straightforward, albeit not always in practice.[54] Rather the main issue here lies on whether transitioning states have any duty to call on corporations to repair, as a matter of law and as part of their overall duties during transition; and to include them, as debtors, in the design and delivery of reparations. In practice, this means that states should

52 *Bodner* v. *Banque Paribas*, 114 F. Supp. 2d 117, 128 (E.D.N.Y. 2000).

53 *Wiwa* v. *Shell*, 2009 U.S. App. LEXIS 11873 (2d Cir.), 3 June 2009.

54 Various barriers might be posed while attributing civil fault. By way of illustration, see those posed by the doctrine of limited liability of shareholders. G. Skinner, 'Rethinking Limited Liability of Parent Corporations for Foreign Subsidiaries' Violations of International Human Rights Law' (2015) 72 *Washington and Lee Law Review* 1769.

include corporations as debtors in administrative reparations schemes or enable relevant adjudication against them. The point of enabling relevant adjudication is raised, because transitional states have often attempted to hinder adjudication. For example, the South African government opposed the apartheid litigation before US courts.[55] Certainly, any such effort should not be interpreted to absolve states from their subsidiary role in providing reparations, if 'the parties liable for the harm suffered are unable or unwilling to meet their obligation'.[56]

In the vernacular of human rights, the inclusion of corporations in reparation measures could be grounded on different approaches. As a springboard, one might investigate potential direct corporate obligations to provide reparations to victims. However, as analysed in Part I, corporate obligations are currently purely theoretical and, given corporate structures, hold limited promise even for the future.[57] Instead, the present attempt focuses on the state, highlighting its role as the key institutional force behind transitional mechanisms and aims to situate corporate reparations, within the state's overall reparative obligations. In other words, the point of departure is state duties. In a scenario, where a corporate entity has engaged in a violation, the state, while not the direct perpetrator, nonetheless assumes responsibility due to its omission to uphold and enforce the violated norm and is, in turn, imbued with an obligation to furnish remedies.

Having state duties as a point of departure, an undemanding way to insert corporate malefactors in the 'reparation formula', would have been

[55] See Section 6.1.

[56] 'Basic Principles', Principle 16 and 17 on the enforcement of domestic and foreign reparations decisions against individuals or entities liable for harm suffered; see also Principle 3, Chicago Principles of Post-Conflict Justice (The International Human Rights Law Institute, 2008), p. 46. Note that the principle of subsidiarity aims to ensure that victims will receive remedies for the harms suffered. Reparations from the state instead of the perpetrator have also been allocated on grounds of social solidarity. See H. Rombouts, *Victim Organisations and the Politics of Reparation: A Case-Study on Rwanda* (Intersentia, 2004), p. 21. In particular, the Truth and Reconciliation Commission of Timor-Leste found Indonesia responsible for violations, but recommended the government of Timor-Leste to provide reparations, due to presumed tardiness on behalf of Indonesia. *Chega!*. Report of the Commission for Reception, Truth and Reconciliation in Timor-Leste (CAVR), 2005 [CAVR Report], Part 11, p. 38. See also Moffett, 'Beyond Attribution'.

[57] They are analysed in this book, limitedly and only to the extent, that they elucidate the main predicament. See Part I Section 2.1 of this book.

to bestow positive obligations on the right to remedy.[58] However, this would presuppose that the right to remedy is an autonomous right,[59] something which is not consistently accepted, as exemplified by the ambivalence in HRC decisions.[60] In some instances, it is accepted as a supporting guarantee,[61] which means that no violation thereof arises, if one is denied a remedy in relation to a right that is not independently guaranteed in the Covenant.[62] In others, it is recognized as autonomously invocable.[63] Notably, a closer examination of the cases that arguably

58 Seemingly in favour of that view, Report of the Special Representative of the Secretary-General on the issue of human rights and transnational corporations and other business enterprises, state responsibilities to regulate and adjudicate corporate activities under the United Nations core human rights treaties: an overview of treaty body commentaries, A/HRC/4/35/Add.1, 13 February 2007, p. 26; Nowak, *UN Covenant on Civil and Political Rights*, pp. 39–40.

59 Note that the autonomy of the right to remedy, or its potential elevation to that status, is also analysed in Section 5.3, but under a different light and within a different context, than the one required here.

60 In the ECHR field, things are clearer, regarding the status of the right to remedy. In the case of *Aksoy* v. *Turkey*, the Court unwaveringly accepted the occurrence of an 'autonomous' violation of Article 13 of the European Convention. In *Kilic* v. *Turkey*, the Court held that 'Article 13 of the Convention guarantees the availability at the national level of a remedy to enforce the substance of the Convention's rights and freedoms in whatever form they might happened to be secured in the domestic legal order'. See ECtHR, *Aksoy* v. *Turkey*, Application No. 21987/93, Judgment of 18 December 1996, paras. 51–53, 95–100; ECtHR, *Kilic* v. *Turkey*, Application No. 22492/93, Judgment of 28 March 2000, par. 91. See also ECtHR, *Mustafa Sezgin Tanrikulu* v. *Turkey*, Application No. 27473/06, Judgment of 18 July 2017, par. 117; ECHR, *Kudla* v. *Poland*, Application No. 30210/96, Judgment of 26 October 2000, paras. 147–149. The Inter-American and the African systems have expressed differing views on the subject (see Sections 5.3.1.3 and 5.3.1.4 of this book).

61 For example, in the *SE* v. *Argentina* case, where relatives of the claimants had disappeared before the entry into force of the Covenant and the Optional Protocol for Argentina, the HRC held that they were unable to claim independently a right to remedy for those disappearances. HRC, *S.E.* v. *Argentina*. See also HRC, *Inostroza et al.* v. *Chile*, UN Doc. CCPR/C/66/D/717/1996, Views of 16 September 1999; HRC, *Vargas* v. *Chile*, UN Doc. CCPR/C/66/D/718/1996/Rev. 1, Views of 24 September 1999.

62 Note that Joseph and Castan argue that the right to remedy means constitutional claims against the state. S. Joseph and M. Castan, *The International Covenant on Civil and Political Rights Cases, Materials, and Commentary* (Oxford University Press, 2013), p. 403, fn. 31 and 871.

63 HRC, *Kazantzis* v. *Cyprus*, CCPR/C/78/D/972/2001, Inadmissibility Decision of 7 August 2003, par. 6.6; HRC, *Faure* v. *Australia*, CCPR/C/85/D/1036/2001, Views adopted on 31 October 2005, par. 7.2; HRC, *Picq* v. *France*, CCPR/C/94/D/1632/2007, Views of 30 October 2008; HRC, *Kibale* v. *Canada*, CCPR/C/93/D/1562/2007, Views of 22 July 2008; HRC, and *Smidek* v. *Czeck Republic*, CCPR/C/87/D/1062/2002, Views of 25 July 2006. See also HRC, *Concluding Observations on New Zealand*, CCPR/C/NZL/CO/5, 7 April 2010.

support its autonomy demonstrate that in fact the violation of the right to remedy was always alleged in combination with another right. It was invoked not in the absence of another violation, but merely to strengthen an ill-founded complaint.[64] This link between the right to remedy and the substantive right violated becomes even more pronounced during periods of transition, where the scale is tipping to the side of the substantial right that was abused and the focus is on healing its grave previous violation, and not merely on providing procedural remedies, as if what needs to be repaired is the absence of remedies. In other words, the predicament is not that the state restitutes a perceived absence of remedies (and unfolds them toward third actors), but rather that through those remedies, it redresses the previous harm. While legally grounded in the right to remedy and reparation, transitional justice's primary aim is to shine a glaring spotlight on the gravity of the harm suffered and, as a result, offer remedies. Bestowing positive obligations on the right to remedy, rather than on substantive rights such as the right to life, would disproportionately highlight remedies, but in isolation, presupposing that the main predicament is to repair the absence of remedies, while downplaying the great harm suffered that led to the transition and to the very need for remedies. It assumes that the state's primary failure is the absence of mechanisms to redress corporate misconduct, whereas the more critical violation was the state's failure to protect individuals from corporate abuse in the first place. That logic also presupposes that one can prove that there were no remedies against corporate abuse, which is highly improbable, given that civil law regulates corporate violations in all countries.

Instead, the approach adopted by this book focuses on the right to remedy, not in isolation, but as intricately associated with the gravest human rights violations that took place during conflict or repression and accordingly scrutinizes states' diverse obligations. A state duty to include corporations, as debtors, in the design and delivery of reparations would mean that the reparative obligation of the state is interpreted as including an obligation to order the third-party abuser to compensate or repair. To unpack it further, for that obligation to be construed in this manner,

[64] In *Picq* v. *France*, the HRC held that 'Article 2, paragraph 3 (b), guarantees protection to persons claiming to be victims if their complaints are sufficiently well-founded to be protected under the Covenant. A State party cannot reasonably be required, on the basis of article 2, paragraph 3 (b), to make such procedures available in respect of complaints which are less well-founded. Since the author of the present complaint cannot claim to be a "victim" of violations of article‘s 14 and 18 of the Covenant, his allegation of violations of article 2 of the Covenant is also inadmissible under article 2 of the Optional Protocol'. HRC, 'Picq v. France', par. 6.4.

first there should be a state obligation to provide redress avenues in domestic law to victims of corporate violations. Secondly, this obligation should form part of the overall reparative obligations of the state. According to international and regional human rights law, the first proposition is true, but in principle not the second. The state obligation to provide domestic redress avenues against corporations can only be traced in the state's protective duties, which precede the reparation ones. Therefore, the state is obliged to fulfil it before embarking on repairing its failure to prevent and redress, and thus strictly speaking cannot form part of transitional justice. In other words, the problem with corporate reparations within transitions lies in that the requisite elements of a potential obligation exist, but can be situated within distinct legal foundations, resulting in them currently not intersecting. As a point of clarification, this logic, at some points, echoes the theory on the horizontal effect of human rights law, which has been used to ground human rights obligations of businesses or to analyse state obligations regarding corporate and other non-state malefactors.[65] Despite its pertinence in systematizing knowledge and jurisprudence of human rights bodies, this theory, unlike this book's proposal, analyses positive state obligations, in isolation and apart from the broader context, and thus, it is insufficient to nest a state duty to call on corporations to repair.[66]

Amidst that background, Chapters 4–8 will argue in favour of a more nuanced understanding and normative interpretation of the sequence of obligations *de lege ferenda*, considering the nature and objectives of transitional justice.[67] It will examine the remedial aspect of states' protective obligations in international and regional human rights law,[68] under the light of theoretical arguments drawing from

[65] For an elaborate account of the theory on human rights' horizontal effect, see L. Lane, 'The Horizontal Effect of International Human Rights Law in Practice: A Comparative Analysis of the General Comments and Jurisprudence of Selected United Nations Human Rights Treaty Monitoring Bodies' (2018) 5 *European Journal of Comparative Law and Governance* 1, pp. 5–88; Knox, 'Horizontal Human Rights'.

[66] In addition, as explained in Section 5.1, the performance of state remedial obligations – whether seen through the lens of horizontal human rights application or not – exerts minimal influence on corporate wrongdoers, stemming from a pragmatic necessity rather than a legally mandated imperative.

[67] There is an ongoing theoretical debate regarding the relationship between interpretation and modification of rules in international law. See n (37) Section 3.2.1, Part II, of this book.

[68] It will be based on the interpretations of human rights bodies. The practice of those organs, in terms of their interpretation, binds states, due to the good faith obligations to respect the treaties that they signed. Simma and Alston, 'The Sources of Human Rights', at 82, 100. Regional human rights courts can also contribute to the development of

different fields that feed into transitional justice. Such examination and systematization is pertinent for various reasons. First, certainty and elaboration brings legality, which is highly valuable in view of the unacceptably large deficits of the legal framework for access to remedies.[69] In the words of the International Commission of Jurists, 'the most acute challenges and needs in the area of business and human rights relate to the deficits both in ensuring the accountability of companies and in access to effective remedies for victims of abuse'.[70] In addition, the analysis of the protective obligations of the state is not a mere iteration of its positive obligations. Unlike traditional business and human rights literature,[71] that examines the preventive aspect of states' positive duties, this book brings to light their remedial angle and argues in favour of their normative linkage to states' overall reparative obligations.

5.3 The State and Corporations as Potential Debtors of Reparations: Alternative Interpretations of International Human Rights Law

5.3.1 *An Unusual Account of Protective Duties: Focusing on the Remedial Aspect of Protection*

5.3.1.1 Human Rights Committee

Under Article 2(1) of the International Covenant on Civil and Political Rights (ICCPR), states are obliged to provide redress avenues in domestic law to victims of corporate violations, as part of their obligation to ensure the rights therein. Among others,[72] this duty to 'ensure' contains redress

custom, through their cumulative and consistent jurisprudence. J. G. Merrills, *The Development of International Law by the European Court of Human Rights* (Manchester University Press, 1993). See also M. Scheinin, 'The Human Rights Committee's Pronouncements on the Right to an Effective Remedy: An Illustration of the Legal Nature of the Committee's Work Under the Optional Protocol', in A. Nisuke (ed.), *Towards Implementing Universal Human Rights: Festschrift for the Twenty-Fifth Anniversary of the Human Rights Committee* (Nijhoff, 2004), pp. 104–105; Nowak, *UN Covenant on Civil and Political Rights*, p. 710.

69 UN Human Rights Council, Report of the Special Rapporteur on extrajudicial, summary or arbitrary executions on armed non-state actors: the protection of the right to life, A/HRC/38/44, 5 June 2018.

70 International Commission of Jurists, Needs and Options for a New International Instrument in the Field of Business and Human Rights, June 2014, p. 15. See also Sánchez et al. 'Roles and Responsibilities of the Private Sector in Transitional Justice'.

71 As well as the literature on the horizontal application of human rights, see Lane, 'The Horizontal Effect of International Human Rights Law in Practice'.

72 Other measures include prevention, investigation and punishment. See HRC, Concluding Observations, *United States*, UN Doc. CCPR/C/USA/CO/3/Rev.1, 18 December 2006,

of abuses,[73] both against public and private agents,[74] including through the establishment of avenues of redress against third-party actors in the domestic sphere.[75] As per the HRC, the protection afforded by paragraph (1) of the article is closely connected to the remedies offered by paragraph (3).[76] Therefore, a state in order to protect a right against private breaches has to enable the necessary redress avenues, either via criminal or civil trial. Besides, under Article 2(2), the state should *give effect to the Covenant rights*. If private actors can detrimentally affect human rights, then 'giving effect' to them would require the existence of a necessary framework that victims can use.[77]

In addition, the obligation to establish domestic avenues of redress against third-party actors is a logical corollary of the obligation to exhaust domestic remedies before filing a case at the Committee.[78] For this to have meaning, the state should have a chain of redress mechanisms available for the victim to use – first against the individual perpetrator and then against the state or its agents, for their omission to ensure. Article 14 on fair trial can also be instructive, insofar as it entails access to judicial institutions able to conduct fair trials in all types of civil and criminal matters and ensure access to those courts.[79] This effectively

par. 13, 14; HRC, Concluding Observations, *Thailand*, UN Doc. CCPR/CO/84/THA, 8 July 2005, par. 21.

[73] See, indicatively, HRC, *Love et al.* v. *Australia*, Communication No. 983/2001, View of 28 April 2003; HRC, *Hopu and Bessert* v. *France*, Communication No. 549/1993, Views of 29 December 1997.

[74] In so far as they are amenable to application between private persons or entities. 'HRC, General Comment 31', para. 8; Joseph and Castan, *The International Covenant on Civil and Political Rights*, p. 43; Nowak, *UN Covenant on Civil and Political Rights*, p. 38.

[75] R. McCorquodale, 'Non State Actors and International Human Rights Law', in S. Joseph and A. McBeth (eds.), *Research Handbook on International Human Rights Law* (Edward Elgar, 2011), p. 105; D. Chirwa, 'State Responsibility for Human Rights', in M. A. Baderin and M. Ssenyonjo (eds.), *International Human Rights Law: Six Decades After the UDHR and Beyond* (Ashgate Publishing Co., 2010), p. 405.

[76] 'HRC, General Comment 31', para. 8.

[77] The Committee has urged states to change their laws to provide remedies against corporate violations, as part of Article 2(2). See HRC, 'Concluding Observations, Germany'; HRC, Concluding Observations, Suriname, UN Doc. CCPR/CO/80/SUR, 4 May 2004, para. 21.

[78] Article 5(2)(b) of the First Optional Protocol.

[79] In *Bahamonde* v. *Equatorial Guinea*, the Committee considered that the notion of equality before courts, enshrined in Article 14, encompasses the very access to the courts. HRC, *Bahamonde* v. *Equatorial Guinea*, Communication No. 468/1991, View of 20 October 1993, par. 9(4). Nowak, *UN Covenant on Civil and Political Rights*, pp. 307, 314. However, Article 14 can legitimately be restricted in cases of enactment of legislation designed to settle the pending legal claim at issue (HRC, *Mahuika* v. *New Zealand*, Communication No. 547/1993, Views of 16 November 2000, par. 9(10)). In addition, as

means that state parties should provide for particular causes of action 'in certain circumstances' and competent courts to determine those causes of action.[80] This is important for corporate involvement in reparations, given that one of the modalities for the distribution of reparations is court procedures.[81] Civil litigation has often been used in cases of corporate accountability,[82] for entities that were named in TRC reports.[83] Consequently, the content of Article 14 and its concomitant access to justice become relevant.

Accordingly, the HRC has expressed concern when states have failed to put in place an effective framework to hold private contractors accountable,[84] including for torture,[85] murder or disappearance of

Joseph notes, the Committee has not specified in what circumstances states are obliged to provide civil causes of action. She concludes that Article 14(1), while guaranteeing a person's access to courts 'in the determination of any criminal charge against him, it does not guarantee civil causes of action per se'. She notes that a state's failure to provide a remedy for an abuse of an ICCPR right would constitute a breach of that right in conjunction with Article 2(3) rather than a breach of Article 14. Joseph and Castan, *The International Covenant on Civil and Political Rights*, p. 403, fn. 31. It should be mentioned at this point that the literature on access to justice, like the one on remedies, is terminologically and conceptually divergent. Francioni classifies Article 2(3) as access to justice, as does Shelton. Conversely, Joseph associates access to justice with Article 14. Francioni opines that the right to remedy goes well beyond mere access to justice, whereas the CoE guide found that the right to remedy is part of access to justice. F. Francioni (ed.), *Access to Justice as a Human Right* (Oxford University Press, 2007), p. 25. Shelton, *Remedies in International Human Rights Law*.

80 HRC, *Avellanal* v. *Peru*, Merits, Communication No. 202/1986, Views of 28 October 1988; HRC, *Concluding observations on Norway* CCPR/C/79/Add.112, par. 16; Joseph and Castan, *The International Covenant on Civil and Political Rights*, p. 403.

81 However, the choice of modality should be contingent on the context of each case. R. Rubio-Marin, 'Women and Reparations' (2007) 1 *International Journal of Transitional Justice* 3, pp. 318–337; J. Malamud-Goti and L. Grosman, 'Reparations and Civil Litigation: Compensation for Human Rights Violations in Transitional Democracies', in P. De Greiff (ed.), *The Handbook of Reparations* (Oxford University Press, 2006).

82 See for example lawsuits brought by Chinese and Korean nationals against Japanese corporations before US Courts on allegations of forced labour during World War II. *In re World War 11 Japanese Forced Litigation*, 164 F. Supp. 2d 1160 (N.D. Cal. 2001); also, claims brought by the Herero community in Namibia against German companies seeking reparations for the enslavement and destruction of their tribe during colonization. *Herero People's Reparation Corp.* v. *Deutsche Bank*, A.G. 125 S. Ct. 508 (D.C. Cir. 2004).

83 M. Gerhart et al., 'Unfinished Business: South Africa, Apartheid, and Truth' (2004) 83 *Foreign Affairs* 3.

84 The Committee has urged states to change their laws to provide remedies against corporate violations, as part of Article 2(2). See HRC, 'Concluding Observations, Germany'.

85 See HRC, 'Concluding Observations USA', par. 13, 14; HRC, Concluding Observations on *New Zealand*, UN Doc. CPR/CO/75/NZL, 7 August 2002, par. 13; HRC, *General*

victims.[86] Furthermore, it has seemingly acknowledged the necessity of complaints mechanisms and remedies for private breaches.[87] It has urged states to strengthen the remedies provided to individual victims of activities of business enterprises and to ensure 'that there are effective means to follow suit against abuses committed by agencies operating outside the military structure'.[88] Numerous Decisions and Concluding Observations highlight the need for states to ensure effective remedies for indigenous peoples affected by corporate activities, particularly those threatening land and cultural resources.[89] Markedly, various instruments and bodies at the UN level have stressed the obligation of the state to facilitate remedies by non-state actors.[90]

As to the form of redress avenues against corporate malefactors and its adequacy for transitions, it should be noted that Article 14 of the ICCPR understands access to justice to be performed before courts, criminal and

Comment No. 20: Article 7 (Prohibition of Torture, or Other Cruel, Inhuman or Degrading Treatment or Punishment), 10 March 1992, par. 2.

86 The HRC concluded that Colombia violated the ICCPR because it failed to investigate effectively the murder or disappearance of the victims, although the perpetrators may have not been state officials. HRC, *Herrera Rubio* v. *Colombia*, Communication No. 161/1983, Views adopted on 2 November 1987, par. 190.

87 Implied in HRC, 'Concluding Observations USA', par. 13. Complaints' mechanisms for private breaches have been deemed appropriate to ensure full protection for migrant workers in Thailand, HRC, 'Concluding Observations Thailand', para. 23; HRC, General Comment No. 16: Article 17 (Right to Privacy), the Right to Respect of Privacy, Family, Home and Correspondence, and Protection of Honour and Reputation, 8 April 1988, par. 10, 11; HRC, 'General Comment No. 20', par. 14; HRC, *Nahlik* v. *Austria*, Communication No. 608/1995, 19 August 1996, para. 8.2; See also HRC, *Rajapakse* v. *Sri Lanka*, Communication No. 1250/2004, Views of 5 September 2006, par. 9.

88 HRC, 'Concluding Observations USA', par. 13. See also HRC, 'Concluding Observations, Germany'. Other reports mention that the HRC has implied that the state should facilitate direct actions against private agencies for reparation. See Report of the SRSG, A/HRC/4/35/Add.1, par. 67.

89 Report of the SRSG, A/HRC/4/35/Add.1, paras. 23, 32.

90 UN General Assembly, Declaration on the Elimination of Violence against Women (Article 4(d)), UN Doc A/RES/48/104, 20 December 1993; Committee on the Elimination of Discrimination against Women, General Recommendation 19: Violence against women, UN Doc A/47/38, 1992, par. 24 (r(i)) and (t(i)); Committee on Economic, Social and Cultural Rights, Statement on the Obligations of States Parties Regarding the Corporate Sector and Economic, Social and Cultural Rights, UN Doc E/C.12/2011/1, 20 May 2011, par. 5; Committee on Economic, Social and Cultural Rights, General Comment 4: The right to adequate housing (Article 11(1)), UN Doc E/1992/23, 13 December 1991, par. 17; 'Guiding Principles', Principle 25; Basic Principles, Principle 15, 22; UN General Assembly, Declaration of Basic Principles of Justice for Victims of Crime and Abuse of Power, UN Doc A/RES/40/34, 29 November 1985, Principle 8.

civil. In addition, it has been interpreted as including other fora,[91] as long as the claim was subject to judicial supervision and control.[92] Thus, presumably, according to Article 14, a Truth and Reconciliation Commission can be a forum where survivors can access justice and obtain redress by corporate malefactors. The same applies to civil courts or any other judicial authority. As for Article 2(3), while it seemingly gives preference to judicial remedies,[93] simple reparation laws can also fulfil the requirements.[94] In cases of summary executions, torture and unresolved disappearances, the state should initiate criminal proceedings, in parallel to the reparation measures.[95] For the rest of the violations, administrative proceedings can suffice.[96] It should be, however, noted that in most jurisdictions, redress against private persons is achieved via private law. In fewer jurisdictions, reparation can be granted in the framework of criminal procedures that provide for *partie civil* and corporate criminal liability or through administrative procedures.[97] A related issue is whether the remedy can be sought against the corporate entity or against individual corporate managers. Given the recognition of corporate entities in private law and the material nature of reparations sought by corporations, this issue would not arise, at least in the pursuit of material reparations.

5.3.1.2 European Court of Human Rights

In addition to the ICCPR, the European Court of Human Rights (ECtHR) creates obligations for state parties to provide redress avenues in domestic law for victims of corporate violations.[98] Pursuant to Article

[91] Nowak commented that while the term court means the usual judicial forum, the juxtaposition to the term tribunal suggests that the latter was meant to encompass other authorities, such as administrative ones, as long as principles of independence and impartiality are satisfied. Nowak, *UN Covenant on Civil and Political Rights*, p. 314.

[92] HRC, *Y.L.* v. *Canada*, Communication No. 112/1981, Views of 8 April 1986, par. 9(1)–9(3); HRC, *Casanovas* v. *France*, Communication No. 441/1990, Views of 7 July 1993, par. 5(2).

[93] Nowak, *UN Covenant on Civil and Political Rights*, p. 64; 'HRC, General Comment 31', para. 15.

[94] HRC, *R. D. Stalla Costa* v. *Uruguay*, Communication No. 198/1985, 9 July 1987, par. 10.

[95] The obligation to investigate, prosecute and punish concurs with the obligation to provide compensation and cannot be substituted by it. Orentlicher, 'Settling Accounts', 2572.

[96] 'HRC, General Comment 31', para. 15.

[97] Malamud-Goti and Grosman, 'Reparations and Civil Litigation'.

[98] M. Fasciglione, 'Enforcing the State Duty to Protect Under the UN Guiding Principles on Business and Human Rights, Strasbourg Views', in A. Bonfanti (ed.), *Business and Human Rights in Europe International Law Challenges* (Routledge, 2018).

1, states bear the obligation to secure the rights of individuals, both in their relations with the state, but also in their private relations.[99] Securing entails adopting preventive measures against violations by non-state actors,[100] as well as establishing avenues of redress against third parties. Providing domestic remedies against private perpetrators is in compliance with the purpose of the Convention to guarantee 'practical and effective' protection.[101] It also stems from the obligation to exhaust domestic remedies before presenting a case at the ECtHR.[102] For the latter to have meaning, the state should offer the necessary domestic remedies, which should be adequate and effective.[103]

It can also be argued that having a domestic remedy against a private perpetrator can be based on Article 13 on the right to remedy.[104] The Court has held that this right entails a domestic remedy and gives 'direct

[99] D. Augenstein and L. Dziedzic, 'State Obligations to Regulate and Adjudicate Corporate Activities Under the European Convention on Human Rights' (2017) *EUI Law* 15. See, indicatively, ECtHR, *X and Y* v. *The Netherlands*, Application No. 8978/80, Judgment of 26 March 1985, par. 23. It is to be noted that the ECHR distinguishes among 'abuses' which are committed by the state and 'violations' committed by non-state actors; see ECTHR, *Cyprus* v. *Turkey*, Application No. 25781/94, Grand Chamber Judgment of 10 May 2001, par. 81; ECtHR, 'Mccann and Others v. The United Kingdom', Judgment, par. 161; ECtHR, *Marckx* v. *Belgium*, Application No. 6833/74, Judgment of 13 June 1979; ECtHR, *Plattform 'Aerzte fuer das Leben'* v. *Austria*, Application No. 10126/82, Judgment of 21 June 1986.

[100] See, indicatively, ECtHR, 'Osman v. the United Kingdom', par. 10, 115; ECtHR, *Kontrová* v. *Slovakia*, Application No. 7510/04, Judgment of 31 May 2007, par. 48. Also, the ECtHR analysed the state's duty to prevent the killings by unknown persons in ECtHR, *Yasa* v. *Turkey*, Application No. 22495/93, Judgment of 2 September 1998. Preventive measures also include adopting effective criminal law measures and investigation of specific cases, by way of illustration; see ECtHR, 'X and Y v The Netherlands', par. 23. See also cases when the violations were not caused by state agents; ECtHR, 'Ergi v. Turkey', par. 79, 82, 365, 398; ECtHR, *97 members of the Gldani Congregation of Jehovah's Witnesses and 4 others* v. *Georgia*, Application No. 48804/01, Judgment of 3 May 2007, par. 97.

[101] ECtHR, *Ouranio Toxo and Others* v. *Greece*, Application No. 74989/01, Judgment of 20 October 2005, par. 37.

[102] Shelton, *Remedies in International Human Rights Law*, p. 124. In *Akdivar* v. *Turkey*, the Court referred to the requirement of exhaustion of local remedies as a reflection of the principle that the machinery of protection established by the Convention is subsidiary to the national systems safeguarding human rights. ECtHR, *Akdivar* v. *Turkey*, Application No. 21893/93, Judgment of 16 September 1996, par. 65.

[103] ECtHR, 'Akdivar v. Turkey', paras. 65–76; ECtHR, 'Aksoy v. Turkey', paras. 51–53; ECtHR, *Mentes and others* v. *Turkey*, Application No. 23186/94, Judgment of 28 November 1997, paras. 57, 59.

[104] The right to remedy has generated several conceptual ambiguities. On occasion of the formulation of the right to remedy in the ECHR, Roht-Arriaza notes that it is not clear

expression to the State's obligation to protect human rights first and foremost within their own legal system, establishes an additional guarantee for an individual in order to ensure that he or she effectively enjoys those rights'.[105] However, it is not entirely convincing, whether this should be interpreted as an obligation of the state to provide internal remedies only against state abuses or against any kind of abuse. An argument in favour of the latter is the gradual development, by the ECtHR, of the right to remedy as an autonomous right.[106] Whereas in the early case law its character was sustained as accessory, in the case of *Aksoy* v. *Turkey*, the Court unwaveringly accepted the occurrence of an 'autonomous' violation of Article 13 of the European Convention.[107] A further argument in favour of that opinion is that lack of access to courts has been deemed to constitute a violation of the right to remedy.[108] Conversely, this means that Article 13 safeguards the existence of domestic remedies against third-party actors, via civil and criminal courts, meaning that the right to remedy should also be enjoyed, in the private sphere against third-party actors.[109]

The right to remedy is closely associated to the right to fair trial, enshrined in Article 6(1) of the ECHR.[110] The ECtHR read in the right

whether the article requires a remedy only when the Committee of Ministers, the Human Rights Court, or a domestic court has already found a violation, as argued by Professors Fawcett and Castberg or whether part of the remedy is precisely a determination of whether or not there has been a violation. J. E. S. Fawcett, *Application of the European Convention on Human Rights* (Oxford University Press, 1987), p. 291; F. Castberg, *The European Convention on Human Rights* (Kluwer Academic Publishers, 1974), p. 158; Roht-Arriaza, 'State Responsibility to Investigate and Prosecute', at 449–513.

105 ECtHR, 'Kudla Versus Poland', paras. 152, 156, 160.

106 A. Cançado Trindade, *The Construction of a Humanized International Law* (Brill, Nijhoff, 2015), p. 559. Note that Section 5.2 discussed the autonomy of the right to remedy, or its potential elevation to that status, but through a different perspective, than the one required here.

107 ECtHR, 'Aksoy v. Turkey', par. 95–100; ECtHR, 'Mustafa Sezgin Tanrikulu v. Turkey', par. 117; ECHR, 'Kudla v. Poland', paras. 147–149.

108 Shelton noted that lack of access to courts, coupled with absence of other remedial processes, violates Article 13. See ECtHR, *Powell and Rayner* v. *United Kingdom*, Application No. 9310/81, Judgment of 21 February 1990; Shelton, *Remedies in International Human Rights Law*, p. 126.

109 However, in this case again, the right to have a remedy against the corporate perpetrator would arise as a primary right and not as part of the secondary obligation of the state to provide compensation in the form of reparation.

110 ECtHR, 'Kudla v. Poland', par. 152. A. Cançado Trindade (ed.), *The Access of Individuals to International Justice* (Oxford University Press, 2011), p. 68. Where the scope of

to fair trial a state obligation to provide access to courts,[111] and a correlative right to institute proceedings before courts in civil matters.[112] Importantly, parliamentary and executive bodies satisfy the requirements of Article 6.[113] Thus, access to justice against corporations, in transitional settings, can be realised via TRCs.

Accordingly, states should ensure that their domestic courts are competent to adjudicate civil claims concerning business-related human rights abuses 'against business enterprises domiciled within their jurisdiction'.[114] Besides, the state would be violating Article 6 if it removes from the jurisdiction of the courts a whole range of civil claims, confers immunities from civil liability on large groups or categories of persons,[115] or omits to fulfil the requirements for the realisation of that right.[116] The Court has held that states should ensure effective access to courts for private disputes,[117] and effective and timely enforcement of domestic judgments against private corporations.[118] As per Article 6, a failure to do so would signal a failure of the state to protect the applicant's

protection of both provisions overlaps, Article 13 ECHR is absorbed by Article 6 ECHR. Augenstein and Dziedzic, 'State Obligations to Regulate and Adjudicate Corporate Activities'; J. H. Gerards and L. R. Glas, 'Access to Justice in the European Convention on Human Rights System' (2017) 35 *Netherlands Quarterly of Human Rights* 1, at 11–30.

111 ECtHR, 'Golder v. The United Kingdom'.

112 ECtHR, *Jelicic* v. *Bosnia and Herzegovina*, Application No. 41183/02, 15 November 2005, par. 38. However, the right of access to court might be limited, as long as limitations do not impair the essence of the right and pursue a legitimate aim under proportional means. See ECtHR, *Ashingdane* v. *UK*, Application No. 8225/78, Judgment of 28 May 1985, par. 57; Shelton, *Remedies in International Human Rights Law*, p. 125. Nowak noted Article 6 of the ECHR is applicable when a dispute exists between the parties to a trial, the outcome of which is directly decisive for the determination of civil rights and obligations. Nowak, *UN Covenant on Civil and Political Rights*, p. 315.

113 ECtHR, *Klass* v. *Germany*, Application No. 5029/71, Judgment, 6 September 1978, par. 75.

114 CoE Committee of Ministers, 'Recommendation CM/Rec (2016) 3 of the Committee of Ministers to Member States on human rights and business' (2 March 2016), par. 34.

115 ECtHR, *Markovic and Others* v. *Italy*, Application No. 1398/03, Judgment of 14 December 2006, par. 97.

116 As was the case with the lack of legal aid, ECtHR, *Airey* v. *Ireland* case, Application No. 6289/73, Judgment of 9 October 1979.

117 ECtHR, 'Golder v. United Kingdom', paras. 34–35; ECHR, *Steel and Morris* v. *United Kingdom*, Application No. 68416/01, Judgment of 15 February 2005, par. 59.

118 ECtHR, *Fuklev* v. *Ukraine*, Application No. 71186/01, Judgment of 7 June 2005, par. 84; ECtHR, *EVT Company* v. *Serbia* Application No. 8024/08, Judgment of 13 January 2015, paras. 31–33.

substantive rights, which is pertinent 'even in cases involving litigation between private individuals or companies'.[119]

5.3.1.3 Inter-American System

Article 1 of the American Convention calls on states to adopt a variety of measures, both preventive and reactive against non-state perpetrators.[120] Therefore, apart from preventive obligations, states should also punish third-party (malef)actors,[121] control and regulate their activities,[122] and provide avenues of redress against their violations. Article 2 of the Convention, by asking states to 'give effect' to the Convention rights, requires the existence of domestic avenues of redress against non-state violators, in the form of civil or criminal trials.[123] This encapsulates an obligation to organise the state apparatus, in a way that is capable of juridically ensuring the free and full enjoyment of human rights.[124] The requirement to exhaust domestic remedies[125] also points to an obligation on behalf of the state to provide redress avenues. This presupposes that domestic remedies exist and that they are not confined in the relationship

119 ECtHR, *Margushin* v. *Russia*, Application No. 11989/03, Judgment of 1 April 2010, paras. 29, 38.

120 C. Anicama, State Responsibilities to Regulate and Adjudicate Corporate Activities under the Inter-American Human Rights System Report on the American Convention on Human Rights, prepared to inform the mandate of the UN Special Representative of the United Nations Secretary-General (SRSG) on the issue of Human Rights and Transnational Corporations and Other Business Enterprises, April 2008.

121 IACtHR, 'Velasquez-Rodriguez v. Honduras', Judgment, par. 174, 177; IACtHR, *Godinex Cruz* v. *Honduras* (Judgment) Series C No. 5, 20 January 1989, par. 182–184, 188; IACtHR, 'Paniagua Morales and Others v. Guatemala, Merits Judgment', par. 91. The IACtHR has repeatedly found that the respect and ensure provision of Article 1(1) of the American Convention of Human Rights presumably applies vis-à-vis all rights. See IACtHR, *Serrano Cruz Sisters* v. *El Salvador* (Judgment Merits, Reparations and Costs), Series C No. 120, 1 March 2005, par. 168. However, scholars have claimed that this is an over-expansion and that the duty to prosecute and punish shall be confined to the most serious violations. Orentlicher, 'Settling Accounts', at 2578.

122 In relation to Article 7, the Court has even ruled that the Convention establishes positive obligations on both state agents and third parties, when they are responsible for carrying out detentions. IACtHR, *Maritza Urrutia* v. *Guatemala* (Judgment, Merits, Reparations and Costs), 27 November 2003, Series C No. 103, par. 71; IACtHR, *Juan Humberto Sánchez* v. *Honduras* (Preliminary Objections, Merits, Reparations and Costs), Series C No. 99, 7 June 2003, par. 81.

123 IACtHR, *Case of Castillo Petruzzi et al.* v. *Peru* (Merits, Reparations and Cost), Series C No. 52, 30 May 1999, par. 205; IACtHR, *Case of Suárez Rosero* v. *Ecuador* (Merits), Series C No. 35, 12 November 1997, par. 98.

124 IACtHR, 'Velasquez-Rodriguez v. Honduras', Judgment, par. 165–166.

125 Shelton, *Remedies in International Human Rights Law*, p. 141.

of the state with the individual, since states are also obliged to protect rights against private transgressors. For it to have meaning, the state should have a chain of redress mechanisms available for the victim to use – first against the individual perpetrator and then against the state or its agents, for their omission to ensure.

It could also be argued that redress avenues against private transgressors can be based on a combined reading of the positive obligations of Article 1, with the right to remedy. The court has held that

> States Parties have an obligation to provide effective judicial remedies to victims of human rights violations (Article 25), remedies that must be substantiated in accordance with the rules of due process of law (Article 8 (1)), all in keeping with the general obligation of such States to guarantee the free and full exercise of the rights recognized by the Convention to all persons subject to their jurisdiction (Article 1).[126]

While it is not entirely certain whether that was meant to cover only state violations, the court has added that Article 25 is intimately linked with the general obligation of Article 1(1) of the ACHR, in conferring functions of protection upon the domestic law of States Parties.[127] Additionally, the right to remedy is often combined with Articles 1 and 8(1),[128] affirming the right of each person to a hearing by competent, independent and impartial tribunals for the determination of their rights.[129] These three articles jointly ensure to each person that those responsible for violations of their rights will be judged and that they can obtain remedies for the damage suffered.[130]

In fact, both the Court and the Commission have recognized the importance of acquiring redress by the corporate perpetrator and not by the individual corporate manager or the state. The Commission has emphasized that victims should be able to claim redress against business

[126] IACtHR, *Velásquez-Rodríguez* v. *Honduras* (Preliminary Exceptions) (1987) 1 (Series C), para. 91.

[127] IACtHR, *Castillo Páez* v. *Peru*, Judgment, Series C No. 34, 3 November 1997, par. 82, 83.

[128] IACtHR, 'Suárez Rosero v. Ecuador', par. 65; IACtHR, 'Blake v. Guatemala', Judgment, par. 102; IACtHR, *Paniagua Morales and others* v. *Guatemala* (Reparations and Costs), 25 May 2001, Series C No. 76; IACtHR, *Loayza Tamayo* v. *Peru (Reparations)*, Series C No. 53, 27 November 1998, par. 169; IACtHR, *Castillo Paez* v. *Peru* (Reparations and Costs), 27 November 1998, Series C No. 34, para. 106; IACtHR, 'Case of the Mapiripán Massacre v. Colombia' Judgment, par. 195. See Cançado Trindade, *The Access of Individuals to International Justice*, p. 54.

[129] IACtHR, *Cantos* v. *Argentina* (Merits, Reparations and Costs), Series C No. 97, 28 November 2002, par. 50, 52.

[130] Shelton, *Remedies in International Human Rights Law*, p. 140.

misconduct based on Article 25 regarding access to judicial remedies[131] via complaint mechanisms, which are transparent and based on access to information.[132] From its part, the Court has evaluated domestic legal remedies against private induced violations,[133] sometimes asking the state to repair 'in conjunction with the company'.[134] This posits that it takes for granted the necessity of domestic remedies against corporate activities.[135]

5.3.1.4 African System

Similarly to the other systems, Article 1 of the African Charter calls on states to adopt legislative or other measures to give effect to the rights enshrined therein.[136] Those measures apply against violations committed by public, and also private actors,[137] and include preventive steps,[138] measures of investigation, and also provision of redress avenues against

[131] IACmHR, Report on the Situation of Human Rights in Ecuador, Chapter IX, OEA/Ser. L/V/II.96, Doc. 10 rev. 1, 24 April 1997; IACmHR, Report on the Situation of Human Rights in Ecuador, Chapter IX, OEA/Ser.L/V/II.96, Doc. 10 rev. 1, 24 April 1997, recommendations.

[132] IACmHR, 'Report on the Situation of Human Rights in Ecuador, 1997'.

[133] IACtHR, *Case of the Saramaka People* v. *Suriname*, Preliminary objections, merits, reparations and costs, Series C No. 172, 28 November 2007, par. 77.

[134] IACtHR, *Kalina and Lokono Peoples* v. *Suriname*, Case 198–107, Report No. 76/07, 25 November 2015, par. 224.

[135] The court has also referred to redress in situations that involve corporate entities. See IACtHR, Case of *Mayagna (Sumo) Awas Tingni* v. *Nicaragua* (Merits, Reparations and Costs), Series C No. 79, 31 August 2001.

[136] See also AfComHPR, 'General Comment No. 4 on the African Charter', par. 73.

[137] Cases before the Commission that involved non-state actors and the respective duty of the state to protect were AfComHPR, 'Commission Nationale des Droits de L'Homme et des libertés v. Chad'; AfComHPR, 'Zimbabwe Human Rights NGO Forum v. Zimbabwe'; AfComHPR, *Amnesty International and Others* v. *Sudan*, Communication Nos. 48/90, 50/91, 52/91, 89/93, Thirteenth Annual Activity Report: 1999–2000; AfComHPR, *S.O.S. – Esclaves* v. *Mauritania*, African Commission on Human and Peoples' Rights, Communication No. 198/97 (1999). The latter case was declared inadmissible not because the state was not the party directly responsible for the alleged violation but due to non-exhaustion of domestic remedies. In *SERAC* v. *Nigeria*, the Commission referred to the state duty to protect against corporate-related human rights violations; AfComHPR, '*Social and Economic Rights Action Centre and the Centre for Economic and Social Rights (SERAC)* v. *Nigeria*'.

[138] Beyond the AfCHPR, developments have taken place before the East African Court of Justice, where a relevant case was filed against South Sudan for its failure to protect human and environmental rights, due to environmental pollution caused by oil exploration companies. The case is currently under mediation. *Hope for Humanity Africa* v. *The Hon. Minister of Justice of the Republic of South Sudan*, Reference Number 9/2020, 27 April 2020.

third-party violators, before resorting against the state.[139] The duty to protect has been deemed to enable individuals to realize their rights, including by ensuring that they have access to remedy, for violations induced by both state and non-state actors.[140] The requirement of exhaustion of domestic remedies, in Articles 50 and 56(5) of the Charter also point to the direction that victims should possess an avenue of redress against private actors, before complaining for state failures. The Commission has stated that national remedies must be 'available, effective and sufficient' to be considered.[141] Lastly, it should be noted that the Charter contains provisions regarding human rights but also regarding the duties of individuals to exercise rights 'with *due regard* to the rights of others' and to respect fellow beings. Despite the fact that it is unsettled whether those duties are enforceable among individuals,[142] they provide useful ground for a potential inclusion of corporations as addressees of the obligation to repair the harm they have caused.

It could lastly be argued that redress avenues against private transgressors can be grounded on a combined reading of the positive obligations of Article 1, with the right to fair trial, under Article 7.[143] Markedly for the current book, the General Comment on the Right to Redress for Victims of Torture foresees that 'in cases where an individual, legal person or other entity is found liable for reparation to a victim, such party should provide reparation to the victim or compensate the State if the State has already provided reparation to the victim'.[144] It also stipulates that sources of funds for reparation include orders, fines, forfeiture, freezing and seizure of property belonging to non-state actors deemed

139 In the *SERAC* case, the Commission cited the Inter-American Court and mentioned that a state has contravened its obligation to protect when it has allowed violations by private persons but also when those violations have been met with impunity. Conversely, anti-impunity and remedies is considered part of protection. AfComHPR, '*Social and Economic Rights Action Centre and the Centre for Economic and Social Rights (SERAC)* v. *Nigeria*', par. 57.

140 AfComHPR, '*Social and Economic Rights Action Centre and the Centre for Economic and Social Rights (SERAC)* v. *Nigeria*'.

141 Shelton, *Remedies in International Human Rights Law*, p. 142; N. Udombana, 'So Far, So Fair: The Local Remedies Rule in the Jurisprudence of the African Commission on Human and Peoples' Rights' (2003) 97 *American Journal of International Law*, p. 2.

142 M. Mutua, 'The Banjul Charter and the African Cultural Fingerprint: An Evaluation of the Language of Duties' (1995) 35 *Virginia Journal of International Law*, at 339.

143 African [Banjul] Charter on Human and Peoples' Rights, adopted on 27 June 1981, OAU Doc. CAB/LEG/67/3 rev. 5, 21 I.L.M. 58 (1982), entered into force on 21 October 1986, Article 7.

144 AfComHPR, 'General Comment No. 4 on the African Charter', par. 33, 73.

responsible for acts of torture and other ill treatment.[145] In addition, according to the General Comment on the Right to Life, accountability encompasses reparation, and states 'must hold to account private individuals and corporations, including private military and security companies, that are responsible for causing or contributing to arbitrary deprivations of life in the State's territory or jurisdiction'.[146] By implication, this means that states should ensure adequate mechanisms for reparations by private persons.

An important development which has not yet materialized is Article 46 of the Malabo Protocol, which vests the African Court on Human and Peoples' Rights (AfCHPR) with international criminal jurisdiction over legal persons.[147] The Protocol allows the Court to order directly the convicted person, natural or legal, to repair victims. In conjunction with the provision on corporate criminal liability, the future court will have the potential to realize not only the right of victims to justice against corporate wrongdoers but also their right to reparation. Article 46M foresees the establishment of a trust fund for the benefit of the victims.

5.3.2 Revisiting the Sequence of State Obligations: A Nuanced Approach or Why States Should Enable Corporate Redress as Part of Reparation Schemes

As per the discussion towards the end of Section 5.3.1, according to international and regional human rights treaties, there is an obligation of states to provide victims with domestic avenues of redress against corporate malefactors. This stems primarily from their positive obligations, attached to the realization of substantial rights, but also from the prerequisite to exhaust domestic remedies, the fair trial rights and in some systems directly from the right to remedy. According to treaty law, that obligation precedes the reparative one. Therefore, the state is obliged to fulfil it before embarking on repairing its failure to prevent and redress. However, in that case, the obligation to provide redress avenues against corporations would fall outside the reparation phase, which would be problematic when one attempts to situate corporate accountability within transitions.

[145] Ibid., par. 75.

[146] AfComHPR, General Comment No. 3 on the African Charter on Human and Peoples' Rights: The Right to Life (Article 4), par. 17 and 18.

[147] Malabo Protocol, Article 46C.

Against this background, there are several reasons in favour of a more nuanced interpretation of the sequence of obligations, particularly so during transitions. Technically, this would mean that states' protection duties (including their duty to provide redress avenues against corporations) should be performed in the context of reparations or that state reparations should involve third-party perpetrators as bearers of the obligation to repair. In other words, based on a novel understanding, transitional states should design reparation schemes in a way that mirrors the responsibility of the perpetrator, either by including it in the administrative reparation programmes or by enabling victims to pursue court procedures against it.[148]

Notably, transitional settings have the comparative advantage of relative exceptionality,[149] understood not as unique arrangements but as existing arrangements adapted to address unique contexts of violations.[150] This opens up a window of opportunity for constructing reparations to mirror the responsibilities of different actors. Theory, practice and vindications of victims and civil society demonstrate shared expectations on the issue of reparations in the framework of transitions, which in turn could gradually lead to the emergence of alternative interpretations of international law, even without 'the formality of treaty arrangements or the specificity of a meaningful legal obligation'.[151]

Furthermore, a combination of protective and reparative obligations could be construed on the dialectical – if not causal – relationship between remedies offered as protection and those leading to state reparation. The latter is triggered only if the former has failed and reparation from the state is enabled, only after the victim did not manage to acquire reparation from the individual perpetrator. The causal relation means that if the state provides the remedies that come first at the causal chain, it is absolved from providing the second. The Human Rights Committee has underlined that the protection afforded by paragraph (1) of Article

[148] The point of enabling relevant adjudication is raised because in the past, transitional states have attempted to hinder that adjudication. For example, the South African government opposed the apartheid litigation before US courts. See Section 6.1 of this book.

[149] Bell and Gray vouch for the exceptional character of transitional justice, as opposed to Posner and Vermeule. Bell, 'Transitional Justice, Interdisciplinarity and the State of the "Field" or "Non-Field"', 21; Gray, 'Extraordinary Justice', 55; Teitel, 'Editorial Note'; Posner and Vermeule, 'Transitional Justice as Ordinary Justice'.

[150] Payne et al., *Archimedes' Lever*, p. 17.

[151] Falk, 'Reparations, International Law, and Global Justice A New Frontier'.

2 is closely connected to the remedies offered by paragraph (3).[152] In the Inter-American system, the right to remedy is often combined with Article 1 and 8(1),[153] which affirms the right of each person to a hearing by a competent, independent and impartial tribunal for a determination of rights.[154] Similarly, in Europe, the right to remedy is linked to the right to fair trial, enshrined in Article 6(1) of the ECHR.[155] Cançado Trindade has argued that Article 6 of the ECHR and Articles 25, 8 and 1 of the ACHR, 'in concrete terms and not as a theoretical abstraction, [leads] to the assertion of the States Parties' duty to take positive measures'.[156] And while an unwilling state might disregard those obligations altogether, it is presumed that upon signing a treaty, each state undertakes to comply with it. It is also presumed that it is preferable to provide domestic remedies against third-party actors than bearing aggravated responsibility both for failing to prevent and for failing to remedy a human right violation.

Additionally, protective and reparative obligations should not be interpreted as constituting watertight categories. Instead, both present flexible and evolving features, approximating one the other. As analysed previously, the primary obligation of the state to protect has been consistently interpreted as entailing traditional remedial measures, such as investigation, punishment and redress. Conversely, the right to remedy often alludes to primary rights and protection underpinnings. In fact, its purely remedial character has been diluted by an overall turn of remedies towards prevention, in view of broader societal aims that they are meant to achieve.[157] The rapidly developing preventive angle of GNRs is the

[152] 'HRC, General Comment 31', para. 8.

[153] IACtHR, 'Blake v. Guatemala', par. 102.

[154] IACtHR, 'Cantos v. Argentina', par. 50, 52.

[155] ECtHR, 'Kudla v. Poland', par. 152. See also Cançado Trindade, *The Access of Individuals to International Justice*, p. 68. Where the scope of protection of both provisions overlaps, Article 13 ECHR is absorbed by Article 6 ECHR. Augenstein and Dziedzic, 'State Obligations to Regulate and Adjudicate Corporate Activities'; Gerards and Glas, 'Access to Justice in the European Convention on Human Rights System'.

[156] Cançado Trindade, *The Access of Individuals to International Justice*, pp. 54, 60. In relation to the Inter-American system, Cançado Trindade also noted that combining the Articles 25, 8 and 1 is a way to confer the function of protection to the domestic law of the States Parties.

[157] The HRC, the Inter-American Court of Human Rights and the ECHR allocate remedies not only as a form of *stricto sensu* reparation to the victims but also as a general measure for the benefit of society or in order to prevent future recurrence of a violation. Schonsteiner, 'Dissuasive Measures and the "Society as a Whole"', pp. 127, 130; A. Seibert-Fohr, *Prosecuting Serious Human Rights Violations* (Oxford University

most illustrative example of this turn.[158] To those, one should factor in the peculiar balance that reparations are meant to preserve. From the one side, presumably, they have departed from their traditional secondary status.[159] From the other, remedies in both the protective and the reparative stage have close ties to the essence of the primary right that was violated. They are invoked on the basis of a substantive right and the latter is crucial in delineating the adequacy of remedies.[160]

That evolving and flexible character of both stages of remedies and their interconnection suggests that they are functionally similar and that a state resorting to its protective duties, while performing its reparative ones, would be in compliance with one of the essential functions of remedies. At a minimum, according to a novel interpretation, protective obligations should inform the way that state reparations will unfold. In a contrary case, where the state sweepingly repairs all violations no matter the perpetrator, then reparations would be reduced to mere transactions, blurring their real essence, namely, to correct the harm suffered, by

Press, 2009), p. 190 *et seq*; Antkowiak, 'Remedial Approaches to Human Rights Violations', p. 382.

158 C. Ferstman, 'Reparation as Prevention: Considering the Law and Practice of Orders for Cessation and Guarantees of Non-Repetition in Torture Cases' (2010) 6 *Essex Human Rights Review* 2, p. 20.

159 Arguably, the right to reparation has evolved into a primary norm of customary international law. Shelton, *Remedies in International Human Rights Law*, p. 238; C. Bassiouni, 'Accountability for Violations of International Humanitarian Law and Other Serious Violations of Human Rights'; C. Evans, *The Right to Reparation in International Law for Victims of Armed Conflict* (Cambridge University Press, 2012), p. 39. However, Tomuschat argues that human rights conventions do not provide the legal basis for an individual right because they are subject to the incorporation in national law. C. Tomuschat, *Human Rights, Between Idealism and Realism* (Oxford University Press, 2014), pp. 293 317; C. Tomuschat, 'Darfur Compensation for the Victims' (2005) 3 *Journal of International Criminal Justice*, pp. 579–589. The right to remedy has generated several conceptual ambiguities. Roht-Arriaza notes that it is not clear whether the ECHR requires a remedy only when the Committee of Ministers, the Human Rights Court, or a domestic court has already found a violation, as argued by Professors Fawcett and Castberg or whether part of the remedy is precisely a determination of whether or not there has been a violation. Fawcett, *Application of the European Convention on Human Rights*, p. 291, and Castberg, *The European Convention on Human Rights*, p. 158; Roht-Arriaza, 'State Responsibility to Investigate and Prosecute'.

160 Zegveld notes that a victim's right to reparation depends in the first place on his rights, as recognized under international law, having been breached. A victim's right to reparation therefore presupposes rights of victims in international law. Zegveld, 'Victims' Reparations Claims and International Courts', pp. 80–85. See also Buyse, 'Lost and Regained?'.

asking 'the responsible actor paying'.[161] It would also lead to 'less rights' for individuals who are adversely affected by corporate activities and to a regulatory gap, whereby corporations evade responsibility.

Similar shifts to the mainly state-centred character of reparations have already taken place when reparations expanded beyond interstate relations to cover violations of human rights norms suffered by individuals.[162] In the field of international humanitarian law, while in principle it was accepted that only states are responsible for reparations for failing to protect individuals,[163] it is being gradually consolidated that ANSAs own reparations as well.[164] The UN has opted for reparations by non-state actors in Liberia[165] and Afghanistan[166] and similar practice has taken place in the Philippines[167] and Peru.[168] In the DRC, mobile courts found local militias liable for reparations due to their involvement in atrocities,[169] and in Colombia, Laws 975/2005 and 1148/2011 foresee the respective obligation of paramilitary forces.[170] Lastly, in Sudan, the

[161] Moffett, 'Transitional Justice and Reparations'.

[162] D. Shelton, 'Righting Wrongs: Reparations in the Articles on State Responsibility' (2002) 96 *American Journal of International Law* 4; Evans, *The Right to Reparation in International Law for Victims of Armed Conflict*, p. 30.

[163] Rule 150 of the ICRC Customary IHL Database, in Henckaerts and Doswald-Beck, *Customary International Humanitarian Law*. Gillard has noted that there are no instances where armed opposition groups have made such reparations in practice, E.-C. Gillard, 'Reparation for Violations of International Humanitarian Law' (2003) 85 *International Review of the Red Cross*, pp. 34–35.

[164] Zegveld, *Accountability of Armed Opposition Groups in International Law*, p. 162; Clapham, *Human Rights Obligations of Non-State-Actors*, p. 41.

[165] UN Security Council Resolution 1083 (1996) on the Situation in Liberia, UN Doc. S/RES/1083, par. 7; UN Security Council, Res. 1071 on the situation in Liberia, UN. Doc. S/RES/1071, par. 346.

[166] UN Commission on Human Rights, Resolution 1997/65 on the Situation of Human Rights in Afghanistan reports on Afghanistan, par. 10. See also UN General Assembly, Res. 51/108 on the situation of human rights in Afghanistan, UN Doc. A/RES/51/108, par. 96.

[167] The Comprehensive Agreement on Respect for Human Rights and IHL in the Philippines foresees the indemnification of victims. See Rule 150 of the ICRC Customary IHL Database, Henckaerts and Doswald-Beck, *Customary International Humanitarian Law*.

[168] The Truth and Reconciliation Commission held that the Shining Path, a non-state armed group was responsible for extrajudicial executions and disappearances. Truth and Reconciliation Commission (CVR) Report, Vol. VIII.

[169] Avocats Sans Frontieres, *Case Study: The Application of the Rome Statute of the International Criminal Court by the Courts of the Democratic Republic of Congo* (2009).

[170] A. Carrillo, 'Truth, Justice, and Reparations in Colombia', in V. M. Bouvier (ed.), *Colombia: Building Peace in a Time of War* (US Institute of Peace Press, 2009), p. 154. Also, in 2016, FARC declared that it would fund reparation programmes in order to

International Commission of Inquiry on Darfur stressed that ANSAs are responsible to pay compensation for their crimes in Darfur.[171] International humanitarian law and the practice in relation to ANSAs can be useful in supporting an analogous development of the obligation to repair in relation to corporate actors.

Another shift in the dominant international law paradigm of state responsibility for reparations is offered by international criminal law. The ICC awards individual or collective reparations, taking into account the scope and the extent of any damage, loss or injury, upon application by the victim.[172] The Trust Fund for the Victims (TVF) implements reparations awards against a convicted person. Importantly, they are to be paid by individual perpetrators, not by states.[173] The TFV is funded by confiscated assets of perpetrators and voluntary contributions, which are used when the number of victims is large, and the perpetrator is indigent.[174] Bestowing the perpetrator with an obligation to repair is important, in so far as corporate managers would be brought before the court to account for harmful activities of their corporations. It is even more significant in orienting the international legal discourse towards subjects, other than the state. It presumably demonstrates a relative consensus on the importance of the perpetrator in the delivery of reparations and can back up the argument made earlier that states should bestow a perpetrator-oriented element on their reparation schemes. The most

become a legitimate political party. See Office of the High Commissioner for Peace, Colombian Peace Agreement, the Opportunity to Build Peace (2022).

171 UN Security Council, International Commission of Inquiry on Darfur, Report to the Secretary-General, 25 January 2005, UN Doc. S/2005/60, paras. 591, 600 and 603.

172 See Article 75 of the Rome Statute and Rules 94 and 95(1) of the Rules of Procedure and Evidence of the International Criminal Court 2002, UN Doc. PCNICC/2000/1/Add.1 (2000).

173 Note that this issue created a lot of controversy. Evans argued that there are inherent dangers in shifting responsibility from states towards individuals, as this may ultimately leave victims without redress. Evans, *The Right to Reparation in International Law for Victims of Armed Conflict*, pp. 86, 100.

174 The Court has ordered individual and collective reparations in the Al Mahdi, Lubanga and Katanga cases. See ICC, *The Prosecutor* v. *Ahmad Al Faqi Al Mahdi*, Reparations Order, No. ICC-01/12-01/15, Appeals Chamber, 8 March 2018; ICC, *The Prosecutor* v. *Thomas Lubanga Dyilo*, Situation en République démocratique du Congo, Appeals Chamber, Judgment on the appeals against the 'Decision establishing the principles and procedures to be applied to reparations' of 7 August 2012 with amended order for reparations (Annex A) and public annexes 1 and 2 ICC-01/04-01/06-3129, 3 March 2015; ICC, *The Prosecutor* v. *Germain Katanga*, Ordonnance de réparation en vertu de l'article 75 du Statut, Trial Chamber II, ICC-01/04-01/07-3728, 24 March 2017. The order is on appeal stage.

significant development in that respect came from the Malabo Protocol on the Statute of the ACJHR, which extended the court's jurisdiction on corporations and at the same time foresaw that reparation can be ordered against the convicted person.

5.4 Rough-Spoken Soft Law

Relevant arguments supporting the interpretation of state obligations, as described in Section 5.3.2, can be drawn by various soft-law instruments.[175] Those instruments, while not *stricto sensu* binding, were all adopted as UN resolutions, and thus presumably reflect emerging state practice or contribute to the formation of *opinio juris*.[176] They bear distinct normative value as they encapsulate the opinion of states with regard to the interpretation of existing international law,[177] whereas some UNSC decisions expressly imposed legal obligations on states.[178] On the other hand, UN declarations have been considered to be an intermediate step towards consolidating legally binding instruments.[179] Notwithstanding their legal effect, those documents – at a minimum – demonstrate an increasing recognition of the role of non-state actors in conflict and repression and the need to include them in processes of redress.[180]

The most important support for the interpretation of a state obligation to include corporate malefactors as bearers of obligations in the reparation phase comes from the Basic Principles and Guidelines on the Right

175 There is an ongoing theoretical debate regarding the relationship between interpretation and modification of rules in international law. See n (37) Section 3.2.1, Part II, of this book.

176 ICTY, *Prosecutor* v. *Tadic*, Decision on the Defence Motion for Interlocutory Appeal on Jurisdiction, Appeals Chamber, Case No. IT-94-1-AR72, 2 October 1995, par. 133.

177 Clapham, *Human Rights Obligations of Non-State Actors*, pp. 104–105; see also B. Sloan, 'General Assembly Resolutions Revisited (Forty Years Later)' (1987) 58 *British Yearbook of International Law* 39; C. Joyner, 'UN General Assembly Resolutions and International Law: Rethinking the Contemporary Dynamics of Norm Creation' (1981) 11 *California Western International Law Journal*, pp. 457, 464.

178 The ones adopted under chapter VII. See J. Burniske, N. Modirzadeh and D. Lewis, 'Armed Non-State Actors and International Human Rights Law: An Analysis of the Practice of the U.N. Security Council and the U.N. General Assembly' (2017) *Harvard Public Law Working Paper No. 17-37*, at 21–29; Clapham, 'Focusing on ANSAs'.

179 United Nations Office of Legal Affairs, *Memorandum of Legal Service*, UN ESCOR, 34th sess, Supp. No. 8, UN Doc E/CN.4/L.610 (2 April 1962), par. 4.

180 Report of the Special Rapporteur on extrajudicial, summary or arbitrary executions on armed non-state actors: the protection of the right to life, A/HRC/38/44, 5 June 2018.

to a Remedy and Reparation for Victims of Gross Violations of International Human Rights Law and Serious Violations of International Humanitarian Law (Basic Principles).[181] They foresee that states should enable access to justice for victims seeking remedies and reparations. In cases where a person, a legal person, or other entity is found liable for reparation to a victim, such party should provide reparation to the victim.[182] Their importance lies in the fact that they were adopted by the UN General Assembly without a dissenting vote,[183] and have been influencing the emergence of international standards on those topics ever since.[184] Importantly, Principle 15 on non-state reparations remained after the long negotiating process before the adoption of the principles.[185] This can be interpreted as evidence of certain recognition by states or at least guidance regarding the future formulation of responsibilities in the realm of corporate responsibility to repair harm inflicted on victims in the context of conflict or repression. Even if the document does not represent customary law in relation to legal entities' duties, at a minimum it can be considered as declaratory of expectations in the area of victims' rights, in particular the right to a remedy and reparation.

The Guiding Principles on Business and Human Rights (UNGPs), adopted by the UN Human Rights Council in 2011, assert that states as part of their duty to protect 'must' take measures to ensure that victims of business-related abuses have access to effective remedy.[186] Given that one

[181] 'Basic Principles'; D. Shelton, 'The United Nations Principles and Guidelines on Reparations: Context and Contents', in K. De Feyter et al. (eds.), *Out of the Ashes: Reparation for Victims of Gross and Systematic Human Rights Violations* (Intersentia, 2005), pp. 11–34; E. Desmet, 'The UN Basic Principles and Guidelines on the Right to a Remedy and Reparation: A Landmark or Window Dressing? An Analysis with Special Attention to the Situation of Indigenous Peoples' (2008) 24 *South African Journal on Human Rights* 1, pp. 71–103.

[182] Basic Principles, Principle 15.

[183] Bassiouni, 'International Recognition of Victims' Rights'.

[184] They have been quoted in the Lubanga case by the ICC. See ICC, *The Prosecutor v. Thomas Lubanga Dyilo*, ICC-01/04-01/06, Decision on Victim's Participation, 18 January 2008, par. 35, 92.

[185] Bassiouni, 'International Recognition of Victims' Rights'.

[186] 'Guiding Principles', UN Doc. A/HRC/17/31, Principle 25. However, the UNGPs have been criticized for not coming with a dedicated accountability mechanism, focusing on non-judicial mechanisms and having permissive rather than restrictive character. S. Deva, 'Treating Human Rights Lightly: A Critique of the Consensus Rhetoric and the Language Employed by the Guiding Principles', in S. Deva and D. Bilchitz (eds.), *Human Rights Obligations of Business: Beyond the Corporate Responsibility to Respect?* (Cambridge University Press, 2013), pp. 78–104; S. Darcy, *Access to Justice and Extraterritorial Obligations, Brainstorming Session on Business and Human Rights 'A*

of the four times that the word 'must' is used in the principles and is in the part concerning access to remedy, it can be assumed that this principle carries increased weight and importance. The remedy system, that the principles envisage, includes judicial and non-judicial grievance mechanisms by the business entity and the state.[187] The substantial relief afforded by UNGP's remedies coincides with that envisaged by all human rights instruments, namely restitution, rehabilitation, compensation, guarantees of non-repetition, punitive sanctions and apologies.[188] In addition, corporations themselves have a duty to remedy. Principle 22 provides that where business enterprises identify that they have caused or contributed to adverse impacts, they should provide for or cooperate in their remediation through legitimate processes. Businesses are under a responsibility to provide non-judicial grievance mechanisms to remedy the harm that they inflict through their operations. This duty is with no prejudice to the primary duty of the state to protect the rights of persons under its jurisdiction, by guaranteeing judicial and non-judicial mechanisms to award remedies.[189] Lastly, the Declaration of Basic Principles of Justice for Victims of Crime and Abuse of Power can also be enlightening in that they indicate the international stance since 1985.[190] They explicitly refer to compensation and restitution as an obligation of the third-party defendant.[191] The consensus that the aforementioned soft-law instruments embody favour and support novel interpretations of respective state duties, whereby part of the state's overall reparative obligation would be to include corporate malefactors as debtors of reparations, showcases the importance of the responsible actor 'paying'.

5.5 The Added Value of Guarantees of Non-repetition for Corporate Accountability

Guarantees of non-repetition are in principle classified as reparation measures, but their added value lies in that they have developed distinct

New Business and Human Rights Instrument?' (Geneva for Human Rights & Friedrich Ebert Stiftung, 2015).

187 Ibid., Principle 22, 27 and Commentary to Principle 25.

188 Ibid., Principle 25.

189 Ibid., Commentary to Principle 25.

190 UN General Assembly, Declaration of Basic Principles of Justice for Victims of Crime and Abuse of Power G.A. Res. 40/34, 40 U.N. GAOR Supp. (No. 53) at 213, UN Doc. A/40/53 (1985), at 201.

191 Ibid.

characteristics, rendering them more responsive to the challenges of business accountability in transitional justice settings. Primarily, this is because the scope of GNRs is increasingly amplified. Early transitional justice initiatives conceptualized GNRs mainly as institutional, security and justice sector reform, as well as demobilization and vetting. For example, the Salvadorian Truth Commission recommended the dismissal of culpable army officers and civil servants from government employment and the disqualification of any other person implicated in wrongdoings, including those investigated by the Commission, from public office.[192] The early transitions of Eastern and Central Europe relied extensively on similar measures.[193]

In contrast, more recent transitions have recognized the significance of addressing the root causes of conflict, as well as the abuse and harm stemming from patterns of violations and recommended measures accordingly.[194] During the Colombian transition, the Unit on Assistance and Integral Reparations to Victims defined GNRs as 'measures, actions and processes to avoid repeating the violations, generate changes in how institutions function, transform the structural factors of violence and achieve positive effects on political culture, with the goal of

192 See Comisión de la Verdad Para El Salvador, Final Report, 15 March 1993, available at www.usip.org/publications/1992/07/truth-commission-el-salvador.

193 For more information on vetting and lustration processes in Poland, Hungary, the Czech Republic and East Germany, see A. Mayer-Rieckh and P. De Greiff (eds.), *Justice as Prevention: Vetting Public Employees in Transitional Societies* (International Centre for Transitional Justice, 2007). On the contrary, this did not happen in South Africa and Argentina.

194 Broad GNRs were also proposed by the Moroccan National Commission for Truth, Justice and Reconciliation. In 2005, it recommended measures concerning executive powers and the judiciary, but went further and proposed development of laws against sexual violence, ratification of the ICC Statute and abolition of the death penalty. See Kingdom of Morocco Justice and Reconciliation commission National Commission for Truth, Justice and Reconciliation, Summary of the Final Report, available at www.cndh.org.ma/an/report-equity-and-reconciliation-commission-ier/summary-final-report-equity-and-reconciliation. Also, in 2005, the Washington-based NGO Nigerian Democratic Movement and Nigeria-based Civil Society Forum unofficially published the report of the Human Rights Violations Investigation Commission of Nigeria. Among others, it recommended combating corruption, a broad consultation of civil society about Nigeria's constitutional structure, better human rights education and monitoring of the social, political and environmental conditions in the Niger Delta. See Nigeria Human Rights Violations Investigation Commission Report (a.k.a. Oputa Panel Report) Nigerian Democratic Movement (NDM), Washington, DC, USA.

strengthening prevention'.[195] The Victims' Law devoted a chapter on them,[196] containing measures to address specific violations, but also wider transformative aims, such as the legal empowerment of victims; strengthening the effective participation of affected and vulnerable populations; and, most importantly, measures for the dismantling of the economic and political structures that have benefited from and given support to armed groups.[197]

Oftentimes, those amplified measures touched upon corporate malefactors. By way of illustration, the Liberian diaspora TRC report recommended to the international community to ensure that transnational corporations and other business enterprises respect human rights and implement the Norms on the Responsibilities of Transnational Corporations and Other Business Enterprises with Regard to Human Rights.[198] The South African Truth and Reconciliation Commission recommended broad measures and socio-political reforms, addressed to various actors, including businesses.[199] Also, the Sierra Leonean Truth and Reconciliation Commission referred to business actors in the context of corruption and called on them to develop a Code of Corporate Governance in order to build a culture of ethical conduct and share information with law enforcement agencies.[200] A similar amplification can be observed in the guarantees of non-repetition ordered by human rights courts and supervisory bodies.[201] While in the beginning they focused mainly in traditional measures of vetting and administrative

[195] Unidad para la Atención y Reparación Integral a las Víctimas, Medidas de No-Repetición, available at www.unidadvictimas.gov.co/index.php/91-intranet/1061-medidas-de-satisfaccion-ygarantias-de-no-repeticion.

[196] Law 1448, 10 June 2011.

[197] Article 150 of the Law 1448, 10 June 2011.

[198] The Advocates for Human Rights, *A House with Two Rooms: Final Report of the Truth and Reconciliation Commission of Liberia Diaspora Project* (2009), p. 484.

[199] Report of the Truth and Reconciliation Commission of South Africa (1998). *Report*, Vol. 4, Introduction.

[200] Sierra Leone Truth and Reconciliation Commission, *Final Report*, 2004, Vol. 2 chapter 3, para. 297–299.

[201] N. Roht-Arriaza, 'Measures of Non-Repetition in Transitional Justice: The Missing Link?' (2016) 160 *UC Hastings Research Paper*, p. 16; Gready and Robins, 'From Transitional to Transformative Justice'; Pietropaoli, *Business, Human Rights and Transitional Justice*, pp. 50–58. See particularly Pietropaoli's analysis of the *Kalina and Lokono Peoples* v. *Suriname* case (IACtHR) and the plaintiffs' arguments in the IAComHR, *Santo Domingo Massacre* v. *Colombia*, Case No. 12.416, 8 July 2011, at 185.

reform, their jurisprudence gradually acknowledged the importance of other measures to ensure future non-repetition of violations.[202]

Notably, GNRs are not just growing in contrast to their previous selves, but also in comparison to other transitional measures. Unlike other mechanisms that are individually tailored, such as prosecutions, GNRs are oriented towards a wider exploration of prior injustice, including root causes of violence or repression, systemic deficiencies in the functioning of democracy and adherence to rule of law. The Liberian Truth and Reconciliation Commission report went beyond specific violations and analysed in depth issues of poverty; greed; corruption; limited access to education; economic, social, civil and political inequalities; land tenure and distribution; the lack of reliable and appropriate mechanisms for the settlement of disputes; and the 'duality of the Liberian political, social and legal systems which polarizes and widens the disparities between the Liberian peoples – a chasm between settler Liberia and indigenous Liberia'.[203] Within that comprehensive account, corporate malfeasance formed part of GNRs, insofar as it intersected with root causes of conflict.

Accordingly, the measures proposed as GNRs have come to include legislative measures which 'identify and attempt to remedy a structural wrong that the court has recognized in its examination of a case',[204] and institutional reforms able to grasp the structural dynamics that supported violence.[205] Again, human rights bodies have aligned to this expansion, have looked at root causes of violations[206] and vouched for broad

[202] See Antkowiak for an overview of the developments in the case law of the HRC, the IACtHR and the AfComHPR. Antkowiak, 'Remedial Approaches to Human Rights Violations', p. 366. In the European system, the adoption of the pilot judgment procedure mirrors an acknowledgement of the need to address structural problems by adopting broad reforms beyond the specific violation.

[203] Liberian Truth and Reconciliation Commission, Consolidated Final Report, Vol. II (2009), p. 16.

[204] Schonsteiner, 'Dissuasive Measures and the "Society as a Whole', p. 147.

[205] When vetting and institutional reforms failed, it was allegedly because they didn't grasp the network that supports and backs the direct violators. Roht-Arriaza, 'Measures of Non-Repetition in Transitional Justice', p. 33.

[206] For the influence of GNRs ordered by human rights bodies in transitional justice, see D. Cassel, 'The Practice and Procedure of the Inter-American Court of Human Rights' (2006). By Jo M. Pasqualucci (Cambridge University Press, 2003), at 503, 507; A. Del Campo, 'Lawyering for Reparations: Inter-American Perspective', in C. Grossman et al. (eds.) *International Law and Reparations: The Inter-American System* (Clarity Press, 2017).

structural[207] and legal reforms.[208] To that, one should add another differentiating qualification of GNRs in relation to other transitional measures, namely their more future-oriented and preventive, rather than remedial, character.[209] This has been applauded both by TRCs and human rights bodies,[210] especially in cases where they ordered or recommended GNRs with the aim to reorganize the state apparatus and structures and make them 'capable of juridically ensuring the free and full enjoyment of human rights'.[211]

In turn, those attributes go hand in hand with a relative loosening of the criteria for the allocation of GNRs. They depart from the strict requirements, typically associated with reparative measures, mandating a direct linkage between the violation, the resultant harm and the reparative action. In addition, respect to the principle of causality[212] and

207 See also the three stages evolution in the Inter-American Court's engagement with reparations described by Antkowiak, 'Remedial Approaches to Human Rights Violations', p. 366; A. Hunneus, 'Reforming the State from Afar: Structural Reform Litigation at the Human Rights Courts' (2015) 40 *Yale Journal of International Law* 1; G. Lessard, 'Preventive Reparations at a Crossroads. The Inter-American Court of Human Rights and Colombia's Search for Peace' (2018) 22 *The International Journal of Human Rights*, pp. 1209–1228.

208 See, for example, ECtHR, *Manole and others* v. *Moldova*, Application No. 13936/02, Judgment of 17 September 2009, par. 117; HRC, *Min-Kyu Jeong et al.* v. *The Republic of Korea*, Communication Nos. 1642-1741/2007, Views adopted 24 March 2011, par. 9; HRC, Guidelines on measures of reparation under the Optional Protocol to the International Covenant on Civil and Political Rights, 30 November 2016, CCPR/C/158; AfComHPR, *Sudan human rights organisation & Centre on Housing Rights and Evictions (COHRE)* v. *Sudan*, Communication Nos. 279/03 and 296/05 (2003); Redress, *Reaching for Justice: The Right to Reparation in the African Human Rights System* (REDRESS, 2013), p. 75.

209 On the contrary, Sullivan argues that the turn of GNRs to prevention rather than remedy has no legitimate legal foundation and infringes the states' sovereignty. According to him, GNRs originate in diplomatic practice and not in the legal arena. He adds that judicial bodies do not give sufficient guidance on the application of GNRs. See S. Sullivan, 'Changing the Premise of International Legal Remedies: The Unfounded Adoption of Assurances and Guarantees of Non-Repetition' (2002) *UCLA Journal of International Law and Foreign Affairs*, 265.

210 See, indicatively, HRC, *M.I.* v. *Sweden*, Communication No. 2149/2012, 26 September 2013, par. 9; IACtHR, 'Suárez Rosero v. Ecuador', par. 106; Redress, *Reaching for Justice*, p. 75.

211 IACtHR, 'Velasquez-Rodriguez v. Honduras', Judgment, par. 166.

212 The allocation of reparations is transpired by the principle of causality, meaning that reparations for a harm suffered are causally related to the violation. IACtHR, *Ticona Estrada and others* v. *Bolivia*, Merits (Reparations and costs), 27 November 2008, Series C No. 191, par. 110.

proportionality[213] is more nuanced in the case of GNRs than in the other forms of reparation, allowing them to be determined on more flexible terms.[214] As Crawford stated, other elements of the breach, such as the wilful misconduct of state organs, should be taken into account, because 'the requirement of a causal link is not necessarily the same in relation to every breach of an international obligation'.[215] GNRs under that more flexible formula build upon patterns of violations[216] that took place during conflict and recommend changes and reforms that would avert the same violations occurring in the future. Their goal is not only to avert future patterns of violence but also to reassure both victims and society that 'reparation is not an empty promise or a temporary stopgap'.[217]

This should not be understood as an absolute dissociation of GNRs from the violations that triggered them and their requirements. The lack of a tight causal link between declared violations and measures awarded by courts does not mean that the latter exceed their competence,[218] or that they 'erode state sovereignty'.[219] Granting GNRs that aim to address structural wrongs can be conceived as a way of materializing the

213 The principle of proportionality is a general principle used by human rights institutions and courts when calculating reparations, meaning that reparations should be proportional to the gravity of violations and the harm suffered. Basic Principles, Principle 15; IACtHR 'Velásquez Rodríguez v. Honduras', Judgment, par. 38.

214 Roht-Arriaza argues that GNRs are not tied specifically to a rights framework. Roht-Arriaza, 'Measures of Non-Repetition in Transitional Justice'.

215 J. Crawford, *The International Law Commission's Articles on State Responsibility: Introduction, Text and Commentaries* (Cambridge University Press, 2002), pp. 204–205.

216 For example, in Albán-Cornejo, based on the violation found by the Court, GNRs concerned training measures linked to violations as they aimed to ensure that people know the laws in relation to patient's rights. IACtHR, 'Albán-Cornejo et al. v. Ecuador', par. 164. The same applies to *Ximenes Lopes* v. *Brazil*, where a mentally ill person was admitted to a mental hospital under 'inhuman and degrading conditions'. The GRNs concerned training for physicians, which also builds up on the specific violation. IACtHR, 'Ximénes-Lópes v. Brazil', par. 250.

217 Magarrell, 'Reparations in Theory and Practice', p. 1.

218 In *Artavia Murillo and Others* v. *Costa Rica*, the Court allegedly awarded GNRs that went beyond the violations declared. It ordered the state to regulate the implementation of in vitro fertilization. It also ordered rehabilitation measures oriented to provide psychological treatment to the victims of the case, free of charge, for up to four years. The state was also ordered to make IVF available within its health care infertility treatments and programmes. IACtHR, *Case of Artavia Murillo et al. (in vitro fertilization)* v. *Costa Rica* (Merits) Series C No. 257, 28 November 2012, paras. 252–255, 336–338. For a critical opinion regarding those measures, see A. Paúl Díaz, 'La Corte Interamericana in Vitro: Comentarios sobre su Proceso de Toma de Decisiones a Propósito del Caso Artavia' (2013) 2 *Revista Derecho Público Iberoamericano* 303, p. 338.

219 Sullivan, 'Changing the Premise'.

protection provisions of treaties and a tangible manifestation of the responsibilities that states assumed when they signed them.[220] Besides, states, by signing a treaty, agree to relinquish some of their sovereignty in favour of the 'object and purpose' of that treaty,[221] namely protection of the rights enshrined therein and prohibition of their violation. As for fears of overexpansion and lack of legal certainty, they can be counterbalanced by the adoption of further criteria for the allocation of GNRs, and not by reducing them back to their merely procedural counterparts.[222] What is more, in transitions, the recommendation of broad GNRs arises out of the need to remedy the victims, but goes beyond mere procedural justice,[223] into establishing a sociopolitical framework that will not allow these violations to happen again.[224]

The different nature of GNRs in comparison to traditional reparations is corroborated by their consolidation and autonomization as a measure of transitional justice. Until recently, the UN conceptualized its work on measures of non-repetition around vetting.[225] In 2011, the UN established the Special Rapporteur on the promotion of truth, justice, reparation and guarantees of non-recurrence, a new Special Procedure of the

[220] Shelton notes that board GNRs is an act of continuous compliance with the treaty itself, especially since compliance procedures are centred on promoting changes in state behaviour rather than merely sanctioning breaches of international obligations. Shelton, 'Righting Wrongs'.

[221] United Nations, Vienna Convention on the Law of Treaties, 23 May 1969, United Nations, Treaty Series, Vol. 1155, Article 31(1).

[222] Those criteria can include GNRs for the core obligations that arise from each right. See, for example, the ESCR Committee, which has supported the existence of a minimum core of obligations regarding rights. UN CESCR, *General Comment No. 3: The Nature of States Parties' Obligations (Article 2, Para. 1, of the Covenant)*, 14 December 1990, E/1991/23; UN CESCR, *General Comment No. 14*: The Right to the Highest Attainable Standard of Health (Article 12), 11 August 2000, E/C.12/2000/4. Otherwise, the criteria can be based on a standard of reasonableness; see, for example, the case *Minister of Health* v. *Treatment Action Campaign*, where the Constitutional Court of South Africa awarded GNRs based on a standard of reasonableness, *Minister of Health* v. *Treatment Action Campaign* (TAC) (2002) 5 SA 721 (CC), par. 135. Lastly, they can be grounded on proportionality concerns. Antkowiak argues that if remedies do not respect certain criteria, they will not be implemented. Antkowiak, 'Remedial Approaches to Human Rights Violations', p. 394.

[223] Teitel refers to this risk. Teitel, 'Transitional Justice and Judicial Activism'; Ferstman, 'Reparation as Prevention', 8.

[224] Zegveld, *Accountability of Armed Opposition Groups in International Law*, 222.

[225] It is to be noted that UN Rule of Law Tools drafted in 2006 dealt only with prosecutions, truth commissions, vetting, consultations, reparations programmes and amnesty. Office of the United Nations High Commissioner for Human Rights, Rule of Law Tools for Post-Conflict States (United Nations, 2006).

Human Rights Council on transitional justice. The terminology used, which allocates to GNRs their own space, is indicative of a distinct conceptualization of this specific field. Similarly, the preparatory works of both the Basic and the Impunity Principles evidence that measures of non-repetition, while initially conceived narrowly, by the time evolved to a self-standing category, connected by their forward-looking, preventive character.[226] In their final version, both sets of Principles understand GNRs' scope as being broader than security and justice sector reform, but also broader than individual violations taking place during conflict or repression.[227]

All those different traits have gained GNRs prominence, at least in theory,[228] and especially so for the topic of corporate accountability. First, they signal that engaging with corporate violations would not be odd, to the extent that their acts could affect the non-repetition outcome.[229] In parallel, by shifting away from a purely remedial purpose, due to their preventive aim and their autonomization, GNRs become more akin to positive obligations to ensure and protect rights.[230] It has been observed that GNRs differ from positive obligations due to the former's ties to a prior violation.[231] Yet this tie tends to fade because of the 'positive reinforcement' of the performance of the right, that GNRs are called to play.[232] The rapprochement of GNRs with positive

226 Roht-Arriaza describes this evolution of GNRs. She mentions that the Basic Principles refer to 'preventing and monitoring social conflicts', a phrase which arguably expands the scope of GNRs to cover the root causes of the conflict. The Impunity Principles refer to codes of conduct, based on international standards, by private economic enterprises and media as well as the state, broadening the universe of potential actors. See Roht-Arriaza, 'Measures of Non-Repetition in Transitional Justice'.

227 Notably the same autonomization of GNRs has taken place in academia. While in 2000 Ruti Teitel classified under GNRs purges, lustration, security sector reform and the like, today academic scholarship analyses a vast array of measures under the heading of GNRs.

228 Lessard, 'Preventive Reparations at a Crossroads'.

229 See Pietropaoli concurring. Pietropaoli, *Business, Human Rights and Transitional Justice*, p. 209 *et seq.*

230 According to Shelton, it may be difficult to distinguish GNRs from other forms of reparation, particularly satisfaction. Shelton, *Remedies in International Human Rights Law*, p. 279. Of further interest is how to distinguish GNRs from positive state obligations to prevent violations in general. See Roht-Arriaza, 'Measures of Non-Repetition in Transitional Justice'.

231 Roht-Arriaza, 'Measures of Non-Repetition in Transitional Justice'.

232 HRC, Report of the Special Rapporteur on the promotion of truth, justice, reparation and guarantees of non-recurrence, Pablo De Greiff, A/HRC/30/42, 7 September 2015; see also 'ILC Articles', Article 30.

obligations can signal, as well, a window of opportunity for the inclusion of corporations in the transitional process, given than positive obligations already reach non-state violators.[233] Fitting corporate accountability under the prevention heading can thus be less controversial than under the remedy heading. In addition, the close affinity of GNRs to positive obligations (evidenced by their consolidation and autonomization as a measure of transitional justice) and their preventive nature create nuances in their secondary status. As SRSG Ruggie noted, the status of GNRs is not easily distinguishable. They are intimately related to the state obligation to prevent violations and so the primary obligation to prevent overlaps with the secondary obligation to guarantee non-repetition where a violation has occurred.[234] In turn, those nuances distance further GNRs from the strict requirements of the right to remedy,[235] that have so far hindered the inclusion of corporate and other third-party malefactors.

Furthermore, those attributes enable GNRs to tackle generalized patterns of corporate abuses and impunity, as they have shifted away from isolated individual violations to navigating overarching dynamics of abuse on a more extensive scale. Accordingly, it would not be unreasonable for a transitional state, ravaged by systemic corporate abuse, to implement GNRs in the form of laws regarding corporate accountability. This can be corporate criminal liability rules for a state that has not yet adopted this kind of rules and thus inclusion of corporations in the justice mechanisms of TJ. It can also translate into their inclusion in the reparation and truth measures, which have been created in order for atrocities not to happen again. Beyond specific pronouncements, GNRs can lead to an obligation of the state to overall include corporations in the transitional process. At the same time, the fact that GNRs against corporate malfeasance will be triggered by corporate violations means that even if in an indirect fashion, they will still be linked to violations.[236]

233 For an analysis, see Bakker, 'Duties to Prevent, Investigate and Redress Human Right Violations by Private Military and Security Companies', p. 130.

234 HRC, Report of the Special Representative of the Secretary-General on the issue of human rights and transnational corporations and other business enterprises, John Ruggie, Addendum, State obligations to provide access to remedy for human rights abuses by third parties, including business: an overview of international and regional provisions, commentary and decisions, A/HRC/11/13/Add.1, 15 May 2009, fn. 89.

235 See also the analogies with the right to accountability as a primary right. Teitel, 'Transitional Justice and Judicial Activism'.

236 In that respect, note Roht-Arriaza's fears that GNRs might become overpromising and vague, similarly, to generalized transformative pronouncements. Roht-Arriaza, 'Measures of Non-Repetition in Transitional Justice', p. 5.

Despite the positive developments in the field of GNRs and their repercussions for corporate accountability, a question lingers as to whether transitional states will respect corporate regulation in the form of GNRs. This can be answered in the positive considering that those GNRs would be related to widespread corporate abuses. But also, the increasing acceptance of corporate accountability in various jurisdictions will presumably demotivate states from breaching an obligation to guarantee non-repetition. According to Henkin's formulation of a cost-benefit analysis for compliance to international legal rules, amidst an international scene where corporate accountability is rising in prominence, there is no advantage for states to diverge from that rule.[237] Also, the increasing acceptability of corporate accountability paves the way for an obligation to provide GNRs in relation to corporations to be perceived as legitimate and thus to be complied with.[238] One could also argue that corporate accountability, via either criminal or civil law, is a concept that emerged out of domestic procedures[239] and thus is sufficiently internalized, something that creates yet another reason for international compliance.

To conclude, even in their narrowest application, GNRs are broader than any other reparative measure. Thus, they can serve for an examination of the root causes of conflict and consequently as a Trojan horse that would insert corporations in the transitional justice discussion and achieve remedy for the existing victims but also regulation of their activities, averting future abuses.

[237] L. Henkin, *How Nations Behave* (Columbia University Press, 1979), p. 49.

[238] T. Franck, *The Power of Legitimacy Among Nations* (Oxford University Press, 1990), p. 25.

[239] Levit, 'Bottom-Up International Law-Making'.

6

Assessing Diverse National Experiences

6.1 Court Reparations: Victims' Herculean Efforts Meeting Barriers

Remedies and reparations can be claimed before civil courts of the transitional or a foreign state, given that civil remedies encompass mechanisms and processes that can lead to the same types of reparations as the ones provided by international human rights law. States themselves have referred to civil remedies as enabling them to fulfil their obligation to protect human rights from abuse.[1] Through civil liability, victims can achieve remedy and reparation for the violations suffered and legal accountability of the perpetrator. Determining whether civil cases against corporations form part of transitional justice can be a complex task. Many of them, like the ones in South Africa, were brought by victims and thus did not form part of a concerted governmental plan but still pertain to a bottom-up approach to transition.[2] From the other hand, some of those cases were brought against corporations which were previously named in TRC reports or as a result of the TRC's 'unfinished business',[3] proving a certain continuity of TJ measures.

Reparation involving corporations can also be achieved in jurisdictions that allow victims to introduce civil claims in the criminal process, the so-called *partie civile*,[4] either in the transitioning forum or in a foreign jurisdiction. Recently a criminal complaint was filed in Austria, which allows *partie civile* claims by Syrian torture survivors against senior

[1] See, for example, Peru's report to the Committee Against Torture (CAT/C/20/Add.6, 12 August 1998, par. 86); Denmark's report to the HRC (HRI/CORE/1/Add.58, par. 60); France's report to the HRC (CCPR/C/76/Add.7, par. 35); and Ireland's report to the Committee on the Elimination of All Forms of Discrimination Against Women (CEDAW/C/IRL/4–5) (2003).

[2] Lundy and McGovern, 'Whose Justice?', at 273, 276–277.

[3] Gerhart et al., 'Unfinished Business', p. 157.

[4] C. Stahn and G. Sluiter (eds.), *The Emerging Practice of the International Criminal Court* (Brill, Nijhoff, 2008), p. 681.

officials in the Assad government.[5] The added value of those cases is the wide international publicity, which can bring a form of relief or recognition to the victims or exercise leverage for effective domestic redress. Furthermore, constitutional and domestic human rights law can provide a cause of action for remedies and reparations against state entities or corporate actors.[6] However, the reparation that will be afforded through those actions is usually symbolic, confined to declaratory relief.

Pursuing litigation allows the victim to regain a sense of control and mastery and an overall agency over his life, which was lost with the violation.[7] It also brings the benefit of strictly defined processes and due process guarantees. Due to the individualized character of legal regulation, court proceedings can lead to decisions tailored to the specific situation, granting reparations proportionate to the harm. Therefore, judicial reparations appear to effectively address the individualized needs of victims, aligning with the highly sought-after victim-centred approach in transitional justice. The pursuit of justice against corporate wrongdoers during transitional periods extends these benefits to corporate victims. Nevertheless, these undertakings are fraught with substantial legal and policy challenges. It is the example of Colombia that stands out, in the positive side, mostly for having more coordinated transitional mechanisms, which take corporate accountability into account.[8] This is evident in the land restitution programme, analysed in Chapter 7. In addition, under the Comprehensive System in the areas of truth, justice and reparation, third parties, including businesspersons, are allowed to voluntarily present themselves before the JEP and admit their illegal actions during the conflict, which might lead to them providing

[5] European Centre for Constitutional and Human Rights, The path to justice leads through Europe – e.g., Austria, Criminal Complaint by Torture Survivors Leads to Investigations against Syrian Intelligence Officials, available at www.ecchr.eu/en/case/the-path-to-justice-leads-through-europe-eg-austria/.

[6] This can be generally against corporations, like Argentina, Portugal, Brazil, Ireland, Nigeria, or limited to cases of corporations exercising public function, like in India, New Zealand and the UK. See International Commission of Jurists, Report of the ICJ Expert Legal Panel on Corporate Complicity in International Crimes: Corporate Complicity & Legal Accountability, Volume 3 Civil Remedies, p. 8.

[7] D. Summerfield, 'Raising the Dead: War, Reparation and the Politics of Memory' (1995) 311 *British Medical Journal*, at 495–497; S. Robins, *Families of the Missing: A Test for Contemporary Approaches to Transitional Justice* (Routledge, 2013), p. 162; The Redress Trust, 'Torture Survivors' Perceptions'.

[8] For an account of the Colombian transitional justice efforts, see Sánchez et al. *Roles and Responsibilities of the Private Sector in Transitional Justice*, p. 56 *et seq*.

reparations, in addition to imprisonment. In many other cases, the limited availability of coordinated reparation mechanisms led victims to independently pursue reparations through their domestic civil courts, but their path to domestic justice is stalled by a wide array of reasons.[9]

To name just a few, in view of the decreased operability of transitional states' institutions, the expediency of court proceedings becomes questionable. Transitional states, usually ill equipped to address a burgeoning number of claims, take a substantial amount of time to adjudicate cases related to conflict or repression. In Argentina, for example, almost forty years after the transition, cases are still pending. Weaknesses of the judicial system are worsened by rife corruption[10] and poor fair trial guarantees.[11] Beyond those, legal hurdles also stymie successful outcomes. In the case against *Techint SA*, in Argentina, although the company's involvement to a worker's disappearance was qualified as crime against humanity, his daughter was denied compensation due to time prescription.[12] In the *Oguru* v. *Shell* case, the structure of the corporate group blocked the process, as the Dutch court applying Nigerian tort law vouched in favour of the parent company's limited liability.[13] In Colombia, threats, violence and intimidation of victims seeking land restitution is omnipresent, on top of increased corporate lobbying and

[9] See generally Zerk, 'Corporate Liability'; W. S. Dodge, 'Business and Human Rights Litigation in U.S. Courts Before and After Kiobel', in D. Baumann-Pauly and J. Nolan (eds.), *Business and Human Rights: From Principles to Practice* (Routledge, 2016); G. Skinner, R. McCorquodale and O. De Schutter, *The Third Pillar: Access to Judicial Remedies for Human Rights Violations by Transnational Business* (International Corporate Accountability Roundtable, 2013); Amnesty International, Injustice Incorporated (2014), p. 136.

[10] Oxford Pro Bono Publico, Obstacles to Justice and Redress for Victims of Corporate Human Rights Abuse: A Comparative Submission Prepared for Professor John Ruggie, 3 November 2008; M. Taylor, R. Thompson and A. Ramasastry, *Overcoming Obstacles to Justice: Improving Access to Judicial Remedies for Business Involvement in Grave Human Rights Abuses* (Fafo, 2010).

[11] See, for example, the Congolese case against Anvil Mining employees, which was condemned by the UN for disrespecting due process guarantees. Global Witness, RAID, ACIDH, 'The Kilwa Trial: a denial of justice', 17 July 2007, available at https://cdn2.globalwitness.org/archive/files/pdfs/kilwa_chron_en_170707.pdf.

[12] Supreme Court of Justice of the Nation, Ingenieros, María Gimena c. Techint Sociedad Anónima Compañía Técnica Internacional s/ accidente – ley especial (9 May 2019).

[13] Judgment of the District Court of The Hague of 30 January 2013 (Oguru/Shell), ECLI:NL:RBDHA:2013: BY9850. Note that the judgment was reversed on appeal. See C. van Dam, 'Breakthrough in Parent Company Liability: Three Shell Defeats, the End of an Era and New Paradigms' (2021) 18 *European Company and Financial Law Review* 5.

power.[14] On top of those, one should not forget that transitioning states frequently sideline the inclusion of corporations in transitional efforts, aiming to avoid risking their presumed contributions to the state's economic development, an issue that will be further analysed in Chapter 8.[15]

An equally difficult bet is resource to foreign courts. Assuming that victims have the necessary legal and financial support to reach a foreign jurisdiction, overpassing jurisdictional barriers is usually arduous. The relatively recent *Kiobel* decision was the final stroke in what concerns ATCA jurisprudence, often used to tackle cases of corporate complicity with violent or repressive regimes.[16] In this case, Nigerian plaintiffs sued Shell company before US courts alleging that members of the Shell group of companies were complicit in torture, extrajudicial killing, arbitrary detention and other violations by the Nigerian government. The court held that the claims do not touch and concern US territory with sufficient force to displace the presumption against extraterritorial application.[17] Similarly, in *Jesner*, it was decided that foreign corporations cannot be sued under the ATCA.[18] The presumption against extraterritoriality was also upheld in the *Daimler* lawsuit, where Argentinian plaintiffs sued Daimler Chrysler AG, on the grounds that its subsidiary Mercedes Benz Argentina collaborated with the Argentinian security forces to kidnap, detain, torture and kill the plaintiffs or their relatives during the junta. The case was dismissed in 2014 due to lack of sufficient ties with the US.[19] In the South African Apartheid litigation, the claims of corporate complicity to Apartheid were also dismissed on the same basis.[20] Further, the separate legal personalities of corporations[21] and the subsequent

[14] Wesche, 'Business Actors and Land Restitution in the Colombian Transition'.

[15] I. Pietropaoli, 'Corporate Accountability and Transitional Justice in Myanmar', Justice Info, 7 March 2016.

[16] United States Congress, 28 U.S. Code Part IV Chapter 85 § 1350. Under the ATCA, the United States has jurisdiction for civil actions brought by aliens for torts, committed in violation of the law of nations or treaties of the United States. A violation of the law of nations is the one which is contrary to a norm of customary international law. *Sosa* v. *Alvarez-Machain* 542 U.S. 692, 734–737 (2004). Even though ATCA is used in tort law cases, it utilizes criminal law standards, and it is one of the main ways of holding companies accountable, albeit increasingly being restricted.

[17] *Kiobel* v. *Royal Dutch Petroleum Co.*, 133 S. Ct. 1659, 1665 (2013), p. 1669.

[18] *Jesner* v. *Arab Bank*, PLC, 584 U.S. (2018).

[19] *Daimler AG* v. *Bauman*, 571 U.S. 117 (2014).

[20] Note that this was not the case for all the lawsuits that were combined in this litigation. *South African Apartheid Litig.*, 617 F. Supp. 2d 228 (S.D.N.Y. 2009).

[21] Joseph, *Corporations and Transnational Human Rights Litigation*, p. 129.

limited liability[22] have been used to insulate corporations from responsibility, as was the case with the tragedy in Bhopal.[23] In the *Oguru* v. *Shell* case, mentioned earlier, the Dutch court held that parent companies have no obligation to prevent their subsidiaries from inflicting damage on others through their business operations.[24]

The doctrine of *forum non conveniens* has also posed challenges to victims of corporate abuse.[25] It has stymied proceedings in the US,[26] and also in Canada. In 2010, Congolese plaintiffs filed a class action against Anvil Mining, for its alleged involvement in a 2004 massacre in Kilwa, the Democratic Republic of Congo, in complicity with the local army. While Anvil acknowledged providing supplies to the army, it argued that the DRC was a more appropriate forum, where the harm occurred, or Australia, where the company's main office is located. Notably, the plaintiffs had already tried the Congolese courts, where their case was conducted in dubious human rights standards, and ultimately failed, as well as Australia, where the case was not pursued by the authorities.[27] While initially the Canadian court accepted to hear the case and found that if it rejected jurisdiction, 'no possibility would exist for the victims to be heard by civil justice',[28] that decision was later overturned. The Court of Appeal reasoned that – among others – the plaintiffs had not proved the impossibility of accessing justice in another jurisdiction.[29] Similarly, in 2008, Palestinian landowners and a Palestinian town sued two Canadian companies before Canadian courts, alleging that their involvement in construction works for illegal settlements entails their complicity in war crimes. The Superior Court of Québec dismissed the claim, stating that the Israeli High Court of Justice would be a more suitable place to argue this case, regrettably noting that 'a great deal of

22 Skinner, 'Rethinking Limited Liability'.

23 In re *Union Carbide Corp. Gas Plant Disaster*, 809 F.2d 195 (2d Cir. 1987).

24 Judgment of the District Court of The Hague of 30 January 2013 (Oguru/Shell), ECLI:NL:RBDHA:2013: BY9850.

25 ICJ Report, Vol. 3, p. 49.

26 The challenge was dismissed in the *Licea* v. *Curaçao Drydock Co., Inc.*, 584 F. Supp. 2d 1355 (S.D. Fla. 2008), but was accepted in *Gulf Oil Corp.* v. *Gilbert*, 330 U.S. 501 (1947); *Aguinda* v. *Texaco, Inc.*, 303 F.3d 470 (2d Cir. 2002).

27 Amnesty International, Injustice Incorporated (2014), p. 131.

28 *Association Canadienne Contre L' Impunite* v. *Anvil Mining Limited* [2011] J.Q. No. 4382, 2011 QCCS 1966 (decision of 27 April 2011), par. 39.

29 *Anvil Mining Ltd.* v. *Association Canadienne Contre L' Impunite* [2012] J.Q. No. 368, 2012 QCCA 117 (decision of 24 January 2012), par. 103.

imagination [is needed] to claim that the action has a serious connection with Quebec'.[30]

Even in successful cases, the enforcement process can present significant difficulties.[31] Victims of human rights abuses, during the Marcos dictatorship in the Philippines, filed ATCA lawsuits initially against Marcos himself, who was replaced by his estate after his death.[32] The court decided in favour of the victims and awarded millions in damages. When they tried to go after Marcos' assets, they sought an injunction on their disposition. At that point, Swiss banks were added in the lawsuit. The plaintiffs alleged that those banks were responsible because they plundered the national treasury, by helping Marcos conceal his wealth and essentially acted as agents of the regime. Although the court held that the banks were in fact agents of the regime,[33] the plaintiffs have been unable to access the funds, in all three countries involved. The Swiss accounts were frozen by a request from the Philippine government in 1986, when the dictator fled the country, and therefore were inaccessible. Switzerland eventually returned the frozen assets to the Philippines, but domestic courts continuously rule against the recovery of Marcos' assets.[34] Lastly, the confiscation of assets by the American branches of Swiss banks was rejected multiple times, on different procedural grounds related to the parent–subsidiary relationship.[35] Additional concerns may revolve around determining liability within the supply chain,[36] selecting the applicable legal framework,[37] dealing with information gaps, grappling with corporate influence within the state,[38] collecting evidence,[39]

30 *Yassin c. Green Park International Inc.*, 2010 QCCA 1455 (CanLII), par. 86.

31 On the difficulties in the enforcement of remedies, see Roht-Arriaza, 'Reparations Decisions and Dilemmas', 166.

32 *Estate of Ferdinand Marcos Human Rights Litigation*, 94 F.3d 539, 542 (9th Cir. 1996).

33 See *Hilao* v. *Estate of Marcos*, 95 F.3d 848, 855 (9th Cir. 1996).

34 Philippine court dismisses case seeking $3.9 billion of Marcos wealth, Reuters, 16 December 2019.

35 Ramasastry, 'Secrets and Lies?'.

36 J. Nolan, 'Human Rights and Global Corporate Supply Chains: Is Effective Supply Chain Accountability Possible?', in S. Deva and D. Bilchitz (eds.), *Building a Treaty on Business and Human Rights: Context and Contours* (Cambridge University Press, 2017), pp. 238–265.

37 Zerk, 'Corporate Liability', p. 50.

38 For an elaborate account of those problems and case studies, see Amnesty International, Injustice Incorporated (2014), p. 136.

39 For example, the Sinaltrainal et al. v. Coca Cola case was dismissed because the court held that the plaintiffs' evidence did not suffice to allege war crimes under international law. *Sinaltrainal et al.* v. *Coca Cola Company et al.*, No. 06-15851, (US District Court, 2009).

the cost of bringing transnational litigation and the enforcement of remedies,[40] the 'non-justiciable political question',[41] or state immunity when public corporations are involved.[42]

To the aforementioned challenges, one should add state opposition to litigation. The South African example illustrates how the state itself dealt a demoralizing blow to the efforts of victims. It is indeed widely acknowledged that businesses played a crucial role in supporting the Apartheid regime.[43] Evidence indicates that some of those businesses not only adopted discriminatory policies internally but also lent a hand in shaping the state's apartheid policies.[44] The involvement of banks, particularly major Western ones, was documented by the UN Special Committee against Apartheid,[45] and even the then US President Reagan was mobilized to ban American companies from conducting business with the South African regime.[46]

Frustrated with the lack of corporate reparations and the TRC's 'unfinished business',[47] victims resorted to US courts. In 2002, an ATCA complaint was filed by the Khulumani Support Group against twenty-three multinational corporations, in oil, armaments, banking, transportation, technology and mining industries, for aiding or participating in the violations of international law by the apartheid regime.[48] In 2003, another lawsuit was filed against Anglo-American and its diamond subsidiary De Beers.[49] The first lawsuit was rejected, after

[40] Roht-Arriaza, 'Reparations Decisions and Dilemmas', p. 166.

[41] For example, the USA case against Chiquita was dismissed on the basis of foreign policy implications. See Sections 3.1.5 and 3.3.2 of this book. Also, the case against Caterpillar before the US courts for complicity in war crimes was dismissed due to concerns that it concerns a foreign policy issue. See Section 3.1.5 on complicity in Part II of this book. See also *Cynthia Corrie et al.* v. *Caterpillar Inc.*, US Court of Appeals for the Ninth Circuit, United States, CV-05-05192-FDB, 17 September 2007.

[42] Zerk, 'Corporate Liability', p. 50.

[43] J. Barnard-Naudé, 'For Justice and Reconciliation to Come: The TRC Archive, Big Business and the Demand for Material Reparations', in F. Du Bois and A. Pedain (eds.), *Justice and Reconciliation in Post-Apartheid South Africa* (Cambridge University Press, 2009), pp. 181–182.

[44] Bond and Sharife, 'Apartheid Reparations and the Contestation of Corporate Power in Africa', at 115–125.

[45] Report of the Special UN Special Committee against Apartheid, General Assembly Official record, thirty-sixth session, Supplement No. 22 (A/36/22), 1981.

[46] Executive Order 12532, Prohibiting Trade and Certain Other Transactions Involving South Africa, 9 September 1985.

[47] Gerhart et al., 'Unfinished Business', p. 157.

[48] Abrahams, 'Lessons from the South African Experience', pp. 161–162.

[49] Diamond industry hit by £3 billion suit, *The Scotsman*, 5 April 2003.

almost ten years of litigation, mainly due to the *Kiobel* precedent.[50] The second was also dismissed in 2004. It was only with General Motors that a settlement was reached.[51] The plaintiffs' claims aligned with the conclusions of the TRC, which, although relatively restrained in its recommendations, had been vocal on how businesses benefited during the apartheid, and the need to commit the sector to a 'focused programme of reparation'.[52]

Throughout their efforts, victims encountered a deliberate and coordinated campaign by the government to undermine and nullify them.[53] President Mbeki openly disapproved the lawsuits, viewing them as damaging governmental policy on reparations.[54] This stance mirrored his previous criticism of the TRC, as attention seeking,[55] and his disregard for its recommendations, only to direct reparation funds to developmental purposes instead of victims' compensation.[56] Even more vigorous was the stance of Penuell Maduna, former Justice Minister and member of Mbeki's cabinet. He vehemently opposed litigation, contending that transitional justice should be the responsibility of the government, not foreign courts. He cited concerns about judicial imperialism and erosion of the people's sovereign rights.[57] The same was also submitted by his successor, Brigitte Mabandla, and interestingly also by the corporations' Joint Memorandum.[58] Those would, of course, be fair arguments, were Maduna not to be, subsequently, hired by the corporations as their lawyer.

Maduna's Declaration on the Apartheid Litigation, where he sets forth the government's view, moved in several axes. Initially, he unequivocally

50 In 'Re South African Apartheid Litigation'. For an analysis of the case, see Michalowski, 'No Complicity Liability for Funding', at 451.

51 Gubbay, 'Towards Making Blood Money Visible'.

52 TRC Report, Vol. 6, Section 2, chapter 5, par. 14, pp. 143–144.

53 Note also that politicians of previous governments were against the litigation. See L. Duke, 'The Price of Apartheid', *Washington Post*, 3 December 2002.

54 Abrahams, 'Lessons from the South African Experience', p. 168.

55 M. Michael, 'Moment of Truth. South Africa's Truth and Reconciliation Commission Closes Its Doors', Worldpress.org, 2 May 2003.

56 Sandoval and Surfleet, 'Corporations and Redress in Transitional Justice Processes', pp. 101–102.

57 Ministry of Justice and Constitutional Development, Republic of South Africa, 'Declaration by Justice Minister Penuell Maduna on Apartheid Litigation in the United States', 11 July 2003, available at www.gov.za/sites/default/files/gcis_document/201409/apartheid1.pdf.

58 Morrisson and Foerster, 'Memorandum of Law in Support of Defendants Joint Motion to Dismiss', 8 December 2008.

exonerated corporations from any responsibility, stating that 'it is the successor government and, as such, bears primary responsibility for the rehabilitation and improvement of the lives of the people whom the claimants claim to represent'.[59] He portrayed the litigation as an attempt to undermine sovereign democratic rights, one that not only encroached on domestic matters but also threatened to disrupt reconciliation efforts.[60] A significant part of the Declaration is dedicated in explaining why the lawsuit was essentially redundant, given that the government had implemented numerous measures for 'the reconstruction and development of the South African economy, accordingly had and continues to have as its central plank the fundamental transformation of South African society'. He went on to enumerate measures for the rehabilitation of those previously disadvantaged, including education, land tenure, pensions and measures against racial inequality. He argued that in any case, reparations had already been adequately addressed by the TRC,[61] for the TRC to rebut that it did not engage with those corporations and that civil law processes did not undermine its work.[62] Finally, he thoroughly assessed the 'meaningful contribution' made by business entities to the South African development, emphasizing their role in 'human capacity building and employment creation' as well as their significant investments. He strongly underscored that the pursuit of litigation has the potential to deter foreign investment, thereby posing substantial risk to the vital goal of advancing towards a more prosperous economic state.[63]

6.1.1 *Finding Hope: Achievements and Insights*

Despite the various challenges discussed earlier, both in domestic transitional as well as foreign settings, there have been positive developments that offer valuable tools and provide insights for transitional justice and its intersection with corporate accountability. The aim of this part is not to establish a hierarchy, determining the superiority of domestic or foreign litigation or vice versa, as this is context dependent. Rather, the

59 Maduna Declaration, par. 6.
60 Ibid., par. 10–13.
61 Ibid., par. 10.
62 Bond and Sharife, 'Apartheid Reparations and the Contestation of Corporate Power in Africa', p. 120.
63 Maduna Declaration, par. 12.

objective is to elucidate the promising aspects of both forms of litigation and draw conclusions on potential lessons learnt.

As a springboard, the example of Colombia is forging new pathways, at least in theoretical terms, its own deficits and criticism notwithstanding.[64] Its Comprehensive System in the areas of truth, justice and reparation allowed third parties, including businesspersons, to voluntarily present themselves before the JEP and admit their illegal actions during the conflict. In case of conviction, on top of imprisonment, they might be asked to provide reparations. The case of Jaime Blanco Maya, former contractor of Drummond, attracted attention. He submitted himself to the JEP, promising to offer truth, reparations and guarantees of no repetition, in order to avoid his previous conviction for the murder of trade unionists.[65] He committed to provide reparations consisting of two conferences in El Paso and Chiriguaná, municipalities in which the Loma Mine, operated by Drummond, is located. Experts in International Humanitarian Law were to attend those pardon activities. He, also, committed to produce two publications seeking pardon in *El Pilón*, the most important newspaper in the province, and build a monument in the area to honour the victims.[66] Those different public activities, with a notable aspect of truth, display the seminal contribution of truth-telling to reparations, often pinpointed in literature,[67] and corroborate the interconnected character of transitional measures,[68] particularly notable in Colombia, where collective memory of the conflict is constructed by all the different mechanisms contributing their own kind of truth.[69]

In addition, individual litigation endeavours brought by victims before transitional fora have, sometimes, yielded positive outcomes, in the overall quest for corporate reparations, and authors note their increased

[64] For an account of the Colombian transitional justice efforts, see Sánchez et al., *Roles and Responsibilities of the Private Sector in Transitional Justice*, p. 56 *et seq.*

[65] 'JEP acepta a Blanco Maya para hablar de asesinato de sindicalistas', El Tiempo, 3 December 2019.

[66] J. Escobar Moreno, 'The Drummond Case Reaches the Special Jurisdiction for Peace', Colombia Support, 18 December 2019.

[67] M. U. Walker, 'Truth Telling as Reparations' (2010) 41 *Metaphilosophy* 4, pp. 525–545; M. Lawry-White, 'The Reparative Effect of Truth Seeking in Transitional Justice' (2015) 64 *The International and Comparative Law Quarterly* 1, pp. 141–177.

[68] On truth mechanisms, see Part IV, Chapter 8, of this book.

[69] L. C. Piedrahíta, 'The Right to Truth in Colombia's Comprehensive System of Truth, Justice, Reparation, and Non-Repetition. A Direct Approach to the Intrinsic Relationship between Its Mechanisms and Objectives' (2022) 18 *Nuevo Derecho* 31, pp. 1–15.

significance in comparison to foreign litigation.[70] In Germany, Norbert Wollheim, former slave labourer at the Auschwitz, sued his corporate owner IG Farben and was granted reparation by the company in 1953.[71] More importantly, pressure from this case led IG Farben to agree with the 'Conference on Jewish Material Claims against Germany' regarding the establishment and management of a reparation fund.[72] Under that scheme, the company paid large amounts of compensation to its former forced labourers.[73] Several other large German businesses followed suit, among which were Krupp, AEG, Siemens, Rheinmetall and Daimler-Benz.[74] Similarly, a civil lawsuit that was filed in Brazil by former employees of Volkswagen, alleging arrest and torture in its factory premises,[75] led the company to negotiate a reparation plan with the government.[76] In Argentina, the wife of a worker who disappeared by the premises of Siderca steel company, during the dictatorship, received compensation for worker safety law violations,[77] and the son of another disappeared victim sued Citibank and the Bank of America for providing loans to the regime while knowing its abuses.[78] The banks rejected the mediation offered, and the case is reportedly ongoing.[79]

[70] Payne et al. conclude that domestic litigation is more promising than foreign litigation; see Payne et al., *Archimedes' Lever*, p. 112.

[71] *Wollheim* v. *IG Farben*, available at www.wollheim-memorial.de/en/das_verfahren_wollheim_gegen_ig_farben.

[72] The Claims Conference was founded in 1951 and represented a coalition of Jewish organizations, seeking compensation agreements with the German government and German corporations. Wollheim Memorial, 'Conference on Jewish Material Claims Against Germany', available at www.wollheim-memorial.de/en/conference_on_jewish_material_claims_againt_germany.

[73] Note, however, that the government enforced a time limit for claims so that Farben would be absolved from subsequent lawsuits. Available at www.wollheim-memorial.de/en/das_verfahren_wollheim_gegen_ig_farben; www.wollheim-memorial.de/en/ vergleichs verhandlungen_en.

[74] Sandt and Moor, 'Peace, Everyone's Business!', p. 72.

[75] 'Brazil: Torture Lawsuit Against VW', Deutsche Welle, 2 November 2015, available at www.dw.com/en/brazil-torture-lawsuit-against-vw/a-18731165.

[76] Sandt and Moor, 'Peace, Everyone's Business!', p. 82.

[77] Payne et al., *Archimedes' Lever*, p. 237.

[78] For banks' liability, see J. P. Bohoslavsky, 'Another Brick in the Uruguayan Transition: Financial Complicity', in S. Michalowski (ed.), *Corporate Accountability in the Context of Transitional Justice* (Routledge, 2013), p. 205.

[79] L. Payne and G. Pereira, 'Accountability for Corporate Complicity in Human Rights Violations: Argentina's Transitional Justice Innovation?', in H. Verbitsky and J. Bohoslavsky (eds.), *The Economic Accomplices to the Argentine Dictatorship: Outstanding Debts* (Cambridge University Press, 2015), pp. 29–44.

Within the diversity of various transitional experiences, shaped by the particularities of each context, there are valuable insights to be gleaned regarding what made some domestic examples to bear fruits, even if limited. An initial observation concerns the growing reliance of victims on domestic litigation, as it has yielded better outcomes compared to cases before foreign courts, making domestic legal avenues a seemingly more viable option.[80] A key contributor to the success of the domestic cases was the use of innovative strategies, like the use of worker safety law at the Siderca case mentioned previously, as well as novel legal arguments based on labour law, slave labour or money-laundering regulations,[81] instead of relying on traditional tort law claims to achieve compensation.[82] Importantly, the infusion of international human rights law into domestic legislation and the foregrounding of arguments blending international and national law have also been instrumental.[83]

Equally important for achieving positive outcomes domestically seems to have been, according to various authors, the role of civil society. Research shows that strong and decisive civil society, supported by transnational activist networks, can exert the necessary pressure and effective advocacy, in favour of justice for victims of corporate abuse.[84] The dynamic of this sort of pressure has been, at the time of this writing, evidenced in the conflicts of Palestine and Ukraine. Domestic, regional and international non-governmental organizations have, from the very beginning of those conflicts, pointed to corporate involvement. Although the conflicts are still ongoing at the time of writing and no court reparations have been allocated, yet, the discussion on corporate reparations has already started.[85] In Latin America, where most successful cases are observed, both civil society advocacy and novel legal strategies were used. Strong civil society, trade unions and various communities persisted in demanding corporate accountability, while plaintiffs did not

[80] Payne et al., *Archimedes' Lever*, pp. 112, 269.

[81] Sandt and Moor, 'Peace, Everyone's Business!', p. 49 *et seq.*

[82] G. Pereira, L. Payne and L. Bermúdez, 'Justice from Below: Corporate Accountability in Argentina' (2022) 26 *The International Journal of Human Rights* 8, pp. 1418–1454.

[83] See Section 2.3.2 of this book.

[84] Payne et al., *Archimedes' Lever*, pp. 229, 261.

[85] See, for example, L. Moffett, 'Reparation Options for the War in Ukraine', Queen's University Belfast, November 2022, available at https://reparations.qub.ac.uk/assets/uploads/Reparation-Options-for-the-War-in-Ukraine-Moffett.pdf.

limit their arguments in traditional tort law vindications but foregrounded diverse and innovative legal arguments.[86]

Drawing broader conclusions, the multiplicity of domestic cases demonstrates that the quest for corporate accountability is beginning to solidly form, shape and strengthen with its roots in the Global South.[87] This is a testament to the significance of localized experience, not only for transitional justice standards but more specifically for the intersection of corporate accountability with transitional justice. Domestic law and experiences have distinct value for the development of a more responsive transitional justice example, as they are better vested to identify and address the root causes of injustice. In what concerns corporate accountability, domestic law becomes especially significant given the absence of an international framework. Similarly, their intersection adopts a distinctly bottom-up approach, through domestic law, sharply contrasting with the predominantly top-down, Northern-led models in these fields.[88] In turn, those domestically rooted experiences have implications for the evolution of the global transitional landscape, in consolidating it towards a more context-specific direction and in setting the stage for the creation of international norms that mirror that direction. What is more, those examples are seminal in paving the way for specific expectations in transitional settings. The greater the number of cases seeking compensation from corporations for pre-transition abuses, the more likely this practice will become replicated, anticipated and normalized,[89] potentially inspiring similar actions in other parts of the world.

In what concerns resource to foreign courts, only a handful of cases turned favourably for the victims, mainly when settled. One such case is the one brought by the Ogoni people of Nigeria against Shell for collaborating with the authoritarian regime's military and police in the murder of political activists.[90] The allegations included summary execution, crimes against humanity, torture, inhuman treatment and arbitrary arrest and

[86] Payne et al., *Archimedes' Lever*, p. 267.

[87] L. Payne, Bernal-Bermúdez, L. and Pereira, G. (eds.), *Economic Actors and the Limits of Transitional Justice: Truth and Justice for Business Complicity in Human Rights Violations* (Oxford University Press, 2022).

[88] J. Gutiérrez Martínez and B. Flores Aricò, 'On the Path to Corporate Accountability: The Global South and the New European Due Diligence Law, Dejusticia', 13 August 2024, available at www.dejusticia.org/en/on-the-path-to-corporate-accountability-the-global-south-and-the-new-european-due-diligence-law/.

[89] Payne et al. analyse how effective legal tools can also be transferable. Payne et al., *Archimedes' Lever*, p. 266.

[90] *Wiwa* v. *Royal Dutch Petroleum Co.*, 96 Civ. 8386.

detention. The case was settled before the hearing for over fifteen million US dollars.[91] Similarly, victims of atrocities of Unocal and Total companies, in complicity with the Burmese junta, were compensated by settling their lawsuits against the companies.[92] Indonesian victims settled their lawsuit against Exxon Mobil, for its complicity to the military's human rights abuses, in May 2023.[93]

Despite the limited success of those cases, they should not be undervalued, at the very least because they stimulated developments internally, by exerting pressure, opening constructive judicial dialogue with domestic counterparts or even catalysing the establishment of reparation funds. The latter took place in favour of Holocaust victims, due to domestic German cases, referred to earlier, but also due to series of lawsuits filed before US courts against Swiss banks,[94] and various German companies, including tech firms, banks and car manufacturers. The companies allegedly concealed assets of Holocaust victims and laundered Nazi loot and profits of slave labour. The pressure from those lawsuits led to the establishment of a settlement fund in 1998,[95] and the fears of economic spillovers pulled the big players in the table, reaching an agreement to compensate former forced labourers and others who have suffered at the hands of German companies during Nazism, in late 1999.[96] A law on 'Remembrance, Responsibility, and Future' was passed in 2000 to put into effect this agreement, paid half by the government and half by the companies.[97]

[91] See Centre for Constitutional Rights, 'Factsheet: The Case Against Shell', 16 June 2009.

[92] Victims filed lawsuits against Unocal before the US courts. The case was settled before the beginning of the trial. *Doe I* v. *Unocal, 403 F.3d 708 [9 Cir. 2005]*. Other Burmese victims filed lawsuits in both Belgium and France, against Total, for violations suffered during the construction and operation of the Yadana gas pipeline. The Belgian lawsuit was dismissed, but the French one was settled. Info Birmanie, la Ligue des droits de l'Homme, Fédération internationale des ligues des droits de l'Homme, 'Info Birmanie, la Ligue des droits de l'Homme et la FIDH dénoncent l'accord intervenu entre Total et Sherpa', 30 novembre 2005, available at https://media.business-humanrights.org/media/documents/files/reports-and-materials/LDH-FIDH-communique-Total-accord-30-nov-2005.pdf.

[93] Al Jazeera, 'Oil Giant ExxonMobil Settles Long-Running Indonesia Torture Case', 16 May 2023.

[94] Holocaust Victim Assets Litigation (Swiss Banks); see official website of the Swiss Banks Settlement, available at www.swissbankclaims.com/overview.aspx.

[95] Kaleck and Saage-Maasz, 'Corporate Accountability for Human Rights Violations Amounting to International Crimes', at 701–702; Sandt and Moor, 'Peace, Everyone's Business!', p. 62.

[96] Statement of Interest of the United States, In *Re Austrian and German Bank Holocaust Litigation.*

[97] P. Dumberry, *State Succession to International Responsibility* (Martinus Nijhoff Publishers, 2007), pp. 388–389. The companies, however, tried tirelessly to secure that

Equally instrumental in catalysing domestic progress have been the legal actions taken against Chiquita Brands in the US regarding their alleged financial support of Colombian paramilitaries. A US Department of Justice investigation for terrorist financing led the company to plead guilty for financing the AUC. It was sentenced to a 25 million fine and an obligation to implement and maintain an effective compliance and ethics programme.[98] In 2007, a class-action lawsuit, seeking compensation for more than 200 victims of paramilitaries, accusing Chiquita of financing torture, war crimes and other human rights abuses, was filed under the ATCA in the United States.[99] As of March 2023, Chiquita was ordered to stand trial.[100] On 10 June 2024, in a groundbreaking verdict, a unanimous jury found Chiquita liable for over thirty-eight million in damages, for financing the murderous activities of AUC.[101] While not yet leading to any reparations, those cases contributed in providing evidence and oral testimonies that led to domestic prosecutions in Colombia.[102] In 2009, another case arising from Colombia was filed under the ATCA. The complaint alleged that Drummond Coal Company was complicit in the killings of union leaders in Colombia and made

no future lawsuits would be filed against them and clarified that those contributions were voluntary. Sandt and Moor, 'Peace, Everyone's Business!', p. 66.

98 US Department of Justice, 'Chiquita Brands International Pleads Guilty to Making Payments to a Designated Terrorist Organization and Agrees to Pay $25 Million Fine', 19 March 2007.

99 Similar lawsuits against Chiquita alleging company's complicity in crimes committed by AUC in Colombia were filed in various other US federal courts, but in 2008 they were consolidated in one multidistrict trial, which transferred six separate lawsuits to the District Court for the Southern District of Florida. In March 2023, Chiquita was ordered to stand trial in US District Court for allegedly financing the paramilitary death squads. Business and Human Rights Resource Centre, 'Chiquita Lawsuits (Re Colombia, Filed in USA by Colombian Nationals)', 14 November 2007, available at www.business-human-rights.org/en/latest-news/chiquita-lawsuits-re-colombia/; Earthrights International, 'Over 200 Colombian Plaintiffs File Claims for Torture and Killings Against Chiquita', 25 March 2020, available at https://earthrights.org/media_release/over-200-colombian-plaintiffs-file-claims-for-torture-and-killings-against-chiquita/. See also Sections 4.2.2 of this book.

100 The court dismissed the ATCA and TVPA causes of action, on the basis of foreign policy implications, but the case is still ongoing on the basis of Colombian law. For an overview of developments, see Earthrights International, 'Doe v. Chiquita Brands International', available at https://earthrights.org/case/doe-v-chiquita-brands-international/.

101 In the re Chiquita Brands International Inc. litigation, US District Court, Southern District of Florida, Case No. 08-MD-01916-MARRA, Verdict.

102 See, for example, the case against Arnulfo Peñuela Marin, director of a private security firm that functioned as an intermediary between the paramilitaries and Chiquita, and the case of Luis Alberto Agudelo Jiménez, in Section 4.2.2 of this book.

payments to the AUC paramilitary group to this end.[103] While the case was eventually dismissed by US courts due to presumed lack of jurisdiction, similar to the Chiquita case, it played a significant role in influencing developments within Colombia.[104]

Lastly, an important foreign case stands out for its ability to uncover historical violence, by corporate actors, with lasting implications. It originates in Guatemala, where a Q'eqchi community leader, Ich Chamán, was severely beaten and shot during a protest against the Fenix mine, operated by Hudbay Minerals. His widow filed a lawsuit, in 2010, before Ontario's Superior Court of Justice.[105] She alleged that the company failed to take the necessary measures to ensure respect of human rights by its security personnel. The shooting took place after the end of the conflict but can be traced to patterns of violence developed back then, particularly by the former owners of the mine. It was back in 1965, when a Canadian company was granted concession to the mine, and land dispossession of indigenous Q'eqchi Mayan communities started, along with brutal massacres by the army, under the company's instructions. Repression and forced disappearances were rife. The Truth Commission reported how the company was 'opening fire from [the company's] cars against the community'.[106] The mine passed in 2004 to Skye Resources and in 2008 to HudBay Minerals. The land ownership issue persisted, and dialogue with the company was fruitless, leading to violent protests and Chaman's killing.[107] This case is important for its snowball effect in bringing more cases by victims, as well as its domestic influence in Guatemala. In March 2011, a group of Guatemalan victims filed a second lawsuit against the same company in Canada, in relation to violations by its security personnel.[108] In December 2011, a third lawsuit was filed for a shooting – again – by Hudbay's security.[109]

[103] The case was finally dismissed due to presumed lack of jurisdiction by the US courts. *Baloco, et al.* v. *Drummond Co., Inc., et al.*, No. 12-15268 (11th Cir. 2014). See also *Doe* v. *Drummond Co., Inc.*, No. 13-15503 (11th Cir. 2015).

[104] See also Section 4.2.2 of this book.

[105] *Choc* v. *Hudbay*, 2013 ONSC 1414.

[106] *Illustrative Case 1149*; see also Níquel: Minería, Militares y Muerte en Guatemala, available at https://cmiguate.org/niquel-mineria-militares-y-muerte-en-guatemala/.

[107] J. Rodríguez, 'Where Impunity Reigns: Nickel Mining in El Estor, Guatemala' (2021) 48 *Latin American Perspectives* 1, pp. 289–299.

[108] *Margarita Caal* v. *HudBay Minerals Inc.* and *Choc* v. *Hudbay Minerals Inc*, 2013 ONSC 1414, 116 OR (3d) 674. For an account in English, see www.chocversushudbay.com.

[109] *German Chub Choc* v. *HudBay Minerals Inc.*, *Choc* v. *Hudbay Minerals Inc.*, 2013 ONSC 1414, 116 OR (3d) 674.

The cases are still ongoing, and in 2021, the security chief of the project admitted guilt for the murder of the indigenous leader before the Guatemalan courts.[110]

Thus, foreign cases, despite being daunting, costly and time consuming, can contribute to domestic processes of transitional justice. By exerting the necessary pressure to prompt domestic developments and by highlighting victims' efforts, such cases support advocacy campaigns not only within national borders but also on the international stage. In addition, foreign cases raise intriguing questions about the nature of transitional justice, its limitations and underlying assumptions. By way of indication, those cases doubt the attachment of transitional endeavours to specific geographic locations and open the way for more fluid efforts, depending on the specificities of each case. Instead of a rigid toolbox with predefined steps to follow, they render transitional justice into an improvised, adaptive process shaped by the unique circumstances of each context, the capacities of relevant actors and the synergies drawn between them. In addition, foreign cases bring a transnational element into the transitional justice discussion, boosting a paradigm that is not confined within the transitioning state, but brings with it a broader framework of norms, institutions and actors.[111] Importantly, this transnational element is brought at the victims' initiative and not as an institutional top-down admonition.

Among others, the previous cases – both domestic and foreign – ought to be remembered for the Herculean efforts of the victims in their pursuit of justice, mobilizing various actors both nationally and internationally, employing innovative strategies, arguments and legal avenues to seek long-awaited justice for corporate abuses during periods of conflict or repression. As Payne, Pereira and Bernal-Bermúdez emphasize, those efforts necessitate more force and support to be extended to the victims,[112] especially so amidst a politico-economic environment, often favouring corporate impunity.[113] In practice, force is materialized by the intellectual or practical support provided by domestic and international

[110] S. Cuffe, 'Guatemala Mine's Ex-Security Chief Convicted of Indigenous Leader's Murder', *The Guardian*, 7 January 2021.

[111] R. Teitel, 'The Universal and the Particular in International Criminal Justice', *Globalizing Transitional Justice: Contemporary Essays* (Oxford University Press, 2014), pp. 11–28.

[112] Payne et al., *Archimedes' Lever*, p. 85.

[113] Note that according to Overy, the environment is not as prone to corporate accountability as it was after the Holocaust. R. Overy, 'The Nuremberg Trials: International Law

activist groups, civil society, international actors engaged in transitional justice and academics working in related fields. This force and support can potentially act, and has in several circumstances acted, as the tipping point that reversed the dynamics and overcame obstacles for victims.

Further to those, the litigation efforts of victims, both domestically and internationally, contribute significantly to the advancement and evolution of transitional justice. First, many of the aforementioned examples highlight the dynamic interplay between domestic and foreign cases, the importance of international and domestic pressure as well as the critical role of truth-telling for reparations, particularly notable in the integrated system of Colombia.[114] In turn, that interplay and dialogue among different fields dislodges the perception of transitional justice as comprised from isolated and watertight mechanisms or legal fields. Instead, it vouches for and emphasizes the interconnectedness and interrelation of transitional mechanisms, tools and relevant legal fields, revealing the importance of holistic approaches for achieving the most effective outcomes.

Second, another contribution is that those efforts imbue transitional justice with the much-desired bottom-up character. Initiated by victims themselves, usually under adverse circumstances, and without any institutional support, those litigation efforts mirror victims' genuine needs for the allocation of justice and reparations, free from any top-down imposition. In addition, even in cases where compensation or other forms of reparation are not secured, the bottom-up character goes hand in hand with a victim-centred approach, a critical aspect, which is not to be taken for granted.[115] Scholars and practitioners often point to the importance of placing victims at the epicentre of transitional justice processes, but the involvement of victims is usually unsatisfactory, resulting in the neglect of their needs, the marginalization of local perceptions of justice and contextual factors.[116]

In turn, the clear expression of victims' genuine desires for court-allocated corporate compensation helps to organically resolve the dilemma of how to fit corporate accountability cases within a context

in the Making', in P. Sands (ed.), *From Nuremberg to The Hague: The Future of International Criminal Justice* (Cambridge University Press, 2003), p. 13.

114 See the case of Jaime Blanco Maya mentioned earlier.

115 See Part I, Section 2.2.1.2 of this book.

116 Longman et al., 'Connecting Justice to Human Experience', p. 206; Engle Marry, 'Transnational Human Rights and Local Activism', pp. 38–51; Mutua, 'Never Again', at 167, 168.

where remedies from responsible political elites are considered more urgent. The perseverance of victims seeking justice for corporate abuses suggests a broader understanding of who constitutes or is related to political elites, as well as a nuanced understanding of what is considered urgent, for reasons of transition. For victims, it seems that political elites are not constrained strictly within politics. Their Herculean efforts against economic actors underscore a perception of connection between political leaders, non-state actors and economic forces. To paraphrase Nagy's words, this understanding seems to run counter to the artificial zones of impunity, sketched by the mainstream paradigm of transitional justice.[117]

A further important contribution of those cases has to do with the law-making processes that transpire corporate accountability, transitional justice and their intersection. The multiplicity of cases brought before domestic and foreign courts constitutes a bottom-up law-making process, departing from 'on the ground experiences' that coalesce and 'gel as law'.[118] In turn, all those developments foster a doctrinal convergence – or at least an expectation thereof – across jurisdictions, which influences other domestic jurisdictions and also general international law.[119] As Payne et al. note, 'a body of practice that holds economic actors accountable emerges'.[120] Borrowing from the concept of recursivity of law, despite the absence of robust international and national frameworks regarding business abuse and access to justice, the law in practice – as demonstrated by these cases – seems to shape to a great extent the expectations and interpretations of what justice should look like, particularly so during transitions.[121] Those cases and the law making processes that they trigger can contribute to close the 'victims' gap' by ensuring that victims' voices are heard and their needs are addressed. At this juncture, the roles of the actors involved in these processes, including academics and practitioners, become critical, given that they also contribute to the evolving understanding of justice in transitional contexts. Despite those achievements and insights, it is important to recognize that the accountability achieved through those processes has not resulted in widespread, tangible outcomes. In light of those limitations and given the ingenuity that

117 Nagy, 'Transitional Justice as a Global Project', p. 276.

118 Levit, 'Bottom-Up International Law-Making', p. 409.

119 See Part I, Section 2.3.1 of this book.

120 Payne et al., *Archimedes' Lever*, p. 271.

121 B. Carruthers and T. Halliday, 'The Recursivity of Law: Global Norm Making and National Lawmaking in the Globalization of Corporate Insolvency Regimes' (2007) 112 *AJS* 4.

transpires transitional engineering, Chapter 7 will investigate the inclusion of corporate wrongdoers into administrative reparation programmes.

6.2 Administrative Reparations

Administrative reparation programmes, usually attached to Truth Commissions reports, grant reparations to victims, through a combination of restitution, rehabilitation and compensation.[122] Their distinguishing feature lies in conveying a more comprehensive message than court reparations, replying to systemic abuses and departing from the assumption that violations were mere exceptions.[123] They come about with a set of benefits, compared to court reparations,[124] as they bolster general perceptions of fairness,[125] relieve victims of litigation costs, employ lower standards of proof and are accessible to a larger amount of population, regardless of their educational, social or financial status.[126] It is reasonable to assume that those benefits are magnified in cases of corporate abuses, in view of the even more acute challenges when accessing courts.

[122] Magarrell, 'Reparations in Theory and Practice', p. 3. For an account of past administrative reparations programmes, see Roht-Arriaza, 'Reparations Decisions and Dilemmas', p. 170. Typically, the amount granted through those programmes does not correspond strictly to the exact level of harm, but is aligned to justice perceptions. P. De Greiff, 'Justice and Reparations', in P. De Greiff, *The Handbook of Reparations* (Oxford University Press, 2006), and Rubio Marin, 'Women and Reparations', p. 332.

[123] De Greiff, 'Justice and Reparations'.

[124] However, note that authors have criticized administrative reparations for abolishing the right of the victims to resort to courts. In South Africa, the amnesty law was appealed because it entailed that the perpetrator could not be criminally or civilly liable, *Azanian Peoples Organisation (AZAPO)* v. *President of the Republic of South Africa*, 1996 (8) BCLR 1015 (CC). Also, the classification of people across strict categories, such as victim and perpetrator, or as a minor or major victim, can be problematic. Moffett, 'Transitional Justice and Reparations'.

[125] Rubio-Marin, 'Women and Reparations', p. 332.

[126] It has been argued that courts entrench the prevalent social biases, which makes them more accessible to educated, urban and well-off victims. P. De Greiff (ed.), *The Handbook of Reparations* (Oxford University Press, 2006), p. 17. For a contrasting perspective on this issue, see Malamud-Goti and Grosman, 'Reparations and Civil Litigation: Compensation for Human Rights Violations in Transitional Democracies', in P. De Greiff (ed.), *The Handbook of Reparations* (Oxford University Press, 2006). The Guatemalan Commission of Historical Clarification itself underlined the inaccessibility of courts for indigenous people. Guatemalan Commission for Historical Clarification (Comision de Esclarecimiento Historico, CEH), Guatemala Memoria del Silencio, 'Denegacion de Justicia', Vol. 3, chapter 16.

Various transitional countries have adopted administrative reparation programmes, in their majority focusing on the state as their debtor and drawing on public resources. The Argentine state paid reparations to, amongst others, victims of forced disappearances and political imprisonment, funding them by issuing public bonds that resulted from different legislative initiatives.[127] In theory, some administrative reparation programmes were to include corporate malefactors. The Sierra Leonean TRC recommended that the Special Fund for War Victims should be financed from 'revenues from the exploitation of mineral resources'[128] which would necessarily touch upon businesses, but such a move was never made by the government.[129] In Liberia, the TRC urged the state to 'aggressively' seek restitution from corporations and to establish a Reparations Trust Fund, funded by taxes on corporations that evaded tax liability under the Taylor regime and confiscated assets from economic criminals.[130] This was also disregarded. The Guatemalan Truth Commission did not engage with corporations, but recommended an administrative programme, financed by universally progressive tax reform, cutting on military expenditure and investing on social issues.[131] The programme that was created in 2002 did not engage with businesses in any way and its implementation failed to meet the expectations.[132] The Truth Commission of East Timor recommended that corporations, who supported the illegal occupation of Timor-Leste, are obliged to provide reparations to victims,[133] but this, also, never materialized.

Likewise, the much applauded South African TRC corroborated that 'business benefited substantially during the Apartheid era either through commission or omission'.[134] It suggested corporate reparations, in the form of a wealth tax; a one-off levy on corporate and private income; a

[127] M. J. Guembe, 'Economic Reparations for Grave Human Rights Violations, the Argentinean Experience', in P. De Greiff (ed.), *The Handbook of Reparations* (Oxford University Press, 2006), pp. 21–54.

[128] Sierra Leone Truth and Reconciliation Commission, Final Report, Volume II, 'Recommendations', par. 227, p. 269.

[129] Sierra Leone Truth and Reconciliation Commission, 'Background to the Recommendations Matrix'.

[130] Republic of Liberia Truth and Reconciliation Commission, Vol. 3, pp. 43–44.

[131] CEH, Memoria del Silencio, Recommendations, Reparatory Measures, No. 19.

[132] D. Martinez and L. Gomez, *A Promise to Be Fulfilled: Reparations for Victims of the Armed Conflict in Guatemala* (Queen's University Belfast, 2019).

[133] Chega! part 11: 'Recommendations', under 12.10 Financing.

[134] Truth and Reconciliation Commission of South Africa (1998), *Report*, Vol. 6, section 2, chapter 5, par. 14, pp. 143–144.

one-off donation of 1 per cent of market capitalization by companies listed on the Johannesburg Stock Exchange; and a retrospective surcharge on corporate profits retrospectively from a time to be agreed. However, those measures were articulated to be owned to all those South Africans whose normal development was impaired by the system of Apartheid,[135] and based on a moral corporate obligation to assist in the reconstruction and development of post-Apartheid South Africa.[136] It also recommended that businesses assume the responsibility for the payment of the previous government's debt,[137] and the creation of the Reparation Trust Fund to be financed by a once-off wealth tax on South African businesses and by contributions of those who benefitted from Apartheid.[138] At the implementation stage, all those proposals failed. Instead, a so-called Business Trust was created, with contributions from over 100 companies,[139] which was ultimately used for generic developmental purposes, and not for repairing victims.[140] The President's Fund that was created in 1995 was financed by the state and the Swiss government, with no corporate involvement.

In effect, it is only in Germany and Colombia, where corporations were involved in administrative reparations. The case of Colombia will be analysed in Chapter 7, as it mainly deals with land restitution. Beyond land issues, corporations are supposed to finance a reparation fund. Initially, Article 54 of the 2005 Law of Peace and Justice provided for a reparation fund to be constituted by assets voluntarily given to the state by members of demobilized illegal armed groups. Article 177 of the 2011 Victims and Land Restitution Law added corporate entities to those debtors.[141] It foresaw that the sources of the fund include, among other, the proceeds of fines imposed on individuals or illegal armed groups in

[135] Ibid., Vol. 6, section 2, chapter 5, par. 3.

[136] It is only in its last sixth addendum report that the TRC used more concrete common law concepts and adds more foundations for the reparation claims, such as unjustified enrichment and illegality in contract law. However, this legal turn cannot be attributed to a change of conceptual premises but rather to an urgency to enforce the reparations. Ibid., Vol. 6, section 2, chapter 5, par. 24, 60.

[137] Ibid., Vol. 5, par. 39, pp. 318–319.

[138] Ibid., Vol. 6, section 5, chapter 7, p. 726.

[139] P. de Vox, 'Khulumani Welcomes Call for a Wealth Tax', constitutionally speaking blog, 16 August 2011.

[140] Sandoval and Surfleet, 'Corporations and Redress in Transitional Justice Processes', pp. 101–102.

[141] Ley de Víctimas y Restitución de Tierras (Victims and Land Restitution Law), No. 1448, 10 June 2011, Article 177.

judicial and administrative proceedings, the amount of the economic conviction of those convicted of conspiracy and the amount established in the judgement as a consequence of the support provided by companies that have financed organized armed groups outside the law.[142] The fund also accepts voluntary private contributions, in the form of donations from companies, but it has seemingly not yet put in operation.

As with the Nuremberg Tribunals, Germany offers rich precedent in terms of reparations. As discussed previously, in the mid-fifties, IG Farben, agreed with the Conference on Jewish Material Claims against Germany, the creation of a reparation fund, to which it provided twenty-seven million German marks, for the compensation of Jewish former slave labourers of Auschwitz, and three million marks for non-Jewish victims.[143] The payments were made, subject to laws granting it immunity from further claims,[144] and putting a time bar to victims for lodging their applications.[145] Compensation was also voluntarily granted by AEG-Telefunken, Siemens, Rheinmetall and Daimler-Benz.[146] A second wave of reparations was initiated with the Green Party's motion before the Parliament, in 1984, to establish a nationwide compensation fund for victims of forced labour, financed by German industry.[147] The motion was dismissed, but pressure started to mount, in the media, and also in courtrooms, where various lawsuits against Swiss Banks and German companies were filed. This pushed representatives of large German companies to accept the creation of a special foundation, along with the German state, with the aim of repairing the harm suffered by forced labourers. The respective law on the creation of the 'Remembrance, Responsibility, and Future Foundation' was adopted in 2000 and the contributions were divided among the state and companies. Again,

[142] N. C. Sánchez León and C. Sandoval-Villalba, 'Go Big or Go Home? Lessons Learned from the Colombian Victims' Reparation System', in C. Ferstman and M. Goetz (eds.), *Reparations for Victims of Genocide, War Crimes and Crimes against Humanity: Systems in Place and Systems in the Making* (Koninklijke Brill, 2020), pp. 547–570.

[143] *Wollheim* v. *IG Farben*, available at www.wollheim-memorial.de/en/das_verfahren_wollheim_gegen_ig_farben.

[144] BVerfG, Order of the First Senate of 7 December 2004 – 1 BvR 1804/03 –, paras. 1–77, p. 303 *et seq.*, available at www.bundesverfassungsgericht.de/SharedDocs/Entscheidungen/EN/2004/12/rs20041207_1bvr180403en.html.

[145] Act on the Notice to Creditors of IG Farbenindustrie Aktiengesellschaft in Abwicklung of 27 May 1957, Federal Law Gazette I, p. 569.

[146] Sandt and Moor, 'Peace, Everyone's Business!', pp. 62–63.

[147] Peer Heinelt, 'Financial Compensation for Nazi Forced Labourers', 2010, pp. 44–45, available at www.wollheim-memorial.de.

payments were described as 'voluntary', giving rise to no further legal obligation.[148] According to the American Jewish Committee, although 255 corporations profited from forced labour, only 17 contributed to the compensation fund.[149]

6.3 Navigating the Complexities of Land Restitution: The Colombian Example

The shift of transitional praxis towards addressing the underlying causes of conflict, including economic, social and cultural rights violations,[150] led to the inclusion of land issues in the context of reparations.[151] This was driven by the understanding that land rights are a primary reason for the onset of conflict in many contexts.[152] Land restitution programmes have been integrated in transitional processes, to a different extent, in various countries; from South Africa,[153] Iraq and Kosovo[154] to the more recent example of Colombia. In most situations, land disputes involved corporate entities, engaging in land grabbing, dispossession and illegal confiscation.[155] Illegal expropriation of land has been linked to corporate

[148] Sandt and Moor, 'Peace, Everyone's Business!', p. 66.

[149] Note that other studies mention six thousand three hundred corporate donations. Payne and Pereira, 'Corporate Complicity in International Human Rights Violations'.

[150] L. Hecht and S. Michalowski, 'The Economic and Social Dimensions of Transitional Justice' (2012) *EJTN Concept Paper*, at 5.

[151] C. Huggins, 'Linking Broad Constellations of Ideas: Transitional Justice, Land Tenure Reform, and Development', in P. De Greiff and R. Duthie (eds.), *Transitional Justice and Development: Making Connections* (Social Science Research Council, 2009), p. 336; B. Atuahene, 'Property and Transitional Justice' (2010) 58 *UCLA Law Review Discourse*, at 65–93.

[152] J. D. Unruh and M. A. Abdul-Jalil, 'Housing, Land and Property Rights in Transitional Justice' (2021) 15 *International Journal of Transitional Justice* 1, pp. 1–6.

[153] F. Du Bois, 'Reparations and the Forms of Justice', in F. Du Bois and A. Pedain (eds.), *Justice and Reconciliation in Post-Apartheid South Africa* (Cambridge University Press, 2008), pp. 116, 128; R. Hall, 'Reconciling the Past, Present, and Future: The Parameters and Practices of Land Restitution in South Africa', in C. Walker et al. (eds.), *Land, Memory, Reconstruction, and Justice: Perspectives on Land Claims in South Africa* (Ohio University Press, 2010), pp. 18–19.

[154] H. Alviar Garcia, 'Transitional Justice and Property: Inextricably Linked' (2021) 17 *Annual Review of Law and Social Science*, at 227–238.

[155] Zoomers defines land grabs as large-scale, cross-border land deals or transactions that are carried out by transnational corporations or initiated by foreign governments. A. Zoomers, 'Globalisation and the Foreignization of Space: Seven Processes Driving the Current Global Land Grab' (2010) 37 *Journal of Peasant Studies* 2, at 429–447.

investments in Myanmar,[156] Colombia, South Africa,[157] DRC[158] and elsewhere.[159]

Land restitution programmes are aligned to public international law, which prioritizes restitution as form of reparation,[160] as well as to international human rights[161] and international criminal law.[162] The Basic Principles also envision the same, stipulating that victims should return to 'one's place of residence' or property.[163] Relevant international legal framework also includes the 1998 Guiding Principles on Internal Displacement[164] and the 2005 UN Principles on Housing and Property Restitution for Refugees and Displaced Persons, known as the Pinheiro principles,[165] which privilege the rights of the displaced and restitution of property, as it was before the conflict.

Unlike Myanmar's or South Africa's failed examples in terms of restitution from private landowners,[166] Colombia offers a unique example of land restitution that touched upon issues of corporate reparations. During the Colombian conflict, more than seven million people were forcibly displaced,[167] either due to violence or because their property was forcibly transferred to other owners. Those lands were usually appropriated by paramilitaries, through systematic violence and intimidation, in some cases in order to gain strategic military advantages. However, in other cases that are of interest here, land was grabbed under the instructions of landowners and elites, who wanted to regain resources

156 UN General Assembly, Report of the Special Rapporteur on the situation of human rights in Myanmar, A/73/332 (20 August 2018), at 22.

157 Pietropaoli, *Business, Human Rights and Transitional Justice*, pp. 200–202.

158 M. Saturnino et al., 'Transnational Land Investment Web: Land Grabs, TNCs, and the Challenge of Global Governance' (2020) 17 *Globalizations* 4, at 608–628.

159 For an overview of land grabs by corporations, see the map created by the Land Matrix Initiative of the International Land Coalition, available at https://landmatrix.org/map/.

160 Permanent Court of International Justice, *Chórzow Factory (Indemnity)* case (*Germany* v. *Poland*), 1928 PCIJ, Series A No. 17, Judgment of 13 September 1928, at 47.

161 International and regional human rights conventions classify restitution as a form of delivering effective remedies and reparations.

162 Rome Statute, Article 75(1).

163 Basic Principles, Principle 18.

164 UN High Commissioner for Refugees, Guiding Principles on Internal Displacement, 22 July 1998, ADM 1.1, PRL 12.1, PR00/98/109.

165 UN Principles on Housing and Property Restitution for Refugees and Displaced Persons, UN Doc. E/CN.4/Sub.2/2005/17 (2005).

166 Pietropaoli analyses the situation of South Africa, Myanmar and Colombia. Pietropaoli, *Business, Human Rights and Transitional Justice*, pp. 200–202.

167 Centro Nacional de Memoria Histórica, *Una nación desplazada. Informe nacional del desplazamiento forzado en Colombia* (Centro Nacional de Memoria Histórica, 2015).

and control lost during the agrarian reforms in the country.[168] Yet in other cases, land was put at the disposal of large agro-industrial and mining projects, again under the instructions of the elites running those projects. In Urabá, for example, companies and primarily Urapalma SA conspired with paramilitaries to force Afro-Colombian communities to cede their titles so that they could develop oil palm monocultures.[169] In other cases, businesses acquired illegally grabbed land from intermediaries,[170] or already abandoned land, way below market prices.[171]

Attempting to grapple with that issue, the state passed the Victims and Land Restitution Law 1448 of 2011.[172] The law relies on both administrative and judicial procedures, initiated by the victim's 'action for land restitution'.[173] The aim of the law is to enable victims of land grabbing, related to the armed conflict, to reclaim their properties. The tools to that end combine human rights principles, along with traditional civil law processes.[174] According to the law, victims submit a request in order to be included in the Registry of Dispossessed and Forcibly Abandoned Lands. The property has to be located within specifically defined zones[175]; the victims need to be owners, possessors or occupants[176]; and the dispossession and other harm need to have been committed within specified time limits, with a nexus to the armed conflict.[177] At this stage, victims need only to make relevant declarations, and it is the Land

168 Wesche, 'Business Actors and Land Restitution in the Colombian Transition', 2, at 98.

169 This is the case of Urapalma in the municipalities of Riosucio and Carmen del Darién, which concerns several companies developing 17.000 hectares of oil palm monocultures, for which there was also a court case. Sandt and Moor, 'Peace, Everyone's Business!'.

170 This is the case of cattle ranchers, which purchased 3.647 hectares of dispossessed land in the municipalities of Turbo and Necoclí. The president of the Livestock Fund (Fondo Ganadero) was found guilty for participating in a criminal enterprise, forced displacement and money laundering.

171 This is the case of Argos, a US- and Colombia-based multinational cement company, whose subsidiary Reforestadora del Caribe, acquired 6.600 hectares to develop teak monocultures in Montes de María. Wesche, 'Business Actors and Land Restitution in the Colombian Transition', at 301.

172 Ley de Víctimas y Restitución de Tierra, Law No. 1448 (10 June 2011).

173 N. Summers, 'Recent Developments: Colombia's Victims' Law: Transitional Justice in a Time of Violent Conflict?' (2012) 25 *Harvard Human Rights Journal* 1, at 232.

174 N. C. Sánchez León, *Tierra en transición: justicia transicional, restitución de tierras y política agraria en Colombia* (Dejusticia, 2017).

175 Law 1448/2011, Article 76.

176 Ibid., Articles 75, 81.

177 Ibid., Article 75.

Restitution Unit that collects the evidence. In case of doubts, they are to be resolved in favour of victims.[178]

If the property is included in the Registry, then victims can proceed with filing a claim before the specialized civil judge.[179] In case of unresolvable dispute between former and current owners, it is then transferred to a magistrate specialized in land restitution within the civil chamber of the higher judicial district courts, who rules in single instance.[180] Before the court, victims are relieved from the burden of proof if they produce prima facie evidence of their relationship with the land and its dispossession.[181] If the victim wins, they are entitled to material and judicial restitution. If the land has been used for agro-industrial purposes, victims can sign a contract with the current owner to continue to exploit the land,[182] or the land is overtaken by the Land Restitution Unit for collective reparation purposes.[183] From the other side, current owners can oppose the process at the judicial stage, and receive compensation if they prove that they acquired it in 'good faith'.[184] Otherwise, they lose their property without compensation.

Although the mechanism does not explicitly target corporate entities or businesspersons, their involvement, due to current ownership, was taken into account by the legislators.[185] Allegedly for this reason, the concept of land dispossession was left quite broad, so as to include land grabbed by violence, and also by seemingly lawful business transactions,[186] notably when land was later acquired below market prices.[187] The law has been praised because it incorporates assumptions, able to

178 Wesche, 'Business Actors and Land Restitution in the Colombian Transition', p. 304.

179 Law 1448/2011, Article 80.

180 Ibid., Articles 79, 86–90.

181 Ibid., Articles 5 and 78.

182 Ibid., Article 99.

183 Ibid., Article 99. According to the constitutional court, such undertaking requires consent of the claimants. Corte Constitucional, Sentencia C-820 de 2012, Bogotá D.C., 18 October 2012.

184 D. L. Attanasio and N. C. Sánchez, 'Return Within the Bounds of the Pinheiro Principles: The Colombian Land Restitution Experience' (2012) 11 *Washington University Global Studies Law Review* 1, at 24.

185 Wesche, 'Business Actors and Land Restitution in the Colombian Transition', p. 301.

186 Law 1448/2011, Article 74.

187 S. R. Chaparro Hernández et al., *La restitución de tierras y territorios. Justificaciones, dilemas y estrategias* (Dejusticia, 2016); A. P. Bolívar Jaime et al., *La buena fe en la restitución de tierras. Sistematización de jurisprudencia* (Dejusticia, 2017), at 21.

grapple with business and human rights challenges.[188] First, it presumes illegal land acquisition, when the land deal involved a person convicted of 'membership, collaboration or financing of armed groups'.[189] Further, it assumes illegal appropriation in cases of vast land acquisitions and large corporate projects. In cases of land transfers in very low value, in areas of massive violence and displacement, with high land concentration, or with major land-use change, it shifts the burden of proof to the current owners.[190] Those have to prove that they took all adequate measures to authenticate the lawfulness of the acquisition.[191] The law has also taken into account the many barriers that victims of business violations face when they try to access judicial remedies. Thus, it provides victims with ample information and gives the possibility of collective actions,[192] it reduces or shifts the burden of proof off the victims[193] and provides for legal aid[194] and victim protection.[195]

However, the law was criticized for its meagre implementation.[196] By the end of July 2023, only 9.8 of the land was restituted, and business cases comprised only a small ratio of that percentage.[197] The Argos Company case is illustrative, as the company admitted to have illegally obtained more than 6,000 hectares of land to develop teak monocultures from victims of forced displacement or through intermediaries,[198] but as of May 2019, only 1.023 of them were returned.[199] According to the foundation Forjando Futuros, between 2012 and 2020, sixty-six

[188] N. C. Sánchez León, 'Corporate Accountability, Reparations and Distributive Justice in Post Conflict Societies', in S. Michalowski (ed.), *Corporate Accountability in the Context of Transitional Justice* (Routledge, 2013), pp. 114, 118.

[189] Law 1448/2011, Article 77(1).

[190] Ibid., Article 77(2).

[191] Including verifying whether the property was subject to forced abandonment or dispossession, on whether the vendors actually constituted its owners and on whether they had acquired it legally, paying a fair price. See Law 1448/2011, Articles 88, 91 and 98.

[192] Ibid., Article 82.

[193] Ibid., Articles 5 and 78.

[194] Ibid., Articles 49–69, 81–84, 154–158.

[195] Ibid., Articles 31, 32, 114–118.

[196] In the absence of agricultural policies, the law is considered insufficient in cases of land-use change to vast monocultures. R. Uprimny-Yepes and N. C. Sánchez, 'Los dilemas de la restitución de tierras en Colombia' (2010) 12 *Revista Estudios Socio-Jurídicos* 2, at 325.

[197] Wesche, 'Business Actors and Land Restitution in the Colombian Transition', p. 312.

[198] Ibid., at 306.

[199] Between 2016 and 2018, twelve judgments were delivered. Forjando Futuros, Empresas, Desplazamiento y despojo de tierras en Colombia (Forjando Futuros, 2018), available at www.forjandofuturos.org/wp-content/uploads/2020/07/596-informe-argos-s-a.pdf.

companies operating in agro-industrial or mining projects as well as banks were sentenced to restitute the land, suspend mining titles and annul the bank mortgages.[200] It is interesting to note the role of the banks in those cases. According to case law, banks contributed to dispossession through confiscation of lands due to unpaid debts, by people who have long abandoned their properties due to violence or forced evictions by corporations. In other cases, the properties were mortgaged by the very people who illegally appropriated them. In 248 cases, the magistrates did not recognize the mortgages in favour of the banks, without compensation and returned the lands to previous owners,[201] due to the fact that well-known acts of violence occurred in those areas at the time, which caused the dispossession of the properties. In the case against the Banco Agrario de Colombia, the court illustratively held that '[a]s a banking entity, aware of the notorious facts of the violence in the municipality of Mutatá, it should have taken into account that said property was located in an area where systematic dispossession occurred, so it is not possible to assume 'good faith without guilt[. . .]'.[202]

6.4 From Reparations as Development to Transformative Justice

Reparations and development have often been analysed in tandem, due to their alleged common features, agendas and objectives, namely to improve lives of individuals – the first through accountability and remedy and the second mainly through equality of socioeconomic opportunities.[203] When it comes to corporate reparations, the confusion with development becomes even more pronounced. This is partially due to the work of some TRCs and respective governments, who, when faced with corporate malfeasance during conflict or repression, prefer to

[200] Forjando Futuros, Empresas, despojo, violencia y concentración de tierras, available at www.forjandofuturos.org/wp-content/uploads/2020/07/boletin-empresas-2-de-junio .pdf; Forjando Futuros, Infografia, Julio 2023, available at www.forjandofuturos.org/wp-content/uploads/2023/06/INFOGRAFIA-JULIO-2023-1.pdf.

[201] Forjando Futuros, Los Bancos y El Despojo De Tierras, 9 September 2020, available at www.forjandofuturos.org/wp-content/uploads/2020/09/Bolet%C3%ADn-BancosYDespojo-5-1.pdf.

[202] Caso Banco Agrario de Colombia, Tribunal Superior Especializado en Restitución de Tierras de Antioquia, 8 October 2018, Radicado: 05045312100120150062500, p. 25.

[203] R. Duthie, *Toward a Development-Sensitive Approach to Transitional Justice* (International Centre for Transitional Justice, 2008), p. 296.

abstain from accountability in the transition phase and replace it with developmental measures on behalf of corporations. Such preferences stem not only from conceptual overlaps of reparations and development or nation-building processes. Most importantly, they result out of competition for investment[204] and the hidden assumption that corporations will divest if some of them are held to account. The resources for transitional states are often limited,[205] the economy and infrastructure might be damaged and thus the compromise between reparations and development will often lean towards the latter.[206] For example, the 2008 Colombian presidential decree on administrative reparations called 'for humanitarian relief already received by victims to be deducted from the amount of reparations they would receive through this program'.[207] In Colombia again, in 2017, the 'Work for Taxes' programme mixed or replaced transitional and developmental goals, leaning to corporations for the latter. The programme foresaw that those entities, whose operations were located in the 'Zones Most Affected by the Armed Conflict', could undertake infrastructure projects for a reduction in their tax liabilities. More often than not, those corporations had long-standing operations in those areas, in collaboration with armed groups.[208] Similarly, the South African TRC suggested generic reparative measures,[209] owned to all those South Africans whose normal development was impaired by the system of Apartheid[210] and based on a moral obligation of the corporations to assist in the reconstruction and development of post-Apartheid South Africa.[211]

204 Sandoval, *Adverse Consequences of Reparations.*

205 P. Arthur, *Identities in Transition: Developing Better Transitional Justice Initiatives in Divided Societies* (International Centre for Transitional Justice, 2009), p. 173.

206 On the debate over how to balance reparations with the government's obligations to encourage development, see R. Carranza, *The Right to Reparations in Situations of Poverty* (International Centre for Transitional Justice, 2009), p. 3.

207 'La reparación que se les da a las víctimas de la violencia en Colombia sí es la debida', El Tiempo, 2 May 2010.

208 N. Jiménez et al., 'Colombia – Work for Taxes: Post-Conflict Development of Rural Zones' (2020) Yale SOM Case 20-026.

209 Truth and Reconciliation Commission of South Africa (1998), *Report*, Vol. 6, section 5, chapter 7.

210 Ibid., Vol. 6, section 2, chapter 5, par. 3.

211 It is only in its last sixth addendum report that the TRC used more concrete common law concepts and adds more foundations for the reparation claims, such as unjustified enrichment and illegality in contract law. However, this legal turn cannot be attributed to a change of conceptual premises but rather to an urgency to enforce the reparations.

But scholars caution that transitional justice and development are essentially different fields and that confusing or substituting the one with the other undermines the victim-centred approach of transitional justice and reduces the latter to a development strategy.[212] Instead, the discourse on transformative justice becomes more relevant. Defined as 'transformative change that emphasizes local agency and resources', it prioritizes process rather than preconceived outcomes and challenges the unequal and intersecting power relationships and structures of exclusion at both the local and the global level.[213] In that context, transformative reparations aim to tackle pre-existing structural inequalities that made individuals vulnerable and prone to victimization,[214] with objectives that prioritize distribution over retribution. In legal terms, it seems centred around the principle of equality, in that it aspires to disrupt and eliminate the patterns of marginalization and exclusion as opposed to transitional justice that is centred on the principle of legality. Transformative justice and thus transformative reparations are characterized by an emphasis on local agency, participation and resources, as well as on the process that is followed to achieve the transformational results and the challenge of structures of exclusion, marginalization or power. Arguably, participation shapes a discourse that encompasses and channels resistance, in a way that the neutrality of a mere human rights discourse cannot.[215] Those elements would presumably manage to consolidate more inclusive democratic regimes.[216]

Truth and Reconciliation Commission of South Africa (1998), *Report*, Vol. 6, section 2, chapter 5, par. 24, 60.

212 Duthie, *Toward a Development-Sensitive Approach to Transitional Justice*, p. 299; International Centre for Transitional Justice, *The Rabat Report: The Concept and Challenges of Collective Reparations* (International Centre for Transitional Justice, 2009), p. 46. Scholars have also argued therefore that reparations should be integrated in larger development and reconstruction agendas or that reparations should be included in development packages for donors to fund. Mani, 'Dilemmas of Expanding Transitional Justice', at 256.

213 Gready and Robins, 'From Transitional to Transformative Justice', p. 340.

214 R. Uprimny and M. P. Saffon, 'Reparaciones transformadoras, justicia distributiva y profundización democrática', in C. Díaz Gómez et al. (eds.), *Reparar en Colombia: los dilemas en contextos de conflicto, pobreza y exclusión* (International Centre for Transitional Justice, 2009), pp. 34–35; Lessard, 'Preventive Reparations at a Crossroads'.

215 Gready and Robins, 'From Transitional to Transformative Justice'.

216 R. Rubio-Marin, 'The Gender of Reparations in Transitional Societies', in R. Rubio-Marin (ed.), *The Gender of Reparations: Unsettling Sexual Hierarchies While Redressing Human Rights Violations* (Cambridge University Press, 2009), pp. 63–120, 66. See

Corporate reparations and accountability seem to be inextricably linked to transformative justice and its aims. Challenging pre-existing structures of exclusion, marginalization and power can only take place by addressing actors who anchored those structures, including economic elites and business malefactors. The presence of specific groups in positions of authority within those structures underscores the need to confront them in order to dismantle power hierarchies. In parallel, tackling systemic socio-economic disparities necessitates confronting those who wield the ability to exploit socio-economic resources and restrict access for other groups. Under a transformative lens that incorporates corporate reparations, socio-economic rights violations are seamlessly integrated in transitional praxis. Those violations often go hand in hand with deeply entrenched structural problems, with business benefiting and exacerbating the situation, through various means, including land appropriation, resource exploitation, exploitative labour practices and discriminatory actions that perpetuate cycles of poverty. In turn, rectifying these violations can only be accomplished through a comprehensive overhaul of socio-economic policies, which will inevitably impact the business-operating environment.

Beyond those, it would be interesting to ponder on the interplay of corporate transformative reparations and historic injustices, such as slavery, colonialism and racial injustice. Various business entities have benefited from slavery,[217] colonialism[218] and racial discrimination,[219] and calls for them to recognize and repair their involvement in those legacies have mounted,[220] in parallel with an overall pressure to recognize the historical damage created by policies and actions that marginalized Black and other communities and deprived them of building

Reparations for Conflict-Related Sexual Violence, UN Guidance Note of the Secretary-General, June 2014.

[217] J. Jolly, 'Barclays, HSBC and Lloyds Among UK Banks That Had Links to Slavery', *The Guardian*, 18 June 2020; Z. Thomas, 'The Hidden Links between Slavery and Wall Street', *BBC*, 29 August 2019. See also the legacies of British slave-ownership database, which includes companies that have benefited from the slave trade at www.ucl.ac.uk/lbs/.

[218] Centre for the Study of Violence and Reconciliation, Transitional Justice and Colonialism, October 2018.

[219] M. K. Marks, '40 Acres and a Mule: Accountability for Corporations to Provide Reparations to Historically Black Colleges and Universities for Profits from Slave Labour' (2023) 10 *Emory Corporate Governance and Accountability Review* 312.

[220] M. Snipe, 'Make Bank of America Pay Reparations, Group Says', *Tampabay*, 13 June 2020, available at www.tampabay.com/florida-politics/buzz/2020/06/12/make-bank-of-america-pay-reparations-demand-protesters/.

intergenerational wealth. Those are accompanied by calls for financial reparations for slavery, colonialism and racial injustice, which have touched upon businesses.[221]

However, with the passing of time, traditional reparations, focusing on individual harm, requiring direct victims and clear evidence, are ill equipped to address those types of harms. Legal cases against them have not been successful,[222] and except for corporate social responsibility initiatives,[223] no reparation has been granted.[224] Instead, transformative approaches have a lot to offer in that respect, for aiming to replace the underlying causes of marginalization and exploitation, with emancipatory dynamics. Transformative reparations are meant to rectify the lingering negative effects of historic injustice. In practical terms, this implies that firms with verifiable historical connections to past injustices will be obligated to undertake reparations and similar redress measures. However, it also entails that recently established enterprises must consider their responsibilities under the UNGPs framework and ensure heightened due diligence to become aware of their potential contributions to exploitation and structural oppression.

Lastly, the focus of transformative justice on participation is in line with the bottom-up approach of the corporate accountability discourse and channels the victims' Herculean efforts seeking justice against corporate abuse in conflict or repressive settings.[225] This focus on

[221] In June 2020, the UN human rights chief called for reparations for slavery and colonialism, with specific reference to the killing of George Floyd in the statement. See 'UN Human Rights Chief Calls for Reparations to Make Amends for Slavery', *The Guardian*, 17 June 2020. See also the Belgian panel on colonial history in the DRC, Rwanda and Burundi; see Burundi demands forty-three billion as reparations from colonial rulers, Bloomberg; for the California 2020 law on investigating reparations for slavery, see N'dea Yancey-Bragg, 'California Considers Slavery Reparations After Historic Law', *USA Today*; and the US Federal Commission to Study and Develop Reparation Proposals for African Americans Act, Commission to Study and Develop Reparation Proposals for African Americans Act, 116 H.R. 40, 116th Cong. (2019).

[222] Business and Human Rights Resource Centre, 'Slavery Reparations Lawsuit', available at www.business-humanrights.org/en/slavery-reparations-lawsuit-re-usa.

[223] Two major British businesses have said they will make undisclosed payments to black and minority ethnic groups to atone for their past owners' involvement in the transatlantic slave trade. Pub group Greene King and insurance broker Lloyd's of London have both apologized for what they respectively call 'inexcusable' actions and 'indefensible wrongdoing'. See C. Hope, 'Exclusive: Top British Firms to Pay Compensation Over Founders' Slavery Links', *The Telegraph*, 17 June 2020.

[224] L. Moffett, 'Slavery Reparations: There's Little Legal Basis to Make Companies Pay for Historic Actions', *The Conversation*, 19 June 2020.

[225] Levit, 'Bottom-Up International Law-Making'.

participation opens also a window of opportunity to reframe the need for corporate liability legislation and regulation. This participatory aspect can materialize only insofar as avenues to seek rights and redress against corporate entities exist and are well functioning. Establishing and enabling corporate accountability in states, where it is not part of the legal system, will enable victims to claim their rights against actors, who are usually more powerful than them, and foster participation and empowerment. Besides, if transformative justice aims to subvert the factors that led to victimization, then in cases of corporate malfeasance, the mere adoption of corporate accountability legislation can be considered transformative, since it will presumably protect victims from being re-victimized by corporations.

Of course, this discourse also comes with its own set of challenges and complexities, in terms of feasibility, implementation in fragile states, legitimacy and weaknesses of the institutions that will have to carry out,[226] the preparedness of local initiatives to challenge macro problems, such as those created by strong multinational entities, as well as too much aspiration. The financial challenges, the entrenched opposing interests and the complexity of the endeavour, especially in relation to historical injustices, might render its practical application quite difficult. In addition to that, one should consider that precedents from post-conflict spaces demonstrate a willingness of corporations to participate in development projects rather than to account for their wrongdoings or to superficially engage in compensation or apologies to absolve themselves from the past.

Despite the obstacles, the transformative perspective appears to hold significant potential for incorporating corporate accountability into transitional praxis. The ongoing efforts to address corporate misconduct in times of conflict or repression can be realized through the convergence of the principles of legality of transitional justice infused with the principle of equality of transformative approaches. Such convergence would balance the transitional character of reparations towards individual victims with future-oriented transformations, able to fully guarantee rights and evade patterns of impunity.[227] Most importantly, initiating a conversation about transformative justice and corporate malefactors, even on a

[226] Regarding, for example, the financing of reparations, Segovia has pointed out that broad reforms and redistribution of resources are more difficult to implement in societies with weak governance. A. Segovia, 'Financing Reparations Programs: Reflections from International Experience', in P. De Greiff (ed.), *The Handbook of Reparations* (Oxford University Press, 2016).

[227] Lessard, 'Preventive Reparations at a Crossroads'.

theoretical level, holds symbolic importance and its own transformational potential. This is because starting a conversation presupposes a level of acknowledgement of prior injustice, while at the same time, it promotes dialogue and shifts public consciousness towards greater understanding of the issue. Those, over time, can contribute towards building a momentum for future reforms, creating a more conducive political environment that can gradually evolve into feasible solutions and act as a catalyst for incremental progress.

Indicative of this shift of the discourse and perception around the role of companies during conflict and their ensuing responsibilities in its aftermath, whose transformative potential should not be underestimated, is the case of Russia, as opposed to prior examples. While it took time and widespread atrocities for the United Nations and various civil society organizations to report on the responsibilities of companies relating to the occupation of the Palestinian territories,[228] in the case of Russia, opposition to the corporate backing of its operations was expressed outright.[229] It took only a month for investors and businesses to voice their concerns about potential corporate involvement in international human rights and humanitarian law violations.[230] In the case of Russia, both consumers and civil society and business organizations came to rapidly accept as reasonable the expectation that companies should take action once they risk being involved in conflicts. While this cannot equate to the predicaments of transformative justice, it still signals a shift in perspective with the potential for significant transformation.

Overall, the transformative element serves as a plea to broaden the conventional boundaries of transitional justice and envision its application under expanding understandings of injustice and responsibility. It is

[228] Human Rights Council, Resolution adopted by the Human Rights Council on 24 March 2016, A/HRC/RES/31/36, 20 April 2016; Al Haq, 'The Case Against Riwal: Corporate Complicity in International Crimes', 16 October 2010, available at www.alhaq.org/advocacy/7137.html; Lawyers for Palestinian Human Rights, 'Business and Human Rights Project', available at https://lphr.org.uk/legal-projects/business-human-rights-project/.

[229] For example, the first UN Forum on Business and Human Rights that took place after the beginning of the Russian invasion had a dedicated panel on business and human rights in conflict, where the issue of Ukraine was discussed. See panel 'Advancing Business Actions on Human Rights in Conflict Situations' at the 11th UN Forum on business and human rights, available at https://2022unforumbhr.sched.com/.

[230] Investor Alliance for Human Rights, 'Investor Alert: Human Rights Risks Related to the Russian Invasion of Ukraine', 3 March 2022, available at https://investorsforhumanrights.org/news/investor-alert-human-rights-risks-related-russian-invasion-ukraine.

also a call to transitional justice itself to critically reflect on its inherent normative and political frameworks, which oftentimes inadvertently perpetuate structural injustices and power imbalances rather than effecting meaningful transformation.[231]

6.5 Concluding Remarks

Corporate wrongdoers are usually excluded from reparation schemes to a greater extent than from other transitional mechanisms, making victims seek compensation through litigation. On top of the usual hurdles and reluctance of transitional states, reparations face an additional legal challenge rooted in their foundation on the right to remedy and reparation, tightly linked to the state. It is the state that is obliged to provide remedies both for its wrongful actions and also for its failure to prevent violations by third actors, including corporate entities. Thus, the inclusion of corporate entities in reparations stumbles upon the state's central role, making it challenging to determine whether transitioning states have any duty to include corporations, as debtors, in the design and delivery of reparations as opposed to providing reparations themselves or hindering victims' efforts for adjudication, as was the case in South Africa.

Part II argued in favour of a novel theoretical framework suggesting that states should interpret their obligation to provide remedies in a way that mirrors the culpable actor – in the context of this book, business actors. This new theoretical framework rests on a novel interpretation of the sequence of state obligations, as it proposes an understanding of the state's overarching reparative obligations, to include a duty to provide redress avenues in domestic law to victims of corporate violations, something which, in principle, is part of the state's protective obligations. In essence, it was argued that transitional states should interpret their obligation to protect – an obligation that already includes enabling redress by the responsible perpetrators and extends to corporate actors – as an integral part of their duty to provide reparations, rather than treating these obligations as separate, sequential tasks. Such a combination or influence of the positive to the reparative obligations is justified, on the basis of their close conceptual and causal relationship, as well as

[231] H. van der Merwe and M. Brinton Lykes, 'Racism and Transitional Justice' (2020) 14 *International Journal of Transitional Justice* 3, at 415–422.

their dialectical development, benefiting from the exceptionality of transitional justice. In addition, this new trajectory in state duties would find support to the vindications of victims and civil society, expressed by the numerous cases that have been filed against corporate abusers. The latter demonstrate shared expectations on the issue of reparations in the framework of transitions, and arguably support alternative interpretations of international law. Soft law instruments like the Basic Principles and the UNGPS, also, seem to support a novel interpretation of the state obligation to enable corporate reparations.

A promising pathway for integrating corporate accountability into transitional justice lies in Guarantees of Non-Repetition (GNR), given their unique characteristics compared to other reparation measures, evidenced, among others, by their consolidation and autonomization as a measure of transitional justice. Notably, GNRs' scope has significantly broadened, from focusing on narrow measures such as demobilization and vetting, to wider transformative ones, few times also addressing corporate actors. In addition, they have come to include legislative measures against structural wrongs, shifting away from isolated individual violations to addressing generalized patterns of corporate abuse and impunity. This bestows them with future-oriented and preventive, rather than remedial, character. In turn, by moving beyond a solely remedial focus, GNRs have become more akin to positive obligations to ensure and protect rights, which could be interpreted as a window of opportunity for the inclusion of corporations in the transitional process, given that positive obligations already reach non-state violators. In other words, the close affinity of GNRs to positive obligations and their preventive nature create nuances in their secondary status and distance them from the strict requirements of the right to remedy, that have so far hindered the inclusion of corporate malefactors.

Important insights regarding the possibility of corporate reparations are also provided by domestic and foreign litigation, as well as by the few land restitution schemes that took account of corporate involvement in land dispossession. The limited availability of coordinated reparation mechanisms usually leads victims to independently pursue reparations through domestic or foreign civil courts. Among the various hurdles faced in their pursuit of justice, it seems that the most demoralizing blow is dealt by governments' opposition, like in the case of South Africa. Its officials, despite the widespread involvement of corporations in the Apartheid, vehemently opposed victims' litigation in the US, exonerated corporations and instead pled for their invaluable support to the country's development.[232]

Nevertheless, both foreign and domestic litigation have, also, promising aspects. Colombia's example, despite its deficits, is heralded for creating a comprehensive system. Under that system, third parties, including businesspersons, can voluntarily present themselves before the JEP and admit their illegal actions during the conflict, for which they might be asked to provide reparations. Beyond Colombia, individual litigation endeavours brought by victims before transitional fora yielded positive outcomes, when victims and their counsels used legal arguments, outside the usual boxes of tort law and blended elements from various domestic and international legal fields. Equally instrumental in achieving positive outcomes domestically has been the role of civil society. The importance of domestic cases against corporations, during transitional times, lies in rooting the integration of transitional justice and corporate accountability in a bottom-up and thus more victim-oriented approach. In turn, and importantly for the future of such practice, those domestic examples attune the global transitional landscape to the need for corporate accountability and create respective expectations in transitional spaces. Accountability of corporations slowly becomes anticipated, and normalized, potentially inspiring similar actions in other parts of the world. Resource to foreign courts has not borne equal fruits, but has contributed to the overall quest for corporate accountability, as it has often catalysed domestic developments. Oftentimes, foreign litigation brought to the global spotlight cases of corporate abuse and stirred advocacy campaigns in favour of victims, beyond national borders.

Altogether, litigation has infused transitional justice with important attributes and has offered new directions for its practical and theoretical development. Litigation efforts, often initiated by victims themselves, typically under challenging conditions and without institutional backing, reflect victims' needs for justice and reparations, free from top-down imperatives. By mirroring victims' desires, they organically address the question of whether corporate accountability should be pursued during periods of transition, where priorities are often perceived to exclude it. The perseverance of victims points to a different, than the mainstream,

232 Ministry of Justice and Constitutional Development, Republic of South Africa, 'Declaration by Justice Minister Penuell Maduna on Apartheid Litigation in the United States', 11 July 2003, available at www.gov.za/sites/default/files/gcis_document/201409/apartheid1.pdf.

understanding of responsibility, one that re-evaluates transitional priorities and challenges rigid perceptions on the identity of perpetrators. Importantly for the future direction of the field, those litigation efforts morph into 'a body of practice that holds economic actors accountable',[233] in turn, fostering a doctrinal convergence or an expectation of such convergence across various jurisdictions, impacting not only other domestic legal systems but also shaping international law. Even in a context where robust regulation is currently missing, the pursuit of justice seems to influence the expectations and interpretations of what justice should look like, particularly so during transitions.

In terms of land restitution, the example of Colombia has been again valuable. It sketched out an intricate scheme, where victims under certain conditions can take back the land lost due to violence and also due to seemingly lawful business transactions. The law has been praised for incorporating assumptions able to grapple with business and human rights challenges, and for shifting the burden of proof to current owners, possibly corporate entities. However, despite its advancements in paper, it has been insufficiently implemented in practice.

A last insight drawn from Part II concerns the often-cited concerns around development and investment, which often serve as arguments against corporate involvement in transitional justice in general, and in reparations in particular. The South African Minister of Justice, Penuell Maduna, in his Declaration on the Apartheid Litigation,[234] appraised the meaningful business contribution to the South African development and emphasized their role in 'human capacity building and employment creation' as well as their significant investments. For him, the pursuit of court-allocated corporate reparations would deter corporate investment and decrease development and prosperity. Maduna represents just one example among numerous TRCs and respective governments, who vouched for corporate-led developmental initiatives while dismissing corporate reparations or other forms of accountability. However, despite this common conflation, the fields of transitional justice and development are distinct, and the aims of the former cannot be subsumed under a development agenda, as they have different objectives, and they are

[233] Payne et al., *Archimedes' Lever*, p. 271.

[234] Ministry of Justice and Constitutional Development, Republic of South Africa, 'Declaration by Justice Minister Penuell Maduna on Apartheid Litigation in the United States', 11 July 2003, available at www.gov.za/sites/default/files/gcis_document/201409/apartheid1.pdf.

legally rooted in different principles. Rather, the transformative justice discourse seems to offer a more suitable framework, as it is better equipped to address the complex challenges of integrating transitional justice with corporate accountability. This is because transformative justice in general, and transformative reparations in particular, aim to tackle pre-existing structural inequalities that left some individuals vulnerable and prone to victimization, but empowered others to commit abuses with impunity. Corporate accountability and reparations can play a crucial role in challenging those pre-existing structures of exclusion, marginalization and power, as they are among the fundamental actors that anchor them, and benefit from the associated socio-economic policies. Transformative approaches, with their commitment to addressing the root causes of marginalization and exploitation, offer a powerful symbolic framework able to support the calls for corporate reparations for historical injustices, including slavery, colonialism and racial discrimination.

PART IV

Truth Mechanisms

7

The Content of Truth

Insights from International Law

Several truth commissions across the world have touched upon the accountability of corporations for different crimes and abuses, including financing violence, participating in illegal detention, torture, extrajudicial killings, forced labour, gender-based violence, profiting from environmental destruction and others.[1] Nevertheless, their impact has been classified as rather poor.[2] As with the other transitional mechanisms, the problem of corporate marginalisation in the work of truth mechanisms is grounded on the lack of understanding of corporate accountability as a feature of transitional justice, in general, and of truth commissions, in particular. Domestic law might not perceive corporate entities as capable of perpetrating offences, and thus their wrongdoing might remain in the shadows. Politicians might perceive truth about corporate violations either as unimportant or as an alternative measure instead of criminal justice and reparations. From its side, international law is unclear regarding the right to truth and its interplay with the revelation of perpetrators' identities. This saddles on the already discussed debate of the capacity of corporate entities to commit criminal and human rights violations.[3]

One could argue that the problem created by the legal inconsistencies mentioned earlier is trivial because, first, truth by definition includes all violations, be they induced by state or non-state actors. However, a meticulous study of the different cases demonstrates that be the truth as it may, yet the work of truth commissions has been targeted on the basis of various legal arguments, including presumption of innocence,

[1] Payne et al., *Archimedes' Lever*, pp. 178–195.

[2] Payne et al. identify several reasons for that, including due to superficial investigation, lack of adequate mandates (except for Chad, Timor-Leste, Kenya and Liberia) or scant recommendations. Payne et al., *Archimedes' Lever*, p. 326 *et seq.*

[3] See Section 3.2.2 of this book.

amnesties and other.[4] It can also be argued that TRCs around the globe have already dealt with corporate accountability, and thus any further examination is redundant. But, again, TRCs have so far touched upon corporate malefactors as a matter of practical necessity, in a rather ad hoc and fruitless way instead of as a matter of law.

Against this background, this chapter and Chapter 8 identify and propose novel frameworks of analysis of state duties and corresponding victims' rights[5] that could address extant and potential challenges regarding the integration of corporate accountability within the purview of Truth Commissions, aligning them with pertinent case studies. Here, two notes are necessary. First, the articulation of a legal rationale for the inclusion of corporate malefactors in transitional schemes is important in that it brings certainty. In turn, certainty brings legality, which is highly valuable in view of the unacceptably large deficits of the legal framework for access to remedies.[6] Secondly, the classification of arguments and case studies was made with the intention to illustrate the main argument, rather than to establish watertight legal classifications. In fact, most of the case studies in this chapter and Chapter 8, and also in general during transitions, are the effect of a multiplicity of factors, actors and challenges.

7.1 The Legal Bases of the Right to Truth and Its Unrestricted Character: Repercussions for Corporate Malfeasance

In transitional settings, different measures aim to achieve accountability for the perpetrator, justice for the victims and reconciliation.[7] The UN independent expert on impunity, Mr Louis Joinet, described truth as an

[4] Aldana-Pindell analyses how the informal setting of TRCs has given alibi to those named in its findings to oppose the work of the TRC on the basis of lack of due process guarantees. Aldana-Pindell, 'In Vindication of Justiciable Victims' Rights', pp. 1443, 1474. See also the case of *Van Rensburg and Du Preez* v. *The Truth and Reconciliation Commission* brought by two persons named in the report of the South African TRC against the Commission, *Van Rensburg and Du Preez* v. *The Truth and Reconciliation Commission* (426/96) [1997] ZASCA 2 (18 February 1997).

[5] There is an ongoing theoretical debate regarding the relationship between interpretation and modification of rules in international law. See n 37, Section 3.2.1, Part II, of this book.

[6] UN Human Rights Council, Report of the Special Rapporteur on extrajudicial, summary or arbitrary executions on armed non-state actors: the protection of the right to life, A/HRC/38/44, 5 June 2018.

[7] United Nations, Guidance Note of the Secretary-General, United Nations Approach to Transitional Justice, March 2010.

inalienable right of every people to know the truth about past events, the circumstances and the reasons, which led, through a consistent pattern of gross violations of human rights, to the perpetration of aberrant crimes.[8] The UN, in the framework of a study on the right to truth almost ten years later, elaborated that truth is the entitlement to know 'the full and complete truth as to the events that transpired, their specific circumstances, and who participated in them, including knowing the circumstances in which the violations took place, as well as the reasons for them'.[9]

Searching for the truth represents an effort to establish a commonly accepted starting point that will enable reconciliation and avert future conflict. TRCs, both as a process and an outcome, are considered to be conducive to reconciliation and peace,[10] by offering individual and collective catharsis[11] and establishing the necessary consensus that will allow society to move forward.[12] According to an official definition, they are 'official, temporary, non-judicial fact finding bodies that investigate a pattern of abuses of human rights or humanitarian law committed over a number of years'.[13] They provide a forum, where victims' voices are brought in the foreground[14] and deliver a report with their findings and respective recommendations. Since by definition they follow periods of serious violations, their material scope has focused on telling the truth

[8] 'Joinet Report', Annex I, Principle 1.

[9] Report of the Office of the United Nations High Commissioner for Human Rights, Study on the Right to the Truth, UN Doc. E/CN.4/2006/91 (2006) ('UN Study on the Right to the Truth'), par. 3.

[10] Leebaw, 'The Irreconcilable Goals of Transitional Justice', 103; J. Méndez, 'The Right to Truth', in C. Joyner and M. C. Bassiouni (eds.), *Reining in Impunity for International Crimes and Serious Violations of Fundamental Human Rights: Proceedings of the Siracusa Conference* (Érès, 1998), p. 270.

[11] Y. Naqvi, 'The Right to the Truth in International Law: Fact or Fiction' (2006) 88 *International Review of the Red Cross* 245, p. 263; IACtHR, 'Case of the Río Negro Massacres v. Guatemala', par. 265.

[12] J. Méndez, 'The Human Right to Truth: Lessons Learned from Latin American Experiences with Truth Telling', in T. A. Borer (ed.), *Telling the Truths: Truth Telling and Peace Building in Post-Conflict Societies* (University of Notre Dame Press, 2006), p. 142.

[13] 'The Rule of Law and Transitional Justice in Conflict and Post-Conflict Societies', UN Doc. S/2004/616, par. 50.

[14] E. G. Salmon, 'Reflections on International Humanitarian Law and Transitional Justice: Lessons to Be Learnt from the Latin American Experience' (2006) 88 *International Review of the Red Cross*, p. 352.

about all gross human rights violations and serious breaches of international humanitarian law.[15]

According to Mendez, Truth Commissions work (or should work) on three levels: first they uncover structural truths, then they address individualized truth telling for each victim and lastly they offer a forum, where the victims can be heard by political and social representatives.[16] The significance of truth mechanisms lies in their ability to influence both the victim and society as a whole.[17] For individual victims, truth processes are fundamental in providing a cathartic forum,[18] leading to a sense of psychological closure and restoration of their dignity.[19] Truth is essential for victims because it signals a shift from conventional criminal justice models towards victim-oriented remedies for both survivors and the society at large.[20] In the macro level, truth mechanisms initiate a public procedure of healing by acknowledging victims' suffering.[21] By establishing a commonly accepted historical record,[22] truth has the potential to fight impunity and avoid recurrence of violations.[23]

15 Méndez, 'Accountability for Past Abuses', p. 255.

16 Méndez, 'The Right to Truth', p. 265.

17 Ruti Teitel, for example, observed that transitional history-making carries transformative potential. See R. Teitel, *Transitional Justice* (Oxford University Press, 2000), p. 71; J. Méndez and J. Mariezcurrena, 'Accountability for Past Human Rights Violations: Contributions of the Inter-American Organs of Protection' (1999) 26 *Social Justice*, at 94. For a detailed classification of the objectives of truth commissions, see P. Hayner, *Unspeakable Truths: Transitional Justice and the Challenge of Truth Commissions* (Routledge, 2011), p. 27.

18 A. Chapman, 'Truth Commissions as Instruments of Forgiveness and Reconciliation', in R. G. Helmick and R. L. Peterson (eds.), *Forgiveness and Reconciliation: Religion, Public Policy, and Conflict Transformation* (Templeton Foundation Press, 2001); M. Freeman and P. Hayner, 'Truth Telling', in D. Bloomfield (ed.), *Reconciliation After Violent Conflict: A Handbook* (International Institute for Democracy and Electoral Assistance, 2003).

19 On the healing potential of TRCs, see Elster, 'Closing the Books'; D. Mendeloff, 'Trauma and Vengeance: Assessing the Psychological and Emotional Effects of Post-Conflict Justice' (2009) 31 *Human Rights Quarterly* 3, p. 619; Aldana-Pindell, 'In Vindication of Justiciable Victims' Rights', at 1439; Naqvi, 'The Right to the Truth', p. 5.

20 R. Teitel, 'Beyond Vienna & Beijing: Human Rights Theory: Human Rights Genealogy' (1997) 66 *Fordham Law Review*, pp. 301, 315.

21 Méndez, 'The Right to Truth', p. 270.

22 C. E. Loyle and C. Davenport, 'Transitional Injustice: Subverting Justice in Transition and Post Conflict Societies' (2015) 15 *Journal of Human Rights* 1, p. 4; Naqvi, 'The Right to the Truth', p. 2.

23 The Inter-American Commission on Human Rights has recognized that the right to know the truth is fundamental for societies in order to avoid repetition of aberrant

Further to that, the documentation of pervasive patterns of abuse allows the state to confront its past and achieve reform.[24] The truth-telling procedure fosters civic trust,[25] reassigns agency and the value of free expression[26] and contributes to the principles of transparency and good governance.[27] Those, in turn, are required for the establishment of rule of law[28] and the functioning of democratic systems.[29] As stated in the Decree establishing the Chilean National Commission on Truth and Reconciliation, 'only upon a foundation of truth will it be possible to meet the basic demands of justice and create the necessary conditions for achieving true national reconciliation'.[30]

In the aftermath of widespread corporate violations during conflict or repression, excluding corporate harm from the scope of Truth Commissions not only undermines the aforementioned benefits but also detracts much of truth's meaning as an entitlement to learn of events, reasons, circumstances and actors that produced harm. Truth about corporate offences seems to be a fundamental part of what is to be registered, insofar as corporate entities committed offences or were implicated in systemic patterns of violence, before the transitional period.

crimes. See Annual Report 1985–1986, OEA/Ser.L/V/II.68, Doc. 8, rev 1, 28 September 1986, chapter V; IACmHR, Report No. 37/00, *Case 11.481, Monsignor Oscar Arnulfo Romero y Galdámez, El Salvador*, 13 April 2000, par. 148. In relation to the Court, see IACtHR, *Case of Ximenes-Lopes* v. *Brazil*, Judgment (4 July 2006), par. 245; see also Joinet Report, Annex I, Principle 1. On the pre-emptive and deterrent character of TRCs, see Loyle and Davenport, 'Transitional Injustice', p. 4; D. Mendeloff, 'Truth-Seeking, Truth-Telling, and Post-Conflict Peacebuilding: Curb the Enthusiasm?' (2004) 6 *International Studies Review* 3, at 361.

24 Aldana-Pindell, 'In Vindication of Justiciable Victims' Rights', p. 1439.

25 T. A. Borer, *Telling the Truths: Truth Telling and Peace Building in Post-Conflict Societies* (University of Notre Dame Press, 2006). On the influence of TRCs on politics, judicial accountability and society, see Bakiner, 'Truth Commission Impact'.

26 L. Laplante, 'The Peruvian Truth Commission's Historical Memory Project: Empowering Truth-Tellers to Confront Truth Deniers' (2007) 6 *Journal of Human Rights*, at 435.

27 'UN Study on the Right to the Truth', par. 46.

28 Truth revealed through adequate investigations increases 'public confidence in their adherence to the rule of law and in preventing any appearance of collusion in or tolerance of unlawful acts'. ECtHR, *El-Masri* v. *The Former Yugoslav Republic of Macedonia*, Application No. 39630/09, Judgment of 13 December 2012, par. 192.

29 Mendeloff, 'Truth-Seeking, Truth-Telling, and Post-Conflict Peacebuilding', 361; T. Olsen, L. Payne and A. Reiter, 'The Justice Balance: When Transitional Justice Improves Human Rights and Democracy' (2010) 32 *Human Rights Quarterly* 4, at 1005; Hayner, *Unspeakable Truths*, p. 105.

30 Report of the Chilean National Commission on Truth and Reconciliation (University of Notre Dame Press, 1993), Vol. I/II, p. 24.

In its absence, the account of the conflict or repression created would lack essential information on perpetrators and circumstances of harm and thus would weaken the TRCs' functions, namely accountability and deterrence[31] for the perpetrators and healing for the victims. In other words, by reducing the account of the narrative publicly recorded, the absence of corporate malefactors would also reduce the very aims that truth seeks to attain.

Furthermore, corporate invisibility would disregard the evolution of human rights law, as evidenced by the work of various international and regional human rights bodies.[32] Although few TRCs[33] and only one international convention[34] specifically mention the right to truth, zooming in different fields of international law lends interesting insights, supporting an interpretation of transitional states' obligations to reveal the truth for every violation, corporate ones included, as a matter of law.

The right to truth and a respective state duty can be traced to a limited extent to public international law,[35] and more extensively to international humanitarian law.[36] Under the ICC Statute, the court has a

[31] Valji, *Trials and Truth Commissions*, p. 3; Fernández Torné, *Accountability, a New Framework to Assess the Impact of Truth Commissions.*

[32] The practice of those organs, in terms of their interpretation, binds states, due to the good faith obligations to respect the treaties that they signed. Simma and Alston, 'The Sources of Human Rights', at 82, 100. Regional human rights courts can also contribute to the development of custom, through their cumulative and consistent jurisprudence. Merrills, *The Development of International Law by the European Court of Human Rights.*

[33] Few truth commissions made explicit references to the right to the truth, namely the Guatemalan, the Peruvian, the Brazilian and the Tunisian. See UN Mission for the Verification of Human Rights in Guatemala, Commission for Historical Clarification: Chapter 1; for Peru, see Supreme Decree No. 065-2001-PCM, 4 June 2001; for Brazil, see Brazil Law No. 12.528 of 18 November 2011, Article 1; for Tunisia, see Draft Organic Law on the Foundations and Organization of Transitional Justice of Tunisia's Instance Verite et Dignite, Articles 2 and 5. Also Articles 4 and 7 of the Colombian Law No. 975 of 25 July 2005 'On justice and peace' referred to the right to truth.

[34] The International Convention for the Protection of All Persons from Enforced Disappearance is the only treaty explicitly providing for a right to know the truth, for the victims and their relatives. See respectively Articles 24 and 18 of the Convention. UN Doc. E/CN.4/2005/WG.22/WP.1/REV.4.

[35] The commentary to Article 37 of the Draft Articles on State Responsibility stipulates that a form of satisfaction for state breaches of international norms is the 'due inquiry into the causes of an accident resulting in harm or injury'. ILC, 'Commentaries on the Draft Articles on Responsibility of States for Internationally Wrongful Acts', Article 33, par. 3.

[36] The First and Second Geneva Conventions stipulate the obligation of the parties to the conflict to search for, ensure adequate care, identify and exchange information about the wounded, sick and dead of the other party to the conflict in the field and at sea. Likewise, the Third and Fourth Geneva Conventions regulate the recording and forwarding of

duty to determine the truth[37] and can sanction those who give false testimony.[38] Truth can also be attained through the participation of victims in the proceedings before the court or upon invitation to share their views regarding potential reparation orders.[39] In the human rights field, said right has been affirmed by respective bodies, or has been inferred, by classifying functionally equivalent information[40] about its constitutive elements, namely investigations,[41] and disclosure of information to the claimants and the general public.[42]

information regarding prisoners of war and civilian persons to the stipulated authorities. The First Additional Protocol to the Geneva Conventions explicitly mentioned the 'right of families to know the fate of their relatives' and accordingly provided for the obligation of the parties to the conflict to 'search for the persons who have been reported missing by an adverse Party'. The International Committee of the Red Cross has affirmed the existence of a customary obligation for the parties to the conflict to provide information for missing persons. Rule 117 in Henckaerts and Doswald-Beck, *Customary International Humanitarian Law*, p. 421.

37 Rome Statute of the International Criminal Court, Article 69(3).

38 Ibid., Articles 69(1) and 70(1)(a). Witnesses are required to take a solemn undertaking before testifying in accordance with Rule 66.

39 Ibid., Articles 68(3) and 75; ICC, Rules of Procedure and Evidence, Rule 97. Note, also, that the review conference recognized that mechanisms to address reparations should help facilitate victims' rights to truth, justice and reparations.

40 On the content of functional equivalence, see Zweigert and Kötz, *An Introduction to Comparative Law*.

41 Note that the use of the term investigation here is broader than the one in the Justice chapter. In the Justice chapter, investigations were subsumed by the overall obligation to criminalize, with the specific challenges entailed. In the current chapter, the focus is on the investigation aspect and not on the criminalization one. As per the International Commission of Jurists, investigation duties form a self-standing category, and face different challenges for the purposes of truth, than for the purposes of criminal justice. In addition, investigative duties are broader because they apply to every violation and not only to those that require criminalisation, whereas they can take forms other than criminal, such as administrative mechanisms. See HRC, 'General Comment 31', par. 15. This is proven by the fact that investigation is the first step for an effective remedy, as stated at the Joinet Report. Criminal investigations will not be analysed further in the current chapter, given that the problems that might arise are the same as those analysed in the Justice chapter. Also, while criminal measures might reveal the truth, it will be argued below that they should run in parallel with truth measures.

42 The publicity of the information revealed through investigations has been put forward by human rights bodies. See, indicatively, IACtHR, 'Juan Humberto Sánchez v. Honduras', par. 186; IACtHR, 'Case of Caracazo v. Venezuela Reparation Judgment', paras. 115, 116; ECtHR, 'McKerr v. the United Kingdom', par. 141; AfrComHPR, *Case Amnesty International et al.* v. *Sudan*, Communication No. 48/90, 50/91, 52/91, 89/93, 15 November 1999, par. 51.

The Human Rights Committee,[43] the Inter-American system,[44] the African Commission of Human and Peoples' Rights[45] and to a lesser extent the ECtHR[46] have constantly touched upon the issue of truth and

[43] HRC, 'General Comment 31', par. 15; HRC, General Comment No. 20 on Article 7, 13 March 1992, HRI/GEN/1/Rev7, par. 14. See also HRC, *Case Hugo Rodríguez* v. *Uruguay*, Communication No. 322/1988, View of 19 July 1994, par. 12(3); HRC, *Case of Lyashkevich* v. *Belarus*, Communication No. 887/1999, Views of 3 April 2003, par. 11; HRC, *Case of Khalilova* v. *Tajikistan*, Communication No. 973/2001, Views adopted on 30 March 2005; HRC, *Case of Valichon Aliboev* v. *Tajikistan*, Communication No. 985/2001, Views adopted on 16 November 2005, par. 6.7; HRC, *Case of Nydia Erika Bautista* v. *Colombia*, Communication No. 563/1993, Views of 13 November 1995, par. 8.6; HRC, *Celis Laureano* v. *Peru*, Communication No. 540/1993, Views of 16 April 1996, par. 10; HRC, *Case Sarma* v. *Sri Lanka*, Communication No. 950/2000, Views of 16 July 2003, par. 11; HRC, *Case of Staselovich* v. *Belarus*, Communication No. 887/1999, Views of 3 April 2003, par. 9.2.

[44] IAComHR, 'Monsignor Oscar Arnulfo Romero y Galdámez v. El Salvador', par. 148; IACtHR, 'Velásquez-Rodríguez v. Honduras', par. 181; IACtHR, Case of *Contreras et al.* v. *El Salvador*, Series C No. 232, Merits, Reparations and Costs, Judgment of 31 August 2011, par. 170; IACtHR, *Case of Las Palmeras* v. *Colombia*, Series C No. 96, Reparations and Costs, Judgment of 26 November 2002; IACtHR, *Case of Gelman v. Uruguay*, Series C No. 221, Merits and Reparations, Judgment of 24 February 2011, par. 243. The state duty to unveil the truth and the respective right of the victim and his family derive from a combined reading of Article 8 on judicial guarantees and 25 on judicial protection of the American Convention. IACtHR, *Case of Bámaca Velásquez* v. *Guatemala*, Series C No. 70, Judgment of 25 November 2000, par. 201; IACtHR, 'Blake v. Guatemala, Judgment', par. 97.

[45] The African Commission on Human and Peoples' Rights, General Comment No. 4 on the African Charter on Human and Peoples' Rights: The Right to Redress for Victims of Torture and Other Cruel, Inhuman or Degrading Punishment or Treatment (Article 5), par. 10; African Commission on Human and People's Rights, Principles and Guidelines on the Right to a Fair Trial and Legal Assistance in Africa, DOC/OS (XXX) 247, Principle C (b)(3), (d); AfComHPR, *Egyptian Initiative for Personal Rights and Interights* v. *Egypt*, Communication No. 323/06, 1 March 2011, dispositive, par. 238; AfCtHPR, *The Beneficiaries of the Late Norbert Zongo, Abdoulaye Nikiema alias Abiasse, Ernest Zongo and Blaise Ilboudo and the Burkinabe Movement on Human and Peoples' Rights* v. *Burkina Faso*, Communication No. 013/2011, Judgment, 28 March 2014; AfComHPR, 'Zimbabwe Human Rights NGO Forum v. Zimbabwe', par. 213; AfComHPR, *Sudan Human Rights Organisation & Centre on Housing Rights and Evictions (COHRE)* v. *Sudan*, Communication No. 279/03–296/05 (2009) AHRLR 153, 27 May 2009, par. 181.

[46] ECtHR, 'Case of El-Masri v. FYROM', par. 191; ECtHR, *Case of Al Nashiri* v. *Poland*, Application No. 28761/11, Judgment, 24 July 2014; ECtHR, *Case of Husayn (AbuZubaydah)* v. *Poland*, Application No. 7511/13, Judgment 24 July 2014. Note that there have been conflicting concurring opinions on whether the right to the truth constitutes a novel human right or just the procedural aspect of the right to life and the prohibition of torture. ECtHR, *Case of El-Masri* v. *FYROM*, Joint Concurring Opinion of Judges Tulkens, Spielmann, Sicilianos and Keller (par. 83) qualified the right to the truth as a well-established reality. Contrary, Judges Casadevall and Lopez Guerra

the state obligation to provide information as part of the right to remedy.[47] The right to know the truth is also stipulated in soft law instruments, such as the Impunity Principles,[48] and the Basic Principles and Guidelines on the Right to a Remedy and Reparation for Victims of Gross Violations of International Human Rights Law and Serious Violations of International Humanitarian Law.[49]

On top of linking truth to remedies, human rights bodies have recurrently framed truth as part of the states' positive obligation to investigate.[50] The HRC has asserted the duty of states to conduct investigations into allegations of gross human rights violations,[51] based on the general provisions to 'respect and ensure' of Article 2 (1) of the ICCPR.[52] The Inter-American organs have also extrapolated the obligation to provide truth from the generic obligations established in Article 1.1 of the Convention.[53] As per the words of the Commission, 'the interpretation

considered an analysis of the right to the truth as redundant. ECtHR, *Case of El-Masri v. FYROM*, joint report concurring opinion of Judges Casadevall and Lopez Guerra.

47 It is to be noted that the HRC, as well as the Inter-American and African human rights organs apply the right to truth and its constituent element of investigations in relation to every human right violation, departing from its initial association to disappearance cases. The ECtHR has been timider in its articulations, recognizing the obligation to investigate serious violations of Articles 2 on the protection of life, 3 on the prohibition of torture and 5 on the right to liberty. For an elaborate account, see T. M. Antkowiak, 'Truth as Right and Remedy in International Human Rights Experience' (2002) 23 *Michigan Journal of International Law* 977, p. 984.

48 'Joinet Report', par. 17–25.

49 'Basic Principles', UN Doc. A/RES/60/147, Principles 7, 15, 22.

50 It is to be noted that the scope of investigations alters depending on the article that has ground the respective obligation of the state. T. Antkowiak, 'Truth as Right and Remedy', 984.

51 HRC, *Concluding Observations on Colombia*, 25 March 2004, CCPR/CO/80/COL, par. 10, 15; HRC, *Concluding Observations on Germany*, CCPR/CO/80/GER, 30 March 2004, par. 15, 16; HRC, *Concluding Observations on Lithuania*, CCPR/CO/80/LTU, 1 April 2004, par. 10.

52 HRC, 'Hugo Rodríguez v. Uruguay', par. 12(3); HRC, *José Vicente and Amado Villafañe Chaparro et al.* v. *Colombia*, Communication No. 612/1995, Views of 29 July 1997, par. 8.8; HRC, *Case Blanco* v. *Nicaragua*, Communication No. 328/1988, Views of 18 August 1994, par. 11.

53 IACtHR, 'Case of Velásquez-Rodríguez v. Honduras', par. 166, 174; IACtHR, *Case of Gomes Lund et al. ('Guerrilha Do Araguaia')* v. *Brazil*, Series C No. 219, Judgment 24 November 2010, par. 173; IAComHR, Report No. 25/98, *Alfonso René Chanfeau Orayce et al., Chile*, Cases 11.505 et al., 7 April 1998, par. 87; IACtHR, *Case of Tibi* v. *Ecuador*, Series C No. 114, Judgment 7 September 2004. See also J. M. Pasqualucci, 'The Whole Truth and Nothing but the Truth: Truth Commissions, Impunity and the Inter-American Human Rights System' (1994) 12 *Boston University International Law Journal*, at 330.

of the generic obligations established in Article 1.1 made by the Court [...] allows for the conclusion that the "right to truth" is a basic and indispensable consequence for every State Party'.[54] The ECtHR has reasoned that investigation into a violation is dictated by the substantive right that was violated, read in conjunction with the state's general duty under Article 1 of the Convention to 'secure to everyone within their jurisdiction the rights and freedoms defined in the Convention'.[55] Lastly, the African Commission has asserted that the essence of a right to truth can be discerned from cases that establish a state's obligation to investigate atrocities as a procedural duty arising out of substantive rights,[56] in conjunction to Article 1 of the African Charter.[57] Conversely, the denial of information regarding violations can amount to a separate violation of human rights.[58]

[54] IACHR, 'Alfonso René Chanfeau Oraycem (Chile)', par. 87.

[55] This has been held in relation to violations of Article 2 on the right to life and 3 on the prohibition of torture. For Article 2, see ECtHR, 'Mccann and Others v. The United Kingdom', Judgment, par. 161; ECtHR, *Case of Öneryildiz* v. *Turkey*, Application No. 48939/99, Judgment of 30 November 2004, par. 90; ECtHR, *Case of Aslakhanova* v. *Russia*, Application Nos. 2944/06, 8300/07, 50184/07, Judgment of 18 December 2012, par. 122. For Article 3, see ECtHR, 'Case of El-Masri v. FYROM', par. 242, 243; ECtHR, *Case of Association 21 December 1989 and others* v. *Romania*, Application Nos. 33810/07, 18817/08, Judgment of 28 November 2011; ECtHR, *Case of Mocanu* v. *Romania*, Application Nos. 10865/09, 45886/07 and 32431/08, Judgment of 17 September 2014, paras. 332–351; ECtHR, *Case of Bouyid* v. *Belgium*, Application No. 23380/09, 28 September 2015, par. 114; ECtHR, *Case of Jeronovičs* v. *Latvia*, Application No. 44898/10, 5 July 2016, par. 103.

[56] In *Gabriel Shumba* v. *Zimbabwe*, the Commission held that lack of investigation of torture is in contravention to Article 5. It recommended to the state to carry out an inquiry and investigation, to bring those who perpetrated the violations to justice. AfrComHPR, *Gabriel Shumba* v. *Zimbabwe*, Communication No. 288/04, 30 June 2017, par. 161. The necessity of investigation as a requirement for the realization of the substance of Articles 2, 5 and 18 was also upheld in the Egyptian Initiative for Personal Rights and Interights v. Egypt case, 'AfrComHPR, Interights v. Egypt', dispositif, par. 163, 167, 209; AfComHPR, *COHRE* v. *Sudan*, par. 145 *et seq.*

[57] AfComHPR, 'Zimbabwe Human Rights NGO Forum v. Zimbabwe', par. 146. In the *Interights* v. *Egypt* case, investigation was also considered as an obligation of the state in accordance with Article 1 of the Charter. AfrComHPR, 'Interights v. Egypt', dispositive, par. 273.

[58] See, indicatively, HRC, *Case Almeida de Quinteros et al.* v. *Uruguay*, Communication No. 107/1981, Views of 21 July 1983, par. 14; IACtHR, *Case of Bámaca Velásquez* v. *Guatemala*, Series C No. 70, Judgment of 25 November 2000, par. 160, 165; ECtHR, *Case of Kurt* v. *Turkey*, Application No. 24276/94, Judgment of 25 May 1998, par. 174; ECtHR, 'Case of El-Masri v. FYROM', par. 233, 240, 249; AfComHPR, 'Amnesty International v. Sudan', par. 54.

If one has to search for the truth, it can reasonably be assumed that this truth will be all-encompassing, including corporate violations, especially in view of the fact that corporate abuses during conflict or repression can rarely be dissociated from systemic patterns of violence that led to the very need for transition. A context abounding with corporate abuses makes those obligations all the more compelling, since the context 'in which the facts took place permeates and conditions the State's international responsibility in relation to its obligation to respect and safeguards the rights embodied in (. . .) the Convention'.[59]

Moreover, truth as a form of satisfaction presents an interesting sequence, in terms of legal obligations, absent from other forms of reparations, in cases where corporate malefactors are in the picture. To illustrate, in the case of compensation, as per international human rights law, when corporations commit wrongs and the state fails to protect against them, then it is the state that will be the debtor of compensation. In the case of truth, the failure of the state to protect against corporate violations will trigger its obligation to investigate. However, this obligation will not be reduced to an investigation of wrongs committed by state agents, namely it will not be confined within the state (or within the secondary state violation), as would be the case with compensation (in an analogous way). Instead, human rights bodies and courts have urged states to investigate the initial violation by the third-party actor,[60] even at the stage of investigation of the state's failure to protect. Putting at the forefront, the positive obligations of states during the remedial phase, in legal terms, consents to the discharge of those obligations against non-state entities, something that has been clearly accepted by human rights bodies.[61] Markedly, the Basic

[59] IACtHR, *Case of Goiburú et al.* v. *Paraguay*, Series C No. 153, Judgment of 22 September 2006, Merits, Reparations and Costs, par. 62.

[60] HRC, 'Almeida de Quinteros et al. v. Uruguay'; see HRC, *Luis Asdrúbal Jiménez Vaca* v. *Colombia*, Communication No. 859/1999, 15 April 2002, par. 9. IACtHR, 'Case of Velásquez-Rodríguez v. Honduras', Reparations and Costs, par. 34; AfrComHPR, '*Zimbabwe Human Rights NGO Forum* v. *Zimbabwe*', Holdings; AfComHPR, *COHRE* v. *Sudan*, par. 229.

[61] See, indicatively, Joseph and Castan, *The International Covenant on Civil and Political Rights*, p. 43; IACtHR, 'Case of Velásquez-Rodríguez v. Honduras', par. 172, 176; ECtHR, *Case of Osmanoglu* v. *Turkey*, Application No. 48804/99, Judgment of 24 January 2008, par.76; AfrComHPR, 'Commission Nationale des Droits de l'Homme et des Libertes v. Chad'; AfComHPR, *Social and Economic Rights Action Centre and the Centre for Economic and Social Rights* v. *Nigeria*, Communication No. 155/96 (2001), 27 October 2001.

Principles list 'verification of the facts and full and public disclosure of the truth' as a measure of satisfaction that is to be provided not only by the state but also from the legal person or entity liable for the harm.[62]

Accordingly, in several communications[63] and concluding observations,[64] the HRC has examined state failures to discharge its positive obligations against acts committed by 'corporate entities' and has ordered investigations.[65] The ECtHR, in *Guerra* v. *Italy* case, located the problem in the lack of sufficient information about the harm inflicted by a chemical fertilizer plant.[66] The Inter-American Court has recently referred to the United Nations Guiding Principles and to the duty of the state to investigate corporate wrongdoing.[67] In the African human rights system, the Commission has acknowledged that states should protect the rights of the Charter by performing their positive obligations against acts committed by corporate entities.[68] In *SERAC* v. *Nigeria*, the Commission appealed to the government of Nigeria to conduct investigations on human rights violations committed by private actors in the oil concessions in Ogoniland and to establish effective and independent oversight bodies for the petroleum industry.[69]

Despite the aforementioned rich legal background, one might argue that disregarding corporate abuses while delivering the truth (or referring

62 Basic Principles, Principles 15 and 22.

63 HRC, 'Love et al. v. Australia', HRC, 'Hopu and Bessert v. France'; HRC, *Ilmari Länsman et al.* v. *Finland*, Communication No. 511/1992, 8 November 1994; HRC, *Chief Bernard Ominayak and the Lubicon Lake Band* v. *Canada*, Communication No. 167/1984, 10 May 1990; HRC, 'Nahlik v. Austria'.

64 HRC, *Concluding Observations, Brazil*, CCPR/C/BRA/CO/2, 1 December 2005, paras. 11 and 14; HRC, *Concluding Observations for Kenya*, CCPR/CO/83/KEN, 29 April 2005, par. 26; HRC, *Concluding Observations, Uzbekistan*, CCPR/CO/83/UZB, 26 April 2005, par. 25; HRC, *Concluding Observations, Suriname*, CCPR/CO/80/SUR, 4 May 2004, par. 21.

65 HRC, *Concluding Observations USA* (2006) UN Doc. CCPR/C/USA/CO/3/Rev.1, par. 14.

66 ECtHR, *Case of Guerra and Others* v. *Italy*, Application No. 116/1996/735/932, Judgment of 19 February 1998, par. 52.

67 IACtHR, *Case of Kaliña y Lokono* v. *Suriname*, Judgement of 25 November 2015 (Merits, Reparations and Costs), par. 224–226; IACtHR, Advisory Opinion (OC-23/17) of 15 November 2017, requested by the Republic of Colombia, par. 154.

68 The General Comment on the Right to Redress for Victims of Torture foresees that 'in cases where an individual, legal person or other entity is found liable for reparation to a victim, such party should provide reparation to the victim or compensate the State if the State has already provided reparation to the victim'. It also considers the truth as a form of reparation. AfComHPR, General Comment No. 4, par. 33.

69 AfrComHPR, 'The Social and Economic Rights Action Centre and the Centre for Economic and Social Rights v. Nigeria', recommendations lit. 1, 2, 4.

to them in a marginal way) amounts to a legitimate restriction of said right, which will presumably enable the transitioning state to move towards the much appraised stage of economic development.[70] However, it should be highlighted that the jurisprudence of international and regional bodies has held that the state duty to investigate, to provide information and truth cannot be restricted by considerations such as confidentiality, public interest or national security.[71] Restrictions that represent 'politically sensitive' approaches, such as for example reconciliation, are also unacceptable, according to the ECHR.[72] If national security cannot hold as a legitimate restriction for the right to know the truth, it is reasonable to believe that neither will economic development, or other common justifications for the exclusion of corporate actors. Notably, the non-derogable character of provisions that the right to truth is linked to, such as the prohibition of torture, also hints to that direction.[73] The UN High Commissioner for Human Rights has further elaborated that 'the judicial remedies that protect fundamental rights, such as *habeas corpus* and *amparo*, which may also be used as procedural instruments to implement the right to the truth, have now come to be understood as non-derogable'.[74]

Even if one argues that truth – as an obligation of means – can be legitimately provided in a partial way, then as Mendez emphasizes, 'the good faith obligation of the Vienna convention closes this gap'.[75] What is important is that the state has initiated adequate processes to reach the truth. Besides, conditioning respect of the right to truth to political exigencies does not seem to be an adequate strategy for transitioning from lawlessness to rule of law. In line with that reasoning, the UN

[70] See also Section 7.2 on the issue of the revelation of identities by TRCs.

[71] IACtHR, *Myrna Mack-Chang* v. *Guatemala*, Series C No. 101, Judgment of 25 November 2003, par. 180, 182 and footnote 258 with reference to the Commission's opinion.

[72] The ECtHR has also excluded national security as a justification for concealing information in relation to criminal state activities. ECtHR, *Case of Varnava and Others* v. *Turkey*, Application Nos. 16064/90 et al., Judgment of 18 September 2009, par. 193.

[73] The judicial recognition of denial of information regarding disappeared persons has been defined as torture, the prohibition of which is non-derogable. HRC, *Almeida de Quinteros et al.* v. *Uruguay*, par. 14; HRC, *Concluding Observations on Uruguay* (1998) CCPR/C/79/Add.90, par. C; ECtHR, 'Staselovich v. Belarus', par. 9.2 and 11; ECtHR, *Khalilova* v. *Tajikistan*; ECtHR, 'Case of Kurt v. Turkey', par. 174; ECtHR, *Case of Cyprus* v. *Turkey*, Application No. 25781/94, Grand Chamber Judgment of 10 May 2001.

[74] 'UN Study on the Right to the Truth', par. 44; HRC, *General Comment No. 29: Article 4: Derogations during a State of Emergency*, 31 August 2001, CCPR/C/21/Rev.1/Add.11.

[75] Méndez, 'The Right to Truth', 270.

asserted that the right to truth is an 'inalienable and autonomous' mandatory right and not subject to limitations.[76] The only restriction of the truth that has gained some legitimate prominence is the one triggered by the potential lack of due process guarantees in the respective fora, such as Truth Commissions. However, TRCs can still validly unveil information about abuses, corporate ones included, on the basis of sufficiently convincing information and respect for due process standards.[77]

7.1.1 The Colombian Commission for the Clarification of Truth, Coexistence and Non-Repetition

The 2016 Colombian Peace Agreement with the FARC-EP established the 'Integrated System of Truth, Justice, Reparation and Non-Repetition', comprising the Commission for the Clarification of Truth, Coexistence and Non-Repetition (CEV), the Special Jurisdiction for Peace (JEP) and the Special Unit for Finding Missing Persons (a.k.a. Missing Persons Unit (MPU)).[78] The mandate of the Commission was to clarify the patterns of human rights and international humanitarian law violations, along with their causes, as well as the relationship between drug trafficking, para-militarism and land dispossession; to promote the victims' recognition and acknowledgement of responsibilities by perpetrators; and to contribute to peaceful co-existence in regions mostly affected by conflict.[79] The CTCN began its work in 2018 and delivered its final report on June 2022.

The significance of this report lies in its alignment to international law, including for cases where non-state actors were involved. It explicitly mentioned that the right to truth forms its basis and clarified that the final report 'constitutes a measure of reparation for the individual and

[76] 'UN Study on the Right to the Truth', par. 4, 41, 44.

[77] For an overview of due process in truth commissions, see S. Szoke-Burke, 'Searching for the Right to Truth: The Impact of International Human Rights Law on National Transitional Justice Policies' (2015), 33 *Berkeley Journal of International Law*, at 561; E. González and H. Varney (eds.), *Truth Seeking: Elements of Creating an Effective Truth Commission* (Amnesty Commission of the Ministry of Justice of Brazil; International Centre for Transitional Justice, 2013), p. 3.

[78] For an overview of the process, see Valiñas, 'The Colombian Special Jurisdiction for Peace', pp. 452–453; Olasolo and Ramirez Mendoza, 'The Colombian Integrated System of Truth, Justice, Reparation and Non-Repetition', p. 1011.

[79] Comisión para el Esclarecimiento de la Verdad, la Convivencia y la No Repetición (CTCN), Régimen Jurídico y Marco Normativo de la Comisión para el Esclarecimiento de la Verdad, la Convivencia y la No Repetición, p. 7.

collective right to truth of victims of the armed conflict in Colombia'. The Commission did not accept any excuse or restriction in releasing names of perpetrators, including corporate ones. It, also, did not confine its work in merely describing wrongful activities of industry sectors, unlike other TRCs, such as the East Timorese one.[80] Instead, it extensively analysed concrete abuses, as well as patterns of abuse, referred to names of both perpetrators and victims, and elaborated on different levels of responsibility for corporate actors.

The lengthy report of the Commission gave a fair and equitable account of the conflict, naming business entities and persons, when they were perpetrators of abuses, and also when they were victimized due to the conflict. It included both individual violations by corporate entities and also brought to light systematic patterns of corporate abuse, which allowed companies to amass economic and political power[81] by exploiting indigenous territories and perpetuating racism, exploitation and abuse, particularly in banana, palm oil and wood-production industries.[82] Extensive land dispossession, particularly in the region of Cesar, was carried out in favour of landowners, ranchers, agro-industrial companies and mega projects.[83] Foreign and local companies, such as Drummond, Glencore and Chiquita, provided financial and logistical support to the AUC, in exchange for dispossessing people of their lands.[84] In the case of Drummond, corporate officials colluded with the military apparatus of the state, as well as paramilitary groups, in order to 'secure' its extractive projects.[85] It is interesting to note that in its testimony, Drummond alleged that Blanco Maya, a former contractor convicted for the company's illegal financing, has falsely tried to incriminate the company.

In other cases, according to the report, extractive projects were carried out without consent by the communities, by corrupting state officials.[86]

[80] See Section 7.2.1 of this book.

[81] CTCN, Final Report, Tomo 11. Colombia adentro: relatos territoriales sobre el conflicto armado, 2022, p. 39.

[82] CTCN, Final Report, Tomo 9. Resistir no es aguantar: violencias y daños contra los pueblos étnicos de Colombia, pp. 48, 53, 62, 110, 392.

[83] CTCN, Final Report, Tomo 4. Hasta la guerra tiene límites: violations de los derechos humanos, infractions al derecho international humanitariano y responsabilidades colectivas, pp. 37 and 447; CTCN, Final Report, Tomo 3. No matarás: relato histórico del conflicto armado interno en Colombia, p. 128.

[84] CTCN, Final Report, Tomo 4, pp. 447 and 953.

[85] Ibid., p. 964.

[86] Ibid., p. 430.

Ecopetrol was mentioned for exacerbating the conflict, by financing paramilitaries, dispossessing people of their land and being involved in the murder of union leaders.[87] Indigenous people were particularly vulnerable to those abuses, as evidenced by the specifically dedicated volume of the report.[88] By way of indication, Urrá Company, in complicity with paramilitary and state forces, persecuted the Emberá people in Córdoba, with the overall aim to curb their opposition to the construction of a hydroelectric plant.[89] The Commission, further, emphasized the privatization of security through agreements with public institutions. It recorded 200 cooperation agreements for security, signed between more than 70 national and foreign mining and energy companies and public institutions. These agreements usually contemplated contributions in money and kind to the institutions in exchange for providing security and surveillance to the companies.[90]

Overall, the Commission registered 258 economic actors, natural persons and companies, national and foreign, that were involved in the Colombian armed conflict by sponsoring, tolerating, facilitating, instigating or committing human rights violations to extract profit, in the petroleum, palm oil, agro-industrial, mining, energy, livestock, financial and real estate sectors.[91] Others ordered paramilitaries to commit human rights violations on their behalf, or participated directly to them, or funded the war and were involved in illicit economies, such as the expropriation of land and the appropriation of natural resources,[92] or took advantage of the conflict to acquire land without respecting human rights due diligence requirements.

The Commission devoted a chapter analysing the responsibility of third parties, and specifically businesses, arising out of the aforementioned situations . It differentiated between two levels of responsibility of economic actors, assessing them against international corporate due diligence standards.[93] The first group of responsible economic actors included those who were directly involved in the conflict, facilitating violations and land dispossession, in a premeditated and decided action in collaboration with armed actors. According to the Commission,

87 Ibid., pp. 430, 960.
88 CTCN, Final Report, Tomo 9, p. 110.
89 CTCN, Final Report, Tomo 4, p. 958.
90 Ibid., p. 950.
91 Ibid., p. 945.
92 Ibid., pp. 943, 945.
93 Ibid., pp. 37, 430.

human rights and humanitarian law violations would have been less serious were it not for those companies' contribution.[94] The second group included those who benefitted from violence and took economic advantage of the armed conflict. This took place through actions or omissions permissive of serious violations of human rights and humanitarian law violations, in particular dispossession and forced displacement in the area of influence of their productive activity.[95] In this scenario, economic actors allowed violations of human rights and humanitarian law by armed groups in the area of their influence, benefited or profited economically from the consequences of the armed conflict or benefitted from supply chains, ravaged by violence.

In terms of recommendations, the report was less daring, with only one direct recommendation being addressed to businesses, namely to reject the armed struggle and demand that different actors put an end to the confrontation.[96] State authorities were urged to prioritize investigations against civilian third parties,[97] including businesspersons, ensure access to justice and resolve land conflicts. In relation to private security companies, the government was asked to ensure effective and efficient control, to strengthen the regime of control and the rules regulating those activities.[98] Explicit reference to corporations was, further, made in the framework of recommendations relating to the sustainable use of lands and territories. Recommendation 56 urges the National Government and the Congress to adopt policies and regulations to prevent, mitigate and repair violations of human, environmental and territorial rights related to business activities, especially in contexts of generalized violence and internal armed conflict.[99] At a minimum, the state was asked to adopt a business and human rights policy that promotes business due diligence in human, environmental and territorial rights, and to establish a company duty to carry out human rights, environmental and territorial impact assessments, and conflict analysis as well as to repair the damage inflicted. Markedly, states were also asked to establish a legal liability regime for non-compliance derived from corporate due diligence, through judicial and non-judicial mechanisms.[100]

[94] Ibid., p. 945.
[95] Ibid., p. 37.
[96] CTCN, Final Report, Tomo 2, Recommendation 6.3, p. 641.
[97] Ibid., Recommendation 34, p. 682.
[98] Ibid., Recommendation 45, p. 700.
[99] Ibid., Recommendation 56, p. 714.
[100] Ibid., Recommendation 56, p. 714.

7.2 The Identity of the Perpetrator as a Key Element of Truth

In transitional contexts, the revelation of identities as part of the truth has sparked debate, because it can exacerbate extant political controversies and hinder reconciliation. The Working Group on Enforced or Involuntary Disappearances (WGEID) in its General Comment on the Right to Truth noted that revealing names of perpetrators is far from common practise, given that 'hiding parts of the truth has been chosen to facilitate reconciliation'.[101] In El Salvador, revealing names of perpetrators raised concerns of triggering a coup.[102] However, the Salvadorian TRC, along with the South African, the Chadian and the Peruvian, chose to name alleged perpetrators in their final reports.[103] In contrast, the Guatemalan did not even have the mandate to do so.[104] The Argentinean and the Chilean TRCs, while under different mandates, chose not to reveal names, but provided information to the judiciary for further investigation.[105] The Moroccan Equity and Reconciliation Commission in Morocco was also not mandated to identify perpetrators, but was reprimanded for that by the HRC.[106]

The controversies over revealing identities of perpetrators become even more acute considering that truth is usually delivered by truth commissions, which, unlike courtrooms, lack strict due process

[101] Working Group on Enforced or Involuntary Disappearances, General Comment on the Right to the Truth in Relation to Enforced Disappearances, UN Doc. A/HRC/16/48, par. 1.

[102] Hayner, *Unspeakable Truths*, p. 128.

[103] Ibid., p. 137; P. Hayner, 'Fifteen Truth Commissions – 1974 to 1994' (1994) 16 *Human Rights Quarterly* 4, pp. 597–655; Truth Commission of El Salvador: From madness to hope – The twelve-year war in El Salvador: Report of the Truth Commission of El Salvador, Security Council, UN Doc. 2/25500, par. 25.

[104] Independent Study on Best Practices, Including Recommendations, To Assist States in Strengthening Their Domestic Capacity to Combat All Aspects of Impunity, By Professor Diane Orentlicher, UN Doc. E/CN.4/2004/88, 27 February 2004, par. 19.

[105] The Argentinean TRC forwarded 1,000 names for investigation. Based on the information provided by it, two former presidents and military leaders were prosecuted. Méndez, 'The Right to Truth', p. 267; J. Malamud-Goti, 'Punishing Human Rights Abuses in Fledgling Democracies: The Case of Argentina', in N. Roht-Arriaza (ed.), *Impunity and Human Rights in International Law and Practice* (Oxford University Press, 1995).

[106] The Human Rights Committee was concerned that 'those responsible for disappearance have still not been identified, tried and punished'. HRC, Consideration of reports submitted by States Parties under Article 40 of the Covenant, Concluding Observations: Morocco, UN Doc. CCPR/CO/82/MAR, 1 December 2004, par. 12.

guarantees.[107] TRCs are considered to be ill suited to provide the guarantees that the attribution of personal guilt requires and, primarily, the presumption of innocence and the right to defend oneself against criminal charges.[108] In turn, this might give an alibi to those named to deny the TRC findings.[109] The South African Truth Commission was brought before the South African courts by two persons named in its report, albeit unsuccessfully.[110] It is also possible that states consider the work of commissions delegitimized and deny to follow their recommendations. In El Salvador, the government considered that the inclusion of names exceeded the Commission's mandate, and denied further cooperation.[111] The majority of scholarship agrees that TRCs should reveal perpetrators' identities,[112] provided that there is sufficiently convincing information and due process standards are respected.

Transposing this debate to cases of corporate abuse, a reasonable question is whether corporate identities should also be revealed, as a matter of law, or if generic references to 'business wrongdoers' might suffice. To that, human rights bodies seem to opt for the former. While they have not ruled specifically on the topic, they have elevated the identity of the perpetrator to a key element of truth's content, from which conclusions on corporate identities can be extrapolated. According to case law, the content of truth includes the identity of the perpetrators, as one of the elements that investigations should reveal,

[107] Zalaquett argues that under no condition should the TRC reveal names because it constitutes a violation of the due process rights of the persons named and an invasion of judicial functions that truth commissions, by definition, do not exercise. Zalaquett, 'Keynote', 51

[108] Naqvi, 'The Right to the Truth', 272.

[109] Aldana-Pindell, 'In Vindication of Justiciable Victims' Rights', 1474.

[110] See the case of *Van Rensburg and Du Preez* v. *the Truth and Reconciliation Commission* (426/96) [1997] ZASCA 2 (18 February 1997).

[111] Aldana-Pindell also adds that many governments have diminished the importance of the commissions' reports by challenging their partiality or by failing to follow their recommendations. Aldana-Pindell, 'In Vindication of Justiciable Victims' Rights', pp. 1441, 1443.

[112] Ambos, 'The Legal Framework of Transitional Justice', p. 46; Naqvi, 'The Right to the Truth', p. 272; see also in favour, J. S. Abrams and P. Hayner, 'Documenting, Acknowledging and Publicizing the Truth', in C. Bassiouni (ed.), *Post-Conflict Justice* (Transnational, 2002), pp. 283–293; González and Varney, *Truth Seeking*, p. 3; Hayner, *Unspeakable Truths*, p. 121. In favour only if no prosecution will follow, see Méndez, 'The Right to Truth', pp. 267–268. Aldana-Pindell opines that prosecutions might be more adequate for revealing identities and addressing issues of individual responsibility. Aldana-Pindell, 'In Vindication of Justiciable Victims' Rights', p. 1474.

namely as constitutive element of the truth. The HRC[113] and the Inter-American organs[114] have confirmed that conclusion. Notably, the Inter-American Commission has stated that 'where a Truth Commission only partially investigates violations, where it is not a judicial body and lacks the power to establish the identity of the perpetrators, to bring them to justice and to award compensation to the victims, such a Commission does not fulfil the obligation of the State under Article 1(1) of the American Convention on Human Rights'.[115] Similarly, the African Commission and the European Court of Human Rights have arguably considered the identity of the perpetrator as an element of the truth, in view of the fact that they require investigations 'able to lead to the prosecution of the authors'.[116] In line with that reasoning, the UN emphasized that truth encompasses 'the events that transpired, their specific circumstances, and who participated in them, including knowing the circumstances in which the violations took place, as well as the reasons for them'.[117] Mendez, a seminal scholar of the field, also corroborates that truth engages a state duty to 'reveal to the victims and society everything known about the facts and circumstances of massive and systematic human rights violations of the past including the identity of the perpetrators and instigators'.[118]

113 HRC, *Concluding Observations on Guatemala*, 3 April 1996, CCPR/C/79/Add.63, par. 25; HRC, 'General Comment 31', par. 18; HRC, 'Rodriguez v. Uruguay', par. 12 (3), 14.

114 IAComHR, 'Monsignor Oscar Arnulfo Romero y Galdámez v. El Salvador', par. 148; IACtHR, case of the *Gómez-Paquiyauri brothers* v. *Peru*, Series C No. 110, Judgment of 8 July 2004; IACtHR, *Case of Tibi* v. *Ecuador*, par. 159 and 257; IACtHR, '*Juan Humberto Sánchez* v. *Honduras*', par. 186.

115 IAComHR, 'Héctor Marcial Garay Hermosilla (Chile)', paras. 74–77. Notably, the Government of Chile, whose amnesty law was criticized in the report, accepted the legal criticism by the Commission. See also IAComHR, Report No. 34/96, *Cases 11.228 et al. (Chile)*, 15 October 1996, par. 72 *et seq.*; IAComHR, *Report No. 25/98, Cases 11.505 et al. (Chile)*, 7 April 1998, par. 66 *et seq.*

116 AfComHPR, 'Amnesty International v. Sudan', par. 51; ECtHR, 'Case of El-Masri v. FYROM', par. 191–192; ECtHR, 'Association 21 December 1989 and Others v. Romania', paras. 133–145; ECtHR, 'Case of Aslakhanova v. Russia', par. 144, 145. For the ECtHR holding that the investigation should be capable of identifying those responsible for the violations, see ECtHR, 'Case of Finucane v. the United Kingdom', par. 69; ECtHR, 'Case of McCann and Other v. the United Kingdom', par. 161; ECtHR, 'Kaya v. Turkey', par. 86; ECtHR, *Case of Assenov* v. *Bulgaria*, Application No. 90/1997/874/1086, Judgment of 28 October 1998, Reports 1998-VIII, par. 102; ECtHR, 'Ogur v. Turkey', par. 88.

117 'UN Study on the Right to the Truth', par. 3.

118 Méndez, 'The Right to Truth'.

Soft law instruments further strengthen that position. The Impunity Principles presumably accept that perpetrators will be named by TRCs, otherwise Principle 9 on guarantees for the persons implicated would not have been included.[119] Naming names seems to be accepted, for cases where the TRC corroborates evidence before publicly naming persons and affords them the opportunity to provide a statement setting forth their version of the facts. Most importantly, the state obligation to investigate and reveal the truth about private entities' abuses is put forward by the Basic Principles, which assert the right of victims and families to know,[120] as a measure of satisfaction.[121] According to the Principles, satisfaction as a reparative measure should be provided not only by the state but also by the legal person or entity liable for the harm.[122] In a similar vein, the Guiding Principles on Business and Human Rights (UNGPs), insofar as they can be of relevance, reaffirm the obligation of states to protect against human rights abuses by third parties, including business enterprises. This requires, among other measures, investigation, punishment and redress of the abuse through effective policies, legislation, regulations and adjudication,[123] presumably also including investigations and its ensuing truth. The UNGPs foresee an element of truth also for business duties, when they urge them to communicate externally on how they address human rights risk in their area of operations and their human rights impacts.[124]

It can reasonably be concluded that the right to truth and the corresponding state obligation are well performed when the identities of perpetrators, including corporate ones, are revealed, within the limits set by due process guarantees. Drawing from Chapter 6 on the unrestricted character of the right to truth, an opposite scenario where corporate identities are concealed would amount to an unacceptable restriction of the right to truth,[125] if not an attack to its constitutive elements. The only restriction of the truth that has gained some legitimate prominence is the one triggered by the potential lack of due process

[119] 'Joinet Report', par. 17–25.
[120] 'Basic Principles', Principle 24.
[121] Ibid., Principles 7 and 22.
[122] Ibid., Principle 15.
[123] 'Guiding Principles', UN Doc. A/HRC/17/31, Principle 1.
[124] Ibid., Principle 21.
[125] Méndez, 'Accountability for Past Abuses', p. 265; Szoke-Burke, 'Searching for the Right to Truth', p. 561; 'Working Group on Enforced Disappearances, General Comment on the Right to the Truth', par. 3.

guarantees in the respective fora, such as Truth Commissions.[126] However, TRCs can still validly unveil names of corporate perpetrators, on the basis of sufficiently convincing information and respect for due process standards. Doubts about respect for due process standards could be eliminated by giving the chance to those named to rebut evidence and information presented before or by the Commission and to cross-examine witnesses, or even by shifting the burden of proof to the Commission, as was the case in El Salvador.[127]

Establishing the obligation of the state to investigate and reveal the truth on corporate malfeasance triggers the question on whether this means that corporate entities should also cooperate during these investigations, especially when carried out by truth mechanisms. In fact, according to human rights instruments,[128] and case law,[129] the state should vest the investigation authorities with the necessary resources and powers to effectively conduct their work, including the power to oblige all involved actors to appear before it. As Mendez notes, the obligation to testify and collaborate is analogous to the obligation to give testimony in civil or administrative cases, in which such a right of not collaborating with the court does not exist.[130]

[126] Zalaquett argues that under no condition should the TRC reveal names because it constitutes a violation of the due process rights of the persons named and an invasion of judicial functions that truth commissions, by definition, do not exercise. J. Zalaquett, 'Keynote', in A. Boraine et al. (eds.), *Dealing with the Past: Truth and Reconciliation in South Africa*, Institute for a Democratic Alternative for South Africa (Clyson Printers, 1994), p. 51; Naqvi, 'The Right to the Truth', p. 272.

[127] Hayner proposes that if TRCs opt for naming names, they should clarify that their conclusions about individual responsibility do not amount to criminal guilt and should thus present them in the form of a summary of the testimony. Hayner, *Unspeakable Truths*, p. 121. For an overview of due process in truth commissions, see Szoke-Burke, 'Searching for the Right to Truth', p. 561; González and Varney, *Truth Seeking*, p. 3.

[128] 'Principles on the Effective Prevention and Investigation of Extra-Legal, Arbitrary and Summary Executions', Principle 10; UN Commission on Human Rights, Declaration on the Protection of All Persons from Enforced Disappearance, 28 February 1992, E/CN.4/RES/1992/29, Article 13(2); UN General Assembly, Principles on the Effective Investigation and Documentation of Torture and Other Cruel, Inhuman or Degrading Treatment or Punishment, Resolution 55/89 of 4 December 2000, Principle 3(a).

[129] AfrComHPR, 'Amnesty International et al. v. Sudan', par. 51; ECtHR, *Hugh Jordan* v. *the United Kingdom*, Judgment of 4 May 2001, Reports 2001-III, par. 127; ECtHR, 'McKerr v. the United Kingdom', par. 124; CoE Guidelines on Eradicating Impunity for Serious Human Rights Violations, Guideline VI; IACHR, *Martin Pelico Coxic et al. (Guatemala)* Merits Report No. 80/07, Case 11.658, 15 October 2007, par. 81; HRC, 'General Comment 31', par. 15.

[130] Méndez, 'The Right to Truth', p. 271.

However, practice shows that such mandate has not been afforded to TRCs. The South African Commission did not oblige businessmen to participate in its proceedings and relied only in their voluntary presence, a fact that presumably undermined its legitimacy and its capacity to clarify the truth. The cooperation of businesses was lacklustre and some of them abstained completely, preferring to be stigmatized for absence than for presumed culpability.[131] As a result, the report was directed towards a voluntary approach to reconstruction and development of post-Apartheid South Africa and avoided the attribution of legal responsibility under strict criteria. The mainly blanket recommendations requiring a once-off wealth tax covering all corporations effectively pointed towards third-order involvement and the requisite perception that corporations were mainly beneficiaries and not direct perpetrators of Apartheid. Similarly, the Colombian Truth Commission, although vested with the power to summon people to contribute to clarifying the truth,[132] its report relied on voluntary testimonies with 300 economic actors, complemented by reports submitted to the Commission regarding the impact of the conflict on them, as victims.[133]

7.2.1 Commission for Reception, Truth and Reconciliation of East Timor

In the aftermath of East Timor's military occupation by Indonesia and internal civil conflict, the United Nations Transitional Authority established the Serious Crimes Unit, in 1999, and the Commission for Reception, Truth and Reconciliation (CAVR),[134] in 2002, mandated to investigate human rights violations committed between April 1974 and October 1999 and recommend prosecutions.[135] The CAVR explained

131 J. Simcock, 'Unfinished Business: Reconciling the Apartheid Reparation Litigation with South Africa's Truth and Reconciliation Commission' (2011) 47 *Stanford Journal of International Law* 1, at 252.

132 Decreto 588 de 2017, 'Por el cual se organiza la Comisión para el Esclarecimiento de la Verdad, la Convivencia y la no Repetición', 5 April 2017, Article 13, par. 3.

133 CTCN, Hay futuro si hay verdad: Informe Final, Tomo 4. Hasta la guerra tiene límites: violations de los derechos humanos, infractions al derecho international humanitariano y responsabilidades colectivas, Primera edition, Bogotá: Comisión de la Verdad, 2022, p. 944.

134 Regulation No. 2001/10 on the Establishment of a Commission for Reception, Truth and Reconciliation in East Timor, UNTAET/REG/2001/10, 13 July, section 13.

135 The Commission was not mandated to provide amnesties. *Chega!* CAVR Report, part 2: The Mandate of the Commission.

early on that corporations would fall under its investigative authority, given that they were often involved in massive violations. It stated that 'often the context of massive violations, which is the object of a Commission's inquiries or investigations, involves not only state actors, such as military and police officers and government officials, but also members of opposition groups, political parties, militias, corporations and other individuals [. . .]'.[136]

The CAVR issued its final report in 2005, after several national hearings. It pioneered in identifying economic, social and cultural rights violations that needed to be addressed as part of the transition.[137] In its report, it acknowledged the role of non-state actors, including corporations, in various violations. In the field of business complicity, the Commission attached corporate complicity liability to businesses who supported Timor-Leste's illegal occupation and thus indirectly allowed violations to take place, or to 'Indonesian business companies, including state owned enterprises, and other international and multinational corporations and businesses who profited from war and benefited from the occupation [. . .] and business corporations who benefited from the sale of weapons to Indonesia'.[138] Special mention was made to British and French arms companies that supplied arms to the Suharto government.[139] It also referred to businesses that were significantly involved in the destruction of natural resources such as sandalwood trees, in complicity with the Indonesian government.[140] Reference was also made to the coffee industry, with various plantations being used as grounds for interrogation, torture and murder.[141]

The CAVR attributed tort responsibility to businesses, presuming that they were indirectly involved to human rights violations, and concluded that they should provide reparations by contributing to a domestic reparation programme, funded by various actors, including state-owned

136 Ibid., point 8.

137 Ibid., parts 7 and 2, Annex A, par. 128–132.

138 Ibid., part 11: Recommendations, point 12.10 on financing of the reparations programme.

139 García Martín, *Transitional Justice, Corporate Accountability and Socio-Economic Rights, Lessons from Argentina.*

140 CAVR Report, part 7, section 1, par. 6 and 11.

141 Ibid., part 2, par. 7.2, p. 1081; par. 824, p. 1119; par. 897(5) and part 3, par. 148. See also T. Van Ho, 'Chapter 18: Business and Human Rights in Transitional Justice: Challenges for Complex Environments', in S. Deva and D. Birchall (eds.), *Research Handbook on Human Rights and Business* (Edward Elgar Publishing, 2020).

enterprises and other international and multinational corporations that profited from the occupation, from selling weapons to Indonesia,[142] or supported the illegal occupation of Timor-Leste.[143] It stipulated that 'member states of the international community, and business corporations who supported the illegal occupation of Timor-Leste and thus indirectly allowed violations to take place, are obliged to provide reparations to victims' due to 'the principle of international responsibility recognized in the international customary law of torts'.[144]

Despite invoking a legally specific rule, namely tort liability, the report lacked specificity in what concerned perpetrators. It refrained from referring to names of either Indonesian or foreign enterprises implicated in the violence, despite widespread knowledge to that effect.[145] Instead, it limited its scope to rather generic descriptions of various industry sectors and their involvement in the occupation and its resulting violations. It was only two Indonesian companies that were specifically named for their association with the military regime.[146] The parliament subsequently disregarded the report, and its implementation remained stranded.[147] In 2005, another Truth Commission was established (the Commission of Truth and Friendship) as a joint effort by Indonesia and Timor-Leste, but it was a priori confined to institutional responsibility,[148] excluding any investigation of corporate malfeasance.

7.3 The Status of the Right to Truth Compared to Other Transitional Predicaments: Truth vs Development

The discourse of corporate accountability in transitional settings abounds of arguments on the necessity of corporations for economic development purposes, which usually overshadow accountability concerns. It was the development priority that presumably halted further corporate

142 CAVR Report, part 11: 'Recommendations', point 12.10 and section 1.8.
143 Ibid., part 11, section 12.10.
144 Ibid., 'Recommendations', under 12.10 Financing.
145 John G. Taylor, *East Timor: The Price of Freedom* (Zed Books, 1999); CAVR Report, part 11: 'Recommendations', point 12.10.
146 Ibid., part 7, chapter 9 on 'Economic and Social Rights', pp. 11, 13, 16.
147 International Centre for Transitional Justice, 'Timor-Leste. Parliament Denies Victims Justice Again', 17 February 2011, available at www.ictj.org/news/timor-leste-parliament-denies-victims-justice-again; Evans, *The Right to Reparation in International Law for Victims of Armed Conflict*, p. 200.
148 Per Memoriam Ad Spem. Final Report of the Commission of Truth and Friendship (CTF) Indonesia - Timor-Leste, Denpasar, 31 March 2008, pp. 13–14 and 295.

accountability efforts in South Africa, beyond the truth commission. More recently, in Tunisia, accountability of corporations, beyond those of Ben Ali and his entourage, was sacrificed in the name of reconciliation, which would create a favourable environment for investment and usher economic growth.[149] Nevertheless, scholars have emphasized that unless framed in remedial terms, corporate contribution to development responds to a separate obligation, namely the right to development.[150] Even within the separate domain of development, the role and capacity of corporations to effect change has been doubted.[151]

Against this background, the status of the right to truth, as it has evolved, hints towards putting it, at least, in an equal footing to developmental or other concerns. Seminal scholars assert an – at least – emerging customary norm,[152] or a general principle of law.[153] That assessment is grounded on resolutions by the Security Council and the

[149] A. Guellali, 'Tunisia: Transitional Justice in the Crosshairs', *Human Rights Watch*, 8 September 2015, available at www.hrw.org/news/2015/09/08/tunisia-transitional-justice-crosshairs.

[150] Laplante, 'On the Indivisibility of Rights', p. 141.

[151] G. Mansuri and R. Vijayendra, 'Community-Based and -Driven Development: A Critical Review' (2004) 19 *The World Bank Research Observer* 1, 1–39; C. Cheng and D. Zaum, 'Corruption and the Role of Natural Resources in Post-Conflict Transitions', in C. Bruch et al. (eds.), *Governance, Natural Resources, and Post-Conflict Peacebuilding* (Routledge, 2017), pp. 461–480.

[152] In scholarship, there are several differing opinions. Naqvi says that it stands 'somewhere above a good argument and somewhere below a clear legal rule'; Naqvi, 'The Right to the Truth'. Méndez argues for an 'emerging' right to truth as part of a 'greater right to justice'; see Méndez, 'The Right to Truth', 260, 263. Ambos says that the right to truth is an emerging customary norm and a general principle of law; see Ambos, 'The Legal Framework of Transitional Justice', p. 36. Also agreeing Pasqualucci, 'The Whole Truth and Nothing But the Truth', 321. Szoke-Burke, 'Searching for the Right to Truth'. Sweeney argues that the right to truth is elusive; J. Sweeney, 'The Elusive Right to Truth in Transitional Human Rights Jurisprudence' (2018) 67 *International and Comparative Law Quarterly* 2, 353–387. Sandoval argues that there is a dispute as to who its right-holder is, what is the scope of such a right and what are states obliged to do; see C. Sandoval, *Briefing Paper Transitional Justice: Key Concepts, Processes and Challenges* (Institute for Democracy & Conflict Resolution, 2011). Orentlicher asserts the existence of the right to know, but without explicitly delineated contours, see Impunity Principles, par. 17.

[153] Note that for human rights norms, customary status is based on the wide acceptance of the norm – in its essence and contours – its repetition in various international instruments, along with its confirmation in national practice. Simma and Alston, 'The Sources of Human Rights', at 82, 100; Merrills, *The Development of International Law by the European Court of Human Rights*. It should be noted that rights that are fundamental for human dignity or that incorporate universally accepted values of humanity require presumably less evidence for their customary status. Regarding general principles, there

General Assembly,[154] as well as decisions by various other international mechanisms[155] and courts,[156] proving a consensus on the existence of the right. At the national level, truth has also been considered as a right by various pieces of legislation[157] and peace agreements.[158] Different courts,[159] across the globe, have sided with that conclusion, including the Human Rights Chamber for Bosnia and Herzegovina,[160] the Constitutional Courts of Colombia[161] and Peru,[162] the Federal Criminal Courts of Argentina[163] and the Constitutional Court of South

are two interpretations. The first derives them from a comparison of the various systems of municipal law. The other uses in addition to municipal law sources, general principles applicable directly to international legal relations. According to Bassiouni, both approaches have been used by the ICJ and the PCIJ. See Bassiouni, 'A Functional Approach to "General Principles of International Law"', 772–773; Thirlway, *The Sources of International Law*, p. 93. See also ICC, *Prosecutor* v. *Katanga/Chui*, Decision on the set of procedural rights attached to procedural status of victim at the Pre-Trial Stage of the Case, 13 May 2008 (ICC-01/04-01/07), par. 32.

154 Naqvi enumerates various UN Security Council and General Assembly resolutions. Naqvi, 'The Right to the Truth', p. 259 *et seq.*

155 'UN Study on the Right to the Truth', par. 55, 60; Working Group on Enforced or Involuntary Disappearances, First Report to the Commission on Human Rights, UN Doc. E/CN.4/1435, 22 January 1981, par. 187; 'The rule of law and transitional justice in conflict and post-conflict societies' S/2004/16; Report of the United Nations Special Rapporteur on the Question of human rights and states of emergency, 26 June 1995, E/CN.4/Sub.2/1995/20, Annex I, par. 39.

156 See to that respect ICC, *Prosecutor* v. *Katanga/Chui*, ICC-01/04-01/07, par. 32.

157 Law on Missing, Bosnia and Herzegovina Official Gazette 50/04. A; Colombian Law No. 975 of 25 July 2005.

158 Agreements on Refugees and Displaced Persons (Annex 7, Article V) and on the Military Aspects of the Peace Settlement (Annex 1A, Article IX) of the General Framework Agreement for Peace in Bosnia and Herzegovina.

159 The decisions of courts are considered only as a 'subsidiary means for the determination of rules', according to Article 38(1)(d) of the Statute of the International Court of Justice (ICJ); they 'play an increasingly important role in the recognition of various human rights as custom', and the cumulative weight of this case law, together with that of the human rights bodies and courts, 'influences and consolidates the development of customary human rights law'. T. Meron, *Human Rights and Humanitarian Law as Customary Law* (Clarendon Press, 1989), p. 93; 'UN Study on the Right to the Truth', par. 22–24.

160 Decision of 11 January 2001, *Palic* v. *Republika Srpska*, Case No. CH/99/3196; Decision of 7 March 2003, 'Srebrenica Cases', Cases Nos. CH/01/8365 et al., para. 220(4).

161 Constitutional Court of Colombia, Judgments of 20 January 2003, *Case T-249/03* and *C-228* of 3 April 2002.

162 Constitutional Tribunal of Peru, Judgment of 18 March 2004, *Case 2488-2002-HC/TC.*

163 Agreement of 1 September 2003 of the National Chamber for Federal Criminal and Correctional Matters, *Case Suárez Mason, Rol. 450* and *Case Escuela Mecánica de la Armada, Rol. 761*; Chamber for Federal Criminal and Correctional Matters, Decision of 18 May 1995, *Case Maria Aguiar Lapacó, Rol. 450*; Supreme Court of Argentina,

Africa.[164] Truth measures are the most frequently resorted measures of transitional justice.[165] While many truth commissions do not often cite the right to truth as their legal basis, their mere establishment on the basis of peace agreements proves a sense of legal obligation.[166] Lastly, the establishment of the mandate of the Special Rapporteur on the Promotion of Truth, Justice, Reparations and Guarantees of Non-Recurrence corroborates further the emergence of truth as distinct and necessary field during transitions.

Recognizing the right to the truth as an autonomous right under customary international law or as a general principle of law has diverse repercussions.[167] While unpacking every angle of these repercussions would be out of scope for this book, offering an initial perspective would be valuable to encourage further reflection and discussion. Particularly, in relation to corporate accountability, such crystallization places an unqualified focus on the importance of revealing the truth, countervailing other considerations invoked in relation to corporations, such as the adequacy of truth commissions to address corporate accountability, and particularly developmental concerns, in line with scholarly caution not to conflate transitional justice with development.[168] Furthermore, that right, having attained the status of emerging customary norm or general principle, seems less exposed to restrictions.[169] Decisions of amnesty,

Judgment of 14 June 2005, S. 1767. XXXVIII, Simón, Julio Héctor y otros s/ privación ilegítima de la libertad, *Case, Rol. No. 17.768*. See 'UN Study on the Right to the Truth'.

164 In the McBride case, the Constitutional Court of South Africa upheld the rights of victims, the media and public to speak the truth about crimes, even if they were not the object of an amnesty. Constitutional Court of South Africa. *The Citizen 1978 (Pty) Ltd and others* v. *McBride*. Case CCT 23/10, 2011, ZACC 11, 8 April 2011.

165 Naqvi, 'The Right to the Truth', p. 261 refers to 30 TRCs worldwide. See also L. Mallinder, 'Exploring the Practice of States in Introducing Amnesties', in Ambos et al. (eds.), *Building a Future on Peace and Justice: Studies on Transitional Justice, Conflict Resolution and Development* (Springer-Verlag Berlin Heidelberg, 2009), p. 160, demonstrating the increase from 1985 to 2005.

166 Naqvi, 'The Right to the Truth', p. 262. See also Méndez, 'Accountability for Past Abuses', p. 263.

167 Typical consequences are that the rule will bind every state and that it will be automatically incorporated in most domestic jurisdictions and protected against derogation by a conflicting domestic statute. At a minimum it will have an increased persuasive normative impact on municipal law. Simma and Alston, 'The Sources of Human Rights', at 86.

168 P. De Greiff, 'Articulating the Links between Transitional Justice and Development: Justice and Social Integration', in P. De Greiff and R. Duthie (eds.), *Transitional Justice and Development: Making Connections* (Social Science Research Council, 2009), p. 58.

169 Szoke-Burke, 'Searching for the Right to Truth', p. 548.

'immunity for testimony'[170] or charge bargaining would necessarily have to be accompanied by some sort of truth telling in order to satisfy the right to the truth.

Also, if the right to truth is customary rule or general principle of international law, so are its elements,[171] and specifically the right to learn the identity of the perpetrator, including that of the corporate entity. It might be a premature conclusion, but it is worth noting that half the truth commissions that have been established worldwide examined corporate involvement in conflict, repression and violations.[172] Thus, if the establishment of TRCs can be indicative of state practise and *opinio juris* – since the commissions are usually foreseen in peace treaties, then the inclusion of corporate malefactors in the work of TRCs can be considered as emerging customary norm or general principle, in the framework of transitions. It can further be argued that since it seems to be a primary right, then states should enable its realization in the field of private relations, like for any other primary right. In practice, this would mean that transitioning states would be obliged to enable the realization of the right to truth against both state agents and corporate entities.

The evolution of truth about corporate violations in an emerging general principle or customary norm would mean that states that 'like to see themselves as contributing to an international lawful order' should adopt measures to show respect to those norms and principles.[173] Especially in cases of transition, where massive crimes took place, a 'government [. . .] can and should be judged by how much it attempts

[170] Before the Special Court for Sierra Leone, a witness may request that testimony delivered in proceedings before that Court will not be used in a subsequent prosecution of that witness (Rule 90(E) of the SCSL Rules of Procedure and Evidence). The rule is derived from Rule 90(E) of the ICTR Rules of Procedure and Evidence, in accordance with Article 14(1) of the SCSL Statute.

[171] Naqvi, 'The Right to the Truth', p. 263; ICC, *Prosecutor* v. *Katanga/Chui*, ICC-01/04–01/07, par. 32; Commission for Reception, Truth and Reconciliation in East Timor; see section 13.2, Regulation No. 2001/10 on the Establishment of a Commission for Reception, Truth and Reconciliation in East Timor, UNTAET/REG/2001/10, 13 July, section 13; 'UN Study on the Right to the Truth', par. 59; HRC, 'Concluding Observations on Guatemala', par. 25; HRC, Resolution 9/11, Right to the truth, A/HRC/RES/9/11, 18 September 2008, p. 2; Méndez, 'The Right to Truth', 255.

[172] Sandt and Moor, *Peace, Everyone's Business!*, p. 34. See also Bakiner stating that half of the TRCs have revealed the identity of the perpetrator. Bakiner, 'Truth Commission Impact', 29.

[173] Méndez, 'Accountability for Past Abuses', p. 263.

to do to comply with these principles',[174] and also to the very functions of custom and general principles.

In essence, if the right to truth is accorded a heightened status, encompassing its constituent elements, notably the disclosure of perpetrator identities, it becomes less amenable to compromises in favour of the oft-cited right to development, a tension that frequently arises and leads to widespread corporate impunity. While the right to development is pivotal, the elevated prominence of the right to truth underscores the imperative of uncovering and acknowledging corporate perpetrators of wrongdoing. Balancing these rights necessitates a nuanced approach, wherein corporate entities are not shielded from liability by overarching developmental imperatives, ensuring that the pursuit of truth remains an indispensable facet in the aftermath of conflict or repression.

7.3.1 Truth and Reconciliation Commission of South Africa

The South African Truth and Reconciliation Commission was established by the Promotion of National Unity and Reconciliation Act 34 of 1995 and was mandated to

> promote national unity and reconciliation in a spirit of understanding which transcends the conflicts and divisions of the past by establishing as complete a picture as possible of the causes, nature and extent of the gross violations of human rights which were committed during the period from 1 March 1960 to the cut-off date, including the antecedents, circumstances, factors and context of such violations, as well as the perspectives of the victims and the motives and perspectives of the persons responsible for the Commission of the violations, by conducting investigations and holding hearings.[175]

It could investigate the identity of all persons, authorities, institutions and organizations involved in such violations, and whether the latter resulted from deliberate planning on the part of the state or any political organization, liberation movement or other group.[176] Under a rather

[174] Ibid.

[175] Promotion of National Unity and Reconciliation Act 34 (1995), chapter 2, Article 3(a). The South African Truth and Reconciliation Commission consisted of three committees: The Human Rights Violations Committee, which was charged with the investigation of human rights abuses; the Reparation and Rehabilitation Committee, responsible for formulating proposals to assist with rehabilitation; and the Amnesty Committee which decided on the granting of amnesty.

[176] Promotion of National Unity and Reconciliation Act 34 (1995), chapter 2, Article 4.

progressive thinking at the time, the Commission dissociated the finding of a gross human rights violation from the prerequisite of state action and paved the way for a more systemic view on Apartheid and crimes against humanity, beyond the narrow scope of the acts that comprise it. Importantly for corporate accountability purposes, amnesty was to be given in relation to criminal and not civil trials.[177]

The Commission made a meticulous account of corporate involvement in the Apartheid regime, which has ever since been the reference point for similar efforts. It classified that involvement under three so-called orders: the first order involvement covered businesses that collaborated directly with the Apartheid regime, especially with its security establishment, and played a central role in helping to design and implement Apartheid policies,[178] such as several mining corporations.[179] Regarding those companies, the TRC concluded that they 'must be held responsible and accountable for the suffering that resulted'.[180] The second order involvement included businesses that profited by engaging directly in activities that promoted state repression, while knowing that their products or services would be used for morally unacceptable purposes.[181] The TRC mentioned specifically the armaments industry and banks. The latter – 'knowingly or unknowingly' – were providing banking services to the Apartheid government,[182] such as covert credit cards, without any investigation of how they will be used despite the well-known violations.[183] The United Bank of Switzerland (UBS) was named as one of the 'important partners of Pretoria during Apartheid [... which] played a central role in marketing South African gold [... and] invested in Apartheid-era infrastructure in South Africa and in the homelands'.[184] For those conclusions, it also used statements by banks themselves, such as the Council of South African Banks, who

177 Simcock, 'Unfinished Business', p. 248.

178 'Formulation of oppressive policies or practices that resulted in low labour costs'. Truth and Reconciliation Commission of South Africa (1998), *Report*, ['TRC Report'], Vol. 4, chapter 2, par. 23.

179 Sandt and Moor, *Peace, Everyone's Business!*, p. 84.

180 TRC Report, Vol. 4, chapter 2, par. 23, p. 24.

181 Ibid., par. 26, 28.

182 Ibid., par. 26, p. 25; par. 75, p. 36. For banks, par. 30.

183 Ibid., par. 31.

184 TRC Report, Vol. 6, section 2, chapter 5; Reparations and the Business Sector, par. 14, p. 144.

acknowledged that being a bank inevitably meant doing business with parts of the Apartheid system.[185]

The third-order involvement included ordinary business activities that benefited indirectly by virtue of operating within the racially structured context of Apartheid society.[186] It did not rely on any intent requirement, or differing levels of culpability and was thus quite broad.[187] It included enterprises involved in extracting and exploiting the country's mineral wealth and benefiting from the provision of a relatively cheap migratory labour force, due to Apartheid laws; the arms industry, which benefited substantially from the Apartheid military requirements; and the banks that lent directly to the regime, and benefited from the relatively high interest rates they were able to charge as a consequence of the international sanctions against South Africa.[188] For this last and broad category of corporations, the TRC condemned the benefits they acquired, and proposed a moral obligation to repair, as opposed to a legal one.[189]

The conclusions of the business hearings used extensively the third category of involvement, and the central finding was that businesses were central to the economy that sustained the South African state during the Apartheid years.[190] The mainly blanket recommendations requiring a once-off wealth tax also indicate the preference to the use of the third category of corporations as beneficiaries. This, actually, meant that for

185 TRC Report, Vol. 6, section 2, chapter 2, par. 29.

186 TRC Report, Vol. 4, chapter 2, par. 32.

187 Barnard-Naudé, 'For Justice and Reconciliation to Come', pp. 181–182.

188 TRC Report, Vol. 6, section 2, chapter 5, par. 3. The TRC named Credit Suisse and UBS banks (par. 17–28), Anglo-American mining corporation (par. 43–60), Tongaat Hulett Sugar company (par. 51), Barlow Rand mining group and Armscor arms company (par. 53). Nevertheless, in other sections, the TRC stated the impracticability of crafting case studies for each private corporation (par. 43). The involvement of the third sector extended to white-owned large-scale agricultural, farming and agri-business enterprises that profited from historical restrictions on black land ownership during the colonial era; banks and financial institutions, which financially supported the military-industrial complex and minerals-energy groups that indirectly gained advantages from the Apartheid.

189 The Commission reiterated its finding that business benefited substantially during the Apartheid era either through commission or omission and have, at the very least, a moral obligation to assist in the reconstruction and development of post-Apartheid South Africa through active reparative measures. TRC Report, Vol. 6, section 2, chapter 5, par. 14.

190 TRC Report, Vol. 4, chapter 2, par. 161–167 and Vol. 6, section 2, chapter 5, par. 3. However, the commission went a bit further for several Swiss banks, which were accomplices to a criminal government that consistently violated international law. See TRC Report, Vol. 6, section 2, chapter 5, par. 26.

the Commission, private entities were more of background players, rather than direct perpetrators of human rights violations.[191] As a result, the Commission engaged in outlining corporate involvement, without clarifying the legal requirements of their mode of participation. In turn, this hindered any judicial consequences for corporate actors with first- and second-order involvement. That approach was criticized for having paralysing consequences on 'creative legal activism – activism that, in its democratic force, would compel the enactment of reparation law'.[192] In addition, the TRC lost the opportunity to consolidate evidence that could be used in future litigation, in the cases where it denied amnesty. The 'beneficiary' approach, in addition to the amnesties granted, seemingly contributed to the absence of corporate accountability cases inside South Africa, to this date.

Based on those findings, or lack thereof, the TRC's recommendations on reparations did not specify the criteria under which the responsible companies would be selected, neither the exact form of reparations, essentially failing to provide for a duty of corporate reparations.[193] It rather stated that businesses should be involved in a wider project of reparation, relating not simply to those identified as victims by the Commission but also to all those South Africans whose normal development was impaired by the system of Apartheid.[194] The measures suggested ranged from a wealth tax on businesses operating in South Africa; a one-off levy on corporate and private income; a one-off donation of 1 per cent of market capitalization by companies listed on the Johannesburg Stock Exchange; a retrospective surcharge on corporate profits backdated to an agreed time; and other.[195] The obligation of the corporations to repair was mainly founded on a moral obligation to assist in the reconstruction and development of post-Apartheid South Africa

[191] Nattrass states that the systemic approach adopted by the TRC directed attention away from those whose involvement with the apartheid regime was of graver moral concern than that of others, and took the heat off wealthy individuals who, by virtue of personal contacts and financial muscle, might have been able to effect change faster had they acted more decisively. N. Nattrass, 'The Truth and Reconciliation Commission on Business and Apartheid: A Critical Evaluation' (1999) 98 *African Affairs*, pp. 373–391.

[192] Barnard-Naudé, 'For Justice and Reconciliation to Come', p. 176. The approach of the TRC is also criticized in that article for lack of stability in the categories of involvement it chose to follow.

[193] T. Bell and D. Buhle Ntsebeza, *Unfinished Business: South Africa, Apartheid and Truth* (Verso, 2003), p. 349.

[194] TRC Report, Vol. 6, section 2, chapter 5, par. 3.

[195] Ibid., Vol. 6, section 5, chapter 7.

through active reparative measures, dissociated from any link among the corporate activity and the victim.[196] It is only in its last sixth addendum report that the TRC used more concrete common law concepts and added more foundations for the reparation claims, such as unjustified enrichment and illegality in contract law.[197]

Subsequently, the government opted for a non-confrontational policy, and President Thabo Mbeki initiated a presidential pardon process on top of the TRC's amnesty process and the amended prosecution policy that provided discretion to abstain from prosecution.[198] Despite the recommendations of the TRC and amid denial by corporations of the concept of corporate reparations, a business trust was established that would help the development and economic prosperity of the country based on voluntary contributions, while the government paid the reparations.[199] The trust received about US$ 143,734,000 from 140 companies, to be used as assistance for the tourism and educational sectors, rather than as individual compensation to victims of the businesses.[200] Another reparation fund, the so-called president's fund, allocating ordinary reparations was created in 2005. It granted lump sum payments to victims who appeared before the TRC and provided for collective reparations focusing on infrastructure projects to 18 out of 128 communities mentioned in the TRC report.[201] As the International Centre for Transitional Justice stated, 'the government has done virtually everything possible to extend amnesty and pardon, and nothing to pursue prosecutions'.[202]

As a consequence of the fact that the business trust was only devoted to educational and tourism purposes and indicative of the frustration of

196 Ibid., Vol. 6, section 2, chapter 5, par. 4 and 14.

197 Ibid., Vol. 6, section 2, chapter 5, par. 24 and 60: 'A reparations claim against corporations like Anglo American would be based on the extent to which decades of profits were based on systematic violations of human rights. In legal terms, this could be based on the principle of "unjust enrichment". "Unjust enrichment" is a source of legal obligation. Actions based on "unjust enrichment" are common to most modern legal systems. These kinds of claims give rise to an obligation in terms of which the enriched party incurs a duty to restore the extent of his/her enrichment to the impoverished party. Put differently, the impoverished party acquires a legal right to claim that the extent of the other's enrichment be restored to him/her if it was acquired at his/her expense'.

198 Sandt and Moor, *Peace, Everyone's Business!*.

199 Sandoval and Surfleet, 'Corporations and Redress in Transitional Justice Processes', pp. 101–102.

200 Ibid.

201 Sandt and Moor, *Peace, Everyone's Business!*, p. 90.

202 P. Seils, 'Devil is in the Detail of Colombian Justice Deal', International Centre of Transitional Justice, 15 October 2015.

the victims that could not achieve corporate reparations for their human rights violations, the Khulumani litigation started in the US under the ATCA.[203] This came as no surprise, considering that President Mbeki previously blamed the TRC for seeking attention,[204] and totally disregarded its recommendations, only to direct reparation funds to developmental purposes instead of victims' compensation.[205] His Justice Minister, Penuell Maduna, on occasion of the Apartheid litigation, emphasized the 'meaningful contribution' made by business entities to the South African development, emphasizing their role in 'human capacity building and employment creation' as well as their significant investments.[206] Any form of corporate accountability, either in the form of prosecutions or reparations was viewed as deterring investment and posing severe risks to the vital goal of advancing towards a more prosperous economic state.[207]

7.4 Collective Truth and Patterns of Corporate Abuse

As evidenced in various occasions throughout this book, corporate abuse during conflict or repression harms victims' individual rights and is also systemically entrenched in patterns of violence and exploitation that perpetuate conflict or repression. Truth mechanisms are seemingly the most adept, among transitional measures, to tackle that systemic aspect of violence, because they materialize the right to truth in its individual but also collective dimension. The collective aspect of truth is a condition *sine qua non* in attaining future-oriented goals, promoting reconciliation and preventing future violations. It involves a comprehensive and inclusive understanding of past violence, particularly pertinent for cases of historical injustice, where deeply ingrained biases prevail. It assists in acknowledging the past and fostering a sense of collective memory and

203 *Khulumani* v. *Barclay National Bank Ltd.*, 509 F.3d 148 2d Cir. (2007).

204 M. Michael, 'Moment of Truth. South Africa's Truth and Reconciliation Commission Closes Its Doors', Worldpress.org, 2 May 2003.

205 Sandoval and Surfleet, 'Corporations and Redress in Transitional Justice Processes', pp. 101–102.

206 Ministry of Justice and Constitutional Development, Republic of South Africa, 'Declaration by Justice Minister Penuell Maduna on Apartheid Litigation in the United States', 11 July 2003, available at www.gov.za/sites/default/files/gcis_document/201409/apartheid1.pdf. See also Section 6.1 of this book.

207 Maduna Declaration, par 12.

responsibility, which is often a step towards reconciliation and healing in a divided society.

The collective aspect of truth has been applauded by legal instruments,[208] and the practice of international and regional institutions.[209] The Inter-American organs have stressed its significance for the 'workings of democratic systems'.[210] In his concurring opinion in the *Bámaca Velásquez* case, Judge Ramirez noted that 'the so-called right to the truth covers a legitimate demand of society to know what has happened, generically or specifically, during a certain period of collective history, usually a stage dominated by authoritarianism, when the channels of knowledge, information and reaction, characteristic of democracy are not operating adequately or sufficiently'.[211] Even the prudent jurisprudence of the ECHR has accepted the importance of truth for society at large, prescribing the right, even of numerous victims, to 'know what happened'.[212]

The collective aspect of the right to truth goes hand in hand with a relative widening of the material scope of the truth itself; while initially focused on individual violations, the concept of truth has expanded to include the examination of systematic patterns and dynamics that

208 'Basic Principles', Principle 22(b); 'Impunity Principles', Principle 2.

209 Working Group on Enforced or Involuntary Disappearances Question of the Human Rights of All Persons Subjected to Any Form of Detention or Imprisonment, Question of Enforced or Involuntary Disappearances, UN Doc. E/CN.4/1990/13, par. 339; See also Joinet Report, Annex I, par. 17.

210 *IACtHR, Case of the Massacres of El Mozote and Nearby Places* v. *El Salvador*, Series C No. 252, Merits, Reparations and Costs, Judgment of 25 October 2012, paras. 298, 317; IACtHR, 'Myrna Mack-Chang v. Guatemala', par. 274; IACtHR, 'Case of Contreras et al. v. El Salvador', par. 173; IACtHR, 'Case of Bámaca Velásquez v. Guatemala', Reparations, par. 76, 77; IACtHR, *Case of 19 Merchants* v. *Colombia*, Series C No. 109, Merits, Reparations and Costs, Judgment of 5 July 2004, par. 261; IACtHR, *Case of Carpio Nicolle et al.* v. *Guatemala*. Merits, Reparations and Costs. Judgment of 22 November 2004, Series C No. 117, par. 128; IACtHR, 'Case of Gomes Lund', par. 200; IACtHR, 'Case of Gelman v. Uruguay', par. 243; IACtHR, *Case of Olmedo Bustos et al.* v. *Chile*, Judgment of 5 February 2001, Series C No. 73, par. 67. For the Commission, see IAComHR, 'Lucio Parada Crea et al. v. El Salvador', par. 151; IACmHR, 'Case Ignacio Ellacuría v. El Salvador', par. 224.

211 IACtHR, 'Case of Bámaca Velásquez v. Guatemala', Separate Concurring Opinion of Judge Sergio Garcia Ramírez, par. 19.

212 ECtHR, 'Case of El-Masri v. FYROM', par. 191–192; ECtHR, 'Association 21 December 1989 and Others v. Romania', paras. 106, 143, 194. But note that in some cases, the right to the truth is perceived as an individual guarantee ensuring the procedural aspect of Article 3. ECtHR, *Affaire Nasr and Ghali c. Italy*, Application No. 44883/09, Judgment of 23 February 2016, par. 262.

enabled those abuses.[213] It has also broadened the goals that the truth is meant to achieve; beyond the victim and its next of kin, collective truth aims to contribute to the mourning process of whole communities.[214] In turn, that enlargement signifies a departure of truth from the strict human rights equation that necessitates a link among the violation, the harm, the victim and the truth measure. The flexibility of that approach is important for corporate accountability, as it can arguably create space – in an otherwise strict state-centric equation – for the accommodation of measures against corporate malfeasance, in the framework of Truth Commissions.

In addition, by broadening its material scope, truth can seemingly cast its net over more generalized patterns of corporate abuses and impunity, which would further contribute to the objectives of truth-telling. Human rights bodies have deemed that truth serves the victim and its family, along with broader aims such as impunity prevention and rule of law. By way of illustration, the Inter-American organs have recognized the importance of the right to information for democracy[215] and the rule of law,[216] as the 'starting-point for the liberation as well as the protection of the human being'.[217] Truth has been also connected to the fight against impunity,[218] which 'fosters chronic recidivism of human rights violations, and total defencelessness of victims and their relatives'.[219] Similarly, the African Commission on Human Rights has vested truth with the goal of addressing root causes of violence.[220] As with the guarantees of non-repetition, the broader scope of truth paves the way for an engagement of TRCs with issues that go beyond individualized justice. Insofar as the aims of truth have also preventive underpinnings,

[213] IACtHR, 'Case of the Rochela Massacre, Judgment', par. 156; 'Case of Contreras et al. v. El Salvador', par. 146. Truth has also been recognized as being held by society as a whole and to constitute a prerequisite for historical clarification of serious human rights violations. IACtHR, *Case of Gudiel Álvarez* v. *Guatemala*, Series C No. 253, Merits, Reparations and Costs, Judgment of 20 November 2012, par. 300.

[214] IACtHR, 'Case of the Río Negro Massacres v. Guatemala', par. 265.

[215] IACmHR, 'Case Ignacio Ellacuría v. El Salvador', par. 224.

[216] IACtHR, Application before the Inter-American Court of Human Rights in Case 11.324, *Narciso González Medina* v. *Dominican Republic*, 2 May 2010, par. 159.

[217] IACtHR, 'Case of Bámaca Velásquez v. Guatemala', Separate Opinion of Judge A. A. Cançado Trindade, par. 29, 32.

[218] IACtHR, *Bulacio* v. *Argentina*, Series C No. 100, Judgment of 18 September 2003, par. 110–120; IACtHR, 'Myrna Mack Chang v. Guatemala', par. 272–277; IACtHR, 'Blake v. Guatemala', par. 97.

[219] IACtHR, 'Paniagua Morales and others v. Guatemala, Merits Judgment', par. 173.

[220] AfrComHPR, '*Zimbabwe Human Rights NGO Forum* v. *Zimbabwe*', dispositif.

the examination of corporate wrongdoing seems fit to contribute to those goals.

As expected, several risks lurk in this approach. The first one, evidenced by the South African TRC earlier, is the risk of belittling business involvement in violence, by placing it as an element of context or historical backdrop of the conflict.[221] In addition, the collective aspect of truth and the extensive patterns of structural inequalities that it is called to elucidate, arguably conflict with the inherently short-term, legalistic and human rights–centred character of transitional experiments.[222] Without degrading the various challenges and inherent limitations of legal approaches, it seems that, at least in cases of corporate wrongdoing, the golden ratio for accountability purposes stands on a thin line between legalism and social justice and, insofar as those two collide, would benefit from combining traditional approaches with more innovative ones.

7.4.1 From Mauritius to Sierra Leone: Stories of Corporate Abuse Enmeshed in Violence

The TRCs that have so far dealt with corporate accountability have also engaged in analysing systematic patterns of corporate abuse and their links to socio-economic violence, inequality and exclusion. The Mauritius Truth and Justice Commission is one such example. Its work was unprecedented in that it covered socio-economic class abuses spanning over more than 370 years, the longest time ever covered by a truth commission.[223] In 2009, the Parliament of Mauritius entrusted the Commission with investigating the history of slavery and indentured labour in the country, that started in 1638, when it was colonized by the Dutch, and lasted until 1835, as well as land dispossession in

[221] L. Laplante and T. Olsen, 'Commentary: On Developing Purposeful Involvement of Business in Reparation Programming within Transitional Justice Setting', 14 January 2022, available at https://nesl.edu/docs/default-source/default-document-library/laplante_olsen_-01-14-22-final.pdf?sfvrsn=13097ca0_2.

[222] Waldorf is apprehensive that transitional justice is inherently short term and legalistic to be able to address socio-economic inequalities. L. Waldorf, 'Anticipating the Past: Transitional Justice and Socio-Economic Wrongs' (2012) 21 *Social and Legal Studies*, p. 171. Zinaida Miller has added that a potentially non-legalistic approach is best suited to address the economic dimensions of conflict. Miller, 'Effects of Invisibility', pp. 266–291.

[223] Hayner, *Unspeakable Truths*, p. 70.

nineteenth-century Mauritius.[224] It was also mandated to determine suitable measures to be extended to descendants of slaves and indentured labourers.

Its report, published in 2011, documented extensively the economics of colonialism, slavery and indentured servitude, the experiences of indentured workers, and living and working conditions on sugar plantations. It revealed patterns of socio-economic exploitation by an interrelated web of economic and political elites[225] who maintained exclusion, poverty and unemployment,[226] as a means to satisfy the demands of a colonial capitalist system. For the Commission, 'the insatiable pursuit of profits and capital accumulation by the Colonial Powers, in particular the traders, the emerging mercantile and industrial bourgeoisie and later by the financial bourgeoisie, of the European Colonial Powers' was linked to colonialism and slave labour. Slavery was

> more than a labour system: it was the most exploitative and socially and culturally oppressive of all economic and social systems. Indentured labour imported from British India and elsewhere was part and parcel of the transformation of the slave system into the new emerging capitalist system: still exploitative and oppressive, though to a lesser extent than slavery, and with wages, albeit very minimal.[227]

The Commission recognized the role of the business sector in the country's history of slavery and labour exploitation. The sugar industry received particular attention, as it was the epicentre of slave labour, with specific laws and power arrangements lending protection to it.[228] Lamentably, a more detailed account of the role of other industries was blocked, first by the vast time lapse and second by the overall approach of the Commission focusing more on their historical role, as opposed to the allocation of concrete responsibilities to modern business community.[229] As with other truth commissions, the Mauritian one rightly situated the business sector within the context of the country's turbulent past, but did so at the expense of attributing concrete responsibility to those actors in a

[224] Truth and Justice Commission Act No. 28, Mauritius, adopted by the parliament on 22 August 2008.
[225] Report of the Truth and Justice Commission of Mauritius, Vol. I, at 4.
[226] Ibid., at 402.
[227] Ibid., Vol. I, p. 59.
[228] Ibid., p. 64.
[229] Laplante and Olsen, 'Commentary'.

way that could form a basis for including them in any future reparation programme.

The Commission put forth a series of recommendations, including the memorialization of slavery, the creation of a comprehensive and inclusive historical narrative, the safeguarding of Mauritius' rich heritage, the eradication of racism and elitism, the promotion of a vibrant and democratic public sphere, the empowerment of individuals with African and Malagasy roots and the implementation of measures aimed at economic and social justice, including land issues and environmental protection. Due to the absence of explicit attribution of blame to companies, the recommendations pertaining to corporate entities remained somewhat imprecise. The Creation of a Special Fund to compensate for the slave system was proposed, to be funded among others by revenues obtained through an increase in corporate taxes from 15 per cent to 20 per cent and by a 2 per cent tax on profits of banks, which have benefitted from related policy decisions.[230] The report proposed audits of public and private employment practices and penalties for employers, who discriminate.[231] It also urged the government to establish an affirmative action programme and anti-discrimination unit to address inequality and institutionalized racism, across different segments of society.[232] The Commission recommended that a 'special class of trainers in small business enterprises' be appointed to support the emerging social class of small business entrepreneurs.[233] As usual, expectations were not met, and the implementation of those recommendations was substandard, leading a former commissioner to accuse the government of using the Commission as 'an eyewash'.[234] To this date, the government and different industry sectors have not taken any action, targeting corporate wrongs in the period investigated by the Commission.[235]

Perhaps the most elaborate account of broader patterns of abuse, violence and inequality was made by the Sierra Leonean Truth and Reconciliation Commission.[236] Its aim was to create 'an impartial

230 Report of the Truth and Justice Commission of Mauritius, p. 437.

231 Ibid., p. 17.

232 Ibid., p. 403.

233 Ibid., p. 413.

234 'Labour and the Truth and Justice Commission', Le Mauricien, 2 May 2015.

235 A. Groëme-Harmon, 'Dépossession des terres: Jean Claude de l'Estrac déterre la "nécessaire réparation" aux exclus', L'Express, 15 December 2020.

236 Article VI(2) of Lomé Peace Agreement of 7 July 1999 provided for the Commission as one of the structures to achieve national reconciliation and consolidation of peace.

historical record of violations and abuses of human rights and international humanitarian law related to the armed conflict in Sierra Leone (...), to address impunity, to respond to the needs of the victims, to promote healing and reconciliation and to prevent a repetition of the violations and abuses suffered'.[237] The investigative tasks of the Commission concerned the causes, nature and extent of abuses, including their antecedents, context and any potential planning, policy or authorization by the government, group or individual, for those acts. The Commission opined that its mandate was not confined to crimes under national or international law,[238] neither to state violations,[239] but extended also to natural persons and corporate bodies,[240] based on the 'growing body of law to support the idea of the involvement of "non-state actors" in violations or abuses of human rights'.[241] It further opined that the word 'abuse' in its founding Act, as opposed to 'violation' in the Lomé Agreement, was a deliberate addition by the Act to cover abuses conducted by non-state actors.[242]

In unpacking the complex factors that led to the conflict, the Commission devoted an entire chapter to the role of mineral resource extraction companies, and particularly diamonds, in the

Article XXVI of the Agreement stipulated that 'a Truth and Reconciliation Commission shall be established to address impunity, break the cycle of violence, provide a forum for both the victims and perpetrators of human rights violations to tell their story, get a clear picture of the past in order to facilitate genuine healing and reconciliation'.

237 The Truth and Reconciliation Commission Act 2000, Part III, Article 6(1).

238 The mandate was 'not confined to violations of human rights that might constitute crimes, under either national or international law, nor is it limited to violations committed by States or governments'. Witness to Truth: Report of the Sierra Leone Truth and Reconciliation Commission (2004), Vol. 1, par. 46 ['TRC Report'].

239 Ibid.

240 Ibid., Vol. 1, par. 45. It is interesting to note that at this point, the Commission suggested that the failure to regulate the corporations involved could be attributed to the corporation's home state. Schabas opines that the Commission's recommendations can be used as an indicator of a trend within international human rights law to include non-state actors as perpetrators of human rights violations. W. Schabas, 'A Synergistic Relationship: The Sierra Leone Truth and Reconciliation Commission and the Special Court for Sierra Leone' (2004) 15 *Criminal Law Forum*.

241 TRC Report, Vol. 1, par. 43.

242 The word 'abuses' was inserted in three different part of the Act, namely the reference to 'human rights violations and abuses' in the Memorandum of Objects and Reasons; the reference to 'child perpetrators of abuses or violations' (Part III, par. 7(4)) and the reference to violations and abuses which were the result of deliberate planning, policy or authorization by any government, group or individual (Part III, section 6(2) (a) (1)). See also TRC Report, Vol. 1, par. 42.

conflict.[243] It found that post-colonial governments misappropriated the diamonds industry and exploited political power to gain economic wealth. Diamond resources were channelled off to other countries, with the complicity of the country's political elite, depriving as such the people from the benefits of their mineral wealth.[244] The international diamond industry, indifferent to the origin of conflict diamonds, encouraged their illicit trade, fuelling further the conflict.[245] Private security firms, such as Executive Outcomes, Sandline International, Lifeguard Security and ArmSec International, partnered with mining companies and the government to provide security services in conflict areas.[246]

The TRC focused on the diamond industry, due to its catalytic role in causing and fuelling the war. It was deemed that the misuse of the diamond resources, in a country with a practically diamond-based economy, generated huge disparities in the socio-economic conditions of people. According to the Commission, the elite and their business associates in the diamond industry enjoyed grandeur and affluence, while poor people lived in deprived communities due to the misuse of collective commonwealth.[247] However, although it accused political elites of plundering the assets of the country, it only named seven corporations,[248] without providing any evidence or specific information on their violations. Even worse, it failed to discern different levels of corporate participation in atrocities, and instead qualified corporate activities generically as indirect causes of the conflict and fuelling factors.

In the recommendations part, the Commission referred to business actors in the context of corruption and called on them to develop a Code of Corporate Governance that would foster ethical conduct and share information with law enforcement agencies.[249] Reparations were considered the primary responsibility of the government, even for human rights violations committed by non-state actors,[250] justified on the state duty to exercise due diligence to prevent them, denying as such any corporate obligation to repair. They were to be implemented by – among others – revenues generated through the exploitation of mineral

[243] TRC Report, Vol. 2, chapter 1, para. 43 and Vol. 3b, par. 6.
[244] Ibid., Vol. 3b, par. 207–210.
[245] Ibid., Vol. 2, chapter 1, par. 44.
[246] Ibid., Vol. 3b, par. 73.
[247] Ibid., Vol. 2, chapter 1, par. 40 and Vol. 3b, par. 4.
[248] Sandt and Moor, *Peace, Everyone's Business!*, p. 107.
[249] TRC Report, Vol. 2, chapter 3, paras. 297–299.
[250] Ibid., Vol. 2, chapter 1, par. 81.

resources as provided for in Article 7 of the Lomé Peace Agreement, which foresaw that all proceeds generated from gold and diamonds are to be used exclusively for social development and economic advancement of the people of Sierra Leone;[251] a once-off tax on local and foreign corporate entities operating in the country; and recovered assets, which were illegally removed during the conflict.[252]

Overall, the Commission vividly described the intricate patterns of socio-economic violence and inequality that triggered and sustained violence, including the role of businesses. Nevertheless, that role was mostly confined in the background, deprived of the features that would enable real reparations by those actors. While corporations were viewed as a source of funding for the implementation of the recommendations, there was no causal link established between corporate wrongs, harm and the subsequent obligation to repair. As usual, the government did not develop any mechanism to use mining revenues for reparation purposes.[253] The only reparations provided were in the form of microcredit, allocated by the governmental National Commission for Social Action, which was designated to implement the post-war rehabilitation to 21,000 beneficiaries.[254] They did not, however, relate to corporate misconduct.

[251] 'The proceeds from the transactions of gold and diamonds shall be public monies which shall enter a special Treasury account to be spent exclusively on the development of the people of Sierra Leone, with appropriations for public education, public health, infrastructural development and compensation for incapacitated war victims as well as post-war rehabilitation and reconstruction. Priority spending shall go to rural areas. The Lomé Peace Agreement, signed by the Government of Sierra Leone and the Revolutionary United Front, Lomé, 7 July 1999, at Article VII, 6.

[252] TRC Report, Vol. 2, chapter 3, par. 506.

[253] Sierra Leone Truth and Reconciliation Commission, 'Background to the recommendations matrix', available at www.sierraleonetrc.org/index.php/background-to-the-recommendations-matrix.

[254] Sandt and Moor, *Peace, Everyone's Business!*, p. 108.

8

Truth as the First Bridge to Cross

Synergies Among Transitional Mechanisms

In transitional settings, it is often the case that TRC's recommendations rarely evolve to actual reparations or prosecutions, the challenge being more acute for those that addressed corporate involvement in conflict or repression. Many TRC reports managed to reveal the truth about corporate involvement in conflicts – to a certain extent – yet prosecutions and reparations were hindered. As such, corporate accountability remained a truth-telling exercise, devoid of any pursuit of criminal liability, compensation or other measure. Practice abounds of examples where TRCs' recommendations were blocked, primarily due to lack of political will or by the so-called corporate veto power.[1] The embryonic state of the concept of corporate accountability and the absence of corporate human rights obligations add to the 'unfinished business' often performed by TRCs.[2] However, the lack of implementation of TRCs' recommendations might also be attributed to the lack of synergies between transitional mechanisms, particularly so in the field of corporate accountability.

In what concerns the relation of truth and reparations, the historic absence of the business sector from the former has been blamed for their omission from the latter.[3] According to empirical evidence, only around one of every four truth commissions has included corporate entities or business persons.[4] Even the TRCs that did include corporate malefactors rarely called for their inclusion in reparation programmes. The Sierra Leonean TRC referred to business involvement in conflict, but rather than requiring reparations from them, it confined the recommendations

[1] Payne et al., *Archimedes' Lever*, p. 113 *et seq.*

[2] *Khulumani* v. *Barclay National Bank Ltd.*, 509 F.3d 148 2d Cir. (2007).

[3] Laplante and Olsen, 'Commentary'.

[4] Ibid., Laplante et al. mention eight out of twenty-nine truth commissions have included corporate entities or business persons, but according to other data, twenty-two out of thirty-nine TRCs recognized corporate accountability issues. See Sandt and Moor, *Peace, Everyone's Business!*, p. 34.

to a Code of Corporate Governance. The El Salvadorian Commission recognized that state and paramilitaries were financed from businesses, but was unable to establish 'all the links existing between private businessmen and the death squads', because of the clandestine nature of their operation.[5] The Uruguayan Peace Commission referred to the assistance of private actors to the regime, but reparations were left to a follow-up secretariat.[6] Rwanda's truth commission analysed the role of the media in inciting hatred and contributing to genocide, but did not make any recommendations on corporate complicity.[7] In contrast, the Paraguayan and Ecuadorian commissions urged for the adoption of norms for transnational and other businesses in relation to human rights, but no implementation of those recommendations took place.[8]

Furthermore, truth commissions, even when they include business actors, do so in an imprecise manner, locating them as a background to describe other violations, as evidenced in the case of Mauritius and Sierra Leone. This essentially absolves corporations from any reparative potential, if not combined with more elaborate links for the attribution of responsibility. Many other commissions, despite putting forward substantial theoretical foundations for their endeavour, omitted to deal in depth with procedural issues of causality and allocation of responsibility. In other words, whereas the TRCs were strong in providing substantial arguments for the inclusion of corporate actors in the transitional justice mechanism, they were weak in procedurally paving the way to enforce that inclusion. They often lacked any details regarding the different modes of involvement, did not refer to names or specific events and did not indicate the link of the victim with the violation. Even the ones that provided details on names and events, like the Liberian one, did not link the violation to a respective reparative obligation. Therefore, they could not substantiate any claim for reparation linked with the corporation, beyond the one of the state. When they did, it was mainly in the form of voluntary contributions, dissociated from the victim's harm and mainly devoted to developmental purposes.

5 It did, however, recommend further investigation of private armed groups. See 'From Madness to Hope: The 12-Year War in El Salvador – Report of the Commission on the Truth for El Salvador', pp. 129, 170.

6 The Commission was mandated to document the fate of those who 'disappeared' between 1973 and 1985. Bohoslavsky, 'Another Brick in the Uruguayan Transition'.

7 Rwanda Truth Commission Report, March 1993, p. 48.

8 Comision Verdad y Justicia de Paraguay, Informe final, Vol. I, pp. 112–113. See Payne et al., *Archimedes' Lever*, p. 327 *et seq.*

In what concerns the relation of truth to justice, this is usually equally strained, with the prevailing narrative in transitional settings often perceiving truth as antagonistic to justice.[9] As will be explored in greater detail further down, truth measures are put forward and immunities from prosecutions are sometimes offered in exchange of testimony, as was the case of the South African and Liberian TRCs. In addition, most TRCs sacrifice robust accountability for the truth. While rightfully providing a systemic view of the patterns of corporate abuse, they fail to herald further prosecutions, and their narrative lacks the necessary specificity that would trigger criminal action. In the Colombian transition, corporations were lured in the truth process in exchange of avoiding the usually harsher penalties of the ordinary justice system.[10] The report of the Guatemalan Commission for Historical Clarification named forty-five companies for their alleged involvement in forced disappearances, either directly or through providing support to paramilitary forces, but was not followed by any criminal or civil proceedings against corporate executives, possibly due to the decision not to attribute individual responsibility.[11] In the case of Liberia, corporations were relieved from prosecution if they provided restitution to the victims.[12] Lastly, the work of the South African TRC, even though groundbreaking, yet it sacrificed the prospects of substantial reparations and domestic prosecutions, in favour of an approach animated mainly by reconciliation and aiming at the truth.[13] Notably, while twenty-two out of thirty-nine TRCs recognized corporate accountability, only twelve of them recommended any

[9] The debate on truth versus justice debate is examined more in detail in Sections 8.1–8.4 and was also investigated in Section 1.3.1 regarding South Africa. Section 3.3 of Part II is also of relevance. For more information, see also Aukerman, 'Extraordinary Evil, Ordinary Crimes'. On retributive approaches to transitional justice, see Orentlicher, 'Settling Accounts'; Malamud-Goti, 'Transitional Governments in the Breach', 6. On restorative approaches, see Sarkin, 'Carrots and Sticks'.

[10] For an overview of the Colombian approach to justice, see Section 4.3.2 of this book. See also M. Freeman and I. Orozco Abad, *Negotiating Transitional Justice: Firsthand Lessons from Colombia and Beyond* (Cambridge University Press, 2020); Valiñas, 'The Colombian Special Jurisdiction for Peace', p. 449; Wesche, 'Business Actors, Paramilitaries and Transitional Criminal Justice in Colombia', 496.

[11] Guatemalan Commission for Historical Clarification (Comision de Esclarecimiento Historico, CEH), *Memoria del Silencio*, example cases 13 and 109.

[12] Truth and Reconciliation Commission, Republic of Liberia, 'Consolidated Final Report', 30 June 2009, p. 370.

[13] Bell and Buhle Ntsebeza, 'Unfinished Business', p. 349.

remedy to be provided and only the Brazilian one explicitly recommended further investigation and prosecution of companies.[14]

What results is an overall minimalist approach to transitional justice, prioritizing truth and amnesties instead of trials and justice,[15] and a narrow view of truth as mere narrative recording instead of a precursor of reparations, criminal accountability and institutional reform.[16] As such, they reject the delivery of holistic transitional justice, which would satisfy the interconnected rights of victims to truth, justice and reparation. Against that precedent, authors vouch for a holistic approach to transitional justice that would allow constructive synergies between judicial and non-judicial mechanisms, to effectively address the multilayered problems of conflict. The adoption of synergistic and holistic approaches to transitional justice means the establishment of truth commissions, reparative measures, trials and guarantees of non-recurrence in a dialectical relation, where the results of the one cross-fertilize and inform the implementation of the other. In this line of reasoning, the Federal Republic of Germany dealt with East Germany's transition, by following a twofold approach of a truth commission and prosecutions.[17] This is because transitional measures can contribute optimally to the transitional goals, when they work in a complementary fashion.

Scholarly contributions have proved the multiplying effect of complementarity, instead of isolated truth commissions' efforts. Olsen et al. have demonstrated that TRCs can have a significant, negative effect on democracy and human rights if not combined with trials and other measures.[18] Evidence from extensive studies demonstrates that the practice of truth commissions does not in fact hinder the work of justice. Only three out of the forty examined TRCs were competent to grant amnesty for

[14] Sandt and Moor, *Peace, Everyone's Business!*, p. 34.

[15] T. Olsen, L. Payne and A. Reiter, 'The Justice Balance: When Transitional Justice Improves Human Rights and Democracy' (2010) 32 *Human Rights Quarterly* 4, at 1005.

[16] For a detailed classification of the objectives of truth commissions, see Hayner, *Unspeakable Truths*, p. 27.

[17] M. Kamali, 'Accountability for Human Rights Violations: A Comparison of Transitional Justice in East Germany and South Africa' (2001) 40 *Columbia Journal of Transnational Law*, at 104.

[18] T. Olsen, L. Payne and A. Reiter, *Transitional Justice in Balance: Comparing Processes, Weighing Efficacy* (United States Institute of Peace Press, 2010), pp. 153–154; Kim and Sikkink also agree that prosecutions increase the effect on truth commissions on human rights conduct. H. Kim and K. Sikkink, 'Explaining the Deterrence Effect of Human Rights Prosecutions for Transitional Countries' (2010) 54 *International Studies Quarterly* 4, at 939–963.

crimes under international law, which means that in practice TRCs support the work of prosecutorial authorities, with half of them contributing to it.[19] Transitional justice mechanisms do not – and probably should not – represent clear-cut and separated fields. Instead, their goals and techniques often intersect, collide or concur.[20] The Kenyan Truth Commission was named 'Truth, Justice and Reconciliation Commission', offering a nominal illustration of collaboration among mechanisms. Under a holistic perspective, well-crafted recommendations of a truth commission should be able to set the stage for symbolic and material reparations,[21] and act as evidentiary basis and constructive precursor to justice.[22] As Bakiner argued, the design of truth commissions, which curtails their judicial powers, accounts for their relative insignificance in judicial processes.[23] Naming specific corporations can provide initial areas for investigation by the judiciary and, in fact, twenty-two companies named in ten TRC reports have faced subsequent judicial action in domestic and foreign criminal and civil courts.[24]

Complementarity and not substitution is dictated, primarily due to the different functions and comparative advantages of each mechanism.[25] Prosecutions are better suited to address individualized guilt with a high degree of reliability due to the strict evidentiary rules. Truth commissions, from the other side, are more fertile forums for the revelation of structural truths,[26] while they require less resources, time and expertise

19 Amnesty International, *Amnesty Research Commissioning Justice Truth Commissions and Criminal Justice* (Amnesty International Publications, 2010).

20 Naqvi, 'The Right to the Truth', p. 2.

21 De Greiff, *The Handbook of Reparations*; A. Du Toit, 'The Moral Foundations of the South African TRC: Truth as Acknowledgment and Justice as Recognition', in R. Rotberg and D. Thompson (eds.), *Truth* v. *Justice: The Morality of Truth Commissions* (Princeton University Press, 2000).

22 For example, Argentina's CONADEP is considered as having facilitated prosecutions. Similarly, the new Federal Republic of Germany decided to deal with East Germany's transition to democracy by choosing a dual approach of a truth commission and prosecutions. Kamali, 'Accountability for Human Rights Violations'.

23 Bakiner, 'Truth Commission Impact'.

24 Sandt and Moor, *Peace, Everyone's Business!*, p. 34.

25 According to Ambos, international criminal law seemingly supports the view that truth measures cannot substitute justice ones because the renunciation of criminal measures in favour of truth ones would indicate inability within the meaning of Article 17(3) ICC Statute on the part of the criminal justice system concerned. Ambos, 'The Legal Framework of Transitional Justice', p. 43.

26 Ibid., p. 41.

and they give the floor to victims.[27] As the Sierra Leonean Truth and Reconciliation Commission summed it up, the TRC can address the 'right to truth' better, whereas the Special Court for Sierra Leone can perform better the 'right to justice'.[28] From their side, reparations can offer not only public acknowledgement but also material and symbolic remedies for the harm suffered. Conversely, prosecutions by seeking the narrow truth of the case[29] cannot really restore the victims' dignity or satisfy society's need for truth.[30] TRCs cannot satisfy the right to justice in view of their lower evidentiary and procedural rules and narrower scope of investigation, and reparations can rarely satisfy retributive goals. As Mendez clearly put it, truth commissions substituting justice efforts would have worse effects 'than doing nothing'.[31]

Instead, ideally, truth should operate as a step towards justice,[32] possibly by allowing the TRC to file the information gathered to the prosecution for further investigation.[33] Besides, truth predicated on the prospect of impunity seems unable to achieve the reconciliatory goals that it was meant to.[34] It should not be forgotten that complementarity among different measures seems also to be at the core of victims' needs and interests.[35] Current evidence on victims' needs seem to corroborate

[27] Méndez, 'Accountability for Past Abuses', p. 277.

[28] Sierra Leone Truth and Reconciliation Commission, Witness to Truth, Vol. 1, p. 44–45, para. 81.

[29] M. Koskenniemi, 'Between Impunity and Show Trials' (2002) 6 *Max Planck Yearbook of United Nations Law* 1, at 32.

[30] Szoke-Burke, 'Searching for the Right to Truth', 553. On the relationship of truth commissions and the ICC, particularly regarding whether a TRC triggers complementarity or not, see S. Stolk, 'The Victim, the International Criminal Court and the Search for Truth: On the Interdependence and Incompatibility of Truths About Mass Atrocity' (2015) 13 *Journal of International Criminal Justice* 5, pp. 973–994; M. Klinkner and E. Smith, 'The Right to Truth, Appropriate Forum and the International Criminal Court', in N. Szablewska and S. Bachmann (eds.), *Current Issues in Transitional Justice: Towards a More Holistic Approach* (Springer Publishers, 2014), pp. 20–24.

[31] Méndez, 'The Right to Truth', p. 275.

[32] Ibid.

[33] This was the case with the TRCs in Chile. See Amnesty International, Chile: Transition at the crossroads – Human rights violations under Pinochet rule remain the crux (AI Index AMR 22/01/96), March 1996.

[34] Méndez, 'Accountability for Past Abuses', p. 269. The Inter-American Commission on Human Rights stated that the value of truth commissions is that they are created, not with the presumption that there will be no trials but to constitute a step towards knowing the truth and, ultimately, making justice prevail. IAComHR, 'Case Ignacio Ellacuría v. El Salvador', par. 229.

[35] Antkowiak, 'Truth as Right and Remedy', fn. 24.

that assertion. The well-known group of mothers of disappeared people in Argentina, the Madres de la Plaza de Mayo, officially rejected reparations lacking any social and historical recognition that their disappeared children had been only political opponents and not criminals.[36] In cases of corporate violations, victims' needs as demonstrated by the multiplicity of foreign lawsuits seems unsatisfied by mere truth. The Khulumani litigation corroborates that,[37] as it took place amidst various barriers, and while the TRC had already told its own truth.

This holistic approach and dialectical relationship find support in legal instruments and the case law of human rights bodies. According to the impunity principles, the right to know for the victims and their families runs in parallel to any legal proceedings.[38] Complementarity and not substitution among transitional mechanisms has been often recommended by human rights bodies.[39] The Committee against Torture found that the efforts of the South African Truth and Reconciliation Commission should be accompanied by justice efforts and other methods of accountability.[40] As Roht-Arriaza notes, 'prosecution constitutes an

[36] Ibid., p. 996.

[37] *Khulumani* v. *Barclay National Bank Ltd.*, 509 F.3d 148 2d Cir. (2007).

[38] 'Joinet Report', par. 17–25.

[39] The HRC upheld that violations committed during the dictatorship in Chile should not only give rise to compensation efforts but also to official investigations to determine direct responsibility. HRC, Concluding observations on Chile, CCPR/C/CHL/CO/5, 17 April 2007, par. 9. See also UN Commission on Human Rights, *Human Rights Resolution 2005/66: Right to the Truth*, 20 April 2005, UN Doc. E/CN.4/RES/2005/66, par. 4; Report of the International Commission of Inquiry on Darfur to the United Nations Secretary-General, pursuant to Security Council Resolution 1564/2004, 25 January 2005, par. 617. According to the Inter-American system, truth obligations should complement the obligation of the state to ensure the judicial determination of responsibilities, IACtHR, *Case of Zambrano Vélez et al.* v. *Ecuador*, Series C No. 166, Judgment of 4 July 2007 Merits, Reparations and Costs, par. 128; IACtHR, *Case of Anzualdo Castro* v. *Peru*, Series C No. 202, Judgment of 22 September 2009, Preliminary Objection, Merits, Reparations and Costs, par. 119; IACtHR, *Case of Radilla Pacheco* v. *Mexico*, Series C No. 209, Preliminary Objections, Merits, Reparations and Costs, Judgment of 23 November 2009, par. 74; IACtHR, 'Case of Gomes Lund', par. 297; IACtHR, 'Case of Contreras et al. v. El Salvador', par. 135; IACtHR, 'Case of the Massacres of El Mozote and nearby places v. El Salvador', par. 298.

[40] UN CAT, Consideration of reports submitted by States Parties under Article 19 of the Convention, Conclusions and recommendations of the Committee against Torture: South Africa, UN Doc. CAT/C/ZAF/CO/1, 7 December 2006, par. 18. See similarly the recommendation that the mandate of the Chilean National Commission for Political Imprisonment and Torture should be extended, to permit criminal proceedings. UN CAT, Conclusions and Recommendations, Chile, 14 May 2004, CAT/C/CR/32/5, par. 6 (g) (vi) and 7 (k) (iv).

important avenue for recounting because it puts the state's resources at the service of truth-telling and identifies those responsible for the disappearance or murder'.[41] As a result, restrictions on the right to truth should not affect the right to justice of the victims. Namely the decision not to release the names of the perpetrators in a truth process should not prevent a prosecution from occurring.[42] In addition, human rights bodies have affirmed that the establishment of truth commissions should complement the obligation of the state to provide reparations and guarantees of non-repetition.[43] Notably, in cases of summary executions, torture and unresolved disappearances, the obligation to provide criminal sanctions concurs with the obligation to provide compensation and cannot be substituted by it.[44] The justification is that investigation and prosecution are required because they are the most effective ways to secure the right to life and the right to be free from torture and forced disappearance.[45] Besides, the complementarity of measures can potentially strengthen each one of them separately. While corporate reparations would be a sign of progress in and of themselves, one might argue that if not combined with prosecutions, they essentially absolve the perpetrator of any public accountability and leave the impetus to commit a crime unaffected. The British ambassador to the Genocide Convention negotiations illustratively held that were the Convention to only include compensation as sanction for perpetrators, it would be rendered valueless, as it would allow genocidaires to escape punishment.[46]

41 Roht-Arriaza, 'State Responsibility to Investigate and Prosecute', pp. 481–482.

42 Working Group on Enforced or Involuntary Disappearances, *General Comment on the Right to the Truth in Relation to Enforced Disappearances*, UN Doc. A/HRC/16/48, par. 8.

43 The Human Rights Committee acknowledged the efforts made by Morocco in the field of data collection and compensation in relation to enforced disappearances but stated that 'those responsible for disappearance have still not been identified, tried and punished'. HRC, Concluding Observations: Morocco, UN Doc. CCPR/CO/82/MAR, 1 December 2004, par. 12.

44 Report of the Human Rights Committee, 37 UN GAOR Supp. (No. 40) Annex V, General comment 7(16), par. 1, UN Doc. E/CN.4/Sub.2/Add.l/963 (1982). For the ECtHR, see 'Jeronovičs v. Latvia', par 105; ECtHR, *Krastanov* v. *Bulgaria*, Judgment, Application No. 50222/99, 30 September 2004; ECtHR, *Grecu* v. *Moldova*, Judgment, Application No. 51099/10, 30 May 2017.

45 Orentlicher states that departures from that requirement and acceptance of administrative inquiries (for example) are allowed only in the face of serious constraints, such as evidentiary ones. Orentlicher, 'Settling Accounts'.

46 H. Abtahi and P. Webb, *The Genocide Convention: The Travaux Préparatoires* (Brill Nijhoff, 2009), p. 1778.

Following this, corporate malfeasance might be better addressed by the complementary work of the three mechanisms, designed to deliver what Mendez calls 'integral' reparations, with truth-seeking measures playing the vital role of 'gateway'.[47] Truth is reasonably the first bridge to cross, since in order to repair and punish, it must be clearly known what should be repaired and punished.[48] Effective TRC reports should be able to set the stage for symbolic and material reparations.[49] TRC reports can also address issues of institutional reform[50] and expedite vetting and lustration processes.[51] Truth can act as the precursor of other mechanisms, insofar as it includes and tackles corporate accountability, in a way that is sufficiently substantiated to trigger reparations or prosecutions.

8.1 Truth Commissions as Gateways to Prosecutions: The Cases of Argentina and Brazil

The Argentinian National Commission on the Disappeared (CONADEP) was created in 1983, to investigate forced disappearances between 1976 and 1983. Its report named companies that were involved in illegal detentions and forced disappearances of trade unionists, during the military regime, and devoted a chapter on trade union activists.[52] Many truth efforts addressing financial complicity to the dictatorship followed suit, including the truth commission established by the province of Rio Negro to investigate corporate complicity during the Argentine dictatorship,[53] and the report drafted by the Ministry of Justice and Human Rights, in 2015, that referred to corporate involvement in forced disappearances and murders,[54] as well as in torture and illegal detention

[47] Méndez, 'The Right to Truth'.

[48] Antkowiak, 'Truth as Right and Remedy'.

[49] De Greiff, *The Handbook of Reparations*; Du Toit, 'The Moral Foundations of the South African TRC'.

[50] Laplante, 'On the Indivisibility of Rights'.

[51] L. Magarrell, 'Reparations for Massive or Widespread Human Rights Violations: Sorting Out Claims for Reparations and the Struggle for Social Justice' (2003) 22 *Windsor Yearbook of Access to Justice*, pp. 85–98.

[52] Comisión Nacional sobre la Desaparición de Personas (CONADEP), Nunca Más, Chapter H: 'Gremialistas', 1984; Sandt and Moor, *Peace, Everyone's Business!*, p. 70.

[53] The Investigative Commission for Memory, the Truth and Justice was approved by law in 2014 and established in 2016. The legislature of the province of Rio Negro, Law No. 4956. See also J. P. Bohoslavsky and J. Letnar Černič (eds.), *Making Sovereign Financing and Human Rights Work* (Hart Publishing, 2014), p. 31.

[54] Dirección Nacional de Sistema Argentino de Información Jurídica, Responsabilidad Empresarial, pp. 406–408.

in car companies' premises.[55] In 2015, a law was approved that established a truth commission on economic complicity.[56]

Argentina is one of the few examples where prosecution and reparation measures capitalized on previous truth efforts,[57] despite governmental efforts to the opposite, with the enactment of two amnesty laws in the 1980s.[58] Evidence demonstrates that Argentina has the highest number of convictions against human rights violators,[59] including against business persons, and CONADEP has been praised as an effective precursor to prosecutions.[60] All the business persons who were prosecuted were identified and indicated in the 2015 report prepared by the Argentine Ministry of Justice and Human Rights, and financial complicity investigations are ongoing.[61] Different reparation measures, funded by the state,[62] were also based on the moral capital of truth efforts.[63]

The Brazilian example was not as fruitful as the Argentinian one, but deserves reference for the effort of the TRC to stir developments in terms of prosecutions and reparations. The Brazilian National Truth Commission (NTC), established in 2011, was mandated to produce a comprehensive account of human rights abuses, recommend measures to prevent further violations, foster national reconciliation and assist the victims.[64] It investigated corporate complicity and named specific companies, such as Mercedes Benz, Ford and Toyota that collaborated with

55 Ibid., pp. 407, 408.

56 Office of the High Commissioner for Human Rights, 'Argentina dictatorship: UN experts back creation of commission on role businesspeople played', 10 November 2015.

57 Payne and Pereira, 'Accountability for Corporate Complicity in Human Rights Violations', pp. 29–46.

58 The first amnesty law was Ley de Punto Final (1986) and the second was the Ley de Obediencia Debida (1987). In 2005, these amnesty laws were struck down by the Argentine Supreme Court. Both were declared null by the Supreme Court in 2005.

59 Verbitsky and Bohoslavsky, *Outstanding Debts to Settle*, p. 2.

60 Sandt and Moor, *Peace, Everyone's Business!*, p. 68 *et seq.*

61 Bohoslavsky and Letnar Černič, *Making Sovereign Financing and Human Rights Work*, p. 31.

62 Office of the United Nations High Commissioner for Human Rights, Rule-of-Law Tools for Post-Conflict States. Reparation programmes, 2008, pp. 11–13.

63 José María Guembe, 'Economic Reparations for Grave Human Rights Violations: The Argentinean Experience', in P. De Greiff (ed.), *The Handbook of Reparations* (Oxford University Press, 2006), p. 11.

64 Pursuant to Article 3 of the Law 12.528 of 18 November 2011 relating to the creation of the National Truth Commission. The previous Special Commission on Deaths and Disappearances and the Amnesty Commission did not refer to corporate involvement. See L. Ghione, 'Addressing Past Violence: The New Brazilian Truth Commission', Peace & Conflict Monitor, 30 March 2012.

the authorities during the dictatorship,[65] and were complicit in detention, torture, disappearances and murders.[66] Although the NTC was deprived from any jurisdictional or prosecutorial capacity, due to the 1979 amnesty law, it did ask the judiciary to establish legal responsibility – criminal, civil and administrative – of those involved in serious, systematic human rights abuses and not to apply the 1979 Amnesty Law.[67] It also recommended reparation measures and the creation of 'an administrative body to [...] continue gathering information and investigating cases, such as [...] the support of businesses'.[68] After the Truth Commission report, various local governments called businesses to testify about their alleged involvement in the dictatorship,[69] but no case has been brought, leading victims of corporate violations to file civil cases against their former employees.[70]

8.2 Truth and Reconciliation Commission of Liberia: Over-Promising but Under-Delivered

The Truth and Reconciliation Commission of Liberia was foreseen in the Comprehensive Peace Agreement of 2003 and established by the 2005 Truth and Reconciliation Commission Act. The mandate of the Commission was to foster truth, justice and reconciliation by determining the root causes of the conflict and identifying those responsible for committing domestic and international crimes against the Liberian people.[71] The scope of its investigations included gross human rights and international humanitarian law violations, including massacres, sexual violations, murders, extrajudicial killings and economic crimes, such as the exploitation of natural resources, between January 1979 and October 2003.[72]

[65] Payne and Pereira, 'Corporate Complicity in International Human Rights Violations', pp. 63–84.

[66] Comissão Nacional da Verdade, Relatório, Volume I, Parte V, Conclusões e Recomendações, pp. 959–973.

[67] Ibid.

[68] International Centre for Transitional Justice, 'ICTJ welcomes the historic final report of the Brazilian National Truth Commission', 10 December 2014.

[69] EFE, 'Brazil Truth Commission Investigates Volkswagen Ties with Dictatorship', *Fox News*, 28 February 2015.

[70] Payne and Pereira, 'Corporate Complicity in International Human Rights Violations'.

[71] Act to Establish the Truth and Reconciliation Commission of Liberia of 12 May 2005, Article IV, Section 4, enacted by the National Transitional Legislative Assembly, 12 May 2005.

[72] Ibid. See also Article IV, Section 4.

At its report, the Commission classified the crimes for which it had to determine responsibility in egregious domestic crimes,[73] gross human rights violations and serious humanitarian law violations.[74] General human rights violations were considered to be mostly, but not exclusively, committed by state actors,[75] leaving the door open to non-state actors. The Commission was also vested to investigate economic crimes and other forms of human rights violations and determine whether they were part of systematic and deliberate patterns or isolated events. It used 'preponderance of evidence' as the appropriate evidentiary standard, differentiating itself from criminal and prosecutorial processes.[76] Importantly, the Commission interpreted the Act as vesting its recommendations with authoritative and binding character, 'which have the weight of law and serve as quasi-judicial directives that must be implemented by the Government of Liberia and the National Legislature'.[77] From hindsight, such power was not attributed to the Commission, as it sparked controversies and was perceived to threaten judicial independence.[78] Regardless, such authoritative power, resembling subpoena powers, could have been beneficial for cases of corporate accountability,

[73] The term egregious domestic crimes covered abuses or crimes beyond the ones of IHRL and IHL, namely those belonging to domestic criminal law. The committee said that the relevant egregious domestic crimes include economic crimes under the Act Adopting A New Penal Law and Repealing Sections 31.3 and 32.1 of the Criminal Procedure Law (19 July 1976), which are as follows: (1) Mercenarism; (2) Official Oppression; (3) Murder; (4) Kidnapping; (5) Rape; (6) Sexual Assault; (7) Fraud on the Internal Revenue of Liberia; (8) Theft and/or Illegal Disbursement and Expenditure of Public Money; (9) Possession, Distribution, Transportation and/or use of Tools and Materials for Counterfeiting Purposes; (10) Misuse of Public Money, Property or Record; and (11) Economic Crime (not a category under criminal law, but one established under Article IV, Section 4(a) of the TRC Act). Truth and Reconciliation Commission, Republic of Liberia, 'Consolidated Final Report', 30 June 2009, p. 54.

[74] Consolidated Final Report, p. 48.

[75] Ibid., 15th additional finding.

[76] The TRC defined 'preponderance of evidence' as a probability test on the basis of the volume and credibility of evidence gathered by it from various primary sources, particularly witnesses' testimonies, and other sources that the accused more likely than not is criminally responsible for committing the violation or crime. 'Consolidated Final Report', twelfth additional finding and p. 16. Although the standard of proof is not a priori remarkable, it could have been useful in cases of corporate violations, when evidence gathering is particularly arduous for victims.

[77] Ibid., p. 332.

[78] Any judicial process must be independent and, as such, devoid of influence from any external actors. Accordingly, the TRC's recommendations to prosecute, or not, particular individuals should not be binding on any criminal investigations and prosecutions for serious past crimes', Human Rights Watch, Justice for Liberia, 10 December 2009.

given that most TRCs have been blamed of making only voluntary suggestions.

The report was the result of elaborate work[79] and attributed to corporate actors both human right violations and economic crimes,[80] which fuelled, exacerbated or prolonged internal and regional armed conflict.[81] It referred to domestic and foreign-owned corporations in several critical economic sectors, such as timber, mining and telecommunications, and were granted illegal benefits in exchange for financial and military support. A massive patronage system was described, comprised of domestic and international economic and political elites that accumulated wealth by looting the country's natural resources.[82] Most notable among them was the lease of one million acres of land on highly favourable terms to the Firestone Rubber Company, which led to the creation of the world's largest rubber plantation, in 1920.[83] Markedly, according to the Commission, the lack of accountability mechanisms and remedies for economic crimes explained the ceaseless plunder, spoilage and waste of public and natural resources, with impunity.[84]

Out of these situations, the TRC named specific companies, corporate representatives and state authorities for sixteen crimes committed during this period, namely aiding and abetting economic criminal actors, corrupt malpractices, bribery, discrimination, environmental crimes, extortion, fraud, government procurement fraud, illegal arms dealings, illegal extraction or sale of natural resources, indigenous spoliation, misuse of public property and funds, money laundering, narcotic drug trafficking, smuggling and other custom violations, and tax evasion. Most importantly, it determined that perpetrators were individuals, but also entities or groups involved in a joint criminal enterprise or conspiracy, who planned, instigated, ordered, commanded, aided or abetted those crimes. All institutions and corporations, including shareholders and corporate

[79] Regarding logging companies, the report was highly detailed as a result of collective work among local civil society, government and international community representatives in the Forest Concessions Review Committee (FCRC), whose data the TRC used. Sandt and Moor, *Peace, Everyone's Business!*, p. 112 *et seq.*

[80] Economic crimes were defined as any prohibited activity with profit purpose by persons and actors whose economic activities contributed to gross human rights and humanitarian law violations in Liberia, perpetuated armed conflict or benefited economically from it. 'Consolidated Final Report', p. 373.

[81] Ibid., pp. 286, 323.

[82] Ibid., pp. 14, 15.

[83] Ibid., p. 15.

[84] Ibid., p. 322.

officers and their agents affiliated with, or aiding and abetting, warring factions or armed groups, were considered responsible for those violations of international humanitarian and human rights law, war crimes and egregious domestic law violations.[85]

The TRC recommended prosecution of specific persons and corporations for the commission of economic crimes during the conflict, as a way to ensure the goals of justice, peace, security, reconciliation and fight against impunity.[86] Regrettably, though, it lacked specificity in linking precise acts with perpetrators and provided only a brief indication of the committed corporate crimes instead of detailed analysis,[87] a shortage that hindered any potential follow-up. It, further, recommended the nationalization, for public good purposes, of all unlawfully acquired corporate assets of complicit corporate persons and the seizure or confiscation of unlawfully acquired individual assets, as proceeds of economic crimes, after respective prosecution for economic crimes. It also suggested the repatriation of assets unlawfully acquired as proceeds of economic crimes, and the criminal liability of natural and legal persons who concealed information or assisted in fraudulent concealment of unlawfully acquired assets.[88]

Regarding reparations, it clarified that the duty to repair falls primarily with the state and development partners, as a long-term peace investment to redress the gross human rights violations committed against victim communities and individuals.[89] For victims of economic crimes, it recommended the establishment of a Reparations Trust Fund, which would be financed by recovering tax arrears from timber, mining, petroleum and telecommunication companies that evaded tax liability under

[85] Ibid., pp. 331, 336. Also in Volume 2, pp. 286–287, the commission mentioned that economic crimes included looting, illegal arms dealing, sexual slavery, human trafficking and child labour.

[86] Ibid., pp. 322, 372. The TRC revealed the names of thirty-five companies for their corporate complicity, and twenty-six corporations were recommended for prosecutions out of a total of forty-five cases. Sandt and Moor, *Peace, Everyone's Business!*, p. 113.

[87] Hayner notes: '[A]nd in particular the lack of specificity as to what acts each person was being held responsible for. Rather than naming perpetrators in the context of specific cases, the report only provides general lists of perpetrators, with a brief indication of the crimes committed (i.e., "massacre, torture, rape")'. Hayner, *Unspeakable Truths*, p. 137.

[88] More specifically, it proposed that anyone (individual or corporation), who concealed information or assisted a perpetrator in the fraudulent concealment or conveyance of unlawfully acquired assets shall be liable for the crime of sabotage and obstruction of justice, for complicity in aiding and abetting a perpetrator in defeating the ends of justice and the public good.

[89] 'Consolidated Final Report', p. 19.

the Taylor regime; funds from economic criminals, sentenced by Liberian courts to pay restitution or other fees; and criminal and civil confiscation schemes in enforcing jurisdictions.[90] It further proposed that restitution paid directly to victims under Liberian criminal law should be redirected to the reparations trust fund and encouraged the state to freeze assets under the UN sanctions scheme and withhold them until the tax arrears are collected. Notably, it suggested to the state to aggressively seek restitution from corporations,[91] but omitted to explicitly link human rights violations with a respective obligation of the corporation to repair. Even worst, despite its clarity in terms of business involvement in economic crimes, yet it allowed corporations to 'make restitution of the full sum of all gains from their engagement in such economic crimes' and thus avoid prosecution[92] and lengthy proceedings. Existing information demonstrate that no company chose to make restitution to avoid prosecution.[93]

Although the TRC's suggestions had the potential to overcome the inability of the state to finance reparations, the government did not implement it and the president opted for collective reparations.[94] Furthermore, the legislation for freezing assets was not adopted, and the UN has got hold of only few illegally obtained assets.[95] Overall, the recommendations of the TRC have not been implemented; nobody has been punished for the crimes described, whereas the Commission and its report were trapped in the swirl of political accusations.[96]

A promising bottom-up transitional effort was the Liberian diaspora TRC report, which devoted a large part to corporate involvement in violence. Its importance lies in corroborating victims' views but also in supporting its narrative with extant legal instruments. It cross-referenced the Norms on the Responsibilities of Transnational Corporations and

[90] Ibid., Vol. 3, title III, pp. 43, 45.

[91] Sandt and Moor, *Peace, Everyone's Business!*, p. 117.

[92] 'Consolidated Final Report', p. 370.

[93] "Although the TRC held a public hearing regarding the role of economic crimes in the conflict, neither asset recovery nor judicial accountability was ever achieved. M Kersten, 'Legacies of Injustice in Liberia: Transitional Justice and Economic Crimes', *Justice in Conflict*, 16 February 2012.

[94] Michalowski, *Corporate Accountability in the Context of Transitional Justice*, pp. 104–105.

[95] Ibid.

[96] Sandt and Moor, *Peace, Everyone's Business!*, pp. 114–115; A. Weah, 'Hopes and Uncertainties: Liberia's Journey to End Impunity' (2012) 6 *International Journal of Transitional Justice* 2, at 5–6.

Other Business Enterprises with Regard to Human Rights,[97] a pivotal instrument of the Business and Human Rights field at the time. Based on the Norms, the report recommended to the international community to ensure that transnational corporations and other business enterprises respect human rights and implement the Norms and other relevant national and international laws.[98]

8.3 The Case of Tunisia: Truth as a Blocking Lever

At the other end of the spectrum stands the example of Tunisia, all the more because it was heralded for its assumed pioneering and brave stance towards corruption. Anti-corruption, as part of a wider demand for socio-economic justice, was the major rallying cry of both the Tunisian uprising and the transition, as it was deemed the main dynamic consolidating economic and political power in the hands of a privileged few, while consigning the majority of society to poverty and unemployment.[99] The Tunisian example is instructive for foreclosing any form of business accountability, with the exceptions that will be analysed further below, despite the various different mechanisms deployed. Truth was recorded eight times, but was seemingly unable to address corporate malfeasance, in its broader form, drifting away the possibilities for corporate accountability by any other transitional mechanism.

All the transitional mechanisms that were established after 2011 focused on the issue of corruption. Eight anti-corruption commissions were established: the 2011 Commission on Corruption and Embezzlement under Ben Ali (Ben Amor Commission),[100] the 2011 National Confiscation Commission, the Commission for the Recovery of Assets Looted and Hidden Abroad, the Commission of Management of Funds and Confiscated Properties,[101] the Tunisian

[97] UN Doc. E/CN.4/Sub.2/2003/12/Rev.2.

[98] The Advocates for Human Rights, *A House with Two Rooms: Final Report of the Truth and Reconciliation Commission of Liberia Diaspora Project*, 2009, p. 484.

[99] Office of the High Commissioner for Human Rights, Report of the OHCHR Assessment Mission to Tunisia, 26 January–2 February 2011 (2011).

[100] Commission on Corruption and Embezzlement under Ben Ali, Decree Law No. 2011-7, 18 February 2011.

[101] Decree Law No. 2011-13, relating to the confiscation of movable and real assets and properties; Decree Law No. 2011-15 establishing the Commission for the Recovery of Assets Looted and Hidden Abroad; Decree Law No. 2011-68 establishing a National Commission of Management of Assets and Funds Subject to Confiscation or Recovery in favour of the state.

National Commission of Investigation on Corruption and Embezzlement, the Truth and Dignity Commission (TDC), including an Arbitration Committee,[102] the Reconciliation Commission[103] and the National Instance of Good Governance and the Fight Against Corruption (IBGLCC).[104] To those, one should add the anti-corruption jurisdiction of the Higher Council for the Fight against Corruption and Assets Recovery and State Assets,[105] the Ministry of Public Service, Governance and the Fight against Corruption,[106] the Specialized Judicial Chambers[107] and the Financial and Economic Judicial Pole,[108] as well as the coordinating role of the Ministry of Human Rights and Transitional Justice.

An overall assessment of those transitional mechanisms demonstrates an exclusive focus on Ben Ali and his entourage,[109] while totally disregarding the corporate counterparts of their misdeeds. The 2011 Ben Amor Commission report listed various corrupt transactions involving him and his clan, in the fields of public procurement, concessions, privatizations, banking and finance, natural resources and the telecommunication sector. It received 10,000 submissions and transferred about 400 to the public prosecutor.[110] The 2018 report of the Truth and Dignity Commission examined corruption and exposed its ramifications on education, economic development, human rights, employment, public debt, business climate and the trust of citizens in the state.[111] It also

[102] Established under the Transitional Justice Law, Organic Law No. 2013-53 of 24 December 2013.

[103] Loi organique No. 2017-62 du 24 Octobre 2017, relative à la réconciliation dans le domaine administrative.

[104] Organic Law No. 2017-59 of 24 August 2017 on the Good Governance and Anti-Corruption Instance (Instance de la Bonne Gouvernance et de la Lutte contre la Corruption).

[105] Decree Law No. 1425 of 2012, issued on 31 August 2012, amending Decree Law No. 3080 of 2010, issued in December 2010, Establishing Higher Advisory Councils.

[106] Decree Law No. 271 of 2016, establishing the Ministry of Public Service, Governance and the Fight against Corruption and Attaching Structures to it, 2 March 2016.

[107] Decree Law No. 2014-2887 creating Specialized Judicial Chambers on transitional justice within first instance courts of Tunis, Gafsa, Gabbs, Sousse, Le Kef, Kasserine et Sidi Bouzid, adopted on 8 August 2014.

[108] Organic Law No. 2016-77 of 6 December 2016.

[109] W. Ferchichi et al., *Transitional Justice in Tunisia: Finally the Law!* (Centre Al-Kawakibi pour la Transition Democratique, 2014), at 14.

[110] Centre for the Study of Violence and Reconciliation, Practitioner Perspectives on Transitional Justice: Tunisia (2015).

[111] Truth and Dignity Commission, Comprehensive Final Report, Part 3 on corruption, pp. 18–30.

referred to the colonial causes of the country's economic decline and requested reparations by the IMF and France for their misdeeds.[112]

All those reports effectively highlighted instances of corruption in various sectors, ranging from procurement to telecommunications. However, responsibility was primarily attributed to members of Ben Ali's family, limiting broader accountability of the business actors involved. The focus of the commissions remained fixed on the 662 companies affiliated with Ben Ali's inner circle.[113] A clear instance of the inclination to simplify the intricate dimensions of corruption to the actions of Ben Ali's close associates is evident in the cases involving corruption within the petroleum sector. These instances were brought to light by both the TDC and civil society groups like IWATCH. Investigations unveiled a complex web of corruption in the oil industry between 2002 and 2012. Foreign entities acquired oil concessions through a network of intermediaries that extended from the inner circle of the clan to bankers, public and private oil companies, politicians and government officials.[114] The British Serious Fraud Office took up investigations related to corruption within Tunisia's petroleum sector.[115] In Tunisia, an inquiry was conducted regarding the Chergui gas field case, which implicated notable figures. Moncef Trabelsi, Ben Ali's brother-in-law, faced charges in 2011. However, business persons and entities outside the immediate Ben Ali family circle, involved in those corrupt activities, such as Amjad Bseisu and Imed Derouiche, managed to avoid repercussions. Instead, they were essentially rewarded with positions in the public domain. Bseisu was appointed as a business ambassador for British trade, while Derouiche was appointed head of the offshore branch of Petrofac Tunisia.

Consequently, numerous other enterprises involved in corrupt dealings remained beyond the scope of truth mechanisms. The reconciliation process involving businesses, overseen by the Arbitration and Reconciliation Committee of the TDC, heavily favoured the business sector, as it did not require any form of apology or structural reform as a condition for reconciliation. The Arbitration and Conciliation

[112] Truth and Dignity Commission, Summary Report, pp. 214, 277.

[113] The Commissions responsible for confiscating, recovering and managing the assets looted by Ben Ali confiscated various assets of the ex-president and his circle, including 486 companies, implicated in corruption instances. Rijkers et al., 'All in the Family: State Capture in Tunisia' (2017) 124 *Journal of Development Economics*, pp. 41–59.

[114] IWatch, 'Petrofac Tunisie Caught Up in a Big Corruption Scandal', 25 November 2016.

[115] Ibid.

Committee, within the TDC, competent to settle corruption cases, received 6,000 applications by 2016 and signed reconciliation settlements with various prominent businessmen close to Ben Ali.[116]

In terms of prosecutions, none of the cases brought before the Specialized Judicial Chambers were directed at a business entity. Convictions due to corruption were pushed – again – only against Ben Ali[117] and his entourage.[118] Although they committed the lion's share of corruption, this is an offence that requires two subjects interacting. Nevertheless, the supply part of corruption, namely multinational corporations, were disregarded, and their legal liability foreclosed. Even though there were legal provisions on corporate criminal liability for money laundering, the Financial and Economic Judicial Pole concluded just twenty-two money-laundering cases by 2016, none of which implicated a corporate entity.[119] Furthermore, any legal proceedings related to corporate wrongdoing in Tunisia occurred in foreign jurisdictions.[120] In terms of confiscations, it was again Ben Ali and his family at the epicentre, without any efforts against corporations that colluded with them. For example, the Tunisian Treasury recovered three and a half million euros from Mohamed Slim Chiboub, a prominent businessman and the spouse of Ben Ali's daughter, through a reconciliation agreement with the Tunisian state.[121] No similar move took place, against foreign or domestic businesses, unaffiliated with Ben Ali.

[116] Organic Law No. 2013-53 of 24 December 2013, Article 45.

[117] He was sentenced, in absentia, to sixteen years of imprisonment for corruption-related charges. Andrieu, 'Civilizing Peacebuilding', at 541.

[118] In the first years after the revolution, more than fifty-two people were prosecuted, for financial corruption, including members of his family. This number corresponds to the first three years of the revolution. The number of cases held against them reached more than 550 in the entire country: while there were 52 abandoned or dismissed cases, 23 cases were presented to the Criminal Division, 45 cases were published before the court's Indictment Division and 62 cases before the court's Appeal Division. Ferchichi et al., *Transitional Justice in Tunisia*, p. 14.

[119] Middle East and North Africa Financial Action Task Force for combating Money Laundering and Terrorist Financing (MENAFATF), Anti-money laundering and counter-terrorist financing measures Tunisia Mutual Evaluation Report, May 2016.

[120] The British Serious Fraud Office has initiated cases against officials of Petrofac and Alstom for corruption offences in Tunisia. Also, a case against Alstom company was initiated in Switzerland for alleged corruption in Tunisia. UK Serious Fraud Office, 'Court orders Alstom Network UK Ltd to pay £16.4 million, Case update', 25 November 2019, available at www.sfo.gov.uk/2019/11/25/sfos-alstom-case-concludes-with-sentencing-of-alstom-network-uk-ltd/.

[121] See 'Transferring an Amount of 3.5 million Euros to Tunisia in the Framework of an Arbitration and Reconciliation File', Truth and Dignity Commission, [Facebook Post], 27 May 2017.

The acknowledgement of the participation of corporations not directly tied to the family in corrupt transactions was limited to situations where it explained corruption involving civil servants or those around Ben Ali.[122] What is more, both legal texts and reports from commissions frequently portrayed corporate entities as victims. This portrayal stemmed from the argument that these entities were coerced into cooperating with Ben Ali due to lack of alternatives. Even after the uprising, business people maintained that they were victimized, this time by a system of extortion involving the handling of reconciliation applications.[123] Research indicates a paradoxical outcome: the economic and business elites grew wealthier through anti-corruption measures by acquiring assets confiscated from Ben Ali.[124] Moreover, they gained access to influential political positions.[125] Notably, the Tunisian business association, UTICA, was awarded the Nobel Peace Prize for its role in facilitating the National Dialogue.[126] Within the discourse of transition, businesses were praised and depicted as both victims and saviours. The focus on reconciliation was emphasized to create a favourable environment for investment and to usher in a new phase of economic growth.[127]

The 2015 preliminary Economic and Financial Reconciliation Bill, which allowed individuals involved in corruption to seek reconciliation,[128] was reportedly influenced by intense lobbying from the business sector. President Essebsi reached an agreement with businessmen to

[122] See the relation between the development of anti-corruption laws and the initiatives to regulate the conduct of multinational corporations. J. Wouters et al., 'The International Legal Framework Against Corruption: Achievements and Challenges' (2013) 14 *Melbourne Journal of International Law* 1.

[123] International Crisis Group, La transition bloquée: corruption et régionalisme en Tunisie Rapport Moyen-Orient et Afrique du Nord, No. 177, 23 (2017), at 24.

[124] M. Oubenal and H. Ben Hamouda, 'The Political Economy of Business Elites in Tunisia: Actors, Strategies and Identities' (2018) Working Papers 1273, Economic Research Forum, p. 10.

[125] Ibid.

[126] Guellali, 'Tunisia: Transitional Justice in the Crosshairs'.

[127] Ibid.

[128] For criticism to the Bill, see European Commission for Democracy through Law, 'Avis intérimaire sur les aspects institutionnels du projet de loi sur les procédures spéciales concernant la réconciliation dans les domaines économique et financier de la Tunisie', Opinion No. 818/2015, 27 October 2015; Rapporteur spécial sur la promotion de la vérité, de la justice, de la réparation et des garanties de non-répétition Pablo de Greiff, Analyse du Projet de loi organique relative aux procédures spéciales concernant la réconciliation dans les domaines économique et financier, Communication OL TUN 2/2016, 1 Juillet 2016.

secure their support during his presidential campaign, as well as to encourage investment and economic development in Tunisia.[129] It is worth noting that similar strategies – excluding the corporate supply of corruption – were employed in anti-corruption endeavours during other transitions, such as in Egypt, where the focus was on prosecuting Hosni Mubarak and his regime members, and in countries like Côte d'Ivoire, where the prosecutions targeted Laurent Gbagbo[130] and his associates, as well as in the Gambia.[131]

8.4 Concluding Remarks

Part III of the book drew from international law and domestic experiences to argue in favour of including corporate wrongdoing in the scope of Truth and Reconciliation Commissions' work. This would support the broader goals of transitional justice, but also uphold the raison d'être of truth-telling, as an entitlement of victims and their families to learn of events, reasons, circumstances and actors that inflicted significant harm on them. Despite the clear advantages of registering truth widely, including for corporate violations, this has often been constrained due to various legal arguments, such as the presumption of innocence, amnesties and other. Furthermore, although truth mechanisms are the ones that have most expansively dealt with corporate wrongdoing, this has often been carried out tangentially, as a matter of practical necessity, and not legal prerogative.

Revealing names of perpetrators during the investigations carried out by truth commissions would legally require that the state duty to investigate is deployed against corporate entities. For truth stemming from the state duty to remedy this would not be a straightforward conclusion, as this duty unfolds between the state and the victim. However, the state duty to investigate unfolds against third actors, when it forms part of the states' positive obligations. To discharge the right to truth or the duty to investigate against corporate malefactors, one would need to put those positive obligations at the forefront, as they already apply against non-state entities. In that line of reasoning, the Basic Principles list the verification of the facts and full and public disclosure of the truth as a

[129] Michalakea, 'Anticorruption and Transitional Justice'.

[130] Maguchu, *Transitional Justice and Socio-Economic Rights in Zimbabwe*, p. 17.

[131] Carranza, *Truth, Accountability, and Asset Recovery*, p. 2.

measure of satisfaction that is to be provided not only by the state but also by the legal person or entity liable for the harm.

Notably, relevant legal sources and case law of human rights bodies underline not only the development of 'a right to truth' in international law but also its unrestricted nature. The right to truth and the associated state duty to investigate have been deemed as not subject to restrictions, for reasons of confidentiality, public interest, national security or for politically sensitive issues. Based on that, it is reasonable to conclude that common justifications for the exclusion of corporate actors, such as economic development and investments, would not constitute acceptable restrictions of the right to truth. In other words, a state could not reasonably argue that its reliance on corporations for future economic development allows it to restrict its duty to investigate and, as a result, withhold names of corporate perpetrators or avoid documenting corporate harm in times of conflict or repression. However, it should be kept in mind that transitional dynamics are fragile and the revelation of identities can spark controversies, particularly in fora that cannot assure due process safeguards in the same way as courts do. Transposing this debate to cases of corporate abuse, a reasonable question is whether corporate identities should also be revealed, as a matter of law, or if generic references to 'business wrong doers' might suffice. Human rights bodies, while they have not explicitly addressed the issue, have elevated the identity of the perpetrator to a key element of truth's content, from which conclusions on corporate identities can be extrapolated.

The Colombian Commission for the Clarification of Truth, Coexistence and Non-Repetition, which issued its final report on June 2022, explicitly based its work on the right to truth and did not accept any excuse or restriction in releasing names of perpetrators, including corporate ones. It registered 258 economic actors and their involvement in concrete abuses, as well as patterns of abuse, and elaborated on different levels of responsibility for corporate actors. However, its recommendations were less daring. In contrast, the 2005 report of the Commission for Reception, Truth and Reconciliation of East Timor was pioneering in identifying economic, social and cultural rights violations that needed to be addressed as part of the transition, acknowledging the role of non-state actors and attributing tort liability to businesses. Yet it refrained from referring to names implicated in violence and limited its scope to rather generic descriptions of various industry sectors.

A further important conclusion is drawn by the evolution of the status of the right to truth, arguably towards the level of an autonomous right under customary international law or a general principle of law. This evolution is important for corporate accountability purposes, as it places an unequivocal emphasis on the importance of uncovering the truth, mitigating other often-cited considerations in relation to corporations, such as developmental concerns, despite the undeniable importance of the latter in reconstruction periods. In essence, if the right to truth is afforded a heightened status, it becomes less amenable to compromises in favour of the right to development, a tension that frequently arises during transitions. This was not the case with the South African Truth and Reconciliation Commission, which meticulously examined corporate involvement in the Apartheid regime and classified involvement under three so-called orders. However, its recommendations balanced business accountability to corporate contribution to development and reconstruction and merely led to two voluntary business trusts, focusing on infrastructure, tourism and educational projects, which remained largely unsuccessful.

A further aspect of truth-telling that can be valuable for advancing corporate accountability within transitional justice is the collective aspect of truth, which has been applauded by legal instruments, and the practice of human rights bodies and truth commissions. The collective aspect of the right to truth develops alongside a gradual widening of the scope of truth itself, from individual violations to more systemic patterns of violence. This widening offers an opportunity for the examination of how corporate abuse is often entrenched within the dynamics that maintain and perpetuate conflict or repression. In addition, it entails its departure from the strict human rights equation that necessitates a link among the violation, the harm, the victim and the truth measure. This more flexible approach is important for corporate accountability, as it can arguably create space – in an otherwise strict state-centric equation – for the examination of corporate malfeasance by TRCs.

A broader and more systemic aspect of the truth was delivered by the Mauritius Truth and Justice Commission, which examined socio-economic abuses spanning over more than 370 years, with a focus on the history of slavery, indentured labour and land dispossession. Its report illustrated the role of the business sector, and particularly the sugar industry, in driving socio-economic exploitation that maintained exclusion, poverty and unemployment. Similarly, the Sierra Leonean Truth and Reconciliation Commission unpacked the complex factors underlying the conflict, including the role of mineral resource extraction companies and their collusion with post-colonial governments and the country's elite. Both Commissions had limited practical success, but prompted a situated understanding of corporate abuse, within broader patterns of violence and inequality, an awareness which leaves a crucial legacy for understanding corporate wrongdoing, beyond isolated instances, as a broader issue of political economy that permeates both the violence itself and also the transitional measures that follow.[132]

Last but not least, another important conclusion concerns the necessary synergies – or the absence thereof – among transitional mechanisms. Oftentimes, TRC's recommendations do not evolve into actual reparations or prosecutions, and the different measures are dissociated one from the other, the challenge being more acute for those that addressed corporate involvement in conflict or repression. More often than not, corporate accountability remained part of the truth narrative, but did not reach the level of tangible criminal or reparative measures. Against this background, legal instruments, the case law of human rights bodies and scholarship vouch in favour of complementarity among measures, due to its multiplying effects. Corporate malfeasance might be better addressed by the complementary work of different mechanisms, where truth is the gateway to justice and reparations, with the goal of delivering integral and holistic justice. If one were to categorize different transitional examples along a spectrum, ranging from the most to the least synergistic ones, then Argentina and Brazil would be at the former end, despite their deficits. In both instances, there were efforts to build both prosecutions and reparations on the moral capital of the truth. The case of Liberia, with the work of its Truth Commission, would stand in the middle, given that despite its meticulous account, the report lacked the necessary specificity that would allow its recommendations on prosecutions to materialize. Lastly, at the opposite end of the spectrum would lie the example of Tunisia. Tunisia's transitional efforts are particularly notable for their bold approach to combating corruption. However, despite the creation of multiple different truth commissions that dealt with that phenomenon, business accountability of the various companies not owned by Ben Ali was foreclosed. The exclusive focus of the truth commissions on Ben Ali and his family structured the narrative accordingly and did not allow for any other effort to materialize.

132 Lai, 'Beyond Context', pp. 385–399.

By Way of Conclusion

Towards Transformative Political Economies of Transitional Justice

Transitional justice consolidated in the early 2000s into what came to be called 'mainstream transitional justice paradigm',[1] amalgamating prosecution, truth, reparations and institutional reform into a toolbox of mechanisms to be deployed in the aftermath of conflict or violence, in different parts of the word, as the most appropriate response to help societies turn the page to past atrocities.[2] That paradigm put the spotlight mostly on state-sponsored atrocities and state-induced human rights abuses, of civil or political nature, during periods of political upheaval or conflict. This standardization of transitional justice came at the expense of a deeper engagement with the dynamics, factors and actors that bred, exacerbated and sustained violence, as well as with the particularities of each setting.[3] Business actors comprise an example of such a prevalent but nevertheless marginalized actor. Their operations, despite widespread knowledge of their involvement in conflict, have remained in the background, and transitional mechanisms have either ignored them or improperly addressed their accountability.

The consolidation of the mainstream transitional paradigm, during the last decades, spawned different criticisms, pinpointing to its weaknesses, blind spots and fallacies.[4] Scholars lamented, among others, the mainly retributive character of the experiment,[5] its technocratic,[6] depoliticizing

[1] Sharp, 'Interrogating the Peripheries'.
[2] Teitel, 'Transitional Justice Genealogy'.
[3] Nagy, 'Transitional Justice as a Global Project'.
[4] Sharp, 'What Would Satisfy Us?'.
[5] M. Minow, *Between Vengeance and Forgiveness: Facing History after Genocide and Mass Violence* (Beacon Press, 1998).
[6] Shaw, Waldorf and Hazan, *Localizing Transitional Justice*; McEvoy, 'Beyond Legalism', 412.

and decontextualizing effects,[7] as well as its liberal orientation, hidden behind ostensibly apolitical technologies.[8] Few critics raised concerns over the narrow scope of different transitional measures, focusing on civil and political rights and state or armed non-state actors, and excluding questions of socio-economic violence[9] and the accountability of economic actors, and particularly corporations.[10] On top of those, the galaxy of different international, regional and domestic documents that have been associated with the business and human rights field deal minimally with transitional justice and its particularities and challenges. As such, the separate development of those fields is consolidated, the one remaining largely insulated from the other.

The absence of corporate accountability from transitional justice theory and practice is in stark contradiction with their actual impact on the ground, particularly so in spaces of conflict, repression and violence. In today's world, corporate entities wield significant economic and political power and are, frequently, implicated in conflicts, enmeshed in the power structures that sustain them, contributing to abuses or benefiting from the prevailing violent conditions. Most conflicts in the world increasingly take place in countries with severe socio-economic inequalities,[11] where corporate malpractices prevail, deepening disparities, fuelling discontent and instability.

This intricate topography of violence, heavily pivoting on economic inequality and on the power of some actors, like corporations to commit abuses, demands a profound reconsideration of relevant frameworks put in place during transitions, and prompts a reassessment of the mechanisms used and their adaptability to address corporate accountability, and the associated socio-economic issues. Key questions emerge: How do we navigate the intricate web of economic interests that may have fuelled or sustained conflict? What role can transitional justice play in dismantling

[7] Leebaw, 'The Irreconcilable Goals of Transitional Justice'; P. McAuliffe, *Transformative Transitional Justice and the Malleability of Post-Conflict States* (Edward Elgar Publishing, 2017), pp. 75–78.

[8] Franzki and Olarte, 'Understanding the Political Economy', pp. 203–204; Bowsher, 'Omnus et Singulatim'.

[9] Miller, 'Effects of Invisibility', p. 266; Arbour, 'Economic and Social Justice for Societies in Transition', p. 1; Cavallaro and Albuja, 'The Lost Agenda'.

[10] Michalowski, *Corporate Accountability in the Context of Transitional Justice*; Payne et al., *Archimedes' Lever*.

[11] P. Collier et al., *Breaking the Conflict Trap, Civil War and Development Policy* (World Bank and Oxford University Press, 2003), p. 53 *et seq*.

the entrenched culture of corporate impunity? How do corporate accountability concerns collide with the boundaries of mainstream transitional justice? What challenges and possibilities can the law offer in that respect? And more generally, what alternative imaginaries can give birth to a fruitful intersection of transitional justice and corporate accountability and what transformational prospects will emerge as a result?

In response to those questions, this book departed from a thorough normative account, consolidating the reasons why transitional justice should consider corporate accountability while having in mind the inherent limitations of the latter. As a springboard, such integration would expand the possibilities for the accomplishment of transitional goals. Insofar as corporate entities were implicated in prior violence, then accountability of the perpetrators, remedies for the victims and ultimately reconciliation can be achieved to the extent that those entities are present in the topography of transition. Research shows that the identification and acknowledgement of the perpetrator is fundamental in allowing remedies, either in the form of criminal justice, reparations, or truth, to unfold their retributive, deterrent and compensatory functions and to contribute to victims' healing.

In addition, holding corporations accountable would respond better to victims' demands and vest the transitional experiment with a bottom-up and victim-centred character. This is because it would bring to the foreground the increasing calls of victims for corporate accountability, as evidenced by the various cases submitted in diverse fora, while simultaneously reducing the influence of top-down expert opinions that currently dominate the field. The value of listening to victims' needs should be assessed under the light of the already existing victims' gap in the field of business and human rights,[12] and the privileged position that corporations find themselves in.

Corporate accountability forming part of the transitional topography would also accomplish a fuller understanding of prior injustice than the one usually acknowledged by the mainstream transitional paradigm. This is because corporate wrongdoing is not only linked to civil and political rights, often at the epicentre of transitions, but also to violations of socio-economic rights and most importantly to the conditions that precipitated violence or repression, the so-called root causes that led, exacerbated or maintained violence and repression. Corporate misconduct can be easily

[12] Ramasastry, 'Corporate Social Responsibility Versus Business and Human Rights'.

understood as a 'root cause' of conflict, in view of the various forms of socio-economic violence in which corporations are enmeshed, enabling the maintenance of systems of abuse.[13] If corporate wrongs are part of root causes of violence, then their accountability can potentially unlock useful discussions on those causes and better equip transitional justice to ensure more sustainable and long-lasting peace and democracy.[14] In reverse, ignoring those deeper inquiries risks the credibility and viability of the whole transitional experiment.[15] Last but not least, corporate accountability within transitions can nuance the presumably apolitical orientation of transitional justice,[16] by reversing the historic exclusion of the economic sphere from transitional contestation. As such, it can stir an honest, in-depth debate on political and economic choices expand the horizon of possibilities for people to choose from and render transitional justice into a truly emancipatory project.

Amidst a variety of TJ scholarship underlining the limitations of legal approaches for transitional goals, and putting forward politics,[17] the book vouched in favour of both transitional justice and of the value of law within that framework, for addressing corporate accountability within transitions. Transitional justice, involving an array of possibilities and variants of responsibility and infused with exceptionality, seems better suited to address the intricate ways in which corporate involvement in conflict or repression plays out, to compromise conflicting priorities and offer new and much needed conceptualizations, while at the same time looking towards the future. Further, focusing on the law has, first, the potential to elucidate persistent epistemic and empirical challenges. Despite high-level paeans to the need for remedies, the precise meaning of the right to remedy corporate-induced violations and its performance during transition times remain contested, poorly understood and thus inapplicable. Second, research affirms the added value of merging international and national legal standards for corporate accountability during transitions.[18] A well-defined international framework in synergy with

13 Schmid, *Taking Economic, Social and Cultural Rights Seriously*.

14 Sharp, 'What Would Satisfy Us?'; Collier and Hoeffler argue that conflicts reignite if the conditions that precipitated violence are not addressed. Collier and Hoeffler, 'On the Incidence of Civil War in Africa', pp. 13, 17.

15 Mani, 'Dilemmas of Expanding Transitional Justice', p. 235.

16 Franzki and Olarte, 'Understanding the Political Economy'; Bowsher, 'Omnus et Singulatim'.

17 McEvoy, 'Beyond Legalism'.

18 Payne et al., *Archimedes' Lever*, chapter 5; Pereira et al., 'Justice from Below', p. 214 *et seq.*

domestic laws is the best tool to trigger international pressure, foster civil society demand and institutional designers' work,[19] in the area of corporate accountability during transitions. Thus, the book engaged in a granular analysis of relevant international and regional law, as well as national practice, transcending conventional silos and blending different regimes, across diverse levels. In addition, instead of theorizing on the yet hypothetical direct human rights obligations of businesses in relation to transitions, the book delved into states' obligations, given that states are the institutional designers and drivers of transitions, as well as in the corresponding rights of victims, whose experiences and demands are paramount for transitional justice. The central legal question of the book concerned whether states have a legal obligation to include corporate malefactors in the design and implementation of transitional measures, as debtors of respective responsibilities.

To address this cardinal question, the book introduced new theoretical approaches, based on *de lege ferenda* perspectives to international human rights and international criminal law. It identified different elements, in scholarship, legal instruments and practice that could support a novel interpretation of state duties to include corporate entities in transitional measures.[20] More specifically, in terms of criminal justice mechanisms, a prerequisite for a potential state duty to investigate, prosecute and punish corporate actors in cases of international crimes would be the existence of corporate obligations under international criminal law. While there are, currently, no relevant corporate obligations, certain elements indicate that the law should evolve in this direction. Those elements include the corporate capacity to commit atrocities and the substantial prohibition of international crimes covering legal persons, in addition to natural ones, despite the absence of a jurisdictional forum to try them. Circling back, if international criminal law is interpreted to bind those entities, then state duties to investigate and prosecute should also cover them when they commit international crimes. Due consideration should also be given to the increasing number of jurisdictions and international instruments that recognize corporate criminal accountability, as they demonstrate an 'expanding web of liability for business entities implicated in international crimes',[21] and emphasize the dissonance of corporate impunity

19 Ibid.
20 There is an ongoing theoretical debate regarding the relationship between interpretation and modification of rules in international law. See n 37, Section 3.2.1, Part II, of this book.
21 Ramasastry et al., 'Translating Unocal', p. 856.

to those developments. The emergence of the right to justice is also instructive for a new theoretical perception of state duties as it entails a departure of accountability from its secondary status, and its approximation to autonomous primary obligations. In turn, this can be interpreted as potentially facilitating its unfolding towards private actors, since primary rights are already protected against acts committed by private persons, through the respective state positive duties.

In terms of reparations, incorporating business wrongdoers into the design and delivery of reparations would presuppose an understanding of the state's overarching reparative obligations, to include a duty to provide redress avenues in domestic law to victims of corporate violations, something which, in principle, is part only of the state's positive protective obligations. The book put forward a novel interpretation of state duties and argued that states' positive obligations should inform the delivery of its remedial duties. This would be justified on the basis of their close conceptual and causal relationship, as well as their dialectical development, benefiting from the exceptionality of transitional justice. In addition, this new trajectory in state duties would find support to the vindications of victims and civil society, expressed by the numerous cases that have been filed against corporate abusers, as well as in different soft-law instruments, like the Basic Principles[22] and the UN Guiding Principles on Business and Human Rights.[23]

In terms of truth mechanisms, despite the inclusion of corporate accountability within the work of truth commissions, legally this would require that the state duty to investigate is deployed against corporate entities. For truth stemming from the state duty to remedy this would not be a straightforward conclusion, but such interpretation could flow from the duty to investigate and the corresponding right to truth that is part of states' positive obligations. To discharge the right to truth or the duty to investigate against corporate malefactors, one would need to put those positive obligations at the forefront, as they already apply against non-state entities. In that line of reasoning, the Basic Principles list the verification of the facts and full and public disclosure of the truth as a measure of satisfaction that is to be provided not only by the state but also by the legal person or entity liable for the harm. Notably, according to case law, the content of truth includes the identity of the perpetrators, as one of the elements that investigations should reveal, namely as

22 'Basic Principles', UN Doc. A/RES/60/147.

23 'Guiding Principles', UN Doc. A/HRC/17/31.

constitutive element of the truth. Lastly, the collective aspect of truth, which has been applauded by legal instruments, and the practice of human rights bodies and truth commissions can be instructive for corporate accountability, for its ability to capture more systemic patterns of violence, and the role that corporations play within them.

Some theoretical insights can also be drawn in relation to development; sometimes invoked as antagonistic to corporate accountability, other times as subsuming it. Regarding the former, it is often the case that victims' rights in relation to corporate accountability are overshadowed by transitional states' eagerness to befriend businesses, seeking their investment to the state's future economic recovery. In what concerns truth, the evolution of the right to truth as an autonomous right seems to be placing an unqualified focus on the importance of truth, including for corporate malfeasance, countervailing developmental concerns, despite the obvious importance of the latter in reconstruction periods. Its heightened status makes it less amenable to compromises in favour of the oft-cited right to development. There are also instances where corporate involvement in transitions is considered exhausted if those corporations contribute to development purposes. However, this approach relies on a conflation of two distinct fields, with different objectives and principles, development rooted in the respective right, while transitional justice being linked to the right to justice. Rather, the transformative justice discourse seems more receptive than the development one, to corporate accountability concerns, as they share similar objectives. Corporate accountability can play a crucial role in delivering the aims of transformative justice, namely challenging pre-existing structures of exclusion, marginalization and power, given that corporations are among the fundamental actors that anchor those structures, and benefit from the associated socio-economic policies. Lastly, transformative approaches, with their commitment to addressing the root causes of marginalization and exploitation, offer a powerful symbolic framework able to support the calls for corporate reparations for historical injustices, including slavery, colonialism and racial discrimination.

The operationalization of corporate accountability through criminal, reparative or truth-seeking measures presents additional challenges. In relation to criminal measures, a first issue relates to the rationale for resorting to transitional courts instead of ordinary ones, in view of the limited resources and increased tensions that are linked to the former. Legally, economic actors should be included in criminal transitional mechanisms only when relegating them to ordinary courts would result in their impunity and they have committed acts to which increased criminal responsibility attaches. However, it is the symbolic value of including corporate malefactors in transitional courts that is more important, because it acknowledges their often-primary role in prior violence and contributes in building a comprehensive judicial narrative about the past. Still, taking into account the fragile compromises during transitions and the fears that corporate prosecutions might overwhelm the already burdened system, it seems plausible to strike a balance between the arguments around peace and justice, in line with the homonymous debate. This balance would include prioritization strategies, on the basis of the gravity of the crime and the contribution of each actor, under a variety of remedies approach,[24] which could maximize the efficacy of each single measure and mitigate their limitations.[25] That being said, the peace versus justice considerations should be invoked with caution so as not to obscure other relevant tensions regarding socio-economic issues. The latter are continuously being sidelined under various pretexts, including the peace versus justice debate, resulting in inadequate future solutions, in the name of a presumed post-political consensus of how peace is achieved.

The cases of Argentina and Colombia illustrate possible choices for transitional engineering. In Argentina, there was no unified prosecutorial strategy or dedicated criminal justice mechanism for transitional justice, and corporate cases were tried by ordinary courts. Colombia's first transitional initiative excluded corporate malefactors, but the second effort allowed economic actors voluntarily to present themselves before the Special Jurisdiction for Peace. This second consolidated effort illustrated the pertinence of specialized criminal justice measures, including for corporate accountability cases, as they are able to create consolidated narratives about prior violence, and avoid the pitfalls of diffusing prosecutorial responsibilities across the ordinary and the transitional systems.

The applicable modes of liability remain a challenging issue in the framework of operationalizing corporate criminal prosecutions. Complicity and particularly aiding and abetting appear more amenable to corporate wrongdoing, due to its knowledge-based *mens rea* requirement under customary international law, as well as the diverse range of actions that can fulfil its *actus reus* requirements, namely provision of material or other assistance, the collusion with repressive governments to

[24] Olsen, *Seeking Justice*, chapter 2.
[25] Kyriakakis, *Corporations, Accountability and International Criminal Law*, p. 177.

extract profits, and financial complicity. The modes of superior responsibility and indirect perpetration as introduced by Article 25(3) (a) of the ICC Statute seem, also, promising for attaching corporate liability. This is because, among others, and insofar as the other requirements are met, the element of control that both include has been used quite flexibly by international courts. A further promising aspect of superior responsibility provided that the theoretical leap from the required military or civilian contexts to the corporate one can be made is its affinity to the theory of *respondeat superior*, which is commonly used for the imputation of crimes to corporate entities, on the basis of unlawful acts committed by employees. The mode that has sparked more controversy seems to be financial complicity, due to the difficulty in establishing the necessary legal link among the harm suffered and the funds provided to regimes violating human rights, as well as due to the misinterpretation of Nuremberg case law upon which the South African Apartheid litigation dismissed the existence of legal links between commercial loans and Apartheid violations.

As for reparations, a promising pathway seems to be offered by guarantees of non-repetition. Unlike other reparation measures, the scope of GNRs has broadened, from mere demobilization and vetting to encompass broader transformative measures. Moreover, they have shifted from isolated individual violations to addressing generalized patterns of corporate abuse and impunity, enhancing their future-oriented character. Those attributes distance them from their remedial focus and create nuances in their secondary status. As a result, they seem to rely less to the strict requirements of the right to remedy, that have so far hindered the inclusion of corporate malefactors. At the same time, GNRs approximate positive obligations to ensure and protect rights, which could be interpreted as a window of opportunity for the inclusion of corporations in their scope, given that positive obligations already reach non-state violators.

Valuable insights regarding the possibility of corporate reparations emerge from domestic and foreign litigation, given that coordinated reparation mechanisms usually ignore business actors, with the exception of Colombia's land restitution programme, which took account of business involvement and facilitated victims' demands – albeit with no sufficient outcomes. Despite the various legal hurdles and the common opposition to litigation efforts by governments, both domestic and foreign litigation present promising aspects for corporate accountability. In domestic cases, success was mostly premised on novel legal strategies and wide civil society support and perseverance. Irrespective of whether they brought tangible remedies to victims, they are important in that they reflect victims' needs for justice and reparations, free from top-down imperatives. Further to that, the multiplicity of domestic efforts paves the way for similar developments on corporate accountability, in the global transitional landscape, and makes relevant cases anticipated and normalized. Resource to foreign courts has not borne equal fruits, but has contributed to the overall quest for corporate accountability, as it has often catalysed domestic developments. Oftentimes, foreign litigation brought to the global spotlight cases of corporate abuse and stirred advocacy campaigns in favour of victims, beyond national borders. Notably, the pursuit of justice seems to influence the expectations and interpretations of what justice should look like, particularly during transitional periods.

Truth mechanisms are the ones among transitional justice measures that have most expansively dealt with corporate wrongdoing, but their practice is quite diverse. While the Colombian Commission for the Clarification of Truth, Coexistence and Non-Repetition registered the misdeeds of more than 200 economic actors and revealed their names, the same did not take place before the CAVR of East Timor, who confined its report in generic references to various industry sectors. Some commissions' reports, like the Mauritian and Sierra Leonean ones, go beyond individual violations into registering a more systemic truth, revealing patterns of abuse and embedded corporate impunity, while others, like the one of Tunisia, remained centred around key figures, like Ben Ali.

Perhaps the most important conclusion that can be drawn from the examination of various truth commissions and the way they address corporate malfeasance has to do with the dependence of corporate accountability on the synergies among mechanisms – or the lack thereof. A close examination of the work of different truth commissions reveals that their limited progress towards actual prosecutions or reparations of corporate entities is often related to the lack of a synergistic approach and the absence of self-identification as part of an interlinked and comprehensive system. Most truth commissions were strong in providing substantial arguments for the inclusion of corporate actors in their scope of work but were weak in procedurally paving the way to enforce that inclusion, either in the form of reparations or prosecutions. As such, corporate accountability remained mostly a truth-telling exercise, devoid of any pursuit of criminal liability, compensation or other measure.

Tunisia is an illustrative example. Despite the establishment of eight anticorruption commissions, business accountability of the broader corporate sector was foreclosed, from the beginning, due to their exclusive focus on Ben Ali's companies.

Instead, it seems that an ecological approach that perceives the different mechanisms as mutually reinforcing and complementary would be able to multiply their effects. In practice, this means that the establishment of truth commissions, reparative measures, trials and guarantees of non-recurrence would unfold in a dialectical relation, where the results of the one cross-fertilize and inform the implementation of the other. This follows a logic of multiple justice modalities that are complementary to each other and seems capable of addressing the complexities of corporate involvement in conflict.[26] In this kind of holistic schemes, and in line with what Méndez calls 'integral' reparations,[27] truth-seeking measures would be the first bridge to cross the gateway that would delineate and clarify what needs to be repaired and what needs to be punished. If sufficiently substantiated, this would pass the baton and act as a precursor to other measures, such as reparation schemes or specialized criminal tribunals.[28]

Overall, the book explored how the integration of corporate accountability and transitional justice can be normatively grounded as well as how it can be translated in the vernacular of legal doctrine, across different transitional mechanisms and informed by diverse legal regimes. It provided a systematic examination of the specific legal avenues and operational limitations for victims of corporate abuses seeking remedies during transitions, along with the related obligations of states as designers of transitional measures.

As we navigate the uncharted territory sketched earlier, it becomes evident that expanding transitional justice to encompass corporate malefactors demands revisiting the applicable law, but also reimagining the interplay between transitional justice, politics and economics, as well as their relation to conflict or violence. A genuine transformative approach to transitional justice would need not only re-evaluating the signifiers, namely laws, mechanisms and tools applied, but also the signified – the aims, ideologies, goals and values that are conveyed through them.

[26] Ibid., p. 216.

[27] J. Méndez, 'The Right to Truth'.

[28] Laplante, 'On the Indivisibility of Rights'.

Inserting corporate accountability within the transitional discourse opens windows of opportunity for debating those elements. Aligned with the commitments of transformative rather than merely transitional justice, such insertion bears the potentiality of subverting the factors that led to violence or repression, of re-evaluating the power dynamics, economic structures and the role of corporations in shaping the prior landscape. It can create space for political contestation and policy experimentation at different levels and with different options of fighting corporate abuse, and ultimately establish transitional justice as a political space of possibilities, where various opportunities for societal transformation can emerge.

To fully grasp these new possibilities offered by inserting corporate accountability, one must first apprehend the connotations and political underpinnings of the current iteration, where corporations are marginalized from transitional purview. Transitional justice, traditionally, works under a presumably apolitical cloak, presenting political questions and the ensuing solutions, as politically and economically neutral.[29] The imperatives of transitional programming are conveyed as neutral, in ahistorical and nonpolitical terms.[30] The bureaucratization of the process and the influx of experts[31] allude to a justice toolkit fit for all political contexts, or rather irrespective of specific political or socio-economic particularities.[32] In such a context, corporate accountability is excluded merely because the subsequent peacebuilding period and the market itself are better adept to address it.[33] This is presented as an undeniable real course of events, empty of political connotations.

However, setting corporate accountability within or outside the boundaries of transitional justice is far from an apolitical choice. Rather, the choice to draw the line around certain issues and insulate them from political debate is itself a political choice. Corporate

[29] Lundy and McGovern, 'Whose Justice?', pp. 273, 276–277; Robins, 'Transitional Justice as an Elite Discourse', p. 3.

[30] Rajagopal, 'Invoking the Rule of Law in Post-Conflict Rebuilding', 1349; Sending, 'Why Peacebuilders Fail to Secure Ownership and Be Sensitive to Context'; Franzki and Olarte, 'Understanding the Political Economy'.

[31] J. Subotic, *Hijacked Justice: Dealing with The Past in The Balkans* (Cornell University Press, 2009); Wilson, 'Anthropological Studies of National Reconciliation', pp. 367–387; Bell et al., 'Justice Discourses in Transition', pp. 305–328.

[32] E. Baines, 'Spirits and Social Reconstruction After Mass Violence: Rethinking Transitional Justice' (2010) 109 *African Affairs* 409, at 414.

[33] M. Pugh, 'The Political Economy of Peace Studies: A Critical Theory Perspective' (2005) *International Journal of Peace Studies* 2, at 25; Sriram, 'Justice as Peace?', p. 591.

accountability, in particular, is intrinsically associated to a range of critical socio-economic issues, notably socio-economic inequality and the uneven global field within which multinational firms, weak transitional states and vulnerable victims meet. As for foreign multinational companies, in many parts of the world, their activities are associated with structures of former colonial economies, their conflictual legacy and the continuation of patterns of exploitation perpetuated by companies headquartered in the formal colonial metropoles.

Thus, along with excluding corporate accountability from the transitional debate, one eliminates the possibility to contest all that range of issues. Instead of being an apolitical coincidence, Marks notes that the tendency to cast off the public discourse issues relating to socio-economic conditions is at its heart a liberal prescription.[34] It serves to marginalize the aspect of 'need' and essentially denies the prospect of economic democracy.[35] By being erased from the transitional agenda, from contestation and experimentation, in reality, the economic aspects of both the conflict and the transitional experiment – aside from state actions in that area – appear to be unconnected to transitional politics.[36] In essence, this marginalization is packed with liberal assumptions, disguising the politically contestable as mere transitional technology, promoting liberal democracy as the only possible choice and depriving the transitional society of the possibility to contemplate, discuss and co-decide different options for its future. What is more, in cases of foreign multinational companies, their exclusion from transitional justice potentially perpetuates the cleavages of former colonial economies and solidifies the development models rooted in colonial relations – that are at times at the heart of conflict or repression.

To further attest its liberal orientation, it has to be noted that marginalizing corporate wrongdoers reflects a pledge to a liberal separation between the public and the private sector, the former in need of discipline, the latter in need of promotion. A common transitional scenario devises a range of measures to confirm the culpability of former state actors, or rebels and other sorts of armed non-state actors, and rightly so, and a parallel exoneration of the private sector. The problem here lies in

[34] Marks, *The Riddle of All Constitutions*, pp. 70–74.

[35] E. Christodoulidis, 'Against Substitution: The Constitutional Thinking of Dissensus', in M. Loughlin and N. Walker (eds.), *The Paradox of Constitutionalism: Constituent Power and Constitutional Form* (Oxford University Press, 2007), p. 199.

[36] Christodoulidis and Veitch, 'Reconciliation as Surrender', pp. 9, 18.

that this inequity in the attribution of responsibility is not an apolitical manifestation, as is principally conveyed. Instead, this discourse reorganizes the political and economic space, in accordance with the prevailing liberal development discourse that promotes the autonomy of the market from political regulation and the simultaneous shrinking of the state. Tunisia is quite an illustrative example in that respect. Transitional mechanisms delegitimized Ben Ali's state due to corruption allegations – justifiably so, but the supply part of his corruption, namely various international and domestic corporations, were presented as mere victims of his corrupt web. The Tunisian business association, UTICA, even received the Nobel Peace Prize for facilitating the National Dialogue.[37] This inequitable allocation of responsibility, in Tunisia and beyond, paves the way for a particular hierarchy, where the state is disciplined and presented as the source of all wrong, whereas the private sector emerges as a victim, absolved from any responsibility and, as a saviour, enforced to seek and deploy the much needed opportunities for investment and economic development.

Thus, the exclusion of economic actors and corporations from the transitional experiment, rather than being neutral or apolitical, is the economic handmaiden of the overall liberal project that mainstream transitional justice envisions and implements. Instead, opening up the transitional discussion to debate corporate involvement in conflict or repression bears the potential of discussing a range of associated issues, primarily issues of socio-economic justice, that lie at the heart of most modern conflicts.[38] Such an endeavour brings about true transformational opportunities, in terms of democratizing the transitional processes themselves and delivering justice to victims.

Debating and experimenting on the issues that are currently foreclosed – the economic system, its colonial roots, the development model and its fallacies, the structures of power and victimhood – means that the prior boundaries of transitional justice will be demarcated not according to a pre-agreed model but according to transitional vindications. Insofar as those vindications posit a reconfiguration of the economic and political landscape, this iteration of transitional justice will be better equipped to deliver it. Enriched with new possibilities in its arsenal, transitional justice could instate itself as a period of contemplation when the fabric of

[37] Michalakea, 'Anticorruption and Transitional Justice', p. 1.

[38] Collier et al., *Breaking the Conflict Trap, Civil War and Development Policy*, p. 53 *et seq.*

society is being weaved instead of merely mended; when transition is not an exercise in reduction but is instead an honest examination of the underlying causes and systemic pathologies of the previous socio-economic structures that led to the need for transition; when the process moves beyond liberal assumptions, towards a paradigm that includes socio-economic justice and empowerment into its very framework.

BIBLIOGRAPHY

Abrahams, C. 'Lessons from the South African Experience', in S. Michalowski (ed.) *Corporate Accountability in the Context of Transitional Justice* (Routledge, 2013)

Abrams, J. S. and Hayner, P. 'Documenting, Acknowledging and Publicizing the Truth', in C. Bassiouni (ed.) *Post-Conflict Justice* (Transnational Publishers, 2002)

Abtahi, H. and Webb, P. *The Genocide Convention: The Travaux Préparatoires* (Brill | Nijhoff, 2009)

Addison, T. 'The Political Economy of the Transition from Authoritarianism', in P. De Greiff and R. Duthie (eds.) *Transitional Justice and Development: Making Connections* (Social Science Research Council, 2009)

Aertsen, Ivo, et al. 'Restorative Justice for Victims of Corporate Violence', in G. Forti et al. (eds.) *Victims and Corporations. Legal Challenges and Empirical Findings* (Wolters Kluwer, 2018)

Aldana-Pindell, R. 'In Vindication of Justiciable Victims' Rights to Truth and Justice for State-Sponsored Crimes' (2002) 35 *Vanderbilt Journal of Transnational Law* 1399

Alston, P. *Non-State Actors and Human Rights* (Oxford University Press, 2005)

Alviar Garcia, H. 'Transitional Justice and Property: Inextricably Linked' (2021) 17 *Annual Review of Law and Social Science* 227–238

Ambos, K. 'The Legal Framework of Transitional Justice', in K. Ambos et al. (eds.) *Building a Future on Peace and Justice: Studies on Transitional Justice, Conflict Resolution and Development* (Springer-Verlag Berlin Heidelberg, 2009)

Treatise on International Criminal Law – Volume 1: Foundations and General Part (Oxford University Press, 2013)

Amnesty International. *Universal Jurisdiction* (2012) www.amnesty.org/es/wp-content/uploads/2021/06/ior530192012en.pdf

Injustice Incorporated (2014) www.amnesty.org/en/wp-content/uploads/2021/06/pol300012014en.pdf

Andrieu, K. 'Civilizing Peacebuilding: Transitional Justice, Civil Society and the Liberal Paradigm' (2010) 41 *Security Dialogue* 537

Antkowiak, T. 'Truth as Right and Remedy in International Human Rights Experience' (2002) 23 *Michigan Journal of International Law* 977

'Remedial Approaches to Human Rights Violations: The Inter-American Court of Human Rights and Beyond' (2008) 46 *Columbia Journal of Transnational Law* 2

Aparac, J. *Business et droits de l'homme dans les conflits armés* (Larcier, 2021)

Arbour, L. 'Economic and Social Justice for Societies in Transition' (2007) 40 *New York University Journal of International Law and Politics* 1–27

Arthur, P. 'How "Transitions" Reshaped Human Rights: A Conceptual History of Transitional Justice' (2009) 31 *Human Rights Quarterly* 321

Identities in Transition: Developing Better Transitional Justice Initiatives in Divided Societies (International Centre for Transitional Justice, 2009)

Attanasio, D. L. and Sánchez, N. C. 'Return Within the Bounds of the Pinheiro Principles: The Colombian Land Restitution Experience' (2012) 11 *Washington University Global Studies Law Review* 1–53

Atteberry, J. 'Turning in the Widening Gyre: History, Corporate Accountability, and Transitional Justice in the Postcolony' (2019) 19 *Chicago Journal of International Law* 333

Atuahene, B. 'Property and Transitional Justice' (2010) 58 *UCLA Law Review Discourse* 65–92

Augenstein, D. and Dziedzic, L. 'State Obligations to Regulate and Adjudicate Corporate Activities Under the European Convention on Human Rights' (2017) *EUI Working Paper Law* No. 2017/15

Aukerman, M. 'Extraordinary Evil, Ordinary Crimes: A Framework for Understanding Transitional Justice' (2002) 15 *Harvard Human Rights Journal* 39–97

Authers, J. 'Making Good Again: German Compensation for Forced and Slave Labourers', in Transition', in P. De Greiff (ed.) *The Handbook of Reparations* (Oxford University Press, 2006)

Avocats Sans Frontieres. *Case Study: The Application of the Rome Statute of the International Criminal Court by the Courts of the Democratic Republic of Congo* (Avocats Sans Frontieres, 2009)

Baars, G. *The Corporation, Law and Capitalism* (Brill, 2019)

Baines, E. 'Spirits and Social Reconstruction After Mass Violence: Rethinking Transitional Justice' (2010) 109 *African Affairs* 409

Bakiner, O. 'Truth Commission Impact: An Assessment of How Commissions Influence Politics and Society' (2014) 8 *The International Journal of Transitional Justice* 6–30

Bakker, C. 'Duties to Prevent, Investigate and Redress Human Right Violations by Private Military and Security Companies: The Role of the Host State', in F. Francioni and Ronziti (eds.) *War by Contract: Human Rights, Humanitarian Law and Private Contractors* (Oxford University Press, 2011)

Ball, H. and Friedman, L. 'The Use of Criminal Sanctions in the Enforcement of Economic Legislation: A Sociological View' (1965) 17 *Stanford Law Review* 197

Bantekas, I. 'The Contemporary Law of Superior Responsibility' (1999) 93 *American Journal of International Law* 573–595

'Corruption as an International Crime and Crime Against Humanity: An Outline of Supplementary Criminal Justice Policies' (2006) 4 *J Intl Criminal Justice* 3, 466–484

Barnard-Naudé, J. 'For Justice and Reconciliation to Come: The TRC Archive, Big Business and the Demand for Material Reparations', in F. Du Bois and A. Pedain (eds.) *Justice and Reconciliation in Post-Apartheid South Africa* (Cambridge University Press, 2009)

Bassiouni, C. 'A Functional Approach to "General Principles of International Law"' (1990) 11 *Michigan Journal of International Law* 768

'Searching for Peace and Achieving Justice: The Need for Accountability' (1996) 59 *Law and Contemporary Problems* 9–28

'Accountability for Violations of International Humanitarian Law and Other Serious Violations of Human Rights', in C. Bassiouni (ed.) *Post-Conflict Justice* (Brill | Nijhoff, 2002)

'Universal Jurisdiction for International Crimes: Historical Perspectives and Contemporary Practice' (2002) 42 *Virginia Journal of International Law* 81

'International Recognition of Victims' Rights' (2006) 6 *Human Rights Law Review* 203

Bassiouni, C. and Wise, E. *Aut Dedere Aut Judicare: The Duty to Extradite or Prosecute in International Law* (Martinus Nijhoff Publishers, 1995)

Beale, S. 'A Response to the Critics of Corporate Criminal Liability' (2009) 46 *American Criminal Law Review* 1481

Becker, D. 'Civil Society and Transitional Justice: Possibilities, Patterns and Prospects' (2003) 2 *Journal of Human Rights* 3, 297–313

Bell, C. 'Transitional Justice, Interdisciplinarity and the State of the 'Field' or 'Non-Field'' (2009) 3 *International Journal of Transitional Justice* 1, 5–27

Bell, C. et al. 'Justice Discourses in Transition' (2004) 13 *Social and Legal Studies* 3, 305–328

Bell, T. and Buhle Ntsebeza, D. *Unfinished Business: South Africa, Apartheid and Truth* (Verso, 2003)

Bernal-Bermúdez, L. and Marín Lopez, D. 'Los Empresarios en la Guerra: Elementos de la Verdad Judicial Sobre la Complicidad Empresarial en Colombia', in N. Sanchez et al. (eds.) *Cuentas Claras* (Dejusticia, 2018)

Bernaz, N. 'Enhancing Corporate Accountability for Human Rights Violations: Is Extraterritoriality the Magic Potion?' (2013) 117 *Journal of Business Ethics* 494

'Establishing Liability for Financial Complicity in International Crimes', in J. P. Bohoslavsky and J. Letnar Černič (eds.) *Making Sovereign Financing and Human Rights Work* (Hart, 2014)

'Corporate Criminal Liability Under International Law: The New TV S.A.L. and Akhbar Beirut S.A.L. Cases at the Special Tribunal for Lebanon' (2015) 13 *Journal of International Criminal Justice* 313–330

Business and Human Rights History, Law and Policy – Bridging the Accountability Gap (Routledge, 2017)

Bhashyam, S. 'Knowledge or Purpose? The Khulumani Litigation and the Standard for Aiding and Abetting Liability Under the Alien Tort Claims Act' (2008) 30 *Cardozo Law Review* 245, 269

Biggar, N. 'Making Peace or Doing Justice: Must We Chose?', in N. Biggar (ed.) *Burying the Past: Making Peace and Doing Justice after Civil Conflict* (Georgetown University Press, 2003)

Bilsky, L. *The Holocaust, Corporations, and the Law: Unfinished Business* (University of Michigan Press, 2017)

Binnie, I. (Justice) 'Legal Redress for Corporate Participation in International Human Rights Abuses' (2009) 38 *Summer Brief* 44

Black, E. *IBM and the Holocaust: The Strategic Alliance between Nazi Germany and America's Most Powerful Corporation* (Crown Publishers, 2001)

Boas, G., Bischoff, J. and Reid, N. *International Criminal Law Practitioner* (Cambridge University Press, 2008)

Bohoslavsky, J. P. 'Another Brick in the Uruguayan Transition: Financial Complicity', in S. Michalowski (ed.) *Corporate Accountability in the Context of Transitional Justice* (Routledge, 2013)

Bohoslavsky, J. P. and Letnar Černič, J. (eds.) *Making Sovereign Financing and Human Rights Work* (Hart Publishing, 2014)

Bohoslavsky, J. P. and Opgenhaffen, V. 'The Past and Present of Corporate Complicity: Financing the Argentinean Dictatorship' (2010) 23 *Harvard Human Rights Journal* 157–203

Bohoslavsky, J. P. and Rulli, M. 'Corporate Complicity and Finance as a 'Killing Agent': The Relevance of the Chilean Case' (2010) 8 *Journal of International Criminal Justice* 3, 827–850

Bohoslavsky, J. P. et al. (eds.) *Pinochet's Economic Accomplices: An Unequal Country by Force* (Lexington Books, 2020)

Bolívar Jaime, A. P. et al. *La buena fe en la restitución de tierras. Sistematización de jurisprudencia* (Dejusticia, 2017)

Bond, P. and Sharife, K. 'Apartheid Reparations and the Contestation of Corporate Power in Africa' (2009) 36 *Review of African Political Economy* 119

Boraine, A. 'Introduction', in A. Boraine et al. (eds.) *Dealing with the Past: Truth and Reconciliation in South Africa* (Institute for a Democratic Alternative for South Africa, 1994)

et al. (eds.) *Dealing with the Past: Truth and Reconciliation in South Africa* (Institute for a Democratic Alternative for South Africa, 1994)

Borch, F. *Military Trials of War Criminals in the Netherlands East Indies 1946–1949* (Oxford University Press, 2017)

Borer, T. A. *Telling the Truths: Truth Telling and Peace Building in Post-Conflict Societies* (University of Notre Dame Press, 2006)

Bosire, L. 'Overpromised, Under-Delivered: Transitional Justice in Sub-Saharan Africa' (2006) 3 *Sur – Revista Internacional de Direitos Humanos* 5

Bowsher, J. '"Omnus et Singulatim": Establishing the Relationship Between Transitional Justice and Neoliberalism' (2017) 29 *Law and Critique* 5, 83–106

Braithwaite, J. *Corporate Crime in the Pharmaceutical Industry* (Routledge & Kegan Paul Books, 1984)

Crime, Shame, and Reintegration (Cambridge University Press, 1989)

Braithwaite, J. and Fisse, B. *Corporations, Crime and Accountability* (Cambridge University Press, 1993)

Buckley-Zistel, S. 'Detained in Hohenschönhausen. Heterotopia, Narratives and Transitions from the Stasi Past in Germany', in S. Buckley-Zistel and S. Schäfer (eds.) *Memorials of Violence in Times of Transition* (Intersentia, 2013)

Burchard, C. 'Ancillary and Neutral Business Contributions to "Corporate-Political Core Crime"' (2010) 8 *Journal of International Criminal Justice* 919

Burniske, J., Modirzadeh, N. and Lewis, D. 'Armed Non-State Actors and International Human Rights Law: An Analysis of the Practice of the U.N. Security Council and the U.N. General Assembly' (2017) *Harvard Public Law Working Paper No. 17–37*

Bush, J. A. 'The Prehistory of Corporations and Conspiracy in International Criminal Law: What Nuremberg Really Said' (2009) 109 *Colom LR* 1094

Buyse, A. 'Lost and Regained? Restitution as a Remedy for Human Rights Violations in the Context of International Law' (2008) 68 *Heidelberg Journal of International Law* 129–153

Caeb, C. 'The Shifting Sands of Corporate Liability Under International Criminal Law' (2016) 49 *The George Washington International Law Review* 351–403

Calderon Meza, J. P. 'ICC Personal Jurisdiction on Corporations for Criminal Liability and/or Civil Liability for Reparations', *Harvard International Law Journal*, 13 May 2021, available at https://journals.law.harvard.edu/ilj/2021/05/icc-personal-jurisdiction-on-corporations-for-criminal-liability-and-or-civil-liability-for-reparations/

Camilo, R. and Villamarin, Q. 'Shredded Colombia 's Special Jurisdiction for Peace in an Increasingly Illiberal Context of Misinformation and Backlash' (2022) 20 *Journal of International Criminal Justice* 1–28

Cançado Trindade, A. (ed.) *The Access of Individuals to International Justice* (Oxford University Press, 2011)

The Construction of a Humanized International Law (Brill | Nijhoff, 2015)

Caron, D. and Schneider, A. 'U.S. Litigation Concerning Japanese Forced Labour in World War II' (2000) 5 *ASIL* 18

Carranza, R. 'Plunder and Pain: Should Transitional Justice Engage with Corruption and Economic Crimes?' (2008) 2 *International Journal of Transitional Justice* 3, 310–330

The Right to Reparations in Situations of Poverty (International Centre for Transitional Justice, 2009)

Truth, Accountability, and Asset Recovery: How Transitional Justice Can Fight Corruption (International Centre for Transitional Justice, 2020)

Carrillo, A. 'Truth, Justice, and Reparations in Colombia', in V. M. Bouvier (ed.) *Colombia: Building Peace in a Time of War* (US Institute of Peace Press, 2009)

Carruthers, B. and Halliday, T. 'The Recursivity of Law: Global Norm Making and National Lawmaking in the Globalization of Corporate Insolvency Regimes' (2007) 112 *AJS* 4

Cassel, D. *The Practice and Procedure of the Inter-American Court of Human Rights* (2006). By Jo M. Pasqualucci (Cambridge University Press, 2003), pp. xlvii, 388, 503–507

Cassese, A. and Gaeta, P. *Cassese's International Criminal Law* (Oxford University Press, 2013)

Castberg, F. *The European Convention on Human Rights* (Kluwer Academic Publishers, 1974)

Cavallaro, J. and Albuja, S. 'The Lost Agenda: Economic Crimes and Truth Commissions in Latin America and Beyond', in K. McEvoy and L. McGregor (eds.) *Transitional Justice from Below, Grassroots Activism and the Struggle for Change* (Hart Publishing, 2008)

Chaparro Hernández, S. R. et al. *La restitución de tierras y territorios. Justificaciones, dilemas y estrategias* (Dejusticia, 2016)

Chapman, A. 'Truth Commissions as Instruments of Forgiveness and Reconciliation', in R. G. Helmick and R. L. Peterson (eds.) *Forgiveness and Reconciliation: Religion, Public Policy, and Conflict Transformation* (Templeton Foundation Press, 2001)

Chen, R. 'Organisational Irrationality and Corporate Human Rights Violations' (2009) 122 *Harvard Law Review* 1931

Cheng, C. and Zaum, D. 'Corruption and the Role of Natural Resources in Post-Conflict Transitions', in C. Bruch et al. (eds.) *Governance, Natural Resources, and Post-Conflict Peacebuilding* (Routledge, 2017)

Chesterman, S. 'The Turn to Ethics: Disinvestment from Multinational Corporations for Human Rights Violations – The Case of Norway's Sovereign Wealth Fund' (2008) 23 *American University International Law Review* 577–615

Chiavario, M. 'Private Parties: The Rights of the Defendant and the Victim', in M. Delmas-Marty and J. R. Spencer (eds.) *European Criminal Procedures* (Cambridge University Press, 2002)

Chirwa, D. 'The Doctrine of State Responsibility as a Potential Means of Holding Private Actors Accountable for Human Rights' (2004) 5 *Melbourne Journal of International Law* 1

'State Responsibility for Human Rights', in M. A. Baderin and M. Ssenyonjo (eds.) *International Human Rights Law: Six Decades After the UDHR and Beyond* (Ashgate Publishing Co., 2010)

Choudhury, B. and Petrin, M. *Corporate Duties to the Public* (Cambridge University Press, 2019)

Christodoulidis, E. 'Against Substitution: The Constitutional Thinking of Dissensus', in M. Loughlin and N. Walker (eds.) *The Paradox of Constitutionalism: Constituent Power and Constitutional Form* (Oxford University Press, 2007)

Christodoulidis, E. and Veitch, S. 'Reconciliation as Surrender: Configurations of Responsibility and Memory', in F. Du Bois and A. Pedain (eds.) *Justice and Reconciliation in Post-Apartheid South Africa* (Cambridge University Press, 2009)

Clapham, A. 'The Question of Jurisdiction Under International Criminal Law Over Legal Persons', in M. Kamminga and S. Zia-Zarifi (eds.) *Liability of Multinational Corporations Under International Law* (Kluwer Law International, 2000)

'The Complexity of International Criminal Law: Looking Beyond Individual Responsibility to the Responsibility of Organizations, Corporations and States', in R. Chandra Thakur and P. Malcontent (eds.) *Sovereign Impunity to International Accountability: The Search for Justice in a World of States* (United Nations Press, 2004)

Human Rights Obligations of Non-State Actors (Oxford University Press, 2006)

'Extending International Criminal Law Beyond the Individual to Corporations and Armed Opposition Groups' (2008) 6 *Journal of International Criminal Justice* 5, 899

'Focusing on ANSAs', in A. Clapham and P. Gaeta (eds.) *The Oxford Handbook of International Law in Armed Conflict* (Oxford University Press, 2014)

Clapham, A. and Jerbi, S. 'Categories of Corporate Complicity in Human Rights Abuses' (2001) 24 *Hastings International and Comparative Law Review* 339

Clinard, M. B. and Yeager, P. C. *Corporate Crime* (Free Press, 2000)

Coffee, J. 'No Soul to Damn: No Body to Kick: An Unscandalized Inquiry Into the Problem of Corporate Punishment' (1980) 79 *Michigan Law Review* 386

Cohen, D. V. 'Ethics and Crime in Business Firms: Organisational Culture and the Impact of Anomy' (1995) 6 *Advances in Criminological Theory* 183

Colleen, D. et al. 'Reparations for Sexual and Reproductive Violence: Prospects for Achieving Gender Justice in Guatemala and Peru' (2008) 2 *International Journal of Transitional Justice* 192–213

Collier, P. and Hoeffler, A. 'On the Incidence of Civil War in Africa' (2002) 46 *Journal of Conflict Resolution* 13

Collier, P. et al. *Breaking the Conflict Trap, Civil War and Development Policy* (World Bank and Oxford University Press, 2003)

Cote-Barco, E. 'Complicidad, responsabilidad penal de directivos empresariales y violaciones de Derechos Humanos cometidas por grupos armados ilegales: lecciones del Derecho Penal Internacional para Colombia' (2019) 68 *Vniversitas* 138

Cox, R. W. 'Social Forces, States and World Orders: Beyond International Relations Theory' (1981) 10 *Millennium – Journal of International Studies* 126–155

Crane, D. 'Dancing with the Devil: Prosecuting West Africa's Warlords: Building Initial Prosecutorial Strategy for an International Tribunal After Third World Armed Conflicts' (2005) 37 *Case Western Reserve Journal of International Law* 1–9

Crawford, J. *The International Law Commission's Articles on State Responsibility: Introduction, Text and Commentaries* (Cambridge University Press, 2002)

Brownlie's Principles of Public International Law, 8th Edition (Oxford University Press, 2012)

Cupido, M. ' Group Acting with a Common Purpose', in M. Cupido et al. (eds.) *Modes of Liability in International Criminal Law* (Cambridge University Press, 2019)

Curtin, D. and Nollkaemper, A. 'Conceptualizing Accountability in International and European Law' (2006) 36 *Netherlands Yearbook of International Law* 3–20

Dancy, G. et al. 'Behind Bars and Bargains: New Findings on Transitional Justice in Emerging Democracies' (2019) 63 *International Studies Quarterly* 1, 1–12

Danner, A. M. and Martinez, J. S. 'Guilty Associations: Joint Criminal Enterprise, Command Responsibility, and the Development of International Criminal Law' (2005) 93 *California Law Review* 75

Darcy, S. *Access to Justice and Extraterritorial Obligations, Brainstorming Session on Business and Human Rights 'A New Business and Human Rights Instrument?'* (Geneva for Human Rights & Friedrich Ebert Stiftung, 2015)

De Greiff, P. (ed.) *The Handbook of Reparations* (Oxford University Press, 2006)

De Greiff, P. 'Introduction Repairing the Past', in P. De Greiff (ed.) *The Handbook of Reparations* (Oxford University Press, 2006)

De Greiff, P. 'Justice and Reparations', in P. De Greiff (ed.) *The Handbook of Reparations* (Oxford University Press, 2006)

'Articulating the Links between Transitional Justice and Development: Justice and Social Integration', in P. De Greiff and R. Duthie (eds.) *Transitional Justice and Development: Making Connections* (Social Science Research Council, 2009)

'Theorizing Transitional Justice', in M. Williams, R. Nagy and J. Elster (eds.) *Transitional Justice* (NYU Press, 2012)

'The Future of the Past: Reflections on the Present State and Prospects of Transitional Justice' (2020) 14 *International Journal of Transitional Justice* 2, 251–259

De Greiff, P. and Duthie, R. (eds.) *Transitional Justice and Development: Making Connections* (Social Science Research Council, 2009)

De Schutter, O. (ed.) *Transnational Corporations and Human Rights* (Hart Publications, 2006)

Dejusticia, *Cuentas Clara: El papel de la Comision de la Verdad en la develacion de la responsabilidad de empresas en el conflict armado colombiano* (Dejusticia, 2018)

Del Campo, 'Lawyering for Reparations: Inter-American Perspective', in C. Grossman, A. Del Campo, and M. Trudeau (eds.) *International Law and Reparations: The Inter-American System* (Clarity Press, 2017)

Desmet, E. 'The UN Basic Principles and Guidelines on the Right to a Remedy and Reparation: A Landmark or Window – Dressing? An Analysis with Special Attention to the Situation of Indigenous Peoples' (2008) 24 *South African Journal on Human Rights* 1, 71–103

Deva, S. 'The Zero Draft of the Proposed Business and Human Rights Treaty, Part I: The Beginning of an End?' Business & Human Rights Resource Centre Blog, 14 August 2018

'Treating Human Rights Lightly: A Critique of the Consensus Rhetoric and the Language Employed by the Guiding Principles', in S. Deva and D. Bilchitz (eds.) *Human Rights Obligations of Business: Beyond the Corporate Responsibility to Respect?* (Cambridge University Press, 2013)

'Protect, Respect and Remedy? A Critique of the SRSG's Framework for Business and Human Rights', in K. Buhmann, L. Roseberry and M. Morsing (eds.) *Corporate Social and Human Rights Responsibilities: Global Legal and Management Perspectives* (Palgrave, 2011)

Diarmuid, J. *Hell's Cartel: IG Farben and the Making of Hitler's War Machine* (Metropolitan Books-Henry Holt and Company, 2008)

Díaz, P. 'La Corte Interamericana in Vitro: Comentarios sobre su Proceso de Toma de Decisiones a Propósito del Caso Artavia' (2013) 2 *Revista Derecho Público Iberoamericano* 303, 338

Diggs, E. et al. 'Business and Human Rights as a Galaxy of Norms' (2019) 50 *Georgetown Journal of International Law* 309

Dinstein, Y. 'Command Responsibility', in F. Lachenmann and R. Wolfrum (eds.) *The Law of Armed Conflict and the Use of Force: The Max Planck Encyclopaedia of Public International Law* (Oxford University Press, 2017)

'Discussion' (2008) 6 *Journal of International Criminal Justice* 5

Dodge, W. S. 'Business and Human Rights Litigation in U.S. Courts Before and After Kiobel', in D. Baumann-Pauly and J. Nolan (eds.) *Business and Human Rights: From Principles to Practice* (Routledge, 2016)

Donais, T. 'Empowerment or Imposition? Dilemmas of Local Ownership in Post-Conflict Peacebuilding Processes' (2009) 34 *Peace and Change* 3

Dörr, O. and Schmalenbach, K. (eds.) *Vienna Convention on the Law of Treaties* (Springer, 2012)

Drumbl, M. 'Collective Violence and Individual Punishment: The Criminality of Mass Atrocity' (2005) 99 *Northwestern University Law Review* 539

Du Bois, F. 'Reparations and the Forms of Justice', in F. du Bois and A. Pedain (eds.) *Justice and Reconciliation in Post-Apartheid South Africa* (Cambridge University Press, 2008)

Du Plessis, M. 'Historical Injustice and International Law: An Exploratory Discussion of Reparation for Slavery' (2003) 25 *Human Rights Quarterly* 3, 624–659

Du Toit, A. 'The Moral Foundations of the South African TRC: Truth as Acknowledgment and Justice as Recognition', in R. Rotberg and D. Thompson (eds.) *Truth v. Justice: The Morality of Truth Commissions* (Princeton University Press, 2000)

Dumberry, P. *State Succession to International Responsibility* (Martinus Nijhoff Publishers, 2007)

Duthie, R. *Toward a Development-Sensitive Approach to Transitional Justice* (International Centre for Transitional Justice, 2008)

'Transitional Justice, Development, and Economic Violence', in D. Sharp (ed.) *Justice and Economic Violence in Transition* (Springer, 2013)

Duttwiler, M. 'Liability for Omission in International Criminal Law' (2006) 6 *International Criminal Law Review* 1

Eide, A. 'Preventing Impunity for the Violator and Ensuring Remedies for the Victim' (2000) 69 *Nordic Journal of International Law* 1–10

Elster, J. *Closing the Books: Transitional Justice in Historical Perspective* (Cambridge University Press, 2004)

Engelhart, M. 'Corporate Criminal Liability from a Comparative Perspective', in D. Brodowski et al. (eds.) *Regulating Corporate Criminal Liability* (Springer, 2014)

Engle Marry, S. 'Transnational Human Rights and Local Activism: Mapping the Middle' (2006) 108 *American Anthropologist* 1, 38–51

Engstrom, P. 'The Inter-American Human Rights System: Notable Achievements and Enduring Challenges', in C. Lennox (ed.) *Contemporary Challenges for Understanding and Securing Human Rights in Practise* (University of London Press, 2015)

Ermann, M. D. and Lundman, R. J. 'Deviant Acts by Complex Organizations: Deviance and Social Control at the Organizational Level of Analysis' (1978) 19 *Sociological Quarterly* 1

Eser, A. 'Individual Criminal Responsibility (Art. 25)', in A. Cassese et al. (eds.) *The Rome Statute of the International Criminal Court: A Commentary* (Oxford University Press, 2002)

European Coalition on Oil in Sudan. Unpaid Debt, The Legacy of Lundin, Petronas and OMV in Sudan, 1997–2003, June 2010

Evans, C. *The Right to Reparation in International Law for Victims of Armed Conflict* (Cambridge University Press, 2012)

Fafo, *Business and International Crimes. Assessing the Liability of Business Entities for Grave Violations of International Law* (Fafo, 2005)

Falk, R. 'Reparations, International Law, and Global Justice: A New Frontier', in P. De Greiff (ed.) *The Handbook of Reparations* (Oxford University Press, 2006)

Farah, Y. 'Toward a Multi-Directional Approach to Corporate Accountability', in S. Michalowski (ed.) *Corporate Accountability in the Context of Transitional Justice* (Routledge, 2013)

Farrell, N. 'Attributing Criminal Liability to Corporate Actors' (2010) 8 *Journal of International Criminal Justice* 3, 873–894

Fasciglione, M. 'Enforcing the State Duty to Protect Under the UN Guiding Principles on Business and Human Rights, Strasbourg Views', in A. Bonfanti (ed.) *Business and Human Rights in Europe International Law Challenges* (Routledge, 2018)

Fawcett, J. E. S. *Application of the European Convention on Human Rights* (Oxford University Press, 1987)

Felstiner, W., Abel, R. and Sarat, A. 'The Emergence and Transformation of Disputes: Naming, Blaming, Claiming' (1980) 15 *Law and Society Review* 3, 631–654

Ferchichi, W. et al. *Transitional Justice in Tunisia: Finally the Law!* (Centre Al-Kawakibi pour la Transition Democratique, 2014)

Fernández, K. and Smart, S. 'Complicity of Companies in Chile's Current Human Rights Crisis', in L. Payne, Bernal-Bermúdez, L. and Pereira, G. (eds.) *Economic Actors and the Limits of Transitional Justice: Truth and Justice for Business Complicity in Human Rights Violations* (Oxford University Press, 2022)

Fernandez Torne, C. *Accountability, a New Framework to Assess the Impact of Truth Commissions* (Institut Català Internacional per la Pau, 2015)

Ferstman, C. 'The Reparation Regime of the International Criminal Court : Practical Considerations' (2002) 15 *Leiden Journal of International Law* 667

'Reparation as Prevention: Considering the Law and Practice of Orders for Cessation and Guarantees of Non-Repetition in Torture Cases' (2010) 6 *Essex Human Rights Review* 2

Fisse, B. and Braithwaite, J. *The Impact of Publicity on Corporate Offenders* (State University of New York Press, 1983)

'The Allocation of Responsibility for Corporate Crime: Individualism, Collectivism and Accountability' (1988) 11 *Sydney Law Review* 468

Forti, G. 'Introduction', in G. Forti et al. (eds.) *Victims and Corporations. Legal Challenges and Empirical Findings* (Wolters Kluwer, 2018)

et al. (eds.) *Victims and Corporations. Legal Challenges and Empirical Findings* (Wolters Kluwer, 2018)

Fortin, K. *The Accountability of Armed Groups Under Human Rights Law* (Oxford University Press, 2017)

Francioni, F. (ed.) *Access to Justice as a Human Right* (Oxford University Press, 2007)

Franck, T. *The Power of Legitimacy Among Nations* (Oxford University Press, 1990)

Franzki, H. and Olarte, M. C. 'Understanding the Political Economy of Transitional Justice', in S. Buckley-Zistel et al. (eds.) *Transitional Justice Theories* (Routledge, 2013)

Freeman, M. *Necessary Evils: Amnesties and the Search for Justice* (Cambridge University Press, 2009)

Freeman, M. and Hayner, P. 'Truth Telling', in D. Bloomfield (ed.) *Reconciliation after Violent Conflict: A Handbook* (International Institute for Democracy and Electoral Assistance, 2003)

Freeman, M. and Orozco Abad, I. *Negotiating Transitional Justice: Firsthand Lessons from Colombia and Beyond* (Cambridge University Press, 2020)

French, P. *Collective and Corporate Responsibility* (Columbia University Press, 1984)

Funk, M. *Victims' Rights and Advocacy at the International Criminal Court* (Oxford University Press, 2010)

Gallagher, K. 'Civil Litigation and Transnational Business' (2010) 8 *Journal of International Criminal Justice* 745

Galtung, J. 'Violence, Peace, and Peace Research' (1969) 6 *Journal of Peace Research* 3, 167–191

García Martín, L. *Transitional Justice, Corporate Accountability and Socio-Economic Rights, Lessons from Argentina* (Routledge, 2020)

Gavron, J. 'Amnesties in the Light of Developments in International Law and the Establishment of the International Criminal Court' (2002) 51 *ICLQ* 91–117

Geneuss, J. et al. 'Core Crimes Inc.: Panel Discussion Reports from the Conference' (2010) 8 *Journal of International Criminal Justice* 3

Gerards, J. H. and Glas, L. R. 'Access to Justice in the European Convention on Human Rights System' (2017) 35 *Netherlands Quarterly of Human Rights* 1, 11–30

Gerhart, M. et al. 'Unfinished Business: South Africa, Apartheid, and Truth' (2004) 83 *Foreign Affairs* 3, 157

Gilbert, G. *Transnational Fugitive Offenders in International Law: Extradition and Other Mechanisms* (Martinus Nijhoff Publishers, 1998)

Gillard, E.-C. 'Reparation for Violations of International Humanitarian Law' (2003) 85 *International Review of the Red Cross* 529–553

Gjølberg, M. 'Explaining Regulatory Preferences: CSR, Soft Law, or Hard Law? Insights from a Survey of Nordic Pioneers in CSR' (2011) 13 *Business and Politics* 2, 1–31

Golden, K. 'License to Kill? Corporate Liability Under the Alien Tort Claims Act?' (2012) 14 *In the Balance* 37–58

González, E. and Varney, H. (eds.) *Truth Seeking: Elements of Creating an Effective Truth Commission* (Amnesty Commission of the Ministry of Justice of Brazil; International Centre for Transitional Justice, 2013)

Goodstein, J. and Butterfield, K. 'Extending the Horizon of Business Ethics: Restorative Justice and the Aftermath of Unethical Behaviour' (2010) 20 *Business Ethics Quarterly* 3, 453–480

Gray, D. 'Devilry, Complicity and Greed: Transitional Justice and Odious Debt' (2007) 70 *Law and Contemporary Problems* 137

'Extraordinary Justice' (2010) 62 *Alabama Law Review* 1, 55–109

Gready, P. and Robins, S. 'From Transitional to Transformative Justice: A New Agenda for Practice' (2014) 8 *International Journal of Transitional Justice* 3, 339–361

Grossman, C., Del Campo, A. and Trudeau, M. *International Law and Reparations: The Inter-American System* (Clarity Press, 2017)

Gubbay, I. 'Towards Making Blood Money Visible: Lessons Drawn from the Apartheid Litigation', in J. P. Bohoslavsky and J. Letnar Černič (eds.) *Making Sovereign Financing and Human Rights Work* (Hart Publishing, 2014)

Guellali, A. 'Tunisia: Transitional Justice in the Crosshairs', Human Rights Watch, 8 September 2015, available at www.hrw.org/news/2015/09/08/tunisia-transitional-justice-crosshairs

Guembe, J. M. 'Economic Reparations for Grave Human Rights Violations: The Argentinean Experience', in P. De Greiff (ed.) *The Handbook of Reparations* (Oxford University Press, 2006)

Haasdijk, S. 'The Lack of Uniformity in the Terminology of the International Law of Remedies' (1992) 5 *Leiden Journal of International Law* 245–263

Hall, R. 'Reconciling the Past, Present, and Future: The Parameters and Practices of Land Restitution in South Africa', in C. Walker et al. (eds.) *Land, Memory, Reconstruction, and Justice: Perspectives on Land Claims in South Africa* (Ohio University Press, 2010)

Hamber, B. 'Repairing the Irreparable: Dealing with the Double-Binds of Making Reparations for Crimes of the Past' (2000) 5 *Ethnicity & Health* 3–4

'The Dilemmas of Reparations: In Search of a Process-Driven Approach', in K. De Feyter, S. Parmnetier, M. Bossuyt and P. Lemmens (eds.) *Out of the Ashes: Reparation for Victims of Gross and Systematic Human Rights Violations* (Intersentia, 2005)

'Narrowing the Micro and Macro: A Psychological Perspective on Reparations in Societies in Transition', in P. De Greiff (ed.) *The Handbook of Reparations* (Oxford University Press, 2006)

Harring, S. 'German Reparations to the Herero Nation: An Assertion of Herero Nationhood in the Path of Namibian Development?' (2002) 104 *West Virginia Law Review* 393

Harwell, E. E. and Le Billon, P. *Natural Connections: Linking Transitional Justice and Development Through a Focus on Natural Resources* (International Centre of Transitional Justice, 2009)

Hayner, P. 'Fifteen Truth Commissions - 1974 to 1994' (1994) 16 *Human Rights Quarterly* 597–655

'The Contribution of Truth Commissions', in B. Duner (ed.) *An End to Torture: Strategies for its Eradication* (Zed Books, 1998)

Unspeakable Truths: Transitional Justice and the Challenge of Truth Commissions (Routledge, 2011)

Hecht, L. and Michalowski, S. 'The Economic and Social Dimensions of Transitional Justice' (2012) *EJTN Concept Paper*

Heinelt, P. 'Financial Compensation for Nazi Forced Laborers' (Wollheim Memorial, 2010), 44–45, available at www.wollheim-memorial.de/files/1066/original/pdf_Peer_Heinelt_Financial_Compensation_for_Nazi_Forced_Laborers.pdf

Helihy, E. D. and Levine, T. A. 'Corporate Crisis: The Overseas Payment Problem', in E. Bittner and S. L. Messinger (eds.) *Criminology Review Yearbook II* (Sage, 1980)

Heller, K. J. 'Retreat from Nuremberg: The Leadership Requirement in the Crime of Aggression' (2007) 18 *The European Journal of International Law* 3, 477–497

The Nuremberg Military Tribunals and the Origins of International Criminal Law (Oxford University Press, 2011)

Henckaerts, J. and Doswald-Beck, L. (eds.) *Customary International Humanitarian Law*, Volume I (International Committee of the Red Cross, 2005)

Henham, R. 'Conceptualizing Accessto Justice and Victims' Rights in International Sentencing' (2004) 13 *Social and Legal Studies* 27

'Some Reflections on the Role of Victims in the International Criminal Trial Process' (2004) 11 *International Review of Victimology* 1

Henkin, L. *How Nations Behave* (Columbia University Press, 1979)

Hinton, A. 'Introduction: Toward an Anthropology of Transitional Justice', in A. Hinton (ed.) *Transitional Justice: Global Mechanisms and Local Realities After Genocide and Mass Violence* (Rutgers University Press, 2010)

Huggins, C. 'Linking Broad Constellations of Ideas: Transitional Justice, Land Tenure Reform, and Development', in P. De Greiff and R. Duthie (eds.) *Transitional Justice and Development: Making Connections* (Social Science Research Council, 2009)

Huisman, W. *Between Profit and Morality: Background Factors of Regulatory Compliance and Violation by Corporations* (Boom Legal Publishers, 2001)

'Corporations and International Crimes', in A. Smeulers and R. Haveman (eds.) *Supranational Criminology: Towards a Criminology of International Crimes* (Intersentia, 2008)

Huisman, W. and van Sliedregt, E. 'Rogue Traders: Dutch Businessmen, International Crimes and Corporate Complicity' (2010) 8 *Journal of International Criminal Justice* 3, 803–828

Hunneus, A. 'Reforming the State from Afar: Structural Reform Litigation at the Human Rights Courts' (2015) 40 *Yale Journal of International Law* 1

Inazumi, M. *Universal Jurisdiction in Modern International Law: Expansion of National Jurisdiction for Prosecuting Serious Crimes under International Law* (Intersentia, 2005)

International Centre for Transitional Justice. *The Rabat Report: The Concept and Challenges of Collective Reparations* (International Centre for Transitional Justice, 2009)

International Commission of Jurists. *Report of the ICJ Expert Legal Panel on Corporate Complicity in International Crimes: Corporate Complicity & Legal Accountability*, Volume 2 (International Commission of Jurists, 2008)

International Crisis Group. La transition bloquée: corruption et régionalisme en Tunisie Rapport Moyen-Orient et Afrique du Nord, No. 177, 23 (2017)

Jackson, M. *Complicity in International Law* (Oxford University Press, 2015)

'Amnesties in Strasbourg' (2018) 38 *Oxford Journal of Legal Studies* 451

'Command Responsibility', in M. Cupido et al. (eds.) *Modes of Liability in International Criminal Law* (Cambridge University Press, 2019)

Jacobson, K. R. 'Doing Business with the Devil: The Challenges of Prosecuting Corporate Officials Whose Business Transactions Facilitate War Crimes and Crimes Against Humanity' (2005) 56 *The Air Force Law Review* 167

Jamieson, K. *The Organisation of Corporate Crime* (Sage, 1994)

Jessberger, F. 'On the Origins of Individual Criminal Responsibility Under International Law for Business Activity: IG Farben on Trial' (2010) 8 *JICJ* 3, 783

Joseph, S. *Corporations and Transnational Human Rights Litigation* (Hart Publishing, 2004)

Joseph, S. and Castan, M. *The International Covenant on Civil and Political Rights Cases, Materials, and Commentary* (Oxford University Press, 2013)

Joyner, C. 'UN General Assembly Resolutions and International Law: Rethinking the Contemporary Dynamics of Norm Creation' (1981) 11 *California Western International Law Journal* Article 11

Kadelbach, S. 'The International Law Commission and Role of Subsequent Practice as a Means of Interpretation Under Articles 31 and 32 VCLT' (2018) 46 *QIL, Zoom-in* 5–18

Kaleck, W. and Saage-Maasz, M. 'Corporate Accountability for Human Rights Violations Amounting to International Crimes: The Status Quo and Its Challenges' (2010) 8 *Journal of International Criminal Justice* 3, 699–724

Kamali, M. 'Accountability for Human Rights Violations: A Comparison of Transitional Justice in East Germany and South Africa' (2001) 40 *Columbia Journal of Transnational Law* 89–142

Kamensky, D. 'Introducing Corporate Criminal Liability in Ukraine: Terra Incognita' (2020) 46 *Stetson Law Review* 89–110

Kaminer, D. et al. 'The Truth and Reconciliation Commission in South Africa: Relation to Psychiatric Status and Forgiveness Among Survivors of Human Rights Abuses' (2001) 178 *British Journal of Psychiatry* 4, 373–377

Karavias, M. *Corporate Obligations Under International Law* (Oxford University Press, 2013)

Karstedt, S. 'From Absence to Presence, From Silence to Voice: Victims in Transitional Justice Since the Nuremberg Trials' (2010) 17 *International Review of Victimology* 9

Keck, M. and Sikkink, K. *Activists beyond Borders: Advocacy Networks in International Politics* (Cornell University Press, 1998)

Kelly, M. 'Prosecuting Corporations for Genocide Under International Law' (2012) 6 *Harvard Law Policy Review* 339–367

Prosecuting Corporations for Genocide (Oxford University Press, 2016)

Kennedy, D. 'The International Human Rights Movement: Part of the Problem?' (2002) 15 *Harvard Human Rights Journal* 101–125

Kim, H. and Sikkink, K. 'Explaining the Deterrence Effect of Human Rights Prosecutions for Transitional Countries' (2010) 54 *International Studies Quarterly* 4, 939–963

Kinley, D. (ed.) *Human Rights and Corporations* (Ashgate Pub., 2009)

Kiss, A. 'Indirect Commission', in M. Cupido et al. (eds.) *Modes of Liability in International Criminal Law* (Cambridge University Press, 2019)

Klein, E. 'Individual Reparation Claims Under the International Covenant on Civil and Political Rights: The Practice of the Human Rights Committee', in A. Randelzhofer and C. Tomuschat (eds.) *State Responsibility and the Individual – Reparation in Instances of Grave Violations of Human Rights* (Martinus Nijhoff Publishers, 1999)

Klinkner, M. and Smith, E. 'The Right to Truth, Appropriate Forum and the International Criminal Court', in N. Szablewska, and S. Bachmann (eds.) *Current Issues in Transitional Justice: Towards a More Holistic Approach* (Springer Publishers, 2014)

Knox, J. 'Horizontal Human Rights' (2008) 102 *American Journal of International Law* 1

Kobrin, S. 'Private Political Authority and Public Responsibility: Transnational Politics, Transnational Firms, and Human Rights' (2009) 19 *Business Ethics Quarterly* 3, 349–374

Kolieb, J. 'Through the Looking-Glass: Nuremberg's Confusing Legacy on Corporate Accountability Under International Law' (2017) 32 *American University International Law Review* 2, 569–604

Koska, G. 'Corporate Accountability in Times of Transition: The Role of Restorative Justice in the South African Truth and Reconciliation Commission' (2016) 4 *Restorative Justice* 1, 41–67

Koskenniemi, M. 'Between Impunity and Show Trials' (2002) 6 *Max Planck Yearbook of United Nations Law* 1

Kramer, R. C. 'Corporate Crime: An Organisational Perspective', in P. Wickman and T. Daley (eds.) *White-Collar and Economic Crime: Multidisciplinary and Cross-National Perspectives* (Lexington Books, 1982)

Kristjansdottir, E. 'International Mass Claims Processes and the ICC Trust Fund for Victims', in C. Ferstman et al. (eds.) *Reparations for Victims of Genocide, War Crimes and Crimes Against Humanity* (Martinus Nijhoff, 2009) 167

Kritz, N. 'Coming to Terms with Atrocities' (1998) 59 *Law and Contemporary Problems* 4, 127–152

Kritz, N. J. 'Progress and Humility: The Ongoing Search for Post-Conflict Justice', in C. Bassiouni (ed.) *Post-Conflict Justice* (Transnational Publishers, 2002)

Kury, H. et al. 'The Position of the Victim in Criminal Procedure – Results of a German Study' (1994) 3 *International Review of Victimology* 1–2, 69–81

Kyriakakis, J. 'Australian Prosecution of Corporations for International Crimes' (2007) 5 *Journal of International Criminal Justice* 809–826

'Corporations and the International Criminal Court: The Complementarity Objection Stripped Bare' (2008) 19 *Criminal Law Forum* 115–151

'Corporate Criminal Liability and the ICC Statute: The Comparative Law Challenge' (2009) 56 *Netherlands International Law Review* 333

'Prosecuting Corporations for International Crimes', in L. May and Z. Hoskins (eds.) *International Criminal Law and Philosophy* (Cambridge University Press, 2010)

'Developments in International Criminal Law and the Case of Business Involvement in International Crimes' (2012) 94 *International Review of the Red Cross* 887

'Article 46C: Corporate Criminal Liability at the African Criminal Court', in C. Jalloh, K. Clarke and V. Nmehielle (eds.) *The African Court of Justice and Human and Peoples' Rights in Context: Development and Challenges* (Cambridge University Press, 2019)

Corporations, Accountability and International Criminal Law, Industry and Atrocity (Edward Elgar Publishing, 2021)

Lachenmann, F. and Wolfrum, R. (eds.) *The Law of Armed Conflict and the Use of Force: The Max Planck Encyclopaedia of Public International Law* (Oxford University Press, 2017)

Lai, D. 'Beyond Context: Taking Political Economy Seriously in the Study of Corporate Accountability' (2024) 29 *New Political Economy* 3, 385–399

Lambourne, W. 'Transitional Justice and Peacebuilding After Mass Violence' (2009) 3 *International Journal of Transitional Justice* 1, 28–48

Lane, L. 'The Horizontal Effect of International Human Rights Law in Practice: A Comparative Analysis of the General Comments and Jurisprudence of Selected United Nations Human Rights Treaty Monitoring Bodies' (2018) 5 *European Journal of Comparative Law and Governance* 1, 5–88

Laplante, L. 'On the Indivisibility of Rights: Truth Commissions, Reparations, and the Right to Development' (2007) 10 *Yale Human Rights and Development Law Journal* 141

'The Peruvian Truth Commission's Historical Memory Project: Empowering Truth-Tellers to Confront Truth Deniers' (2007) 6 *Journal of Human Rights* 433–452

'Transitional Justice and Peace Building: Diagnosing and Addressing the Socioeconomic Roots of Violence Through a Human Rights Framework' (2008) 2 *International Journal of Transitional Justice* 3, 331–355

Laplante, L. and Theidon, K. 'Truth with Consequences: Justice and Reparations in Post-Truth Commission Peru' (2007) 29 *Human Rights Quarterly* 228–250

Lawry-White, M. 'The Reparative Effect of Truth Seeking in Transitional Justice' (2015) 64 *The International and Comparative Law Quarterly* 1, 141–177

Layús, R. F. 'Just Collateral Damage? Accountability of Economic Elites in Peacebuilding and Transitional Justice in Colombia' (2024) 49 *Peace & Change* 3, 1–19

Leebaw, B. A. 'The Irreconcilable Goals of Transitional Justice' (2008) 30 *Human Rights Quarterly* 1, 95–118

Lefranc, S. and Vairel, F. 'The Emergence of Transitional Justice as a Professional International Practice', in L. Israël and G. Mouralis (eds.) *Dealing with Wars and Dictatorships: Legal Concepts and Categories in Action* (Springer, 2013)

Lessa, F. et al. 'Overcoming Impunity: Pathways to Accountability in Latin America' (2014) 8 *International Journal of Transitional Justice* 1, 75–98

Lessard, G. 'Preventive Reparations at a Crossroads: The Inter-American Court of Human Rights and Colombia's Search for Peace' (2018) 22 *The International Journal of Human Rights* 1209–1228

Levit, J. 'Bottom-Up International Law-Making: Reflections on the New Haven School of International Law' (2007) 32 *Yale Journal of International Law* 393–420

Lira, 'Policy for Human Rights Violations in Chile', in P. De Greiff (ed.) *The Handbook of Reparations* (Oxford University Press, 2006)

Llewellyn, J. and Philpott, D. (eds.) *Restorative Justice, Reconciliation, and Peacebuilding* (Oxford University Press, 2014)

Longman, T. et al. 'Connecting Justice to Human Experience: Attitudes Toward Accountability and Reconciliation in Rwanda', in E. Stover and H. Weinstein (eds.) *My Neighbor, My Enemy: Justice and Community in the Aftermath of Mass Atrocity* (Cambridge University Press, 2004)

Loyle, C. E. and Davenport, C. 'Transitional Injustice: Subverting Justice in Transition and Post conflict Societies' (2015) 15 *Journal of Human Rights* 1, 126–149

Lundy, P. and McGovern, M. 'Whose Justice? Rethinking Transitional Justice from the Bottom Up' (2008) 35 *Journal of Law and Society* 265

Lutz, E. 'After the Elections: Compensating Victims of Human Rights Abuses', in E. Lutz et al. (eds.) *New Directions in Human Rights* (University of Pennsylvania Press, 1989)

Lutz, E. and Sikkink, K. 'The Justice Cascade: The Evolution and Impact of Foreign Human Rights Trials in Latin America' (2001) 2 *Chicago Journal of International Law* 1, 1–34

Macdonald, A. 'From the Ground Up: What Does the Evidence Tell Us about Local Experiences of Transitional Justice?' (2015) 1 *Transitional Justice Review* 3, Article 4

Macklem, P. 'Corporate Accountability under International Law: The Misguided Quest for Universal Jurisdiction' (2005) 7 *International Law Forum du droit international* 281–289

Madlingozi, T. 'On Transitional Justice Entrepreneurs and the Production of Victims' (2010) 2 *Journal of Human Rights Practice* 2, 208–228

Magarrell, L. 'Reparations for Massive or Widespread Human Rights Violations: Sorting Out Claims for Reparations and the Struggle for Social Justice' (2003) 22 *Windsor Yearbook of Access to Justice* 85–98

'Reparations in Theory and Practice' (2007) *ICTJ Reparative Justice Series* 85–98

Maguchu, P. *Transitional Justice and Socio-Economic Rights in Zimbabwe* (T.M.C. Asser Press, 2019)

Malamud-Goti, J. 'Transitional Governments in the Breach: Why Punish State Criminals?' (1990) 12 *Human Rights Quarterly* 1

'Punishing Human Rights Abuses in Fledgling Democracies: The Case of Argentina', in N. Roht-Arriaza (ed.) *Impunity and Human Rights in International Law and Practice* (Oxford University Press, 1995)

Malamud-Goti, J. and Grosman, L. S. 'Reparations and Civil Litigation: Compensation for Human Rights Violations in Transitional Democracies', in P. De Greiff (ed.) *The Handbook of Reparations* (Oxford University Press, 2006)

Mallinder, L. *Amnesty, Human Rights and Political Transitions: Bridging the Peace and Justice Divide* (Hart, 2008)

'Exploring the Practice of States in Introducing Amnesties', in K. Ambos et al. (eds.) *Building a Future on Peace and Justice: Studies on Transitional Justice, Conflict Resolution and Development* (Springer-Verlag Berlin Heidelberg, 2009)

Mamdani, M. 'Reconciliation Without Justice' (1996) 46 *South African Review of Books* 3–5

Mani, R. *Beyond Retribution: Seeking Justice in the Shadows of War* (Cambridge University Press, 2002)

'Dilemmas of Expanding Transitional Justice, or Forging the Nexus between Transitional Justice and Development' (2008) 2 *International Journal of Transitional Justice* 253

Mansuri, G. and Vijayendra, R. 'Community-Based and -Driven Development: A Critical Review' (2004) 19 *The World Bank Research Observer* 1, 1–39

Maravall, J. and Przeworski, A. (eds.) *Democracy and the Rule of Law 68* (Cambridge University Press, 2003)

Marks, M. K. '40 Acres and a Mule: Accountability for Corporations to Provide Reparations to Historically Black Colleges and Universities for Profits from Slave Labour' (2023) 10 *Emory Corporate Governance and Accountability Review* 312

Marks, S. *The Riddle of All Constitutions. International Law, Democracy and the Critique of Ideology* (Oxford University Press, 2000)

Martinez, D. and Gomez, L. *A Promise to Be Fulfilled: Reparations for Victims of the Armed Conflict in Guatemala* (Queen's University Belfast, 2019)

May, L. 'Reparations, Restitution, and Transitional Justice', in L. May and A. Forcehimes (eds.) *Morality, Jus Post Bellum, and International Law* (Cambridge University, 2012)

Mayer-Rieckh, A. and De Greiff, P. (eds.) *Justice as Prevention: Vetting Public Employees in Transitional Societies* (International Centre for Transitional Justice, 2007)

McAuliffe, P. 'Transitional Justice's Expanding Empire: Reasserting the Value of the Paradigmatic Transition' (2011) 2 *Journal of Conflictology* 2, 32–44

'Rhetoric and Realpolitik: Interrogating the Relationship between Transitional Justice and Socio-Economic Justice' (2012–2013) 23 *Finnish Yearbook of International Law* 239–307

Transitional Justice and Rule of Law Reconstruction: A Contentious Relationship (Routledge, 2013)

Transformative Transitional Justice and the Malleability of Post-Conflict States (Edward Elgar Publishing, 2017)

McBeth, A. 'Crushed by an Anvil: A Case Study on Responsibility for Human Rights in the Extractive Sector' (2008) 11 *Yale Human Rights and Development Law Journal* 127

'Every Organ of Society: The Responsibility of Non-State Actors for the Realization of Human Rights' (2008) 30 *Hamline Journal of Public Law and Policy* 1, 33–88

McCarthy, C. 'Victim Redress and International Criminal Justice Competing Paradigms, or Compatible Forms of Justice?' (2012) 10 *Journal of International Criminal Justice* 351–372

McCorquodale, R. 'Non State Actors and International Human Rights Law', in S. Joseph and A. McBeth (eds.) *Research Handbook on International Human Rights Law* (Edward Elgar, 2011)

McEvoy, K. 'Beyond Legalism: Towards a Thicker Understanding of Transitional Justice' (2007) 34 *Journal of Law and Society* 4, 411–440

McEvoy, K. and McGregor, L. 'Transitional Justice from Below: An Agenda for Research, Policy and Praxis', in K. McEvoy and L. McGregor (eds.) *Transitional Justice from Below, Grassroots Activism and the Struggle for Change* (Hart Publishing, 2008)

Meeran, R. 'Tort Litigation against Multinational Corporations for Violation of Human Rights: An Overview of the Position Outside the United States' (2011) 3 *City University of Hong Kong Law Review* 1–41

Mendeloff, D. 'Truth-Seeking, Truth-Telling, and Post-conflict Peacebuilding: Curb the Enthusiasm?' (2004) 6 *International Studies Review* 3, 355–380

'Trauma and Vengeance: Assessing the Psychological and Emotional Effects of Post-Conflict Justice' (2009) 31 *Human Rights Quarterly* 3, 592–623

Méndez, J. 'Accountability for Past Abuses' (1997) 19 *Human Rights Quarterly* 255–282

'The Right to Truth', in C. Joyner and M. C. Bassiouni (eds.) *Reining in Impunity for International Crimes and Serious Violations of Fundamental Human Rights: Proceedings of the Siracusa Conference* (Érès, 1998)

'The Human Right to Truth: Lessons Learned from Latin American Experiences with Truth Telling', in T. A. Borer (ed.) *Telling the Truths: Truth Telling and Peace Building in Post-Conflict Societies* (University of Notre Dame Press, 2006)

'Victims as Protagonists in Transitional Justice' (2016) 10 *International Journal of Transitional Justice* 1

Méndez, J. and Mariezcurrena, J. 'Accountability for Past Human Rights Violations: Contributions of the Inter-American Organs of Protection' (1999) 26 *Social Justice* 84–106

Meron, T. *Human Rights and Humanitarian Law as Customary Law* (Clarendon Press, 1989)

Merrills, J. G. *The Development of International Law by the European Court of Human Rights* (Manchester University Press, 1993)

Merwe, H. and Brinton Lykes, M. 'Transitional Justice and Corporate Accountability: Introducing New Players and New Theoretical Challenges' (2022) 16 *International Journal of Transitional Justice* 1–7

Mettraux, G. *The Law of Command Responsibility* (Oxford University Press, 2009)

Michalakea, T. 'Article 46C of the Malabo Protocol: A Contextually Tailored Approach to Corporate Criminal Liability and Its Contours' (2018) 7 *International Human Rights Law Review* 2, 225–248

'Anticorruption and Transitional Justice: A Distinction Without a Difference' (2022) 22 *Human Rights Law Review* 2, 1–17

Michalowski, S. 'No Complicity Liability for Funding Gross Human Rights Violations?' (2012) 30 *Berkeley Journal of International Law* 451

(ed.) *Corporate Accountability in the Context of Transitional Justice* (Routledge, 2013)

'The Mens Rea Standard for Corporate Aiding and Abetting Liability Conclusions from International Criminal Law' (2014) 18 *UCLA Journal of International Law and Foreign Affairs* 2, 237–274

'Doing Business with a Bad Actor: How to Draw the Line Between Legitimate Commercial Activities and Those That Trigger Corporate Complicity Liability' (2015) 50 *Texas International Law Journal* 403

'Approaches to Criminal Responsibility of Economic Actors in Transitional Justice Processes: Lessons from Colombia' (2024) 55 *Columbia Human Rights Law Review* 2, 444–508

Michalowski, S. and Cardona Chaves, J. P. 'Responsabilidad corporativa y justicia transicional' (2015) 11 *Anuario de Derechos Humanos* 173–182

Michalowski, S. et al. *Entre coacción y colabouración. Verdad judicial, actores económicos y conflicto armado en Colombia* (Centro de Estudios de Derecho, Justicia y Sociedad, Dejusticia, 2018)

Los terceros complejos: la competencia limitada de la Jurisdicción Especial para la Paz 50 (Dejusticia, 2019)

Guía De Orientación Jurídica, Terceros Civiles Ante La Jurisdiccion Especial Para La Paz (Dejusticia, 2020)

Middle East and North Africa Financial Action Task Force for combating Money Laundering and Terrorist Financing (MENAFATF). Anti-money laundering and counter-terrorist financing measures Tunisia Mutual Evaluation Report, May 2016

Miller, Z. 'Effects of Invisibility: In Search of the "Economic" in Transitional Justice' (2008) 2 *International Journal of Transitional Justice* 3, 266–291

Minow, M. *Between Vengeance and Forgiveness: Facing History After Genocide and Mass Violence* (Beacon Press, 1998)

Mitchell, C. *Aut Dedere, aut Judicare: The Extradite or Prosecute Clause in International Law* (Graduate Institute Publications, 2009)

Moffett, L. 'Beyond Attribution: Responsibility of Armed Non-State Actors for Reparations in Northern Ireland, Colombia and Uganda', in N. Gal-Or, C. Ryngaert and M. Noortmann (eds.) *Responsibilities of the Non-State Actor in Armed Conflict and the Market Place: Theoretical Considerations and Empirical Findings* (Brill, 2015)

'Transitional Justice and Reparations: Remedying the Past?', in D. Jacobs et al. (eds.) *Research Handbook on Transitional Justice* (Edward Elgar Publishing, 2017)

Reparations and War: Finding Balance in Repairing the Past (Oxford University Press, 2023)

Moon, C. 'Who'll Pay Reparations on My Soul? Compensation, Social Control and Social Suffering' (2012) 21 *Social and Legal Studies* 2, 187–199

Moreno Ocampo, L. 'Building a Future on Peace and Justice', Keynote Address at the Building a Future on Peace and Justice Conference, Office of the ICC Prosecutor, 24 June 2007

'Transitional Justice in Ongoing Conflicts' (2007) 1 *International Journal of Transitional Justice*

Muchlinski, P. 'The Impact of the UN Guiding Principles on Business Attitudes to Observing Human Rights' (2021) 6 *Business and Human Rights Journal* 2, 212–226

Murphy, C. *The Conceptual Foundations of Transitional Justice* (Cambridge University Press, 2017)

Murphy, J. and Brindusa Albu, O. 'The Politics of Transnational Accountability Policies and the (Re)construction of Corruption: The Case of Tunisia , Transparency International and The World Bank' (2018) 42 *Accounting Forum* 1, 32–46

Murray, D. *Human Rights Obligations of Non-State Armed Groups* (Hart Publishing, 2016)

Musila, G. *Rethinking International Criminal Law: Restorative Justice and the Rights of Victims in the International Criminal Court* (Lambert Academic Publishing, 2010)

Mutua, M. 'The Banjul Charter and the African Cultural Fingerprint: An Evaluation of the Language of Duties' (1995) 35 *Virginia Journal of International Law* 339

'The Ideology of Human Rights' (1996) 36 *Virginia Journal of International Law* 589

'Never Again: Questioning the Yugoslav and Rwanda Tribunals' (1997) 11 *Temple International and Comparative Law Journal* 167

Nagy, R. 'Post-Apartheid Justice: Can Cosmopolitanism and Nation-Building Be Reconciled?' (2006) 40 *Law and Society Review* 3, 623–652

'Transitional Justice as a Global Project: Critical Reflections' (2008) 29 *Third World Quarterly* 2, 275–289

Naqvi, Y. 'Amnesty for War Crimes : Defining the Limits of International Recognition' (2003) 85 *International Review of the Red Cross* 583–626

'The Right to the Truth in International Law: Fact or Fiction' (2006) 88 *International Review of the Red Cross* 245

Nattrass, N. 'The Truth and Reconciliation Commission on Business and Apartheid: A Critical Evaluation' (1999) 98 *African Affairs* 373–391

Nerlich, V. 'Core Crimes and Transnational Business Corporations' (2010) 8 *Journal of International Criminal Justice* 3, 895–908

Nesiah, V. 'Transitional Justice Practice: Looking Back, Moving Forward', Scoping Study, Impunity Watch Research Report (May 2016)

Neuborne, B. 'Holocaust Reparations Litigation: Lessons for the Slavery Reparations Movement' (2003) 58 *N.Y.U. Annual Survey of American Law* 615

Nigeria Human Rights Violations Investigation Commission Report (Aka Oputa Panel Report). Nigerian Democratic Movement (NDM), Washington, DC, USA

Nino, C. S. 'The Duty to Punish Past Abuses of Human Rights Put Into Context: The Case of Argentina' (1991) 100 *The Yale Law Journal* 8, 2619–2640

Nolan, J. 'The Corporate Responsibility to Respect Human Rights: Soft Law or Not Law?', in D. Bilchitz and S. Deva (eds.) *Human Rights Obligations of Business: Beyond the Corporate Responsibility to Respect* (Cambridge University Press, 2013)

'Human Rights and Global Corporate Supply Chains: Is Effective Supply Chain Accountability Possible?', in S. Deva and D. Bilchitz (eds.) *Building a Treaty on Business and Human Rights: Context and Contours* (Cambridge University Press, 2017)

Nollkaemper, A. and Van der Wilt, H. (eds.) *System Criminality in International Law* (Cambridge University Press, 2009)

Nowak, A. C. 'Accommodating Social Justice into Transitional Justice Mechanisms: the Case of Northern Uganda' (2011) 1 *International Journal of Rule of Law, Transitional Justice and Human Rights* 107

Nowak, M. *UN Covenant on Civil and Political Rights: A Commentary* (Engel, 1993)

UN Convention Against Torture: A Commentary (Oxford University Press, 2008)

Ochoa, S. J. *The Rights of Victims in Criminal Justice Proceedings for Serious Human Rights Violations* (Brill | Nijhoff, 2013)

O'Connell, J. 'Gambling with the Psyche: Does Prosecuting Human Rights Violators Console Their Victims' (2005) 46 *Harvard International Law Journal* 295

O'Donnell, G. *Modernization and Bureaucratic-Authoritarianism: Studies in South American Politics* (Institute of International Studies, University of California, 1973)

Olasolo, H. *The Criminal Responsibility of Political and Military Leaders as Principles to International Crimes* (Hart Publishers, 2009)

Olasolo, H. and Ramirez Mendoza, J. 'The Colombian Integrated System of Truth, Justice, Reparation and Non-Repetition' (2017) 15 *Journal of International Criminal Justice* 1011–1047

Olsen, T. *Seeking Justice: Access to Remedy for Corporate Human Rights Abuse* (Cambridge University Press, 2023)

Olsen, T., Payne, L. and Reiter, A. 'The Justice Balance: When Transitional Justice Improves Human Rights and Democracy' (2010) 32 *Human Rights Quarterly* 4, 980–1005

Transitional Justice in Balance: Comparing Processes, Weighing Efficacy (United States Institute of Peace Press, 2010)

Orentlicher, D. F. 'Settling Accounts: The Duty to Prosecute Human Rights Violations of a Prior Regime' (1991) 100 *Yale Law Journal* 2537–2615

'Settling Accounts' Revisited: Reconciling Global Norms with Local Agency' (2007) 1 *International Journal of Transitional Justice* 1, 10–22

Osiel, M. *Making Sense of Mass Atrocity* (Cambridge University Press, 2009)

Oubenal, M. and Ben Hamouda, H. 'The Political Economy of Business Elites in Tunisia: Actors, Strategies and Identities' (2018) Working Papers 1273, *Economic Research Forum*

Overy, R. 'The Nuremberg Trials: International Law in the Making', in P. Sands (ed.) *From Nuremberg to The Hague: The Future of International Criminal Justice* (Cambridge University Press, 2003)

Panepinto, A. 'The Right to the Truth in International Law: The Significance of Strasbourg's Contributions' (2017) 37 *Legal Studies* 739–764

Paris, R. 'Peacebuilding and the Limits of Liberal Internationalism' (1997) 22 *International Security* 54–89

'International Peacebuilding and the "Mission Civilisatrice"' (2002) 28 *Review of International Studies* 637

'Saving Liberal Peacebuilding' (2010) 36 *Review of International Studies* 337

Park, A. 'Peacebuilding, the Rule of Law and the Problem of Culture: Assimilation, Multiculturalism, Deployment' (2010) 4 *Journal of Intervention and Statebuilding* 4, 413–432

Pasqualucci, J. M. 'The Whole Truth and Nothing But the Truth: Truth Commissions, Impunity and the Inter-American Human Rights System' (1994) 12 *Boston University International Law Journal* 297–361

Paul, G. and Schonsteiner, J. 'Transitional Justice and the UN Guiding Principles on Business and Human Rights', in S. Michalowski (ed.) *Corporate Accountability in the Context of Transitional Justice* (Routledge, 2013)

Paulon, V. 'Acindar and Techint: Extreme Militarization of Labour Relations', in H. Verbitsky and J. P. Bohoslavsky (eds.) *Outstanding Debts to Settle: The Economic Accomplices of the Dictatorship in Argentina* (Cambridge University Press, 2015)

Paust, J. 'Human Rights Responsibilities of Private Corporations' (2002) 35 *Vanderbilt Journal of Transnational Law* 801

Payne, L., Bernal-Bermúdez, L. and Pereira, G. (eds.) *Economic Actors and the Limits of Transitional Justice: Truth and Justice for Business Complicity in Human Rights Violations* (Oxford University Press, 2022)

Payne, L. and Pereira, G. 'Accountability for Corporate Complicity in Human Rights Violations: Argentina's Transitional Justice Innovation?', in H. Verbitsky and J. P. Bohoslavsky (eds.) *Outstanding Debts to Settle: The Economic Accomplices of the Dictatorship in Argentina* (Cambridge University Press, 2015)

Payne, L., Pereira, G. and Bernal-Bermúdez, L. *Transitional Justice and Corporate Accountability from Below: Deploying Archimedes' Lever* (Cambridge University Press, 2020)

Pensky, M. 'Amnesty on Trial: Immunity, Accountability and the Norms of International Law' (2008) 1 *Ethics and Global Politics* 1

Pereira, G. and Payne, L. 'Corporate Complicity in International Human Rights Violations' (2016) 12 *Annual Review of Law and Social Science* 63–84

Pereira, G., Payne, L. and Bernal-Bermúdez, L. 'Justice from Below: Corporate Accountability in Argentina' (2022) 26 *The International Journal of Human Rights* 8, 1418–1454

Phillips, T. and Albon, M. 'When Prosecution Is Not Possible: Alternative Means of Seeking Accountability for War Crimes', in B. Cooper (ed.) *War Crimes: The Legacy of Nuremberg* 244 (TV Books, 1999)

Piedrahíta, L. C. 'The Right to Truth in Colombia 's Comprehensive System of Truth, Justice, Reparation, and Non-Repetition. A Direct Approach to the Intrinsic Relationship Between Its Mechanisms and Objectives' (2022) 18 *Nuevo Derecho* 31

Pieth, M. and Ivory, R. 'Emergence and Convergence: Corporate Criminal Liability Principles in Overview', in M. Pieth and R. Ivory (eds.) *Corporate Criminal Liability: Emergence, Convergence, and Risk* (Springer, 2011)

Pietropaoli, I. *Business, Human Rights and Transitional Justice* (Routledge, 2020)

'Obligations of Third States and Corporations to Prevent and Punish Genocide in Gaza', Al Haq Organization, 5 June 2024

Posner, E. and Vermeule, A. 'Transitional Justice as Ordinary Justice' (2004) 117 *Harvard Law Review* 3, 761–825

Pugh, M. 'The Political Economy of Peace Studies: A Critical Theory Perspective' (2005) 2 *International Journal of Peace Studies* 23–41

Punch, M. 'Suite Violence: Why Managers Murder and Corporations Kill' (2000) 33 *Crime, Law and Social Change* 243

'Why Corporations Kill and Get Away With It: The Failure of Law to Cope With Crime in Organizations', in A. Nollkaemper and H. Van der Wilt (eds.) *System Criminality in International Law* (Cambridge University Press, 2009)

Raftopoulos, B. and Mlamba, A. (eds.) *Becoming Zimbabwe: A History from the Pre-Colonial Period to 2008* (Weaver Press, 2009)

Rajagopal, B. 'Invoking the Rule of Law in Post-conflict Rebuilding: A Critical Examination' (2008) 49 *William & Mary Law Review* 1347

Ramasastry, A. 'Secrets and Lies? Swiss Banks and International Human Rights' (1998) 31 *Vanderbilt Journal of Transnational Law* 325

'Corporate Complicity: From Nuremberg to Rangoon – An Examination of Forced Labour Cases and Their Impact on the Liability of Multinational Corporations' (2002) 20 *Berkeley Journal of International Law* 91

'Corporate Social Responsibility Versus Business and Human Rights: Bridging the Gap Between Responsibility and Accountability' (2015) 14 *Journal of Human Rights* 2, 237–259

Ramasastry, A. and Thompson, R. *Commerce, Crime and Conflict: Legal Remedies for Private Sector Liability for Grave Breaches of International Law* (Fafo, 2006)

Ramasastry, A. et al. 'Translating Unocal: The Expanding Web of Liability for Business Entities Implicated in International Crimes' (2009) 40 *George Washington International Law Review* 841–902

Ratner, S. 'Corporations and Human Rights: A Theory of Legal Responsibility' (2002) 111 *Yale Law Journal* 443

Redress. *Reaching for Justice: The Right to Reparation in the African Human Rights System* (The Redress Trust, 2013)

Rehabilitation as a Form of Reparation under International Law (The Redress Trust, 2009)

Reintegration and Reparation for Victims of Rendition and Unlawful Detention in the War on Terror: A European Perspective (Workshop Report, 2008)

Torture Survivors' Perceptions of Reparation Preliminary Survey (The Redress Trust, 2001)

Richmond, O. 'The Romanticisation of the Local: Welfare, Culture, and Peacebuilding' (2012) 44 *The International Spectator* 149

Rijkers, B. et al., 'All in the Family: State Capture in Tunisia' (2017) 124 *Journal of Development Economics* 41–59

Robins, S. 'An Assessment of the Needs of Families of the Missing in Nepal' (2009) *SSRN Electronic Journal* 1

'Transitional Justice as an Elite Discourse: Human Rights Practice: Where the Global Meets the Local in Post-Conflict Nepal' (2012) 44 *Critical Asian Studies* 1, 3–30

Families of the Missing: A Test for Contemporary Approaches to Transitional Justice (Routledge, 2013)

'Failing Victims? The Limits of Transitional Justice in Addressing the Needs of Victims of Violations' (2017) 2 *Human Rights and International Legal Discourse* 41–58

Robinson, D. 'Serving the Interests of Justice: Amnesties, Truth Commissions and the International Criminal Court' (2003) 14 *European Journal of International Law* 3, 481–505

Rodríguez, J. 'Where Impunity Reigns: Nickel Mining in El Estor, Guatemala' (2021) 48 *Latin American Perspectives* 1

Roht-Arriaza, N. 'State Responsibility to Investigate and Prosecute Grave Human Rights Violations in International Law' (1990) 78 *California Law Review* 449–513

'Reparations Decisions and Dilemmas' (2004) 27 *Hastings International and Comparative Law Review* 166

'The New Landscape of Transitional Justice', in N. Roht-Arriaza and J. Mariezcurrena (eds.) *Transitional Justice in the Twenty-First Century* (Cambridge University Press, 2006)

'Why Was the Economic Dimension Missing for So Long in Transitional Justice? An Exploratory Essay', in H. Verbitsky and J. P. Bohoslavsky (eds.) *Outstanding Debts to Settle: The Economic Accomplices of the Dictatorship in Argentina* (Cambridge University Press, 2015)

'Measures of Non-Repetition in Transitional Justice: The Missing Link?' (2016) 160 *UC Hastings Research Paper* 1–42

Roht-Arriaza, N. and Mariezcurrena, J. (eds.) *Transitional Justice in the Twenty-First Century* (Cambridge University Press, 2006)

Rombouts, H. *Victim Organisations and the Politics of Reparation: A Case-Study on Rwanda* (Intersentia, 2004)

et al. 'The Right to Reparation for Victims of Gross and Systematic Violations of Human Rights', in K. De Feyter et al. (eds.) *Out of the Ashes: Reparation for Victims of Gross and Systematic Human Rights Violations* (Intersentia, 2005)

Rubio-Marin, R. 'Women and Reparations' (2007) 1 *International Journal of Transitional Justice* 3, 318–337

'The Gender of Reparations in Transitional Societies', in R. Rubio-Marin (ed.) *The Gender of Reparations: Unsettling Sexual Hierarchies While Redressing Human Rights Violations* (Cambridge University Press, 2009)

Ryngaert, C. *The Principles of Extraterritorial Criminal Jurisdiction* (Oxford University Press, 2008)

'Accountability for Corporate Human Rights Abuses: Lessons from the Possible Exercise of Dutch National Criminal Jurisdiction Over Multinational Corporations' (2018) 29 *Criminal Law Forum* 1–24

Salmon, E. G. 'Reflections on International Humanitarian Law and Transitional Justice: Lessons to Be Learnt from the Latin American Experience' (2006) 88 *International Review of the Red Cross* 862, 327–353

Sánchez León, N. C. 'Corporate Accountability, Reparations and Distributive Justice in Post Conflict Societies', in S. Michalowski (ed.) *Corporate Accountability in the Context of Transitional Justice* (Routledge, 2013)

Tierra en transición: justicia transicional, restitución de tierras y política agraria en Colombia (Dejusticia, 2017)

Sánchez León, N. C. and Sandoval-Villalba, C. 'Go Big or Go Home? Lessons Learned from the Colombian Victims' Reparation System', in C. Ferstman and M. Goetz (eds.) *Reparations for Victims of Genocide, War Crimes and Crimes Against Humanity: Systems in Place and Systems in the Making* (Koninklijke Brill, 2020)

Sánchez, N. C. and Uprimny, R. *The Challenges of Negotiated Transitions in the Era of International Criminal Law in Beyond Binary Securing Peace and Promoting Justice after Conflict* (Dejusticia Collection, 2019)

Sánchez, N. et al. *Roles and Responsibilities of the Private Sector in Transitional Justice Processes in Latin America, The cases of Colombia, Guatemala, and Argentina* (Due Process of Law Foundation, International Coalition of Sites of Conscience, 2020)

Sanders, A. 'New Frontiers in the ATS: Conspiracy and Joint Criminal Enterprise Liability After Sosa' (2010) 28 *Berkeley Journal of International Law* 619

Sandoval, C. (ed.) *Adverse Consequences of Reparations Briefing Paper No. 6* (Essex Transitional Justice Network, 2011)

Briefing Paper Transitional Justice: Key Concepts, Processes and Challenges (Institute for Democracy & Conflict Resolution, 2011)

Sandoval, C. and Surfleet, G. 'Corporations and Redress in Transitional Justice Processes', in S. Michalowski (ed.) *Corporate Accountability in the Context of Transitional Justice* (Routledge, 2013)

Sandt, J. and Moor, M. (eds.) *Peace, Everyone's Business! Corporate Accountability in Transitional Justice: Lessons for Colombia* (PAX, 2017)

Sarkin, J. *Carrots and Sticks: The TRC and the South African Amnesty Process* (Intersentia, 2004)

Sarkin, J. and Davi, T. 'Examining the Criticisms Levelled against Transitional Justice: Towards an Understanding of the State of the Field' (2017) 11 *Human Rights & International Legal Discourse* 7, 12

Saturnino, M. et al. 'Transnational Land Investment Web: Land Grabs, TNCs, and the Challenge of Global Governance' (2020) 17 *Globalizations* 4, 608–628

Schabas, W. 'A Synergistic Relationship: The Sierra Leone Truth and Reconciliation Commission and the Special Court for Sierra Leone' (2004) 15 *Criminal Law Forum*

'Enforcing International Humanitarian Law: Catching the Accomplices' (2001) 83 *International Review of the Red Cross* 842

Scheffer, D. 'The Impact of the War Crimes Tribunals on Corporate Liability for Atrocity Crimes Under US Law', in C. Walker-Said and J. Kelly (eds.) *Corporate Social Responsibility? Human Rights in the New Global Economy* (University of Chicago Press, 2015)

Scheinin, M. 'The Human Rights Committee's Pronouncements on the Right to an Effective Remedy – An Illustration of the Legal Nature of the Committee's Work under the Optional Protocol', in A. Nisuke (ed.) *Towards Implementing Universal Human Rights: Festschrift for the Twenty-Fifth Anniversary of the Human Rights Committee* (Nijhoff, 2004)

Schmid, E. *Taking Economic, Social and Cultural Rights Seriously in International Criminal Law* (Cambridge University Press, 2005)

'War Crimes Related to Violations of Economic, Social and Cultural Rights' (2011) 71 *Heidelberg Journal of International Law* 3, 540

Schonsteiner, J. 'Dissuasive Measures and the "Society as a Whole": A Working Theory of Reparations in the Inter-American Court of Human Rights' (2011) 23 *American University International Law Review* 1, 127–164

Schwöbel-Patel, C. 'The Core Crimes of International Criminal Law', in K. Jon Heller et al. (eds.) *The Oxford Handbook of International Criminal Law* (Oxford University Press, 2020)

Scott, S. W. 'Note, Taking Riggs Seriously: The ATCA Case Against a Corporate Abettor of Pinochet Atrocities' (2005) 89 *Minnesota Law Review* 1497

Segovia, Alexander. 'Financing Reparations Programs: Reflections from International Experience', in P. De Greiff (ed.) *The Handbook of Reparations* (Oxford University Press, 2006)

Seibert-Fohr, A. *Prosecuting Serious Human Rights Violations* (Oxford University Press, 2009)

Seils, P. *Squaring Colombia's Circle: The Objectives of Punishment and the Pursuit of Peace* (International Centre for Transitional Justice, 2015)

Sending, O. J. 'Why Peacebuilders Fail to Secure Ownership and Be Sensitive to Context' (2009) 8 Norwegian Institute of International Affairs: Department of Security and Conflict Management, Security in Practice Working Paper No. 755

Sharp, D. 'Toward a Positive-Peace Paradigm for Transitional Justice' (2012) 35 *Fordham International Law Journal* 796

'Beyond the Post-Conflict Checklist: Linking Peacebuilding and Transitional Justice through the Lens of Critique' (2013) 14 *Chicago Journal of International Law* 1, Article 6

'Economic Violence in the Practice of African Truth Commissions and Beyond', in D. Sharp (ed.) *Justice and Economic Violence in Transition* (Springer, 2013)

'Introduction: Addressing Economic Violence in Times of Transition', in D. Sharp (ed.) *Justice and Economic Violence in Transition* (Springer, 2013)

'Interrogating the Peripheries: The Preoccupations of Fourth Generation Transitional Justice' (2013) 26 *Harvard Human Rights Journal* 149

'What Would Satisfy Us? Taking Stock of Critical Approaches to Transitional Justice' (2019) 13 *International Journal of Transitional Justice* 3, 570–589

Shaw, R., Waldorf, L. and Hazan, P. (eds.) *Localizing Transitional Justice: Interventions and Priorities After Mass Violence* (Stanford University Press, 2010)

Shelton, D. 'Private Violence, Public Wrongs, and the Responsibility of States' (1989) 13 *Fordham International Law Journal* 1, 17

'Righting Wrongs: Reparations in the Articles on State Responsibility' (2002) 96 *American Journal of International Law* 4, 833–856

Remedies in International Human Rights Law (Oxford University Press, 2005)

'The United Nations Principles and Guidelines on Reparations: Context and Contents', in K. De Feyter et al. (eds.) *Out of the Ashes: Reparation for Victims of Gross and Systematic Human Rights Violations* (Intersentia, 2005)

Sherman, L. *Scandal and Reform* (University of California Press, 1978)

Shover, N. 'Defining Organisational Crime', in M. D. Ermann and R. J. Lundman (eds.) *Corporate and Governmental Deviance: Problems of Organisational Behaviour in Contemporary Society* (Oxford University Press, 1978)

Sikkink, K. *The Justice Cascade: How Human Rights Prosecutions Are Changing World Politics* (Norton, 2011)

'The Age of Accountability: The Global Rise of Individual Criminal Accountability', in F. Lessa and L. Payne (eds.) *Amnesty in the Age of Human Rights Accountability: Comparative and International Perspectives* (Cambridge University Press, 2012)

Evidence for Hope: Making Human Rights Work in the 21st Century (Princeton University Press, 2017)

Sikkink, K. and Joon Kim, H. 'The Justice Cascade: The Origins and Effectiveness of Prosecutions of Human Rights Violations' (2013) 9 *Annual Review of Law and Social Science* 1, 269–285

Simcock, J. 'Unfinished Business: Reconciling the Apartheid Reparation Litigation with South Africa's Truth and Reconciliation Commission' (2011) 47 *Stanford Journal of International Law* 1, 239

Simma, B. and Alston, P. 'The Sources of Human Rights: Custom, Jus Cogens and General Principles' (1989) 12 *Australian Year Book of International Law* 82

Skinner, G. 'Rethinking Limited Liability of Parent Corporations for Foreign Subsidiaries' Violations of International Human Rights Law' (2015) 72 *Washington and Lee Law Review* 1769

Transnational Corporations and Human Rights: Overcoming Barriers to Judicial Remedy (Cambridge University Press, 2020)

Skinner, G., McCorquodale, R. and De Schutter, O. *The Third Pillar: Access to Judicial Remedies for Human Rights Violations by Transnational Business* (International Corporate Accountability Roundtable, 2013)

Sloan, B. 'General Assembly Resolutions Revisited (Forty Years Later)' (1987) 58 *British Yearbook of International Law* 39

Slye, R. 'Corporations, Veils, and International Criminal Liability' (2008) 33 *Brooklyn Journal of International Law* 955

Snyder, J. and Vinjamuri, L. 'Trials and Errors: Principle and Pragmatism in Strategies of International Justice' (2004) 28 *International Security* 5–44

Spiga, V. 'Non-Retroactivity of Criminal Law: A New Chapter in the Hissène Habré Saga' (2011) 9 *Journal of International Criminal Justice* 1, 5–23

Sriram, C. 'Justice as Peace? Liberal Peacebuilding and Strategies of Transitional Justice' (2007) 21 *Global Society* 4, 579–591

Stahn, C. 'Complementarity, Amnesties and Alternative Forms of Justice: Some Interpretative Guidelines for the International Criminal Court' (2005) 3 *Journal of International Criminal Justice* 695–720

Stahn, C. and Sluiter, G. (eds.) *The Emerging Practice of the International Criminal Court* (Brill | Nijhoff, 2008)

Stephens, B. 'The Amorality of Profit: Transnational Corporations and Human Rights' (2002) 20 *Berkeley Journal of International Law* 45

Stewart, J. *Corporate War Crimes: Prosecuting Pillage of Natural Resources* (Open Society Foundations, 2010)

Stewart, J. G. 'Complicity in Business and Human Rights' (2015) 109 *Proceedings of the ASIL Annual Meeting* 181

Stoitchkova, D. *Towards Corporate Liability in International Criminal Law* (Intersentia, 2010)

Stolk, S. 'The Victim, the International Criminal Court and the Search for Truth: On the Interdependence and Incompatibility of Truths About Mass Atrocity' (2015) 13 *Journal of International Criminal Justice* 5, 973–994

Subotic, J. *Hijacked Justice: Dealing with the Past in the Balkans* (Cornell University Press, 2009)

Suhrke, A. and Samset, I. 'What's in a Figure? Estimating Recurrence of Civil War' (2007) 14 *International Peacekeeping* 195

Sullivan, S. 'Changing the Premise of International Legal Remedies: The Unfounded Adoption of Assurances and Guarantees of Non-Repetition' (2002) 7 *UCLA Journal of International Law and Foreign Affairs* 265

Summerfield, D. 'Raising the Dead: War, Reparation and the Politics of Memory' (1995) 311 *British Medical Journal* 495–497

Summers, N. 'Recent Developments: Colombia 's Victims' Law: Transitional Justice in a Time of Violent Conflict?' (2012) 25 *Harvard Human Rights Journal* 1, 219

Sunga, L. S. *The Emerging System of International Criminal Law, Developments in Codification and Implementation* (Kluwer Law International, 1997)

Sveass, N. and Lavik, N. J. 'Psychological Aspects of Human Rights Violations: The Importance of Justice and Reconciliation' (2000) 69 *Nordic Journal of International Law* 35–52

Sweeney, J. 'The Elusive Right to Truth in Transitional Human Rights Jurisprudence' (2018) 67 *International and Comparative Law Quarterly* 2, 353–387

Szoke-Burke, S. 'Searching for the Right to Truth: The Impact of International Human Rights Law on National Transitional Justice Policies' (2015) 33 *Berkeley Journal of International Law* 561

Taylor, J. *East Timor: The Price of Freedom* (Zed Books, 1999)

Taylor, M., Thompson, R. and Ramasastry, A. *Overcoming Obstacles to Justice: Improving Access to Judicial Remedies for Business Involvement in Grave Human Rights Abuses* (Fafo, 2010)

Teitel, R. 'Beyond Vienna & Beijing: Human Rights Theory: Human Rights Genealogy' (1997) 66 *Fordham Law Review* 301

Transitional Justice (Oxford University Press, 2000)

'Theoretical and International Framework: Transitional Justice in New Era' (2003) 26 *Fordham International Law Journal* 4, 893

'Transitional Justice Genealogy' (2003) 16 *Harvard Human Rights Journal* 69

'Transitional Justice and Judicial Activism – A Right to Accountability?' (2006) 48 *Cornell International Law Journal* Article 4

'Editorial Note, Transitional Justice Globalized' (2008) 2 *International Journal of Transitional Justice* 1–4

'The Universal and the Particular in International Criminal Justice', in R. Teitel (ed.) *Globalizing Transitional Justice: Contemporary Essays* (Oxford University Press, 2014)

The Advocates for Human Rights. *A House with Two Rooms: Final Report of the Truth and Reconciliation Commission of Liberia Diaspora Project* (2009)

Thirlway, H. *The Sources of International Law* (Oxford University Press, 2015)

Thoms, O. N. T. and Ron, J. 'State-Level Effects of Transitional Justice: What Do We Know?' (2010) 4 *International Journal of Transitional Justice* 329

Thoms, O. N. T., Ron, J. and Paris, R. *The Effects of Transitional Justice Mechanisms: A Summary of Empirical Research Findings and Implications for Analysts and Practitioners* (Centre for International Policy Studies, 2008)

Tobar Torres, J. A. 'Responsabilidad corporativa en procesos transicionales de paz: Entre la judicialización y la autorregulación. Elementos de análisis desde el caso colombiano' (2019) 17 *Estudios constitucionales* 2, 121–140

Tomuschat, C. 'Reparation for Victims of Grave Human Rights Violations' (2002) 10 *Tulane Journal of International and Comparative Law* 157–184

'Darfur – Compensation for the Victims' (2005) 3 *Journal of International Criminal Justice* 579–589

Human Rights, Between Idealism and Realism (Oxford University Press, 2014)

Udombana, N. 'So Far, So Fair: The Local Remedies Rule in the Jurisprudence of the African Commission on Human and Peoples' Rights' (2003) 97 *American Journal of International Law* 1–37

Unruh, J. D. and Abdul-Jalil, M. A. M. 'Housing, Land and Property Rights in Transitional Justice' (2021) 15 *International Journal of Transitional Justice* 1–6

Uprimny, R. and Saffon, M. P. 'Reparaciones transformadoras, justicia distributiva y profundización democrática', in C. Díaz Gómez et al. (eds.) *Reparar en Colombia: los dilemas en contextos de conflicto, pobreza y exclusión* (International Centre for Transitional Justice, 2009)

Uprimny-Yepes, R. and Sánchez, N. C. 'Los dilemas de la restitución de tierras en Colombia' (2010) 12 *Revista Estudios Socio-Jurídicos* 2, 305–342

Urueña, R. 'Prosecutorial Politics: The ICC's Influence in Colombian Peace Processes, 2003–2017' (2017) 111 *AJIL* 104

Vaccari, E. and Van Ho, T. 'Insolvency Law Through the Lens of Human Rights Theories', in E. Ghio et al. (eds.) *Re-Examining Insolvency Law and Theory. Perspectives for the 21st Century* (Edward Elgar Publishing, 2023)

Valiñas, M. 'The Colombian Special Jurisdiction for Peace' (2020) 18 *Journal of International Criminal Justice* 449

Valji, N. *Trials and Truth Commissions: Seeking Accountability in the Aftermath of Violence* (Centre for the Study of Violence and Reconciliation, 2004)

Van Dam, C. 'Breakthrough in Parent Company Liability: Three Shell Defeats, the End of an Era and New Paradigms' (2021) 18 *European Company and Financial Law Review* 5

Van den Herik, L. 'The Difficulties of Exercising Extraterritorial Jurisdiction: The Acquittal of a Dutch Businessman for Crimes Committed in Liberia' (2012) 9 *International Criminal Law Review* 211–226

Van den Herik, L. and Letnar Černič, J. 'Regulating Corporations under International Law: From Human Rights to International Criminal Law and Back Again' (2010) 8 *Journal of International Criminal Justice* 725–743

van der Merwe, H. and Brinton Lykes, M. 'Racism and Transitional Justice' (2020) 14 *International Journal of Transitional Justice* 3, 415–422

Van der Wilt, H. 'Genocide, Complicity in Genocide and International v. Domestic Jurisdiction: Reflections on the van Anraat Case' (2006) 4 *Journal of International Criminal Justice* 239–257

'Corporate Criminal Responsibility for International Crimes: Exploring the Possibilities' (2013) 12 *Chinese JIL* 43

Van Dyke, J. 'Promoting Accountability for Human Rights Abuses' (2005) 8 *Chapman Law Review* 153

Van Ho, T. 'Chapter 18: Business and Human Rights in Transitional Justice: Challenges for Complex Environments', in S. Deva and D. Birchall (eds.) *Research Handbook on Human Rights and Business* (Edward Elgar Publishing, 2020)

Van Sliedregt, E. *The Criminal Responsibility of Individuals for Violations of International Humanitarian Law* (T.M.C. Asser Press, 2003)

Van Sliedregt, E. and Yanev, L. 'Co-Perpetration Based on Joint Control over the Crime', in M. Cupido et al. (eds.) *Modes of Liability in International Criminal Law* (Cambridge University Press, 2019)

Vandegiste, S. 'Reparation', in D. Bloomfield et al. (eds.) *Reconciliation After Violent Conflict: A Handbook* (International Institute for Democracy and Electoral Assistance, 2003)

Ventura, M. 'Aiding and Abetting', in M. Cupido et al. (eds.) *Modes of Liability in International Criminal Law* (Cambridge University Press, 2019)

Verbitsky, H. and Bohoslavsky, J. P. (eds.) *Cuentas Pendientes Los Complices Economicos de La Dictadura* (Siglo Veintiuno Editores, 2013)

(eds.) *Outstanding Debts to Settle: The Economic Accomplices of the Dictatorship in Argentina* (Cambridge University Press, 2015)

Vest, H. 'Business Leaders and the Modes of Individual Criminal Responsibility Under International Law' (2010) 8 *Journal of International Criminal Justice* 3, 851–872

Vinjamuri, L. and Snyder, J. 'Law and Politics in Transitional Justice' (2015) 18 *Annual Review of Political Science* 303

Waldorf, L. 'Anticipating the Past: Transitional Justice and Socio-Economic Wrongs' (2012) 21 *Social and Legal Studies* 171

Walker, M. *Moral Repair* (Cambridge University Press, 2006)

What Is Reparative Justice? (Marquette University Press, 2010)

Walker, M. U. 'Truth Telling as Reparations' (2010) 41 *Metaphilosophy* 4, 525–545

Wallace, D. *Human Rights and Business* (Brill | Nijhoff, 2014)

Weah, A. 'Hopes and Uncertainties: Liberia's Journey to End Impunity' (2012) 6 *International Journal of Transitional Justice* 2, 331–343

Weigend, T. 'Perpetration Through an Organization: The Unexpected Career of German Legal Concept' (2011) 9 *Journal of International Criminal Justice* 1, 91–112

'Societas Delinquere Non Potest? A German Perspective' (2008) 6 *Journal of International Criminal Justice* 5, 927–945

Wells, C. *Corporate Criminal Liability*, Paper written for the ICJ Expert Legal Panel on Corporate Complicity in International Crimes, 2008

Corporations and Criminal Responsibility (Oxford University Press, 2005)

Werle, G. *Principles of International Criminal Law* (TMC Asser, 2005)

'Individual Criminal Responsibility in Article 25 ICC Statute' (2007) 5 *Journal of International Criminal Justice* 953–975

Werle, G. and Jessberger, F. *Principles of International Criminal Law* (Oxford University Press, 2014)

Wesche, P. 'Business Actors, Paramilitaries and Transitional Criminal Justice in Colombia' (2019) 13 *International Journal of Transitional Justice* 478

'Business Actors and Land Restitution in the Colombian Transition from Armed Conflict' (2021) 25 *The International Journal of Human Rights* 2, 295–322

Wettstein, F. *Multinational Corporations and Global Justice* (Stanford Business Books, 2009) 18

'Duty to Protect: Corporate Complicity, Political Responsibility, and Human Rights Advocacy' (2010) 96 *Journal of Business Ethics* 33–47

'Silence as Complicity: Elements of a Corporate Duty to Speak Out Against the Violation of Human Rights' (2012) 22 *Business Ethics Quarterly* 37–61

Whyte, D. (ed.) *Crimes of the Powerful: A Reader* (Open University Press, 2008)

Williamson, J. A. 'Command Responsibility in the Case Law of the International Criminal Tribunal for Rwanda' (2002) 13 *Criminal Law Forum* 365–384

Wilson, R. A. 'Anthropological Studies of National Reconciliation Processes' (2003) 3 *Anthropological Theory* 3, 367–387

Wippman, D. 'Atrocities, Deterrence, and the Limits of International Justice' (1999) 23 *Fordham International Law Journal* 473

Wouters, J. et al. 'The International Legal Framework Against Corruption: Achievements and Challenges' (2013) 14 *Melbourne Journal of International Law* 1, 209–280

Yanev, L. 'Joint Criminal Enterprise', in M. Cupido et al. (eds.) *Modes of Liability in International Criminal Law* (Cambridge University Press, 2019)

Yom, S. et al. 'Youth Politics in the Middle East and North Africa' (2019) 16 *Project on Middle East Political Science* 3

Yusuf, H. 'Peace Versus Justice and Rule of Law Debates in Transitions', in H. Yusuf and H. van der Merwe (eds.) *Transitional Justice Theories, Mechanisms and Debates* (Routledge, 2021)

Zahar, A. 'Command Responsibility for Civilian Superiors for Genocide' (2001) 14 *Leiden Journal of International Law* 591–616

Zalaquett, J. 'Balancing Ethical Imperatives and Political Constraints: The Dilemma of New Democracies Confronting Past Human Rights Violations' (1992) 43 *Hastings Law Journal* 1425

'Keynote', in A. Boraine et al. (eds.) *Dealing with the Past: Truth and Reconciliation in South Africa*, Institute for a Democratic Alternative for South Africa (Clyson Printers, 1994)

Zegveld, L. *Accountability of Armed Opposition Groups in International Law* (Cambridge University Press, 2002)

'Victims' Reparations Claims and International Criminal Courts' (2010) 8 *Journal of International Criminal Justice* 79

Zerk, J. 'Corporate Liability for Gross Human Rights Abuses: Towards a Fairer and More Effective System of Domestic Law Remedies', Report prepared for the Office of the UN High Commissioner for Human Rights (2014)

Zimmermann, A. 'Violations of Fundamental Norms of International Law and the Exercise of Universal Jurisdiction in Criminal Matters', in C. Tomuschat and J.-M. Thouvenin (eds.) *The Fundamental Rules of the International Legal Order. Jus Cogens and Obligations Erga Omnes* (Martinus Nijhoff Publishers, 2006)

Zoomers, A. 'Globalisation and the Foreignization of Space: Seven Processes Driving the Current Global Land Grab' (2010) 37 *Journal of Peasant Studies* 2, 429–447

Zunino, M. *Justice Framed: A Genealogy of Transitional Justice* (Cambridge University Press, 2019)

Zweigert, K. and Kötz, H. *An Introduction to Comparative Law* (Oxford University Press, 1998)

INDEX

For EU product safety concerns, contact us at Calle de José Abascal, 56–1°,
28003 Madrid, Spain or eugpsr@cambridge.org.

www.ingramcontent.com/pod-product-compliance
Lightning Source LLC
Chambersburg PA
CBHW071946101225
36481CB00033B/107
* 9 7 8 1 0 0 9 6 7 6 8 2 3 *